Praise for
The Heart of Wisdom Tea

MW00610019

Robin Sampson has put together a jewel of a package. many different learning methods using Charlotte Mason's philosophy of learning, ... Bible first philosophy, and the biblical Hebraic method of education. The creative way of melding Charlotte Mason and the four basic learning styles has produced a approach that is truly a conduit to life-long learning. Robin gently leads us to this place of light yet highly encourages delight-directed learning at the same time. When you ignite a spark of interest in your child, lay aside the schedule/timetable and watch them fly! Children who are learning by choice will retain and enjoy so much more than those who are forced to study topics of no interest to them. There are comprehensive helps on making timeline books and portfolios, all with lots of illustrations and examples. Robin has obviously spent time in prayer and more prayer while she prepared these studies. Her writings are thoughtful, insightful and joyful and have been a labor of love from her whole family, I'm quite sure! Enjoy the four-steps—Excite, Examine, Expand, and Excel! You may never go back to any other way of learning.—Heidi Shaw, *The Old Schoolhouse Magazine*

Robin Sampson has her own approach for sparking the love of learning in your child's heart. If you are a Charlotte Mason fan, you should love the way the lessons are presented. She combines Charlotte Mason's time-tested approach with Marilyn Howshall's ideas. The Heart of Wisdom approach adds the 4Mat System of learning and you have a method that appeals to all learning styles. If you like combining unit studies and the Charlotte Mason approach, with a heavy emphasis on Bible study, then you'll love the Heart of Wisdom approach—**Mary Pride, *Practical Homeschooling Magazine.***

Using Heart of Wisdom has been a life-changing experience for our entire family. We spend more time together in God's Word and are growing in our understanding together! Learning Israel's history has been a tremendous benefit to understanding all of history—past, present, and future. Also, learning about our Hebrew roots has brought new life to our relationship with God through Jesus Christ. We are just beginning the Wisdom unit and are gleaning so much already. I know that God orchestrated Heart of Wisdom becoming part of our homeschooling.—**Customer**

We are very excited about this "renewed" style of learning and the Hebrew-based education that has become the center of our lives. We are so very grateful for everything that Robin has created within Heart of Wisdom. The books she has written and the resources that are shared within Heart of Wisdom are phenomenal. Heart of Wisdom has paved the way to many an enlightened discussion in our Bible studies and around our lunch and dinner tables. Thank you for such enrichment.—**Customer**

The Heart of Wisdom Teaching Approach

Bible-Based Homeschooling

by Robin Sampson

Heart of Wisdom Publishing Inc

Homeschool-Books.com

HeartofWisdom.com

Statement of Faith

We believe the Scriptures to be the verbally inspired Word of God, without error in the original writings, the complete revelation of His will for the salvation of men, and the only absolute authority for genuine faith and practice.

We believe in one God, Creator of all things, infinitely perfect, Who eternally rules His universe and is bringing all things to their proper end according to His glorious plan of redemption.

We believe that Jesus Christ is the Messiah, is true God and true man, having been conceived by the Holy Spirit and born of the virgin Mary. He died on the cross as a perfect sacrifice for our sins and He rose bodily from the dead, later ascending triumphantly into heaven where he intercedes for us in God's presence.

We believe that the primary ministry of the Holy Spirit is to glorify the Lord Christ, our Messiah. To accomplish this, He convicts men of sin, indwells, guides, instructs and empowers believers for godly living and service.

We believe that man, originally created perfect in God's image, fell into sin in Adam, and consequently we are all by nature under God's wrath, and subject to both sin and death if left to our own dispositions and designs.

We believe that unless man accepts the Jesus the Messiah as his Savior, he is condemned to eternal damnation. We believe that salvation is by God's free gift of grace through faith. No man can do anything to earn salvation.

We believe we should uphold all of the commandments of God if we love Christ with all our heart (John 14:15, Romans 3:31, 7:22, Galatians 3:21–22, I John 5:1–3) and teach others to do so (Matthew 5:17–19, Revelation 22:13–14).

We believe that Christ will return to the earth with power and glory to bring earthly history to its close according to His wise plan of redemption. We believe that all men will be resurrected bodily, believers to everlasting blessedness in the presence of God.

Disclaimer

Heart of Wisdom is nondenominational, functioning entirely apart from any denominational agenda. The main objective and focus of our publications are on students and parents learning God's Word and establishing a relationship with Him. Resources and links are provided as a service to our customers. Many scholars with varying doctrinal opinions may contribute to specific areas of research. This does not mean the author or publisher is in complete doctrinal agreement with authors of contributed scholarly text or recommended resources.

Dedication

To the Glory of God

To My Loving Husband Ronnie

To My Children
Tammy, Belinda, Rebecca, Victoria, Daniel, Connie, Regina,
Anthony, Michael, David and Christopher.

To My Grandchildren
Jennifer, Abigail, Ann Marie, John, Joseph,
Stephen,Timothy, Brandon,
Tiffany, Sierra, Kaitlyn,
Jordan,
and those yet to be born.

To All Those Reading this Book
Who Hunger and Thirst After Righteousness
My Prayer for You:

For this cause I bow my knees unto the Father of our Lord Jesus Christ,
of whom the whole family in heaven and earth is named,
that he would grant you, according to the riches of his glory,
to be strengthened with might by his Spirit in the inner man;
that Christ may dwell in your hearts by faith;
that ye, being rooted and grounded in love,
may be able to comprehend with all saints what is the
breadth, and length, and depth, and height;
and to know the love of Christ, which passeth knowledge,
that ye might be filled with all the fulness of God.
Now unto him that is able to do exceeding abundantly
above all that we ask or think, according to the power that worketh in us,
unto him be glory in the church by Christ Jesus
throughout all ages, world without end. Amen.

(Ephesians 3:14)

About the Author

Robin Sampson is a home schooling mother of eleven, grandmother of twelve, and author of several acclaimed books including *What Your Child Needs to Know When*, *A Family Guide to the Biblical Holidays*, and *Ancient History: Adam to Messiah*. See over a dozen unit studies by Robin on pages 376–378.

Robin has been writing and speaking, covering a broad spectrum of home school topics, from education philosophies to Biblical studies for over eightteen years. Robin has authored articles for magazines such as *Homeschool Today*, *Teaching Home*, *Home School Digest*, *The Old Schoolhouse*, and *Restore Magazine*.

Robin actively lives her subject as she continues to home-educate her youngest children. Most of Robin's children are grown, married, and homeschooling their own children. Robin's husband, Ronnie, is a deputy director for Homeland Security in Washington, D.C. They reside in northern Virginia.

The Heart of Wisdom Teaching Approach: Bible-Based Homeschooling
First Edition © April 2005. Heart of Wisdom Publishing Inc.
ISBN: 0970181671

Acknowledgments

I must first thank my dear husband and family for their encouragement and patience as I wrote and rewrote this book. Special thanks to my husband for his editing. It is my hope that my grandchildren and their children will glean much wisdom from this book.

The Heart of Wisdom teaching approach is a combination of several different methods, philosophies, and teaching ideas. I owe appreciation to a number of people.

I am especially thankful to David Mulligan, author of *Far Above Rubies, Wisdom in the Christian Community* which laid the foundation for the Heart of Wisdom teaching approach. Mr. Mulligan graciously gave me permission to use anything I felt necessary for this work.

I'd like to express particular thanks to Marvin Wilson, author of *Our Father Abraham,* for his invaluable and balanced teachings on the Hebraic roots of the Christian faith.

I am deeply appreciative to Dr. John Garr for providing fruitful discussions which helped me clarify several ideas comparing Greek and Hebrew thought patterns.

I am extremely grateful to Dr. Ruth Beechick for all her wonderful advice in each of her books, particularly in *You Can Teach Your Child Successfully*. Her efforts made teaching my children much easier.

I am thankful to the late Charlotte Mason whose love for children is now helping a new generation of homeschoolers understand her many unique and delightful teaching methods.

I am thankful to Marilyn Howshall for her unique Lifestyle of Learning ideas.

I am appreciative of Dr. Bernice McCarthy's work in learning styles and the 4Mat System™ which I have adapted and termed the Four-Steps.

I'd like to give special thanks to Dolores Woodrum for editing this work. Thank you for all your encouragement and for polishing my rough spots.

I'm grateful to Julie Chuande for her prayers and daily help with my children. Without her help this book would not be possible.

Others authors to whom I am indebted for useful information include Tim Hegg, Robert L. Lindsey, Dave Bivin, Cheryle Holman, Alfred Edersheim, Dr. Francis and Edith Schaeffer, Dr. Albert Green, Dwight A. Pryor, Brad Young, James Charlesworth, Richard Booker, Harro Van Brummelen, Valerie Bendt, Clay and Sally Clarkson, Barb Shelton, and Cindy Rushton.

Several others have given me the opportunity to present preliminary versions of my ideas and to benefit from their support, advice, and encouragement including Peggy Jones, and Brandon and Victoria Phillips.

Contents

Section Four: Heart of Wisdom Directions

Section Five: Resources

Preface

What is a Heart of Wisdom?

The Heart of Wisdom teaching approach begins with the Bible as the center of education, with all subordinate studies taught through the light of God's Word. A Bible framework provides the structure and stability with which to approach all of life. Academics play an important part, but they are secondary. This approach is a combination of several popular methods and can be utilized for all ages with any curriculum. The purpose of this book is to provide inspiration and motivation for you to make God's Word the primary focus of your day, every day.

We adopted the name, Heart of Wisdom, from Psalm 90, verse 12:

> *Teach us to number our days aright, that we may gain a heart of wisdom.*
> —*Psalm 90:12*

Psalm 90 was written by Moses, making it the oldest of all the Psalms (possibly written in conjunction with the events of Numbers 13-14). Let's consider each of these three terms in this verse: *number our days aright; heart;* and *wisdom.*

Number Our Days Aright

In verse ten of this psalm, Moses declared: *The length of our days is seventy years—or eighty, if we have the strength.* Seventy or eighty years is all that we are likely to be given, and that means that we have somewhere between 25,550 and 29,200 days on this earth. If you could imagine a timeline of eternity, a lifespan of eighty years would be a small speck. James wrote: *You are a mist that appears for a little while and then vanishes* (James 4:14). We have only a fleeting existence on this earth, yet God's mighty love can bring joy into the lives of His people and make life meaningful and worthwhile, if we seek Him.

What if you discovered that you had only one day left to live? What would you want to teach your children before you died? Serious illness and death of those near us have a way of instantly putting our priorities into focus. When my two-week-old daughter was dying of pneumonia, my priorities instantly came into focus. Two months earlier, I was fretting over what color to paint the nursery and dealing with a teething toddler, an unexpected guest, and our budget. But my daughter's illness made all of my other anxieties disappear. (She did die, and God miraculously brought her back to life, but that's another story—she is now 27 and mother of three boys.)

When we become aware of how short our time on earth is, we become conscious of what is truly important in life and what is merely trivial. So often we look up and realize that time has passed us by. The things we promised we'd accomplish remain undone. Before we know it, days have become weeks; weeks, months; and months, years. We so often miss the opportunities that God places in our path, and we need to learn to number our days aright.

Heart

The Bible never speaks of the brain as the center of consciousness, thought, or will. The Hebrews thought in terms of subjective experience rather than objective, scientific observation, and thereby they avoided the modern error of over-compartmentalization. It was essentially the whole man, with all of his attributes—physical, intellectual, emotional, psychological, and spiritual—of which the Hebrews thought and spoke, and the heart was conceived of as the governing center for all of these. It is the heart that makes a man or a beast what he is and governs all of his actions (Proverbs 4:23).

The Heart is the Center of Our Intellect:

- We can understand with our heart. (Deuteronomy 8:5).
- We can pray in our heart (Isaiah 1:12–13).
- We can meditate in our heart (Psalm 19:14).
- We can hide God's Word in our heart (Psalm 119:11).
- We can doubt in our heart (Mark 11:23).
- We can ponder in our heart (Luke 2:19).
- We can believe in our heart (Romans 10:9).
- We can sing in our heart (Ephesians 5:19).
- The heart provides wisdom (1 Kings 3:12).

The Heart is the Center of Emotions:

- Joy (Deuteronomy 28:47; Acts 2:26)
- Grief (Psalm 13:2)
- Ill-temper (Deuteronomy 15:10)
- Love (Deuteronomy 6:5; Philippians 1:7)
- Courage (2 Samuel 17:10; Psalm 27:14)
- Fear (Genesis 42:28)
- Gladness (Exodus 4:14)

The Heart is the Center of Our Will:

- The heart can be yielded to God (Joshua 24:23).
- We can discern good and evil with our heart (1 Kings 2:44).
- We can request a pure heart (Psalm 51:10; Matthew 5:8).
- The heart can be devoted to seeking God (1 Chronicles 22:19).
- The heart receives from God (Psalm 21:1–2).
- The heart can be turned toward God's statutes (Psalm 119:36).

Character, personality, will, and *mind* are modern terms that all reflect something of the meaning of *heart* in its biblical usage.[1]

Wisdom

Before exploring how a person acquires wisdom, it is important to understand the Bible speaks of different types of wisdom. The wisdom (*sophia*) of this world is foolish. Only when a person abandons what seems wise by human standards and accepts God's viewpoint can he or she be truly wise.

> *The wisdom of this world is foolishness in God's sight. As it is written: "He catches the wise in their craftiness"; and again, "The Lord knows that the thoughts of the wise are futile."*—1 Corinthians 3:19–20

At the time of the writing of the Bible there were two types of popular wisdom: that from God sought after by the Hebrews, and that of the world sought after by the Greeks. Biblical wisdom is the teaching of a personal God who is holy and just and who expects those who know Him to exhibit His character in the many practical affairs of life. This perfect blend of the revealed will of a holy God with the practical human experiences of life is also distinct from the speculative wisdom of the Greeks. The ethical dynamic of Greek philosophy lay in the intellect; if a person had perfect knowledge he could live the good life (Plato). Knowledge was virtue. The emphasis of Bible wisdom is that the human will, in the realm of practical matters, is to be subject to divine causes. Therefore, Hebrew wisdom was not theoretical and speculative. It was practical, based on revealed principles of right and wrong, to be lived out in daily life.[1]

According to the Bible, a wise person is known by actions which honor God, by choices based on mature spiritual understanding and a desire to instruct others in the way of wisdom. To become wise is to take on the character of God in love and concern for His people and His creation. True wisdom is found only in God. The amazing thing about Godly wisdom is once you begin to grow in it you realize it was always there. It is more like it needs to be recognized rather than learned. God's Spirit reveals it to you as you become open to receiving it.

The word wisdom we refer to (from Heart of Wisdom) is *chokmah*, which is used in 157 instances to describe an exalted form of insight and understanding, which is usually related to God or to godly people. When Moses laid his hands on Joshua he received this wisdom (Deuteronomy 34:9). Moses commanded Israel to be obedient to God so that their *chokmah* would be seen as a witness to other nations. This is the type of wisdom which was given by God to Solomon (I Kings 4:29), possessed by David (I Samuel 18:14) and characterizes the Messiah (Jeremiah 23:5; Isaiah 52:13). This wisdom is an attribute of God Almighty. We are advised by Solomon to seek this wisdom above all other values. *Wisdom is supreme; therefore get wisdom. Though it cost all you have, get understanding.* (Proverbs 4:7). We need this wisdom:

Oh, the depth of the riches of the wisdom and knowledge of God! How unsearchable his judgments, and his paths beyond tracing out!—Romans 11:33

Happy is the man that findeth wisdom, and the man that getteth understanding. For the merchandise of it is better than the merchandise of silver, and the gain thereof than fine gold. She is more precious than rubies.—Corinthians 3:13–15a.

My son, if thou wilt receive my words, and hide my commandments with thee; so that thou incline thine ear unto wisdom, and apply thine heart to understanding; yea, if thou criest after knowledge, and liftest up thy voice for understanding; if thou seekest her as silver, and searchest for her as for hid treasures; then shalt thou understand the fear of the Lord, and find the knowledge of God.—Proverbs 2:1–5.

Receive my instruction, and not silver; and knowledge rather than choice gold. For wisdom is better than rubies; and all the things that may be desired are not to be compared to it.—Proverbs 8:10–11.

The second section of this book will examine the difference between worldly wisdom and wisdom from God. This section explains that a major requirement on the way to wisdom is an unswerving commitment to and reliance upon God. As we abide in Him and rely upon the Holy Spirit, we will grow to be more and more like Christ.

Summary

Moses' petition to God was to help us recognize how brief our time on earth is so that we might discern the true meaning of life. He was praying (paraphrase), Lord, number our days and make our lives count. Give us grace to consider how little time we have to live in this world. Help us to not waste our lives' precious time with useless endeavors. Help us seek the one needful thing: true wisdom from the Creator of the universe. Open our eyes and our souls to see and make true wisdom our first priority. Create a desire in our intellect, our emotions, and our will to keep our focus on God at all times.

Matthew Henry's commentary on Psalm 90:12 eloquently explains:

> Those who would learn true wisdom, must pray for divine instruction, must beg to be taught by the Holy Spirit; and for comfort and joy in the returns of God's favor. They pray for the mercy of God, for they pretend not to plead any merit of their own. His favor would be a full fountain of future joys. It would be a sufficient balance to former griefs. Let the grace of God in us produce the light of good works. And let divine consolations put gladness into our hearts, and a luster upon our countenances. The work of our hands establish thou it; and, in order to do that, establish us in it. Instead of wasting our precious, fleeting days in pursuing fancies, which leave the possessors forever poor, let us seek the forgiveness of sins, and an inheritance in heaven. Let us pray that the work of the Holy Spirit may appear in converting our hearts, and that the beauty of holiness may be seen in our conduct.[2]

Introduction

The simplest way to understand the Heart of Wisdom teaching approach is to compare it to a cookbook of recipes. I have worked on these recipes for over fifteen years; I have altered the ingredients, measurements, and methods and finally came up with nourishing and satisfying results that work well for my family. You can use my recipes as outlined, or adapt them to your family's preferences.

This cookbook not only provides the recipes but also gives a detailed account of the background of the ingredients and cooking methods to help you make the best use of them. Before you skip ahead to the directions I encourage you read through the book to discover the history and reasoning behind each of the the methods and ingredients.

A cookbook and a teaching approach are both resources which include many kinds of information—from ingredients and sources, to proportions, methods of mixture and preparation, to particular kinds and uses of utensils.

	Cooking Recipe	Teaching Approach
Ingredients	Food items: main ingredients, seasonings, etc. to make various dishes—main dish, side dish, dessert, etc.	Resources: Books, Internet, videos, etc. to teach various subjects—Bible, history, science, life skills.
Methods	Cooking methods used to combine the ingredients above. i.e. sift, chop, mix, bake, stir, sauté, etc.	Teaching methods used to combine the ingredients above, i.e. 4-step unit studies, creating a portfolio, copy work, narration, time line book, etc.
Outcome	Presentation and consumption of nutritious and appealing meals.	Presentation and consumption of healthful and nourishing ideas—Wisdom.

There are general recipes in this book. The main dish you will use daily, it is a recipe for studying God's Word. The side dish recipes include history, science, and life skills unit studies which you will adapt depending on the unit (like a basic casserole recipe or pie recipe that you adapt, depending on the filling.) The recipes provide useful step-by-step instructions on how to complete a desired task and can be easily modified if you have special desires. You don't have to follow my recipes exactly.

The Main Course: Bible Study

The main recipe is an outline for making God's Word the primary focus of the school day. The Bible is the chief ingredient. This recipe provides step-by-step methods (chronological readings divided into four steps) of mixture and preparation, with various seasonings (Bible study tools), but does not provide exact measurements. The recipe is more like a grandmother's rough-guide cooking instruction, "a little bit of this, a pinch of that." The purpose of this recipe is to serve as an inspiration to the parent/teacher by presenting a variety of teaching ideas.

Side Dish Recipes: Unit Studies Based on God's World

The other recipes include instructions on how to study God's world through history, science, and life skills unit studies. The Bible is the most important ingredient for each of these recipes as well. Other ingredients include living books, videos, and the Internet. Using these recipes you will be able to teach the following subjects: Bible, history, science, geography, composition, agriculture, religion, government, economics, and many more. The methods of mixture and preparation include learning styles, the four-step cycle of instruction and delight-directed studying.

This book includes recipes for creating your own unit studies, and also gives you the option of saving time by using a prepared unit study. The Heart of Wisdom teaching approach includes a four-year plan (meal plans), which is to be repeated three times for a total twelve-year program. If you decide to use the Heart of Wisdom teaching approach, you can utilize Heart of Wisdom unit studies or create your own unit studies using and/or adapting the recipes provided.

Planning Your Meals

If you use these recipes, you will need to add side dishes of your choice (math, phonics, foreign language, and other electives), based on your preferences, to create a complete balanced meal. Each student has a wide diversity of strengths, weaknesses, ambitions, and goals. I provide enough direction so you know what's essential to keep the recipes from failing, but I also give you enough room to let you discover for yourself the best balance of ingredients for your family.

As you learn about this approach, remember that your family cannot thrive on menus, recipes, or analysis of the food—you must spend time preparing the dishes that will feed your family. When you do this, as long as you don't leave out the main ingredient—the Bible—your outcome will be a success.

Sections of this Book

Section One: Lessons from Exodus

The first section of this book describes recipes and methods I tried that failed, and how I came to create the Heart of Wisdom recipes. The main problem with all the previous recipes I tried had to do with the fear ingredient. In this section you'll learn that fear is actually a poison! Any recipe that includes fear will result in disaster. I addresses the common fears of homeschoolers in this section by turning to the story of the Exodus, with the hope of preparing the hearts of homeschooling parents to wait and depend on God for all of their needs—and to be anxious for nothing.

Section Two: Rethinking Education

The second section explains the historical and cultural backgrounds of my recipes. Here you will learn how it is necessary to sift the proper ingredients and methods by looking at other recipes that have been tried through history. This section includes the origins and development of our traditional educational methods, from ancient times until today, with an appeal to return to biblical methods.

Section Three: Heart of Wisdom Methods

Section Three includes comprehensive descriptions of the ingredients and preparation methods you'll be using in the recipes. Here the most popular homeschool teaching philosophies and little-known methods are described.

Section Four: Heart of Wisdom Instructions

The fourth section contains the cooking directions—how to decide on a meal plan, actually combine and prepare the ingredients, and then present the finished product to your students. In this section you will learn about the Heart of Wisdom four-year plan and philosophies for teaching each subject, as well as how to create your own unit studies.

Section Five: Resources (Ingredients)

The fifth section includes book lists contained in the Heart of Wisdom four-year plan. This section explains the equipment that should be in every kitchen (books that should be in every homeschool library) and provides hundreds of books by grade level to teach the unit studies. Includes everything you need to teach Bible, literature, history, science, geography and more for twelve years (the four year plan three times).

Section 1

Lessons from Exodus

In This Section:

The first chapter in this section focuses on our personal homeschool journey, comparing our escape from the public school system with the Israelites' Exodus from Egypt. The next three chapters are lessons I have learned from the Exodus story that speak to the common fears of homeschoolers. My hope is that they will prepare your heart to wait and depend on God for all of your needs—and to *be anxious for nothing.*

Chapter 1

Our Homeschool Journey

Escape from Public School

In This Chapter

◆ How the homeschool journey is similar to the Exodus from Egypt.

◆ Why homeschool mothers are frustrated and complain.

◆ How to tell if you are on the right path.

◆ Why just bringing your children home is not the answer.

◆ How you can depend on God to direct your homeschool.

Our homeschool journey has many parallels to the Exodus story. Just as Israel escaped from Egypt, our family escaped from the public school system. We left "Egypt" to teach our children God's Word and the necessary academics to prepare them for life. At that time, there were four school-aged children and a toddler in our family. We were excited about our new direction!

In the Latin language, the Greek word *exodus (exodos)* means "the way out"—literally, "the road out."[1] The Exodus story explains Israel's bondage in Egypt and the wonderful deliverance that God gave them. Another important word related to the Exodus is *redemption*, because "to redeem" means "to set free." According to the *Enhanced Strong's Lexicon*, it pertains to "an object or person who has been delivered from danger by being purchased from indenture or slavery, with a focus on the relationship to the new master."[2] The Exodus story is a portrait of our salvation through Christ.

Liberated!

Once on the far side of the Red Sea, the liberated Hebrews united in song and grateful praise, acknowledging their powerful, providing God.

> *When the Israelites saw the great power the LORD displayed against the Egyptians, the people feared the LORD and put their trust in him and in Moses his servant. Then Moses and the Israelites sang this song to the LORD: "I will sing to the LORD, for he is highly exalted." —Exodus 14:31–15:1a*

Once our family gathered in our new homeschool classroom, we united in grateful praise, acknowledging our powerful, providing God. We felt well-prepared to go forth on our journey. We had a curriculum and a schedule. The classroom was equipped with bookshelves, a miniature desk for the toddler, a child-sized desk for each of the older children, a teacher's desk, textbooks, pencils, papers, notebooks, and even an American flag. Each child had a separate Bible workbook, history textbook, science textbook, math book, spelling workbook, vocabulary workbook, handwriting workbook, and English workbook.

> Once our family gathered in our new homeschool classroom, we united in grateful praise.

In the Wilderness

Only a few weeks after their liberation, the Hebrews began complaining and exhibited hearts of unbelief. They met new difficulties as impossibilities.

> *In the desert the whole community grumbled against Moses and Aaron. The Israelites said to them, "If only we had died by the LORD's hand in Egypt! There we sat around pots of meat and ate all the food we wanted, but you have brought us out into this desert to starve this entire assembly to death."—Exodus 16:2–3*

A few weeks into our new school experience, I began complaining and exhibited a heart of unbelief like the Israelites. I met new difficulties as impossibilities. When my childrens' papers reflected a lack of comprehension, I panicked. I lost faith in God. I spent each evening planning six subjects for four grade levels. During the day I sat at my desk, graded papers and spent countless hours writing scores in miniature boxes in a teacher's lesson-plan book and, if I had time, I answered questions about schoolwork. I enforced school rules, not allowing the children to talk to each other or to me unless they raised their hand. I was exhausted and irritable. I spent so much time planning and doing paperwork for

> A few weeks into our new school experience, I began complaining and exhibited a heart of unbelief like the Israelites.

school that I did not have time to interact with my children. As a result, "school" became little more than a sticky note on the outside of a textbook or workbook telling each student what pages to accomplish for the day. I was frustrated because I was looking back to the ways of the public school system (Egypt). I spent months researching and documenting state standards and objectives. I increased our school time, but it only made for longer and more boring days. It became evident that I needed a better way.

> *Do not put your trust in princes, in mortal men, who cannot save. When their spirit departs, they return to the ground; on that very day their plans come to nothing. Blessed is he whose help is the God of Jacob, Whose hope is in the LORD his God.*
> —*Psalm 146:3–5*

God Provides

The Lord told Moses that He would rain bread from heaven for them. He provided the Israelites with manna, a new food that appeared with the dew each morning as small, white, round pieces. It tasted sweet, like wafers made with honey. The Israelites baked, boiled, and prepared the manna in many other ways. It was always fresh, and they never had to worry about being hungry (see Exodus 16:1–31).

Trusting that God would provide our family with the nourishment we needed in this seeming wilderness of education, I began to read everything I could find on learning styles and teaching methods. When I read about thematic unit studies and Charlotte Mason's approach, I knew I had found direction that would make homeschooling much easier.

Thematic unit studies allowed me to teach Bible study, history, and science to all of my children at the same time, and then work separately with them on math and language arts. Suddenly, my planning and grading time was drastically reduced. I combined Charlotte Mason's approach with the unit studies by adding

> Thematic unit studies allowed me to teach Bible study, history, and science to all of my children at the same time.

narration and copy-work methods and reading real "living books." Now the children and I interacted with each other. We read aloud together and worked on projects together—and they were really learning! We shelved the boring textbooks and began to build a home library with real books. The children were beginning to do well academically, and our school day was much more interesting. The children began to actually enjoy school. Learning became sweet, like manna.

Failure to Enter the Promised Land

God provided all that the Hebrews needed. He had taken them through these difficulties to show them that He would always care for them. But when it came time for God to give them what they wanted—a place of their own, a land full of food, freedom as a nation—they were too afraid to believe that He would provide. At the entry to the Promised Land, twelve spies brought reports to the Hebrews about the land and the people living there. Ten of these spies gave negative reports about the possible problems that the Hebrews would encounter, and the Hebrews became afraid. They focused on the negative reports and looked to themselves for solutions—relying on themselves, not on God. God punished them by causing them to wander in the desert for forty years (see Numbers 13–14 and Deuteronomy 1:19–46).

God provided everything that our family needed. He had taken us through many difficulties to show us that He would always care and provide for us. But when it came time for God to give us what we wanted—true wisdom—we were too afraid to believe that He would provide. Like the Hebrews, I was not trusting God; I was still looking to "Egypt" for the answers. I was worried that I wasn't doing enough. I was relying on myself, not God. Somewhere along the way, I found that I had replaced Bible study time with academics. The multi-level unit study teaching that I had adopted was much more effective for academics, but a quick evaluation of our school time showed a great lack of Bible study. Our curriculum was Christian and we read an occasional Bible verse, but we were not spending sufficient time in God's Word. I was so busy with academics that some days we didn't start the day in prayer! We were not seeking true wisdom. The whole reason we had begun homeschooling was to teach our children God's Word, and yet we were completely overlooking it.

> The whole reason we had begun homeschooling was to teach our children God's Word, and yet we were completely overlooking it.

I wasn't the only homeschool parent on the wrong path. Many others had joined the "Exodus from Egypt" and were also stuck in the wilderness! As I spoke to new and veteran homeschoolers at homeschool meetings and conferences, the most frequently asked question was, "How do I know if I am doing enough?" It seemed as if everyone, including myself, was looking back to "Egypt," more than we were looking forward to the "Promised Land."

I believe this happens to most homeschoolers. They leave "Egypt" with the best of intentions—to teach their children what God commands us to teach them. But out of fear, their goals gradually change to teaching what the state, or "world," requires. This happens simply because parents were taught that academics equals school. Their heart desires the "Promised Land," but their minds can't shake "Egypt," and they remain in the wilderness because of fear.

It was during this time, when I was seeking the state's standards, that I wrote my first book, *What Your Child Needs to Know When*. It contained a checklist of standards for grades kindergarten through eighth grade. *What Your Child Needs to Know When* quickly became a homeschool bestseller. Sadly, most homeschoolers were purchasing this first edition out of fear—fear of the state's requirements.

Entering the Promised Land

The answer to my homeschool problems and fears was the same answer that God gave to Joshua. After the death of Moses, God told Joshua:

> *"No one will be able to stand up against you all the days of your life. As I was with Moses, so I will be with you; I will never leave you nor forsake you. Be strong and courageous, because you will lead these people to inherit the land I swore to their forefathers to give them. Be strong and very courageous. Be careful to obey all the law my servant Moses gave you; do not turn from it to the right or to the left, that you may be successful wherever you go. Do not let this Book of the Law depart from your mouth; meditate on it day and night, so that you may be careful to do everything written in it. Then you will be prosperous and successful. Have I not commanded you? [And He repeats:] Be strong and courageous. Do not be terrified; do not be discouraged, for the LORD your God will be with you wherever you go."*—Joshua 1:5–9

For emphasis I repeat: *Do not let this Book of the Law depart from your mouth; meditate on it day and night.* **Day and night!** I had thought that 15 minutes in a Bible workbook was an accomplishment!

By reexamining my goals and praying earnestly, I finally set aside my striving and anxiety and purposed to teach our children who Christ is. We began to spend time sitting at His feet and feasting at the table of His mercy, forgiveness, and peace. We stopped using Bible workbooks and began studying God's Word—really studying—reading from His Word, and using Bible study tools. We began to learn to *know* God. We prayed for and began to obtain godly knowledge and true wisdom. I found that true wisdom is available only by spending a significant amount of your homeschool time studying and teaching God's Word.

> True wisdom is available only by spending a significant amount of your homeschool time studying and teaching God's Word.

For the word of God is living and active. Sharper than any double-edged sword, it penetrates even to dividing soul and spirit, joints and marrow; it judges the thoughts and attitudes of the heart.—Hebrews 4:12

After this revelation I rewrote and expanded *What Your Child Needs to Know When,* and added two hundred pages to put the state's standards and achievement tests in proper perspective. The new edition explained that academic standards should not be separated from spiritual standards, and that we need to teach the whole child according to the child's individual God-given gifts.

Many years have passed since we first began our homeschool journey. At the time of this writing, we have eleven children and twelve grandchildren. For years I struggled to stay out of "Egypt," and even more so out of "Greece" (more on this in Section 2), but whenever I stopped and listened to the Lord, He always reminded me of Proverbs 3:5–6:

Trust in the LORD with all your heart
and lean not on your own understanding;
in all your ways acknowledge him,
and he will make your paths straight.

None of us is capable of seeing the big picture of God's plan, because, for one thing, it extends into eternity. God alone knows what He has planned and how He intends to accomplish it. One thing I am certain of, however, is that God will remain powerful, all-knowing and everywhere present. His goodness, righteousness, love, mercy, grace, and all-powerful holiness are sufficient. He promises to supply all our needs, and His nature will never change.

A Message of Faith and Hope

God redeemed Israel by destroying the Egyptian forces. The Exodus story is full of God's redemptive activities, much as our stories are today. He who caused light to shine out of darkness has made His light shine in the hearts of believers today so that they become new creations (see 2 Corinthians 5:17).

The story of the Exodus is a story of justice, mercy, and grace. Despite Moses' objections, God used him—an ordinary, weak man—to free His people. I believe that the same God who spoke to Moses wants to motivate homeschoolers, not just to leave "Egypt," but to go the distance, to travel into the "Promised Land" of milk and honey. God reveals His purposes to those who seek Him. We need only to follow. God will show us how to teach our children if we seek Him.

God is the *principal thing* we should seek. He is the principal of our school; we are only His teaching assistants. We need to meet with Him daily to seek His direction. He promises that if we acknowledge Him in all our ways, He will direct our paths. Academics (math, language arts, history, and science) are important, but only as they sharpen our focus on the Kingdom of God and His righteousness.

> God is the *principal thing* we should seek

Academic subjects are important tools—but they are only tools. These are neither the destination nor the goal. The moment academics begin to redirect you, cloud your view, or to any degree slow your pursuit of God and His righteousness, the more they move from being helpful tools to what Jesus calls the "cares of this life."

God says:

> *"For my thoughts are not your thoughts, neither are your ways my ways...*
> *As the heavens are higher than the earth, so are my ways higher than your ways*
> *and my thoughts than your thoughts."*—Isaiah 55:8–9

> *Great is our Lord and mighty in power; his understanding has no limit.*
> *The LORD sustains the humble...Sing to the LORD with thanksgiving; make music to*
> *our God on the harp.*—Psalm 147:5–7

Renewing of the Mind to Gain a Heart of Wisdom

I have continually analyzed changes made during our Exodus journey to understand the changes that occurred in our homeschool program. The curriculum change and different teaching methods were helpful, but these were only surface changes. The biggest change was the one made in me—I experienced a paradigm shift in my thinking. Spending time in God's Word brought to me a new perspective of my abilities and God's willingness to lead and provide. Over the years, my thoughts and opinions about school have changed drastically into new realizations about school, teaching, learning, education, and wisdom.

> Spending time in God's Word brought to me a new perspective of my abilities and God's willingness to lead and provide.

A paradigm shift is a change from one way of thinking to another. It's a revolution, a transformation, a sort of metamorphosis. A paradigm is a set of assumptions, concepts, values, and practices that constitutes a way of viewing reality for the community that shares them, especially in an intellectual discipline. [3]

The Hebrews watched as God redeemed them by destroying the Egyptian forces. The Hebrew people as a whole experienced a paradigm shift as they traveled through the wilderness: They renewed their minds and changed their thinking about themselves and about God, and eventually they entered the Promised Land.

I experienced a paradigm shift by spending time in God's Word and getting to know God. The richness of this experience is expressed by the Hebrew phrase *da'at Elohim*, or the "knowledge of God."[4] This term can only be understood fully when it is viewed from the Hebrew perspective. From our Western view, gaining "knowledge of God" is akin to examining the Bible in order to prove God's existence or to work out a theology about God's character.

To the Hebrews, the "knowledge of God" meant living life in relationship with Him—true spiritual wisdom—to know the Lord's will and live it out. Lois A. Tverberg, Ph.D., director of the En-Gedi Resource Center, explains in *Listening to the Language of the Bible*:

> The Hebraic view is that true spiritual wisdom is *da'at Elohim* (knowledge of God), which comes from experiencing a life in relationship with Him. A Greek will discuss God with abstract terms like *immutable, unchanging, steadfast,* etc. But a Hebrew would tell the story of God's care for Israel in the desert through forty years of constant complaining. While the Greek form of spiritual wisdom can be abstract and divorced from relationship, the Hebrew form is experiential, coming from real interactions between God and people. That is why the Bible is a book of stories of God's dealings with people, not just a theological treatise on the nature of God.[5]

The rest of the Exodus story reveals God's redemptive activities on many levels. The rest of this section (Section 1) will examine three "Lessons from Exodus," in the hope that they will help to bring about a paradigm shift in your thinking. It is my prayer that through this change, you and your children will all obtain a "heart of wisdom."

Section 2 will examine the paradigm shift that is needed as we view education. Sections 3, 4, and 5 will give you what is needed to help your children gain a "heart of wisdom."

Chapter 2

God Called You to Be a Part of His Plan

In This Chapter

◆ Fear is common among homeschoolers.

◆ Moses was fearful when he was called.

◆ Whom God calls, He equips.

In my years of traveling to speak at homeschool conventions, as well as through email and message boards, I have talked to thousands of homeschoolers. One obstacle that always comes up is fear—fear that they are making the wrong choice in homeschooling their children. Fear that they won't be able to give their children the education they deserve. Fear that they won't be able to accomplish this task to which God has called them.

During the writing of this book I received tragic, devastating news that could alter our family's life forever. Neither details nor the event are important. My reaction in the first minutes after receiving the news taught me a significant lesson.

The information was so overwhelming that I literally felt sick to my stomach. I experienced physical pain. The circumstances at that moment were such that I was unable to consult with my husband or family. Decisions had to be made. I sat down and began to mentally evaluate the possible options. Within minutes I realized that no matter what option I took, it would gravely impact everyone in my family—our eleven children, our twelve grandchildren—and everyone in our business. I grew more traumatized by the second. There was no easy answer, no quick way out. This was one of the biggest tribulations I had ever faced in my life. The options and possible results of each were swimming in my head. I was so mentally shaken, the burden was so heavy I could not stand up, I had to lie down. Finally, I went to my heavenly Father; I laid down on my face, sobbing out to God.

As I turned to the Creator of the universe, He instantly and lovingly reminded me through His Spirit that He had a plan. I went from terror to joy in less than 30 seconds! Suddenly this overwhelming idea of making these momentous decisions was gone. I didn't have to make a choice. My Father had a plan. He was in control and He knew the outcome! James 1:2–5 became so real to me:

> *Consider it pure joy, my brothers, whenever you face trials of many kinds, because you know that the testing of your faith develops perseverance. Perseverance must finish its work so that you may be mature and complete, not lacking anything. If any of you lacks wisdom, he should ask God, who gives generously to all without finding fault, and it will be given to him.*

The atmosphere in the room went from panic to calm. All I had to do was to seek Him, ask for wisdom, and follow His lead. My heart was flooded with unspeakable joy and I felt the peace that passes all understanding. I was now actually looking forward to seeing how God was going to work out this problem!

Next I felt guilt. I asked myself how I could have spent a full 15 minutes wallowing in this predicament alone. I'm a Christian author; I am involved in hours of Bible study every day. I go to God daily for the smallest matters. How could I possibly not turn to God immediately in such an enormous crisis? I asked God to forgive me for not directly turning to Him. Then my Father lovingly reminded me that He is made strong in my weakness. I again was filled with joy and began singing, "Because He lives I can face tomorrow, because He lives all fear is gone; because I know He holds the future, and life is worth the living—just because He lives."

> When God gives a mission, as He did to Moses, He supplies the means to complete that mission!

Once I became conscious that God was going to bear my burden, I could not only function again, but function with purpose and happiness, looking forward to watching Him work. What joy we have available in Christ!

Humble yourselves under the mighty hand of God, that He may exalt you in due time, casting all your care upon Him, for He cares for you. —I Peter 5:6–7.

In spite of being in the midst of great trauma, I received the gift of joy. This was not resignation about things over which I had no control; it was a holy joy, a divine enabling to rejoice in the Lord. The object of my joy was the God of my salvation. In Christ, our salvation, we have divine power to overcome any infirmity. By following Christ in simplicity and faith, the paths in which he leads us all end in glory and immortality. The paths are not always smooth but lead to *the city which hath foundations, whose builder and maker is God* (Hebrews 11:10).

Later in this book, I address differences in worldviews and the impact of our worldviews on our decisions concerning education. Here is a brief preview of the differences our worldview can make when we receive bad news:

Problem	Results/Christian	Results/Non-Christian
Death in Family	Trust in God producing peace	Fear producing worry and anxiety
Serious Illness	Trust in God producing peace	Fear producing worry and anxiety
Job Loss	Trust in God producing peace	Fear producing worry and anxiety
Etc.	Trust in God producing peace	Fear producing worry and anxiety

How sad to think of those who do not have a personal relationship with Christ! We all get tragic news sometime in our lives. We Christians can choose to turn to Christ, make that an integral part of our daily living, and in all circumstances we can experience joy.

If this joy and peace is available during tragedies, how much more is it available in our decision to homeschool our children? The worry and anxiety we experience come from a variety of sources. First there is the overwhelming number of choices: which teaching approach, which curriculum, which math, which science, which schedule, which child should be taught by what learning style, etc. Then the nagging questions: what about college, what about socialization, what about calculus, etc. Then there are the well-meaning relatives and neighbors telling us the many problems with homeschooling, and the people who find out that we homeschool who loudly proclaim, "Oh. I could never do that!" If anyone has reason to be anxious it would be a homeschooler. But God's Word says *Do not be anxious about anything, but in everything, by prayer and petition, with thanksgiving, present your requests to God. And the peace of God, which transcends all understanding, will guard your hearts and your minds in Christ Jesus.* (Philippians 4:6–7). So what is the answer? Make your request known to God, and He will take care of it!

God wants us to develop patience, endurance, and the ability to keep going when things are tough (Romans 5:3–4). The answer to all of our challenges is faith—and God provides the faith! *So then faith cometh by hearing, and hearing by the word of God* (Romans 10:17). *God hath dealt to every man the measure of faith* (Romans 12:3b).

Look at how ironic this situation is: We are worried about homeschooling. We need faith. Faith comes from spending time in God's Word. Homeschooling gives us the opportunity to spend time in God's Word daily. If we homeschool by following God's plan, our faith grows, our worry diminishes and we teach our children! Problem solved! *God has given us all spiritual blessings in Christ* (Ephesians 1:3), but we must step out by faith and claim them. We must walk forward by faith and claim new territory for the Lord. Like Moses, we must move ahead toward the Promised Land.

> Look at how ironic this situation is: We are worried about homeschooling. We need faith. Faith comes from spending time in God's Word. Homeschooling gives us the opportunity to spend time in God's Word daily. If we homeschool by following God's plan, our faith grows, our worry diminishes and we teach our children! Problem solved!

Moses' Fear

Many of the people whose stories were recorded in the Bible faced similar fears, but Moses was arguably one of the most terrified when it came to receiving his calling from God.

When God called Moses to the most difficult undertaking of his life—leading the children of Israel out of Egypt—He gave him his instructions through a burning bush. As He did so, He told Moses of the many great things He would do to deliver His people.

> *"Go, assemble the elders of Israel and say to them, 'The LORD, the God of your fathers—the God of Abraham, Isaac and Jacob—appeared to me and said: I have watched over you and have seen what has been done to you in Egypt. And I have promised to bring you up out of your misery in Egypt into the land of the Canaanites, Hittites, Amorites, Perizzites, Hivites and Jebusites—a land flowing with milk and honey.'*

> *"The elders of Israel will listen to you. Then you and the elders are to go to the king of Egypt and say to him, 'The LORD, the God of the Hebrews, has met with us. Let us take a three-day journey into the desert to offer sacrifices to the LORD our God.' But I know that the king of Egypt will not let you go unless a mighty hand compels him. So I will stretch out my hand and strike the Egyptians with all the wonders that I will perform among them. After that, he will let you go.*

"And I will make the Egyptians favorably disposed toward this people, so that when you leave you will not go empty-handed. Every woman is to ask her neighbor and any woman living in her house for articles of silver and gold and for clothing, which you will put on your sons and daughters. And so you will plunder the Egyptians."—Exodus 3:16–22

> Many of the people whose stories were recorded in the Bible faced fears, but Moses was arguably one of the most terrified when it came to receiving his calling from God.

What was Moses' answer to these amazing promises?

Moses answered, "What if they do not believe me or listen to me and say, 'The LORD did not appear to you'?"—Exodus 4:1

Moses said to the LORD, "O LORD, I have never been eloquent, neither in the past nor since you have spoken to your servant. I am slow of speech and tongue."—Exodus 4:10

Moses was anxious about his calling, and he gave two objections to the Lord: fear that the Hebrews would not listen (4:1), and a lack of eloquence (4:10). Sound familiar? God patiently dealt with Moses' fear, giving him miraculous powers to authenticate him as God's messenger, and He dealt with Moses' perceived lack of eloquence, giving him Aaron to speak for him. When God gives a mission, as He did to Moses, He supplies the means to complete that mission!

Why did you decide to homeschool? Did God call you to homeschool? Is homeschooling your children a conviction or a preference? God's will is to lead us to the Promised Land of our homeschool journey, but we'll only relax and enjoy this journey if we understand His plan for getting us there. A lack of understanding will result in confusion and bewilderment.

The key to understanding God's plan for the journey is in learning His ways, and how He thinks. God doesn't think in the same way we do, but we often try to relate to Him according to our way of thinking; but He'd rather we understand the way He thinks so we can better enjoy fellowship with Him. God describes His way of thinking in Isaiah:

"For my thoughts are not your thoughts, neither are your ways my ways," declares the LORD. "As the heavens are higher than the earth, so are my ways higher than your ways and my thoughts than your thoughts. As the rain and the snow come down from heaven, and do not return to it without watering the earth and making it bud and flourish, so that it yields seed for the sower and bread for the eater, so is my word that goes out from my mouth: It will not return to me empty, but will accomplish what I desire and achieve the purpose for which I sent it."—Isaiah 55:8–11

> Homeschooling your children isn't nearly as hard as Moses' task was, and God is just as sufficient for the task He has given you as He was for Moses.

Without a doubt, God has called you to homeschool the children under your care, and God has placed this book in your hands and has you reading these words to encourage you! Homeschooling your children isn't as hard as Moses' task was, and God is just as sufficient for the task He has given you as He was for Moses.

Let's take a closer look at Moses' call.

Moses was so fearful of what God was calling him to do that he asked God for a sign, to prove that He was who He said He was and He would do what He said He would do. Have you been so fearful of homeschooling your children that you've been begging God for a sign that you are on the right track? Wouldn't it be nice if we all were so full of faith from the start that we never questioned God or asked Him to prove Himself? Unfortunately, there are few such giants of faith among us—and Moses wouldn't have been included either, at first!

Interestingly, God calls us in the ways in which He needs us in this world—*but He also calls us in the ways in which we need to be called*. Moses needed miraculous signs to be able to believe the calling of God on his life. He needed the burning bush, the staff that turned into a snake, and the hand that turned leprous. Moses also needed help in speaking—but God gave him everything he needed. And God will give you what you need as well!

Reverend Robert C. Wisnewski, Jr., has this to say about God's call: "The manner in which God calls us is an interesting mixture of power and compassion. He calls us because He needs for us to do something, yet He calls us in ways to which we can respond."[1]

God calls each one of us—not just the pastors, prophets, and priests among us—and He has called you to the task of homeschooling your children. And because He has called you, He will equip you accordingly! God came to His chosen servant, Moses, and made Himself known. As the presence of God was acknowledged—*the place where you are standing is holy ground* (Exodus 3:5), God then acted to give Moses what he needed to carry out his calling.

Begin to pray and acknowledge the presence of God in your life. Say "yes" to His calling on your life, especially to the calling to homeschool your children, and then trust Him to give you what you need. This trust should not include a demand on God to give you certain things before you take steps toward your calling; instead, you should step out in obedience and faithfulness to the call, and allow God to meet your needs in the way He chooses—which always will be best for you.

Again, Rev. Robert C. Wisnewski, Jr., illustrates this concept:

> Begin to pray and acknowledge the presence of God in your life. Say "yes" to His calling on your life, especially to the calling to homeschool your children, and then trust Him to give you what you need.

We play a little game at our house; not a fine kind of game, but a game where we know our parts, and we keep playing out the same scenario. I ask my children to do something, and they resist my request. "I'll do it after this show is over." "I've got homework to do." "I was just going out to play." "Daddy, that's too heavy." "I can't do that." It's funny how a child can ride a bike like the wind up and down the street and then complain that it's too heavy to put in the shed. My all-time favorite line, and one I used myself as a child, is "I have to do everything," or its close cousin, "I never get to do what I want to do."

I play the game, too. Very rarely, but sometimes, I do the right thing. I'll gently assure them of their great favor in my eyes, convey to them in an imaginative way that what I've asked them to do is both important to me and good for them. I'll use the interchange to spend more time with them and teach them without a long lecture about family and responsibility. We'll grow closer together in that moment, and they will do what I have asked, and all will be perfect. But, as I say, that's a rare occurrence. What usually happens, and this is why the game continues, is that I will get exasperated, raise my voice, and say, "Never mind, I'll do it myself." It's a lot easier that way. In fact, it would be easier if I never asked them to do anything. I'd avoid a lot of conflict. But here, the easy way is not the right way.

Perhaps you've noticed that when God calls us to action and we resist with statements like, "That's too heavy," or "I have to do everything," God doesn't then say to us, "Never mind, I'll do it myself." He usually finds a way to inspire us to do what He wants, brings us closer to Him, and accomplishes His purpose. God does not the easy thing, but the right thing.

Moses complains that he won't be able to tell the people about who has told him to do these things. God says, "Tell them *I AM* sent you," giving Moses the name of God, *Yahweh,* that will endure throughout their history.

> God has called you to do a mighty work—to teach His precious children—so don't proclaim yourself to be weak!

He complains more and says the people won't believe him. God turns his staff into a serpent and then back again. "I'll do that to help you convince them," God says. Or, "I'll afflict your hand with leprosy and then heal you right in front of everybody." "If need be,

I'll turn the water of the Nile into blood just to convince the people for you."

Moses keeps whining, but God keeps assuring. "I'm not eloquent. I'm slow of speech and of tongue." "I've already thought of that," God says. "I'm sending Aaron along with you so he can speak to the people for you." And at this point, God makes it clear that He's had about enough of the whining and He's ready to set the process in motion.

The story ends with Moses' being sent out. God uses Moses to free the people from Egypt. It's not easy, but He does it, and He uses Moses, His chosen servant.[2]

God has called you to do a mighty work—to teach His precious children—so don't proclaim yourself to be weak!

God wants us to *walk by faith and not by sight* (see 2 Corinthians 5:7). Peter learned this lesson the hard way: *Peter got down out of the boat, walked on the water and came toward Jesus. But when he saw the wind, he was afraid* (Matthew 14:29–30). Peter first focused on his Lord, not the wind and waves. He stepped out in recognition of Christ's authority over the sea, and he walked on the water. Only when he began to look at the circumstances did he falter and begin to sink.

As we grow in our love relationship with the Lord, we begin to realize in part the magnitude of His love. One sign of Christian maturity is the ability to stop focusing on ourselves and launch out in faith. When we first experienced salvation, our viewpoint was altered—our focus changed; our desires became new, and old things lost their power over us. *If anyone is in Christ, he is a new creation; the old has gone, the new has come!* (2 Corinthians 5:17). Worry, fret, and discouragement will cease when our attitude has grown to complete focus and dependence on God.

> Worry, fret, and discouragement will cease when our attitude has grown to complete focus and dependence on God.

God Always Provides

When we ask anything according to God's will, He will provide. This remarkable promise is found over and over in God's Word. God knows everything. We can only see a glimpse of our future—therefore, our faith should be in the One who knows all of the facts and everything

> We can only be as strong in faith as we are in direct communication with God—it is then that He will work in us the fullness of Christ.

in the future. We must have *faith*—faith that
God will perfect His work in our lives.

God has said, *Be still, and know that I am God*
(Psalm 46:10). When we are quiet and still, God
can come in and do His work in our hearts. The
root of our weakness will always lie in not
trusting in God, step-by-step, moment-by-
moment. We can only be strong in faith as we are in direct communication with God—it
is then that He will work in us the fullness of Christ. In our weakness He is strong. God
can and will do all.

> God knows what your children will
> face in the future, and He will give
> you what you need to educate them
> in the way they need to be educated.

As He did for Moses, God will do for you. Those whom He calls, He equips. He knows
what your children will face in the future, and He will give you what you need to
educate them in the way they need to be educated. Just trust in Him for what you need.
When we rely on Him, we are on our way to creating in ourselves and in our children
what Moses termed *a heart of wisdom* (Psalm 90:12).

Chapter 3

Focus on God, Not on Circumstances

In This Chapter

◆ The importance of a right view of God.

◆ The faith of two of the twelve spies.

◆ Another kind of fear.

How do you view God? Do you envision Him as a harsh taskmaster with a lightning bolt in hand, always judging, requiring perfection, and waiting to punish wrongdoing? Or do you regard Him as a compassionate Father? Without a proper balanced view of God, you will never have a correct view of man. God is holy, just, righteous, and supreme, as well as loving, generous, merciful, and available. God desires an intimate personal relationship with each of His children, and He will bless us when we live in accordance with His instruction. Those who have a balanced view of God will also have a right relationship with Him through Jesus Christ.

Having a right view of God will allow you to trust Him completely in every area of your life. When you realize that He wants you to live an abundant life, you will be able to trust Him to guide you on your homeschool journey.

God uses the Bible to teach us about life—what He wants to do here and now for, in, by and through those who trust Him. The entire Bible is about the victory of faith and the glory that comes to God when His people trust and obey Him.

Let's return to the story of the Hebrews in the wilderness to discover the importance of faith (Numbers 13 and 14).

> *There are eleven days journey from Horeb, by the way of mount Seir, unto Kadesh-barnea. —Deuteronomy. 1:2*

The route of the Israelites' wilderness journey between the Exodus and their entry into the Promised Land is listed in Numbers 33:1–50. That detour was due to their deplorable lack of faith in God's conquering power.[1] The journey that should have taken eleven days turned into a forty-year detour in the desert. (The first time they arrived at the border of the Promised Land took almost a year; and their lack of faith resulted in another 39 years of wandering.)

Twelve Spies

When the Hebrews first came to the border of Canaan, Moses sent twelve spies into the land to see what it was like—and what sort of opposition they were likely to meet. When the twelve spies returned forty days later, they brought glowing reports of the land, but ten of the men were terrified of Canaan's inhabitants. They were afraid that the Canaanites were too strong to be conquered (see Numbers 13:31–33). On the other hand, they had evidence of the fruitfulness of the land—they returned with figs, pomegranates, and enormous clusters of grapes. Imagine how delightful fresh fruit would have seemed after such a long time in the wilderness! God had promised the people a land flowing with milk and honey (milk and honey are symbols of prosperity and abundance. See Isaiah 60:16 and Joel 3:18).

> *"I have promised to bring you up out of your misery in Egypt into the land of the Canaanites, Hittites, Amorites, Perizzites, Hivites and Jebusites—a land flowing with milk and honey."*—Exodus 3:17

> The Hebrews were firsthand witnesses to so many miracles...and there they were, ready to enter the Promised Land, but all they could see were the difficulties.

The Israelites had been redeemed from slavery by God's great power. They were at the doorway to the Promised Land, but unbelief blinded them. They forgot God's promises and His many mighty acts and proofs of His power. How could they have forgotten? The evidence was there. God had done everything He promised. The Hebrews were firsthand witnesses to so many miracles—the ten plagues, the opening of the waters of the Red Sea, the destruction of Pharaoh's army, water from a rock, bitter water turned sweet, manna and quail from heaven—and there they were, ready to enter the Promised Land, but all they could see were difficulties.

The children of Israel focused on the obstacles and their fears instead of God's promises and His power, and the more they focused on their circumstances, the more they became vulnerable to mental exaggeration and emotional devastation. Can you imagine? They had been promised a land of milk and honey—you'd think their hunger would have pushed them forward. It wasn't that long ago that they had been yearning for the leeks in Egypt! Their fear was due to their lack of faith. And the God who had brought harsh judgments on Egypt now judged Israel. Only Caleb and Joshua—the two believing spies—and the next generation of Hebrews were allowed to enter into the Promised Land, while the unbelieving generation never knew rest from their wanderings and died in the wilderness.

A major statement about God can be found in this portion of Scripture:

> *The LORD is slow to anger, abounding in love and forgiving sin and rebellion. Yet he does not leave the guilty unpunished.* —Numbers 14:18

God is love—but we are still responsible to Him for our choices. God's people were facing challenging circumstances, getting ready to enter into a new land and face new enemies. All they had ever known was slavery in Egypt, but now each of their decisions would have a profound impact on the entire congregation. Read the passage below as you imagine yourself and your family as a part of the apprehensive tribes awaiting the report about the new land.

> *They came back to Moses and Aaron and the whole Israelite community at Kadesh in the Desert of Paran. There they reported to them and to the whole assembly and showed them the fruit of the land. They gave Moses this account: "We went into the land to which you sent us, and it does flow with milk and honey! Here is its fruit. But the people who live there are powerful, and the cities are fortified and very large. We even saw descendants of Anak there. The Amalekites live in the Negev; the Hittites, Jebusites and Amorites live in the hill country; and the Canaanites live near the sea and along the Jordan."*

> *Then Caleb silenced the people before Moses and said, "We should go up and take possession of the land, for we can certainly do it."*

> *But the men who had gone up with him said, "We can't attack those people; they are stronger than we are." And they spread among the Israelites a bad report about the land they had explored. They said, "The land we explored devours those living in it. All the people we saw there are of great size. We saw the Nephilim there (the descendants of*

Anak come from the Nephilim). We seemed like grasshoppers in our own eyes, and we looked the same to them." —Numbers 13:26–33.

The land was fertile, as the grapes they had brought back proved. God had promised them it would be a land flowing with milk and honey but it was more than He had promised. God always gives more than He promises! But the ten spies saw themselves as tiny grasshoppers that would be crushed by the giants. The people focused on the giants instead of the fruit, the evidence of God's promise, and then they wept and complained:

> God always gives *more* than He promises!

That night all the people of the community raised their voices and wept aloud. All the Israelites grumbled against Moses and Aaron, and the whole assembly said to them, "If only we had died in Egypt! Or in this desert! Why is the LORD bringing us to this land only to let us fall by the sword? Our wives and children will be taken as plunder. Wouldn't it be better for us to go back to Egypt?" And they said to each other, "We should choose a leader and go back to Egypt." —Numbers 14:1–4

They wanted to return to Egypt, the land devastated by plagues, to the very people who had so mistreated and enslaved them! It's hard to imagine their frame of mind. Did they really believe that Pharaoh's wrath would be better than facing the giants in Canaan?

Once the people became conscious of their mistake, they tried to set the problem right. Numbers 14:26 through 35 tells of God's judgment upon the Israelites because of their unbelief and initial failure to possess what He had provided. Numbers 14:40 tells how the people responded:

Early the next morning they went up toward the high hill country. "We have sinned," they said. *"We will go up to the place the LORD promised."*

But Moses responded: *"Do not go up, because the LORD is not with you. You will be defeated by your enemies"* (verse 42). Moses later announced that, as punishment for their rebellion, they would wander in the wilderness until a new generation arose to go up and possess the land.

What was Israel's sin? They failed to believe the promises of God. They wanted to go back to Egypt. What was the consequence of their sin? They were not permitted to enter into God's rest (see Joshua 1). *The Lord disciplines those He loves, and He punishes everyone He accepts as a son* (Hebrews 12:6). *God disciplines us for our good, that we may share His holiness* (Hebrews 12:10).

The unbelieving Hebrews had the same mindset as many of today's fearful homeschoolers, especially those who begin to think of returning their children to public school. (There is a joke about the frustrated homeschool mother ready to chase the yellow school bus to send the children back to public school.) Going back to Egypt is familiar; following God's path is, quite often, unfamiliar. But those who put their faith in God will be rewarded!

> Going back to Egypt is familiar; following God's path is, quite often, unfamiliar. But those who put their faith in God will be rewarded!

> *Blessed is the man that trusteth in the LORD, and whose hope the LORD is. For he shall be as a tree planted by the waters, and that spreadeth out her roots by the river, and shall not see when heat cometh, but her leaf shall be green; and shall not be careful in the year of drought, neither shall cease from yielding fruit.* —Jeremiah 17:7–8 KJV

Whom Do You Fear?

Two of the spies, Joshua and Caleb, had confidence that God would give Israel the land of Canaan, despite its dreadful inhabitants. Joshua and Caleb were not afraid of their circumstances—instead, they experienced the fear of the Lord, a reverent fear that comes from spiritual maturity. The fear of the Lord is a fear that has been joined with love and hope; it is not a slavish dread, but rather it is a filial reverence: a fear of not doing what God leads you to do, a fear of not being in God's will. I hope this is the fear you are experiencing, because the fear of the Lord is the beginning of wisdom!

> *The fear of the LORD is the beginning of wisdom; all who follow his precepts have good understanding. To him belongs eternal praise.* —Psalm 111:10

> *The fear of the LORD is the beginning of wisdom, and knowledge of the Holy One is understanding.* —Proverbs 9:10

The Fear of the Lord

The fear of the Lord refers to the awe that a person ought to have before God (see Proverbs 5:7 and Ecclesiastes 12:13). This is represented by the fear and trembling with which Paul encouraged the Philippians to work out their salvation (see Philippians 2:12).

Dr. Lois Tverberg explains how an understanding of the Hebrew meaning of fear, and the rich Jewish thinking about the fear of the Lord can shed a great new light on this issue in *Listening to the Language of the Bible*:

> Understanding the Hebraic idea of "fear" is to know that like many Hebrew words, it has a much broader sense of meaning than we have in English. To us, "fear" is always negative—it is the opposite of trust, and its synonyms are fright, dread and

terror. In Hebrew, it encompasses a wide range of meanings from negative (dread, terror) to positive (worship, reverence), and from mild (respect) to strong (awe). In fact, every time we read "revere" or "reverence," it comes from the Hebrew word *yirah*, literally, to fear. When fear is in reference to God, it can be either negative or positive. The enemies of God are terrified by him, but those who know him revere and worship Him, all meanings of the word *yirah*.

How Should We Fear the Lord?

Many Christians understand the fear of the LORD as the fear of the punishment that God could give us for our deeds, and it is true that everyone should realize that they will stand at the judgment after they die. But a Christian who knows that his sins have been forgiven should not have this kind of fear of God anymore, although some do. People who have been steeped in this kind of punishment mindset have a very hard time loving God. This is what John speaks against when he says, *There is no fear in love; but perfect love casts out fear, because fear involves punishment, and the one who fears is not perfected in love"* (1 John 4:18).

Interestingly, in rabbinic thought, fearing God's punishment is also understood to be an incomplete and inferior understanding of the term *Yirat Adonai* (fear of the Lord). At its core is self-centeredness—what will happen to me because of God's knowledge of my deeds? Knowing the broader implications of the word fear in Hebrew, the rabbis came to a different conclusion—that the best understanding of the term *Yirat Adonai* is the idea of awe and reverence for God that motivates us to do His will.[2]

> Fearing God's punishment is also understood to be an incomplete and inferior understanding of the term Yirat Adonai (fear of the Lord). At its core is self-centeredness—what will happen to me because of God's knowledge of my deeds?

God has called us to keep our focus on Him. Jesus said:

"I tell you, my friends, do not be afraid of those who kill the body and after that can do no more. But I will show you whom you should fear: Fear him who, after the killing of the body, has power to throw you into hell. Yes, I tell you, fear him."—Luke 12:4–5

After this stern warning, Jesus then reassured His listeners—and us—with these beautiful words: not a sparrow falls, or a hair of our head is lost, without God's knowledge.

> Not a sparrow falls, or a hair of our head is lost, without God's knowledge.

"Are not five sparrows sold for two pennies? Yet not one of them is forgotten by God. Indeed, the very hairs on your head are all numbered. Don't be afraid; you are worth more than many sparrows."—Luke 12:6–7

When we love God and obey Him, His incredible power is used for us, not against us. We stand in fear and awe of God, not because He will destroy us, but because He loves us. We are important to Him!

"Therefore I tell you, do not worry about your life, what you will eat or drink; or about your body, what you will wear. Is not life more important than food, and the body more important than clothes? The pagans run after all these things, and your heavenly Father knows that you need them. But seek first his kingdom and his righteousness, and all these things will be given to you as well."—
Matthew 6:25, 32–33

Anxiety caused by a fixation with acquiring wealth or worldly wisdom in order to gain or protect worldly treasures reflects a lack of trust in God (see Matthew 6:19–21, 25–33). Such anxiety is not productive: can worrying add an hour to your life, or anything to your height? (see Matthew 6:27; Luke 12:25). This sort of anxious grasping can be likened to the pursuit of the pagans who do not know that God is aware of their needs. But those who put God's Kingdom-matters first not only have their needs met, but receive God's gifts, including the Kingdom.

> Anxiety caused by a fixation with acquiring worldly wisdom in order to gain or protect worldly treasures reflects a lack of trust in God...this sort of anxious grasping can be likened to the pursuit of the pagans who do not know that God is aware of their needs.

The Bible records six times Caleb *hath fully followed the Lord*, writes Bible teacher Henry Lockyer. "What magnificent adverbs are used to describe Caleb. He followed faithfully, wholly, fully. He never lowered his standards, but was perpetually wholehearted." Faith cannot be full without steady, enduring fellowship with the Lord.

As you focus on spiritual matters, God will take care of all of your homeschool needs. He will give you the energy, resources, and opportunities to teach your children what they need to know for their unique future. You need only to trust Him: His thoughts are so much more far-reaching, so much more fertile, so much higher than your own.

> As you focus on spiritual matters, God will take care of all of your homeschool needs. He will give you the energy, resources, and opportunities to teach your children what they need to know for their unique future.

"For my thoughts are not your thoughts, neither are your ways my ways," declares the LORD. "As the heavens are higher than the earth, so are my ways higher than your ways and my thoughts than your thoughts. As the rain and the snow come down from heaven, and do not return to it without watering the earth and making it bud and flourish, so that it yields seed for the sower and bread for the eater, so is my word that goes out from my mouth: It will not return to me empty, but will accomplish what I desire and achieve the purpose for which I sent it.—Isaiah 55:8–11

Read this powerful passage again. Commit it to memory. His thoughts and ways are far superior to our thoughts and ways. His Word will accomplish what He says it will. God's word is like rain that waters the earth and brings it to abundant vegetation. God's Word bears fruit! His Word brings forth spiritual life accomplishing His purpose! Those who wait on God will share in a harvest of everlasting joy! (This illustration is examined further in the Weather unit study).

Waiting on God

The Bible tells us much about waiting. The word wait is used seventy-six times in the Old Testament, with twenty-five different phases or degrees of meaning, and twenty-one times in the New Testament, with eight different meanings. John Wright Follette includes a study on waiting on God in his book, *Broken Bread*.[3] The many uses of the word wait may be divided and grouped under four general divisions, giving the word four general meanings, discussed below.

Silence

The first meaning of "wait" is silence; to be silent. Silence is rare in our high-tech, fast-paced world. The psalmist made use of this meaning of the word wait:

Truly my soul waiteth upon God; from him cometh my salvation. My soul, wait thou only upon God; for my expectation is from him.—Psalm 62

We are living in an age of intense activity. Our hearts are frequently distressed and burdened. We pray, Lord, give me patience—and I want it NOW! But contrary to what we might think, being silent before God is not wasted time. This time is needed now more than ever for proper adjustment to Him, to get our vision properly focused, our hearts hushed, and our minds subdued. When we quietly wait in His presence, we can hear Him whisper to us.

Expectation and Hope

The second meaning of "wait" is expectation and hope. Twenty-two times we find this use of the word in the Scriptures. To wait upon God means to expect something from God. A real "waiting meeting," according to Scripture, is an "expectation meeting." It implies dependence on Him. How necessary it is today that we wait upon God—and expect to receive from Him! We want to be self-sufficient, but this desire is contrary to the teaching of the Word. If we will submit to His orders, He will reduce us and strip us of all of our self-sufficiency, until, with the psalmist of old, we cry, "My expectation is from him" (Psalm 62:5).

To Watch, Observe, and Take Notice

The third meaning of "wait" is to watch, observe, and take notice. This means that all our spiritual senses must remain expectant. To wait means that we are to be near to God, in His Word and in prayer; and to be still means that we become sensitive enough to catch the faintest whisper and be able to quickly discern His voice. This meaning is clearly shown in Proverbs 8:34:

Blessed is the man who listens to me, watching daily at my doors, waiting at my doorway.

He who tends a fig tree will eat its fruit and he who looks after his master will be honored. — Proverbs 27:18

Proverbs 27:18 is referring to a person, maybe a servant or soldier, who is waiting at a door or gate. He does not know the moment when his master will open the door to require his service, or perhaps to give him a gift. Be it one or the other, it does not matter to the waiting man. His duty is to wait—to watch or to take notice.

We will not watch long or keenly observe the movements of God for a great length of time before He has some word for us. We will hear Him as He bids us to come or go on some mission; or to speak, write, pray, or visit someone; or even to sing for Him. Why? Because we are near enough to feel what is on His heart, and so we are able to enter into fellowship with Him in service.

Many people do not understand the movement of God in the world as He is speaking to us in present conditions, because they are not near enough or still enough to observe Him. We have seen, and continue to see, God's hand in it all; and because of a peculiar and holy response in our hearts, we know that God has risen up and that our redemption draws nigh.

To Serve or Minister

The fourth meaning of "wait" is to serve, or to minister. This meaning is clearly taught in 2 Samuel 23. David had many mighty men, but three among them were chief. What special service made them chief, and not the others? One day when David was being hunted, as he said, like a partridge, on the mountains of Israel (see 1 Samuel 26:20), when he was very far from the throne and only faith could see him as king, the garrison of the Philistines was in Bethlehem. His longing prompted him to say: "*Oh, that someone would get me a drink of water from the well near the gate of Bethlehem!*" (2 Samuel 23:15). It was not a command, but three men heard the wish that had been breathed out of David's heart, and, risking their lives, they broke through the host of Philistines, drew water out of the well by the gate, fought their way back again, and presented the water to David. They were near enough and still enough to hear David's sigh, and that sigh was to them a command.

Such wonderful blessings hang upon this one condition—to wait. Do we wait? Are we silent before God? Is our expectation from Him, or is it from ourselves, our friends, or our circumstances? Do we watch for His movements so that we may serve Him?

Wait for the LORD; be strong and take heart and wait for the LORD.—Psalm 27:14

They that wait upon the LORD shall renew their strength; they shall mount up with wings as eagles; they shall run, and not be weary; and they shall walk, and not faint.—Isaiah 40:31

Look at the four blessings you will receive when you wait on God:

1. Renewed strength!

2. The ability to mount up with wings as eagles!

3. The ability to run and not being weary!

4. The ability to walk and not faint!

Are you prepared wait on God? You are now armed to go into His presence with much to talk about. The Bible has provided you with a list of priorities. I hope you'll discover real power and passion as you pray according to these realities. As a result, may you grow to be more like Christ.

Wait for the Lord and keep his way. He will exalt you to inherit the land. —Psalm 37:34.

Chapter 4

Only Be Strong and Very Courageous

In This Chapter

◆ Three requirements for courage.

◆ Joshua's humility.

◆ Rahab's trust in YHWH.

◆ God uses those who trust Him.

Our third lesson takes us back to the border of the Promised Land, only this time we are fast-forwarding to forty years after the story of the twelve spies. The Jews were weary from forty years of wilderness wanderings; but God would give them rest in the Promised Land. When Moses instructed the people, he told them: "*You have not yet reached the resting place and the inheritance the LORD your God is giving you*" (Deuteronomy 12:9). This Promised Land rest is a picture of the rest that Christian believers experience when they yield to Christ and claim their inheritance by faith.

After the death of Moses, the servant of the Lord, Joshua became the leader of God's people. Joshua had grown in his faith and leadership abilities—and God promised to be with him: "*As I was with Moses, so I will be with you*" (Joshua 1:5).

Charles Stanley explains the Lord spoke to Joshua three times about courage:

> This Promised Land rest is a picture of the rest that Christian believers experience when they yield to Christ and claim their inheritance by faith.

1. *"Be strong and courageous, because you will lead these people to inherit the land I swore to their forefathers to give them"* (Joshua 1:6).

2. *"Be strong and very courageous. Be careful to obey all the law my servant Moses gave you; do not turn from it to the right or to the left, that you may be successful wherever you go"* (Joshua 1:7).

3. *"Have I not commanded you? Be strong and courageous. Do not be terrified; do not be discouraged, for the LORD your God will be with you wherever you go"* (Joshua 1:9).

Note the three things that required Joshua to have courage:

1. To make decisions that affected the people under his leadership;

2. To keep the laws and commandments, even as changes were occurring; and

3. To remember continually that the Lord was with him, the implication being in spite of what circumstances might indicate to the contrary.[1]

Matthew Henry comments on God's words to Joshua:

Only be strong and very courageous. And he concludes with this (v. 9): *Be strong and of a good courage; be not afraid, neither be thou dismayed.* Joshua had long since signalized his valor, in the war with Amalek, and in his dissent from the report of the evil spies; and yet God sees fit thus to inculcate this precept upon him.

Those that have grace have need to be called upon again and again to exercise grace and to improve in it. Joshua was humble and low in his own eyes, not distrustful of God, and His power, and promise, but diffident of himself, and of his own wisdom, and strength, and sufficiency for the work, especially coming after so great a man as Moses; and therefore God repeats this so often, "*Be strong and of a good courage; let not the sense of thy own infirmities dishearten thee; God is all-sufficient. Have not I commanded thee?*"

[1.] "I have commanded the work to be done, and therefore it shall be done, how invincible so ever the difficulties may seem that lie in the way." Nay,

[2.] "I have commanded, called, and commissioned, thee to do it, and therefore will be sure to own thee, and strengthen thee, and bear thee out in it."

Note, when we are in the way of our duty we have reason to be strong and very courageous; and it will help very much to animate and embolden us if we keep our eye upon the divine warrant, hear God saying, "Have not I commanded thee? I will therefore help thee, succeed thee, accept thee, reward thee." Our Lord Jesus, as Joshua here, was borne up under his sufferings by a regard to the will of God and the commandment he had received from his Father (John 10:18).[2]

How does this story relate to homeschooling in a practical way? The book of the Law was Joshua's guide, his instruction book in godly living, and so the Bible is for us today. Through God's Word, He leads us, warns us, comforts us, and assures us. When we pray and seek direction, we should ask God to speak to us through His Word and give us advice to clarify our direction. As we meditate upon the Word with our request or decision in mind, God will often lead us to a specific Bible story, a passage, or even a single verse that will show us the way. It is our job to ask and then listen.

Joshua Sends Spies

> Rahab was motivated by a sincere fear of God and a belief that He would cause the children of Israel to be victorious over her city.

Joshua's first step was to secretly dispatch two spies into enemy territory—and they wound up in a prostitute's chamber! (Possibly because nobody would suspect them there.) Rahab was an unlikely hero—she was a harlot living in the wall of the city. But she showed more faith in the God of Israel than the ten spies had previously. In fact, she trusted in the God of Israel more than she trusted her own king, the king of Jericho.

When the king's men came looking for the spies, Rahab hid them from the soldiers and then helped them to escape from Jericho by sliding down a rope from a window of her home (which was built against the city wall). Rahab was motivated by a sincere fear of God and a belief that He would cause the children of Israel to be victorious over her city. She had asked the men to swear to her that they would spare her family when they returned (see Joshua 2:12–13, 17–18). She later tied a crimson cord to her window to signal the Hebrews when they returned to conquer the city, so that they would remember her favor and not harm her or her family. God promises peace, healing, direction, comfort, and an attitude of praise to those who have faith in Him (see Isaiah 57:18–19).

Interestingly, both Joshua (the great leader of God's chosen people) and Rahab (a foreigner and a harlot) received similar rewards of God's peace, comfort and direction.

Joshua understood miracles, after following God on trails all the way from the Exodus through forty years in the desert. His faith was undeniably strong. But Rahab had only heard what God had done for Israel at the Red Sea, and she demonstrated an astonishing faith by receiving the spies and sending them out another way. The Bible includes many stories of Gentiles who had faith in God. God accepts each person as he is, whether a foreigner or from a Hebrew bloodline, if they have faith in Him, and He brings them all together in the New Covenant. Those who were

> It is unimaginable that God would give His Son to die for us and not leave us directions on how to live our lives in a way that is pleasing to Him.

once excluded from citizenship in Israel and who were foreigners to the covenants of the promise, without hope and without God in the world, have now been brought near through the blood of Christ (see Ephesians 2:12–13). Many scholars believe that Rahab later became the wife of Salmon, a prince of the tribe of Judah and that she was part of the lineage of Christ (see Ruth 4:21; 1 Chronicles 2:11; Matthew 1:5).

The message is, God uses those who trust in Him, no matter what their bloodline, their position, their gender, or their past. He will use you when you trust Him. Rahab's faith was based on who *God* was, not who *she* was. Don't ever, ever, ever let who you are keep you from discovering who God is!

Many homeschoolers today, trapped by fear in the wilderness of overachieving, need a new beginning. After forty years of wandering in the wilderness, Israel claimed her inheritance and enjoyed the blessings of the land that God had prepared for her, as the days of heaven upon the earth (see Deuteronomy 11:21). God wants us to experience these same blessings today. Jesus Christ, our Joshua, wants to lead us in conquest and share with us all the treasures of His wonderful inheritance. *He has blessed us...with every spiritual blessing in Christ* (Ephesians 1:3), but too often we live like defeated paupers.[3]

> Jesus Christ, our Joshua, wants to lead us in conquest and share with us all the treasures of His wonderful inheritance.

The mature Christian understands that God has a purpose for his life. God has a purpose—a reason, an intention, a plan—for *your* life (see Ephesians 2:10). Before you were even conceived, God knew you. He created you! He has a plan for you and each of your children. You may choose your direction in life because you have free will, but God has a specific plan for your life He wants you to follow. You will know you are on the right road when you fully view yourself as a person placed here by almighty God, a person whose life has meaning, and when you begin to seek that meaning. God has a planned path for each of His children, and we must deeply desire to follow that path wherever it leads.

Jeremiah supplies us with encouragement for this journey:

> *"For I know the plans I have for you," declares the LORD, "plans to prosper you and not to harm you, plans to give you hope and a future."* —Jeremiah 29:11

God has clearly revealed His purposes for our lives throughout the Bible. It is unimaginable that God would give His Son to die for us and not leave us directions on how to live our lives in a way that is pleasing to Him. We are not our own; we have been purchased with a price (see 1 Corinthians 6:19–20). Our loving Father has a perfect plan for each of us, and He reveals this plan in His Word. (Isn't it amazing how many people who know that the Bible reveals God's plans don't even bother to read it?)

> God accepts each person as he is, whether a foreigner or from a Hebrew bloodline, if they have faith in Him, and He brings them all together in the New Covenant.

> *For we are God's workmanship, created in Christ Jesus to do good works, which God prepared in advance for us to do.*—Ephesians 2:10

We were all born with talents (see Psalm 139:13–18), and then we received further gifts when we accepted Christ as Lord. There was a time when we were dead in our sins, a time when we were foreigners to God's promises; we were estranged, excluded, and alienated from God. That was a time of no hope, a time without God. But now, what beautiful words describe our relationship to Him:

> *Remember that at that time you were separate from Christ, excluded from citizenship in Israel and foreigners to the covenants of the promise, without hope and without God in the world: But now in Christ Jesus you who once were far away have been brought near through the blood of Christ.*—Ephesians 2:12–13

When we walk in His wisdom, we can confidently say: *The Lord will fulfill his purpose for me* (Psalm 138:8). Our journey through life may not be an easy one, but it will always be a fulfilling one if we walk in His will. In God's sight, you are *complete in Him* [Jesus Christ] (Colossians 2:10). Even now you are *accepted in the beloved* (Ephesians 1:6).

The Promised Land Is a New Beginning

The Promised Land was the destination, but not the end for the Israelites; the Promised Land was actually just the beginning. Just as the Promised Land is a beginning so is acquiring a heart of wisdom. Once the transformation takes place—within your heart and mind—you begin to view the world with a renewed mind—the mind of Christ. It is then you can go forth to inherit the land and enjoy its blessings.

The wilderness wanderings represent the experiences of believers who do not claim their spiritual inheritance in Christ. The generation that surrendered to fear and rebelled were dead in the wilderness. The generation that experienced a paradigm shift—trusted God—went forth to inherit the land and enjoy its blessings.

Five times Psalm 37 speaks of inheriting the earth or inheriting the land. This Hebrew word for inherit (Strong's number 3423) is *ya-raysh* and means "to occupy by driving out previous tenants and possessing in their place, to seize, to expel..." We need to get to work and take hold of our inheritance! Our inheritance is all that was represented by the Promised Land and more. As believers we inherit the kingdom of God (Matthew 25:34; 1 Corinthians 6:9–10; 15:50; Galatians 5:21; Ephesians 5:5; James 2:5). We inherit salvation (Hebrews 1:14), a blessing (1 Peter 3:9), glory (Romans 8:17–18), and incorruption (1 Corinthians 15:50). Additionally, this is an inheritance that can never be lost (I Peter 1:35)!

Be strong and of good courage, and remember that believers are partakers:

1. Of the inheritance—competency (Colossians 1:12)

2. Of His promise in Christ—salvation (Ephesians 3:6)

3. Of the divine nature through regeneration (2 Peter 2:4)

4. Of the heavenly calling our position in Christ (Hebrews 3:1)

5. Of Christ's sufferings through discipleship (1 Peter 4:13)

6. Of fatherly chastisement through discipline (Hebrews 12:6)

7. Of the glory which is potential (1 Peter 5:1)

It is my prayer that these lessons from Exodus will encourage you:

> *...that your love may abound more and more in knowledge and depth of insight, so that you may be able to discern what is best and may be pure and blameless until the day of Christ, filled with the fruit of righteousness that comes through Jesus Christ to the glory and praise of God.*—Philippians 1:9

Let us begin the renewing of our minds by moving to the next section: Rethinking Education.

Suggested Reading

Gaining Confidence to Teach: Forty-Two Confidence Builders to Encourage Christian Homeschoolers by Debbie Strayer ⊶

Reading the pages of this book made me feel like I do when I've had the opportunity to be with Debbie in person—I immediately felt the warmth and concern and encouragement. Debbie speaks from her heart to deal with topics such as the call to homeschool, relatives, support groups, test results, curriculum, relationships, facing changes, and enduring trials. This is a much-needed homeschool book.

Waiting on God by Andrew Murray ⊶

This is a powerful little book by the best-selling author Andrew Murray. He addresses one of the most difficult lessons of the Christian life—how to patiently wait on God. Here you will discover how God's presence and love can refresh the weary heart when one waits on Him. Murray's thirty-one heartfelt meditations are life-changing. His writings help renew our vision and quicken our desire to turn to the Lord for His quiet, peaceful strength. With Murray's insights you will learn to make waiting on God a true joy in your life.

The Kneeling Christian by an unknown Christian ⊶

My Grandmother gave me this book soon after I became a Christian. I read it over and over, amazed at the source of power available to us through prayer. Prayer, communication with the Creator of the universe, must be a central part of our day to prepare us for daily life. I urge you to spend time reading this book aloud with your family. Since its first publication, *The Kneeling Christian* has helped hundreds of thousands of believers discover the key to God's treasure house of blessing. This classic book on prayer, written by "An Unknown Christian" sometime before the 1930's, answers the most basic and often-asked questions Christians have about prayer: "How shall I pray?" "What is prayer?" "Must I agonize?" "Does God always answer prayer?" "Who may pray?" All real growth in the spiritual life—all victory over temptation, all confidence and peace in the presence of difficulties and dangers, all repose of spirit in times of great disappointment or loss, all habitual communion with God—depends upon the practice of secret prayer.

Section 2

Rethinking Education

In This Section:

This section considers the foundation of Christian education by defining wisdom and education, and by exploring the roots of our educational methods from ancient times until today. We also examine the difference between Christian and secular worldviews, and Hebrew and Greek worldviews, with an appeal to return to biblical methods.

Chapter 5

What is Education?
What is Wisdom?

In This Chapter

◆ We need a paradigm shift in our thinking about education.

◆ Man's initial search for wisdom.

◆ The primary purpose of education.

◆ Christ our Wisdom.

In Section One of this book I described a paradigm shift that took place in my thinking about my abilities and God's provision, relative to homeschooling my children. In this section I will present another necessary paradigm shift—the way we look at education.

In paradigm theory, it is taught that how we perceive reality is dependent on the way we have been programmed. If you have been homeschooling for any length of time, you will begin to see this as it relates to the topic of education. A paradigm of school would include the basic assumptions, values, goals, beliefs, expectations, theories, and knowledge that a community had acquired about school.

We all have underlying assumptions that affect how we think about education and many other areas of our lives. For example, think about the traditional Thanksgiving meal. Do you assume that turkey, cranberry sauce, and pumpkin pie were on the table of the first Thanksgiving? If you answered yes, you assumed wrong. Your preconceived ideas about Thanksgiving have been shaped by traditions which were reinforced by the entertainment and news media, retailers and public school—in other words, by our Western culture. The historical fact is that the first Thanksgiving meal did not include squash, cranberry sauce or pumpkin pie; and it's quite possible there was no turkey! John Ahern explains that many of our ideas about this American holiday are false:

> Each Thanksgiving our children draw pictures of Native Americans and Pilgrims sitting around a table: The Native Americans are wearing war bonnets; the Pilgrim men and boys have silver buckles on their belts and shoes, and with knives and forks ready, are posed to eat cranberries and turkey. In reality, although the Pilgrims were surrounded by cranberry ponds, at that time in history the Pilgrims did not eat cranberry sauce. More probably, the hosts and guests shared a common pot that everyone dipped into, because there were no forks in Plymouth. An accurate picture of the feasts should show the slain deer brought by the Native Americans, as well as cod and eel. It is quite unlikely that the Pilgrims, who were simple people, were wearing silver buckles. Historians have found no mention of such items in the Pilgrims' detailed wills. More likely, such buckles were owned by the more prosperous Puritans of the Massachusetts Bay Colony—and the Pilgrims were not Puritans. The Native Americans at this feast did not wear war bonnets, which was the headdress of the Plains Indians. [1]

To clarify, I don't think it's wrong to carry on the Thanksgiving traditions of our parents. About twenty years ago I began my own Thanksgiving tradition, making cookies in the shape of turkeys from chocolate candy, fudge striped cookies and candy corn, for our family and friends. I am proud to say that my daughters still make the same cookies with their children, but it is safe to assume there was no chocolate candy, fudge striped cookies, nor candy corn at the first Thanksgiving!

Second Timothy 2:15 explains the attitude we should have in approaching the Bible: do not assume anything; do not take anything for granted; lay aside any preconceived notions:

> *Do your best to present yourself to God as one approved, a workman who does not need to be ashamed and who correctly handles the word of truth.*

God requires us to think about the way we do things, to become Christ-like in our attitudes and clear in our beliefs. Sometimes, because we assume one kind of answer, we are blinded from seeing other possible ways of responding; we are blocked by our preconceived notions.

This investigation of our educational assumptions will help us to see if we are on God's path. You have now taken a giant step in this direction by choosing to investigate homeschooling. Once you took the step to consider homeschooling, you abandoned the assumption most people have that public or private school is the best way to receive an education. However, we all have other assumptions about school and education which also have a great impact on how we teach our children.

Throughout this section I hope to inspire you to take a fresh look at education with a focus on the advantages and benefits of returning to the ancient paths revealed in the Bible (Jeremiah 18:15). I will show you how to build a strong foundation on the Rock, Jesus Christ. To do this, you will first need to examine history, various worldviews, and traditional teaching methods with new eyes, to renew your mind concerning education.

Understanding Historical Culture and Language

In addition to understanding our preconceptions concerning the Bible, we too must understand the culture and language of the time. Let us look at an example of understanding the culture of a different time period. Why, for example, did Yankee Doodle stick a feather in his hat and call it macaroni? What do feathers in a hat have to do with pasta? Have you ever wondered about this folk song?[2]

The answer is understanding the culture and language of the pre-Revolutionary time period in American history. This famous song was a put-down of the Americans, penned by the British. American troops wore ragged farm clothes while fighting against the decked-out British Red Coats. During this time there was a fashionable group known as "the Macaronis," who dressed and spoke in an outlandish manner. Anything that was fashionable was considered "very macaroni." The word macaroni came to denote the people who dressed in high fashion, with stripes and tall, powdered wigs with a little hat on top. So macaroni meant fancy and overdressed, and also implications of one being a slave to fashion and overly concerned with appearance. A "doodle" was a country bumpkin. The pony was a knock too, because a "real" man would be riding a horse, not a pony. In summary, the country bumpkin stuck a bird feather in his hat and believed that this addition made his hat stylish. The Americans took the song and made it their own; apparently their way of thumbing their noses at the British!

As we scrutinize education, wisdom, and worldviews throughout this section, we will be doing so through the magnifying glass of Bible hermeneutics. Hermeneutics comprises all the rules, principles, theories, and methods of interpreting the Bible. Differences in understanding can be greatly reduced when we examine Scripture hermeneutically and look seriously at the nature of the writings, the situations from which they were taken and the purposes for which they were written.

Looking to the Hebrews in the Bible

Today it is popular to look back to traditional methods for better methods. Some look back to the ancient Greeks and some look back to the Puritans. We will examine the ancient Hebrew world in which Christianity was first planted, and uncover the roots of our American ideas and assumptions about education. You may be somewhat surprised by some portions—surprised due to preconceived notions that anything having to do with the Jews has to do with legalism and nothing to do with Christianity—so, I encourage you to keep an open mind. As I use the term Hebrew throughout this book, it is a reference to the Hebrews in both the Old and New Testaments. Although the Hebrews were not always in harmony with God's will, God used both their obedience and disobedience to teach them, and both are examples from which we can learn. Please prayerfully pursue this study and set aside any preconceived assumptions that could prevent you from learning about—and benefiting from—our rich Hebrew heritage.

Studying Scripture from our Western/American/Greek view is like looking for gold in a dark mine with a dim pen light—you can see enough to stumble around but you need more light to see clearly. A good grasp of ancient Hebraic customs and terminology will enable you to reexamine Scripture in a more powerful floodlight, exposing intricate details and treasures. [3]

Striving for Balance

The historical Church is rooted in ancient Greek culture and thought; therefore, much of what you will learn in this section promotes the study of our Hebrew roots in order to gain a more comprehensive and balanced understanding of our faith. An almost exclusive focus on Greek ways has led to unbalanced perceptions about the Bible. We need to examine this problem—in balance—and not go too far in the other direction.

I can compare this dilemma with the quandary between biblical teachings on submission and the woman's liberation movement. The women's lib movement came about partially from a false teaching that biblical submission equals slavery. True biblical submission is being taught in the Church today to correct this unbalanced view. However, there are times when the teaching goes too far in the the other direction and women are treated like doormats.

God has a plan for the harmonious functioning of the family. The Bible is clear that women are to be submissive to their husbands and that their husbands are to be submissive to God. A balanced teaching includes the command that men are to love their wives as Christ loves the Church—sacrificially, giving honor to their wife as to the weaker (more fragile and valuable) vessel. When complete and balanced views of biblical marital roles are practiced, the fruit will be seen in both husbands and wives as they demonstrate love, joy, peace, and kindness. When an unbalanced view of submission is practiced, the fruits can lead to abuse, fear, guilt, rigidity, defensiveness, and discouragement.

When we recognize the amount of pagan Greek philosophy in the Church today, a commitment to study and to understand the Hebrew roots of our faith will bring back a proper perspective. When a balanced view of our Hebraic roots is understood the fruit will be love, joy, peace, and kindness, and motivation to be a better disciple of Christ. When an incomplete and/or unbalanced view of our Hebraic roots is accepted, the fruit will be likely at one extreme; rigid legalism (Judaizing); or at another extreme anti-Semitism, avoidance, animosity, hostility, prejudice, etc.

Please pray before and during your reading of this section. Ask God for wisdom and understanding, and B-A-L-A-N-C-E! Ask Him to help you set aside your preconceived ideas and assumptions, and to give you vision that seeks truth.

What is Wisdom?

Scripture defines two types of wisdom. The wisdom of God is all pure, undefiled, peace-loving, considerate, gentle, willing to yield to reason, full of compassion and good fruits; it is wholehearted, straightforward, impartial and free from doubts, wavering, and insincerity, and is shown by a good life and deeds done the humility that comes from wisdom. Superficial, worldly wisdom is full of selfish ambition, confusion, jealousy, disharmony, pride, and all sorts of evil practices. As James gives us a choice between the two, will it be God or the world?

> When the fruit of wisdom is pride it is false wisdom—wisdom of the world.

> *Who is wise and understanding among you? Let him show it by his good life, by deeds done in the humility that comes from wisdom. But if you harbor bitter envy and selfish ambition in your hearts, do not boast about it or deny the truth. Such wisdom does not come down from heaven but is earthly, unspiritual, of the devil. For where you have envy and selfish ambition, there you find disorder and every evil practice. But the wisdom that comes from heaven is first of all pure; then peace-loving, considerate, submissive, full of mercy and good fruit, impartial and sincere. Peacemakers who sow in peace raise a harvest of righteousness.—James 3:13.*

To most people, wisdom is academic ability. Learning and education are viewed purely as pursuits to prepare one for an occupation. There is the possibility of pride and arrogance in academic achievement, when it is viewed as a status symbol (we've all seen the bumper stickers depicting honor roll students). When the fruit of wisdom is pride it is false wisdom—wisdom of the world.

We do not dare to classify or compare ourselves with some who commend themselves. When they measure themselves by themselves and compare themselves with themselves, they are not wise.—2 Corinthians 10:12.

The Bible presents man as a unified whole, never separating academic learning from spiritual wisdom. The Hebrews did not recognize secular occupations nor sacred ones; every Hebrew views their "God-given vocation—whether it be that of farmer, herdsman, fisherman, tax collector, teacher or scribe—as a means of bringing glory to God by the very privilege of work itself."[4] This aspect of Hebrew thought is clearly stated in the words of the psalmist: "*I have set the LORD always before me*" (Psalm 16:8). The ancient Hebrews viewed study not as a status symbol but as a form of worship. In the Introduction to *Wisdom: An Internet-Linked Unit Study*, I give the following parable.

Wisdom Parable

Once upon a time there was a village far away in a remote location, which had experienced a hard year of severe weather. A group of missionaries worried that the villagers' crude huts would not be able to withstand the strong weather any longer. The missionaries wanted to help by taking supplies to the village, but there were no accessible roads for a car trip and there was no landing field for a plane.

The missionaries decided to have a small plane air-drop supplies over the area until they could get there themselves. They sent food and tools (shovels, saws, hammers, screwdrivers, etc.). The missionaries hoped that the villagers would use the tools to build new homes sturdy enough to resist the rough weather.

It took several months to repair the necessary roads to get to the village. Once the missionaries arrived, they noticed that the villagers had rebuilt the same crude handmade huts. They were surprised to see tools tied on the tops of stakes about eight feet tall in front of each new hut. The tools were badly rusted and had never been used. Instead of working with the tools to build new homes, the tools became a status symbol; the villagers worshiped them. The villager with the most tools hung over his hut was viewed with awe and admiration.[5]

In this parable the tools represent credentials. Academic subjects studied in school and colleges are tools meant to help a person in life. A Christian should use these tools to better himself and to become the person God wants him to become—a wise person. When one has an unbalanced view of education, the tools are viewed as the end result instead of an apparatus to be used to reach the goal. A diploma on a wall or the ability to recite facts is not wisdom; the ability to change someone's opinion with a logical argument is not wisdom; and the ability to speak several languages or read philosophical literature is not wisdom.

Scripture often uses the words knowledge, understanding, and wisdom interchangeably, but occasionally they are spoken of as though they are separate and distinct. Thus, it may be useful to attempt to define the differences in their meanings: Knowledge is recognition of the facts; understanding is to perceive the meaning of the facts, and wisdom is knowing what to do with the knowledge.

> Wisdom begins when man humbles himself before God in reverence and worship and is obedient to His commands.

Those with knowledge are able to collect, remember, and access information. They "know" the Scriptures. God's Word is literally "in them." They are scholars. However, it is possible to have knowledge and yet lack understanding and wisdom; that is, you may have the facts but not comprehend their meanings and/or have no clue as to what to do with them.

When Christian parents begin to consider what sort of educational training would be best for their children, they must first answer a few fundamental questions:

- What is education, really?

- What goals for my child's education should I set—and which ones should take the highest priority?

- What is the purpose of my child's education?

- What do I believe is more important: knowledge or wisdom?

- How best can my child's educational needs be met?

These are not easily answered, but they must be carefully considered if a satisfactory choice is to be made—one that best fits the needs of your child, and follows what the Bible instructs us to do with regard to the education of our children because it is an extremely important matter. The Heart of Wisdom philosophy is unique among educational philosophies in that it causes a paradigm shift: an entirely new way of thinking about education—a complete change in focus from the common educational philosophies in today's American school systems.

Let's consider these important questions in the light of the Heart of Wisdom educational philosophy.

What Is Education, Really?

The definition of *education* is seemingly easily understood: most people believe they know what education means—at least, the way our society commonly defines it. The

> "We must avoid the artificial and unbiblical compartmentalzation of life that keeps religion in one room only and allows secular standards to reign everywhere else."

Random House Dictionary reflects modern society's views of education, providing this straightforward definition of *education:*

...the act or process of imparting or acquiring general knowledge, developing the powers of reasoning and judgment, and generally of preparing oneself or others intellectually for mature life.[5]

America's school systems, along with many Christian parents and teachers, would find this to be an accurate definition. Larry Richards states:

In our society, education implies school.... To teach or to learn, education focuses on knowledge and on the intellect.... School systems teach reading and writing, history and science, business and law, so learners will be "prepared intellectually for the mature life." In our society, teaching is imparting knowledge and processing information; learning is acquiring knowledge and using information.[6]

The key phrase used to define education in the *Random House Dictionary* is: "preparing oneself or others *intellectually* for mature life"[7] (emphasis mine). Our modern educational system certainly prepares students academically for life beyond the classroom—but Christian parents must ask themselves the critical question: Is an academic education all that is needed? What about the emotional—and more importantly—the spiritual education of the child? We are doing our children a grave disservice when we think that the spiritual education they gain from Sunday school classes once a week and vacation Bible school once a year are adequate to prepare them for life as a mature Christian adult.

In biblical times the concept of education was completely different from what modern society perceives it to be. The Hebrews did not separate the child's need for education into categories, such as spiritual, mental, emotional and physical. The Jewish worldview was holistic—one in which mind, body, and spirit functioned together, each part as much in need of education as the others. David Mulligan explains that the Bible teaches that holiness involves the whole life, "We must avoid the artificial and unbiblical compartmentalzation of life that keeps religion in one room only and allows secular standards to reign everywhere else."

The Scripture provides a wonderful example of this concept when it describes how the boy Jesus grew, learned, and matured: *And Jesus grew in wisdom and stature, and in favor with God and men* (Luke 2:52). Jesus Himself, our perfect example in so many other ways, followed the Hebraic model of education as He grew into manhood. He grew in *wisdom*—notice the Scripture does not say intellectual knowledge. Certainly, Jesus became intellectually educated, but the ultimate result of that education was wisdom. He also grew in stature, indicating His physical development; in favor with man, indicating His emotional and social development; and in favor with God through His spiritual education and maturation. *Each of these categories was important in Jesus' life—just as they are in the lives of our children today!*

> The primary purpose of education should be to train the whole person for lifelong, obedient service in the knowledge of God—the same purpose that was in place in Bible times.

In *Train Up a Child: Educational Ideals in the Ancient Worlds*, William Barclay provides insight into the Hebraic educational model, where the primary purpose was to bring about *holiness* in the life of the child, to teach them a lifestyle that was pleasing to God:

> The very basis of Judaism is to be found in the conception of holiness. *"You shall be holy for I the Lord your God am holy." "And ye shall be holy unto Me: for I the Lord am holy, and have severed you from other people that ye might be Mine."* That is to say, it was the destiny of the Jewish people to be different. Holiness means difference [among other things]. And their whole educational system was directed to that end. It has been precisely that educational system which has kept the Jewish race in existence. The Jew is no longer a racial type; he is a person who follows a certain way of life, and who belongs to a certain faith. If Jewish religion had faltered, or altered, the Jews would have ceased to exist. First and foremost, the Jewish ideal of education is the ideal of holiness, of difference, of separation from all other peoples in order to belong to God. Their educational system was nothing less than the instrument by which their existence as a nation, and their fulfillment of their destiny, was ensured.[8]

Therefore, what is true education for the Christian student? A truly biblical education includes more than Bible stories and Scripture memorization—it certainly encompasses those elements, but education is much more—an education based on the biblical model will teach children, first and foremost, how to live a life that is pleasing to God. The spiritual education of the child must be the primary purpose in the mind of the parent or teacher, with the intellectual education placed as a secondary goal.

This is the paradigm shift of the Heart of Wisdom educational philosophy: viewing the spiritual education of our children as fundamental, as the basis upon which all other forms of education—intellectual, social, physical—are founded. This paradigm shift is critical! Luke 6:46–49 explains the difference between the foolish and wise builders—the wise builder begins with a foundation on a rock. Our children's education must begin on the foundation of Christ. We are stewards of our children's minds and talents. We must not neglect the spiritual education of our children in our pursuit to provide them the best intellectual education possible. Without a solid foundation destruction is certain.

Man's Initial Search for Wisdom

The initial search for wisdom recorded in the Bible resulted in the Fall of man and the entrance of sin into the world:

Now the serpent was more crafty than any of the wild animals the LORD God had made. He said to the woman, "Did God really say, 'You must not eat from any tree in the garden'?"

The woman said to the serpent, "We may eat fruit from the trees in the garden, but God did say, 'You must not eat fruit from the tree that is in the middle of the garden, and you must not touch it, or you will die.'"

"You will not surely die," the serpent said to the woman. "For God knows that when you eat of it your eyes will be opened, and you will be like God, knowing good and evil."

> Christ our Wisdom is available to our children—but we must make His teachings, and His educational goals for our children, a priority in our lives.

When the woman saw that the fruit of the tree was good for food and pleasing to the eye, and also desirable for gaining wisdom, she took some and ate it. She also gave some to her husband, who was with her, and he ate it.—Genesis 3:1–6.

Satan promised Eve that her *eyes would be opened*—that she would have so much more of the power and pleasure of contemplation, a larger compass in her intellectual views, a greater vision and insight into the world around her. The serpent spoke as if Eve were shortsighted and narrow in comparison to what she could be if she would only disregard God's command. But partaking of the Tree of the Knowledge of Good and Evil did not bring godly wisdom—it brought the ability to know both good and evil—and guilt, fear, and separation from God.

Eve was deceived by the serpent's lie and attracted to the fruit's alluring but false promise of wisdom. She was faced with the decision to believe either God or the serpent. She chose the serpent. Adam also chose to ignore God's warning and join Eve in believing the serpent rather than the loving Creator who had given him the freedom to choose to obey (see 1 Timothy 2:14). The sins of Adam and Eve were the first in the world, but all of us have sinned since that time (see Romans 3:23). We all have been given the same decision to make: we must choose either to believe our flesh and the wisdom of the world or the wisdom of God.

Both Colossians 2:3 and 1 Corinthians 1:30 explain that Christ is the source of all truth and wisdom; in Him is the secret, hidden treasure of knowledge. When we neglect to feed our spirits and drift away away from God and His ways, the things of this world quickly become desirable to us, but true wisdom comes from giving our attention to the truthful teachings of God's Word.

> *My purpose is that they may be encouraged in heart and united in love, so that they may have the full riches of complete understanding, in order that they may know the mystery of God, namely Christ, in whom are hidden all the treasures of wisdom and knowledge.*
> —Colossians 2:2–3.

> Following the ways of biblical wisdom will help to bring us all into harmony with God, because these ways are in accordance with His will, as revealed in the Bible, and they are pleasing to Him.

> *It is because of him that you are in Christ Jesus, who has become for us wisdom from God—that is, our righteousness, holiness and redemption.*—1 Corinthians 1:30.

The great Bible commentator Matthew Henry once said:

> We prosper when we have clear knowledge of the truth as it is in Jesus....Knowledge and faith make a soul rich. The stronger our faith, and the warmer our love, the more will our comfort be.

> The treasures of wisdom are hid, not *from* us, but *for* us, in Christ. We cannot be built up in Christ, or grow in him, unless we are first rooted in him, or founded upon him.[9]

Can we teach our children the Scriptures, by word and by deed, to the extent that they will be able to recognize evil and automatically—without even thinking about it—turn away? Can we teach our precious ones to automatically respond in kindness to an unkind deed done to them? The encouraging answer is: Yes, we can!

True Wisdom

True wisdom is the ability to judge correctly and to follow the best course of action, based on both knowledge and understanding. If you truly desire to teach your children this wisdom, spend a significant amount of your homeschool time studying and teaching God's Word. You won't be disappointed, for as Hebrews 4:12 declares:

> *For the word of God is living and active. Sharper than any double-edged sword, it penetrates even to dividing soul and spirit, joints and marrow; it judges the thoughts and attitudes of the heart.*

The ultimate desire for Christians should be for their children to have a heart of wisdom—true wisdom from God.

Although academic school requirements are included in the Heart of Wisdom curriculum, the main objective and focus is on learning God's Word and establishing a vibrant and active relationship with God Himself while also developing a love of learning.

> Jesus' role as a teacher and His teaching methods were distinctly Hebrew in nature.

Author Marilyn Howshall explains that we must consider the problems confronting us as Christian homeschoolers:

> We come from a generation that was not taught to learn. Few Christians know how to access the Word of God for themselves, and fewer still know how to access the Lord for themselves in an intimate way. Many parents were, themselves, not given a love of learning as children and are now lacking in purpose, and training their children in the same way.

> With only the raw material of our fragmented lives to work with, we attempt to implement our new godly desires and goals into our existing lifestyles and systems. In so doing, we create an additional problem: burnout! We use the world's methods and means to produce something they were not designed to produce. When we finally accept the truth that the old way will not produce the results we want, we are ready to receive the suggestion of a new way. Now we are ready to learn. That is what a *lifestyle of learning* is all about—a new way, a new system—and a fresh beginning for the entire family.[10]

God's Word promises that wisdom can be attained by all who seek and follow it. Those who keep God's moral and ethical laws will be rewarded with long life, health, possessions, respect, security, and self-control (see Proverbs 3:2–4).

This wisdom begins when man humbles himself before God in reverence and worship and is obedient to His commands.

This is quite different from ancient Greek and contemporary American views of wisdom, sought through philosophy and by using man's rationale to explain the mysteries of the existence of the universe.

Christian wisdom may appear to be foolishness to the people of the world, but it is actually wiser than the philosophies of this age which ultimately will come to nothing. True wisdom is revealed by God and received through His Spirit, and therefore, Christians have the highest and most complete wisdom in Christ:

> For it is written: "I will destroy the wisdom of the wise; the intelligence of the intelligent I will frustrate."

Where is the wise man? Where is the scholar? Where is the philosopher of this age? Has not God made foolish the wisdom of the world? For since in the wisdom of God the world through its wisdom did not know him, God was pleased through the foolishness of what was preached to save those who believe. Jews demand miraculous signs and Greeks look for wisdom, but we preach Christ crucified: a stumbling block to Jews and foolishness to Gentiles, but to those whom God has called, both Jews and Greeks, Christ the power of God and the wisdom of God. For the foolishness of God is wiser than man's wisdom, and the weakness of God is stronger than man's strength.

Brothers, think of what you were when you were called. Not many of you were wise by human standards; not many were of noble birth. But God chose the foolish things of the world to shame the wise; God chose the weak things of the world to shame the strong. He chose the lowly things of this world and the despised things—and the things that are not—to nullify the things that are, so that no one may boast before him. It is because of him that you are in Christ Jesus, who has become for us wisdom from God—that is, our righteousness, holiness and redemption. Therefore, as it is written: "Let him who boasts boast in the Lord."—1 Corinthians 1:19–31

Requirements for Receiving Wisdom

The only real requirement for receiving this kind of wisdom is a true desire to follow and imitate God as He has revealed Himself in Jesus Christ, without self-reliance, and especially not in a spirit of pride:

Let the wise listen and add to their learning, and let the discerning get guidance—for understanding proverbs and parables, the sayings and riddles of the wise. The fear of the LORD is the beginning of knowledge, but fools despise wisdom and discipline.
—Proverbs 1:5–7

The person who diligently seeks wisdom will receive understanding:

For the LORD gives wisdom, and from his mouth come knowledge and understanding. Thus you will walk in the ways of good men and keep to the paths of the righteous.
—Proverbs 2:6, 20

The Fruit of True Wisdom

The wonderful fruits of wisdom are plentiful, and the book of Proverbs describes many of them. In New Testament terms, the fruits of wisdom are the same as the fruit of the Holy Spirit: *But the fruit of the Spirit is love, joy, peace, patience, kindness, goodness, faithfulness, gentleness and self-control. Against such things there is no law* (Galatians 5:22–23).

Let's continue to teach our children the true wisdom that comes from God, and then watch the fruit of that wisdom develop in their lives!

> *The wisdom that comes from heaven is first of all pure; then peace-loving, considerate, submissive, full of mercy and good fruit, impartial and sincere. Peacemakers who sow in peace raise a harvest of righteousness.* —James 3:17–18

The Primary Purpose of Education

> Christ is the source of all truth and wisdom; in Him is the secret, hidden treasure of knowledge.

The primary purpose of education should be to train the whole person for lifelong, obedient service in the knowledge of God—the same purpose that was in place in Bible times. God never changes. He continues to have the same desire for us to know Him intimately.

Our first goal must be to teach our children God's ways and His paths. Homeschooling parents must not become so worried about fractions or spelling that they neglect sitting at the feet of our Master in Bible study and prayer. We can attempt to prepare our sons and daughters for what we discern their gifts to be, but God still may take them in another direction. Only He knows the end from the beginning, and He knows the training they will need for their futures of serving Him.

The teaching and learning of true wisdom can only take place when both teacher and student are operating in humble dependence upon God: *Trust in the LORD with all your heart and lean not on your own understanding* (Proverbs 3:5).

True wisdom acknowledges that the reverence of the Lord is the fountain of life (see Proverbs 14:27). Our ultimate goal in teaching must be to help our children discover God's instructions for life and then respond in loving obedience.

Following the ways of biblical wisdom will help to bring us all into harmony with God, because these ways are in accordance with His will as revealed in the Bible, and they are pleasing to Him. This is a far different calling than the standards set forth by the states with regard to education!

True learning means learning something to a degree that it becomes second nature. The subjects of reading and math are good examples from the academic world; most adults have learned to read without thinking about how to sound out the letters, and most of us know the multiplication tables without having to stop and calculate in our heads. These concepts have become second nature to us. This type of true learning can be applied to all areas of life. Our number-one goal should be to instill God's Word into our children so that it becomes second nature to them.

Christ, Our Wisdom

What does all of this mean for us today as we attempt to develop a Christian view of education? Let's return to the basics: Jesus of Nazareth and how He taught.

Jesus' role as a teacher and His teaching methods were distinctly Hebrew in nature. He sometimes functioned as a prophet, using object lessons to teach moral truths (see especially His driving out of the money–changers from the Temple, as recorded in Matthew 21, Mark 11, and Luke 19). In addition to His role as a prophet, Jesus' role as a Rabbi, or teacher, was the most prominent. Jesus' most frequently used title in the Gospels, Teacher, was used forty-five times, the more specific title of Rabbi being used fourteen of those times.[11] Jesus' heart was to teach the people the ways of God, and He taught the Scriptures with authority.

For the students of Jesus, school did not take place in a traditional classroom, with desks, paper, and pencils. Rather, Jesus taught wherever there was a lesson to be learned—in the fields, on a mountain, along the seashore. He taught people from all walks of life, whatever level they were. People even followed Him from town to town to hear more of His teachings.

Jesus' teaching methods were wide and varied—and they enabled people to learn at many different levels. He taught in parables, or stories, to illustrate a point; He used object lessons to help people understand and remember His teaching; He used dialogue, comparisons (similes and metaphors), poetry, hyperbole, and even puns to teach the lessons He wanted people to learn.

David Mulligan discusses how the Master Teacher learned when He was a child—and how we must teach our children today. Christ our wisdom is available to them—but we must make His teachings and His educational goals for our children a priority in our lives.

> When we speak of Christian education, we must mean, above all else, doing what we can to give our children "the mind of Christ." We must searchingly ask ourselves whether the education we are giving our children would equip them to sit there with Christ [as a twelve-year-old child] at the rabbis' feet and demonstrate anything like the same wisdom He was showing. At that time Jesus was the age of a seventh-grader.
>
> Is there anything in our educational format or standards that corresponds to the wisdom with which Jesus astounded His teachers?

> Once you understand the difference between Christian and secular worldviews, you can better define and shape your own educational purposes and goals.

Or to ask it in another and possibly more telling way: is there anything in the wisdom of Jesus that would guarantee His academic success in another type of educational setting? Would Jesus have been the head of His class if He had to attend the Greek grammar school at Sephoris? What would He have done with Homer, Herodotus, and Aeschylus? Or how would He have fared at the Academy of Plato or the Lyceum of Aristotle? More to the point, how would Jesus do today in our schools? Would He recognize their distinctly Christian orientation? Would He be the student to receive consistently high grade-point averages, graduating *summa cum laude* to the infinite joy of His proud parents?

> "One who acquires knowledge but knows not what to do with it is no more than a donkey carrying a load of books."

If wisdom has anything to do with education, and if Jesus is demonstrating the meaning of wisdom to us, our schools need a serious reworking in their approach to learning. Education as we know it is most certainly knowledge oriented—more now than ever—but knowledge is not the same as wisdom. It has been said in Jewish literature, "One who acquires knowledge but knows not what to do with it is no more than a donkey carrying a load of books."

Do we not want our children to walk through childhood with Christ? He was six, ten, twelve, sixteen...Every age our children are, Christ was that age also—and even then He was wise. Would we not want it said of our children what was said of our Lord—that they are "strong in spirit and filled with wisdom"? Our children do not have to be extraordinary, astonishing their elders—that's not the point—but they should, from their youth up, be pursuing the same path trod by our Lord during His childhood years.

And lest some (the parents of adolescents!) despair, St. Luke tells us the wisdom demonstrated by Christ before He was twelve increased during His teenage years (Luke 2:52). As our Lord matured physically, He matured in wisdom as well. There is a way for our teenagers to walk in this world, but during those wondrous times of adolescence, the roadway of wisdom must be most clearly marked out. That, too, is the task of Christian education.[12]

Christian education seeks to impart the wisdom of God into the lives of young students—but secular education as a whole has an entirely different mission. To understand the contrast between Christian and secular views of education, we next present a brief history of education.

Suggested Reading

Far Above Rubies: Wisdom in the Christian Community by David Mulligan ✍
This book is the foundation for the Heart of Wisdom teaching approach. Mulligan and others on a school board for a Christian school were dissatisfied with the classical curriculum and were looking for better answers. They felt that is not enough simply to borrow a curriculum of the Western tradition and sprinkle it with Christian words. They needed something "more Christian" but didn't know what. This quandary led Mulligan to volunteer to search out God's purpose and standards for education. He found that the question of Christian education is a deep subject, intensely interconnected with Scripture, theology, history and culture. From the courts of Charlemagne to the academy of Plato; from the university of Paris to the Yeshivoth of Yavneh, from the libraries of the Vatican to the spare classrooms of Salem Congregationalist. Along the way he became familiar with Alcuin, Boethius, Cassiodorus, Aquinas, Aristotle, Herodotus, John Milton, Cotton Mather, Jonathan Edwards, and many more.

In this book Mulligan explains that God has appointed wisdom to be the structure, method and goal of our learning and that wisdom is far above all other educational goals, even a good-paying job or socialization. Mulligan's book urges us to return to biblical standards for education, to become a holy generation set afire by truth and inspired for our daily lives, bearing the power to turn the world upside down again. The result of his quest involves several new and unique ideas for Christian education.

He explains that his book is complete but the task is undone, as there is room for expansion—and this is where I came in. I combined many of Mulligan's ideas with popular homeschool methods the outcome is the Heart of Wisdom approach and the book in your hand. His idea of a two-side curriculum base, God's Word and God's world, is the foundation of the Heart of Wisdom approach.

Far Above Rubies is divided into five parts: Part 1, "The Redemptive Setting,"examines true wisdom. In Part 2, "The Historical Setting," he takes a detailed look at the history of education beginning with Christianity and Classicism, and moving on to the ancient Greeks and Romans and Medieval Christendom. In Part III, "The Wisdom Setting," he investigates Christian education, the wisdom tradition, and models for Christian education. Part IV, "The School Setting," he highlights the fine points of educational goals in Scripture, the three gates of learning (knowledge, understanding and wisdom) and an outline for the seven pillars of Christian curriculum. Messenger Publishing.

Reclaiming the Future of Christian Education by Albert Green ✍
Dr. Green has spent over 40 years in Christian education. In this book he explains the true purpose of Christian education is to prepare young people for a complete life under the Lordship of Jesus Christ. *Reclaiming the Future of Christian Education* is a walk through

the philosophical and cultural history of education. It is a call to affirm in the teaching-learning process the central role and validity of God and Truth. The insights in this book are valuable for all teachers. Association of Christian Schools International.

Walking With God in the Classroom: Christian Approaches to Learning and Teaching by Harro Van Brummelen ⌐○
Van Brummelen presents a comprehensive view of teaching and learning while explaining that knowledge is not value-free. The book discusses common views of teaching and presents a Christian alternative. It develops a model of learning based on the biblical view of the person. Written for Christian teachers this book can be used as a college textbook but offers insight to the homeschool parent. Alta Vista College Press.

Wisdom: An Internet-Linked Unit Study by Robin Sampson ⌐○
This unit study was designed for grades 7–12. Suppose you wanted to go to a city in Texas but you were given a map to Florida mislabeled Texas? Following the directions would not work even if you changed your attitude, tried harder or increased your speed. You would still be lost because the map is not the territory; it's merely an explanation of certain aspects of the territory. The problem is that you have the wrong map! Many homeschoolers are following the wrong map on their homeschool journey. They follow the state's standards, curriculum, scope and sequence or SAT benchmarks. This unique unit study is a map to true wisdom. In this study you will learn that true wisdom is understanding and knowing God. The moment we begin to understand and know God—to see His holiness—His purposes, His love love for us—we know who God is so there's never any hesitation to obey Him. This study is one of the most important things you will ever do with your children! Heart of Wisdom Publishing.

Chapter 6

A Brief History of Education

In This Chapter

◆ Education in ancient Greece, Rome and Israel.

◆ Education in the Middle Ages, Renaissance, Reformation, Enlightenment.

◆ Education in America from the Puritans until modern times.

◆ The Modern Return to Classical Education.

It is not possible to provide an exhaustive history of education in just one short chapter, but a brief overview is necessary for an adequate understanding of the importance of a homeschool education for your children. Our public schools are what they are today because of the historical background from which they have sprung. God has a different way—a better plan—in mind for your children.

Education in Ancient Greece

The most influential culture on the education systems present in modern-day America is ancient Greece. The Greek civilization can be traced back to the Iron Age and in the beginning was organized as a loosely joined group of city-states, two of which—Sparta and Athens—later developed distinct philosophies of education at almost opposite ends of the spectrum.

> The most influential culture on the education systems present in modern-day America is ancient Greece.

The Spartan way of life was greatly influenced by its location and citizenship. Three of the most famous philosophers in human history emerged in Greece during this period: Socrates, his student Plato, and Aristotle. All three influenced the educational system of their time, encouraging human wisdom and reasoning skills, argument and rhetoric, and political thought. The classical education approach developed in the Middle Ages is based primarily on the philosophies of these men.

The city of Athens was only a day's journey by foot from Sparta, but the views of each city-state toward education could not have been more different. Athens populace was more of a peaceful, agricultural society, and their lack of insurrection and violence allowed them to pursue a higher form of education. Literacy was extremely important to Athenians, as was higher thinking in realms such as mathematics, literature, art, and philosophy.

Tom Eldridge, author of *Safely Home*, describes the Greek state education:

> The care of children's minds (the most time-consuming responsibility of the family) was turned over to institutions outside the family and often to the state. In the quiet power struggle between the family and the state, the state welcomed the opportunity to train the children of future generations. This trend continued until the public finally came to view public control over education as essential for the future security of prosperity.

> Once a boy reached the age of sixteen, he was to be educated in the gymnasium. It was at the gymnasium the boy would learn to become an athlete, a warrior, and a communicator. The state controlled the system of education to ensure uniformity of doctrine and thought. It is important to note that the very word gymnasium comes from the Greek word meaning excise naked. The word athlete comes from the Greek goddess Athena, the goddess of wisdom, skills, and warfare... Another purpose for the gymnasium was to create an entire nation of soldiers...The final use of the gymnasium was for the development of oratory, which consisted of not only of learning the techniques of voice projection and elocution but emphasized logic and rhetoric... The driving religious philosophy behind the Greek system was the worship of man. Their system did produce great knowledge, but it also produced pride, immorality, nakedness, institutionalism, dependence on government, a militaristic philosophy, and a destruction of family cohesiveness and love. [1]

> It is important to note that the very word gymnasium comes from the Greek word meaning to exercise naked. The word athlete comes from the Greek goddess Athena, the goddess of wisdom, skills, and warfare.

This was the path the Greeks followed. Indeed, their adoration of the naked body, the education of boys in the gymnasiums (where young and old exercised together in the nude), and the tutelage of young boys by older men (other than the boys' own fathers) combined to reap for them the great number of homosexuals for which the Greeks are remembered. In the final stages of this downward trend, children were left standing without the protection and provision of the family. Even custodial care of children became a public instead of a private concern. The role of the family was replaced by the state, and each person lived his life clamoring selfishly for his share of government services and rights.

> ...because of Hellenization, the Greek form of education endorsed by Aristotle could soon be seen in schools throughout the known world.

After the philosophies of Plato and Socrates were popularized, the Greeks moved from a non-familistic culture to an anti-familistic culture, represented by the individual and the state alone. It could be said that the Greek civilization committed suicide. When they destroyed the family, they destroyed the only institution that had any spiritual meaning to it—that contained any meaningful relationships. Without this, there was no reason to bring children into the world. As a result they could not even provide their armies with enough soldiers to protect their civilization. In short, without the family they were dead.

With the rise of Alexander the Great, the process of Hellenization, or the spreading of the Greek way of life, began, especially in areas newly conquered by the leader. Alexander the Great had been strongly influenced by the views of Aristotle, and because of Hellenization, the Greek form of education endorsed by Aristotle could soon be seen in schools throughout the known world.

Education in Ancient Rome

During the time of the Roman Empire, the Christian Church was founded and the first Christian educational philosophies were formed. Early Rome (600–250 B.C.) was primarily an agricultural state and, because of the early Romans' concern about survival and conquest, the education during that time was similar to that which was developing in Sparta—rigid, disciplined, physical, and strongly concerned with all things military. Little formal schooling took place, but a Roman boy who lived during this time could expect to learn farming skills and other crafts and then be introduced into the military training that would often define his identity later in life. Only members of the privileged class during that time had the luxury of studying reading, writing, and history.

However, with the spread of Hellenism, beginning around 300 B.C Greek scholars were becoming more of an influence throughout the Roman world. Rome and Greece had been consistently involved with one another through commerce, but when Rome conquered the Greek city of Tarentum and brought back its citizens as slaves, the Greek influence began to take hold. Some of these slaves were eventually freed, and they began to translate Greek scholarship into Latin, intriguing their Roman neighbors. Soon, the

> The family remained the primary institution of education, and Hebrew fathers considered the education of their children to be their most important responsibility.

study of literature—both Greek and Roman—became highly popularized, and Roman schools were both founded and adapted to incorporate the new disciplines of Greek grammar, literature, and composition.

When Cicero, a lawyer in Rome around 60 B.C, wrote his work on the importance of rhetoric and oration, *De Oratore*, oratory skills became an important part of Roman education. Cicero's idea was to raise up a generation of orators who would influence the government and legal system of the empire for the good—but the effects of his influence lasted much longer than one generation. His emphasis on the ethical character of future orators led to an enduring focus on the virtues of honesty, selflessness, and discipline in education.

Both the Greeks and the Romans have had a profound influence on the educational systems present in America today. As David Mulligan states:

> Where the Roman was practical, the Greek was speculative; where Rome was conservative, the Greek, innovative; where the empire best expressed the Roman spirit, the Greek stressed individuality. The Greek sought after freedom—of thought, of expression, of self-government. His was a world of the ideal. The virtuous man was he who contemplated the unchanging things of the spirit, rising above the animal passions that dominated lesser men. The Greek world expressed itself most clearly in its literature, for there the ideal could be portrayed...The Roman world was a world of actions; the Greek world was a world of ideas.[2]

Education According to the Hebrews

Because Christianity should, ultimately, reflect the culture God designed, it is important to take a look at the history of Hebrew education.

God's promise and instruction to Abraham was very specific in regard to the education of his children:

> *For I have chosen him, so that he will direct his children and his household after him to keep the way of the LORD by doing what is right and just, so that the LORD will bring about for Abraham what he has promised him.*—Genesis 18:19

Abraham and the people of his time were nomadic, meaning they traveled from place to place without permanent lodgings. Education occurred in the home, as children learned important lessons about life, their religion, and vocational responsibilities from their parents. After the children of Israel conquered the Promised Land and began to dwell in permanent dwellings, this system of education continued. The family remained the primary institution of education, and Hebrew fathers considered the education of their children to be their most important responsibility. It was during this time that the Mosaic law and oral traditions of the Hebrews were being meticulously passed down through the generations—and preservation of this history was a father's supreme responsibility.

> Hebrew education was practical—and primarily religious in nature.

Hebrew education focused on religion first— and then on teaching the children a trade they could use later in life. The tribe of the Levites was established by God to help further the religious education of the people. This was the first—and primary—public educational service for the Hebrew people, and it is worth noting that it was religious in nature.

In addition to the Levites (priests), prophets also were raised up by God to teach the people, again with religious themes in mind. The prophets spoke primarily of God's justice, mercy, judgment, and grace, but there were also schools of prophets who were believed to have preserved these prophetic traditions and provided training for future prophets.

Hebrew education was practical—and primarily religious in nature. Children were taught to observe the various religious feasts and festivals, which in turn taught them the history of their people and positioned them to know and remember all that God had done for them. Their educational methods were experiential in nature, allowing children to live life and experience what they were learning to the fullest degree. In addition, memorization and repetition of Scripture and oral traditions helped children learn to read, and firmly implanted the ways of God into their hearts.

The Babylonian exile dispersed the Hebrew people throughout the known world. Because most of the people exiled during this time were from the tribe of Judah, they became known as the Jews. During the exile, the Jews could no longer focus on Jerusalem as the center of their religion, and therefore they began to create meeting places called synagogues in local Jewish communities across the region. These synagogues continued the Hebrew religious education and remained in place until Jesus' day.

Interestingly, the primary purpose of the synagogue was education, not worship. Synagogue leaders were known as scribes and rabbis, educational positions of the day. The word rabbi means "teacher."[3] It is a title of dignity given by the Jews to their doctors of the law and their distinguished teachers. It is

> ...the primary purpose of the synagogue was education, not worship.

sometimes applied to Christ (Matthew 23:7, 8; Mark 9:5; John 1:38, 49; 3:2; 6:25, etc.) Eventually, religious education at the synagogue became compulsory for Jewish boys— and this free elementary education was available to all. Teaching in the synagogue was similar to the instruction the children continued to receive at home: repetition and memorization were of primary importance, and older students studied the *Mishnah*, the

Talmud, and the *Gemara*, all religious writings about the laws that had been given by God to His people.

There was a great decline in the Hebrew education after Alexander the Great took over Jerusalem. Some of those in Jewish society readily embraced Hellenistic culture and began teaching their children in the Greek ways. However, the vast majority of the Jews remained loyal to God, angering the Greeks as they felt this rejection was a form of rebellion. Thus began a cultural war.

The climax of this cultural war can be seen in the mid-second century B.C. (in-between the Testaments). Antiochus Epiphanes issued a decree to ban the teaching and practice of Judaism. The book of the Maccabees describes it: "Not long after this, the king sent an Athenian senator to compel the Jews to forsake the laws of their fathers and cease to live by the laws of God, and also to pollute the Temple in Jerusalem and call it the Temple of Olympian Zeus." (II Maccabees 6:1–2). The horrid Greek persecutions of the Jews triggered the first religious war in history—the Maccabean revolt. Ultimately, the Greeks were defeated and Judaism survived, and the miracle is remembered as the story of Chanukkah.

The Period of the Early Church

The influence on the early Church did not come from the Roman empire but from the Greeks. Roman power and Roman law controlled the military, political, social, and economic life of the empire, but it was the Greek way of thinking that controlled the minds of the people. The Greek philosophers tried to find the meaning of life and the world to come, and to affect the practical life of men in all realms: in politics, law, art, social relations, intellectual knowledge and religion. The influence of Hellenic philosophy can be seen in the lives of well-educated men from the very beginning of the Christian Church. As a result, soon after the time of Christ the early Church turned away from Hebrew teaching methods and began combining Christian education with pagan Greek philosophies.

Encarta Encyclopedia names the some of the doctors (eminent theologians) of the Church as four Western Fathers, including Saints Ambrose, Augustine, Pope Gregory I, and Jerome, and four Eastern Fathers, including Saints Athanasius, Basil, John Chrysostom, and Gregory of Nazianzus. The earlier Eastern Fathers, including Clement of Alexandria, St. Justin Martyr, and Origen, were strongly influenced by Greek philosophy. Clement of Alexandria (c.150-220) brought reason to the support of faith by trying to make Christianity more intellectually respectable.The Western Fathers, however, including Tertullian and Saints Gregory I and Jerome, generally avoided the synthesis of pagan and Christian thought. Tertullian (150–225) wrote, "With our faith, we desire no further belief. For this is our faith that there is nothing which we ought to believe besides." [4]

Philo of Alexandria, a Hellenized Jew, merged Hebrew thought with Greek philosophical thought in the first century. Christian apologists like Athenagoras, Theophilus, Justin Martyr, and Origen followed. Philo was thoroughly educated in Greek philosophy. He had a deep reverence for Plato and referred to him as "the most holy Plato." The split from Jewish roots and the merging of Platonism caused disastrous changes in the Church's understanding of Scripture.

> *No one can serve two masters. Either he will hate the one and love the other, or he will be devoted to the one and despise the other.*—Matthew 6:24.

A good deal of false teaching and incorrect biblical exegesis spread. Paul spent much of his life in the Hellenistic world. He warned the Church about those promoting Greek philosophy. He argued to both Jews and Gentiles that Christ is crucified was the wisdom of God (I Corinthians 1:18–25). By the middle of the second century, Christianity ultimately accepted and used Greek philosophy.[5]. Paul's warnings to the Gentiles about pride in Romans 11 were ignored. From the second through the fourth centuries a spirit of arrogance arose. The Gentiles began to believe that they had replaced Israel.

Kevin Lawson, author of *Historical Foundations of Christian Education*, explains the Greek education methods were used in the early Church schools: By the late second century, some of the catechumenal schools began to expand their curriculum to include higher theological training as well as philosophy, logic, and rhetoric....In 179, Pantaenus became head of the school in Alexandria, Egypt. To this religious instruction he added Greco-Roman philosophy and classic literature as well as other disciplines.[6]

The Christian educational movement grew and gained government support. Justin Martyr, Cyril of Jerusalem, and Augustine of Hippo influenced the catechetical schools. Augustine's reason and faith teachings became the root of the Lutheran and Counter-Reformation catechism. *Encarta Encyclopedia* describes the merge and results:

> The process of reconciling the Greek emphasis on reason with the emphasis on religious emotion in the teachings of Christ and the apostles found eloquent expression in the writings of Saint Augustine during the late 4th and early 5th centuries. He developed a system of thought that, through subsequent amendments and elaborations, eventually became the authoritative doctrine of Christianity. Largely as a result of his influence, Christian thought was Platonic in spirit until the 13th century, when Aristotelian philosophy became dominant. Augustine argued that religious faith and philosophical understanding are complementary rather than opposed and that one must "believe in order to understand and understand in order to believe." Like the Neoplatonists, he considered the soul a higher form of existence than the body and taught that knowledge consists in the contemplation of Platonic ideas as abstract notions apart from sensory experience and anything physical or material.

The Platonic philosophy was combined with the Christian concept of a personal God who created the world and predestined (determined in advance) its course, and with the doctrine of the fall of humanity, requiring the divine incarnation in Christ. Augustine attempted to provide rational understanding of the relation between divine predestination and human freedom, the existence of evil in a world created by a perfect and all-powerful God, and the nature of the Trinity. Late in his life Augustine came to a pessimistic view about original sin, grace, and predestination: the ultimate fates of humans, he decided, are predetermined by God in the sense that some people are granted divine grace to enter heaven and others are not, and human actions and choices cannot explain the fates of individuals. This view was influential throughout the Middle Ages and became even more important during the Reformation of the 16th century when it inspired the doctrine of predestination put forth by Protestant theologian John Calvin. [7]

What was the fruit of the early Christian education merger with Greek philosophy and literature? The catechumenical schools grew in the fourth and fifth centuries; however, they gained reputations as the seedbeds of heresy. Loyalty to the Catholic Church and its doctrines became more important than the study of Scripture.[8]

Education in the Middle Ages

During the Middle Ages, philosophy merged with theology and spawned what we now call the classical educational method that would be the standard of learning for the next one thousand years. David Mulligan sums it up with a family analogy: The Medieval world has parents—Christianity and Greco-Romanism—that did not, could not always agree. The one, Christianity is perfect—no sorting necessary there. But the other, the classical world, was a potpourri of good, bad, false and true. The Middle Ages accepted both parents with equal ease. They sometimes accepted a falsehood with the same loyal obedience as they did the truth. The Middle Ages was a time to search through ancient heritage in order to glean truth. Some children of the Middle Ages went bad, as children will; but others recognized the essential good of their parentage, and only tried to improve on it. [9]

Mulligan goes on to explain the changes the Church had gone through up to the time of the Middle Ages: By the time the Church confronted the issue of education on an institutional level, several important events had occurred:

1. The Church had transferred from Jewish to Gentile soil.

2. The standard of orthodoxy was moving in a more theological direction.

3. The Judaic roots of Christianity were radically de-emphasized as the Gospel message was universalized.

4. The biblical wisdom tradition was exchanged for Greek education.

5. Wisdom was redefined in classical terms.

6. As the Church became more and more Gentile, and less and less Judaic, a church educational system arose. The biblical standards that would have caused friction with the classical paideia [education] had retreated into the distance. The Church had undergone a strange and deadly transformation. [10]

> The Medieval world has parents—Christianity and Greco-Romanism—that did not, could not always agree. The one, Christianity is perfect—no sorting necessary there. But the other, the classical world, was a potpourri of good, bad, false and true. The Middle Ages accepted both parents with equal ease.

Medieval society was divided into three sects—the clergy (priest and monks) who were to pray for all the people; the nobility (nobles and knights), who were to govern and protect them; and the commoners (merchants, peasants, laborers), who were to feed all of them. Basic instructions were given to commoners: Ten Commandments, Seven Deadly Sins, and the Lord's Prayer. The education for nobility included basic reading and writing, military skills, government, religion, and Latin. Those in the schools for the clergy received instruction in reading, writing, arithmetic, prayers, and the Scriptures.

Around 500 the Roman Catholic Church prescribed that boys destined for the clergy should be instructed in the cathedral schools under the supervision of the bishop. The obligation of parish churches and cathedral churches to maintain schools was set forth time after time by church councils and by the Pope. A council held in Rome in 853 decreed that elementary instruction should be given in all parishes and that schools for instruction in the liberal arts should be established in all cathedrals. [11]

Charlemagne (742–814) was king of the Franks and Emperor of the Holy Roman Empire. His educational and religious reforms changed the history of Europe. He required the clergy to improve their ability to read and write and to raise the level of their scholarship in general so that they could write good letters. He thus required schools for teaching reading to be established.[12] Charlemagne required all priests to learn classic Latin. His purpose was to insure that church services were always conducted in the proper form, with correct pronunciation and grammar. The education of the priests also served to provide Charlemagne with a growing number of educated people for his administration, and gave his kingdom a unified written language that could be passed on throughout all of Western Europe.[13] The education system used by Charlemagne's scholars was very similar to that of classic Greek and Roman scholars.

Birth of the Trivium

In the eleventh and twelfth centuries the cathedral schools developed into universities. The sciences of grammar and rhetoric were brought into union with the science of dialectics (logic), and were amalgamated into the seven liberal arts (based on Plato's writings): grammar, rhetoric, dialectics, arithmetic, music, geometry, and astronomy. The first three became known as the Trivium, the remaining four the Quadrivium. The division is derived from St. Augustine. As the universities grew there was more focus on using Aristotle's logical method to understand Church doctrine. In the later Middle Ages many challenged this approach, believing that God is known by faith, not logic. The Hebrews rejected the classical approach, continuing in the biblical method that God had given them.

The Medieval Church used the textbooks from ancient Greece and Rome and never saw a need for writing new ones. That was not because the Church accepted paganism, but because it assumed, in many cases, the basic curricula of certain structures had been worked out in the ancient world and did not need to be written again. The link between theology and the sciences was broken, and man began to work out an understanding and explanation of life that was independent of religion, independent of God. Secularism was born. [14]

In Western Europe during the Middle Ages, education was typically a charge of the Catholic Church: monastic schools and universities were the chief centers of learning. The trend to blend philosophy and religion birthed the movement of Scholasticism, ultimately bringing about such thinkers as Anselm, Abelard, Lombard, and, perhaps the most well known Catholic scholastic, Thomas Aquinas (1225–1274).

Aquinas is considered the most important scholar and thinker of the Middle Ages. He was a philosopher and fundamentally an Aristotelian. His received a secular trivium education that complemented sacred doctrine as learned from the Bible. His writings on theology were somewhat mystical. His suggestions were condemned by a commission appointed by the Bishop of Paris but were later lifted; he was canonized and eventually was given the title of Common Doctor of the Church (patron saint of education). He considered faith and reason both to be reliable forms of knowing; he was one of the first to declare that faith and reason should remain supreme, and he was one of the first to insist that education be available for all people—that it was a basic human right. [15] His Sucamma Theologica was the most comprehensive effort at a synthesis of Aristotelian humanism and biblical thought ever attempted. [16]

The era of Scholasticism did much to forge together the realms of religious faith and scholastic education. David Mulligan describes this relationship, as well as what the decline of these ideas has meant for modern education:

> The Medieval Church regarded right philosophy as the guardian of the realm of reason. The Church was insistent that each department of the philosophical sciences be fully developed so that it formed a boundary to man's intellectual pursuits. Because of this extreme carefulness, the Middle Ages were looked upon with scorn by the Renaissance men who, according to their perspective, named them the Dark Ages. The first modern men ridiculed the era of the Middle Ages for the stifling use of philosophy, and the [secular] man of today ridicules it for having used philosophy at all. The Christian [of today] particularly finds in medieval philosophy a blatant

compromise with the world, a watering down of theology with the humanistic and pagan doctrines of pre-Christian Greece.

> Aquinas was arguably the most important scholar and thinker of the Middle Ages and later became the patron saint of education.

The Medieval scholar would have been surprised to hear that. For him, philosophy was the handmaid of theology, a noble servant who mediated between the natural and supernatural orders of knowledge. "If philosophy is to be destroyed," he would say, "then what is to keep the sciences from creating their own view of the world in opposition to that given by revelation?" And apparently he would have been right, for as soon as philosophy (as the Middle Ages knew it) was discredited, the natural sciences began to take the place of philosophy and ranged themselves as a secular order against the supernatural order of revelation.[17]

Between 1200 and 1500, the Middle Ages melted into the past. Between 1347 and 1350, the Black Death killed 23,840,000 people—nearly one-third of Europe's population. The Hundred-Year War dragged on. Corruption reigned in churches. In 1409, the Council of Pisa decided that the Church did not need the Pope's approval to make binding decisions. The people of Europe were confused about the identity and teachings of true Church. At this time, the Roman Catholic Church taught that only they could understand the Scriptures.

Education in the Renaissance

Between the fourteenth and seventeenth centuries, two milestones occurred in Western history affecting education: the Renaissance and the Reformation. The Renaissance was a cultural movement, a change in the way a number of different disciplines approached their work. It embodied all art forms, the sciences, and philosophy.

The leaders of the Renaissance, which embraced humanism and rationality to the exclusion of the Christian faith, were predominantly educated in the classical manner, with the heavy influence of Greek and Roman philosophers. According to *A History of Christian Education*:

> Renaissance humanists elevated individual human values above the Church. They studied classical literature and culture and sought to revive ancient learning. Humanists rejected medieval asceticism and rejected scholastic Aristotelianism. Yet there were significant differences among humanists. Many humanists, particularly those in Italy, virtually abandoned Christianity in their passion for ancient culture. On the other hand, most humanists in northern Europe were Christians. These Christian humanists also studied Latin, Greek and other ancient languages, but they were interested in biblical and patristic studies as well as the Greek and Roman classics.[18]

As Timothy Paul Jones explains in his book *Christian History Made Easy,* in 1453 the Ottoman Turks seized Constantinople, and by 1460 they controlled most of Greece. Thousands of Greeks went into exile in Christian Europe, where they had an important influence on the European Renaissance.

> Hundreds of eastern schools fled west. They carried with them their most precious possessions—ancient Greek manuscripts. For centuries, Roman Christians had neglected the ancient authors. The manuscripts from the east caused a rebirth—a Renaissance—of interest in ancient Greek rhetoric, art and writing. Renaissance art, like medieval art, portrayed life from a human perspective. Renaissance humanists, like ancient orators, stressed practical language and actions. Poignant words became more important than precise logic.
>
> Christian humanists applied these insights to Scripture. They focused on the original intent and the original language of each biblical text. Much of the rebirth was made possible by a printer named Johann Gutenberg. In 1453 Gutenberg discovered how he could use movable metal type. For the first time, printers could mass-produce books. The price of books plummeted. Greek and Roman classics, as well as Bibles, flooded Europe.
>
> The popes supported classic books and Renaissance art. However, most of them neglected the most important aspect of the Renaissance—the renewed focus on Scripture. Roman bishops came increasingly corrupt. Indulgences remained a booming business. The Spanish Inquisition used the Church's power to persecute myriads of Muslims, Jews, and heretics. Reform became unavoidable.[19]

During this period, John Wycliffe (called the Morning Star of the Reformation) entered the scene. He criticized abuses and false teachings in the Church, urging people to understand the Bible for themselves! Wycliffe was the first person to translate the Bible into English. Pope Alexander V promulgated a bull (made a law), ordering the surrender of all books written by England's John Wycliffe. Bohemia's archbishop publicly burned some 200 volumes of Wycliffe's writings. He was posthumously declared a heretic, and his body was exhumed and burned in 1428.

The Scientific Revolution began in the 1600s with the discoveries of Kepler, Galileo, and others. During this time the worldview of rationalism became prominent. The rationalism wordview is where scientific reason and logical thought is valued over and above everything else including spirituality, religion, and faith.

Education During the Reformation

Several individuals figure prominently in the Reformation period. Martin Luther, a Roman Catholic priest, sparked the Reformation when he nailed his ninety-five theses opposing the Catholic Church on the church door at Wittenberg, Germany, on October

31, 1517. Luther experienced a conversion based on grace through faith, and that truth became a motivation for him throughout his life. Luther stressed a return to the Scriptures as the ultimate authority in the believer's life. This period marked a return to a study of the Scriptures, particularly with the publication of the Greek New Testament by Erasmus.[20]

Luther had the most impact on Christian education during this period. He wanted to keep the cause of God clear of the entanglements of worldly prudence and worldly power. Luther's schools required the study of Greek and Hebrew. He credited his own language skills to his deliverance from the Catholic Church. Luther also promoted singing and required each school to have a cantor. Luther wrote many hymns about the Christian faith. He established vernacular primary schools that offered a basic curriculum of reading, writing, arithmetic, and religion. Luther's educational methods included oral language, an apprenticeship plan to teach trades, the use of catechisms, (primary books that summarized their religious doctrine, in a question and answer format) and other practical approaches. Luther encouraged parents to teach their children to read, to pray together, to read the Bible, study the catechism, and practice a useful trade.

Other reformers began schools during the period of the Reformation. Most had catechisms and hymns. John Calvin (1509–1564), followed Luther's education principles. His theology has been recognized as lying in the Pauline-Augustinian tradition. [21]

The Protestant reformers retained the dual-class school system that had developed in the Renaissance. Vernacular schools provided primary instruction for the lower classes, and the various classical humanist and Latin grammar schools prepared upper-class males for higher education. [22] The Roman Catholic Church responded to the Protestant rebellion by beefing up their own schools. Ignatius of Loyola founded the Society of Jesuits, which had a somewhat militaristic structure. The teachers were skilled in dialogue, debate, speeches, and games. Jesuit colleges and universities were established all over the world and continue to this day.

The Education of the Puritans

The Pilgrims were a small band of English people who came here in 1620 on the Mayflower and settled in Plymouth, Massachusetts. The Puritans refer to a much larger group of English immigrants, led by John Winthrop (1588–1649), who came here ten years later and started the Massachusetts Bay Colony. Both groups left England because of religious persecution and found religious freedom in Holland and then sailed to North America where they could build a new biblical commonwealth. They returned to the Hebrew heritage of the early Church and follow it as a model for teaching their own children. In his book, *Our Father Abraham*, Marvin Wilson explains:

During the period of the Protestant Reformation (in the 16th century), some signs of the re-Judaization of the Christian faith began to surface, as certain Hebrew categories were rediscovered. The Reformers put great stress on *sola scriptura* (Scripture as the sole and final authority of the Christian). The consequent de-emphasis on tradition brought with it a return to the biblical roots. Accordingly, during the two centuries following the Reformation, several groups recognized the importance of once again emphasizing the Hebraic heritage of the Church. Among these people were the Puritans and the leaders who pioneered American education.

The Puritans came to America deeply rooted in the Hebrew traditions, most even bearing Hebrew names. Our Pilgrim fathers considered themselves to be like the children of Israel fleeing "Egypt" (England), crossing the "Red Sea" (the Atlantic Ocean), and emerging from this "Exodus" in their own "Promised Land" (America). The Pilgrims thought of themselves as "all the children of Abraham," and thus, they lived under the covenant of Abraham.

In 1783, the president of Yale College used these words before the governor and general assembly of the state of Connecticut: "Their [the Puritans'] influence on American society was not soon forgotten: More than a century and a half after the first Puritan settlers reached New England, the American people were referred to in a State Assembly as 'God's American Israel.'"[23]

The International Institute for Christian Studies reports: Just as in Europe, with the birth of the earliest universities, the Christian worldview, more than any other system of thought, dominated American intellectual development during the colonial period... Regardless of the vocation for which a student was preparing, the colonial college sought to provide for him an education that was distinctly Christian...If colonial higher education operated from a Christian foundation, it did so primarily because such an intellectual framework also characterized the European institutions that served as models for the colonial college founders.... Thirty-five of the university men in early New England, including a large majority of the Harvard founders, had attended Emmanuel College of Cambridge University.[24]

Education, for the early Puritans, had to have at its heart the purpose of creating character and producing leaders for the New World. The hornbook, Primer, Psalter, and Bible were used as textbooks. The hornbook contained the alphabet, a shortened syllabary, the invocation, and the Lord's Prayer. The Primer was a book of prayers for the laity. What God would work inside of a person was to be processed through his thinking and out into his daily life. The teacher's role was to draw out that which God was putting into the student.

The first colleges in America were founded to spread the Gospel of Christ. One hundred and six of the first 108 colleges were started on the Christian faith. By the close of 1860 there were 246 colleges in America. Seventeen of these were state institutions; almost every other one was founded by Christian denominations or by individuals who vowed a religious purpose.[25] The Bible was their first textbook. In 1636 Harvard students were to follow three rules:

> Education, for the early Puritans, had to have at its heart the purpose of creating character and producing leaders for the New World.

> 1. Students were to consider the main goal of their studies to know God and eternal life through Jesus Christ.

> 2. Recognizing the Lord gives wisdom, every student was to pray and seek wisdom from God.

> 3. Every student and teacher was to exercise reading of the Scriptures twice a day.

Other great universities had similar aims. The president of Princeton said, "Cursed be all learning that is contrary to the cross of Christ." Yale University was started by Congregational ministers in 1701, "for the liberal and religious education of suitable youth…to propagate in this wilderness, the blessed reformed Protestant religion…." Noah Webster wrote, in the preface to the first English dictionary (1828), "In my view, the Christian religion is the most important and one of the first things in which all children, under a free government ought to be instructed."

The first college, Harvard, was established for "Christ and the Church." In his bequest of the first large gift to what is now Harvard University, John Harvard said: Let every student be plainly instructed and earnestly pressed to consider well the main ends of his life and studies; to know God and Jesus Christ, which is eternal life, and therefore to lay Christ in the bottom as the only foundation of all knowledge and learning and see that the Lord only giveth wisdom. Let everyone seriously set himself by prayer in secret to see Christ as Lord and Master. Above Harvard's gates are etched today these words: "After God had carried us safe to New England, and we had built our houses, provided necessities for our livelihood, reared convenient places for God's worship, and settled the civil government; one of the next things we longed for, and looked after was to advance learning, and perpetuate it to posterity; dreading to leave an illiterate ministry to the churches, when our present ministers shall lie in the dust."[26]

Unfortunately, during the 1700s, Harvard University, began moving away from its orthodox Christian roots to become thoroughly Unitarian by the early 1800s.

The Puritans knew that the Greek classical educational system, which was pagan in both origin and tradition, could ruin America. Look at these excerpts written by John Wesley from his sermon *The Education Of Children*:

> And education under Pythagoras or Socrates had no other end, but to teach children to think and act as Pythagoras and Socrates did. And is it not reasonable to suppose that a Christian education should have no other end but to teach them how to think, and judge, and act according to the strictest rules of Christianity?

Let it be carefully remembered all this time, that God, not man, is the physician of souls; that it is He, and none else, who giveth medicine to heal our natural sickness; that all *the help which is done upon earth, he doeth it himself*; that none of all the children of men is able to *bring a clean thing out of an unclean*; and, in a word, that *it is God who worketh in us, both to will and to do of his good pleasure*. But is generally his pleasure to work by his creatures; to help man by man. He honors men to be, in a sense, *workers together with him*. By this means the reward is ours, while the glory redounds to him.

Ye that are truly kind parents, in the morning, in the evening, and all the day beside, press upon all your children, *to walk in love, as Christ also loved us, and gave himself for us*; to mind that one point, *God is love; and he that dwelleth in love, dwelleth in God, and God in him.*[27]

John Wesley often quoted William Law. Review the excerpt below from Law's writing, *A Serious Call to a Devout and Holy Life*, first published in 1728. In all of the Puritan writings, God—not academics—is the primary source of wisdom.

Devotion is neither private nor public prayer; but prayers, whether private or public, are particular parts or instances of devotion. Devotion signifies a life given, or devoted, to God.

He, therefore, is the devout man, who lives no longer to his own will, or the way and spirit of the world, but to the sole will of God, who considers God in everything, who serves God in everything, who makes all the parts of his common life parts of piety, by doing everything in the Name of God, and under such rules as are conformable to His glory.

We readily acknowledge that God alone is to be the rule and measure of our prayers; that in them we are to look wholly unto Him, and act wholly for Him; that we are only to pray in such a manner, for such things, and such ends, as are suitable to His glory.[28]

The Age of Enlightenment

Education in the 17th and 18th centuries began to reveal a trend away from the religious roots of the Puritans and back toward Greek philosophy. The Enlightenment was a term used to describe a new vision based on the inferred reliability of human reason and the scientific revolution in Europe and the American colonies before the French Revolution. Philosophical rationalists René Descartes and Baruch Spinoza, the political philosophers Thomas Hobbes and John Locke, new discoveries in science and the spirit of exploration and discovery ushered in the idea the men were emerging from centuries of darkness and ignorance into a new age enlightened by reason, science, and a respect for humanity.

Enlightenment rationalism created a climate of skepticism toward Christianity. The claims of the Bible were made subject to the scientific method of proof. A division developed between faith and reason. Religion was considered blind and ignorant superstition, while science attempted to explain away God's position in nature.

With the expansion of science, philosophers finally began to openly condemn the authority of the Church and engage in what became known as "free thought." In this era the rationalist optimistically anticipated that the darkness would be dispelled and reason would oversee all human activity, religious, civil, and artistic.

The goal of education shifted from biblical understanding to achieving success in life, particularly economic success.[29] Unbelievers discarded the concept of sin as irrelevant. In this godless view there are no sins, only sicknesses, misfortunes, mistakes, or the outworking of one's environmental, hereditary and biological input (Western terminology) or of one's fate or karma (eastern). Alternatively, sin is acknowledged to exist, but only as defined in one's culture—cultural relativism thus negates the biblical concept of sin as absolute wrong. [30]

Modern Education

Two radical events took place in 1859. Charles Darwin published his work titled *The Origin of Species,* and John Dewey (1859–1952) was born.

> *For certain men whose condemnation was written about a long ago have secretly slipped in among you. They are godless men, who change the grace of our God into a license for immorality and deny Jesus Christ our only Sovereign and Lord.* (Jude 4)

Darwin introduced the myth of evolution and Dewey introduced pragmatism into the American public school system at turn of the twentieth century. Pragmatism argues that the best way to determine whether or not to embrace a certain proposition is not by its truthfulness but by its usefulness. Essentially, it makes no difference if the proposition you are considering is true or moral; the important thing is whether or not it works. Education that was once devoted to perpetuating truth changed into shaping minds for the supposed betterment of society. The philosophy of pragmatism and expedience began to infiltrate our school systems and affect the mindset of educators throughout the country.

Pragmatism was formulated by Charles Pierce (1839–1914) and popularized by William James (1842–1910) but it had its roots in the Greek thinking of Heraclitus (ca. 540–470 B.C.). He wrote: "All things flow; nothing abides. One cannot step twice into the same river. Into the same rivers we step and do not step; we are, and we are not." Because of the philosophy that everything is in a constant state of change, the studies of science and mathematics became more appealing as a way to control, or at least understand, the constant change in the universe.

Pragmatism is a form of radical empiricism (the view that experience, especially of the senses, is the only source of knowledge). It postulates that reason alone cannot be a source of knowledge, because knowledge is derived from experience such as discernable facts and actions rather than from logical proofs or abstract principles.

> The public schools are the way they are today because of the historical background from which they have sprung.

Pragmatism replaces the authority of the Word of God for establishing the truth about God, with the authority of the practical results of an experience for establishing the truth to live by, leading people to seek truth via practical experience rather than the Bible. An example of pragmatism in society is the testimony, "I gave up Christianity because it didn't work for me." But absolute truth about God should not be abandoned just because Christianity doesn't appear to work in one's life. Although personal testimonies of genuine change in a Christian's life after conversion are God-glorifying, Christianity is true, regardless of what works, and the propositions that support its truth are not based on personal testimonies.[31]

Gradually, more emphasis on science and math—as well as practical skills such as carpentry, printing, farming, furniture building, and engraving—began to infiltrate the curriculum of the American school system. This pragmatism was fostered by the frontier lifestyles of Americans in the nineteenth century. Rather than sitting and reminiscing about the past through the study of history and literature, an American in the 1800s had more practical problems to solve: how to grow food, how to survive Indian attacks, how to build a life for the children, grandchildren, and great-grandchildren of tomorrow.

Unfortunately, into this educational environment was launched a controversial idea that would forever change the landscape of America's school curriculum: Darwin's *The Origin of Species.* John Childs remarks:

> First, the conception of evolution in which species arise and disappear implies that reality is not a static, closed system, but a dynamic process of change and development.... Second, the evolutionary view brings man and all his cultural achievements within a natural process of development, and thus cuts the ground from the theory of special creation and the "two-world" outlook associated with it.... Third, the pragmatists rejected the notion that evolution applied to the body of man but not to his mind.[32]

In other words, Darwin's claims fostered the pragmatic spirit in America and marked the beginning of the secularization of this country's school system.

It was into this burgeoning secularism that John Dewey's educational philosophies made its debut. Dewey's book entitled *Democracy and Education* (1916) has been called "the most influential book ever written on American education."[33] Unfortunately, as a "critical naturalist," Dewey "accepted natural knowledge as the total of everything; therefore, the Divine Being was not responsible for creation." While Dewey's idea that children should receive a hands-on education—in other words, "education through activity"—had some merit, ultimately the pragmatism he endorsed has had a negative impact on education in this country.

For centuries education had been subject-centered. The teacher was the authority and most eminent person in the classroom. The pragmatist thought the opposite idea was the best for the educative process: instruction was to be child-centered. The teacher was a corporate problem-solver.

In religious education the Sunday School movement of the twentieth century has experienced change as a result of the progressive education emphasis. Sunday school teachers, especially with preschoolers and children, have in many settings turned more attention to the child and less to biblical content.

Although some churches desire more pragmatic activities than others, the tools for measuring results have changed during the last century. Some believe this pragmatic approach is short on Christian depth and content. Curriculum planning has also changed noticeably in Church educational programs. Under a more practical arrangement, lessons are grouped in units with projects to support the basic content.

John Dewey's progressive movement has influenced all phases of American education. Seeking numerical results, many churches have "baptized" his ideas. Whether this action is best, only time will indicate.[34]

A Modern Return to Classical Education

In recent years, there has been a surge of interest in returning to classical methods in both secular and Christian education. "We need to return to the traditional literary culture, the classical standards of the past," experts contend. Insistence on "getting back to the basics" of "reading, writing, and arithmetic" has again become popular.

The Washington Times, September 2, 2003, reports, "More and more students are returning to the classics in home schooling, charter schools, and private Christian schools. Dissatisfied with traditional public education, they've left it behind as they trade in their secondary-source textbooks for original works by intellectual staples such as Plato, Shakespeare and Nietzsche. "The movement for classical education has evolved out of the academic crisis that everyone is admitting that we have in our schools today," says Gene Veith, dean of the School of Arts and Sciences at Concordia University in Wisconsin and co-author of *Classical Education: Towards the Revival of American Schooling*."

The failure of the public school system is the reasoning behind returning to the classical approach. Then why are homeschoolers seeking such methods? Homeschooling has been successful for years. Homeschool students score significantly higher than their public, and private school counterparts in every subject and at every grade level.[35] Studies also show that homeschoolers are more emotionally and mentally mature, and they are better socialized, than are students who who are sent to public school.[36]

Some today seek the classical methods to be educated like the American founders were educated. Many of the founders did receive a classical education. Two of the main ideals that influenced the Founding Fathers were the Natural Rights Theory and Classical Republicanism. Strong Christian men like Patrick Henry, Richard Henry Lee and Samuel Adams recognized the Greco-Roman humanist influences and fought against the Constitution. Somewhere between the Puritans and Constitution the focus went from God back to Greco-Roman values. Dennis Woods explains in *Discipling The Nations*:

> The United States Constitution breaks with the tradition of previous civil documents that were forthright covenants with the God of the Bible. The Constitution is a secular document, which ignores God and represents therefore, a breach in earlier national covenants with Him. Reinforcing the secular nature of the Constitution is its denial of a religious test for office. This was a basic feature of most of the earlier documents and a biblical imperative. These fundamental flaws were recognized by strong Christians of the founding era, who strenuously resisted its passage.

> It is well known that many of those attending the Constitutional Convention were church members and Christian, at least in the nominal sense. However, because of their failure to reason self-consciously from the Bible, we are forced to conclude that their Christianity was seriously compromised by the natural law humanism of the 18th Century Enlightenment. Noted social commentator Otto Scott put it this way:

> The United States was a government whose constitution claimed no higher authority than its own laws. That was essentially a lawyer's concept of civilization, and could be traced **not to the church, but to Roman tradition.**[Emphasis mine.]

> The novelty of a nation without an official religion was not fully appreciated in 1830 for no land was as crowded with churches and no people more prone to use religious terminology and Christian references in everyday speech in their writings, and in their thinking, than the Americans. There was no question of the piety of millions. There was equally little doubt that they did not fully realize that a land with no religious center is a land where religion is what anyone chose to claim.

> Far from being the ideal document hailed and heralded in a sea of campaign oratory, the Constitution was a lawyer's contract that claimed no higher law than its managers, who represented themselves as reflecting the will of the people. Since such a will was undefined and undefinable, lawyers made up the rules and procedures of government as they went along, within limits that were often ignored, slyly subverted, or poorly guarded. In effect, the Founders had recklessly placed the government in the position of what ancient Greeks called a 'tyrant' which, in its original sense, meant a rule **without divine authority.**

> We gain little by clinging to an interpretation of history that pretends the founders and the document they produced are something other than what they really were. We need to take what is good from the Constitution, admit the problems, and then

move forward to correct them. Until we acknowledge the problems, we will never be able to move on to the desperately needed solutions.

Classical Education Has a Controversial History

Classical education in early America was very controversial. Commentary Magazine 1998 states, "There is a long tradition in America of resistance to the wisdom of the Greeks: Thomas Paine, Benjamin Franklin, and Noah Webster all judged the classics to be of scant use. "[37]

The Protestant Quarrel with the American Republic said Webster defended "primitive Christianity" and warned against dependence on classical morality.[38] Noah Webster received a classical education but expressed concerns with the classical philosophy in a letter to his cousin Daniel which was published in 1837. Noah Webster was praised by the Congregationalist New Englander for his writing as an insightful attack on classical morality—because he chastised an American weakness for "self-admiration." Just months before his death in 1843, Webster acknowledged that pleas for "intelligence and virtue" had become a political shibboleth [group] so tied to classical thought in general that it could only produce "fallacious hopes."[39]

Patrick Henry was among the most forthright Christian statesmen. He did not receive a classical education, he was homeschooled. This self educated attorney, had little respect for Greek philosophy. While Patrick Henry was dying, he spoke: "I am much consoled by reflecting that the religion of Christ has, from its first appearance in the world, been attacked in vain by all the wits, philosophers, and wise ones, aided by every power of man, and its triumphs have been complete." [40]

This insistence reflects a desire to go back to the fork where the American educational system supposedly took the wrong turn. But is this really the solution? David Mulligan explains that when we hear the phrase *returning to traditional methods*, we need to ask, "Whose tradition?"

> In reacting against modernist educational failure comes an instinctive turning to traditional schooling. What does this mean? Does the bare use of 19th century educational material safeguard the essential Christianity of our school? There is a nagging sensation that we have not yet gotten down to the bottom of things. What is traditional education? What is the tradition? It isn't modernism. We know that traditionalism offers another way to look at the world. We know that, but what is it? Where did it come from? Is it just a haven for Christians playing modernist Babylon? We just want to be sure, lest we be like the man who, to escape the lion, ran into the house and was bitten by a serpent. [41]

Classical Greek education methods became the standard in the Church through the influences of men like John Chrysostom (a fourth-century Greek theologian). The Greek/Western worldview sees truth as ideas that can be reduced to printed pages and considered in abstraction in a classroom. The education model we follow must be defined by God, not man. Wisdom can only be established and recognized in Christ. This wisdom comes with admitting there are questions to which we do not know and will never know the answer. Reason does not recognize these limits. Reason operates under the assumption that everything can be explained. This is a form of idolatry in that it is a worldview which everything can be measured in human terms.

> The Greek classical education model focuses on *pagan literature* and *logic*. The biblical Hebraic education model focuses on *God's Word* and *faith*.

In the biblical worldview truth is personal: Truth is not only something we can know intellectually; Truth is someone we can know—the person of Jesus Christ, who said, "*I am...the Truth...*" it is also something we can and must "do" (see 1 John 1:6). God's truth is only communicated truly in the context of relationship. God did not just give us the written Word of truth—He gave us His Son and fills us with Himself: *If anyone acknowledges that Jesus is the Son of God, God lives in him and he in God.* (1 John 4:15).

In 2 Corinthians 6:15–7:1 God calls His people to come out from among the masses and be holy (separate) from the world. Earl and Diane Rodd's article titled "Questioning Secular Classical Education" explains how merging Christian and classical methods can lead to worldliness: "The history of the Church is full of examples of educational movements and institutions which began with Spirit-led vision and distinctly Christian purposes, and [which were] then compromised in the use of classical curriculum, and slowly lost their entire Christian orientation. Strong Christian thinkers may be able to digest classical material as scholars without compromising their faith, but history shows that classical learning soon dominates. Some modern Christian colleges began as strong Bible-based training centers for missionaries and Christian workers, but as they have sought and gained academic "respectability," they have become virtual clones of non-Christian institutions in much of their teachings and practice.[42]

This occurs through a process similar to that of natural phenomena like the accumulation of dust, the decay of ripened produce, the growth of mold, etc., and must be prevented through the same methods as in nature—ongoing inspection for impurities, cleansing, and rejection of rot.

The Emperor is Naked!

In the last five years there has been a growing trend which is reflected in the availability of numerous Greek mythology and philosophy books in homeschool catalogs and curriculum fairs. I feel like the little boy who felt that he must point out the obviously lack of clothing on the Emperor. Well-intentioned Christians have combined classical Greek educational methods with Bible-based curricula, which is exactly the same error that the early Church committed!

To take every thought captive to the obedience of Christ means that we must be discerning about what goes into our minds and the minds of our children. The classical book list entitled the "Great Books of the Western World" contains the writings of Plato, Sophocles, Aristotle, and other men who declare that the answers to life's mysteries and problems are found in men and not in God. Our children should be immersed in the sixty-six great books in God's Word, not in writings by men who knew not our Lord.

> "There is a long tradition in America of resistance to the wisdom of the Greeks: Thomas Paine, Benjamin Franklin, and Noah Webster all judged the classics to be of scant use."

Three Approaches to Classical Literature—and Our Alternative

Currently there are three different approaches to literature by using with the classical approach:

1. With the traditional focus on mythology and Greek philosophy.

2. Using the classical methods but rejecting the material written by pagans.

3. Immersion into the classic literature from a critical viewpoint.

1. Traditional Focus on Classics

The focus of the traditional classical approach is on Greek mythology, philosophy, logic, and Latin. The current best-selling homeschool book on the classical approach focuses on creating a student Plato would be proud of. Students of all ages beginning with kindergartners are immersed in stories about the Greek gods. Mythology and philosophy are encouraged while there is no emphasis on Bible study and only a scant mention of religion. The authors suggest reading the Bible during history studies because it "ought to be treated as a serious philosophical document."

There is legitimate cause for concern when a curriculum's focus is on mythology and philosophy rather than the Bible. Proponents of classical education defend the study of mythology (which is really the study of false gods, idols, and/or demons) by saying that the myths are an integral part of our Western literary heritage. [43]

It is short-sighted to use the argument that children need to study mythology in order to be adequately aware of the world; the same argument would imply that our children should be immersed in books on New Age philosophies, astrology, witchcraft, reincarnation, or Harry Potter. A well-grounded Christian adult with discernment may safely choose to study these subjects, but we should be careful not to feed these as entertainment to our children. Jesus said, *"Therefore be as wise as snakes and as innocent as doves"* (Matthew 10:16).

2. Adoption of Classical Methods but Rejection of Classical Literature

Some using the classical approach avoid the pagan literature. There are Christian homeschoolers who use the classical approach because they view the Trivium: grammar, logic, and rhetoric as a worthy form of structure but reject the writings by the pagan authors (which is somewhat like trying to order a cheeseburger without the cheese). There is nothing inherently wrong with acknowledging the three discernible stages of learning: grammar, logic, and rhetoric—it is only common sense that children go through certain basic learning stages that build upon each other. It seems somewhat ironic to me, though, that one would use the classical methods designed by the classical authors but reject the classical authors' writings. But I applaud their efforts to avoid evil.

3. Focus on the Classic Literature From a Critical Viewpoint

There are other Christians using the classical approach that focus on Bible. They immersing students in the "Great Books" but are doing so from a critical viewpoint——to teach their children about the positive and negative influences these books have had on our culture—an understandable endeavor. But this too seems an irony—that one would use the classical methods designed by the classical authors to teach students the deficiencies of the writings of the classical authors. But I am glad to see they are evaluating the writings from the standpoint of Scripture.

Heart of Wisdom's Alternative

To ignore the classics would be like a doctor disregarding symptoms of a serious disease. We need to understand the classics for ourselves and to teach our children the impact of these works on our history and philosophy. We can reject the classical teaching approach as the Hebrews did but study the impact of classical literature on our culture. Our children need to understand the world's philosophy so they can recognize and avoid it, just as a doctor must study to recognize disease.

However, when a doctor studies a disease he takes precautions, lest he catch the disease. He does most of his studies at a distance. When he does examine a patient with the disease he does so with limited exposure. We can teach spiritually mature students, from a biblical worldview, about the influences of the classical authors sufficiently, with historical analysis and brief excerpts, without immersing them in pagan writings. I don't accept any rationale to introduce these writings to young children.

The Great Conversation: A Biblical Analysis of the Great Books of Western Civilization by Dennis Woods is a resource designed to introduce students to classical literature by analyzing excerpts from a biblical standpoint. You can use this study to incorporate the study of classical authors into the Heart of Wisdom plan, see page 384. In Section Five I address more about classical literature and the so-called "Great Books" (see page 358).

> Our children should be immersed in the sixty-six great books in God's Word, not in writings by men who knew not our Lord. The education model we follow must be defined by God, not man. Wisdom can only be established and recognized in Christ.

Measure by Fruit, Not Appearance

God's Word commands us to discern good from evil, and fruit. Fruit is the standard by which we should measure. The virtues of the fruit of the Spirit—love, joy, peace, patience, kindness, goodness, gentleness, faithfulness, self control—are based on relationships (with God and others). The focus of the Greek classical methods was on shallow and superficial knowledge based on pride, whereas the fruit of the Spirit are based on humility. The god of the Greek philosophers was intellectualism (supreme egotism). Any philosophy which is focused on men rather than in God is bound to be false and destructive. The important thing about any teaching is its origin: Did it come from God or from man? Paul gives a serious warning for discernment concerning this intellectualism:

> *See to it that no one carries you off as spoil* or *makes you yourselves captive by his so-called philosophy* and *intellectualism and vain deceit* (idle fancies and plain nonsense), *following human tradition* (men's ideas of the material rather than the spiritual world), *just crude notions following the rudimentary* and *elemental teachings of the universe and disregarding* [the teachings of] *Christ* (the Messiah).
> —Colossians 2:8 (The Amplified Bible)

The Greek classical schools, with their naïve belief that it is possible to produce, and their arrogant belief that they are capable of producing perfect citizens through education, have produced only artificial and cruel societies. Natural-born men still look back on Greece's "golden days" for personal and cultural inspiration, but they fail to realize that the true nobility that they aspired to was never attainable through any humanistic premise. True nobility, which to some extent the Greek and Roman ideal correctly identified, is only available through obedience to the Gospel of Jesus Christ, with its requirement of our recognition, confession and repentance of sin and its promise of sanctification. This is not possible through the self-effort of education, but rather through the free grace and mercies of Christ our Savior and the power of God's Holy Spirit.

Samuel Taylor Coleridge asked the question: "Is it fitting to run Jesus Christ in a silly parallel with Socrates—the Being [Christ] whom thousands of millions of intellectual creatures, of whom I am a humble unit, take to be their Redeemer—with an Athenian philosopher, of whom we know nothing except his glorification in Plato and Socrates?"

J. Vernon McGee comments that "If you were to follow the history of philosophy beginning with Plato, including many of the church fathers, and coming down to more recent times (including Kant, Locke, and Bultmann, who seems to be the craze with some theologians right now), you would find that none of them have a high view of the inspiration of the Word of God. They are looking for answers to the problems of life, but they will not be found in philosophy. A true philosopher is a seeker after truth, but truth is not found in human wisdom. Christ is the answer, the answer to philosophy."

Every level of Christian education must be built, line upon line and precept upon precept, on the foundation of Scripture. That is the way of education that God gave the Hebrews, the example that the Bible's record of them has given us, and it is the example we must follow.

Chapter 7

Christian Versus Secular Worldviews

In This Chapter

◆ The differences between Christian and secular worldviews.

◆ The answers to four questions will define our worldview.

◆ Our worldview affects our education choices.

There are great differences between the way Christians and non-Christians view the world. A person's perception of the world is called their worldview. It comprises the sum total of a person's beliefs about the world. What we believe and trust in profoundly shapes our worldview.

Every action we take can be interpreted from a spiritual worldview, as having spiritual consequences, especially what we study. Once you understand some of the differences between Christian and secular worldviews, you will be better able to define and shape your own educational purposes and goals.

A worldview can be considered a grid through which each person looks at the world around them. Every individual, whether a Christian or not, begins with certain assumptions, or presuppositions, about the nature of reality.

A non-Christian views the world through a grid based on man's word, which is derived from the carnal sin nature. A Christian views the world through a grid based on the Word of God (see Psalm 119:128), which is holy and spiritual in nature. A person's worldview will govern every dimension of life. It affects how we think about and relate to our family, how we look at other people, how we handle money, how we vote, and so on. There is no area of life that is exempt from our basic assumptions about how the world works—our worldview. Our worldview determines our priorities in life. In short, our worldview determines how we think in every area of life. And how we think in principle determines how we act in the practical.[1]

Christians understand the world through the stories of Creation, the Fall, and God's plan of redemption. In their book, *Transforming a Vision*, Brian Walsh and Richard Middleton suggest that we can identify our basic faith commitments by answering four questions:[2]

Secular Worldview	Christian Worldview
1. Who am I?	**1. Who am I?**
I am an animal of the human species which evolved from the apes.	I am a human being created by an awesome, wonderful, loving God. He put me here for a specific reason.
2. Where am I?	**2. Where am I?**
I am on Earth, a planet that just happened by accident. The accident is called "the big bang."	I am on the earth created by God. This earth is so marvelously created that if it were placed differently in the universe—only one percent more or less away from where it is—it could not support life.
3. What is wrong?	**3. What is wrong?**
People lack self-esteem, education and sufficient money, and therefore they are frustrated, disappointed and defeated.	Sin, which is disobedience to God. When the first humans sinned, it severed their relationship to the only source of eternal life and truth, and all of their descendants have remained in this estranged condition because all have sinned.
4. How can it be fixed?	**4. How can it be fixed?**
Better self-esteem, education and money can fix most of the world's problems.	God sent His Son, Jesus Christ, to pay for our sins, to reverse the curse that sin brought on the world, and to redeem us back into fellowship with Himself. Each person must agree to the terms of restoration, which is to accept Christ's sacrifice for their own sin, and to trust and obey Him each day.

The person with a secular worldview faces all of the same questions as the person with a biblical worldview, but he will respond with different answers. A person's answers are shaped by his beliefs about how things began, what powers are in control, how we should live, what is right and wrong, and how to solve the problems of mankind.

> There is no area of life that is exempt from our basic assumptions about how the world works—our worldview.

There are several elements of our worldview, expressed by these four questions, that provide the foundation for the rest of our beliefs and for how we live our lives, including how we educate our children. American public schools teach from a secular, humanistic worldview. Christians must evaluate the subjects in a curriculum in a radically different way from that of a secular humanist. What we believe about our purpose and worth in this life will reflect or determine the values we place on our families and our beliefs about education.

Question One: Who Am I? (Secular View)

Can a person who thinks his life is an accident, or who thinks he is a descendant of apes, have a worthy self-esteem? Could this mindset be the deeper reason behind America's high abortion and suicide rates? Could this kind of thinking lead to legalized, wide-spread euthanasia?

While doing research for this book, I began reading *Assumptions That Affect Our Lives* by Christian Overman. I had just begun reading chapter 14, "Greek Assumptions and Unwanted Children," when some interesting things occurred. This particular chapter in the book explained that in ancient Greek society, the value of a child was based on his or her worth as it was perceived by the entire community. If the child was viewed to be a detriment to the "good life" of Athens, he was eliminated. If he was seen as a hindrance to the strength of the city-state of Sparta, his life was terminated. The chapter went on to compare the ancient Greeks' attitudes with Hitler's quality-of-life formula, which was used by a group of doctors in Nazi Germany to decide whether certain babies should live or die.

While I was reading, my snuggly, cuddly toddler climbed into my lap. Looking at his beautiful face, I found it absolutely inconceivable that anyone could have this mindset. About this time, I took a break from my research to watch the television program *48 Hours*. Imagine my surprise when I saw that anchor Dan Rather was interviewing Peter Singer, a professor of human values at Princeton University (I had just read about Singer in Overman's book). Singer's philosophy went hand-in-hand with that of the ancient Greeks—and Hitler. Peter Singer is a philosopher who has become famous for asserting that all of life is equally precious. In fact, he argues that the lives of animals are not inferior to the lives of humans; he declares that it might be ethical to kill handicapped babies; and he claims that most people choose their own enjoyment over the needs of starving children. Singer would allow dangerous experiments to be performed on certain humans: "I think that there perhaps are some things which could be done with people who are no longer conscious at all, and will never recover consciousness," declared Singer. He continued:

> It would be ethically justifiable to approach the relatives and to say, "Look, we want to find out whether certain drugs produce adverse reactions in human beings. Do you have any objections to us doing this test on your relative, who can no longer suffer from it because he or she can no longer feel anything at all?[3]

In one explosive essay, he wrote, "Killing a disabled infant is not morally equivalent to killing a person. Very often, it is not wrong at all."[4] Singer told Dan Rather:

> *Killing a disabled infant is sometimes not wrong,* given that the infant, like any infant, is not a person, *as I see it.* I think that it's ethically defensible to say we do not have to continue *its* life. *It does not have a right to life.* And we can choose to end *its* life on the grounds that the future otherwise will be very bleak for that child.[5] [Italics mine].

Protesters shouted disapproval when Singer was hired to teach at Princeton, but Howard Shapiro, the president of the university that had hired him, said: "Controversy is a part of academic life—the marketplace of ideas does live, and is alive here at Princeton."[6] Amazingly, Princeton University was established by the "New Light" (evangelical) Presbyterians, and it was originally intended as a training ground for ministers, but this purpose has gradually disappeared as secular philosophies of higher education have gained a foothold. I believe that the founders of Princeton would be more than slightly upset at this godless philosophy.

Singer's ethical views aren't just mere philosophical ramblings. Singer was a strong supporter of Dianne Arnder, mother of twenty-nine-year-old Tina Cartrette. Tina had been afflicted with cerebral palsy, severe mental retardation, and seizures since infancy. Her mother wanted to end Tina's life; the hospital agreed; and Singer supported her, one hundred percent. But an advocacy group for the disabled, Not Dead Yet, asked a judge to intervene to keep Tina alive.

In November, 2001, a judge gave Tina's mother (who only visited Tina twice a year) the power to decide what was best for her daughter. Tina was not in the process of dying. She did not have a terminal condition but she was denied food and fluids for three days before the state's Governor's Advocacy Council for People with Disabilities intervened. Dianne Arnder was removed as her daughter's legal guardian, and Tina's food and fluids were reinstated. Dan Rather, the anchor of *48 Hours*, reported on this incident in

February of 2002, titling the show "Unconventional Wisdom."[7] Later, another judge gave the power to decide back to Tina's mother, and she chose to terminate Tina's life support. Tina died in August of 2002.

Question One: Who Am I? (Biblical View)

A Christian should answer the "Who am I?" question with something like this: I am, as every person is, a unique individual created by God in His image. Man should behave according to the principles of moral absolutes of right and wrong, and have a general awareness of being different from the rest of the creative order of animals.

An interesting comparison can be made between Professor Singer's views stated in the previous pages and the views of a professor who taught at Princeton a century earlier. Benjamin B. Warfield was a renowned theologian who taught at Princeton Seminary for almost thirty-four years. Francis Landey Patton, president of Princeton Theological Seminary at that time, and ex-president of Princeton University, commented on Dr. Warfield in the memorial address which he delivered by invitation of the faculty of Princeton Theological Seminary, in the First Presbyterian Church of Princeton on May 2, 1921. "Dr. Warfield," he said, "was a most imposing figure." He continued:

> "What most impresses the student of Warfield's writings—apart from his deeply religious spirit, his sense of complete dependence on God for all things, including especially his sense of indebtedness as a lost sinner to His free grace—is the breadth of his learning and the exactness of his scholarship.[7]

Many people are aware of Warfield's famous books, including *The Inspiration and Authority of the Bible.* [8] The real fruit of Warfield's life is shown in his marriage. In 1876, at the age of twenty-five, he married Annie Pearce Kinkead and took a honeymoon to Germany. During a fierce storm Annie was struck by lightning and permanently paralyzed. If Warfield had the same worldview as Singer, Annie's paralyzed state would have been grounds to end her life. But Warfield, a man of God, valued life. After caring for Annie for thirty-nine years, Warfield laid her to rest in 1915. Because of her extraordinary needs, Warfield seldom left home for more than two hours' time during all those years of marriage....

> When Warfield came to write his thoughts on Romans 8:28, [*And we know that all things work together for good to them that love God, to them who are the called according to his purpose*], he said...."All that comes to you is under His controlling hand.... Though we are too weak to help ourselves and too blind to ask for what we need, He will so govern all things that we shall reap only good from all that befalls us."[9]

What a world of difference between these two men! Both Singer and Warfield are considered wise by the standards of the world, but only one produced the fruit of true wisdom in his life. The fruits of wisdom are many, and the book of Proverbs describes the benefits and value of wisdom. In New Testament terms, the fruits of wisdom are the same as the fruit of the Holy Spirit:

> *The fruit of the Spirit is love, joy, peace, patience, kindness, goodness, faithfulness, gentleness and self-control. Against such things there is no law.*—Galatians 5:22–23

> *The wisdom that comes from heaven is first of all pure; then peace-loving, considerate, submissive, full of mercy and good fruit, impartial and sincere. Peacemakers who sow in peace raise a harvest of righteousness.*—James 3:17–18

> *Blessed is the man who finds wisdom, the man who gains understanding,*
> *for she is more profitable than silver and yields better returns than gold.*
> *She is more precious than rubies; nothing you desire can compare with her.*
> *Long life is in her right hand; in her left hand are riches and honor.*
> *Her ways are pleasant ways, and all her paths are peace. She is a tree of life to those who embrace her; those who lay hold of her will be blessed.* —Proverbs 3:13–17

Question Two: Where Am I? (Secular View)

If you were educated in America's public school system any time after 1960, you probably heard a scientific explanation of our origins similar to this one: *The creation of the universe occurred billions of years ago when two atoms collided to create a supernova.* (Too bad there wasn't someone in the class to ask, "Where did the first two atoms come from?"!) This great explosion, or big bang, expanded across the universe. The hot, fiery matter later cooled to give us the complex universe of stars and planets. Life then evolved from a primeval "soup," which then, through natural selection—from beneficial mutations—changed into animals, plants, and eventually, man. Our public schools pour these godless theories into young minds before they have any reasoning skills to question them.

According to chemist Dr. John Grebe, "[The fact that] organic evolution could account for the complex forms of life in the past and the present has long-since been abandoned by men who grasp the importance of the DNA genetic code."[10] Researcher and mathematician I.L. Cohen said:

> At that moment, when the DNA/RNA system became understood, the debate between evolutionists and creationist should have come to a screeching halt.... The implications of the DNA/RNA were obvious and clear. Mathematically speaking, based on probability concepts, there is no possibility that evolution was the

mechanism that created the approximately 6,000,000 species of plants and animals we recognize today.[11]

> The big bang theory is not science, but an atheistic, secular faith.

Even evolutionist Michael Denton said:

> The complexity of the simplest known type of cell is so great that it is impossible to accept that such an object could have been thrown together suddenly by some kind of freakish, vastly improbable event. Such an occurrence would be indistinguishable from a miracle.[12]

The big bang scenario suggests our ordered universe randomly resulted from a gigantic accidental explosion. Never in the history of human experience has a chaotic explosion been observed that has produced such an intricate order that operates purposefully. An explosion in a print shop does not produce an encyclopedia. Sir Fred Hoyle, the eminent astrophysicist compared random accidents producing higher organisms with this excellent image: "A tornado sweeping through a junkyard does not assemble a Boeing 747. No building contractor dumps his materials on a vacant lot, attaches dynamite, and then waits for a completed house to be built from the resulting bang. The very idea is absurd. The big bang theory is not science, but an atheistic, secular faith.[13]

Question Two: Where Am I? (Christian View)

God created created the universe out of nothing, by His word, and He continues to govern the operation of the universe. A purposeful Designer and Creator gives meaning and purpose to life. Purposeful design does not occur without a designer! The Bible tells us that God created this planet to be inhabited (see Isaiah 45:18). The apostle Paul, a wise and educated man, wrote:

> A purposeful Designer and Creator gives meaning and purpose to life. Purposeful design does not occur without a designer!

> *For since the creation of the world God's invisible qualities—his eternal power and divine nature—have been clearly seen, being understood from what has been made, so that men are without excuse.*—Romans 1:20

He also said that:

> *God has not left himself without testimony: He has shown kindness by giving you rain from heaven and crops in their seasons; he provides you with plenty of food and fills your hearts with joy.*—Acts 14:17

Astonishingly, everywhere we look we can see evidence of God's existence in the design of the earth. The Bible begins by affirming that the heavens and the earth were created by God alone. There is no other god, and everything that exists is from His hand. God does not share His rule with other so-called gods, and as the sole Creator of all things, He is supreme in the universe.

Isaac Asimov wrote, "The Bible describes a universe created by God, maintained by him, and intimately and constantly directed by him, while science describes a universe in which it is not necessary to postulate the existence of God at all."[14]

> If our young people have no concept of a Christian worldview...they will be totally unprepared to defend their beliefs.

God expects His people to seek earnestly for the truth. As the apostle Paul faced the humanists of his day, so the faithful and aware Christian must also face the humanists of our day if he is to truly follow Christ. Our children will eventually be in company with those who are taught totally humanistic values in the public school system. If our young people have no concept of a Christian worldview (as is the case with the vast majority of young people these days), they will be totally unprepared to defend their beliefs. It is of vital importance for our children to study and understand the different worldviews being taught today. If we Christians are going to be salt and light in our world, we must understand how non-Christians think. The study of philosophy, theology, and ethics should not be reserved for the conversation of learned academics; the price for ignorance of these subjects could be our lives—or, more importantly, our very souls.

The ambition of Christian parents must be to encourage their children to *bring every thought captive to the obedience of Christ* (see 2 Corinthians 10:5), *in whom are deposited all the treasures of wisdom and knowledge* (see Colossians 2:3).

> *By wisdom a house is built, and through understanding it is established; through knowledge its rooms are filled with rare and beautiful treasures.*
> —Proverbs 24:3–4

Question Three: What Is Wrong? (Secular View)

The secular answer to the question, "What is wrong?" will vary, depending on whom you ask. Most non-Christians believe ethical issues are the problem. Ethical issues pertain to a body of moral principles or values held by or governing a culture, group, or individual, while moral issues are concerned with the difference between right and wrong as defined by God.

Ben Franklin (a deist) attempted to attain perfection by practicing thirteen virtues: temperance, order, silence, resolution, frugality, industry, sincerity, chastity, justice, moderation, cleanliness, tranquility and humility. Late in life he admitted he fell far short of perfection.

Non-Christians begin with the assumption that man is basically good. They believe that anything that impedes a person's autonomy and progress in terms of economic growth, and/or threatens their sense of world mastery, is the problem. Ethical standards are determined by means of a universal absolute that can be known by studying the effect of an action upon our social and economic systems (i.e., utilitarianism). With this view man believes he can save himself.

> ...the problems with today's American school children are not in spite of their schooling, but largely because of what (and how) they are taught in school.

Psychology blames, among other things suffering and guilt. People search for what is wrong by lying on a couch analyzing their dreams, fears, and their relationship with their mothers.

In each non-biblical worldview man attempts to find out the cause of man's problems by using man's reasoning. When you start with the premise that man evolved from an animal with no real purpose, it is logical that you must look out for yourself because eventually all the lower races will be eliminated. The result is unrestrained mass selfishness.

With this view, pride and selfishness are actually considered virtues because man needs to be both proud and selfish to redeem himself. You may think pride and selfishness are overstating the specifics but think about some of the popular terms used today: you need to feel good about your self, self-esteem, respect, personal worth. Pride and selfishness are seen as the answers to fulfillment—the same motivation as original sin. It is difficult to convince the "powers that be" that the problems with today's American school children are not in spite of their schooling, but largely because of what (and how) they are taught in school.

An extreme example of this view are those who followed Darwin's "survival of the fittest" ideas, resulting in eugenics and natural selection. Adolph Hitler had the idea of artificially selecting who should have children, which led to the idea of eliminating "unfit" people like the ancient Greeks did. This line of reasoning led Nazi Germany to embrace mass murder and mass forced sterilization.

Margaret Sanger—esteemed as an American heroine—believed that man must save himself by ridding the human race of all unfit members. She called the unfit "human weeds" (which in her definition was anyone who was poor, uneducated or mentally handicapped) that should not be allowed to reproduce. By only allowing the fit to reproduce, the world would develop to perfection. She founded Planned Parenthood, the largest abortion provider in the world. [15]

Question Three: What Is Wrong? (Christian View)

The Christian view of what is wrong with the world is simple: the basic problem of mankind is sin. All mankind stands guilty before God (see Romans 6:23). Sin is a defiance of God's orders and it has separated us from Him. It all began in the Garden of Eden with, interestingly, an offer of wisdom:

Now the serpent was more crafty than any of the wild animals the LORD God had made. He said to the woman, "Did God really say, 'You must not eat from any tree in the garden.'?"

The woman said to the serpent, "We may eat fruit from the trees in the garden, but God did say, 'You must not eat fruit from the tree that is in the middle of the garden, and you must not touch it, or you will die.'"

"You will not surely die," the serpent said to the woman. "For God knows that when you eat of it your eyes will be opened, and you will be like God, knowing good and evil."

When the woman saw that the fruit of the tree was good for food and pleasing to the eye, and also desirable for gaining wisdom, she took some and ate it. She also gave some to her husband, who was with her, and he ate it.—Genesis 3:1–6

In the form of a serpent, Satan deceived Eve when he promised that she would not surely die, and that her eyes would be opened—that is, she would have so much more of the power and pleasure of contemplation and a larger compass in her intellectual views. Satan spoke as if she were shortsighted in comparison to what she could be. However, partaking of the Tree of the Knowledge of Good and Evil did not bring godly wisdom; instead, it brought guilt, fear, and separation from God (spiritual death).

Eve was attracted to the fruit's alluring promise of wisdom. Why should she have to wait for God to reveal knowledge to her when she could simply eat some fruit, have her eyes be opened, and receive the knowledge firsthand? She had to decide whether to believe God or the serpent. Adam had a choice also, and he chose to believe the woman rather than the loving Creator who had given him the freedom to choose to obey (see 1 Timothy 2:14). The sin of Adam and Eve is the origin of the sin of all of us (see Romans 3:23).

Thankfully, when a person recognizes sin as the fundamental problem in the world, he is then in a position to hear God's call and understand how the problem has been remedied, and how he can receive the benefit of that remedy.

Question Four: What Will Make Things Better? (Secular View)

Humanists believe that science, reason, logic, and historical experience are sufficient guides for figuring out what is right or wrong in any situation. Their standards and values are relative. They believe that scientific and technological breakthroughs, with corresponding economic and social reforms, are ways for man to evolve, and they support getting rid of any traditions or superstitions that may impede their progress.

Ultimately, secular humanists believe that education is the answer to all problems. There are 25,300 public high schools, both junior- and senior-high, in the United States. They enroll 19 million students and carry a million teachers on their payrolls. To maintain this educational establishment—from elementary schools to colleges—taxpayers will spend over $150 billion per year.[16] And prayer to God, our Creator, is not allowed in these institutions!

Psychology blames suffering and guilt for humanity's problems so they try to remove the guilt and suffering to make people feel good about themselves, but the result only validates people's inherent selfishness by condoning it. No therapy can make unredeemed man feel good about himself, because man is not basically good. Darwin's followers, mentioned previously, such as Hitler and Margaret Sanger, believed forced sterilization and abortion were necessary and practical methods to properly stock future generations, ultimately leading to perfection.

The New Age movement believes that all things are divine, or a part of God: people, rocks, trees, stars, etc. Since everything and everyone is a part of God we have to get in touch with the "god within" to achieve total cosmic unity. Some adherents of Cosmic Humanism resort to channeling, meditation, Ouija boards, or hallucinogenic drugs to contact the god within. (In a very real way, these methods are the "sacraments" of the New Age religion.)[17]

In all non-biblical worlviews man attempts to fix man's problems with man's answers, but answers that exclude Christ will never work.

Question Four: What Will Make Things Better? (Christian View)

Only Christianity provides true redemption—a restoration to the original created state and the hope of eternal peace with God. No other worldview has identified the source of the problem—the stain of sin on our souls—and no other worldview can set our tormented souls free.[19]

The only way to fix the problem of sin is through God's Messiah. Jesus overcame sin to set us free from sin and death. God accepted the ultimate sacrifice, Christ's death, for our sin. Because Jesus took our place, we can live eternally with Him. Through Him we are saved from the punishment we deserve. However, salvation is not only the forgiveness of our sins; it also involves the total transformation of our lives.

> The only way to fix the problem of sin is through God's Messiah. Jesus overcame sin to set us free from sin and death.

High quality spirituality is celebrated in the practice of its disciplines—praise, thanksgiving, worship, prayer, solitude, silence, sacrificial giving, meditation on God's Word, and service to others. There is nothing we can do to earn salvation; it is God's merciful, loving gift of His Son, who paid the price for our sins. We receive this gift from God through His mercy by faith.

Salvation, however, is only the beginning. Jesus of Nazareth came that we might have the fullness of a God-intended, Word-directed, and Spirit-empowered life. We must dedicate ourselves to the study, observance, and teaching of His message.Christ, the living Word of God, is the only source of all truth and of wisdom, and *in Him is hidden the treasures of knowledge* (see Colossians 2:3 and 1 Corinthians 1:30). When we wander away from God, then the things of this world become desirable, but wisdom comes from learning, and learning comes from paying attention to the truthful teachings in God's Word.

The Kingdom of God is the domain ruled by Jesus. He primarily used the phrase "the Kingdom of God" to describe the body of His followers, among whom God is present in power. Jesus spoke of this Kingdom in Matthew 7:21: *"Not everyone who says to me, 'Lord, Lord,' will enter the kingdom of heaven, but only he who does the will of my Father who is in heaven."* Jesus' emphasis was on the importance of keeping God's commandments, but Jesus' use of the phrase "Kingdom of heaven" speaks of God's Kingdom being rooted in the confession of His authority and the doing of His will.

> *My purpose is that they may be encouraged in heart and united in love, so that they may have the full riches of complete understanding, in order that they may know the mystery of God, namely Christ, in whom are hidden all the treasures of wisdom and knowledge.*
> —Colossians 2:2–3

We prosper when we have a clear knowledge of the truth as it is in Jesus. The combination of knowledge and faith will make a soul rich. The stronger our faith, and the warmer our love, the more our comfort will be. The treasures of wisdom are hidden—not from us, but for us—in Christ. We cannot grow to be like Christ unless we are first rooted in Him.

Summary

By lining up the Christian faith against other worldviews, we can see that the Bible offers the only real answers to the basic questions and problems of life. No other worldview identifies the real problem of sin, and no other worldview provides real redemption and eternal peace—*shalom*—with God.

A biblical worldview teaches that:

1. We are individuals who have been created by God for a specific reason.

2. We were placed here on His earth, on which all things are maintained by Him.

3. The problems of the world began with sin.

4. The way to solve the problems of mankind begins with salvation through Christ and righteous living.

The Rest of the Story...

The biblical worldview of Creation, the Fall of man, and God's plan of redemption, is all-inclusive. It explains who we are, where we are, what is wrong, and what the remedy is. But there is a problem. If the biblical view is so uniquely different from the secular view, why doesn't our life show a radical difference? How is it that Christians fit so well into the secular culture? Why do we view life as being so divided? Why do we tend to view our religion as only a small part of life? Our lives today, as well as our relationships, are generally divided into four basic categories:

1. Religious—a few hours each week spent at church,

2. Educational—time spent in school or in acquiring training for a career,

3. Professional—time spent in the workplace, usually about forty hours a week, and

4. Leisure—time spent enjoying hobbies, family time, and other activities.

Does this sound like the lifestyles of the godly men and women in the Bible? The answers to these questions lie in understanding the differences between Greek and Hebrew worldviews. We look at these differences in the next chapter.

Suggested Reading

Transforming a Vision, Brian Walsh and Richard Middleton. ᴑ
Wash and Middleton explain that a worldview is the perspective which governs how one sees and perceives all things. "A worldview is more than a vision *of* life, it is a vision for life. It motivates the individual to work to make that future a reality. It guides the individual as he works toward that goal." The authors explain dualism has caused us to compartmentalized life into two convenient and practical sections. We have one part that has to do with the spiritual, which leaves all the rest of life to be secular. Such a view contradicts the clear teaching of the Word of God that He created all of life, and that Jesus Christ is Lord of all. The authors urge Christians need to have their dualistic world view converted to a single worldview. Instead of a combined spiritual and secular world view it must be converted to a unified and comprehensive Christian worldview.

The Deadliest Monster: An Introduction to Worldviews by J.F. Baldwin ᴑ
This book is part worldview handbook and part theological primer. In an exciting journey that begins with our assumptions about the nature of man, *The Deadliest Monster* explores the impact that such assumptions have on our beliefs about God, truth, morality, psychology and politics. Not surprisingly, the initial assumption colors all other beliefs, so that the book is a fascinating catalogue of the ways in which the Christian perspective matches reality.

In *How Should We Then Live?: The Rise and Decline of Western Thought and Culture* by Dr. Francis A. Schaeffer ᴑ
Drawing upon forty years of study in theology, philosophy, history, sociology and the arts, Dr. Schaeffer traces the causes and effects of human thought and action as they are played out in life and society. From his depth of knowledge and Christian commitment, Dr. Schaeffer contemplates the reasons for modern society's very sorry state of affairs, and presents the only viable alternative: living by the Christian ethic, acceptance of God's revelation, and total affirmation of the Bible's morals, values and meaning.

Understanding the Times: The Religious Worldviews of Our Day and the Search for Truth by David A. Noebel ᴑ
A comprehensive guide from Summit Ministries to the most popular worldviews of our day: secular humanism, Marxism/Leninism, and the New Age movement. These worldviews are then compared to biblical Christianity. Noebel provides a biblical perspective of philosophy, science, psychology, sociology, law, economics, politics, and history.

Chapter 8

Greek Versus Hebrew Worldviews

In This Chapter

◆ The Greco-Roman civilization had a profound impact on education.

◆ Dualism is the primary reason our worldview is at odds with the Scriptures.

◆ The Biblical model views life in its entirety, not divided into categories.

A popular book of the early 1990s is entitled *Men Are From Mars, Women Are From Venus.* The author uses the Mars/Venus metaphor to illustrate how very differently men and women view and think about the same issues, and how different our conclusions are. In the same way, the Greco-Roman worldview is very different from the biblical worldview. The lens through which we modern-day Americans view the world has been colored by years of the influence of ancient Greek thought; Homer, Thales, Socrates, Plato, and Aristotle's thinking and teachings have had a profound impact on how we think today.

In the previous chapter, we examined and compared secular and Christian worldviews; but to fully understand how we think about education, we must also scrutinize the two most significant historical influences in the development of Western culture and Christianity—the Greco-Roman civilization and philosophies, and the God-given Hebrew standards revealed in the Bible.

Digging through the Layers

Archaeologist dig through various layers of debris and sediment to discover what life was like in ancient times. As each layer is uncovered, it must be removed to reveal the clear evidence beneath it. To truly understand the views of those who lived in Bible times, we must first dig through the layers of the cultural influences of men, shoveling off and discarding man's secular and superstitious traditions, theories, interpretations, and philosophies that were mixed in from ancient Greek and Roman societies—especially from Constantine, Marcion, and Roman Catholicism.

During the Reformation, men such as Wycliffe, Luther, and Calvin had the right idea of digging up and discarding many theological errors that had been added to the Scriptures, and they discovered the truth (which had actually been there all along) that God's plan of salvation was by His grace through faith in His Son. Unfortunately, various layers of tradition and Greek and Roman thought still remained—and layers of traditions and misinterpretations still need to be removed. Only then will we have a clear view of the lifestyle of the early Christians.

This examination is crucial if we are to understand that we have acquired distorted beliefs about education which are detrimental to our children. The roots of modern America's educational system and traditions come from the ancient Greeks. They were the first to separate academics from religion in formal education settings—and they were the first humanists. Humanism is the primary reason that many Christians are bringing their children back home to educate them. If we are taking our children out of the American school systems in order to avoid the corrupting influences of secular humanism, it behooves us to understand the roots and background history of this ideology, lest we unwittingly duplicate it at home.

The humanist manifesto itself regards humanism as a religion. The very first sentence declares that it has been present since ancient civilizations: "Humanism is a philosophical, religious, and moral point of view as old as human civilization itself."[1] There is a religion found in public schools today that has a view of God—that He does not exist. Secular humanism, like the ancient pagan Greeks, declares that there is no God. Charles Francis Potter, a signer of the first Humanist Manifesto and honorary president of the National Education Association, has this to say about public school education: "Education is thus a most powerful ally of humanism, and every American public school is a school of humanism."[2]

Mike and Sue Dowgiewicz explain:

> The basis for humanism is found in the Greek philosophical spirit. The common thread for both belief systems requires man—not God—to be the measure of all things. Greek philosophy and humanism place man as the ultimate evaluator of

everything. The outgrowth of this view is that there are no God-given standards. Everything changes and evolves. Ethics and morality are based on the whims of man, not on the holy will of God. [3]

Under the Greek system, learning begets goodness, but under the biblical system, goodness begets learning. All non-biblical education operates under the assumption that man can become learned without God, but a biblical education makes knowledge of God the foundation of learning.

We must beware of Satan's counterfeits. He has counterfeit Christians (see 2 Corinthians 11:26), who believe a counterfeit Gospel (see Galatians 1:6–9). He encourages a counterfeit righteousness (see Romans 10:1–3), and even has a counterfeit church (see Revelation 2:9). At the end of the age, he will produce a counterfeit Christ (see 2 Thessalonians 2:1–12).[5] The ancient Greek humanistic philosophy is a counterfeit religion, and it has pervaded the American public educational system. God's command to parents is to plant truth in the hearts of their children. We must oppose Satan and expose his lies, and we must also sow the Word of God and bear fruit in the place where He has planted us.

In *Our Father Abraham*, Marvin Wilson said, when examining the concept of knowledge, one of the main differences between these worldviews becomes pronounced. Norman Snaith effectively summed up the issue:

> The object and the aim of the Hebrew system is *da'ath elohim* (knowledge of God). The object and the aim of the Greek system is *gnothi seauton* (Know thyself). Between these two there is the widest possible difference. The is no compromise between the two on anything like equal terms. They are are poles apart in attitude and method. The Hebrew system starts with God. The only true wisdom is knowledge of God. "The fear of God is the beginning of wisdom." The corollary is that man can never know himself, what he is, and what is his relation to the world, unless he first learns of God and is submissive to God's sovereign will. [4]

The Greek system, on the contrary, starts from the knowledge of man, and seeks to rise to an understanding of the ways and nature of God through the knowledge of what is called "man's higher nature." According to the Bible, man has no higher nature unless he is born of the Spirit.

We find this approach of the Greeks nowhere in the Bible. The whole Bible, the New Testament as well as the Old Testament is based on the Hebrew attitude and approach.

Greek and Hebrew Thought

The differences between the way the ancient Greeks and Hebrews viewed the world, time, life, nature, etc., have been sources of discussions for scholars and theologians for centuries. As previously explained, the ancient Greeks were generally humanistic (man-centered) in their worldview, as opposed to the God-centered worldview of the Hebrews.

Today we read the Hebrew Bible from a 20th-century American cultural viewpoint, which grew out of ancient Greek thought. To develop a biblical educational approach, as well as to be able to understand the Bible better, we must examine some of the differences between ancient Greek and Hebrew thought.

> To develop a biblical educational approach, as well as to be able to understand the Bible better, we must examine some of the differences between ancient Greek and Hebrew thought.

The entire Bible is a Hebrew book. The New Testament is a Hebrew book that was written in the Greek language, and, due to the language, the New Testament does inevitably convey certain conceptual ideas from the ancient Greek language and culture.

A quick example of the difference between Greek and Hebrew thought is the word peace. In Greek thought peace is a lack of confusion or commotion, or lack of war. In Hebrew thought, shalom or peace is wholeness or completeness. Notice that in the Greek way of thinking, peace is what remains when there is an absence of something, but in the Hebrew, peace is the presence of something. When a person is fully submitted to God he is at peace.

Another example is pain. Greek philosophers often taught that one should ignore pain; Paul taught that pain should drive one to trust God for help.

The main difference between the Western, Hellenistic (ancient Greek) mindset and the Hebrew mindset is found in the area of knowing versus doing. William Barrett explains:

> The distinction...arises from the difference between doing and knowing. The Hebrew is concerned with practice, the Greek with knowledge. Right conduct is the ultimate concern of the Hebrew, right thinking that of the Greek. Duty and strictness of conscience are the paramount things in life for the Hebrew; for the Greek, the spontaneous and luminous play of the intelligence. The Hebrew thus extols the moral virtues as the substance and meaning of life; the Greek subordinates them to the intellectual virtues...the contrast is between practice and theory, between the moral man and the theoretical or intellectual man.[5]

Western/Greek Approach	Hebraic Approach
Life analyzed in precise categories.	Everything blurs into everything else.
A split between natural and supernatural.	Supernatural affects everything.
Linear logic.	Contextual or "block" logic.
"Rugged Individualism."	Importance of being part of group.
Equality of persons.	Value comes from place in hierarchies.
Freedom orientation.	Security orientation.
Competition is good.	Competition is evil (cooperation is better).
Man-centered universe.	God/tribe/family-centered universe.
Worth of person based on money/material possessions/power.	Worth derived from family relationships.
Biological life sacred.	Social life supremely important.
Chance + cause and effect limit what can happen.	God causes everything in His universe.
Man rules nature through understanding and applying laws of science.	God rules everything, so relationship with God determines how things turn out.
Power over others achieved through business, politics and human organizations.	Power over others is structured by social patterns ordained by God.
All that exists is the material.	The universe is filled with powerful spirit beings.
Linear time divided into neat segments. Each event is new.	Cyclical or spiraling time. Similar events constantly reoccur.
History is recording facts objectively and chronologically.	History is an attempt to preserve significant truths in meaningful or memorable ways whether or not details are objective facts.
Oriented to the near future.	Oriented to lessons of history.
Change is good = progress.	Change is bad = destruction of traditions.
Universe evolved by chance.	Universe created by God.
Universe dominated and controlled by science and technology.	God gave man stewardship over His earthly creation. Accountability to God.
Material goods = measure of personal achievement.	Material goods = measure of God's blessing.
Blind faith.	Faith based knowledge.
Time as points on straight line ("at this point in time…".	Time determined by content ("In the day that the Lord did…").

Abstract vs. Concrete Thought

The ancient Greeks perceived and understood the world predominantly through the mind and abstract thought. The Hebrews of the Bible perceived and understood the world predominantly through the senses and concrete thought. This concept is explained at the Ancient Hebrew Research Center by Jeff Brenner:

> To develop a biblical educational approach, as well as to be able to understand the Bible better, we must examine some of the differences between ancient Greek and Hebrew thought.

Concrete thought is the expression of concepts and ideas in ways that can be seen, touched, smelled, tasted and/or heard. All five of the senses are used when speaking and hearing and writing and reading the Hebrew language. An example of this can be found in Psalm 1:3; *He is like a tree planted by streams of water, which yields its fruit in season, and whose leaf does not wither.* In this passage we have concrete words expressing abstract thoughts, such as a tree (one who is upright, righteous), streams of water (grace), fruit (good character) and an unwithered leaf (prosperity).

Abstract thought is the expression of concepts and ideas in ways that cannot be seen, touched, smelled, tasted or heard. Hebrew never uses abstract thought as English does. Examples of abstract thought can be found in Psalm 103:8; *The LORD is compassionate and gracious, Slow to anger, abounding in love.* As you noticed I said that Hebrew uses concrete and not abstract thoughts, but here we have such abstract concepts as compassionate, gracious, anger, and love in a Hebrew passage. These are actually abstract English words translating the original Hebrew concrete words. The translators often translate this way because the original Hebrew makes no sense when literally translated into English.

The Greek culture describes objects in relation to the object itself. The Hebrew culture describes objects in relation to the Hebrew himself.

Using the example of the pencil, the Greek description portrays the pencil's relationship to itself by using the word is. The Hebrew describes the pencil in relation to himself by saying "I write." Because Hebrew does not describe objects in relation to themselves, the Hebrew vocabulary does not have the word "is."

A Greek description of God would be "God is love" which describes God in relation to God. A Hebrew description would be "God loves me" describing God in relationship to myself.[6]

Philosophy, Logic, Reasoning, and Rhetoric

The three products of the Greek mind were abstract metaphysics (philosophy), logic (the principles of reasoning), and rhetoric (the study of literature and literary expression). The addition of Greek rhetoric into Christianity brought great emphasis on the cultivation of literary expression and quasi-forensic argument.[7]

The impersonal rhetoric-lecture so common in churches today began with the Greek influence in the early Church causing a turn away from preaching, teaching, and the ministry of the Word. Into its place moved the "art of the sermon" that was more involved with rhetoric than with truth. The Greek "sermon" concept fast became a significant tradition. Mike and Sue Dowgiewicz explain: When Greek oratorical skills replaced Judeo-Christian role modeling; the Church lost its Hebraic approach to life's difficulties: practical application of biblical truth. Greek rhetoric, the structure and style of what is taught, became the main teaching pattern in the Church.[8]

To the Hebrews growing in wisdom was learning to think God's thoughts. In 1 Corinthians chapters 1 and 2 Paul pointed out the differences between man's ways of thinking and God's ways of thinking. Paul's whole argument is a warning to the church at Corinth—and to us—that we must learn to look at issues from the divine viewpoint. We must realize that God doesn't think the same way we do. We must be willing to surrender our own way of thinking and earnestly search out His. How? God has revealed His thoughts "in words taught by the Spirit" (1 Corinthians 2:13). And God has given believers the Holy Spirit to interpret the written Word (vv. 9–15). In the Word and in the Spirit we have been given an astounding gift: *We have the mind of Christ* (v. 16). Searching the Word, guided by the Spirit, we are to learn God's way of thinking (His wisdom), and gradually learn to evaluate all things from His unique perspective.

This is why a tracing-the-argument approach to Bible study is so important. We're prone to grasp a single verse or teaching, and then try to make it fit our way of thinking. We're apt to use the Bible to try to prove our point of view, or to disprove another's. But Paul here teaches us to study the Scripture so we can learn to abandon our own points of view, and submit ourselves instead to God's. By disciplining ourselves to trace the argument of a section of Scripture, we guard against our natural tendency to misuse, and we set ourselves to grasp the very thoughts of God.

Dualism

Dualism is one of the most profound influences on how we view spiritual life, yet most Christians are not even aware of it. The American ethic is a result of the combined ideals of the Jews, Greeks, and Romans. Approximately 200 B.C., the Greeks began to move south which resulted in a coming together of the Greek and Hebrew cultures. This was a very chaotic time as these two immensely different cultures collided. Over the next 400 years the Greek culture took over and nearly eliminated the ancient Hebrew culture. This ancient Greek culture influenced many subsequent civilizations, including the Roman and European cultures, our own American culture, and even the modern Hebrew culture in Israel today.

Plato's doctrine of dualism has had a greater effect on the way Americans—including Christians—think and view the world today than the teachings of any other single man in history. Plato hypothesized that life is divided into two realms: spiritual and material. He said that the spiritual realm is good and the physical (material) realm is evil. Church fathers Origen, Justin and Clement were greatly influenced by Greek thought. Werner Jager said, "...the most important fact in the history of Christian doctrine was that the father of Christian theology, Origen, was a Platonic philosopher at the school of Alexandria...he built into the Christian doctrine the whole cosmic drama of the soul, which he took from Plato."

> A biblical view of work negates dualism. One can love God with all his heart whether he is a missionary, pastor, butcher, baker, or candlestick maker. God calls all Christians to full-time Christian service.

Many Greek-minded Christian converts spend time merging Plato's and other philosophers' teachings with the Bible. According to their views, everything in the world is constantly changing and evolving, and so there are no fixed moral standards or absolutes. Morality is based on man's opinion, not the will of God.

Dualism can be seen throughout Christian literature. The battle over this issue penetrates into the core of Christianity. The ancient Greeks regarded the body as a prison of the soul. The goal of the wise was to gain deliverance from all that is bodily in order to liberate the soul. One must restrain oneself from physical pleasures because they may become a hindrance to spiritual growth.

In stark contrast, the Hebrews viewed all of life as good and each person as a complete unit of body and soul. Instead of trying to flee this world and focus on the world to come, the Hebrews passionately desired to serve God in this physical world created by God, who called it good.

When we divide life into spiritual and material categories, it causes greater value to be placed on the pursuit of spiritual things over the pursuit of earthly things. This becomes obvious when we look at the hierarchy within the Christian community. We consider a seriously devoted Christian will become a foreign missionary; a less devoted Christian will stay close to home and become a pastor, while others who are even less devoted will work in the material world. A biblical view of work negates dualism. One can love God with all his heart whether he is a missionary, pastor, butcher, baker, or candlestick maker. God calls all Christians to full-time Christian service. There is no sacred part of life that can be separated from a secular part.

Augustine's dualism views marital sex negatively, and elevates celibacy as the highest way of life. He viewed all sexual acts as shameful because, in his view, all sex was rooted in lust. This dualistic view created problems for Christians, because Mary physically gave birth to Jesus. The Roman Catholic solution was to proclaim Mary sinless and holy, and deny that she had other children. The Catholics viewed bread and wine as too earthly to be the blood and body of Christ and therefore made rules that only clergy could control the sacraments so these physical elements could be spiritualized.

The Protestant Christian world also is steeped in dualism. Christian mothers feel pressure from this dualistic view because tending to children is seen as a lower type physical job and not as spiritual as ministry or other church activities, while in a truly biblical view, motherhood is highly esteemed as the greatest contribution a woman can make to the human race.

A biblical view of curriculum also opposes dualism. Love for God and neighbor encompasses all of life and therefore all subjects. We should not worship God during Bible study and leave Him out of all other subjects. Dualism profoundly affects modern Christians in America. Dr. Albert Green explains this in his book *Reclaiming the Future of Christian Education*:

> Historically, the change that separated the sacred from the secular took place in two principle steps. During the early centuries of our era, Christian theology was considerably influenced by Greek philosophy. Augustine, for example, was touched by neo-Platonism. Gradually the view of Christian thinkers, commonly known as scholasticism, came to carry a good many ideas derived from the pagan Greeks rather than from the Bible. The development of scholasticism came to a head in the thirteenth century, when the writings of Aristotle first found their way into the newly established universities of Western Europe. Aristotle was much more concerned with the physical world than Plato had been. The question now was, "Can Christian thinkers accept the teachings of Aristotle?" The answer given by Thomas Aquinas at the University of Paris was that this was permissible as long as it was remembered that Aristotle was dealing with ordinary things, and grace, spiritual ones. In the spiritual area Christ was Lord and the Bible was needed. In ordinary things human reason was all that was necessary. This concept, growing out of the Roman Catholic view that the fall of man hurt his will but not his reason, resulted in a form of idolatry. In spiritual things Christ is Lord: in ordinary things, reason is. This view puts reason, something created, in the place of God. Thus, it is idolatrous.[9]

Americans embrace dualism. For example, President Clinton won at least one of his two elections after his true character was revealed, proving that most voting Americans believed that Bill Clinton could be untruthful and unfaithful in his personal life, yet somehow that would not affect his public life. Jesus taught that a good tree produces good fruit and a bad tree produces bad fruit, and whoever can/can't be trusted with little can/can't be trusted with much (see Luke 16:10).

Gnosticism

Gnosticism was born out of Greek dualism. During the second century after Christ, several systems of Gnosticism grew in Alexandria and the Mediterranean area, most of which were closely related to Christianity. The word *Gnosticism* is derived from the Greek word for "knowledge," *gnosis*, referring to the idea that there is special, hidden knowledge (esoteric knowledge) that only a few can possess.[10] In the second and third centuries, orthodox Christian believers defended the biblical worldview against the widely popular heresy known as Gnosticism. Gnostics believed that the "divine spark" resided within each person, and people were saved from material incarceration in a physical body by the knowledge (*gnosis*) of their essential divinity. Much of New Age humanism is simply a modern rehash of ancient Gnosticism. Gnostics denied the goodness of creation, the reality of the Incarnation, and the eternal value of this world. The orthodox Church stood its ground, however, ultimately prevailing over the Gnostic degradation of the goodness of creation.[11]

As *Nelson's New Illustrated Bible Dictionary* explains:

> The Gnostics accepted the Greek idea of a radical dualism between God (spirit) and the world (matter). According to their worldview, the created order was evil, inferior, and opposed to the good. God may have created the first order, but each successive order was the work of anti-gods, archons, or a demiurge (a subordinate deity).

> The Gnostics believed that the earth is surrounded by a number of cosmic spheres (usually seven) that separate human beings from God. These spheres are ruled by archons (spiritual principalities and powers) who guard their spheres by barring the souls who are seeking to ascend from the realm of darkness and captivity that is below, to the realm of light that is above.

> The Gnostics also taught that every human being is composed of body, soul, and spirit. Since the body and soul are part of people's earthly existence, they are evil. Enclosed in the soul, however, is the spirit, the only divine part of this triad. This spirit is asleep and ignorant; it needs to be awakened and liberated by knowledge.

> According to the Gnostics, the aim of salvation is for the spirit to be awakened by knowledge so that the inner person can be released from the earthly dungeon and

return to the realm of light where the soul becomes reunited with God. As the soul ascends, however, it needs to penetrate the cosmic spheres that separate it from its heavenly destiny. This, too, is accomplished by knowledge. One must understand certain formulas that are revealed only to the initiated.[12]

> While truth can be expressed in the statements of Scripture, it is always connected to life and conduct.

Wash and Middleton's book *Transforming the Vision: Shaping a Christian Worldview* details dualism from Plato to Aristotle to Aquinas, into the Renaissance. They show how dualism opened the door to humanistic secularism. They explain the negative influence of ancient Greek dualism by stating, "To put it bluntly: if it were not for the medieval nature/grace dualism, modern secularism might never have risen at all."[13]

Judaism Was Not Originally Dualistic

The Hebrews' Scriptures did not depict Yahweh and his enemies as being outside the world, but, on the contrary, very much a part of it. In response to Greek and other influences Judaism became more dualistic over time. By the time of Jesus, the Jews were bitterly divided on the subject, with the Sadducees defending the older view against Greek influences and the Pharisees advocating modern dualistic ideas.

Many think Paul taught dualism when he used the term flesh but in most of Paul's uses of the term flesh he was speaking of the sin nature (Romans 7:18, 25; 8:7–8; 1 Corinthians 3:1–3; Galatians 5:17; 6:8; Colossians 2:18, 23; 1 John 2:16; 1 Peter 2:11; 2 Peter 2:10).

Understanding the Culture of Bible Times

In *How to Study the Bible*, John MacArthur explains the importance of understanding Scripture in light of the culture:

> The cultural gap must be bridged, because cultures can be very different. If we don't understand the culture of the time in which the Bible was written, we'll never understand its meaning. For example: *In the beginning was the Word, and the Word was with God, and the Word was God* (John 1:1). What does that mean? Why didn't he say, "In the beginning was Jesus"? Well, he used "the Word" because that was the vernacular at that time. To the Greeks the term Word was used to refer to a floating kind of cause, a kind of ethereal, spatial kind of energy that was floating around. John said to the Greeks that that floating cause, that thing which caused everything, that spatial energy, that cosmic power, is none other than that Word which became flesh (1:14).

To the Jew, the term Word was always the manifestation of God, because "the Word of the Lord" was always God emanating His personality. So when John said "the Word was made flesh and dwelt among us," he was identifying Jesus Christ, the incarnate Christ, as the very emanation of God. In the text, therefore, he meets the Greek mind and Hebrew mind with the right word that grabs both at vital points. And this goes on all through the Bible. If you don't understand the Gnosticism existent at the time of the writing of Colossians, you won't understand the book. If you don't understand the culture at the time the Judaizers were moving into the Gentile churches, you can't understand the book of Galatians. If you don't understand the Jewish culture, you can't understand the book of Matthew. There must be cultural comprehension to fully understand the Bible. [14]

> "What has Athens to do with Jerusalem?"

Suggested Reading

Assumptions That Affect Our Lives by Christian Overman ⌐○
Overman explains the clash and contrast between Greek philosophy and Hebrew wisdom and their roles in shaping Western Christianity. The visible actions of people are first shaped by invisible thoughts, deep in the unseen recesses of the human mind and heart. What factors influence those invisible ideas? For people who live in the Western world, the answers can be found by examining the two major roots of Western thought—the ancient Greeks and the ancient Hebrews. This book takes the reader back to the roots of the modern conflict between Christianity and secular humanism through a comparison of ancient Greek and Hebrew culture. What the reader will discover is that the current tension between evangelical Christians and the non-biblical ideas with which they are surrounded is an age-old conflict. By viewing the current situation in the context of the ancient Greeks and Hebrews, contemporary Christians can be better equipped to deal with the challenges of living in a predominately Greek-based culture today. An excellent book that should be read by every Christian.

Bless You! Restoring the Biblically Hebraic Blessing by Dr. John Garr ⌐○
This book is a a systematic, comprehensive study of the biblical concept of blessing. God has forever focused on confirming his covenantal blessings and bringing this good news to all humankind. God himself composed and prescribed the blessing for his children, a benediction that also places God's personal name on the one who is blessed. This powerful dynamic can now be experienced in every Christian home and in every corporate worship experience. You, too, can restore this vital part of the Hebraic faith of Jesus and the Apostles and bring God's blessings upon yourself and your family.

Christianity is Jewish by Edith Schaeffer ⌐○
Edith Schaeffer, wife of Francis Schaeffer, wrote this inspirational book to explain how the Bible is a story of love. Exploring the historical and spiritual significance of the Jewish race, this treatment presents the Bible as a unified document in which God has progressively unfolded the plan of salvation. "By recorded words on stone, parchment, and paper, God has unfolded all the facts of the past history we need to know—all the essential teaching we need to have, all the understanding of how we are to get rid of sin and how we may come into His presence, become His people, look forward to a time of complete restoration."

Our Father Abraham: Jewish Roots of the Christian Faith by Dr. Marvin Wilson ⌐○
Although the roots of Christianity run deep into Hebrew soil, most Christians are regrettably uninformed about the rich Hebrew heritage of the Church. This volume delineates the link between Judaism and Christianity, between Old and New Testaments, and calls Christians to examine their Hebrew roots. Since it was first published, *Our Father Abraham* has reverberated loudly through any Jewish-Christian dialogue that is

concerned with developing a better understanding between these two faiths. Touching on areas of history, Jewish thought and tradition, this book seeks to help Jews and Christians better understand one another and attempt to build bridges regarding our sizable pool of common belief. Dr. Wilson, Professor at Gordon College, warns that once the Church strays from its Jewish heritage, distortion is bound to follow. He illustrates this with selected studies on community, family life and discipleship. In each of these areas he shows how the Church has lost sight of the biblical ideal. This is a stunning achievement and a life-changing book!

The Hebrew Education Model

What would Jesus do? is a popular question today. We should also ask questions like, How did Jesus teach? What kind of education did Jesus receive? What were Abraham and Sarah's educational goals for their children? What about Isaac and Rebekah's educational goals for their children? What were Mary and Joseph's educational goals for Jesus? Would Jesus have been at the head of His class if He had attended the Academy of Plato? How was Paul taught?

Education has always been of primary importance to God's people. The Bible does not specifically describe the type of education Jesus received, but we do have evidence from history that demonstrates what the education of the Hebrews was like during Christ's time here on earth. Jesus was a Jew living in Israel. He grew up in a Jewish home with Jewish parents, whom we assume were like all good Jewish parents, and that they taught Him from the Torah.

Jesus' parents obeyed the Law first by having Him circumcised when He was eight days old (Luke 2:30). We know that Jesus appeared in the temple at the age of twelve, discussing the Torah and its application to daily life with the Jewish elders. From the Mishnah we learn that a typical boy in Jesus' day would have been studying the Torah from the age of five:

At five years of age, one is ready for the written Torah, at ten years of age for the study of the oral Torah, at thirteen for bar mitzvah [coming of age], at fifteen for the study of halachot [rabbinic legal decisions]...at twenty for pursuing a vocation, at thirty for entering one's full vigour."[1]

The Jewish philosopher Philo wrote that the Jews...were from their swaddling clothes, even before being taught either the sacred laws or the unwritten customs, trained by their parents, teachers, and instructors to recognize God as Father and as the Maker of the world.[2]

We also know from the writings of Josephus that: From their earliest consciousness, [the Jews] learned the laws, so as to have them, as it were, engraven upon the soul.[3]

The book of Deuteronomy mandates who, what, when and where the Hebrews were to teach their children. The purpose of the book of Deuteronomy is to inspire loyalty to God through a review of His guidance and protection in times past, and through a description of His holy precepts. When Jesus was called upon to summarize the divine requirements, He cited as "the first and great commandment" a passage from Deuteronomy (6:5). When tempted by Satan in His own wilderness (Matthew 4), Jesus quoted from this great book three times. The dominant themes in Deuteronomy are love toward God and toward fellow men.

Deuteronomy consists largely of words spoken by Moses on the east of the Jordan River, just before the people of Israel entered the land God was giving them. Deuteronomy was written by Moses and given to Israel with a command to read it publicly and entirely every seven years (31:10–13). Moses commanded the Hebrews to discipline themselves and their children by diligence in learning and teaching the words of God.

Only be careful, and watch yourselves closely so that you do not forget the things your eyes have seen or let them slip from your heart as long as you live. Teach them to your children and to their children after them.—Deuteronomy 4:9–10.

On four separate occasions, God commanded parents how to answer the questions of their sons and daughters, in Exodus 13:14, Deuteronomy 6:20, and Joshua 4:6, 21. Let's look at the first two passages now, and later in this chapter we will look at the two passages in Joshua.

In days to come, when your son asks you, "What does this mean?", say to him, "With a mighty hand the Lord brought us out of Egypt, out of the land of slavery."
—Exodus 13:14.

Hear, O Israel: The Lord our God, the Lord is one. Love the Lord your God with all your heart and with all your soul and with all your strength. These commandments that I give you today are to be upon your hearts. Impress them on your children. Talk about them when you sit at home and when you walk along the road, when you lie down and when you get up. Tie them as symbols on your hands and bind them on your foreheads. Write them on the doorframes of your houses and on your gates.—Deuteronomy 6:4–8.

From these passages we know the following about Hebrew education:

- Who—Parents are to teach their children
- Where—In the home
- What—The commands of God
- When—Sitting, walking, rising up and lying down, i.e., all throughout the day
- How—Diligently (asking and answering questions, and using object lessons)

Who—Parents Are to Teach Their Children

The first aspect of the biblical model is that the home is to be considered the center of education and spiritual growth. Children are to receive parental instruction in the safety of their own homes. As Proverbs 4:3–4 states: *When I was a boy in my father's house, still tender, and an only child of my mother, he taught me and said, "Lay hold of my words with all your heart; keep my commands and you will live."* This passage clearly outlines two facts about education at that time: First, learning took place *in my father's house*; and second, the head of the household did the teaching (*he taught me*). Deuteronomy 6:6–7 declares: *These commandments that I give you today are to be upon your hearts.* **Impress them upon your children when you sit at home** *and when you walk along the road, when you lie down and when you get up.* (Emphasis mine).

In biblical times, the family home was set apart for something special. In the original Hebrew language, the word used for *sanctuary* is the word *miqdash*,[4] which means a consecrated thing or place, a holy place, a hallowed part. Another term used for the word *sanctuary* in the Bible was *tabernacle*. In Exodus 25:8, God said to Moses: *"And let them make me a sanctuary, that I may dwell among them."* The Hebrew word *ma`at* (meh-at') means "little" (see Ezekiel 11:16).[5] The home was referred to as the *miqdash me'at*, or, a little sanctuary. The home was to be a house of prayer, worship, and the study of both academics and spiritual life.

From early biblical times, the center of education was found in the home. Both parents shared responsibility in this task, although the father bore the chief responsibility for the instruction of the children (see Deuteronomy 11:9). In biblical times, it was the father—not textbooks, audiovisual aids, or brightly colored bulletin boards—who was the main focal point of the learning process. As the primary teacher of his children, the father served as a living and dynamic communicator of divine truth.

> The dinner table was meant to be a place to gather, not just for food, but to study God's Word, to pray, to praise, and to worship.

Christians need to reassess this concept. The primary sphere of religious activity should be in the home, not in the Church. The dinner table was meant to be a place to gather, not just for food, but to study God's Word, to pray, to praise, and to worship (see Deuteronomy 8:3). The home was more important in Jewish culture than even the synagogue: it was the center of all training—religious, academic, and familial.

The Hebrew word for parent is very similar to the word for teacher. It is *horeh*, which is from the root word *yarah*,[6] and it means to cast, to throw, or to shoot. The Bible commands the father, the priest of this little sanctuary, to instruct the children (see Deuteronomy 6). The father is to diligently impart both knowledge and wisdom to his children.

What—The Commands of God

To what commands does Deuteronomy 6 refer? In a previous passage (5:1–33), Moses repeated the Ten Commandments, the basis for God's moral law. In fact, the rest of the book of Deuteronomy is actually an amplification and application of these commandments. Israel was to hear, learn, keep, and do these laws (v. 1), for in obeying the Law they would be honoring God and opening the way for victory and blessing.[7]

The first part of Deuteronomy 6—*Hear, O Israel: The Lord our God, the Lord is one. Love the Lord your God with all your heart and with all your soul and with all your strength* (Deuteronomy 6:4–5)—is known by the Jews as the *shema*. The *shema* is the official Hebrew declaration of faith. When Jesus was asked for the first commandment, He answered with the commandment of the *shema* (see Matthew 23:37).

Listening to the Language of the Bible: Hearing It Through Jesus' Ears, by Lois Tverberg, is a wonderful book that explains the depth and meaning we can find in the Bible when we enter the minds of its ancient authors. Here Tverberg explains the Hebrew word *shema*:

The word that means "hear" or "listen," *shema* (pronounced "shmah") is an excellent example of the difference between Hebrew, which stresses physical action, and Greek and Western culture which stresses mental activity.

Listening, in our culture, is a mental activity, and hearing just means that our ears pick up sounds. But in Hebrew, the word *shema* describes hearing and also its effects—taking heed, being obedient, doing what is asked. Any parent who yells at their children, "Were you listening?" when they ignore a command to pick up their rooms understands that listening should result in action. In fact, almost every place we see the word obey in the Bible, it is translated from the word *shema*.

The word *shema* is also the name of the "pledge of allegiance" that Jesus and other observant Jews up until this day have said every morning and evening. It is the first word of the first line, *Hear* (shema), *O Israel! The LORD is our God, the LORD alone. You shall love the LORD your God with all your heart and with all your soul and with all your might.* (Deuteronomy 6:4–5). By saying this, a Jew would remind himself of his commitment to love God, to dedicate himself to following God and doing His will. Some Jews teach their children the *shema* as soon as they learn to talk! It is the central affirmation for a Jewish person of his or her commitment to the Lord. The word *shema* here again means, take heed or listen and obey!

This gives us a clue as to why Jesus said, *"He who has ears to hear, let him hear!"* He is calling us to put His words into action, not just listen. He wants us to be doers of the word, and not hearers only (James 1:22). We Westerners put all our stress on what is in our minds, and tend to consider action as dead works. But Hebrews understood that we have not truly put what we have heard into our hearts until it transforms our lives as well.[8]

In the second part of Deuteronomy 6, God's people were commanded to meditate on "these commandments" (the Torah) and to keep the Law in their heart. Parents were in a position to impress them on their children's hearts. The moral and biblical education of children was accomplished best as the natural topic of a conversation which might occur anywhere and anytime during the day, rather than in a formal teaching format. Again we need to view the Scriptures in their Hebraic setting to discover beautiful nuggets of new meaning. Here Lois Tverberg explains the Hebrew word torah in *Listening to the Language of the Bible:*

> Protestant Christians tend to have a negative attitude about the word *law*,
> feeling that it refers to oppressive and arbitrary regulations. But the word
> that we translate as law, *torah*, has a very different emphasis and connotation
> in Hebrew.

> Torah could best be defined in English as instruction, that is, God's instruction to man.

Torah is derived from the root word *yarah* which literally means to flow as water. Figuratively it means to point out, to teach, inform, instruct, show. *Torah* could best be defined in English as instruction, that is, God's instruction to man. When it is used to speak of God's instruction, there is an understanding that whatever God teaches us, we are obligated to obey. Therefore, the word law is within the bounds of the definition of *torah*, but is not really its main emphasis. Our translations tend to reinforce our thinking, by translating *torah* as law most of the time. The Jewish translations like the *JPS Tanakh* instead translate *torah* as teaching most of the time.

We see evidence of *torah* as teaching rather than law when we notice that the first five books of the Bible are called the *Torah*, but they contain much more than laws. The *Torah* contains the story of the Creation and Fall, God's covenants, His rescue of His people from slavery, and His training them to be His people in the desert. All of the *Torah* teaches us about God's ways and purposes, and about the nature of man. But only part of it is actually law. The Penteuch is specifically called the *Torah* because it is understood to be the teaching given through Moses, but the word *torah* is often used in a larger sense to describe all of Scripture.

This emphasis helps us see God in a more positive light. Now the word *Torah* reminds us that, rather than being primarily a lawgiver or a policeman waiting to punish us, God is a loving Father instructing His children in how to live. Jesus, who instructed His disciples and the crowds, was simply imitating His Father in teaching us how to have life, and have it more abundantly.[9]

For you to teach your child God's law you need to know it yourself or learn it as you teach your child. Charles Spurgeon's devotional on Psalm 37:31 sheds light on the meaning of the law of God: *The law of his God is in his heart; none of his steps shall slide.*

Put the law into the heart, and the whole man is right. This is where the law should be; for then it lies, like the tables of stone in the ark, in the place appointed for it. In the head it puzzles, on the back it burdens, in the heart it upholds.

What a choice word is here used, "the law of his God"! When we know the Lord as our own God His law becomes liberty to us. God with us in covenant makes us eager to obey His will and walk in His commands. Is the precept my Father's precept? Then I delight in it.

We are here guaranteed that obedient-hearted man shall be sustained in every step that he takes. He will do that which is right, and he shall therefore do that which is wise. Holy action is always the most prudent, though it may not at the time seem to be so. We are moving along the great highroad of God's providence and grace when we keep to the way of His law. The Word of God has never misled a single soul yet; its plain directions to walk humbly, justly, lovingly, and in the fear of the Lord are as much words of wisdom to make our way prosperous as rules of holiness to keep our garments clean. He walks surely who walks righteously.[10]

When—All Throughout the Day

The moral and biblical education of children was accomplished best, not in a formal teaching period each day, but when the parents, out of concern for their own lives as well as their children's, made God and His Word the natural topic of a conversation which might occur anywhere and anytime during the day.[11]

"…*When thou walkest by the way…*"(Deuteronomy 6.) To walk means to go along with, to follow a course of action or to live, follow a way of life.

Alfred Edersheim explains in *Sketches of Jewish Social Life at the Time of Christ*:

When we pass from the heathen world into the homes of Israel, even the excess of their exclusiveness seems for the moment a relief. It is as if we turned from enervating, withering, tropical heat into a darkened room, whose grateful coolness makes us for the moment forget that its gloom is excessive, and cannot continue as the day declines. And this shutting out of all from without, this exclusiveness, applied not only to what concerned their religion, their social and family life, but also to their knowledge. In the days of Christ the pious Jew had no other knowledge, neither sought nor cared for any other—in fact, denounced it—than that of the law of God.[12]

How—Diligently

The Hebrews have always placed God's Word at the center of their education. Modern religious Jews (especially Hasidic Jews) continue to focus on God's Word. The book *The Chosen*, by Chaim Potok, is an absorbing novel about two Jewish boys, Reuven and Daniel, which takes place in New York in the late 1940s just after World War II. It's a deep, heartfelt novel about the struggles of overcoming religious differences, with several lessons on Jewish history and traditions skillfully woven in along the way.

The novel begins with Danny and Reuven as high-school boys and concludes with their graduation from college. God's Word was consistently the priority in the boys' education. Throughout the book, both boys regularly studied the Torah with their fathers, especially on the Shabbat, usually for several hours at a time. Once they entered college, they studied the Torah from 9 a.m. to 3 p.m., and then they began academic studies at 3:15 p.m. to 6 or 7 p.m.!

What a lesson in priorities—and what a story of fruit! The Hebrew education methods of diligent Bible-focused study has been passed down over thousands of years. The unbelieving Jews don't have the Messiah nor the Holy Spirit but they focus their study on God's Word. Compare this fruit with the fruit from the Greek classical methods used in Christianity. How many hours a day do we devote to God's Word?

The American Jewish community is famous for academic attainment. Twenty to forty percent of students at Ivy League schools are Jewish.[13] In the 20th century, Jews, more than any other minority, ethnic or cultural, have been recipients of the Nobel Prize, with almost one-fifth of all Nobel laureates being Jewish. Twenty-two percent of Nobel Prizes in all categories awarded between 1901–2003 were Jewish. This is an astonishing percentage for a group of people who add up only *a twenty-fourth of one percent* of the world's population. [14]

Marvin Wilson explains,

> There is no shortcut method to a sound education. If spiritual training is to be a priority in your children's education, you will be required to make a major commitment of your time and your resources. As the psalmist wrote: *His delight is in the law of the Lord, and on his law he meditates day and night* (Psalm 1:2). Although ancient Israel had no formal system of schooling, learning and knowledge were considered the greatest goals in life—parents today would be wise to make the spiritual education of their children just as high a priority.

> So strongly did the early rabbis feel about the priority of education that they said it should not be interrupted, even for the rebuilding of the Temple. Israel was to acknowledge the Lord's authority in every circumstance and turn of the way (see Psalm 16:8 and Proverbs 3:5–6). The ultimate prophetic vision in the Bible was that *all peoples of the earth may know that the Lord is God and that there is no other* (1 Kings 8:60).[15]

Dwight Pryor explains the Hebrew's view of learning for life:

> Shortly before his death, the exemplar Moses reminded Israel that the Torah's guidance and instruction *are not just idle words for you—they are your life. By them you will live...* (Deuteronomy 32:47). To study God's Word so as to obey it was the greatest joy and chief duty of any son of Abraham. Study was supremely important because Torah (teaching) was supernaturally given. The process of diligently engaging and wrestling with the sacred text enlivened and sanctified all of one's existence. Learning was for life and life

was for learning.... Study leading to obedience was an act of devotion that engaged the whole person—heart, soul, mind and might—not just the intellect.[12]

William Barclay describes methods of instruction in *Educational Ideals in the Ancient World*:

> Methods of instruction were largely by repetition; the Hebrew verb "repeat," came to mean both "learn" and "teach." Mnemonic devices such as acrostics were therefore employed. Scripture was the textbook, but that other books were not unknown is evidenced by Ecclesiastes 12:12. The value of rebuke was known (Proverbs 17:10), and an emphasis on corporal chastisement is to be found in Proverbs and Ecclesiastes, but discipline was much milder in Mishnaic times.
>
> Until comparatively late times, it was customary for the pupil to sit on the ground at his teacher's feet, as did Paul at Gamaliel's (Acts 22:3). The bench was a later invention.
>
> Jewish education's whole function was to make the Jew holy and separate from his neighbors, and to transform the religious into the practical. Such, then, was normal Jewish education; but undoubtedly there were schools after a Greek pattern, especially in the closing centuries B.C., and indeed Ecclesiastes may have been written to combat deficiencies in such non-Jewish instruction. Hellenistic schools were found even in Palestine, but of course more frequently among Jewish communities elsewhere, notably in Alexandria.
>
> In the infant church, child and parent were told how to behave towards one another (Ephesians 6:1, 4). Church officers had to know how to rule their own children. There were no Christian schools in early days; for one thing, the church was too poor to finance them. But the children were included in the church fellowship, and doubtless received their training there as well as in the home.[17]

Object Lessons

God teaches through object lessons. God commanded His children to put up stones as a reminder in Joshua 4. The stones were specifically put up in order to prompt children's questions. *When your children shall ask their fathers in time to come, saying, What mean these stones?* The parent's response is to explain what he has done for them. The lesson is that God cares for His people and provides for them.

And those twelve stones, which they took out of Jordan, did Joshua pitch in Gilgal. And he spake unto the children of Israel, saying, When your children shall ask their fathers in time to come, saying, What mean these stones? Then ye shall let your children know, saying, Israel came over this Jordan on dry land. For the LORD your God dried up the waters of Jordan from before you, until ye were passed over, as the LORD your God did to the Red sea, which he dried up from before us, until we were gone over: That all the people of the earth might know the hand of the LORD, that it is mighty: that ye might fear the LORD your God for ever.—Joshua 4:20–5:1.

We need reminders and we need to remind our children. The Hebrews have a tradition of placing a mezuzah on the doorpost of their homes (Deuteronomy 6:4–9 and 11:13–21). It is customary, upon entering or leaving a residence, to touch the mezuzah. This reverence acknowledges belief in the shema: *Hear, O Israel, the LORD our God, the LORD is one.*" In Jewish tradition teachers introduced letters of the alphabet on a slate covered with honey; the child then licked the slate so that the words of the Scriptures might taste as sweet as honey.

In Numbers 15:28 God told His people to wear tassels or fringes on the four corners of their garments to remind them of God's commandments. *Speak to the Israelites and say to them: "Throughout the generations to come you are to make tassels on the corners of your garments, with a blue cord on each tassel. You will have these tassels to look at and so you will remember all the commands of the LORD, that you may obey them and not prostitute yourselves by going after the lusts of your own hearts and eyes. Then you will remember to obey all my commands and will be consecrated to your God."* Today, many Jews wear a prayer shawl, or tallit to fulfill this commandment. It has fringes called tzitzit which are tied to its four corners; the tassels are tied into knots, as a reminder of all 613 of the laws of Moses (248 prohibitions and 365 positive commands). The numerical value of the letters of the word tzitzit is 600; there are eight threads in each fringe, and five knots; add these all up and you get 613. The shawl is often worn in religious services.

Reminders are a form of teaching. Some people wear a mustard seed pendant as a reminder of Jesus' words, *If ye have faith as a grain of mustard seed, ye shall say unto this mountain, Remove hence to yonder place; and it shall remove; and nothing shall be impossible unto you* (Matthew 17:20). The rainbow is a reminder of God's covenant with Noah. I have a friend who uses each shirt she irons as a reminder to pray for that family member. I have another friend who uses the days of the week as a reminder to pray for a specific grandchild. I use the photographs on my refrigerator, dresser, and fireplace mantle as reminders to pray for our twelve grandchildren (I go through the list by chronological age and occasionally reverse the order to make sure every child receives equal time). The superstition of walking under a ladder being considered bad luck actually began as a reminder of God because medieval theologians suggested that a ladder leaning against a wall forms a triangle and, therefore, is a symbolic reminder of the Holy Trinity.

In this century, most Americans don't have much interaction with God's creation. Our forefathers worked the soil, took care of animals, depended on the weather and interacted daily with the natural elements. Psalm 23 is more meaningful to a sheep farmer because he understands the profound and insightful parallels of the role of the shepherd in the lives of sheep—as a leader, comforter, caregiver, provider, guardian, and owner—to Jesus' role in the life of the believer.

John 15 records one of Jesus' last messages to His disciples before His death. Jesus chose a vine and branches to show us the way to a life of fruitfulness. My family's interaction with a vineyards is limited, so I've attempted use the décor of my house as a reminder like the stones in Joshua. Our home is decorated with rich colors of the vineyard—deep purple, burgundy, and greens. My kitchen and dining area are decorated with a vineyard theme. Drying the dishes with grapevine-decorated dish towels or setting the table grapevine decorated dinnerware are prompts for several Bible lessons. The dependence of the branch on the grapevine is a model of our relationship with Christ. The vineyard reminds us that we must stay in Jesus to bring forth good fruit. If we keep His commandments, we will remain in His love. As we abide in Jesus we see more and more of Him and grow more and more like Him. Our job is simply to remain. To remain is to hold fast and stay in loving obedience. We are not just staying with Him, standing nearby, watching what is going on—we are connected to Him, grafted into Him. Our identity and existence are bound up in Him.

> **Object Lesson in a**
> **Heart of Wisdom Unit Study**
>
> Sample from the Light unit study. The Lesson is "Lenses: Bigger and Better" Step 1 discussion:
>
> Did you know one of our jobs as Christians is to be a lens? In Phillipians 1:20 Paul said Christ was magnified. Warren Wiersbe explains: Does Christ need to be magnified? After all, how can a mere human being ever magnify the Son of God? Well, the stars are much bigger than the telescope, and yet the telescope magnifies them and makes them appear closer. The believer's body is to be a telescope that brings Jesus Christ close to people. To the average person, Christ is a misty figure in history who lived centuries ago. But as the unsaved watch the believer go through a crisis, they can see Jesus magnified and brought so much closer. To the Christian with the single mind, Christ is with us here and now. The telescope brings distant things closer, and the microscope makes tiny things look big. To the unbeliever, Jesus is not very big. Other people and other things are far more important. But as the unbeliever watches the Christian go through a crisis experience, he ought to be able to see how big Jesus Christ really is. The believer's body is a "lens" that makes a "little Christ" look very big, and a "distant Christ" come very close.[18]

Israel is also God's vine or vineyard; see Isaiah 5:1–7, 27:2–6; Jeremiah 2:21, 12:10; Ezekiel 17:5–6; Hosea 10:1; Joel 1:7; Psalm 80:8–16. The word vine is used to describe both the Jewish people and its Messiah, and reinforces the close identification of Jesus with Israel (Matthew 2:15). God's remnant, the Hebrews and grafted-in Gentile Christian branches (Romans 9:6ff., 11:1–10, 17–24) will obey God's commands, stay attached to the true vine, and have the true vine's power and strength to bring forth good fruit (Matthew 7:16–19).

The law of sowing and reaping teaches that a successful harvest must be preceded by timely planting and ongoing care (watering, weeding, etc.). A similar principle applies in our lives: things we value take time and maintenance. There's no quick fix for healthy, lasting, relationships in a marriage, family or elsewhere. If we neglect them now, we can't expect positive results later. In any living vine the function of a branch is to bear fruit, but it cannot fulfill its purpose unless it remains in intimate connection with the vine. Without that cherished "remain in Me" relationship, it will never fulfill the purpose for which it was created. The Christian who fails to remain in the Vine is as unfulfilled as that of a branch that has been torn from the vine, with no prospect for fruit bearing. There are many more such lessons but I'll save them for the *Plants* unit study. When we are aware of teaching moments, these are the type of lessons that should be taught through out the day.

The Bible is full of these object lessons. Jeremiah spoke of honey jars in his object lesson about the destruction of the nation of Judah (Jeremiah 19:1, 10). Hosea was commanded by God to marry a prostitute (Hosea 1:2–9). This was an object lesson of the sin of the harlotry of Israel in rejecting God and serving pagan gods, and how God would continue to love them and use them as His special people. The book of Jonah is full of object lessons. Most are obvious but some aren't. God used the loss of the leafy gourd plant that had shaded Jonah's hut from the blazing sun to ask Jonah that, if he cared about a plant, not wanting to see it die, should not God care about a whole city of people, not wanting to see them die? Another lesson is the comparison of Jonah's being rescued from a fate he deserved, with the Ninevites' rescue from a fate they deserved.

Object lessons in Jeremiah include the linen girdle (13:1–11), the potter's vessel (19:1–12), a basket of figs (24), and bonds and yokes (27:2–11; 28). In Ezekiel: illustrations on a tile (4:1–3), shaving the head (5), moving household items (12:3–16), eating and drinking sparingly (12:18–20), sighing (21:6, 7), a boiling pot (24:1–14), widowhood (24:16–27). More examples include the ram substitute (Genesis 22:1–19), a pot of manna (Exodus 16:32), shedding of blood (Leviticus 16 and Hebrews 8–9), bird's nest (Deuteronomy 22:5), sackcloth (Isaiah 20:1), grass (Isaiah 40:6–8), almond tree (Jeremiah 1:11–12), little children (Matthew 18:5), a coin (Matthew 22:17), the fig tree (Mark 11:13–20), foot washing (John 13:1–20), a sheet (Acts 10:10–16).

The Bible's object lessons provide the answers to mankind's fundamental questions about life. Jesus' entire life, teaching, death and resurrection are all object lessons. As a teacher it is your responsibility to know God's Word well enough to teach these types of lessons to your children, not only during daily Bible study but by seizing teachable moments throughout the day.

Each of the biblical holidays listed in Leviticus 23 is an object lesson to remind us of God's mercy and faithfulness. The biblical holidays are very exciting studies revealing Christ.

The Biblical Holidays

The biblical holidays were given by God to His people as special days set apart as appointed times and object lessons for His people to remember. Most people think of these observances as Jewish holidays but God calls them His feasts:

> *And the LORD spake unto Moses, saying, "Speak unto the children of Israel, and say unto them, concerning the feasts of the LORD, which ye shall proclaim to be holy convocations, even these are **my feasts**."*––Leviticus 23:1. [emphasis mine]

The *Condensed Biblical Cyclopedia* explains that the law required the Hebrews to give a large amount of their time to His service. Seventy-five days of one year (twenty percent) were to be set aside, devoted to observing special times:

To the Passover: They were required to give six days to the feast of the Passover and Unleavened Bread each year (Leviticus 23:4–8).

To the Feast of the Weeks: They were required to give one day to this feast each year. (Leviticus 23:15–21.)

To the Feast of Tabernacles: Counting out one day for the Sabbath, they were required to give six days to this feast each year. (Leviticus 23:34–42).

To the weekly Sabbath: They were required to give fifty-one days to the Sabbath each year. (Leviticus 23:3).

To the Day of Atonement: They were required to give one day to the Atonement each year. (Leviticus 23:26–32).

To the Feast of New Moons: Counting out one day for the Feast of Trumpets, they were required to give eleven days to this feast each year. (Numbers 28:11–15; 29:1–5 Amos 8:5).[18]

The Hebrew word for feasts is mow`ed which means appointed time. These holidays are a picture—more than any other subject in the Bible—to teach historical, spiritual, and prophetic lessons. God commands the observance of seven feasts on specific days of specific months. His instructions are recorded by Moses in Exodus 12:1–57, Leviticus 16:1–34, 23:1–44, Numbers 9:1–14, and Deuteronomy 16:1–17.

In Deuteronomy 16:1–7 Moses explained that all male Israelites were to attend three of the seven annual feasts (16:16). If possible their families were to go along (16: 11, 14). These feasts gave the Israelites opportunities to teach their children to know God as both their Deliverer and Provider.

The instructions demonstrated that worshiping God should be a joyful experience in which the participants gratefully share in the bounty of His blessings (Deuteronomy 16:11, 14–15; 12:7, 12, 18; 14:26). These feasts provide weekly, monthly, and yearly rests from the common routines of daily life. They also offer a schedule for reflection and worship. These special days are sacred convocations that give everyone a time to remember the holiness, power, and love of God.

In a Period of Seven Years

1. Sabbaths, three hundred and six days (Leviticus 23:3)
2. Feast of Passover and Unleavened Bread, counting out one day each year for the Sabbath, thirty-six days (Leviticus 23:4–8)
3. Feast of Pentecost, six days (Leviticus 23:15–21)
4. Feast of Trumpets, six days (Leviticus 23:23–25)
5. Atonement, six days (Leviticus 23:26–32)
6. Feast of Tabernacles, counting out one day each year for the Sabbath, thirty-six days (Leviticus 23:34–42)
7. The first of every month, counting out one day each year for the feast of Trumpets, sixty-six days (Numbers 28:11–15; Amos 8:5)
8. The seventh year, three hundred and sixty days (Leviticus 25:1–7).

(306 + 36 + 6 + 6 + 6 + 36 + 66 + 360 = 822). They therefore gave eight hundred and twenty-two days to their religion in seven years.[14]

Paul wrote to the Gentile believers in Colossians 2:16–17 that the holidays *are a shadow of things to come*. Each of the spring holidays is a picture of Christ's first coming: Jesus was sacrificed for our sins on Passover, buried on Unleavened Bread, and arose on Firstfruits. Fifty days later the Holy Spirit was given on Pentecost (the celebration of the receiving of the Law). The fall holidays are a picture of His second coming and the beginning of the Messianic reign (although we don't know on which of the fall feasts he will actually return).

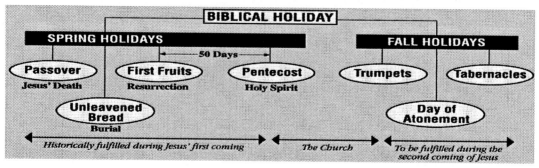

The Spring Feasts

The first three of the four spring holidays are celebrated within an eight–day period: the combined holidays of Passover, Unleavened Bread, and Firstfruits. The fourth and final spring feast is the Feast of Weeks (Shavuot or Pentecost). The Feast of Weeks is held seven weeks or fifty days following the day after the Sabbath of Passover (the day the Law was given on Mount Sinai in the Old Testament, and the Holy Spirit was given in the New Testament.)

The Passover dinner eaten with unleavened bread is full of object lessons. Each part of the meal tells an important part of the story of the Exodus.

> *Then Moses said to the people, "Commemorate this day, the day you came out of Egypt, out of the land of slavery, because the LORD brought you out of it with a mighty hand. Eat nothing containing yeast. Today, in the month of Abib, you are leaving. When the LORD brings you into the land of the Canaanites, Hittites, Amorites, Hivites and Jebusites—the land he swore to your forefathers to give you, a land flowing with milk and honey—you are to observe this ceremony in this month: For seven days eat bread made without yeast and on the seventh day hold a festival to the LORD. Eat unleavened bread during those seven days; nothing with yeast in it is to be seen among you, nor shall any yeast be seen anywhere within your borders. On that day tell your son, 'I do this because of what the Lord did for me when I came out of Egypt.' This observance will be for you like a sign on your hand and a reminder on your forehead that the law of the LORD is to be on your lips. For the LORD brought you out of Egypt with his mighty hand. You must keep this ordinance at the appointed time year after year." (Exodus 13:3–10).*

The Fall Holidays

The fall holidays are the Feast of Trumpets (Rosh HaShanah), Day of Atonement (Yom Kippur), and the Feast of Booths or Tabernacles (Sukkoth). The Feast of Trumpets is the major fall holiday. Since the spring festivals so clearly prophesied the first coming of Messiah, it stands to reason that the fall festivals are also prophetic of His second coming. (Hanukkah and Purim are also celebrations in the Bible to remember God's work but are not commanded by God).

The fall forty-day season called Teshuvah (which means return or repentance) begins on Elul 1 and ends on the Day of Atonement (Tishri 10). This forty-day season is a time for each one to annually examine his life and restore relationships with both God and man. The first thirty days of this season are the thirty days of the month of Elul. The last ten days of this forty-day season are the Feast of Trumpets and Day of Atonement, or the ten High Holy Days (Days of Awe).

The Jews start the celebration of the Fall Holidays thirty days prior to the Feast of Trumpets, which falls on the first day of the seventh month. For thirty days the shofar is blown every morning in the synagogue to remind the people that the holy days are approaching, and that they should prepare themselves. Their preparation consisted of confessing their sins and seeking forgiveness, and going back to fix mistakes made during the year. The ten days between the Feast of Trumpets and the Day of Atonement (Yom Kippur) are called the Days of Awe.

The long period between The Feast of Weeks and the Feast of Trumpets is symbolic of the long period between the formation of the Church at the Feast of Weeks and the regathering of Israel to the trumpet blast calling all believers.

For more details about the these holy days see my publication *A Family Guide to the Biblical Holidays* or visit my Web site, http://BiblicalHolidays.com.

How Did Jesus Teach?

Now that you have a sense of how Jesus was taught, let's investigate how Jesus taught. What sort of teacher was Jesus? What were His methods? What can we learn from Jesus' teaching methods? What was the manner of this teaching? We know that He was a marvelous teacher, because the crowds would stay all day to listen to Him.

First, we know that Jesus' methods were natural and spontaneous, not formal. Jesus did not give a prepared address that was to be delivered on a formal occasion. He frequently taught in the homes of His friends or disciples. Many of Christ's messages were delivered out in the open, or beside the sea, or in a desert place. There was nothing stilted or formal about His teaching. Mark painted a picture of this relaxed tone when he described Jesus' return to Capernaum after the first journey through the villages of Galilee: *A few days later, when Jesus again entered Capernaum, the people heard that he had come home. So many gathered that there was no room left, not even outside the door, and he preached the word to them* (Mark 2:1–2). Even when Jesus taught huge crowds, the manner of the gathering remained informal and intimate, in the give-and-take of mealtime conversation, or in answering questions for people.

Jesus gave object lessons. We gave some examples in the previous pages. He used a coin to teach about taxes (Mark 12:16–17). He used the stones of the Temple to explain the end of the age (Mark 13:1–4). He used a fig tree to illustrate both faith and His return

(Matthew 21:21; 24:30–36). Jesus taught in such a way that people could not forget. He taught and trusted them to share His messages with following generations. He guided His pupils to discover, understand, and live His truth. He involved them in the learning experience.

> Jesus did not use the common, logical Greek methods of His day...
>
> He never aimed at a systematic and logical presentation of his teaching.
>
> ...His thought was picturesque, full of figures, illustrations, striking expressions...

Many people assume that Jesus was a philosopher and a teacher, something after the nature of Confucius or Socrates, and they read His teachings as if they had been carefully prepared and organized for educational purposes. But these assumptions are incorrect. Harvie Brascomb explains that Jesus did not use the common, logical Greek methods of His day:

> Jesus' teachings were popular, not logical. Jesus apparently never aimed at a systematic and logical presentation of his teaching. He did not speak to the crowds of fisher folk and peasants in the logical manner of a professor lecturing a classroom. Nowhere do you find definitions of terms used, premises laid down, deductions drawn. He did not attempt to transform men by syllogisms. These things are the mechanics of speech; they are difficult to follow and almost inevitably convey a sense of artificiality. Certainly the deepest things of life are not determined by an argument. That is probably due to two things. On the one hand, the ordinary person always feels that if clever enough, he might find a flaw in the argument. There is a vague general feeling that one cannot believe everything that one may not be able to answer. But there is, I think, a deeper reason than this. Logic divides a subject into its parts, dissects its different phases, and deals with them separately. Never the whole is before the eyes. Analysis—with the average man, at least—is not the method by which people are stirred to great decisions.

> Jesus' method was fundamentally different. He appealed to the intellect—note the controversies with the Pharisees in particular—but so far as our records go he never set himself to present his view of God and man and duty in a systematic theology. Instead, what he does is to present a very few central and basic truths, in such fashion that men may see them whole and feel their drawing power. In the longer discourses which are recorded he takes some basic principle of conduct, presents it now from this side, now from that, illustrates it by a parable, shows its application to life in a concrete example, returning thus ever again and again to the main thought with which he is dealing.

> ...the deepest things of life are not determined by an argument...
>
> Logic divides a subject into its parts, dissects its different phases, and deals with them separately. Never the whole is before the eyes. Analysis—with the average man, at least—is not the method by which people are stirred to great decisions.

Of this manner of teaching, the Sermon on the Mount in Matthew is the clearest illustration. The theme is the nature of Christian righteousness. First it is pictured in the character of those who are truly blessed; then we have it set forth by way of contrast with the Jewish ideal; next Jesus shows what it actually means in practice, taking such familiar illustrations as alms giving, prayer, fasting, the laying up of riches, and criticizing others; there then follows a section on the complete trust in God which is characteristic of the righteous individual; and finally it is closed with parables of warning and exhortation. This is not a logical or piecemeal treatment: the whole subject is constantly before the mind and is exemplified by various means. Several times one finds verses which seem to state the whole Christian ideal with such completeness as to seem to leave nothing further to be said, only to pass on to further illustrations and presentations. That was always Jesus' method. He did not divide his subject into its proper divisions and present his views systematically. Instead he constantly holds up before his hearers the ideal of the good life in all its completeness and perfection.

Jesus' teachings were metaphoric. Many people have made mistakes in trying to understand Jesus because they have failed to take this fact into consideration. Jesus was in the best sense of the word a popular teacher. His thought was picturesque, full of figures, illustrations, striking expressions, all of which made the meaning so clear that even the most ignorant could understand. "*I send you as sheep amid wolves.*" "*Be ye wise as serpents, and harmless as doves.*" "*I saw Satan fallen as lightning from heaven.*" "*O, Jerusalem, Jerusalem...how often would I have gathered thy children together, even as a hen gathereth her chickens under her wings.*" "*Ye are the salt of the earth.*" One could go on and on with such striking similes and metaphors. It was his method of speaking and teaching.

In the best sense of the word Jesus was a popular teacher. Crowds of ordinary people would stay all day listening to him, even forgetting their lunch in the eagerness with which they hung upon his words. From that fact alone we might infer that what he said was lucid and clear, easy to understand. The recorded teaching bears this out. What could be simpler or clearer than Jesus' statement of the chief commandment? Or the summary of Christian duty which is called the Golden Rule? Or the parable of the Good Samaritan?[19]

Jesus' teaching methods include five broad types:

1. Straightforward
2. Questioning
3. Proverbs
4. Parables
5. By example

Jesus' straightforward teaching, such as the "Sermon on the Mount" (Matthew 5:1–7:29; Luke 6:20–49), needs no real explanation. Now let's examine how Jesus used questions, proverbs, and parables. We'll look at Jesus teaching by example later in this chapter.

> "That was always Jesus' method. He did not divide his subject into its proper divisions and present his views systematically....
>
> His thought was picturesque, full of figures, illustrations, striking expressions, all of which made the meaning so clear that even the most ignorant could understand."

Jesus Used Questions to Teach

Jesus used questions to teach in more than half of the conversations he had which are recorded in the Gospels. He got people to talk, established a relationship, and made them receptive to what He had to say. He used questions to confront people, to draw people into spiritual awareness, for self-confrontation, and for growth. His questions caused people to stop and think. Jesus especially used questions when dealing with a hostile audience.

For example: While Jesus was teaching in the temple courts, He asked, *"How is it that the teachers of the law say that the Christ is the son of David? David himself, speaking by the Holy Spirit, declared: 'The Lord said to my Lord: "Sit at my right hand until I put your enemies under your feet."' David himself calls him 'Lord.' How then can he be his son?"* (Mark 12:35–37).

The rest of verse 37 states, *The large crowd listened to him with delight.* Wouldn't it be great if your children listened to you with delight? A good teacher uses questions either to review old material or to introduce new material. When introducing new material, be sure to ask questions to find out what the student already knows and to evoke their interest in the topic.

Questions allow you to evaluate the level of understanding, but they also provide opportunities to elicit feedback; for example: "What was that story about?" and "How did you come up with that answer?" Ask open-ended questions instead of questions that can be answered with a simple yes or no. Sometimes being quiet can be an important teaching technique. Probe your child

Some Questions Jesus Asked

- Can the children of the bride chamber fast while the bridegroom is with them? Mark 2:19
- Couldn't you stay awake? Mark 14:27–42
- How can Satan cast out Satan? Mark 3:23
- Do you believe that I am able to do this? Matthew 9:28
- Do you love Me more than these? John 21:15
- Don't you understand? Mark 7:1–23
- Which will you choose: good or evil, life or death? Mark 2:23–3:6
- Have ye not read what David did? Matthew 12:3
- How much then is a man better than a sheep? Matthew 12:10
- How much more are ye better than the fowls? Luke 12:24
- How many loaves do you have? Mark 6:30–46

- Know ye not this parable? Mark 4:17
- Is a candle brought to be put under a bushel, or under a bed? Mark 4:21
- Were there not ten cleansed? but where are the nine? Luke 17:17
- What did Moses command? Mark 10:2–12
- What do you want Me to do for you? Mark 10:32–45
- What good is it for a person to gain the whole world, yet forfeit his soul? Mark 8:6
- What is easiest to say? Mark 2:1–12
- What shall, therefore, the lord of the vineyard do? Matthew 21:41
- Which of you shall have an ass or an ox fallen into a pit, and will not straightway pull him out on the sabbath day? Luke 14:4
- Wilt thou be made whole? John 5:6

- Who are you looking for? John 20:1–18
- Who do you say that I am? Mark 8:27–38
- Who is my mother? and who is my brethren? Mark 3:33
- Who Then can be saved? Luke 18:26
- Whose likeness is on this coin? Mark 11:27–12:17
- Why are you so afraid? Mark 4:35–41
- Why do you bother her? Mark 14:1–11; 43:44
- Why do you call Me good? Mark 10:17–31; 39:16
- Why do you call Me, "Lord, Lord," and not do what I say? Luke 6:46
- Why do you weep? Mark 5:35–43
- Why have You forsaken Me? Mark 15:22–41
- Why did you doubt? Luke 12:28

with thoughtful questions and then be quiet and wait. When answers are not spoon-fed, the student must work to find them; in fact, the student must define the answer.

Jesus Taught with Proverbs and Parables

The kind of teaching that Jesus practiced poses a sharp contrast to the didactic styles of most instruction that took place in ancient Greece and Rome. Jesus' distinctive use of parables represented a type of *mashal*, which was part of the wider Rabbinic tradition.[20]

The parables Jesus used are from the Hebrew tradition of *meshalim* (plural of *mashal*), including proverbs, riddles, aphorisms, and allegories. The words parable and proverb are from the same Greek and Hebrew root word meaning laying by the side of or a casting alongside, thus a comparison or likeness, allegory or metaphor. Parables are terrific teaching tools as they provoke interpretation and curiosity. They make students wonder and think.

The *mashal* is the beginning point of learning. The word *mashal* is variously translated as a proverb, a parable, an allegory, a metaphor, or a discourse. The explanation of a parable is called a *nimashal*. In Samuel, Nathan reproved King David and convicted him of his sin of committing adultery with Bathsheba using a mashal:

Mashal	Nimshal
The Lord sent Nathan to David. When he came to him, he said, "There were two men in a certain town, one rich and the other poor. The rich man had a very large number of sheep and cattle, but the poor man had nothing except one little ewe lamb he had bought. He raised it, and it grew up with him and his children. It shared his food, drank from his cup and even slept in his arms. It was like a daughter to him. Now a traveler came to the rich man, but the rich man refrained from taking one of his own sheep or cattle to prepare a meal for the traveler who had come to him. Instead, he took the ewe lamb that belonged to the poor man and prepared it for the one who had come to him." David burned with anger against the man and said to Nathan, As surely as the Lord lives, the man who did this deserves to die! He must pay for that lamb four times over, because he did such a thing and had no pity.—2 Samuel 12:1–4	Then Nathan said to David, "You are the man! This is what the Lord, the God of Israel, says: "I anointed you king over Israel, and I delivered you from the hand of Saul. I gave your master's house to you, and your master's wives into your arms. I gave you the house of Israel and Judah. And if all this had been too little, I would have given you even more. Why did you despise the word of the Lord by doing what is evil in his eyes? You struck down Uriah the Hittite with the sword and took his wife to be your own. You killed him with the sword of the Ammonites. Now, therefore, the sword will never depart from your house, because you despised me and took the wife of Uriah the Hittite to be your own.—2 Samuel 12:7–10

The *mashal* comes in many forms, depending on its usage and the occasion. Here is an example of a *mashal* and *nimshal* in Jesus's teachings:

Mashal	Nimshal
Jesus told them another parable: The kingdom of heaven is like a man who sowed good seed in his field. But while everyone was sleeping, his enemy came and sowed weeds among the wheat, and went away. When the wheat sprouted and formed heads, then the weeds also appeared. The owner's servants came to him and said, "Sir, didn't you sow good seed in your field? Where then did the weeds come from? "An enemy did this," he replied. The servants asked him, "Do you want us to go and pull them up?" "No," he answered, "because while you are pulling the weeds, you may root up the wheat with them." Let both grow together until the harvest. At that time I will tell the harvesters: First collect the weeds and tie them in bundles to be burned; then gather the wheat and bring it into my barn.—Matthew 13:24–30.	His disciples came to him and said, "Explain to us the parable of the weeds in the field." He answered, "The one who sowed the good seed is the Son of Man. The field is the world, and the good seed stands for the sons of the kingdom. The weeds are the sons of the evil one, and the enemy who sows them is the devil. The harvest is the end of the age, and the harvesters are angels. As the weeds are pulled up and burned in the fire, so it will be at the end of the age. The Son of Man will send out his angels, and they will weed out of his kingdom everything that causes sin and all who do evil. They will throw them into the fiery furnace, where there will be weeping and gnashing of teeth. Then the righteous will shine like the sun in the kingdom of their Father. He who has ears, let him hear.—Matthew 13:36–42.

In our Western view we see Matthew's Gospel as a biography of Jesus—which it is—however, it is much more. There are forty-seven stories that are common to Matthew and Luke, yet only one of these stories is placed in the same order by both writers. Matthew used literary patterns to give us the nimshal—an explanation or better understanding—of the seven kingdom parables in his Gospel. On the surface, only two of the seven parables include nimshal; however, if you understand the parallel literary patterns you can see the remaining nimshal in Matthew. Here is an example from Jeff Curry's book *The Parable Discovery*[21]:

Matthew Parables	Hidden Nimshal	Hidden Nimshal
1. Parable of the Sower 2. Parable of Wheat and Tares 3. Parable of the Mustard Seed 4. Parable of Leaven 5. Parable of Hidden Treasure 6. Parable of the Pearl 7. Parable of Fish	1. Sowing seed from Abraham to Jesus (1:1–17) 2. Landowner comes to field (1:18–25) 3. Infant King (2:1–8) 4. Following instructions (2:9–12) 5. Hiding Jesus in Egypt (2:13–15) 6. Herod tries to find Jesus (2:L16–18)7. Jesus sent to fish (2:119–23)	1. John sowing (3:1–4) 2. Promise of separation (3:5–12) 3. Foreshadow of Jesus death' and resurrection (3:13–17) 4. Refusing satan (4:1–11) 5. Jesus is hidden (4:12–16) 6. Cost of the Kingdom (4:17) 7. Fishers of men (4:18–22)

Jesus Himself explained His reasons for this in His answer to the inquiry of His disciples: "Why do you speak to the people in parables?" (Matthew 13:10; see Matthew 13:13–15; Mark 4:11–12; Luke 8:9–10). Jesus was following the rule of the divine procedures, as recorded in Matthew 13:13: *Jesus said, "This is why I speak to them in parables: 'Though seeing, they do not see; though hearing, they do not hear or understand.'"*

Most of us learn best by analogy. In one theological workbook of the Old Testament, A.S. Herbert observes that the *mashal* clearly has a recognizable purpose. The idea of the *mashal* is to bring one thing alongside another in order to force a comparison. The student then moves from something well-known to something less known or unknown. This forced comparison brings light into darkness.

Literary Patterns

In our Western culture we have been trained to think and outline in a linear fashion. By reading the Bible as literature and history (Greek logical methods) you can only see part of the message. The Hebrews used literary parallel patterns. These literary patterns are found through the Bible. Here is an example of a parallel pattern in Genesis 1-11 from *The Literary Structure of the Old Testament*.

Creation Story	Flood Story
1. Beginning (1:1–2:3)	1. New beginning (6:9–9:19)
2. Sin, nakedness (2:4–3:24)	2. Sin of Ham, nakedness (9:20–29)
3. Younger righteous son, no Descendants (4:1–16)	3. Descendants of younger righteous son (10:1–5)
4. Descendants of sinful son Cain (4:17–26)	4. Descendants of sinful son Ham (10:6–20)
5. Descendants of choosen son Seth (5:1–32)	5. Descendants of choosen son Shem (10:21–32)
6. Divine judgement (6:1–4)	6. Divine judgement (11:1–9)
7. Introduction of Noah—through him God will bless humankind (11:10–26)	7. Introduction of Abram—through him God will bless humankind (11:10–26).

Tony Robinson (RestorationofTorah.org) explains literary schemes arranged as a parallelism. In a parallelism, the themes of the first half of the story are repeated in the second half of the story in the same order as the first half of the story. Here is an example of the parallels in Exodus 14-16 and Joshua 3-5.

Crossing the Jordan	Crossing the Red Sea
A. Joshua 3:9–10: Joshua said, "He shall <u>destroy the inhabitants</u>; you shall know the living God is among you"	A. Exodus 14:13–14: Moses said, "Dont fear... stand still and see the salvation of YHVH...He will <u>destroy the Egyptians</u>; He will fight for you"
B. Joshua 3:11–14: Joshua told the people ahead of time what would happen; <u>the ark of the covenant went before the people</u>;	B. Exodus 14:15–20: Adonai told Moshe ahead of time what would happen; <u>the angel of God and pillar of cloud that went before them</u>, went behind them
C. Joshua 3:15–17: The priests <u>feet dipped into the edge of the Jordan</u>; the <u>water split</u>; the people crossed on <u>dry ground</u>; the priests stood on dry ground in the <u>midst of the Jordan</u>	C. Exodus 14:21–22: Moses stretched out his <u>hand over the sea</u>; Adonai turned the sea into dry land; the waters were <u>divided</u>; Am Yisrael went into the <u>midst of the Red Sea on dry ground</u>; the water was a heap on the left and right
D. Joshua 4:15: Adonai commanded Joshua <u>what to do so that the water would return</u>	D. Exodus 14:26: Adonai commanded Moses <u>what to do so that the water would return</u>
E. Joshua 4:16–18: As the priests feet touched the dry ground the <u>water returned</u>	E. Exodus 14:27–28: Moses stretched his hand over the sea and the <u>water returned</u>
F. Joshua 4:19–24: Tell your children Israel <u>crossed on dry ground</u>; Adonai dried up the water of the Jordan	F. Exodus 15:8 and 19: The waters heaped up; the deep congealed; Am Yisrael <u>walked on dry ground</u>.
G. Joshua 5:1: The Amorite and Canaanite kings <u>heard</u> how Adonai dried up the Jordans waters <u>and feared</u>	G. Exodus 15:14–15: The people <u>heard and feared</u>; may they fear the greatness of Your mighty arm
H. Joshua 5:12: The manna ceased	H. Exodus 16:4: The manna began coming down

David Dorsey points out that in our culture children delight in listening to stories laid out in parallel patterns such as *The Three Little Pigs, Henny Penny,* and *Goldilocks and The*

Three Bears. By the time the wolf in the *Three Little Pigs* arrives at the second pig's house, we can guess what he will do and in what order; and certainly by the time he reaches the third pig's house we know what to expect.

There are several advantages to parallel patterns. One is that its repetitiveness makes it easier to remember, both for the speaker and the audience. Literary patterns are fascinating. They don't change the meaning of Scripture, but instead, provide even more meaning and deeper insight.

There is a wide variety of literary pattern arrangements: linear: a-b-c; parallel: a-b-c-a'-b'-c'; and symmetric: a-b-c-b'-a'. And there are variations. such as a-a'-b-b'-c-c'. The most common parallel pattern is the seven-part chaism scheme. a-b-c- (d or X for the climax)-c'-b'-a', which resembles a menorah design.

A chiasm is a reverse-parallel in literary structure. The word chiasm comes from the name of the Greek letter chi, which looks like the English letter X. An outline of a verse, a paragraph, or even a book which conforms to such a shape is called chiastic. In a chiasm, two or more lines work into the center and then work out again. These can be very elementary, or complex. In its simplest form the chiastic outline could be diagrammed A-B-C-B-A. Think of a chiasm as a sandwich. The meat is found in the center and the outer layers of bread are on either side (in a more complex form, layers of tomatoes, lettuce, and mayonnaise would be on either side of the meat in the same order.

Chiasm Sandwich
A. Bread
B. Mayo
C. Lettuce
D. Tomato
X Meat
D' Tomato
C' Lettuce
B' Mayo
A' Bread

Here is an example of a chiasm discovered by D. C. Fredericks:

Chiasm in Ecclesiastes 11:3-12:2
A Clouds and Rain (11:3)
B Light and Sun (11:7)
C Consider the days of darkness (11:8a)
D All that comes is breath (11:8b)
E Enjoy your Youth (11:9a)
X But know ... God will bring you to judgment (11:9b)
E' Enjoy your Youth (11:10a)
D' All of youth is breath (11:10b)
C' Consider God before the days of darkness (12:1)
B' Sun and Light (12:2a)
A' Clouds and Rain (12:2b)

Dr. William D. Ramey Web site IntheBeginning.org has an "X-File" section where you can download dozens of papers explaining literary patterns. Here are two examples:

Chiasm in the Joseph Narrative

Introduction (37:1–2)

A. Hostility of brothers to Joseph (37:3–11)

  B. Apparent death of Joseph, Jacob mourns (37:12–36)

  C. Interlude: Judah and Tamar (38:1–26)

   D. Unexpected Reversals (38:27.39:23)

   E. Wisdom of Joseph (40:1.42:57)

   F. Movement to Egypt (43:1.46:7)

    X. The Genealogy of Israel (46:8–27)

   F' Settlement in Egypt (46:28.47:12)

   E' Wisdom of Joseph (47:13–26)

   D' Unexpected Reversals (48:1–22)

  C' Interlude: Jacob blesses his sons (49:1–28)

  B' Death of Jacob, Joseph buries him (49:29.50:14)

A' Joseph reassures brothers (50:15–26)

Chiasm in Deuteronomy 1:19-46

A. Geographical note: the people went from Horeb to Kadesh-barnea (1:19)

 B. The Command: "Go up, take possession" of the Promised Land and "Do not fear or be dismayed" (1:20–21)

  C. Twelve spies are sent out and bring back fruit from the land (1:22–25)

   D. The people are rebellious and not willing to fight (1:26–28)

    E. The LORD states that He will be with them when the people go up to possess the land (1:29–31)

     F. The people did not trust the LORD (1:32–33)

      G. None of these shall see the Promised Land (1:34–35)

      H. Caleb will see the land (1:36)

       X. MOSES WILL NOT ENTER THE LAND (1:37)

      H' Joshua will enter the land (1:38)

      G' Children shall enter and inherit the Promise Land (1:39)

     F' The people go up to fight (1:40–41)

    E' The LORD states He will not be with the people if they now go up to possess the land (1:42)

   D' The people are rebellious and act presumptuously (43)

  C' The people are pursued out of the land and are crushed [like fruit] (44)

 B' The Response: the people returned and wept before the LORD, but He did not listen to them (1:45)

A' Geographical note: the people dwelled many days in Kadesh[-barnea] (1:46)

For more information see *The Literary Structure of the Old Testament* by David Doresy. *The Parable Discovery* by Jeffrey Curry. Also see IntheBeginning.org and RestorationofTorah.org.

Mashalic Method

David Mulligan explains the mashalic method in *Far Above Rubies: Wisdom in the Christian Community:*

> The mashalic method of teaching then is one that emphasizes the likeness between things and the created world. It is teaching by analogy rather than analysis. If, for example, we say that malicious thoughts in the mind are like noxious weeds in a garden, we are teaching by an analogy. By contrast, we could approach the subject of the human mind analytically. The human mind is composed of two aspects: the intellect and the will. The analytical seeks to label the distinct units of some portion of reality, compile them into similar categories and then describe the interrelationships between the units as part of the synthetic whole, in other words, determine where the units fit into the system. There is nothing wrong with that way of thinking and learning and teaching; it is a God-given ability and serves an important purpose in any educational program. But it has a tendency to go wrong by replacing the true nature of reality with the finally constructed system of logic. Logic and reality are *not* the same [like a map and the territory it represents are not the same]. Logical consistency does not always mean truth. Even when we have a true system of thought, one that genuinely reflects the real state of things, it is not exactly identical with reality. It is an abstraction, and men who mistake it for reality (for example, those who leave God for theology) often wake too late to see the vast difference between them.
>
> Analogical thinking as it is used in the *mashal* presents life as the picture. It deals with things in their real settings. It is a narrative rather than science. It treats the whole of things as they actually appear to us, and reveals their inner nature by comparison with something in which that inner aspect is more evident.
>
> Consider the following example: An argument is like a fire. As a fire needs heat, combustible materials, and oxygen to burn, so does an argument need inflamed passion, a real or imagined something to argue about, and words to fan the flames. Take away any of these components and the fire goes out. We can see fire, and we can understand it, and so it helps us to comprehend that great human mystery, the argument. We can also see how analysis feeds analogy. The components of fire—flame, combustibles, and oxygen—become part of the *mashal*. Analogy consumes that analysis like a flame consumes combustibles, and as real life consumes our thoughts about it.

There are two fundamental ways of thinking about life: the literary and the scientific. The two find little comfort in each other's company. The scientist sees the storyteller as an amusement, but little better, in the realm of the cold, hard facts of truth. Literature finds science to be lifeless and abstract, destructive to the sensibilities. There is something to be said for the argument on either side.

> The idea of the mashal is to bring one thing alongside another in order to force a comparison. The student then moves from something well-known to something less known or even unknown. This forced comparison brings light into darkness.

Science does tend to turn the "starry heavens" into a neat list of constellations and chemical interactions. But then again, the romantic poet might find a rainbow still the roadway for the goddess Isis, something that it certainly is not. Or take the sun, for instance: Is it, as the poet tells us, Apollo in his fiery chariot, or is it merely a great ball of burning helium? You can see the problem. The literary approach is often strongly personal but wrong, while the scientific approach is correct but dead. To state it in another way, the literary method is correct in approach, but wrong in estimation, while the scientific method is correct in estimation, but wrong in approach. The sun is not Apollo, but neither is it merely helium. Both methods arise from a sense of wonder. The scientific mind looks at the world and says, I wonder, why? It seeks answers, categories, and lists. The literary mind, on the other hand, looks at the world and says, It is full of wonders. It seeks to magnify experience and participation.

Both of these approaches were once unified in unfallen Man. In the holy Scriptures, they come together again. The Word of God brings together the personal and the mechanistic views of the universe, giving precedence to the personal. The rainbow is caused by reflected light, but it exists because God created it as a covenant sign. The sun is composed of helium and other elements, but it is created and appointed by God to rule over the day (Psalms 136:8).

The proper approach to education is a Hebrew mashalic approach. We are free to use logic, analysis, and other scientific methods, but always as pieces that fit into the whole picture. It is the whole picture that is the most important to the student. By illustration, by example, by metaphor, by figurative language, by dwelling on the resources of nature, art, human conduct, and by any of a thousand means, the true picture of this creative world is brought before a student's mind. He is guided into the path of wisdom, where the real can be embraced and the unreal cast aside.[22]

What Type of Education Did Paul Receive?

As a Pharisee, Paul was a learned product of Judaism, a man well-versed in Jewish thought and in Scripture (see Philippians 3:4–6). Paul speaks of himself in both Acts and Philippians: "I am a Jew, born in Tarsus of Cilicia, but brought up in this city. Under Gamaliel I was thoroughly trained in the law of our fathers and was just as zealous for God as any of you are today" (Acts 22:3–4); "[I was] circumcised on the eighth day, of the people of Israel, of the tribe of Benjamin, a Hebrew of Hebrews; in regard to the law, a Pharisee; as for zeal, persecuting the church; as for legalistic righteousness, faultless" (Philippians 3:5–6); "The Jews all know the way I have lived ever since I was a child, from the beginning of my life in my own country, and also in Jerusalem. They have known me for a long time and can testify, if they are willing, that according to the strictest sect of our religion, I lived as a Pharisee" (Acts 26:4–5).

Paul was brought up in Jerusalem and taught by the Rabbi Gamaliel. He studied to become a teacher of the Law. As a son in an educated and perhaps aristocratic home, Paul probably began to learn the Law by the time he was five years of age, and the oral Torah by the age of ten. He was probably sent to pursue training to teach the Law sometime after he turned thirteen. We don't know at what age he was sent to Jerusalem for his education, but some scholars believe it was before the age of twelve.[19] At whatever age he began this formal education in the Law, Paul studied with passionate devotion to the Law. In The Letter Writer, Tim Hegg explains:

> Paul's studies as a young boy would have begun with learning the Hebrew alphabet, using the Torah as the primer both for letters and reading [copy work!]. He most likely would have begun with the Shema and then progressed to the recognized liturgy... He would have memorized prayers, as well as other portions of the Torah, learning to read and write in Hebrew and Aramaic.[20]

Paul's teacher, Gamaliel, was the son of Rabbi Simeon, and grandson of the famous rabbi, Hillel. He was noted for his learning and was president of the Sanhedrin during the reigns of Tiberius, Caligula, and Claudius. He died, it is said, about eighteen years before the destruction of Jerusalem. When the apostles were brought before the Council, charged with preaching the resurrection of Jesus, as a zealous Pharisee, Gamaliel counseled moderation and calmness. By a reference to well-known events, he advised them to "refrain from these men." If their work or counsel was of man, it would come to nothing, but if it was of God, they could not destroy it, and therefore they ought to be on their guard lest they should be "found fighting against God" (Acts 5:34–40). This passage of Scripture also refers to Gamaliel, the teacher of the Law, "who was honored by all the people." It appears that Paul learned his love for and responsibility to the Gentiles from his famous teacher (he taught love by example).

The Life and Letters of Paul the Apostle explains that Paul probably did not receive a Greek education:

> Paul was born in Tarsus. His ancestry was Hebrew, and he was by birth, by inheritance, and by education a Hebrew. His city was a Greek city in its atmosphere, though under Roman domination. It was a famous university town; it was claimed in that time that the university was greater than that of Alexandria. It was not only a university town, but notable for Greek scholarship, perhaps scarcely less so than Athens itself, possibly even more so. Thus this boy breathed a Grecian atmosphere in his boyhood. But he did *not* receive a Greek education. His knowledge of Greek literature would be something like the knowledge which a Huguenot boy might get in Paris in the time of the Revolution respecting the literature of Diderot and Voltaire; for the Hebrews regarded Greek literature, and with some show of reason, as grossly immoral. A Hebrew would no more have set his boy to the study of the Greek poets and dramatists than a Puritan in the reign of Charles II would have set his boy to study the dramatic literature of that age. There are three or four citations from the Greek poets in Paul's writings, but they are simply popular proverbs such as any man might pick up in common intercourse in society.[21]

In other words, Paul knew about Greek philosophy the way a Christian-educated child knows about evolution. Paul learned about the pagan philosophies and how to counter them from his Hebrew teacher, Rabbi Gamaliel. You can easily learn about Homer, Socrates, and Plato, just as you can learn who Darwin is, without becoming absorbed in their writings. We should study the influence these writers have had on Western civilization, but we should study how Christian writers explain these philosophies from a Christian perspective. It will help us to sharpen our ability to witness and to evangelize. But we should learn of them through the eyes of Abraham and not through the eyes of Plato. This is a good time to ask that famous question, "What would Jesus do?" Do we really think that He would have read the pagan writers for wisdom or for entertainment?

The United States Treasury Department has a special group of men whose job it is to track down counterfeiters. Naturally, these men need to know a counterfeit bill when they see it. How do they learn to identify fake bills? Oddly enough, they are not trained by spending hours examining counterfeit money. Rather, they study the real thing. They become so familiar with authentic bills that they can spot a counterfeit by looking at it or, often, simply by feeling it. [22] The best way to detect error is to know truth. Your children will be able to recognize worldly wisdom and false doctrines by constant exposure to God's Word. Our goal in studying is to recognize counterfeits (just as a a doctor needs to recognize healthy and ill person). To specifically study Greek thought, in order to

> What is there in common between Athens and Jerusalem? What between the Academy and the Church? What between heretics and Christians?

recognize the counterfeits, use a Christian book like *Assumptions That Affect Our Lives* by Christian Overman or *Our Father Abraham* by Marvin Wilson,

Around 200 A.D., Tertullian, a Christian writer, penned these words:

It is this philosophy which is the subject matter of this world's wisdom, that rash interpreter of the divine nature and order.... What is there in common between Athens and Jerusalem? What between the Academy and the Church? What between heretics and Christians? Away with all projects for a "Stoic," a "Platonic," or a "dialectic" Christianity! After Jesus Christ we desire no subtle theories, no acute enquires after the Gospel.[23]

Paul made no distinction between the so-called sacred and secular areas of life. He taught—just as his Hebrew forebears did—that all of life is God's domain of activity. Every detail of life, therefore, must be set aside and consecrated to the glory of God. So Paul wrote to the Corinthians: *So whether you eat or drink or whatever you do, do it all for the glory of God* (1 Corinthians 10:31). Paul later wrote to the Colossians: *Whatever you do, whether in word or deed, do it all in the name of the Lord Jesus, giving thanks to God the Father through him* (3:17).

How did Paul teach?

But when they departed from Perga, they came to Antioch in Pisidia, and went into the synagogue on the sabbath day, and sat down. And after the reading of the law and the prophets the rulers of the synagogue sent unto them, saying, Ye men and brethren, if ye have any word of exhortation for the people, say on. Then Paul stood up, and beckoning with his hand said, Men of Israel, and ye that fear God, give audience. —Acts 13:14–16.

Paul taught much like Jesus, to the people in informal settings and in the synagogue. Paul preached Jesus from the Old Testament. The people of Jerusalem and their rulers did not recognize Jesus, yet in condemning him they fulfilled the words of the prophets that are read every Sabbath. Paul taught them using the Psalms. (See Acts 13:27–29).

Paul taught using word pictures: analogies and metaphors that are effective when the audience is familiar with the illustration. In 2 Timothy Paul uses several word pictures in this chapter to illustrate and encourage endurance:

Thou therefore endure hardness, as a good soldier of Jesus Christ. No man that warreth entangleth himself with the affairs of this life; that he may please him who hath chosen him to be a soldier. (3–4) And also if anyone competes in athletics, he is not crowned

unless he competes according to the rules.
(5) The hardworking farmer must be first to
partake of the crops (6). ... Remember ...
Jesus Christ. ... I endure all things for the
sake of the elect. ... If we endure, we shall
also reign with Him.

> Away with all projects for a "Stoic," a "Platonic," or a "dialectic" Christianity! After Jesus Christ we desire no subtle theories, no acute enquires after the Gospel.

He begins with the analogy of a soldier (v. 3–4) then compares the field of athletics (5) then changes the nature of his illustrations to farming (6). In I Corinthians 5, Paul addresses a Gentile congregation using the analogy of leaven to make important spiritual points about sin.

Paul taught for long periods. In Acts 19:9, where it is asserted that Paul withdrew from the synagogue in Ephesus and began instruction in the hall of Tyrannus. from the fifth to the tenth hour (11:00 a.m. to 4:00 p.m.), a time not usually utilized by teachers of morality of this era for systematic instruction.[24]

The Most Important Method: Teaching by Example

Jesus and Paul taught in many effective ways, but the most important of all the methods we've mentioned is teaching by example. Too often there is a gulf between the things we teach and the things we do.

Jesus taught obedience by choosing to obey not just once but thousand of times during His lifetime on earth. God became man to teach us by example!

> God became man to teach us by example!

Jesus commanded us to follow Him, to learn of Him so we can become like Him. Jesus taught by example when He healed the sick, forgave the sinner, ate with outcasts, taught His followers to love-to love God, to love one another, and to love the lost. We must teach obedience by example. Our first lesson should be to teach to love God with our whole being. Children learn more from what parents do than from what they say. Do your children see you studying God's Word? Do they see you showing kindness to the unkind? Our children will handle problems the way they see us handling problems-by dropping to our knees in prayer, or by falling apart.

Teaching by example is the perfect illustration of how the Hebrew method is superior to the Greek method (teaching by lecture). Any doctor or nurse will tell that you they learned more in a few months of internship working in a hospital than they did from years of sitting in a classroom.

How would you go about teaching your child to cook a meal? Would you sit in the school room explaining the theory of cooking or would you bring them in the kitchen and let them interact as you cook the meal? Obviously the answer is the latter. Children learn by doing. They retain information when they are engaged in hands-on, enjoyable activity with a purpose. We know children learn how to do physical things in daily life such as cooking, setting the table, making a bed, throwing a ball or walking, but for some reason we think school subjects should be isolated to the classroom. The apprenticeship approach is far superior to the lecture approach.

I see myself in my adult daughters each time I speak to them—good and bad. Most of the qualities I see in them are things I taught that I didn't realize I was teaching them. I see it in how they speak to their husbands and children, how they volunteer for church work, how they react to unexpected company, when they offer hospitality, how they react to someone who disagrees with them or when a friend disappoints them, how they hold and speak to their babies, how they cook, how they sew, how they read, how they study, how they spend money, how they show love, how they show anger, how they show forgiveness, how they laugh, etc.

I rarely see fruit from anything I taught them during our school time (except maybe the three Rs). The things I see (things that shout at me) are what they learned from my own examples. And now this is my lesson—it is a cycle of instruction. I now learn from their behaviors, responses, and actions. I learn how better to teach my younger children. I have learned I need to persist in some areas and try to improve many areas in my life because my actions are more of a lesson than anything I say—to my children and to everyone else in my life.

Ours is an enormous responsibility. Christ is made strong in our weakness. I encourage you to pray for wisdom daily. Pray your children will learn from you as they see Christ in you.

Summary of the Hebraic Teaching Methods

The Hebrews taught their children in the home. The father was the primary teacher. The Word of God was the primary focus and was used to teach both morality and worship, as well as both reading and writing. Hebrew education stressed the importance of recognizing and remembering the acts and events of divine providence throughout history through the example of the parents and through object lessons. Hebrew education also stressed the responsibility that individuals have toward God and others, the accountability of human behavior, and the need for disciplined training in making right choices. Learning was for life, and life was for learning. Study was considered a form of worship. The Heart of Wisdom teaching approach seeks a reproduction of these elements found in biblical teaching methods:

- The Bible is the primary subject. All other subjects are studied through the light of God's Word. (2 Timothy 3:16–17)

- Parents are to diligently instruct their children to love God; obey His law; be thankful for His blessings; and separate from the worship of pagan gods. (Deuteronomy 6:1–9)

- Parents are to teach by example, modeling Bible standards in daily living—loving God and loving others, and by being in prayer and God's Word daily. (Proverbs 23:26)

- God will provide the abilities and the resources we need to teach our children. (Matthew 6:25–34)

- Teaching involves using object lessons to help children recognize that all of the creation reveals God's handiwork and presence. (Psalm 19)

- Teaching involves using parables or metaphors (*mashal*) by using something familiar to the child so they can relate by a comparison. (Matthew 13:13)

- History is viewed as His story as we recognize and remember the acts, events, land, and the people of God. (Genesis 15:18)

- Reading, writing, speaking, and all topical studies should bring glory to Christ. (I Peter 4:11)

- Special weekly and annual days are set apart for worship, and as reminders of God's acts of protection and provision. (Leviticus 23)

- We are to grow in wisdom, learning is for life and life is for learning, and study is a form of worship. (I Peter 1:5–18)

- Our ultimate goal is to be to be conformed to the image of God's Son. (Romans 8:29)

Suggested Reading

Christian Education: Seeking to Become Like Jesus Christ by Lawrence O. Richards ⋈
Richards biblical and theological analysis conveys an excitement that makes Christian education a mission, not just a responsibility. And still his approach is eminently practical, insightful, and motivational.

Family Sanctuary Restoring the Biblically Hebraic Home by Dr. John Garr ⋈
A provocative look at the modern home that offers clear answers for families in crisis and for those who want to restore their families to biblical foundations. This book is a systematic, comprehensive study of the biblically Hebraic concepts of family. By helping you understand—as the ancient Hebrews did—that your home is a mikdash me'at (a temple in miniature).

The Life and Times of Jesus the Messiah (Updated) by Alfred Edersheim ⋈
This is Edersheim's classic, his most well-known, scholarly, yet exceedingly practical and highly readable book. What was it really like to live when Jesus lived? Portrays the streets, the marketplaces, the religious conflicts, the people, and the places of Jesus' earthly ministry.

The Method and Message of Jesus' Teachings (Revised) by Robert H. Stein ⋈
This useful and practical book is a much-needed introductory guide on the "how" (method) and the "what" (message) of Jesus' teachings.

Our Father Abraham: Jewish Roots of the Christian Faith by Dr. Marvin Wilson ⋈
See full description on page 129.

Paul: The Jewish Theologian by Brad H. Young ⋈
The book explains Saul of Tarsus was a man who, though rejected in the synagogue, never truly left Judaism. It dispels the skewed notion that Hellenism was the context which most influenced Paul's communication of the Gospel. Only when one rightly recognizes Paul as rooted in his Jewish upbringing and Pharisee training can he be correctly interpreted.

The World Jesus Knew by Anne Punton ⋈
This superb introduction to the culture of Jesus's time explains the beliefs and customs that are the background of the gospels. Each chapter covers distinct aspect of the life of Jesus: his home, childhood, education, clothes, language, prayers, customs, festivals, and much more. The author spent 12 years in Israel and lectures extensively on the Jewish roots of the Hebrew faith. Includes over 60 maps and photographs. This is a fantastic book to use during Bible study readings as well as during the Messiah and Ancient Israel unit studies. This is an invaluable reference tool.

Why Christians Reject Hebrew Ways

In previous chapters we examined the ancient Greek roots of modern education as we know it, and the vast differences between Greek and biblical thought. Hopefully by now this will have brought you to the obvious question, "Why do Christian homeschoolers look to the Greeks instead of the Bible for education answers?" or as the early church father Tertullian once asked, "What has Athens to do with Jerusalem?"

For the first one hundred years, the Church was comprised mostly of Jews. In 1700 of the last 2000 years of Church history, attempts to teach about the Jewish roots of the Christian faith have produced negative results, from contempt to death penalties. It has only been within the last 200 years that it has become acceptable to examine and discuss the subject rationally. In this chapter we are going to examine this part of Church history which has been long shunned. We'll examine why the Church has rejected the Hebrews' ways. This is not to say that if we all were Jewish everything would be perfect; we must always keep our focus on Christ, who is our true wisdom. But the Church has made many mistakes by walking in the flesh instead of in the Spirit and it is necessary to look at these mistakes to make sure we don't repeat them. Please read this chapter prayerfully—this section of Church history may be new to you, and some of it may disturb you. Remember we are discussing Bible times—Old and New Testament times. Some people hear the term Hebrew and think it only refers to the Old Testament.

In this chapter we will examine how and why important values and teachings from the Hebrews were rejected in favor of pagan cultures and Greek philosophies, and how those mistakes affect us today.

In all of mankind's history, Israel is the only nation to ever have been established with all three of these things dependent on God:

1. Education—the purpose and mode of instruction used by a society to educate the upcoming generation into the values and habits of the society as well as to train them to be self-supporting, contributing members of society.

2. Religion—practices, consciously or unconsciously held, that enshrine the highest and most transcendent values of the society.

3. Law—positive and negative precepts that reward culturally accepted norms and punish deviation from those norms. God gave Israel the Law through their religion.

You could take religion from Greece or Rome and there would still be plenty of the culture left, but take religion from Israel, and Israel would be dissolved. For Israel, not only was religion their religion, but education and law were integral parts of their religion. Certainly Israel was not perfect. Sin was present, but the Hebrews believed in God and taught His ways. The nation of Israel is a people of God by God's choice. Their culture was provided to them by revelation from heaven. Even the name Israel was revealed by God.

Hebrews, Jews, or Israelites?

"Hebrew People" is an ethnic term designating the lineage of the nation of Israel and the Jewish people, Abraham's descendants through Isaac and Jacob. The Hebrews, long called "The Chosen People," are descendants of Abram (renamed Abraham), who was a Semite, a descendant of Noah's son, Shem. Abraham was the first Hebrew (Genesis 14:13). His son Isaac had a son, Jacob (renamed Israel), who had twelve sons that were known as Hebrews (Genesis 40:15; 43:32). Israel's twelve sons were called the Children of Israel, Israelites, and/or the Twelve Tribes of Israel. One of the tribes was named after

Jacob's son Judah, whose descendants were called Jews (2 Kings 16:6; 25:25; Jeremiah 32:12; 38:19; 40:11; 41:3), in distinction from those belonging to the kingdom of the ten tribes, who were called Israelites. During the Babylonian Captivity, and after the Restoration, the name, however, was extended to all the Hebrew nation without distinction (Esther 3:6, 10; Daniel 3:8, 12; Ezra 4:12; 5:1, 5).

Easton's Bible Dictionary explains there are three names used in the New Testament to designate this people:

1.) Jews, as regards their nationality, to distinguish them from Gentiles.

2.) Hebrews, with regard to their language and education, to distinguish them from Hellenist, i.e., Jews who spoke the Greek language.

3.) Israelites, as respects their sacred privileges as the chosen people of God.[1]

Abram's call began a new chapter in God's plan to redeem mankind. From Abram's family would come a people who would know how to teach and keep the ways of the Lord. God made an everlasting covenant of promise with Abraham. Both Christians and Jews have their spiritual roots in Abraham and God's great, everlasting covenant with him: *And I will establish my covenant between me and thee and thy seed after thee for generations for an everlasting covenant…* (Genesis 17:7). According to the New Testament we, as believers in Christ, have been grafted into the commonwealth of Israel—we have become a part of Israel (Romans 9, 10, and 11). In this covenant, God promised numerous offspring and great blessings to Abraham, and the land of Canaan to his seed.

The *New Bible Commentary* describes God's promises to Abraham and explains these promises were framed in a covenant and confirmed with an oath, providing four major promises:

> • **A relationship with God.** *I will establish my covenant as an everlasting covenant between me and you and your descendants after you for the generations to come, to be your God and the God of your descendants after you.* (Genesis 15:1; 17:7; 26:3; 28:13, 15).

> • **A land.** *Go, walk through the length and breadth of the land, for I am giving it to you* (Genesis 13:17). The Land of Canaan is specifically intended (Genesis 15:18–21) but the New Testament indicates that Abraham and his offspring received the promise that he would be heir of the world (Romans 4:13).

> • **A people.** Abraham's descendants will become a countless multitude. *I will make your offspring like the dust of the earth.* (Genesis 13:16), *I will make you into a great nation.* (Genesis 12:2), *I will make your descendants as the stars in the sky and as the sand on the seashore.* (Genesis 22:17).

• **The nations blessed in Abraham's seed.** The Hebrew word seed (offspring, Genesis 22:18), can refer either to all descendants or to just one offspring. All nations will share the blessings promised to Abraham; his seed will bring this about. This is the promise of Christ Jesus, Abraham's seed and the light of the world (John 1:9; 9:5; Galatians 3:16).[2]

The covenant promise continued through Abraham's son Isaac, and then through Isaac's son Jacob. Jacob's name was changed to Israel. The name Israel means "he who strives with God" (Genesis 32:28). Israel had twelve sons, who began the twelve tribes of Israel, the Israelites. Jesus was born through the tribe of Judah (the Jews).

The scepter will not depart from Judah, nor the ruler's staff from between his feet, until He comes to Whom it belongs, and the obedience of the nations is His—Genesis 49:10.

God gave the Hebrews the Torah, or the Law. The word law in the Bible actually means instruction. The Torah, the Law of God, teaches or instructs believers how to live before God and with their fellow man in ethical and moral harmony. Most people believe that the law Moses received was only the Ten Commandments, but he received the whole Torah *shebikta*, which consists of the instruction contained in the five books of Moses— Genesis, Exodus, Leviticus, Numbers, and Deuteronomy. God revealed to Moses and the children of Israel His divine system for praise, worship, service as well as hygiene, dietary practices, civic laws, etc..

One common misconception in the Church is that the Jews/Israelites/Hebrews are no longer God's chosen people because they rejected Jesus. But we can't say the Jews rejected Jesus anymore than we can say the Gentiles accepted Him (if we mean *all* of them). According to the New Testament the Jewish people were of divided opinion about Jesus, not united in hostile rejection. The first century Church was first predominately Jewish. In Romans 11:1–5 Paul strongly states that God has not rejected His chosen people. He has maintained His relationship with the Jewish people through the centuries, and has promised to always do so. (For more on this see http://Heartofwisdom.com/Replacementtheology.htm)

So why don't we look at the examples God gave through the Hebrews for instruction on how to live in all three areas—education (training our children), as well as law (morality) and religion (fellowship and worship)?

Christians Are Grafted Into Abraham's Family

Christians are a part of Abraham's family through adoption. When a person accepts Christ as Savior they are grafted into Abraham's family tree—the cultivated olive tree of Israel. In Romans chapter 11, verse 11 tells us that through the Jews' fall, salvation came unto the Gentiles: *I say then, Have they stumbled that they should fall? God forbid: but rather through their fall salvation is come unto the Gentiles, for to provoke them to jealousy.* Verse 25 says that the Jews were blinded in part until the fullness of the Gentiles came in: *For I would not, brethren, that ye should be ignorant of this mystery, lest ye should be wise in your own conceits; that blindness in part is happened to Israel, until the fulness of the Gentiles be come in.* Paul encourages regenerated Gentiles not to boast in themselves as they consider Israel's present rejection by God, because the nation as a whole has been divinely hardened for a time.

Romans 11:17–21 says *And if some of the branches be broken off, and thou, being a wild olive tree, wert grafted in among them, and with them partakest of the root and fatness of the olive tree; Boast not against the branches. But if thou boast, thou bearest not the root, but the root thee. Thou wilt say then, The branches were broken off, that I might be grafted in. Well; because of unbelief they were broken off, and thou standest by faith. Be not highminded, but fear: For if God spared not the natural branches, take heed lest he also spare not thee.*

The Abrahamic covenant is important because it is a picture of God's relationship with His people, including a picture of God's mercy and our salvation. God made His covenant with Abraham and He cannot deny or change it. Thus, it is God's promise to Abraham that sustains Israel today. Paul pictured them as branches broken off the tree. But he saw an amazing thing taking place—other branches were being grafted into the tree to share in the life of the tree. These branches were the Gentiles.

Look at the parallels: Abraham being willing to sacrifice his son is a picture of God's willingness to sacrifice His only Son. God provided Abraham with a substitute sacrifice just as He provided His Son to take our place as a sacrifice; and not for our sins only, but the sins of the whole world! Legalism has no place in the covenantal relationship with God. We all must enter into a relationship with God in the same way that Abraham did, by faith in God through His sacrificial substitute, the Messiah.

Matthew Henry's commentary on 1 Peter 2:9 explains that the Jews were "exceedingly tender" of their ancient privileges, of being the only people of God, taken into a special covenant with Him, and separated from the rest of the world. *But ye are a chosen generation, a royal priesthood, an holy nation, a peculiar people; that ye should shew forth the praises of him who hath called you out of darkness into his marvelous light.* The epithet, "a peculiar people" is derived from the Latin *peculium,* and denotes "a people for God's own possession," a special possession or property. The blessings of Abraham have come to the Gentiles through Jesus Christ... (Galatians 3:14). "A peculiar people" applies to both the nation of natural Israel and to spiritual Israel, made up of all believers, both Jews and non-Jews.[3]

Dr. John Garr explains in his book, *Restoring Our Lost Legacy*:

> Millions of believers in the Jewish Messiah have been deprived of their rightful heritage in biblical Judaism as a part of the faith race of Abraham. A vast legacy of knowledge of the eternal God and the opportunity to worship and praise him in the manner which best pleases him have been lost to them, buried in nearly two millennia of Gentile tradition." [4]

When we Christians lost our Hebraic heritage, false doctrines infiltrated and corrupted the Church throughout the centuries. We also lost one of the crucial elements necessary to provoke Israel to jealousy (see Romans 10:19; 11:11 and 14).

Why Many Christians Shy Away From Things Jewish

Many Christians shy away from the terms Jewish or Hebraic. I could have easily used the term biblical or scriptural instead of Hebrew or Jewish to avoid tension, but then we would miss the critical point that we have been saved by a Jewish Messiah and grafted into a Hebrew covenant! If we renew our thinking, we can begin to pray and act in such a way that our relationship with the Jewish people and the nation of Israel will finally, after so many centuries, take the form that God intended from the beginning.

Knowledge of our Hebraic roots will give us a richer understanding of the Bible, the ministry of Jesus, and the writings of Paul, as well as prompt us into a deep study of God's Word to follow the command to *study to show thyself approved* (2 Timothy 2:15). When we investigate and learn how the early believers lived their faith in a hostile pagan world, we can better teach our children how to live in America today.

Why do so many Christians think that if something is Jewish, it's contaminated or cursed? The answer is in the history of cultural anti-Semitism in the Church that caused the separation from its Hebraic heritage.

To understand our estrangement from our Hebraic roots, we need to look at the Christian-Jewish relationship throughout the Church's history. Gentile Christians have often shown resentment that the Jews were God's Chosen People, that they have occupied the center of a story whose focus Gentile Christians have longed to be. Jesus taught that we are to practice love, humility, and goodwill among the brethren, but when carnal Gentile Christians came to political power over the Church, we saw centuries of terror and persecution committed in the name of Christ.

This is a vast subject and this portion of this chapter is by no means an in-depth study, but only a brief overview of anti-Semitism as it manifested in different time periods of history. For more information, see the end of this chapter for reading recommendations.

The Separation Begins (First—Third Centuries)

The original Church was entirely Jewish. Jesus and all of the disciples and apostles were Jewish. All of the writers of the Old Testament, as well as the New Testament, with the exception of possibly Luke, were Jewish. They worshiped on Shabbat (Saturday, the seventh day) according to the fourth commandment, kept the seven annual God-ordained festivals, and attended synagogue. Before the first Jewish revolt, the Church was actually a sect within Judaism.

Alexander Kimel, a Holocaust survivor, explains that anti-Semitism began in the first century:

> In the first century, Christianity was considered a branch of Judaism; Jews and Christians prayed together and shared synagogues. Almost from the beginning, Christianity split into two competing sects; the Jewish sect called Ebionites, headed by James the brother of Christ, and Gentile churches headed by Paul from Tarsus. The two groups competed for converts, but there was no hatred. In the writing of St. Paul, the Jews were not made responsible for the crucifixion of Jesus. Paul was sent to the Gentiles; compare what Peter, the apostle to the Jews, said in Acts 2:23, Acts 2:36, Acts 3:14. [5]

Peter's sermon on the Day of Pentecost was to an entirely Jewish group who had come Jerusalem to observe Shavuot. The 3000 people who were saved that day would all have been Jewish. (Acts 2:1–41, 47; 4:4; 6:7; 9:31; 21:20). Very few Gentiles were converted before Peter and Paul were sent out (circa 65 AD) to spread the Gospel. When God miraculously showed the believing Jews that Jesus was the Messiah for both Jew and Gentile alike, then Gentiles from every nation began to pour into this Jewish faith. All followers of Christ, whether Jew or Gentile, were seen as one family. Both groups considered themselves part of Israel. The Gentiles saw themselves as grafted into Israel (see Romans chapter 11), not replacing Israel. The word Christian was not used until A.D. 42 in Antioch (Acts 11:26), and was originally a term of contempt. Later it was adopted to set apart Jews believing in Jesus from unbelieving Jews. Ultimately it became an identity for the entire Church.

In Acts 15, the question arose in the Church as to whether Gentile (non-Jewish) believers in Jesus as the Messiah would be required to follow Jewish religious customs as proselytes before being accepted as Christians. The Church leaders ruled that they would not have to observe circumcision but would commit to following the seven Noahide Laws: 1. Not to deny God. 2. Not to blaspheme God. 3. Not to murder. 4. Not to engage in incestuous, adulterous, bestial or homosexual relationships. 5. Not to steal. 6. Not to eat a limb torn from a living animal. 7. To set up courts to ensure obedience to the other six laws.

As a result of the ruling on this issues, and the extensive missionary efforts of the apostle Paul to the Gentiles, the ethnic composition of the first-century Church began to rapidly change from a Jewish majority to a Gentile majority. To mainstream Jews, this change appeared as a willingness on the part of the early Church to be a lawless society. They also feared that this would allow pagan influences into Jewish-Christian circles and eventually, Israel. [6]

Paul made it clear that Gentiles who trust in Jesus and become children of God are equal partners with believing Jews in the Body of Messiah, and are declared righteous by God without their having to adopt any further Jewish distinctives (Romans. 3:22–23, 29–30; 4:9–12; 10:12; 11:32; 1 Corinthians 12:13; Ephesians 2:11–22; 3:6; Colossians 3:11) [7]

After the destruction of the Jerusalem Temple in the year 69 A.D., it became expedient for the Church to renounce Judaism and diminish the guilt of the Romans for the crucifixion by passing the guilt onto the Jews. The Jews became known as God killers. Many new Gentile Christians assumed the destruction of the Temple was a sign that God had rejected the Jews because they had rejected His Messiah.

By the second century, Gentiles had taken control of the Church and started the process of removing Jewish influences. There was a growing resentment toward non-believing Jews and Jewish customs. The first seeds of anti-Semitism were thus sown. As the Church grew, it became increasingly Hellenized (Greek) and Latinized (Roman) because of the Roman occupation of Israel and the Greek cultural influence. Both Judaism and Christianity were trying to distinguish themselves from the other in the eyes of Rome's political system. Christianity came to be regarded as an illegal sect and was no longer under the protective umbrella of the legal status of Judaism.

The era from A.D. 66 to A.D. 135 was the most difficult for both Israel and the Church. Jerusalem and the Temple were both destroyed; that which had provided an important unifying tie between both groups was now lost. Intense persecution of Jews and Christians led both groups to develop a defensive attitude about themselves. The Jewish people could not overlook the fact that the Church had forsaken the revolt against Rome. The Church, at the same time, began to discover that it was politically and socially advantageous to represent itself as independent of Israel, and began to embrace a universal (catholic, or non-national) identity. More and more, as men from Gentile backgrounds came to leadership positions in the Church, the tie with Israel was further weakened.

Also during the second century, Marcion, a heretic who twisted Paul's writings, fabricated a radical opposition (dualism) between the Law and God's grace, as revealed in the Gospels and other New Testament books. He recommended that the entire Old Testament be omitted from the Church's official canon of Scripture. He broke away from the Roman church in 144 and set up his own very successful group. Polycarp referred to

Marcion as "the son of Satan." Marcion believed that the God revealed in the Old Testament was cruel, so he refused to acknowledge the God of the Old Testament and embraced only the portions of the New Testament that expressed God's love. Marcion created a reduced version of the New Testament consisting of Luke and parts of Paul's letters—purposely leaving out all Jewish interpolations.

Marcion's anti-Jewish churches spread throughout the Roman Empire until the fifth century. Greek influence brought a heavy reliance on natural human reasoning. By the third century, the Church, which had been founded on revealed Truth, fitted neatly into the mold of human thought.

From Disassociation to Anti-Semitism (Fourth Century)

By the fourth century, the rise and eventual domination of Christianity throughout the Western world had taken hold. The discrimination against Jews on religious grounds had become virtually universal, and systematic and social anti-Judaism had appeared.

Eusebius wrote that the promises of the Hebrew Scriptures were for the Christians and not the Jews, and that the curses were for the Jews and not the Christians. He argued that the Church was the continuation of the Old Testament [God's Chosen People] and thus superseded Judaism. The young Church declared itself to be the true Israel, or "Israel according to the Spirit," heir to the divine promises, and found it essential to discredit the "Israel according to the flesh" to prove that God had cast away His people and transferred His love to the Christians.[8]

The Council of Nicea (A.D. 325) endorsed several anti-Jewish Church positions, including the false belief that the Jews were solely responsible for the crucifixion of Christ. This Council was convened by Constantine, Emperor of the Roman Empire. Constantine, a sun-god worshiper, claimed conversion to Christianity and proclaimed himself the head of the Christian church (he had his son and wife executed after his claimed conversion). Suddenly, things changed drastically for Gentile believers. They were no longer persecuted. It became an economic advantage to be a Christian. Constantine also blended the symbols and ceremonies of paganism with Christianity. In 314 he placed the symbol of the cross on his coins with the marks of Sol Invictus and Mars Conservator (Roman gods). Constantine retained the title of chief priest of the state cult until he died.

Under Constantine, life became easier for the Gentile Christians; however, now the Gentile Christians persecuted the Jewish believers. Jews who accepted Jesus as the Messiah were forced to give up all cultural ties with Judaism—Jewish practices, Jewish friends—anything Jewish. Constantine issued laws forbidding Jewish believers to keep Saturday as the Sabbath, circumcise their children, celebrate the Passover, etc. The punishments for disobedience included imprisonment and even death.

When Greek dialectic, dualistic thinking and oratorical methods replaced Judeo-Christian role-modeling, the Church lost the Hebraic approach to life—practical application of biblical truth. A fourth-century theologian from Antioch, John Chrysostom (who studied under the famous pagan professor Libanius), made Greek rhetoric the main teaching pattern in the Church. Modern seminary oratorical skills find their roots in the ancient Greek teaching tradition, not in the early first-century Church. The impersonal rhetorical lecture replaced teaching by example.

In 365, the Council of Laodicea (which decided what would and would not be included in the Bible and/or read in church) banned the keeping of the Jewish Sabbath by Christians. The Council of Orleans in 538 commanded Christians not to take part in any Jewish feasts such as Passover, and Jewish people were not allowed to appear in public during the Easter season.

The Roman Catholic theologian who is considered a father of the Church, St. Augustine, (354 to 430 A.D.) said, "The true image of the Hebrew is Judas Iscariot, who sells the Lord for silver. The Jew can never understand the Scriptures and forever will bear the guilt for the death of Jesus."

Mike and Sue Dowgiewicz explain the Greek and Roman influence that took place in the early church in *Restoring the Early Church*:

> The first major turning point in the church was the widespread influx of Gentiles and Hellenistic thought into the body resulting in the loss of the churches' Hebraic roots and the rise of anti-Semitism. The second turning point was the merger of the state and church.... The state church became so far removed from the teaching of Jesus and the apostles, and so politically dogmatic, that it led into the corruption and ignorance of the Dark Ages. The Roman church forbade any printing of the Bible in any language other than Latin. Therefore the populace was totally dependent upon the educated clergy for any religious instruction.

> Sacerdotalism, the system of ordained priests who mediate between God and man, became firmly established. This practice emulated the pagan practice pattern of an elevated hierarchy of priests.... From Constantine onward the glory of the Church was not found in intimate relationship with God but in its riches and forms. Church leaders were held in great awe as great men on earth; over the centuries men bowed to them. Their power represented the power of men, enforced, if need be by, the sword.... Dependence on human wisdom excluded more and more the Spirit-revealed wisdom of God, resulting in ever increasing darkness. [9]

The Middle Ages

Christians and Jews lived side by side in Rome for several centuries until Church officials enforced legislation to keep them apart. The Roman Catholic Church commenced a series of holy wars (the Crusades) from 1096–1272 to liberate the Holy Land from the people who are now known as Muslims. The Crusades, sanctioned by the Papacy, intended to make Jerusalem a Christian city.

Tragically, some of the Crusaders committed horrible atrocities, raping, murdering and plundering Jews, Muslims and other Christians en route to Palestine. The Crusaders massacred all who refused to be baptized into Christianity. The majority of Jews preferred to die for their faith rather than convert. Under this violent threat of death for refusal to convert to Christianity, the Jews in Europe were known to commit mass suicide, with parents killing their children as an act of piety. In a six-month period in 1096, over ten thousand Jewish women, children, and men (almost one-third of the entire Jewish population) were slaughtered in northern France and Germany by mobs produced by the Crusades.

Between the 11th and 15th centuries medieval Jews experienced a dramatic deterioration of their status in Europe. Jews were viewed as the devil's agents, Europe's greatest sinners, rapacious usurers, malicious murderers of Christian children (ritual-murder defamation), drinkers of Christian blood (blood libel), conspirators who sought to destroy Christianity (poisoners of wells), and continued enemies of Jesus Christ (desecraters of the Host). These frequent defamations against Jews were not borne out by the facts. Nevertheless, whole Jewish communities were slaughtered as a result of the animosity behind these charges [10]

In 1135 French scholar Pierre Abelard wrote "No nation has ever suffered so much for God. Dispersed among all nations, without king or secular ruler, the Jews are oppressed with heavy taxes as if they had to repurchase their very lives every day. To mistreat the Jews is considered a deed pleasing to God. Such imprisonment as is endured by the Jews can be conceived by the Christians only as a sign of God's utter wrath. The life of the Jews is in the hands of their worst enemies. Even in their sleep they are plagued by nightmares. Heaven is their only place of refuge. If they want to travel to the nearest town, they have to buy protection with the high sums of money from the Christian rulers who actually wish for their death so that they can confiscate their possessions. The Jews cannot own land or vineyards because there is nobody to vouch for their safekeeping. Thus, all that is left them as a means of livelihood is the business of money-lending, and this in turn brings the hatred of Christians upon them." [11]

In 1348 the bubonic plague (also known as the Black Death) in Europe killed as many as twenty-five million people. Accusations began circulating that the reason for the plague was God's anger towards sinners, and, more specifically, the Jews. As a result, throughout Germany and in many other places, Jews were murdered and their communities destroyed. On a single day in 1349, 2000 Jews were burned to death by a mob in Strasbourg. The canton of Basel (a general council of the Roman Catholic church called by Pope Martin V) in Switzerland gathered all 4500 of its Jews in a specially-built structure on an island in the Rhine and burned them to death; afterwards the town fathers passed a law forbidding Jewish residence in the canton for 200 years.

The Reformation

The Reformation was the 16th-century religious revolution that established the Protestant churches and ended the supremacy of the Pope in Western Christendom. Martin Luther (1483–1546), known as the father of the Reformation, was the German leader of the Protestant Reformation. On October 31, 1517, he published ninety-five theses and nailed them to the door of the Castle Church in Wittenberg, inviting debate on matters of practice and doctrine. These theses contained things like propositions opposing the release from temporal penalties for sin through the payment of money to the Church (called indulgences). Luther's action was movement for reform. He was a wise and insightful Church leader who initially favored the Jews, hoping that they would accept the Christian faith.

Luther, expecting mass conversions of the Jews, wrote: "The Jews are blood-relations of our Lord; if it were proper to boast of flesh and blood, the Jews belong more to Christ than we. I beg, therefore, my dear Papist, if you become tired of abusing me as a heretic, that you begin to revile me as a Jew."

However, when the Jews did not convert, his attitude changed dramatically. In a sermon shortly before his death, he called for the immediate expulsion of all Jews from Germany. Here are some of his statements:

- "All the blood kindred of Christ burn in hell, and they are rightly served, even according to their own words they spoke to Pilate..."

- "Verily a hopeless, wicked, venomous and devilish thing is the existence of these Jews, who for fourteen hundred years have been, and still are, our pest, torment and misfortune. They are just devils and nothing more."

- "Firstly, their synagogues should be set on fire.... Secondly, their homes should likewise be broken down and destroyed.... Thirdly, they should be deprived of their prayer-books and Talmuds.... Fourthly, their rabbis must be forbidden under threat of death to teach any more.... Fivthly, passport and traveling privileges should be absolutely forbidden to the Jews.... Sixthly, they ought to be stopped from usury…. Seventhly, let the young and strong Jews and Jewesses be given the flail, the axe, the hoe, the spade, the distaff, and spindle, and let them earn their bread by the sweat of their noses…. We ought to drive the rascally lazybones out of our system…. Therefore away with them…."[12]

- "To sum up, dear princes and nobles who have Jews in your domains, if this advice of mine does not suit you, then find a better one so that you and we may all be free of this insufferable devilish burden—the Jews."

It's hard for us to understand how Luther could have done such mighty work during the Reformation and later have had such a drastic reversal of his attitude toward God's people.

The Inquisitions

The first Inquisition was established by the papacy during the Middle Ages in 1233 to suppress heresy. Inquisitors could bring suit against any suspect person. Suspects would have a trial with witnesses from both clergy and laity, to assist the court in arriving at a verdict. Punishment could include anything from excommunication to the death penalty. Galileo was tried and condemned under this Inquisition in 1633.

The Spanish Inquisition was independent of the Medieval Inquisition. The Spanish Inquisition (1481-1820), established at the request of King Ferdinand V and Queen Isabella I, was designed to drive out Jews, Protestants, and other non-Catholics from Spain. Converted Jews [13] were punished for secretly retaining their Jewish values and culture. Over 350,000 Jews suffered punishment. Between 2,000 and 4,000 were condemned to death as heretics or "crypto-Jews" (or *marranos*).[14]

Eastern Europe

The Jews tried to escape the Crusades and Inquisitions by moving east, but they faced persecution in Russia and Poland as well. Between 1648 and 1656, an estimated three hundred thousand to five hundred thousand Jewish people were slaughtered in Poland and Ukraine alone.

The Holocaust

The Holocaust which took place during World War II (1939–1945) was the worst genocide in history. Without anti-Semitism in the Church, the Holocaust could not have happened.

The Nazis explicitly intended to totally destroy the Jewish people. They ordered the violent murder of almost six million Jews, including two million children. The Nazis referred to this butchery as the "Final Solution." The slaughter was carried out mainly by mobile killing squads, in ghettos, labor, and death camps.

There were hundreds of labor and death camps located in Germany, Austria, Belgium, Poland, Finland, France, Holland, Italy, Lithuania, Norway, Russia and Yugoslavia. In the ghetto and labor camps people were worked to death. They died from beating, torture, liquidation of the sick by an injection of phenol into the heart, execution or disease, including infectious diseases such as typhus, tuberculosis and dysentery. The death camps had a more direct approach. They were created "to solve the Jewish question" completely. Their function was to kill the people who arrived there as quickly as possible. At the Auschwitz-Birkenau camp more than 20,000 people could be gassed and cremated each day.

In my teens my grandmother gave me *The Hiding Place* by Corrie ten Boom and *Tortured for Christ* by Richard Wurmbrand (both books about the Holocaust). To say I was horrified is an understatement. I was ignorant about World War II. I did not have a grasp of the time period. When I realized both authors were still alive and the Holocaust happened during my mother's lifetime I was shocked.

This was just a few years before I was born! Imagine: just a few years before I was born, almost six million Jews were systematically and brutally executed while most of the world silently stood by. It was during this century that a massive organization of special divisions was set up specifically to deal with the administrative and technical needs of an enormous plan to wipe out God's people. It wasn't very long ago that babies were used as target practice, men and women were used as human guinea pigs by doctors and other scientists, and human beings were shot in front of ravines to fall into mass graves in layer upon layer of corpses. The compassion I gained at fourteen years of age has grown into a deep love for the Jewish people.

After the defeat of Hitler, the slaughter of Jews seemed over; however a dictator in Russia named Joseph Stalin continued Hitler's work. The Russians, led by Stalin, also massacred many Jews, calling them terrorists and simply lying to justify their murder.

Modern Times

Anti-Semitism continues today through out the world. There are some who have the same diabolical intent to destroy Israel which is found among some Arabs, Soviets, and extremists; and then there are those in a different category—Christians who believe that they have replaced Israel (see http://Heartofwisdom.com/ReplacementTheology.htm). In America, organizations like the Ku Klux Klan, the John Birch Society, the Liberty

Lobby, the Institute of Historical Research, and neo-Nazi splinter groups remain anti-Semitic; which, until recently, have attracted few adherents.

Since the September 11, 2001 disaster, public expressions of anti-Semitism have abounded. An article by Rafael G. Grossman entitled "9-11 and Anti-Semitism" summarizes, "In an article appearing in London's Daily Telegraph, Petronella Wyatt, a non-Jewish British journalist, wrote, 'Since September 11, anti-Semitism and its open expression has become respectable at London dinner tables.'"

Today there are hundreds of [Internet] sites and links to vile anti-Semitism [tragically, some by so-called Evangelicals]. It can also be heard from pulpits and read in many local, especially rural, newspapers across the United States. Arab propagandists have ignited this hateful fire and stirred the otherwise latent, but pre-existent, age-old canard: Jews are to blame for anything that goes wrong."[15]

Phyllis Chesler, who is a highly regarded activist, writer, and teacher in Jewish world affairs, recently wrote *The New Anti-Semitism*. In it she explains that after September 11, Osama bin Laden called the assault on America "blessed attacks" against the "infidel...the new Christian-Jewish crusade." He explained that the Twin Towers had fallen because of American support for Israel. Islamic reactionaries and Western intellectuals and progressives, who may disagree on every other subject, have agreed that Israel and America are the causes of all evil. Israel has fast become the Jew of the world, scorned, scapegoated, demonized, and attacked.[16]

The Beginning of a Decline in Christian Anti-Semitism

Scholars like Alfred Edersheim, Dr. Marvin Wilson, Dr. Dwight A. Pryor, Dr. John Garr, Dr. Brad Young, Dr. Robert L. Lindsey, David Bivin (Jerusalem Perspective), Joseph Frankovic and many others are bringing an exodus from eighteen centuries of Judaeophobia, anti-Judaism, and anti-Semitism. Edward H. Flannery says that a new era in Jewish-Christian understanding has caused a general decline in Christian anti-Semitism:

> The emergence of a revisionist Christian theology of Judaism in recent years promises to become a potent factor in the decline and disappearance of Christian anti-Semitism. Though begun in the pioneering efforts of a mere handful of scholars in the '30s and '40s, its present impetus has derived in the main from the growth of the ecumenical spirit in the '50s and '60s, the establishment and survival of the State of Israel, and from a postwar realization of the horrors and implications of the Holocaust. These crucial events brought some Christian theologians and scholars to the recognition that the anti-Judaism of Christian teaching and [a misreading of the] Scriptures played a crucial role in the origin and growth of anti-Semitism throughout

the Christian centuries and, if to a lesser degree, contributes to its course. It became evident that a revised Christian theology of Judaism was imperative, not for the defeat of anti-Semitism alone but for the integrity of the Christian message as well.

Though still in its infancy, this new theology has increasingly attracted a broad and reputable band of theologians, and more recently has enlisted the attention of some first-rank theologians of international reputation. The objective these theologians have set for themselves is the correction and emendation of Christian theology of a kind to excise as far as possible the anti-Judaic elements of traditional teachings and to accord Judaism its proper theological validity and importance from a Christian perspective. Thus far the beginnings of a consensus have materialized. Virtually all agree that any Christian theological consideration of Judaism must include a full appreciation of the Jewish heritage of Christianity, the Jewishness of Jesus and the primitive Church; the rejection of offensive teachings, such as the deicide accusation and the divine repudiation and replacement of Judaism; invidious comparisons of Christianity with Judaism; and repudiation of anti-Semitism as sinful and unchristian.

The blueprint for the extinction of Christian anti-Semitism is, ostensibly, already on paper. It is to be found in the statements and guidelines of the churches and in the work of revisionist theologians. When this corpus will have been sufficiently disseminated and implemented on all ecclesial levels, Christian anti-Semitism will for all practical purposes have come to naught, or become wholly absorbed in its disowned offspring, secular anti-Semitism. Regrettably, the present pace of its dissemination and implementation is slow. Most of the Christian populace has not been reached.[17]

Christians' Hebrew Roots

Paul tells Gentile believers in Messiah in Romans 11:18 that anyone who repents of their sins and receives Jesus as Savior and Lord is grafted into Israel (pictured as an olive tree) and is made a partaker of its rich root. They are made partakers of the promise to Abraham and become fellow citizens of the commonwealth of Israel (Ephesians 2:19).

Paul wrote concerning the Church in Galatians 3:7–9, *Know ye therefore that they which are of faith, the same are the children of Abraham. And the Scripture, foreseeing that God would justify the heathen* [Gentiles] *through faith, preached before the Gospel until Abraham, saying, in thee shall all the nations be blessed!* This is why Christianity has historically been referred to as the Judeo-Christian faith. Our faith is rooted in the Bible—in biblical Judaism.

> *Paul said…do not boast over the branches. If you do, consider this: You do not support the root* [Israel], *but the root supports you* [the Church]—Romans 11:18.

Christians have faith in and serve a Hebrew Lord, who had Hebrew disciples; and, through Christ, we are grafted into a Hebrew family. All the patriarchs and all the prophets were Hebrew, from Abraham to John the Apostle. We study a Hebrew book—the Bible was written entirely by Hebrews (with the possible exception of Luke), and we should desire to follow the first-century Church, which was predominately Hebrew. It makes perfect sense for Christian parents to study how the Hebrews taught their children.

The themes of the Old and New Testaments are the same—God's holiness, righteousness, and mercy, man's alienation and estrangement from God through disobedience, and God's provision of a Savior. It might surprise you to learn that the Jewish people do not rely on works for salvation; they know that the only way to salvation is through believing and trusting in the Messiah. The basic message of the New Testament is uniquely a Jewish one—the fulfillment of the Messianic hope. There is nothing in the New Testament that is non-Jewish or anti-Jewish. Quite the contrary, Al Brickner explains that Jesus' entire message taught that:

> Only the merciful were to receive mercy, only the forgiving could expect forgiveness and that love would be the sign of His true disciples. Our adoption as Christian believers into the commonwealth of Israel, concurrent with initial salvation, was a blood-bought possession. Jesus died not only to save humanity from sin, but also to gain for us a heritage in Abraham through whom the commonwealth of Israel was produced. This heritage from Abraham has been brought to us by a birthright acquired through faith in Jesus the Messiah—not through DNA or a genetic connection to Abraham. From this birthright, we obtain spiritual citizenship in the commonwealth of Israel, perpetuated through the eternal kingdom that was produced by the Messiah in the Spirit. The nature of this Abrahamic heritage properly shapes our world view, our concept of destiny, our worship system, our political views, our civic responsibilities, our domestic life, our personal conduct, and last but not least, our understanding of the eternal God himself.

The Messianic Covenant not only brought redemption, but guaranteed all men, both Jews and Gentiles, the right of equal access to the promises of God through Abraham. In his book *Traitor*, Dr. Jacob Gartenhaus makes this insightful remark:

> …false Christianity—as is nominal Christianity—and false Judaism—as is nominal Judaism—are not and cannot be reconciled, can never be blended together. But true Christianity and true Judaism are one and the same thing. When this is fully understood and the tendency to fear Jews and things Jewish is eliminated, the Church is will see an accelerated restoration of Judeo-Christian values manifested in the lives of its people. The occasional indictments of being Judaized will diminish because it will be clearly understood that the blood of Christ is the only answer to

the sin question. Authentic Judeo-Christianity is the only source of biblically sound praise, worship, and teaching.

Most Gentile Christians infer that the Jews' rejection of Jesus is analogous to their rejection of the Messiah. Nothing could be further from the truth. The fact is that the Jews have always believed in the Messiah, and they still do. It was because of their unwavering expectation of the Messiah's coming that the words of God declaring his advent were delivered and preserved. It was for us Gentiles and for our salvation that Israel was blinded in part and did not recognize Jesus as the Messiah. As a result of their partial blindness, we, the wild olive tree, were grafted into the tame olive tree. We Gentiles who did not know the ways and precepts of God were given access to this life and knowledge, the rich sap of the olive tree (the system of Judaism), because of our faith in the Jewish Messiah, Jesus. The tree of the Jewish way of life has become to us a tree of life through Jesus.[18]

Finding Our Way Home

We have lost so much since the Church's separation from her first-century roots and the parting of the ways between Jew and Gentile. Christians have lost a beautiful legacy and instead experienced Judaeophobia and anti-Semitism. But God is doing a mighty work! Many Gentile Christians all over the world are rediscovering and reconnecting to our biblical roots and heritage, forsaking the ancient Greco-Roman dualistic worldview. We are learning to obey Paul's letter to the Ephesians:

> *Endeavoring to keep the unity of the Spirit in the bond of peace. There is one body and one spirit; just as you were called in one hope of your calling; one Lord, one faith, one baptism; one God and Father of all, who is above all, and through all, and in you all.*—Ephesians 4:3–6.

Christians are recognizing and ridding themselves of prejudices and becoming aware of our Hebrew heritage. This exciting movement spans all denominations of Christianity. Again, I reiterate the importance of B-A-L-A-N-C-E. As Dr. John Garr explains, "We cannot allow the pendulum to swing from the extreme of the antinomianism[19] of the Christian past to the other extreme of legalism, where we seek to acquire or maintain status before God by obedience to the law rather than by grace through faith only in the shed blood of Jesus Christ." The Bible is a Jewish document, it is Hebraic, but not all things Hebraic are necessarily biblical. Many of today's Jewish practices are at odds with Scripture.

We must keep our eyes focused on Christ and obedience to His commands of loving God and loving others. *Knowledge of the truth leads to godliness* (Titus 1:1). *May our words mirror the spirit of Christ who came into the world not to condemn but to save.* (John 3:17).

Suggested Reading

Resources About Our Biblical Heritage

Fellow Heirs by Tim Hegg 🖛

Tim Hegg is a homeschool father and an excellent, balanced author. I believe he understands Romans 11 adoption more than most of us because he has both adopted and natural children. *Fellow Heirs* seeks the biblical perspective on identity within the family of God as Jews have begun to discover their Messiah, and non-Jewish believers have begun to discover the Torah.

Listening to the Language of the Bible: Hear it Through Jesus' Ears by Dr. Lois Tverberg 🖛

The Bible speaks in words and phrases that come from a very different culture, place and time. Sometimes its Hebraic ideas and imagery sound foreign to our ears, but when we enter the minds of its ancient authors, we discover wonderful new depth and meaning. Join this author to learn from the Bible's rich phrases and imagery, and gain new insight on its words for your life. This book is an excellent guide to discovering the richness of the Scriptures in their Hebraic setting. Using the tools of language and culture, it unearths beautiful nuggets of new meaning from the Bible's ancient words. From seemingly odd phrases, it shares rich insights that do not translate well from culture to culture. The book examines many topics from the perspective of the ancient writers, including prayer, family and the promised Messiah. It also looks at the powerful sayings of Jesus in light of the Jewish culture of His time. The book contains more than 60 brief, illustrated devotional articles that unpack the meaning of biblical words and phrases for our lives. Excellent!

The Mystery of the Gospel: Jew and Gentile and the Eternal Purpose of God
by D. Thomas Lancaster 🖛

Ultimately, the mystery is about the identity of Gentile believers and their relationship to Israel through the Messiah. *The Mystery of the Gospel* provides long-sought answers for everyone who is confused about where they fit in the House of Israel and the Torah of God. A great introduction to the Hebrew Roots of Christianity and a wealth of new material for those familiar with our heritage. Exciting!

Restoring Our Lost Legacy: Christianity's Hebrew Heritage by Dr. John Garr 🖛

Millions of believers have been denied their biblical legacy, the riches of the Hebrew foundations of their faith. Christian Judaeophobia, anti-Judaism, and anti-Semitism have conspired to rob them of the treasures of their inheritance. Dr. Garr urges the Church to recover its Hebrew heritage and its connection with the Jewish matrix which produced it. These pages call Christians back to the Bible, to the roots of faith that enrich lives and equip believers to achieve greater spiritual maturity through a more comprehensive understanding of Jesus.

Resources About Anti-Semitism in the Church

God's Plan for Israel: A Study of Romans 9–11 by Steven A. Kreloff ↜
The first-century Church was almost exclusively Jewish. Its faith was in the Jewish Messiah. It believed in a message taught in a Jewish land. It looked to the Old Testament Scriptures for spiritual understanding of New Testament truth. Then the picture changed. Severe persecution arose and the believers were scattered across the Roman empire. Jews became bitter opponents of Christianity and multitudes of Gentiles turned to Christ for salvation. Jewish believers were puzzled. What would happen to the promises made to Israel. Would Israel be cast aside for the Gentile church. These were the questions Paul had in mind when he wrote Romans chapters 9–11. A small but excellent book—hard to find—but worth looking for.

Our Hands Are Stained with Blood by Dr. Michael Brown ↜
From the first 'Christian' persecutions of the Jews in the fourth century to the unspeakable horrors of the Holocaust, from Israel-bashing in today's press to anti-Semitism in today's pulpits, this shocking and painful book tells the tragic story of the Church and the Jewish people. It is a story every Christian must hear." Brown does a good job explaining the false doctrine of replacement theology (the teaching that the Church has replaced Israel). He shares how God's promises made directly to the people and nation of Israel were unconditionally everlasting!

The Road to Holocaust by Hal Lindsey ↜
This book could have been titled *The Danger in the Homeschool Movement!* This is Hal Lindsey's most shocking revelation ever: the disquieting facts about a spiritual movement—found in many homeschool books and promoted by many homeschool speakers—that would take over our churches and government and lead us to disaster. This movement, commonly known as Christian Reconstructionism or Dominion Theology, reintroduces an old error that brought catastrophe to the Church and the Dark Ages to the world—the same error that founded a legacy of contempt for the Jews and ultimately led to the Holocaust of Nazi Germany.

What Price Prejudice?: Anti-Semitism in the Light of the American Christian Experience
by Frank E Eakin ↜
What Price Prejudice? examines the long tradition of anti-Semitism by giving an overview of the history of Jewish-Christian relations. Frank Eakin's work will help Christians to reflect seriously and objectively upon history and theology—and their impact on Jewish-Christian relations. Discussion questions follow each chapter to stimulate discussion and encourage further reflection on the issues addressed.

Where Was Love and Mercy? by Clarence Wagner ↜
Addresses the long and painful history of the Church and its attitude toward Jews and Judaism. It presents the biblical and historical facts that put Israel, the Jewish, and the Church into context, encouraging Christians to redress our historical error, reconnect to our Hebraic roots, and stand with Israel and the Jewish people in the relationship invisioned in the New Testament.

Section 3

Heart of Wisdom
Methods

In This Section:

The previous sections explain why we need to change our ideas about education. This section explains how to change our methods.

In this section we examine the many different methods and approaches that are components of the Heart of Wisdom teaching approach: Learning Styles and the Four-Steps, Delight Directed Learning, Charlotte Mason's Ideas, Unit Studies, and Writing to Learn.

Learning Styles and the Four-Step Process

There is a story about a man who once had three horses: a racehorse, a plow horse, and a pony. The man made up a schedule whereby he could get the most work out of his horses. On Mondays, Wednesdays, and Fridays, all three horses worked in the fields, hooked up to a plow. On Tuesdays and Thursdays, the man took all three horses to a racetrack so that each horse would learn how to run fast. On the weekends, he used all three horses to give pony rides to children. At the end of the week, the man complained that not a single one of the horses had met his expectations.

The racehorse turned to the man and said, "I could not run properly when my back ached from plowing. If you had let me stay at the racetrack all week, I could have spent time doing and improving at what I do best."

The plow horse said, "If my feet were not so swollen from racing, I could have pulled the plow straighter and farther. If you had allowed me to stay in the fields all week, I could have spent time doing and improving at what I do best."

> No one person can learn everything there is to know, and God has given us all very different gifts and talents.

The pony said, "I have had it! If I didn't ache all over from doing things I was not made to do, I wouldn't have been so grumpy to all the children who rode on my back. If you had only allowed me to give rides to children all week, I could have spent time doing and improving at what I do best."

Each of our children has different gifts and talents. Who was the person who decided that educational goals should consist only of certain subjects, some of which are only used by a small percentage of the population? Is the goal of education to make everyone the same? Should the goal of education be to make everyone the same? You can't make everyone be the same by forcing them all to learn the same thing. No one person can learn everything there is to know, and God has given us all very different gifts and talents. The metaphor used by the apostle Paul (see 1 Corinthians 12:12–31) that the Church is the body of Christ illustrates this perfectly. We can't all be the arms, or the eyes, or the ears, or the feet. We need each others' gifts and talents in order to be the most effective people we can be.

God knows more about our children than the public school system! And we can trust Him with our children's futures. God's Word promises that if we acknowledge God in all our ways, He will direct our path (see Proverbs 3:6). We know that God has made each of our children for a specific purpose. If we teach them what He commands us to teach them, He will guide us to prepare them for the plan that He has for them—knowingly or unknowingly.

God can prepare us for the future in many ways. Just think of your life right now. What had to happen in your past to prepare you and place you where are and for what God has called you to do and be today? Did you learn what you needed to know in school? From your parents? At church? From different situations or relationships? God uses all things for good—for the people who love Him (Romans 8:28). All of life is a classroom. God can and often does use bad situations to help us turn our weaknesses into strengths.

> Seventy percent of children do not learn well in the way that most schools teach—through lectures, textbooks, and tests.

Each of our children is different from any other child who is currently being educated—or has ever been educated throughout history, for that matter—but there are four basic learning styles that will apply to them, and which you should keep in mind when you begin to design your own personal homeschooling curriculum.

> All of life is a classroom.

Four Different Learning Styles

The most important thing to know about learning styles is that none of them is any better than the other. We all have different intellectual strengths. No one will fit into a box—we are all unique individuals who have been created by God—but each of us is a combination, more or less, of the four basic types, with strong tendencies in one or two of the categories. Studies have shown that seventy percent of children do *not* learn well in the way that most schools teach—through lectures, textbooks, and tests—most students need more.[1]

There are many ways to categorize learning styles. Most of us are familiar with the visual, auditory, and kinesthetic modes of learning—visual learners prefer to learn primarily by seeing and watching demonstrations; auditory learners prefer to learn primarily through verbal instructions; and kinesthetic learners prefer to learn primarily by doing, through their own personal direct involvement.

In the last twenty years or so, neurosurgeons have discovered that each of the two hemispheres of the human brain is responsible for different modes of thinking and specializes in certain skills. Studies reveal that the left brain is mostly responsible for logic, sequence, and rational thinking. The right brain is mostly responsible for random, unordered, and intuitive creativity.

Other categories relate learning styles to genetic personality types, while a student's age, home environment, and experiential background are also factors.

> Anything you read about learning styles should line up with God's Word and should never be used as an excuse for sin or other shortcomings.

Christians should be cautious when studying learning-style theories. As with other truths, non-believers can take a discovery of a natural law, as the secular world often does, and distort the principle to fit their secular worldview. New Age philosophies, as well as the field of psychology, take things like learning differences and brain dominance and use them as an excuse for sin. Sigmund Freud and Carl Jung are responsible for most of the teachings about the four personality types, and both of these men were not only unbelievers, they were downright anti-Christian. The psychology teachings that are creeping into our churches today are not in line with biblical principles, are not of God, and are, therefore, ultimately destructive. Any time the word psychology or the names Freud or Jung come into play, a red flag should wave in your mind.[2]

This does not mean that we must discount certain facts just because they were discovered by non-believers. We would not discount inventions such as eyeglasses or the automobile, which we use every day, just because atheists invented them. The Bible reveals that different people are given different gifts and talents by God. Anything you read about learning styles should line up with God's Word and should never be used as an excuse for sin or other shortcomings. The fact is, we all have different preferences in all areas of life. Some of us like broccoli, and some of us like spinach. Some of us prefer the color red, and some prefer blue. Some of us prefer discussion and interaction, and some prefer to have quiet time alone. And, of course, we change as we go through the different stages of our lives—and our preferences change as well.

The scientific studies which prove that we learn in different ways should *not* be used to categorize or label children. They should be used, instead, to realize the benefits of teaching new concepts through different modes of learning and to help children who have difficulty grasping or retaining information. In fact, we should not teach exclusively to any particular style—else the student would only learn in one mode. We need to teach children to recognize their strengths and endeavor to improve on their weaknesses.

Scientific studies show that people take in, or perceive, information differently—and that they also process this information differently. Some learners need to perceive things concretely (through their five senses) in order to be able to understand the information. Other learners can understand information abstractly—that is, mentally understand what cannot be perceived concretely.

How we *process* what we learn is the way we *use* the information. Some learners process reflectively, while other learners process actively. When we combine the various ways information can be perceived and processed, we get four basic learning styles. Bernice McCarthy (teacher for twenty-two years) revealed the remarkable similar results amongst learning styles researchers. Dr. McCarthy outlined and classified the similarities of eighteen researchers. A few are shown in the table below[3].

Carl Jung	Alexis Lotas	Barbra Bree Fischer	David Merrill	Anthony Gregorc	Elizabeth Wetzig
Feelers	Affective One Learner	Emotionally Involved	Amiable	Abstract Random	Assister
Thinkers	Cognitive Two Learner	Incremental	Analytical	Abstract Sequential	Posturer
Sensors	Cognitive One Learner	Sensory Generalist/Specialist	Driver	Concrete Sequential	Resister
Intuitors	Affective Two Learner	Intuitive	Expressive	Concrete Random	Percerverator

Based on these findings the McDonald's Corporation funded a conference for eight researchers to discuss the ramifications of the research connections in Chicago in 1979. The conference included: Dr. Bernice McCarthy, Dr. Joseph Bogen, Dr. Bill Bergquist, Dr.

Betty Edwards, Dr. David Kolb, Dr. Anthony Gregroc, Dr. Louis Fisher, Dr. Barbara Fisher, Dr. Bill Hazard, Elizabeth Wetig, and Dennis Detzel. The result of this conference was the conception of and development of the 4Mat System™ designed to teach to all four learning styles in a cycle of instruction. Since the development of this teaching approach, Dr. McCarthy has achieved national recognition as a leader in the instructional field. The 4Mat System™ is being used by hundreds of thousands of teachers throughout the country to design and develop lesson plans for every age group: kindergarten, elementary school, middle school, high school—even college, law school, and medical school.

In documented field studies of the 4Mat System™, the following outcomes have been found to recur consistently:

- Improved retention
- Higher achievement
- Increased motivation
- Improved thinking skills
- Lower remediation

McCarthy explains the four learners in her book *The 4Mat System: Teaching to Learning Styles with Right/Left Mode Techniques*[4].

The Four Learners

Type 1: The Innovative Learner

A type-one learner is one who primarily perceives information concretely, and processes by thinking it through. Innovative learners are "people-people." They learn by listening, sharing ideas, and personalizing information. They need to be personally involved in learning. They often tackle problems by thinking about it by themselves then brainstorming with others. They do well then they can view concrete situations from many perspectives. They show appreciation for other people and model themselves after those people whom they respect.

Type 2: The Analytic Learner

A type-two learner is one who primarily perceives information abstractly and processes actively by working with it consciously. Analytic learners are mainly interested in acquiring facts in order to deepen their understanding of concepts. Schools are generally made for this type of learners, who are eager to think through and understand ideas. They are thorough and industrious, and they excel in traditional learning environments. They are do well organizing details and thinking sequentially. They tackle problems rationally and logically, and they are often more interested in concepts than in other people.

Type 3: The Common-Sense Learner

A type-three learner is one who primarily perceives information abstractly and processes by thinking it through. Common-sense learners are primarily interested in finding out how things work. Ninety-five percent of engineers tested were type-three learners. They excel in down-to-earth problems and are common-sense people. They have little patience for unclear ideas; they prefer to experiment and fiddle with concrete objects. They undertake problems by acting (often without confer with others), and they need to discover, maneuver, and practice things in order to understand how they work.

Type 4: The Dynamic Learner

A type-four learner is one who primarily perceives information concretely and processes actively by working with it. Dynamic learners are chiefly concerned with self-directed discovery. They seek to influence others, and they often learn by trial and error. They thrive on challenge, take pleasure in change and easily adapt to it. They tend to take chances and are at ease with other people. They perceive many things through their emotions, and they process information by enthusiastically doing something with it. They have a strong need to be able to use what they have learned in other situations.

Homeschooling and Learning Differences

When I first began homeschooling, I quickly discovered how differently each of my children learned. With the best of intentions, I started out by using a traditional school textbook approach. Each day, I would assign reading passages, and then test my children weekly for comprehension—because that is how the schools taught and it seemed like the best thing to do. But it wasn't long before even I became bored with the textbooks, and discouraged because my children were frustrated and did not enjoy learning.

About that time, I began reading about learning styles. I recalled the times in my life when I actually enjoyed learning—and none of those times were when I was in school! The truth was, I was almost entirely self-taught by being an avid reader. I am a strong type-four learner, and I eventually discovered that it was okay to learn differently from the way the school system taught. I refocused my homeschooling goals and began to concentrate on having my children actually learn the material—not just on duplicating school at home. You don't get any brownie points for teaching or learning something in the most boring way possible!

One example of the difference between the various learning styles can easily be seen when comparing my two oldest daughters (who are now adults). My oldest daughter, Belinda, is a combination type-one and type-four learner. She is creative, friendly, and full of energy. Belinda did not learn well using a textbook approach—she needed more. My second daughter, Rebecca, is a strong type-two learner. She is quiet, organized, and systematic. Rebecca flew through all of her textbooks, gaining a fair grasp of every concept with very little effort.

Both girls had talents that God had given them, and they both excelled in different areas. By traditional school standards, Rebecca seemed more intelligent because she outshone Belinda academically in every subject; but I knew that Belinda was not a slow learner. At 16 years of age she could make a dress without a pattern, speak fluent Spanish, and cook a gourmet meal for twenty people on a moment's notice. She picked up concepts easily, but only if they were relevant to her interests. If she did not see a meaningful purpose in what she was studying, she had a difficult time staying focused.

Eventually, we switched over to a unit-study curriculum that utilized McCarthy's 4Mat System™, which shows how to teach to all learning styles. Before delving into the details of a certain subject, the curriculum guided us to discuss, interact, and create a genuine interest in the subject and how it related to our children's lives.

This made an incredible difference for Belinda. It was as if she suddenly woke up and discovered that learning could be not only interesting, but downright fascinating! Meanwhile, Rebecca was discovering further possible applications of the concepts she was learning about, and she developed more creativity. To this day, Belinda loves to read, study, and write about things that interest her. She occasionally tutors algebra, which she learned well because she found a reason to learn it—she enjoys teaching it! I am convinced that if we had stayed on the frustrating road of textbook-only learning, she would not enjoy reading and studying as she does today.

The Four Steps to Learning

The Heart of Wisdom approach begins with a two sided curriculum base: God's Word and God's world. Each lesson in this approach are based on a simplified version McCarthy's 4Mat System™ merged with Delight Directed Learning and Charlotte Mason's methods. The four step system, I termed Excite, Examine, Expand, and Excel is a way to teach to all four learning styles—whichever ones might be present in your children. This system does not isolate any one particular type of learning, but instead, teaches in four different ways so that students can ultimately relate to the subject in the way they feel the most comfortable—and, at the same time, learn how to learn in other ways.

Step	Step Description	Activities
Step 1: **Excite** To create an interest	This is a critical step that is, unfortunately, skipped in many schools. The idea is to motivate students by making the lesson meaningful to their lives. Discuss what the children may already know about the subject and what they would like to find out.	• Mind mapping • Brainstorming • Watching a video • Discussing the topic • Making lists • Drawing tentative conclusions
Step 2: **Examine** To find out the facts	This is the step most often used in traditional education. The idea is to find out the facts—but not necessarily with a textbook. We suggest utilizing real books, Internet Web sites, and videos.	• Researching on the Internet • Reading an interesting book on the subject • Reading a classic • Looking the topic up in an encyclopedia • Referring to a commentary • Viewing maps • Interviewing an expert • Interacting with computer software
Step 3: **Expand** To do something with what has been learned	The idea is to reinforce the lesson by completing an assignment or creating a project based on what has been learned. Projects can be simple ten-minute activities or elaborate three-day endeavors. HOW lessons tend to focus on writing assignments. To retain the material, a student must do something with what has been learned.	• Mind mapping • Completing a writing assignment (a letter from or to a character in a book; a newspaper article; etc.) • Creating illustrations for a book • Making a salt-dough model • Performing a science experiment • Creating a diorama • Writing songs or poetry • Tracing a journey on a map • Making a booklet, pamphlet, or poster
Step 4: **Excel** To pull everything together and share what has been learned with someone else	The idea is for the student to share what he has learned, usually through narration (verbally or in writing) and through the creation of a portfolio. When a student can teach someone else what he has learned, he knows the subject.	• Creating a portfolio • Narrating the subject • Sharing and explaining a project • Giving a report • Sharing writing activities • Explaining the portfolio • Creating artwork • Sharing oral stories • Reciting poetry • Sharing a song

The four steps may be utilized to plan a balanced curriculum. Students need all four processes of learning for perceptive and engaged response and action. These four steps have grown out of extensive research in learning styles, brain research, and research on creativity. They were designed with the understanding that different people have different learning preferences, and that these differences can be addressed through a specific sequential cycle of instruction. Let's take a look at each of these four steps in detail.

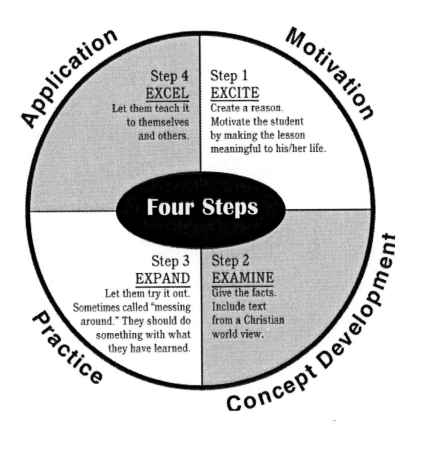

Step One: Excite

Step One is arguably the most important step in the process, and yet it is completely overlooked in traditional education. Most

> The teacher's job is not just to present the material—the teacher's job is to cause the student to learn!

schools skip ahead to Step Two, but as we use the four steps, instead of diving into the subject at hand, the parent/teacher spends a few minutes relating the subject to the student's life—to create an interest about what they are about to learn in Step Two.

Objectives: To create an interest in the topic to be studied; to enter into and connect personal meaning with experience.

Activities: Brainstorming, interacting, reading Bible verses, observing, imagining, watching a video, discussing, making lists, drawing tentative conclusions.

Preference: Type-one learners feel most comfortable in this phase because they benefit the most from personal involvement and interaction. They need their learning to be based on personal issues that are relevant to them.

Why Step One Is Important: Most teachers assume that their job is to present the material (often by lecturing or assigning textbooks to read), and the student's job is to learn. But the teacher's job is not just to present the material—the teacher's job is to cause the student to learn! One of the more graphic words that is translated "to teach" from the Hebrew language is the verb *shanan*.[5] It appears to be derived from the root meaning to sharpen, to whet. The Hebrew noun *shen*, or tooth, also derives from this root, giving force to the idea of being sharp, to pierce, or to prick.[6] The student's responsibility is to learn the material, but the teacher's job is to cause them to *want* to learn the material. Unfortunately, the most important step—to create an interest, to motivate, or to cause to learn—is missing from most school curricula.

How Jesus Taught Using Step One: Jesus always created an interest in what He was teaching. He used various ways to relate to people in their personal and social situations—right where they were. When He spoke to shepherds, He taught about sheep. When He spoke to farmers, He spoke about farming—planting, sowing, and reaping. When He spoke to fishermen, He spoke about fish. He spoke of things familiar— buildings, birds, food, etc. He began with the people where they were and made the subject meaningful to their lives in some way.

An Example: I taught my children a lesson on rocks. During step one, the children were told to gather a variety of rocks from outdoors, as well as a paper clip, a piece of glass, a glass of water, and a penny. We then brainstormed as to how we could use these materials to group the rocks into categories. The children loved it. They scraped and poked and soaked the rocks until they were able to classify them by strength, weight,

Education in Bible Times

Step 4
Israel was to instruct all nations in divine holiness and redemption as Yahweh's instrument of light to the nations.

Step 1
Motivation—
Israel's mandate was to diligently teach their children to love God, and to know and obey his statutes and ordinances (Deut 6:1-9).

Step 3
Oral and written recitation. Repetition in observation, experiential learning (doing), listening, reciting, and imitating.

Step 2
The aim of education was ethical and religious, centering on the Torah and recognizing and remembering events of divine providence in history.

Modern-day science may have come up with the 4Mat System™, but is it really a new way to teach or have we had this pattern all along?

Ultimately, biblical education is instruction in a lifestyle.

you ... know all about my teaching, my way of life ... continue in what you learned...
(2 Timothy 3:10,14).

Not only is biblical education a lifestyle
—it is a lifetime!

The four-step lessons are designed so that all learning styles are addressed, in order that more than one type of student may be permitted to both shine and stretch. Each lesson contains something for everybody, so each student not only finds the mode of greatest comfort for him/her, but is challenged to adapt to other, less comfortable but equally valuable modes.

How Jesus Taught

Step 4
He asked them to go and tell others. "Go ye therefore, and teach all nations..."

Step 1
He took the people where they were and made the lesson meaningful to their lives in some way. He spoke to shepherds about sheep, farmers about planting, fishermen about fish, etc.

Step 3
He asked them to do something with what they learned—to actively respond—doing and practice are vitally connected with knowing.

Step 2
He brought in the facts—Scripture, "It is written,..."

size, and appearance. In Step Two, we moved on to learn the various procedures that scientists use for classifying rocks—which is by strength, weight, size, and appearance.

In Step Two we learned scientist classify rocks depending on the nature of the mineral grains, including their composition and size and relationship to surrounding grains; the way the rock occurs; how uniform it is; its hardness; how it reacts with acid; its color; and the way in which it breaks. This information "clicked"because in Step One we first tried classifying the rock ourselves.

> Before delving into the details of a certain subject, the curriculum guided us to discuss, interact, and create a genuine interest in the subject and how it related to our children's lives.

Step Two: Examine

Examining the topic is what most teachers feel most comfortable doing. This is the step that traditional schools emphasize most frequently—and it is important in order to learn the facts and concepts of a certain topic.

Objectives: To classify theories and concepts; to combine personal experience with conceptual understanding.

Activities: Finding out what experts think, reading text, looking up the topic in an encyclopedia, reading historical fiction, reading a classic novel, watching a video, using computer software, interviewing experts.

Preference: Type-two learners feel most comfortable working at this step. They enjoy detailed and definite knowledge; they like to classify, reason things out, and think through ideas.

Why Step Two Is Important: Specific, well-organized instruction must follow the first step. This phase emphasizes careful conceptual development. In this step, concepts are organized, presented, and explained. Step Two is an important step but it should not be overemphasized, simply because it is the step on which most schools focus. Strive for a balance between all four phases of learning.

How Jesus Taught Using Step Two: By using Step One, Jesus created an interest, but in Step Two, He brought in the facts, usually by quoting Scripture: "It is written..." or, "You have heard it said that..."

Examples: Step two in a history or science lesson would be find out the facts by: reading or listening to text from a reference book, interviewing an expert, utilize the Internet, researching an encyclopedia, reading a novel about the time period, or by watching a video.

Let's look at an example of the second step in the "Evolution: A Theory" lesson from the Heart of Wisdom's *Creation* unit study.

Step 2 Examine

Over 150 years ago, a British scientist, Charles Robert Darwin (1809-1882) wrote *The Origin of Species*. He laid the foundation of modern evolutionary theory with his concept that God did not create things; they arose through natural processes. He taught that microbes, over billions of years, changed into trees, animals, and men. His work was of major influence on the life and earth sciences. There are three major problems with Darwin's theory of evolution.

> #1. A thing cannot evolve from nothing. If there was nothing in the beginning how did something evolve?

> #2. There is no scientific law for non-living things coming to life. A tree or a rock cannot become an animal.

> #3. There is no fossil record to prove a creature turned naturally into a completely different kind. There are "missing links." There are no fossils representing evolving species making the leap from ape to man (although several hoaxes that attempted to show a monkey to man fossils but all later proved to be hoaxes) Today our museums "contain in excess of 250,000 different fossil species represented by tens of millions of catalogued fossils (the Smithsonian Natural Museum contains 40 million fossils)."[1] But not one of these fossils shows a concrete transition from one species to another.

Darwin's work was far more than a biological concept; the theory of evolution constitutes the underpinnings of a dishonest philosophy that has held sway over a great number of people since its introduction. For example, Karl Marx taught that Darwin's theory provided a solid ground for materialism and thus for communism. Darwin was well aware that his theory faced many problems. He confessed this in his book in the chapter "Difficulties of the Theory."

Darwin's ideas were theorized and used as important "scientific ground" for racism. Darwinism was even adapted to the social sciences, and turned into a conception that came to be called "social Darwinism." Social Darwinism contends that existing human races are located at different rungs of the "evolutionary ladder," and that the European races were the most "advanced" of all. Nazism openly proclaimed its dependence on Darwin.[1] According to Nazism's interpretation of social Darwinism, it was right and moral for the strongest race to survive; to have pity for the weak was to defy nature's laws.

> The Big Bang scenario suggests that the marvelously ordered universe randomly resulted from a gigantic explosion. Never in the history of human experience has a chaotic explosion been observed producing an intricate order that operates purposefully. An explosion in a print shop does not produce an encyclopedia. A tornado sweeping through a junkyard does not assemble a Boeing 747. No building contractor dumps his materials on a vacant lot, attaches dynamite, and then waits for a completed home from the resulting "bang." The idea is absurd. (*The Big Bang Theory vs. God's Word*, Wayne Jackson) The Big Bang theory is not science, but an atheistic, secular faith.

Research Charles Darwin's theory. Use any resource (an encyclopedia, a nonfiction book, or the Internet). We recommend the following:

ı

4-8	9-12
Unlocking the Mysteries of Creation "Good Science Bad Theory" (64-96).	
It Couldn't Just Happen "The Mystery of the Moths" (73-81).	
The Origin of the Universe (Video) It seems to be blindly accepted as an "unproven fact" by most scientists and educators, but did the universe really result from a "big bang?" This program reveals that the universe is far too complex and well designed to have originated simply by time and chance. There is clear evidence of an intelligent "master designer," while there is also abundant evidence that evolution is impossible. Length: Thirty minutes. Order from Eden Communications (Films for Christ): 1-800-332-3261. Age level: Teens & Adults.	
	The Lie: Evolution Chapter 8 "The Evils of Evolution" (83-96).

Internet Sources

Evolution's Illusions: How the Disguise Works
Article for children explains belief that animals evolved into completely different types of creatures persists because of a myth and an illusion. htp://www.users.big-pond.com/rdoolan/illusion.html

Scientific Case Against Evolution
Article by Henry M. Morris, Ph.D. from the Institute for Creation Research.
http://www.icr.org/bible/tracts/scientificcaseagainstevolution.html

The Crucial Failure of Darwin: Design in Nature
Chapter from *The Handy Evolution Refuter.*
http://www.parentcompany.com/handy_dandy/hder2.htm

Step Three: Expand

When Step Three has been reached, the child will have really begun to grasp the concepts and ideas that are being learned.

Objectives: To do something with what has been learned and reinforce the concepts learned in Step Two.

Activities: Experimenting, writing stories, writing poems, writing essays, coloring in instructional books, playing games, using interactive computer software, mind mapping, cooking, writing songs.

Preference: Type-three learners usually prefer Step Three. They feel most comfortable here because they like to solve problems, and they prefer well-defined, focused tasks. They enjoy using what they have learned in useful situations.

Why Step Three Is Important: During Step Three, the student begins to actually do something with what they are learning. If a student does not do something with the material, he will forget it. The material only becomes meaningful when the student reformulates the main concepts. They must do more than just repeat back to the teacher what has been presented. Students must actively respond to what they have learned by adding something of themselves in the form of a project or a writing assignment.

How Jesus Taught Using Step Three: Jesus first created an interest, and then He brought in the facts of Scripture. Third, He always asked people to do something with what they had learned from Him. They were to listen (*He that hath ears to hear, let him hear*—Matthew 11:15); to show faith (*Arise and walk*—Matthew 9:5); and to obey (*Come out onto the water*—Matthew 14:29; *Go and sin no more*—John 8:11).

Examples: Writing activities or hands-on crafts are good Step Three options to demonstrate learning. Here are some of examples from the "Evolution: A Theory" lesson:

Step 3 Expand

Choose and complete one of the following activities:

❶Activity 1: Write a summary of each of the five "fundamental fallacies" in *Unlocking the Mysteries of Creation*: 1. "It All Started with a Big Bang" 2002 (70-71) 2003 (80-81). 2. "Non-Living Matter Produced Life" 2002 (72-73) 2003 (90-91). 3. "Time the Magic Factor" 2002 (74-77) 2003 (82-83). 4. "Random Chances Result in All Complexity of Things" 2002 (78-83) 2003 (86-87). 5. "Simple Forms Develop into Complex Forms of Life in Time" 2002 (84-96) 2003 (96-97). Refer to "Writing Summaries" in *Writers Inc.*

❷Activity 2: Write a paper that responds to this concept: If scientists say that an idea is probably true, then it should be accepted as true, at least until a better idea comes along. Refer to "Writing to Persuade" in *Writers Inc.*

❸ Activity 3: Write an editorial about how teaching evolution as fact has affected our society. Be clear about why you hold the opinion that you do. Use examples from your experience to support your claims. Refer to "Writing to Explain" in *Writers Inc.*

❹ Activity 3: Fill in a contrast and compare chart or venn diagram listing and comparing the main features of creationism and evolution. List important aspects for each one. Ask yourself questions beginning with who, what, where, when, why and how. Find graphic organizers at http://HeartofWisdom.com/helps.htm.

Step Four: Excel

Step Four can be easily overlooked, but it is important in order to complete the cycle of learning for the student.

Objectives: To evaluate for application; to bring students to the point where they can teach themselves; to have students share the material with others.

Activities: Choosing, planning, and exhibiting projects; sharing notebooks, artwork, stories, poems, music, or other completed work.

Preference: Type-four learners feel the most comfortable in this phase, primarily because they enjoy teaching themselves, and they like to learn by trial and error.

Why Step Four Is Important: Step Four is an essential and integral part of meaningful learning. All learning must eventually proceed to this step in which the student uses what he has learned. Unfortunately, this step is almost always left out of traditional classroom teaching. Passing a test should not be the ultimate goal; the ultimate goal should be to take what has been learned out into the real world and use it In this step, the student is given the opportunity to offer the result of the information they have learned to others in a variety of ways.

How Jesus Taught Using Step Four: Jesus created an interest, brought in the facts, and asked people to then do something with what they had learned. After that, He consistently asked people to "go and tell others."

An Example: From the "Evolution: A Theory" lesson:

Share information about the evolution vs. creation debate with a group or your family. Add corrected written work or any illustrations to your portfolio.

- ❏ Correct all written work to demonstrate correct punctuation and spelling.
- ❏ Correct all written work to demonstrate correct and effective use of grammar.
- ❏ Add to your Writing Notebook the rules for all punctuation and grammar errors you corrected.
- ❏ Record any misspelled words in your Spelling Notebook.
- ❏ Add to your Vocabulary Notebook any new words encountered in this lesson. Include a definition for each word. Use each vocabulary term in a sentence orally or in writing.
- ❏ Add corrected written work or any illustrations to your Portfolio.
- ❏ Add any important people or events to your Time Line Book.
- ❏ Share with a friend or family member an activity you completed for this lesson. Explain to them what you have learned.

In the next chapter we see how to use the structured four steps with the Delight Directed methods.

The Animal School

The following parable, much like the story of the three horses at the beginning of this chapter, illustrates the importance of identifying the various learning styles and teaching in a way that encompasses all of these styles.

Once upon a time, the animals decided they must do something heroic to meet the problems of "a new world," so they organized a school. They adopted an activity curriculum consisting of running, climbing, swimming, and flying. To make it easier to administer the curriculum, all of the animals were to take all of the subjects.

The duck was excellent in swimming; in fact, he was even better than his instructor. But he made only passing grades in flying, and he was very poor in running. Since he was so slow in running, he had to stay after school to practice running, and soon he had no time to swim. This kept up until his webbed feet were so badly worn out from trying to run that he became only average in swimming. Fortunately, average was acceptable in this school, and so no one really worried about the duck.

The rabbit started at the top of the class in running, but before the end of the school year, he had a nervous breakdown because of so much makeup work he had to do in swimming class.

The squirrel was excellent in climbing; that is, until he became too frustrated in the flying class, where the teacher made him start from the ground up rather than the treetops down. When he developed a charley horse from overexertion, he ended up with a C in climbing and a D in running.

The eagle became known as a problem student when, in the climbing class, he beat all the other students to the treetop—but only by using his own methods to get there.

At the end of the year, an abnormal, retarded gopher that could swim exceedingly well, and also run, climb, and even fly a little, managed to beat the system—and became the valedictorian.

Suggested Reading

About Learning by Bernice McCarthy
About Learning presents the profound differences in how people learn and how these differences can be combined to create high performance learning programs. Discover the consistent and replicable forces behind all quality learning programs and how to put them to work in a variety of settings.

The 4Mat System: Teaching to Learning Styles with Right/Left Mode Techniques by Bernice McCarthy
A book about the wonderful differences in people, and how to capitalize on these differences. It explains the current research on learning styles and right and left brain processing in clear understandable language. This is a book for anyone interested in how people learn.

Learning Styles: Reaching Everyone God Gave You to Teach by Marlene LeFever ↜
Foreword by Bernice McCarthy. Lefever explains a learning style is the way in which a person sees or perceives things best and then uses that knowledge. When we understand learning styles and adjust our teaching or parenting to those styles, we begin reaching everyone God gives us to teach. wonderful book capable of teaching us how we learn and what to do with all that knowledge once we've learned it. Effective learning follows a natural four-step process that answers these four questions:

1. Why do I need this?
2. What does the Bible say about my need?
3. How does what the Bible teaches actually work?
4. How will I use what I have learned?

By answering each of these questions, we will appeal to the four learning styles: Imaginative, Analytic, Common Sense, and Dynamic. Review: "What a mother lode of resources this is! Imaginative, thorough, engaging, and accessible—characteristic of Marlene's own teaching style. Lights will come on in your head, and you'll never be the same teacher, or student, again."—Jerry B. Jenkins, Moody Bible Institute.

Most books are available from Homeschool-Books.com. Books from a Christian perspective are marked with a ↜

204

Delight-Directed Studies

All children love to learn—at least before they go to school! Anyone who has been around babies, toddlers, and preschool children has seen that they are constantly seeking out new things to explore—to see, hear, touch, smell, and especially taste! But by the time a toddler becomes a teenager, all too often, their love of learning has been squelched, many times leaving a sullen student, slumped in the back of a classroom while a teacher tries to pour meaningless facts into their mind.

A delight-directed study is like a wonderful fire in the mind of a student. It starts small, but as it grows, it begins to consume vast amounts of information until it bursts into a roaring blaze of insight, understanding, and creativity. It takes on a life of its own.

—Gregg Harris

> The forced learning that takes place in many of our schools today can destroy the natural love for learning that all children are born with.

The forced learning that takes place in many of our schools today can destroy the natural love for learning that all children are born with. Children and teenagers who are locked into studying something they find boring behave no differently than adults who are locked into boring, irrelevant meetings at work. If adults cannot see the relevance of the material covered in a meeting, they will either tune out or drop out—in much the same way that children will if they do not see how the subject being studied relates to the concerns of their lives. Would you, for example, be reading this book if it were entitled *Basic Plumbing Concepts*? Probably not— unless your kitchen sink were leaking or you had a basement full of water! If that were the case, you would probably be participating in a delight-directed study of your own!

A large part of the Heart of Wisdom philosophy of education involves the concept of delight-directed studies. This is an active, learner-centered approach. There is an interactive relationship between teachers, learners, and the resources used that involves learners in making significant decisions about how and what they will learn, how they will assess what they learn, and how they will use what they have learned in meaningful ways. In sum, your children's education needs to be guided by what delights them, not just by a textbook or a set curriculum. This will not only stimulate them in the here and now, but will foster within them their inborn natural love of learning, and inspire them to make learning a lifelong pursuit.

Delight-directed learning places students in charge of their own learning process, helping them to discover what they want to accomplish and then giving them the tools they need to get it done. The delight-directed approach uses the student's own natural curiosity as a strong motivator, and basic skills such as reading, writing, and researching are learned during the process of examining the topic of interest. Less control by the parent or teacher can actually mean more learning!

Gregg Harris describes the delight-directed approach, "The child's delight is the spark that ignites everything. Once established, like a fire, it is self-sustaining. The student begins to study for his own personal satisfaction, and the fruits of his study begin to flow outward to others. This approach is especially helpful for the child who has become burned out on school because it can reignite his love for learning. But delight-directed study is more than just a method of remedial instruction; as we shall see, it is the foundation for all true scholarship. Once the basic concepts of delight are understood, the approach is easy to implement."[1]

Remember, the core focus in the Heart of Wisdom approach is God-directed, and the central focus of each day is Bible study. We blend the delight-directed method with the four-step lessons (in the study of both God's Word and God's world) by allowing learners to make choices that grow out of their interests and concerns. Learners of all ages can and will make good choices and contribute meaningfully when they are regularly given, with proper preparation and within developmentally appropriate boundaries, opportunities to participate in making decisions that will affect their lives.

If we allow our children free choice in what they want to learn, they can then concentrate on learning what they may actually need in their lives; and freedom to choose what not to study provides the freedom to learn more about what they care about, including the freedom to explore new interests.

Defining Delight-Directed Learning

Marilyn Howshall provides one of the best definitions and explanations of delight-directed learning:

> To delight in something is *to take a high degree of pleasure or satisfaction of mind in something.* Delight is of a permanent nature as opposed to fun, or a sudden burst of joy which lasts for the moment. There is no moral nature to delight. It is neither good nor bad. Rather it is the object of delight that will determine its moral quality or educational value. Children will delight in something whether it is fruitless, divertive entertainment, or something of educational value. With this in mind, delight as a vital sign must be viewed with the goal that the thing delighted in has dimension, substance, quality, and purpose.

> The child's personal interests in life should not be looked upon as having mere fringe educational benefits, but should be recognized as central to his development.

> The child's personal interests in life should not be looked upon as having mere fringe educational benefits, but should be recognized as central to his development. These interests can give direction to his future studies, and provide current opportunities for rich spiritual lessons. Likewise, the parent can draw from the child's interests for the content needed to develop his language skills. As one interest is allowed to develop, it will begin a natural overflow into other areas of interest and into a more mature expression as the child develops. *You will not reap a learning delight in your children if you attempt to prematurely expect all their activities to yield a polished product.* Quality products that are a true outgrowth of the child's learning pursuits require time to surface...

> Delight's counterfeit comes in the form of anything that is fun for the moment. Enjoying or simply being agreeable to an activity that has been

> The Scriptures instruct parents to recognize that each child is a unique individual, with a way of learning already established and grounded within him...

parent-generated is not the same as taking delight in it. Often the parent is making stabs in the dark in her effort to provide educational experiences for her child. In fact, too many activities of this nature, in which the child never goes beyond surface curiosity or interest, may actually keep the void in his life from being recognized and effectively addressed.

Destructive forces of boredom may be present within the home. If this is true, then it may be necessary to begin tempering less desirable interests and indulgences, while at the same time directing activity into more fruitful areas. This can be a challenge with adolescents whose value systems are already set. Approaching change within the context of their personal relationship with God is the best place to begin. A pure, teachable heart is essential to developing a learning delight and [delight in the] learning process—first in ourselves, then in our children.[2]

Delight-Directed Studies Are Biblical

When the indulgence factor is removed from delight-directed study, it becomes a highly biblical form of education. The Scriptures instruct parents to recognize that each child is a unique individual, with a way of learning already established and grounded within him that needs to be recognized, acknowledged, and encouraged by means of the truth of Scripture.

> *Train a child **in the way he should go**, and when he is old he will not turn from it.*
> —Proverbs 22:6 (emphasis mine)

This verse reveals that a parent's training of their children must be based on knowing their children. In the original Hebrew text, a personal pronoun is attached to the noun *way*, and it actually reads *his way*, not simply in *the way he should go*. The word *way* here is the Hebrew word *derek*, which means way, road, journey, or manner.[3] Parents need to recognize the way, or manner, each of their children is bent by the way or manner God has designed each of them. If parents fail to recognize this in their children, they may also fail to launch their children into God's plan for their lives.

Get to Know Your Children

Because delight-directed studies build as much of the child's education as possible on their interests rather than a set course of study from a generic textbook or workbook, it is imperative for a parent to get to know their children—to begin to see them with new eyes of understanding.

It is imperative for a parent to get to know their children—to begin to see them with new eyes of understanding.

Learn what makes your child tick. What is that activity or interest that they tend to gravitate toward time after time? What motivates them to learn? What is truly the inner delight of their life? What gifts and talents has God given to them that are unique to them alone? *Who has God created them to be?*

God has a unique plan for your child's life—and He has breathed into them the gifts and talents that they will need to accomplish His purpose. The challenge is in discovering them—unearthing them from beneath the piles of textbooks and curricula that threaten to squelch them out of existence—and then developing them for the glory of God.

> *For we are God's workmanship, created in Christ Jesus to do good works, which God prepared in advance for us to do.* —Ephesians 2:10

God has prepared unique works for your child to perform. Your job is to prepare the child to complete those tasks, and the best way to do that is through delight-directed studies. The spark that God has placed within your child will be the thing that evokes their own enthusiasm for certain topics and ideas—and you can then begin to prepare them for their life ahead by fostering that enthusiasm and causing it to grow.

How Can You Use This Method With a Structured Plan?

Is it possible to allow a child to study what he wants and still be sure you cover all the bases? Can you instruct using the delight-directed method with a structured curriculum plan? Yes, and yes. The delight-directed method flows beautifully with the four-step cycle of instruction in all Heart of Wisdom unit studies.

The spark that God has placed within your child will be the thing that evokes their own enthusiasm for certain topics and ideas.

Each lesson can be skimmed, covering the basic concepts, while allowing the time needed to dwell on the things that delight the student. It's like introducing new foods—the child won't know if he likes or dislikes a food until he tries it. If it's not his cup of tea, you can move quickly on to the next lesson, always looking for a spark of interest. Once you notice the spark, fan it until it grows into a flame.

> *Consider what a great forest is set on fire by a small spark.* —James 1:5.

Planning and Looking for the Spark

Delight-directed learning, with a set plan like Heart of Wisdom unit studies, begins by allowing children to be a part of the planning process. During the planning phase, allow the student to participate in choosing the resources for that unit (fiction novel, colorful reference book, video, Internet site, interactive multi-media, etc.). It's very possible that a child might balk at the unit as a whole but later find a spark in one of the individual lessons. To continue with the food analogy, a child might, say, groan over something he sees cooking, but after a taste, finds it pleasing to his palate.

Example

Mother is teaching Jenny (fifteen), John (thirteen), and Joseph (ten) a unit on the Middle Ages. During the unit planning the three decide together on the resources. They look through the resources at Homeschool-Books.com or in the back of this book at the Middle Ages Resources. The three choose *Kingfisher Illustrated Encyclopedia*, and *Eyewitness Medieval Life* from their home library. Mother orders a novel, *The Door in the Wall* (from the library or a vendor) to read aloud during the unit. While reviewing the lessons the children show the most interest in knights, castles, and medieval feasts. Before the unit begins they will pick up books on these topics from the library.

Several opportunities will occur during the steps in each lesson to bring into play the delight-directed methods. Let's look at an example of how each of the three children might discover their own level of interest in the lesson on knights.

Unit: Middle Ages. Lesson: Knights

1. In Step One (Excite) Mother is watching each student for a spark. Step One activities evoke feedback which shows how interested each child is in the topic and suggests the possible duration of the lesson. As they brainstorm to make lists, John and Joshua both show an intense interest in this topic.

2. In Step Two, Mother reads the provided text in the unit, and then turns to the resources chosen during the unit planning phase. She reads aloud from the suggested pages in the *Kingfisher Illustrated Encyclopedia* and *Eyewitness Medieval Life*. John and Joseph spend time reading through the suggested web sites and library resources, and print out several illustrations of a knight's armor and weapons. Jenny also browses the Internet sites and chooses an image of a knight to add to her portfolio, but she leaves the boys to explore the sites as she moves on to Step Three assignments.

3. In Step Three, Mother allows each child to choose an activity:

- John (13) chooses to complete a writing assignment. Mother encourages this assignment because he needs more writing practice and he enjoys this topic. John writes a separate draft paragraph for each of several topics: tournaments, jousting, suits of armor, crossbows, and the Crusades. He searches or uses the Internet to find illustrations for each summary.

- Joseph (10) chooses to create a shield with a coat of arms. He uses colored pencils to design a coat of arms similar to those he viewed from the resources. He then makes the shield from cardboard and pastes or glues the coat of arms onto the shield.

- Jenny is not as interested in this topic so she copies a paragraph from *Eyewitness Medieval Life* and moves on to a math lesson (more about Jenny later).

4. In Step Four the students choose how they will share their work.

- During this step, Mother and John are busy revising and correcting John's drafts. After the corrections John glues illustrations to the summary pages and includes them in his portfolio. He chooses to add more on this topic to his portfolio and shares it with his grandparents.

- Joseph shows his shield to his father and explains his coat of arms.

- Jenny adds her writing and illustrations to her portfolio and shares the work with her brothers.

In this example all three children have learned about knights. John has obviously learned the most. We know all three have learned significantly more than they would in a typical school where the children would read perhaps one boring paragraph about knights.

John and Joseph will continue on this topic in the coming weeks by choosing a novel and/or illustrated reference books from the library on knights, or by learning more from the Internet. Their wise mother will continue to fan the flame as long as the fire burns (weeks or months). If no spark had appeared during this lesson the amount of time spent on this lesson would have been dramatically different.

Jenny did not do a lot with the lesson on knights because she did not have a spark of interest. Later, however, Jenny's spark shows up in the "Food in the Middle Ages" lesson. She ends up spending several hours researching and planning an authentic medieval feast for her family. She designs an elaborate menu for her portfolio and reads the library book *Medieval Feasts* to Joshua.

Four-Steps Summary

1. During Step One, look for the spark.

2. In Step Two, the spark will be your signal to encourage your student(s) to go on to more resources. If the lesson ignites a spark for one child and not another (which will probably be the case) don't force all the students into spending time on further study. Take a trip to the library, or order books, or allow computer time for Internet research.

> While your children are given the freedom to choose their courses of study, they are also given parameters within which they must work.

3. In Step Three, allow each child to choose the activity in which to do something with what he or she just learned.

4. In Step Four, allow each child to choose how to share the material.

Teaching is much more than providing facts—real teaching means causing to learn. The delight-directed methods work when we provide opportunities for meaningful experiences, and then wait and watch for moments when children's eyes light up. Then they're off and running, determined and motivated to learn!

Delight-Directed Does Not Equal Indulgence!

An immediate misconception arises in many parents' minds when they hear the term *delight-directed,* and that misconception will remain unless and until the term is defined properly. To allow your child's education to be delight-directed does not mean that you as the parent/teacher will no longer have any say in what will be studied!

In the Heart of Wisdom teaching approach the parent presents the material and looks for the spark at the same time. It is essential to maintain a consistent routine. We do not encourage allowing children to follow just any path of learning that delights them, with no rhyme, reason or pattern to guide them. While your children are given the freedom to choose their courses of study, they are also given parameters within which they must work.

Terry Camp explains the freedom in the delight-directed approach in her delightful book *Ignite the Fire*:

> FIRE stands for Freedom Is Real Education. What do I mean by freedom? I do not mean allowing our children to have ultimate liberty. I do not mean that we allow our children to play computer games ceaselessly. I do not mean our children are allowed

to watch movies, even "good" movies all day
long. The History Channel has some great
educational programs on it, but it will not
teach our children to think and grow for
themselves. Instead, it will develop in them a
passive learning process. An occasional show
or two will not harm them, but if it becomes
your habit to "see if there's something good
on," then your children are missing out. I would rather they never watch anything
than that they become educational vegetables.

> Delight-directed does not mean
> indulging every whim and fancy of
> the child. Godly child training
> includes a disciplined—not a hap-
> hazard—lifestyle.

The freedom that I refer to is a freedom that comes only from following God. *Now
the Lord is the Spirit and where the Spirit of the Lord is, there is freedom.*
—II Corinthians 3:17

Galatians chapter 5 is a great chapter on freedom. It begins, *It is for freedom that Christ
has set us free. Stand firm, then, and do not let yourselves be burdened again by a yoke of
slavery* (5:1). Verses 13 through 15 say, *You, my brothers, were called to be free. But do not
use your freedom to indulge the sinful nature; rather, serve one another in love. The entire
law is summed up in a single command. Love your neighbor as yourself. If you keep on biting
and devouring each other, watch out or you will be destroyed by each other.*

What does this mean for me in light of homeschooling? It means that I have had my
yoke taken from me. Christ has set me free from my burdens. As a homeschooling
mom trying to follow a standard curriculum, I found myself bound. I found myself
burdened. It wasn't until I gave up our homeschooling to Jesus, that I once again
found that freedom.

I often found myself wanting to study a certain area with my children, but I felt
confined by the books I was using. I felt like I was giving them more work in what I
felt was an already overloaded day. I was finding myself struggling with the
promptings of the Holy Spirit in my life. He would prompt me to study a certain
area with the children, and I would reason that there just wasn't enough time.

Now that I am turning to the Lord FIRST, I find the promptings from Him get done.
It's a great feeling knowing that your children are learning what the Holy Spirit
wants them to learn.[4]

Children need boundaries, and they need guidance in the learning process. Delight-
directed does not mean indulging every whim and fancy of the child. Godly child
training includes a disciplined—not a haphazard—lifestyle. Delight-directed studies
need to take place in a routine—however flexible—that is orderly and makes sense.

In addition, it is important to note that the delights that this chapter refers to are not necessarily objects (such as dolls, Legos, or bicycles), but they are those ideas, activities, and interests that spark the child's enthusiasm about learning something new.

Individualized Education

In *Engines for Education*, Roger Schank, from The Institute for the Learning Sciences, explains the importance of individualized education:

> Depending on an individual's situation and goals, there are many things that might be worth learning. In order to give a very detailed prescription for what knowledge a student should acquire, we must take into account that not every child will need or want to do the same things. A curriculum must therefore be individualized. It must be built around an understanding of what situations a particular learner might want to be in, or might have to be in later in life, and what abilities he will require in those situations.
>
> Nevertheless, for many people, the notion of mandating the same knowledge for every student is appealing. Building lists of facts that one claims everyone should know is relatively simple to do. Furthermore, there is the attraction of providing standards that can be easily measured. But from the perspective of the teacher and the student, this approach spells trouble. Each mandated bit of knowledge removes more local control and drives the system towards fixed curricula and standardized tests, which not only diminishes teacher flexibility but also student choice, and therefore, student interest and initiative.

> When we ask how our children are doing in school, we usually mean, "Are they measuring up to the prevailing standards?" rather than, "Are they having a good time and feeling excited about learning?"

> In public schools from first through twelfth grades, much of the classroom routine is shaped by an emphasis on rote learning, a strict adherence to standardized textbooks and workbooks, and a curriculum that is often enforced with drill and practice. The methods and the curriculum are molded by the questions that appear on the standardized achievement tests administered to every child from the fourth grade on. Success no longer means being able to do. Success comes to mean "academic success," a matter of learning to function within the system, of learning the "correct" answer, and of doing well at multiple-choice exams. Success also means, sadly, learning not to ask difficult questions. When we ask how our children are doing in school, we usually mean, "Are they measuring up to the prevailing

standards?" rather than, "Are they having a good time and feeling excited about learning?"

We should purpose to be flexible in the way we try to tap into our children's innate interests. When we are interacting with the student we can evaluate whether learning has taken place. If one approach doesn't work, we can drop it and try another.[5]

Delight-Directed Learning in Real Life

All of this may sound wonderful to you, but you may be asking, "How can I make this work in real life?" We all want the education of our children to have meaning beyond just circling the correct answer on an exam or filling in the blanks correctly in a workbook. *Delight-directed learning in real life means to look at the entirety of life as your child's curriculum*, to help them find what they are interested in, and then allow them to dig in as deeply as they want. Learning this way is never dumbed down, and children can rise quickly to levels beyond a traditional high-school education. Because the learning process belongs to them, they begin to care about developing skills like writing and reading comprehension. They *want* to improve and know more about the subjects that interest them, and they spend most of their waking hours actually learning.

> Delight-directed learning in real life means to look at the entirety of life as your child's curriculum, to help them find what they are interested in, and then allow them to dig in as deeply as they want to.

This type of learning is not inferior to a traditional education in any way—in fact, it is superior, because a love of learning is being fostered rather than rote facts being memorized. In real life, however, it can take more dedication on the part of the parent/teacher to make it work, because the education of every child in the family will be very different, based on their talents, interests, and speed of learning.

> ...it is superior, because a love of learning is being fostered rather than rote facts being memorized.

Doesn't delight-directed learning sound like fun? The good news is—it is, and it should be fun! That's what delight-directed study is all about: putting the delight back into the educational process and fostering children who love to learn and who will make learning a lifelong avocation.

Suggested Reading

Ignite the Fire! by Terri Camp. ⟜
Terri Camp gives parents a vision for their child no matter how much or little they excel academically. She also provides a long list of ordinary household items and their usefulness in educating children. This book is full of practical, easy-to-implement ideas. Prepare to be inspired. *Ignite the Fire!* will ignite the fires in your children so what they learn is both enjoyed and retained.

Get to Know Your Children—Develop Interests through Three Seasons of Your Child's Development by Marilyn Howshall ⟜
This book will clearly show how you can develop God-designed purpose in your children while they are still young that can extend into vocational expression as they mature. Marilyn uses examples from her son John's life (up through the ages of 13 to 14) to show how many of his interests were sparked and allowed to develop because of the opportunity he was given to "focus." Focus is vision's counterpart and a principle that must be present in the child's daily training in order for his personal life purpose and vision to unfold. She is attentive to the peculiar traits and underlying motivations as they manifested through his interests. Knowing the child's motivations will significantly contribute to the parents' ability to direct his learning process and his future vocation. You will "see" her son's informal learning process unfold. Next, she shows how her daughter Kathryn's primary interest in horses was encouraged and developed throughout the seasons of her development, even though their family was never around horses. She then shows how this interest is being developed toward an entrepreneurial purpose and shares the answers to prayer and provision that came along the way. Various types of notebooks, entrepreneurial, and apprenticeship structures are discussed using actual examples. As you read, you may find yourself seeing your children with tender "eyes of love" in deeper ways than ever before.

Most books are available from Homeschool-Books.com. Books from a Christian perspective are marked with a ⟜

Chapter 13

Unit Studies

In This Chapter

◆ Defining thematic unit studies.

◆ Studying the whole, not just the parts.

◆ Teaching several ages together.

◆ Choosing unit studies.

Unit studies, sometimes called thematic units or integrated studies, have become very popular with homeschoolers. They usually use a hands-on approach for effective learning—the child learns by actually experiencing and discovering through different methods and activities, rather than by just reading from a textbook. Studies have shown that children using unit study methods retain the information longer and better than children who are taught using a traditional approach.

Unit studies, or thematic units, take a topic and live with it for a period of time, integrating multiple subjects—such as science, social studies, language arts, math, and fine arts—as they apply.

For example, a unit study about horses could include the following:

• *Literature*: Reading stories such as *My Friend Flicka*, *Misty of Chincoteague*, etc.

- *Composition*: Writing stories about horses (includes paying attention to writing mechanics such as spelling, capitalization, punctuation, and grammar).

- *Language Skills*: Copying or dictating passages about horses (correcting any spelling, capitalization, punctuation, and grammar mistakes).

- *Vocabulary*: Learning new words about horses such as *bit, bridle, equine, colic, ligament, stallion, vaulting*, etc.

- *Science*: Learning about the zoological classification of horses.

- *Geography*: Learning about which breeds live in which parts of the world.

- *Biblical Study*: Reading about horses in the Bible.

- *History*: Examining man's relationship with and dependence on horses in different time periods in history.

Later in this book I will teach you how to create a unit study. We'll be using the example of a horse unit study.

Pizza, Anyone?

The unit study concept can probably best be explained by using a food analogy: Traditional school formats can be compared to a meat-and-vegetables meal, while a unit study is more like a pizza.

Traditional school subjects do not interact. Using our food analogy, we see that a dinner plate contains meat, potatoes, and one or two types of vegetables, all separated from each other. Likewise, in traditional education, science, history, Bible study, and language arts are taught independently of one another, in separate time slots, with no apparent relationship to one another.

Unit studies, however, are interactive. This approach is similar to the way we learn things as adults in everyday life. The focus of the unit study is on a specific topic which can be seen as the pizza "crust," with different "toppings" from other subject areas mixed together all over it. Made with a variety of ingredients, what makes pizza special is the overall taste of the mixture. With unit studies, students see and experience the interrelatedness of the information while focusing on a specific topic. The unit might focus on a history or a science topic (seen as the "sauce"), and then incorporate various "toppings," such as Bible study, language arts, or fine arts. The focus is on the whole effect, not the individual ingredients. This approach uses large blocks of time, sometimes an entire day, to look at many different aspects of one subject; and this is the way that life is generally experienced—integrated, not as isolated subjects.[1]

The "crust" of the Heart of Wisdom unit study is always the Bible. The "sauce" may be history, science, or life skills. Various "toppings," such as Bible study, language arts, and fine arts, etc., are all included.

Pizza	Heart of Wisdom Unit Studies		
Crust	BIBLE		
	GOD'S PLAN	GOD'S WORLD	GOD'S KINGDOM
	History Units	Science Units	Life Skills Units
Sauce	History/Culture (Ancient Egypt, Civil War, etc.)	Science (Light, Zoology, etc.)	Theology, Husbandry, Economics, etc
Varied Toppings	Bible study, history, science, language arts, fine arts, etc.		

Each Heart of Wisdom unit study is divided into easy, bite-sized (pardon the pun) lessons, each focusing on a main topic. Each unit has a clear thematic focus to provide the framework for the objectives. Students learn how the various aspects interrelate, and the themes go beyond the topic studied, directing the students to other areas of personal development. The focus is on the whole "dish," not on the individual "ingredients."

Studying the Whole, Not Just the Parts

More and more school systems are beginning to use unit studies, due to the tremendous positive response from students. Children enjoy studying subjects that are related other across the curriculum and their enjoyment means their attention will be engaged, they will delight in learning, and they will truly become educated.

America's traditional Greek educational system is failing from rigidity and stagnation (as well as from ungodly cultural influences such as profanity, vulgarity, violence, etc.). The ancient Greeks are responsible for the subject divisions we see in our school curricula today. They took a topic and divided it into isolated parts, taking away its relationship to the Creator; and such divisions don't always make sense: for example, under what "subject" should the sun be studied? Yes, the sun usually falls under the subject of science, in the subdivision of astronomy. But the study of the sun could encompass so much more:

- *Art*: Colors of the spectrum, reflection and refraction, sunlight, beautiful photos or paintings of sunsets and sunrises.

- *Bible Study*: Creation of the sun, scientific discoveries in Bible times, symbolism (Jesus is the light of the world; Christians are to be carriers and reflectors of His light in the world).

- *Biology*: The need of humans, animals, and plants for light and heat.

- *Chemistry*: Chemical reactions of light and heat from the sun in plants, animals, etc.

- *Composition*: Reading and writing poetry and classics about day and night, dark and light, emotions the sun can evoke.

- *Ecology*: The greenhouse effect, solar energy.

- *Geology*: The sun's effect on the earth's environment.

- *Geometry*: Spheres, orbits, rotation.

- *Geography*: The sun's effect on different locations of the globe, time zones, the effects of little or no sunlight in certain parts of the earth.

- *Health*: Light, vitamins provided by sunlight, burns, sunscreen, sleeping patterns.

- *History*: Theological beliefs about the sun in different time periods (ancient, Middle Ages, modern times), including the Egyptian culture and the Aztecs; scientific discoveries in each time period.

- *Language Arts*: Similes, metaphors, and idioms related to the sun; dictated passages learned about the sun for handwriting practice; reading assignments about the sun.

- *Literature*: Reading fiction, myths, and fables about the sun.

- *Math*: Calculations of distance, radius, calendars, speed of light, etc.

- *Meteorology*: How the sun relates to weather, climate zones, evaporation, etc.

- *Physics*: Light waves, microscopes, mirrors, bending light, photon theory of light, the "Big Bang" and other false theories.

- *Political Science*: Government regulations concerning times of day and day/night.

- *Studying and Thinking Skills*: Research, referencing, reasoning, recording, and problem-solving various aspects of all of these subjects, as they relate to the sun.

Teaching Several Ages Together

As previously stated, children learn better when unit studies are used rather than the subject-by-subject traditional method of education. But there are other benefits that are important to home school education:

If God had meant for children to learn with only other children of their same age, He would have given us children in litters! Fortunately, through unit studies, successful home school study can take place with children of different ages and levels learning together. The one-room-schoolhouse multi-age teaching method works. Research studies show that children in multi-age classrooms have more positive attitudes toward school, themselves and their peers. They also support that students often do better cognitively.[2]

Consider two families, each with three children—one in first grade, one in third grade, and one in sixth grade.

Mother A teaches using textbooks and workbooks to teach three children seven different subjects each; that's a *whopping* twenty-one subjects to prepare and teach. She has one child studying the Civil War, another learning about ancient Rome, while still another is studying the American Revolution—all under the one subject of history! In the subject of science, one child might be studying plants, another the planets, and still another, reptiles. In Bible study, one child might be studying Moses, another studying Joseph, and another, Paul. Even the most committed parent can easily become overwhelmed with such a system!

Mother B uses unit studies so she can teach history, geography, art, music, science, and Bible studies together to all ages. Each child studies the topic at hand at his or her own level, which can save up to half of the parent's teaching and preparing time. All children can go on field trips together, many projects can be done together, and writing assignments and vocabulary words can be on the same topic—just on different levels. For example, while studying animals, a younger child may be able to classify birds, mammals, and insects, while an older child would classify them in much more detail, such as arachnids, crustaceans, and so on. The older child learns and helps to teach the younger, while the younger learns from the older.

Let's use an example of a unit study taught by Mother B: she prepares to teach a study of the human body to all three children—grades one, three, and six. All of the children will look at the creation of man, human anatomy, medical discoveries throughout history, and so on. All three children will interact with one another, teaching each other, and reading and writing at their own levels in more detail. Each child learns as much as they are able, but they are not limited in what they can learn. For example: All three children can learn that God created man, that human beings have a sinful nature, that we are hindered by the lusts of the flesh, and so on. The first grader goes on to learn about the five senses, about illnesses, about doctors in pioneer days. The third grader begins to learn about the body's systems and about major medical discoveries in the last two hundred years. The sixth grader learns how each body system functions and further details about medical discoveries and how they have affected people's lives in different time periods.

From the previous examples, which mother do you think spends more time planning and which one spends more time teaching?

As you can see, unit studies are extremely beneficial to home schooling parents who are teaching more than one child.

Teaching Children with Different Learning Styles

Unit studies also work extremely well with children who have different learning styles. Most unit studies give several optional ways to learn about a topic. For example, for the study of the history of slavery in the United States, you can let your children choose how they want to study the subject, and how they want to demonstrate what they've learned. Here are some options:

- Read about slavery in the encyclopedia.
- Read about slavery in a textbook.
- Research slavery from reference books in the library.
- Read a historical novel about slavery.
- Read a biography of a slave.
- Watch a documentary on slavery.
- Write a letter, pretending that you are a slave owner.
- Write a poem about slavery.
- Create and act out a play with a slave owner and his slaves.
- Do an Internet search on slavery.

- Create a shadowbox scene depicting a plantation with slaves.
- Draw or sketch a scene depicting a plantation with slaves.
- Interview someone that has knowledge about slavery in their family history.
- Illustrate a scene depicting slavery (paint, water color, chalk, ink, pencil, etc.).

With so many different options to choose, all four learning styles are addressed, and children have the opportunity to learn in the way most effective and beneficial for them. In the chapter on "Creating and/or Purchasing Unit Studies" chapter you'll learn how a unit study is made.

Chapter 14

Charlotte Mason's Educational Philosophies and Methods

In This Chapter

◆ Who was Charlotte Mason?

◆ Mason's ideas: Narration, dictation, copy work, time line and Creation notebooks.

◆ Combining Mason's methods with the four-step process.

◆ Popularity of Charlotte Mason in the homeschool movement.

Charlotte Mason's educational teachings are worthy of great attention and respect. She criticized the tendency to "play down" to children, and emphasized their claim to be regarded as "persons" and to be treated accordingly. She provided a curriculum based on the best literature, and on direct contact with whatever is good and beautiful and interesting in the child's environment. Miss Mason laid stress on a teaching method, which she called "narration" which consists essentially in making the child reproduce in his own words the substance of what he has read or heard. In order to provide teachers and governesses to carry out her ideas she founded in 1892 a House of Education at Ambleside. She also provided courses of instruction by correspondence for mothers who wished to educate their children at home.

I was thrilled to find Charlotte Mason's philosophies and methods because they completely transformed our homeschool. I'm especially fond of her ideas in regard to living books, dictation, copywork, narration,

> Charlotte Mason's educational ideas were years ahead of her time.

time line books, and daily walks. However, I feel that I should mention that I'm not in 100% agreement with all of her philosophies, and that I adapt her methods accordingly. I should also say that I have not read the entire original Mason series because they are difficult to read, and I'm grateful for the homeschool authors who have adapted Mason's writings for today's readers (see end of this chapter for suggested reading). That being said, there is much to glean from Charlotte Mason's methods.

Charlotte Mason believed parents should be the primary source of a child's learning, and that learning should be a fun—and lifelong—process. This view went counter to the educational system that was in place at that time. According to a Worldwide Education Service (WES) pamphlet, she lived in the era when

> they practiced reading, writing, and arithmetic, sitting bolt upright on hard chairs (no slouching was allowed!) and writing on a piece of slate which could be wiped clean and used again. They were often given long lists to learn by heart, such as capital cities or dates from history, or hard spellings. If they did not learn their work they were punished, sometimes by caning...[1]

Charlotte Mason's educational ideas were years ahead of her time. One of her many biographers, Jenny King, wrote: "Charlotte Mason was probably the first educationalist to advocate visits to museums, galleries, concerts...and the children were free to relate their own impressions after the visit."[2]

Charlotte Mason believed that children should be educated through a wide curriculum, using a variety of real, "living" books. ("Twaddle," meaning dumbed-down literature, and "living books," meaning the original works of literature, are terms that were first coined by Mason.) The living books that children ought to be reading, she believed, would absorb the reader. They are well-written and engaging, and the narrative and the characters seem to come alive. Living books are actually the opposite of the cold, dry textbooks that were used in the schools of her day. Charlotte Mason said:

> Upon the knowledge of these great matters—History, Language, Nature, Science, Art—the mind feeds and grows. It assimilates such knowledge as the body assimilates food, and the person becomes what is called magnanimous, that is, a person of great mind, wide interests, incapable of occupying himself much about petty, personal matters. What a pity to lose sight of such a possibility for the sake of miserable scraps of information

about persons and things that have little connection with one another and little connection with ourselves![3]

Charlotte Mason was born in 1842 and died in 1923. When she was eighteen years old, she began attending one of the only colleges existing at that time for the education and training of teachers. Interestingly, this college had begun teaching that the *performer* (the child) was of more importance than the *performance* of the child. These ideas were new to that time, but they have become the basis for much of the popularity of homeschooling in our own time. Charlotte Mason learned of the philosophies of Matthew Arnold and John Ruskin, which promoted going beyond the "three Rs"—reading, writing, and arithmetic—and including the study of literature, poetry, religion, art, and nature in a child's curriculum. Obviously, these philosophies played a huge role in influencing Charlotte's ideas on education, and she made her determination: a liberal education was as important for children as it was for adults, which was a revolutionary idea for her time, and she worked for the rest of her life to see this philosophy come to life for the children of England.

During Charlotte's life, she taught school, lectured at Bishop Otter Teacher Training College in Chichester, England, founded a training school for governesses that later became Charlotte Mason College, was a popular public lecturer, established the Parent's National Education Union (PNEU) and was the chief editor for its magazine, *Parent's Review*. Charlotte Mason also held retreats and taught classes for parents on building the family. It would be nearly impossible to compress all of her philosophies into just one chapter in this book, for in her lifetime she filled six large volumes with her writings on the topic of education alone!

> She had a deep love of children and the deep concern that they would develop a lifelong love of learning.

Charlotte was ill for much of her life, and her health problems no doubt influenced her sympathy and care for the disadvantaged children of her day. A touching description of the struggles Charlotte faced has been recorded, and even though she was ill, the historian Sir Michael Thomas Sadler (1780–1835) noted, her face did not show any signs of weariness or pain:

> Children were to deal directly with the best books, music, and art—not read about them in some secondary source.

Her face was full of light, of wide sympathy and understanding, of delicate humor and gentleness and love. When she talked with you she brought out the best that was in you, something that you did not know was there.... She caught you up to her level, and for the time you stayed there; and you never quite fell back again.[4]

He went on to say:

> In any difficulty she always saw the right way. With few words. Always perfectly chosen, yet coming naturally and without trace of effort, she said what you knew at once to be the right thing, though you had groped long and had not found it.... It is not yet the time to measure up her full achievement. The full harvest is not yet. But there is enough to justify the confidence that posterity will see in her a great reformer, who led the children of the nation out of a barren wilderness into a rich inheritance.... The children of many generations will thank God for Charlotte Mason and her work.[4]

Charlotte Mason believed that children should be educated through a wide curriculum, using a variety of real, "living" books.

Ideas from Charlotte Mason

Mason had much respect for children. She felt the need of three essential instruments explained in *The Original Homeschooling Series* Volume 3:

1. Atmosphere: By the saying, *education is atmosphere*, it is not meant that a child should be isolated in what may be called a "child environment," especially adapted and prepared; but that we should take into account the educational value of his natural home atmosphere, both as regards persons and things, and should let him live freely among his proper conditions. It stultifies a child to bring down his world to the "child's" level...my object is to show that the chief function of the child—his business in the world during the first six or seven years of life—is to find out all he can, about whatever comes under his notice, by means of his five senses; that he has an insatiable appetite for knowledge got in his way; and that...the endeavor of his parents should be to put him in the way of making acquaintance freely with nature and natural objects; that, in fact, the intellectual education of the young child should lie in the free exercise of perceptive power...and the wisdom of the educator is to follow the lead of nature in the development of the complete human being.

2. Discipline of habit. By *education is a discipline* is meant the discipline of habits formed definitely and thoughtfully, whether habits of mind or body. Physiologists tell us of the adaptation of brain structure to habitual lines of thought—i.e., to our habits.

3. Presentation of living ideas. In the saying that *education as a life*, the need of intellectual and moral as well as of physical sustenance is implied. The mind feeds on ideas, and therefore children should have a generous curriculum.... Therefore children should be taught, as they become mature enough to understand such teaching, that the chief responsibility which rests on them as persons is the acceptance or rejection of initial ideas. To help them in this choice we should give them principles of conduct and a wide range of the knowledge fitted for them.

Here are some other revolutionary concepts that she espoused, which are important to incorporate in homeschool programs today:

Twaddle: *Twaddle* is a term coined by Charlotte Mason that refers to dumbed-down literature—watered-down versions of classic works, which should be avoided at all costs. Using twaddle is like serving fast-food to your children rather than healthy balanced meals.

Living Books: Mason recommended that children learn from real books instead of dry, boring textbooks. When is the last time you curled up with a good textbook? Living books are real books that hold a child's interest. The resources in the back of this book include hundreds of excellent living books. Most people think of historical novels, classic literature and biographies when they hear the term living books. I believe Charlotte would have included colorful information type reference books—full of great photographs and illustrations like *Eyewitness, Usborne,* etc.)—in her description of living books (if they had been available in her lifetime) because they also hold a child's interest and motivate them to want to learn more.

Whole Books: Whole books are the entirety of the book that the author actually wrote. If the author wrote a book, then the entire book should be read, not just an excerpt. The usual classroom approach is to study a textbook that is essentially an anthology, including snippets from other works, such as a chapter from Dickens, another chapter from Hawthorne, etc.

Short Lessons: Charlotte Mason recommended spending short, focused periods of time on a wide variety of subjects. In the early years of a child's education, only ten to fifteen minutes should be spent on a subject at a time, which should be progressively increased as the child matures, until the lessons approximate an hour in length for high-school students.

Nature Walks: Despite the usual rainy, inclement weather in Great Britain, Charlotte Mason insisted on going out once a week for an official "nature walk," allowing the children in her care to experience, observe and appreciate the natural environment [God's Creation] firsthand. It is important to note, however, that these should be *nature walks*—allowing the child to experience nature for himself—rather than *nature talks*, in which the child primarily gets to listen to the teacher tell about nature.

Charlotte Mason's philosophies not only breathe new life into the home-schooling curriculum, but they are also inexpensive and adaptable to just about any homeschool program.

Daily Walks: In addition to the weekly nature walks, Charlotte Mason also recommended that children spend large quantities of time in the outdoors each day, no matter what the weather. Take a daily walk for fun and fresh air. Said Mason, "That the child should be taken daily, if possible, to scenes—moor and meadow, park, common, or shore—where he may find new things to examine, and so observation should be directed to flower or boulder, bird or tree; that, in fact, he should be employed in gathering the common information which is the basis for scientific knowledge."[9]

Nature Notebooks: Mason used the term Nature notebook, I prefer using the term Creation notebook. Nature with a capital N may not have carried the same implication during Mason's time as it does today. Using the term Creation is a constant reminder there is a Creator. Children should keep Creation notebooks, artist sketchbooks that contain pictures they have personally drawn of plants, wildlife, or any other object found in its natural setting. These nature journals can also include nature-related poetry, prose, detailed descriptions, weather notes, Latin terms, etc.

Narration: Narration is literally "telling back" what has been learned. Once you know you'll be telling back you pay much better attention. This process involves sorting, sequencing, selecting, connecting, rejecting, and classifying. Narration increases the mind's ability to remember. Narration from ages four to nine should be done orally and casually by age 10 children begin to write out their narrations. The parent reads aloud from the Bible, text from a suggested resource, or content from a web site. Keep the reading about 10 to 13 minutes in length to keep their full attention on each reading. Don't stop to explain or define words unless the child asks for a definition. The children "tell" what they have heard, either orally or in writing. Its a simple process, you read, they tell, you listen. You can also use this method after a child has read a passage. This process works well. The emphasis is placed on what they do know versus what they do not know. This training in essay-style examinations is a good preparation for college.

Copy Work: Mason taught that a child learns grammar best by copying selections from fine literature into a notebook. Have your child keep a notebook specifically for copying down noteworthy poems, prose, or quotations. Each day, choose a paragraph, sentence, or page—depending on the age of the child—and have the child practice writing it out perfectly during his copy work time. Copy work is underrated. It provides ongoing practice for handwriting, spelling, grammar, etc. as well as providing good exercises for teaching accuracy and attention to detail. Students discover things about the text they are copying that they would be unlikely to notice otherwise. Students learn correct spelling, capitalization, punctuation, and other language mechanics when they compare their work to the original and correct mistakes.

Dictation: In dictation the parent speaks as the student writes. As with copy work you begin by choosing a paragraph, sentence, or page—depending on the age of the child. Dictate the words to the student as the child writes. Make sure he is following punctuation and capitalization accurately. This is an excellent method for memorizing Bible passages.

Journaling: There is great value in keeping a personal journal. Encouraging the child to keep a record of activities, thoughts, feelings, favorite sayings, and favorite poems encourages self-reflection and descriptive writing.

Book of the Centuries: A "book of the centuries," as Charlotte Mason called it, was a glorified timeline, usually a notebook consisting of one to two pages per century. As children learn historical facts, they make notes in their book on the appropriate century's page about famous people, important events, inventions, wars, battles, and so on.

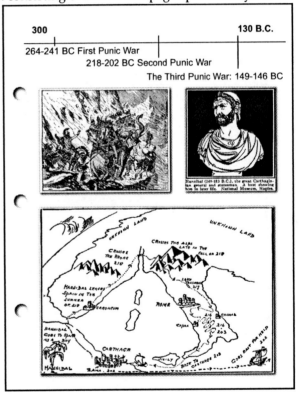

Art Appreciation: Children can be brought into direct contact with the best art ever created without too much difficulty. Choose one artist at a time, and six paintings per artist. Study one painting per week—even taking as little as fifteen minutes per week. Allow the child to look at the work intently for a period of time, such as five minutes, taking in every detail. Then take the picture away and have the child narrate (tell back) what he saw in the painting. It helps to have on hand a selection of prints that are copies of famous paintings.[6]

Free-Time Handicrafts: Charlotte Mason advocated finishing all daily academics in the morning hours, allowing the afternoon hours to be free to pursue crafts, hobbies, and other activities of personal interest.

Step	Four-Steps	Charlotte Mason Method
1. Excite	Motivating students	Motivate the student by making the lesson interesting on his/her level—not dumbed down.
2. Examine	Teaching ideas and facts	Give the facts from living books, Creation, and humanities.
3. Expand	Experimenting with concepts and skills	Get the student to do something with what he has learned, such as copy work, dictation, or adding to a nature notebook or timeline.
4. Excel	Integrating new learning into real life	Get the student to tell back—share with others—what he has learned (narration).

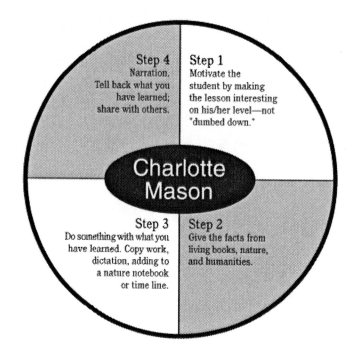

Charlotte Mason's Ideas and the Four-Step Process

Charlotte Mason's method of education focused on the formation of good habits: reading a variety of books, narration, copy work, dictation, nature diaries, spelling notebooks, and timeline books. The Heart of Wisdom teaching approach combines each of Mason's unique methods into a four-step process:

1. Motivation
Students are reached at their level, not with a dumbed-down approach that treats them as if they are not capable of understanding or that the information is too far above them, which induces boredom.

2. Teaching Ideas and Facts
Ideas and facts should be gleaned from the things that spark your child's interest, as discussed in the Delight-Directed Studies chapter.

3. Experimenting with Concepts and Skills
Copy work and dictation teach accuracy and attention to detail, and students discover things about the text they are copying that they would be unlikely to notice otherwise. In dictation, the parent reads aloud as the child writes. In copy work, the child copies the material from a book or another resource. Students learn correct spelling, capitalization, punctuation, and other written language mechanics when they compare their work to the original and correct their mistakes. In addition, Charlotte Mason recommended preparing a handmade "book of the centuries," or timeline book.

4. Integrating New Learning into Real Life
Through narration, concepts are integrated into the real life of the child. Narration is simply the telling back of what has been learned. Students are instructed to read a passage from the Bible, text from a suggested resource, or content from a Web site, and then tell what they have learned, in their own words, either orally or in writing. This is a wonderful activity, and one which you will find frequently in both the third and fourth steps of the four steps in each Heart of Wisdom unit study. The mental process required for telling back involves comprehension and memory, as well as sorting, sequencing, selecting, connecting, rejecting, and classifying the information that has been learned. Mason always advocated the idea that if narration is used correctly and consistently, review of the material becomes almost unnecessary. Narration increases the mind's ability to remember.

Mason's Methods Have Changed Homeschooling

Charlotte Mason's educational ideas were timeless, stretching far beyond her generation, and appeal to a diverse group of people from all levels of the current homeschool movement that has been sweeping across our country for the last several years. One of the greatest reasons for its appeal is Charlotte Mason's gracious respect and love for children that still touches the hearts and minds of her modern-day followers. She had a deep love of children and the concern that they would develop a lifelong love of learning. Her philosophy was based on the Latin word for education *educare*, which means "to feed and nourish."[1]

This nourishment is achieved through a wide and diverse curriculum that uses a variety of books and resources in the education of the child. Charlotte's methods advocated a liberal—that is, a generous—education. It has its basis in certain core subjects, but also incorporates the fine arts and whatever else sparks the child's interest. Children are to deal *directly* with the best books, music, and art—not read *about* them in some secondary source. Students are to be trained in the practice of narration, of telling back what they have learned, and sharing their knowledge with others. The emphasis—contrary to the educational models of her time—is to always be placed on what the children *do* know and not on what they do *not* know.

One of the fastest growing methods of homeschool education around the United States is that of Charlotte Mason's philosophies. It is easy to see why: Not only do they breathe new life into the homeschooling curriculum, but they are also inexpensive and adaptable to just about any homeschool program. There are other reasons as well, as Charlotte Levison has stated:

> All methods of home schooling enhance the parent's knowledge and understanding as they teach their children. Most of us find that to be a rewarding side benefit—for awhile. Eventually, though, as the years come and go, we find ourselves repeating core teaching with each child as they advance in age. Depending on the number of children in your home, you're apt to teach reading, handwriting, grammar, phonics, adding, subtracting, dividing, and fractions more than once or twice—and it might be nice if you covered the Revolutionary War at some point.

> Burnout is a sad state of affairs. It has several causes, and one of them is simply growing weary of teaching the same core information over and over again. Burnout can be such a hopeless condition that it is far better to avoid it than to have to find a way out of it.

> Charlotte Mason's ideas and techniques rescued me from burnout. In addition, they have enriched my life as no other home school method ever could. Parents must continue to teach the core subjects—this is mandatory. However, if you can accomplish that to everybody's satisfaction and still have ample time to go on to art and music appreciation, nature study, classic literature, poetry, a better understanding of history, and foreign languages, you will find your own education has been enriched along with the children's.

Typically, public school graduates (which most of us are) did not receive a rich, abundant education. Worse than that, no one seemed to care if we enjoyed the learning process or not. In the Charlotte Mason method, we care deeply that the children develop a love for learning. Mason warned the parent not to kill that love. At the same time we expose the children to a wide, generous, lively smorgasbord of an education. We learn along with them because in most cases we, as students, were not exposed to such a wide variety.[10]

Her work has aided not just the generation of children in her own lifetime, but successive generations that have followed and are yet to come. Her gravestone is a telling memorial to her accomplishments and spirit:

In loving memory of Charlotte Maria Shaw Mason. Born Jan 1 1842, died Jan 16 1923, Thine eyes shall see the King in His beauty. Founder of the Parents National Education Union, The Parents Union School and The House of Education. She devoted her life to the work of education, believing that children are dear to our heavenly Father, and that they are a precious national possession. Education is an atmosphere, a discipline, a life. I am, I can, I ought, I will. For the children's sake.

Suggested Reading

Charlotte Mason Companion by Karen Andreola ⌐⊂
A thorough chapter-by-chapter overview of the inspiring teaching principles of Christian educator Charlotte Mason, this book reveals the practical day-by-day method of how to teach "the Charlotte Mason way." Karen offers friendly advice and humor, along with the joys and struggles of real homeschool life.

Charlotte Mason Education: A How-to Manual by Catherine Levison ⌐⊂
Catherine Levison has collected the key points of Charlotte Mason's methods and presents them in a simple, straightforward way that will allow families to quickly maximize the opportunities of homeschooling. With weekly schedules, a challenging and diverse curriculum will both inspire and educate your child. *A Charlotte Mason Education* is the latest tool for parents seeking the best education for their children.

Charlotte Mason's Original Homeschooling Series by Charlotte Mason ⌐⊂
This is the complete works of the turn-of-the-century British educator, Charlotte Mason. The six-volume set includes over 2,400 pages of the finest material ever written on education, child training and parenting. Recognized as the pioneer in home education and major school reforms, Charlotte Mason's practical methods are as revolutionary today as when they were first written. (If you have trouble reading material written during Mason's time you would do better to choose from the other books in this list.)

For the Children's Sake by Susan Schaeffer Macaulay ⌐⊂
Susan Schaeffer Macaulay shows how education can be a wonderful, life-enriching, joyous

experience. This book is about what education can be—for your child, in your home, and in your school. It is based first on a Christian understanding of what it means to be human—to be a child, a parent, a teacher—and on the Christian meaning of life. At the same time it is very practical. Many of the central ideas have been tried and proven true over a century in almost every kind of educational situation. The ideas are, in fact, so true that they can be applied equally at home, in different schools, in Africa, in the inner city, and in your own community. But they are also ideas which Susan and her husband Ronald Macaulay have tried and proved in their own family and school experience.

A Literary Education by Catherine Levison ▷
Catherine shares her favorite resources for many areas of homeschooling, including math, poetry, art, science, literature and more. Through detailed descriptions and age-appropriate suggestions, homeschoolers have an abundance of recommended resources to complement their homeschools.

More Charlotte Mason Education by Catherine Levison ▷
Offers broad advice about scheduling, selecting materials, teaching methods, and Mason's philosophy of education. It also includes using Mason's methodology with high schoolers, creating a "century book," and lengthy, recommended book lists.

When Children Love to Learn: A Practical Application of Charlotte Mason's Philosophy by Elaine Cooper ▷
A love of learning—isn't that what it is all about? It can't be denied—children have an inherent desire to know. Teachers and parents can either encourage this natural inquisitiveness or squelch it. There is joy in the classroom when children learn—not to take a test, not to get a grade, not to compete with each other, and not to please their parents or their teachers—but because they want to know about the world around them! Both Christian educators and parents will find proven help in creating a positive learning atmosphere through methods pioneered by Charlotte Mason that show how to develop a child's natural love of learning. A practical follow-up to *For the Children's Sake,* this book follows a tradition of giving serious thought to what education is, so that children will be learning for life—and for everlasting life. Elaine covers a lot of ground to show how easy it can be to make learning enjoyable.

See excerpts from several of the books listed at http://Homeschool-Books.com.

Most books are available from Homeschool-Books.com. Books from a Christian perspective are marked with a ▷

234

Writing To Learn

In This Chapter

◆ Defining writing to learn.

◆ Types of writing.

◆ Correcting written work.

One of the best ways for a student to understand a topic is to write about it. To write successfully, students must comprehend the material, restructure the new information, and then share their new understanding. The concept of writing to learn is more than just an accumulation of reports that the student must write; rather, writing to learn helps students to think carefully and learn completely.

Writing assignments are not only about creating ideas, but learning. All writing is an exercise in thinking, an exercise through which we learn new connections and see new directions to take with our ideas. During writing assignments, students learn how to assess information and determine its appropriateness for inclusion, how to evaluate and compare, analyze and discern, add their own feelings to the material, organize information, and communicate their conclusions. Through these processes, students learn to manage and use information to solve problems, interrelate knowledge, and effectively communicate.

Excellence will be learned by continually practicing clarity, accuracy, relevance, prioritizing, consistency, depth, and breadth through writing activities. Diligence will be developed by producing the required quality assignments.

Cafi Cohen, author of *What About College*, explains her children's writing experience:

As teenagers, our kids seldom did grammar exercises and never wrote reports and term papers. According to some in the educational establishment, they ought to be poor writers. Not so. Both got A's in their college freshmen English classes. Friends now often ask them for help editing assignments. Both enjoy writing, and they produce credible pieces for college classes as well as for real-life purposes.

"I had to ask myself why I was trying to improve my (adult) writing one way (reading good writing, reading about writing, and writing and editing my work), and my teenagers' writing another way (with grammar exercises and pointless papers). And, of course, I had no good answer. "

Successful authors, it turns out, never recommend diagramming sentences, memorizing verb tenses, taking spelling tests, and identifying parts of speech in random sentences. And they seldom advise using textbook writing techniques, like identifying predicates and combining sentences by creating subordinate clauses. Instead professional writers discuss developing leads, writing and rewriting, writing for real purposes, avoiding clutter, and choosing words. They talk about their writing toolkits—those practices that help them produce clean, informative, and entertaining poetry and prose.

Most significantly, successful authors describe writing as a process, not a product. Each writer says that his process, developed over a long period of time, is idiosyncratic; that is, his approach, often established through trial and error, is peculiar to him.

In reading about the practices of professional writers, I had to ask myself why I was trying to improve my (adult) writing one way (reading good writing, reading about writing, and writing and editing my work), and my teenagers' writing another way (with grammar exercises and pointless papers). And, of course, I had no good answer. So I made a command decision: no more grammar exercises, punctuation drills, or assignments to write papers on meaningless topics. It was time to catalog and USE with my kids the techniques suggested by successful authors.[1]

One of Charlotte Mason's narration methods for younger children involves "telling back" favorite stories read to them by their parents. As children grow older, they can progress to reading passages on their own and then telling back what they've learned in verbal or written form. Talking about what they have learned, whether aloud or on paper, helps students learn to think and remember more effectively.

Many teachers in traditional school environments use writing as a way of testing. They use it to find out what students already know, rather than as a way of encouraging them to learn. But the active processes of seeking information, compiling notes, and evaluating, analyzing, and organizing content, as well as personal reflection, choosing and constructing words, and expressing ideas in writing, are valuable learning tools which students will use for the rest of their lives.

Catherine Copley compares writing to baking bread in *The Writer's Complex* (another food analogy!):

> Writing provides food for thought—it enables you to knead small, half-baked words and sentences into great big loaves of satisfying thought that then lead to more thoughts. Developing ideas involves getting some ideas—in whatever form—onto paper or screen so you can see them, return to them, explore them, question them, share them, clarify them, change them, and grow them. It really is almost like growing plants or kneading bread and waiting for the results: plant the seed, start the process, and then let your mind, including your unconscious, take over. Go to sleep and let your dreaming continue to develop your ideas. Humans were born to think; it's almost impossible to stop us. Writing helps us to bring all that activity into consciousness, helps to clarify and direct our thinking, and generate more thinking. Writing, thinking, and learning are part of the same process. [2]

Before you Begin

Before you give any writing assignment, your student should have a clear understanding of the writing process. The writing process and writing to learn is explained in detail in the suggested writing handbooks available from our web site in the Language Arts/Writing category: *Writers Express* (grades 5–6), *Write Source 2000* (grades 6–8), and *Writers Inc* (grades 9–12).

Various Writing Activities

There are countless ways to encourage your children's writing skills and incorporate writing to learn into your homeschool curriculum. Good writing assignments always start with a clear goal. Ask yourself, "What do I want to my child to learn from this?" By defining your goal you'll be able to give detailed guidelines about both the writing task and the final written product. Use these principles:

- Keep in mind the specific goals.

- Remind the student of the audience, purpose, writing situation.

- Make all basics of the task clear.

- Break down the task into manageable steps.

The next pages give a few example activities.

Writing Summaries: A Narration Method

Several activities in Heart of Wisdom unit studies recommend that the student read passages from the Bible or other literature and then write a summary. This is an excellent way to tell how well one understands something they have read. This method is almost always required preparation for deeper thinking, and is an important tool for research writing. Adding summary writing to your student's routine will increase his or her ability to understand and remember.

Knowing how to write a summary is an essential skill for studying and writing in college. A student has written a good summary when he or she has portrayed the real meaning of a piece of writing in his or her own words. While writing summaries the student will learn sources and integrate the ideas and information of others into their own thinking. The length of a summary is determined by the student's purpose and audience. Students must first have a basic understanding of the material and then carefully paraphrase the selection. One reading will not, in all likelihood, enable them to write a good summary. Writing a summary is for conveying the meaning of what was read in one's own words (paraphrasing), with the fewest number of words and sentences, and without a biased opinion. Summaries are to be objective, explaining what the author stated, not the student's feelings or personal evaluation of the material. Explain to your students the steps in writing a summary:

1. Read the work.

2. Reread the work several times, using various reading strategies such as previewing, skimming, and scanning.

3. Locate the main idea in each paragraph. Highlight and then write down the main ideas, in order, on a separate piece of paper.

4. Write and rewrite the information, condensing and arranging the summary in the best fashion.

5. Rewrite and reread; select, eliminate, and add information until satisfied that the summary is complete, clear, concise and correct.

Informal or Free Writing

Informal or free writing is probably the easiest to implement of all writing-to-learn activities. In its basic form, free writing is simply writing down everything that comes to mind, usually for five or ten minutes without stopping. Focused free writing, which uses some kind of prompt (a term, an issue, a question, or a problem) is useful for the thematic units in this curriculum. This type of writing is unconstrained by any need to appear correct in public (similar to brainstorming). It is not yet arranging, asserting, or arguing. It is still reflecting and questioning. This is probative, speculative, generative thinking that is written in class or at home to develop the language of learning, and it may not even be read by a teacher.

Specifically, informal written language will help your student to:

- Develop the ability to define, classify, summarize, question, generate criteria, establish inferences, imagine hypotheses, analyze problems, and identify procedures.

- Improve methods of of observing, recording and reporting, organizing and structuring data into generalizations, formulating theories, and recognizing and applying the methods themselves.

- Learn about central concepts such as problem solving, thinking, learning, communicating, and knowledge itself.

- Develop the ability to question, create problems and solutions, wonder, and think for oneself.

- Understand one's own beliefs and attitudes toward learning, knowing oneself, one's work, one's own and others errors, the knowledge and opinions of others, and the attitudes that affect behaviors.

Journals and Blogging

Students can journal in a learning log or other type of journal. A more formidable type of journal is the double-entry or dialogic journal. Students copy down thoughts, quotes, facts, or impressions from the unit study in one column or on one page and write responses, questions, and insights in the next column or on the facing page. In this way the writer engages in a continuing dialogue with the material. Journaling can be an important part of life in any field or profession.

Blogging (short for web logging) is a type of journaling that is popular on the Internet (weblogs, online diary, chronicling events and thoughts). There are blogs on just about any interest (media, food, personal diaries, policy, Bible views, etc.). It's fairly easy to start a blog. All you need is access to a computer and the Internet, and feel the need to communicate. If this is something your student may be interested in there are several free places to blog online.

Writing About Bible Passages

When writing about Bible passages, students should ask questions about every section of text. They are: *Who, What, When, Where, Why,* and *How.*

- Who?   Who are the participants, the author, and the intended listeners or first readers? If there is a command, who must obey it?

- What?   What happened or will happen? If there is a command, what should be done? What does the text say about God, Jesus, people, Satan, angels, demons, etc.? What ideas are discussed, and what is said about them?

- When?   When did (will) it happen? (Time lines line are helpful.) If there is a command, when must it be done? If the text is a prophecy, has it been fulfilled?

- Where?   Where did (will) it happen? (Bible maps are helpful.) If there is a command, where must it be performed?

- Why?   Why was (is) this done? Why did (will) this happen? Why should it be done?

- How?   How was (is) it done? How should it be done?

Other Types of Writing Assignments

Other types of writing assignments could include:

- Writing a letter to a person studied in a unit.

- Keeping a diary or journal as if written by someone studied in a unit.

- Writing a newspaper article about an event studied in a unit.

- Creating a Web site about the unit.

- Making a mind map about the unit theme.

- Writing a summary of a concept learned during the unit study.

Correcting Written Work

An important part of writing to learn is learning through mistakes. For this to happen, the parent/teacher must be able to accurately proofread and check their child's work. When this is done correctly, the student will learn:

- *Writing Skills*: Context, form, mechanics, editing, and revision.

- *Spelling Skills*: Improved through the creation of a personal spelling notebook.

- *Vocabulary*: Increased through the creation of a personal vocabulary notebook.

- *Handwriting Skills*: Improved through the practice of writing out Bible verses.

- *Critical Thinking Skills*: Problem-solving, interrelating information, effectively communicating learning outcomes.

- *Character Development*: Developed through attentiveness, decisiveness, commitment, faithfulness, perseverance, responsibility, assignment completion, promptness, efficiency, confidence, and self-control.

Because the correction of written work is such an important part of the learning process, every unit in the Heart of Wisdom curriculum utilizes the *Writers Inc* handbook, which allows the parent to correct spelling, capitalization, punctuation, grammar, sentence structure, subject/verb agreement, consistency in verb tense, and word usage, by marking the error with a number that corresponds with a rule in the handbook. The student can then refer to the rule in the book, correct his paper, and turn it back in. The *Writers Inc* handbook is the one that Heart of Wisdom recommends, but you can purchase a similar type of handbook at bookstores around the nation.

My Access! Online Writing Coach

We provide an online program for a minimal annual fee that will grade and analyze your children's written work. MYAccess!™ is a prompt-driven, web based writing environment that scores essays instantly and provides diagnostic instruction that engages and motivates students to want to improve their writing proficiency. MYAccess! allows students to write essays, submit them via the internet and receive immediate and meaningful feed-back employing Vantage Learning's remarkable IntelliMetric™ automated essay scoring technology. Parents can access student writing portfolios online to monitor progress, provide additional feedback and tailor instruction to address the specific needs of their children. For details go to HeartofWisdom.com/MyAccess.html. Vantage Learning's MYAccess! is designed for students in the 4th grade through seniors in college.

Suggested Reading

Nurturing the Write Relationship by Mary Ann Froehlich Edited by Robin Sampson ᴦᴏ
In this book you'll learn how to inspire writers of all ages, from a four-year-old expressing her thoughts through pictures in a notebook, to a ten-year-old creating a memory by journaling about a birthday celebration, to a teenager venting her views and recording her spiritual growth in a conflict journal, to a mother communicating her grief over the loss of her child, to a professional writer who is collecting ideas for stories. Each of those examples involves an outpouring of emotions and personal experience. Teaching your child to write about life can help them adapt to new challenges and nurture relationships at the same time.

Mary Ann Froehlich, an established author, taught her children to write using a real-life approach, following the rules of a writing group. She posed as a mock publisher to lead her children through the writing process, from query letters to contracts and finished publications, complete with book signings and marketing techniques. Her process is outlined in this book. Froehlich explains that when writing assignments are viewed as academic exercises, the adventure of writing is lost. She will show you how families working on individual and joint writing projects can motivate children to catch the excitement of meaningful writing. They come to understand that the art of writing is a also powerful life tool.

This book is much more than a guide to writing groups. In it you will learn how writing activities and rituals can be woven through the day, year, and even throughout life. Froehlich's ideas go hand in hand with Charlotte Mason-type methods, in that she encourages copy work and journaling. Activities include ideas for family journaling, letter writing, Bible journaling, goal journaling, celebration journaling, and more. This book is not about the educational nuts and bolts of writing, but is intended to inspire and celebrate writing in the home. Nurturing the Write Relationship will help you develop a writing lifestyle and tradition in your own family. Ebook or paperback.

Writing to Learn by William Zinsser
This is a book on how to write clearly about any subject and how to use writing as a means of learning. It is an engaging personal journey, written with warmth and humor as Zinsser takes the reader into many surprising corners of knowledge and demonstrates that every field has accessible literature.

On Writing Well by William Zinsser
This book is for everybody who wants to learn how to write or who needs to do some writing to get through the day, as almost everybody does in this age of email and the Internet. Whether you want to write about people or places, science and technology, business, sports, the arts or about yourself in the increasingly popular memoir genre, On Writing Well offers you fundamental principles as well as the insights of a distinguished writer and teacher. With more than a million copies sold, this volume has stood the test of time and remains a valuable resource for writers and would-be writers.

Most books are available from Homeschool-Books.com. Books from a Christian perspective are marked with a ᴦᴏ

Critical Thinking and Logic

Logic and rhetoric are extremely popular and enthusiastically sought after by those in the homeschool community today, as well as in our public schools. The words logic, classical, philosophy, dialectic, and reasoning sound extremely intelligent to our Greek-conditioned ears. It is understandable that homeschoolers want their children to become critical thinkers. We want to be able to defend the Gospel logically. We want our students to learn to evaluate their beliefs and the beliefs of others before they take a course of action.

But logic and reality are not the same,
and logical consistency does not always produce truth.

Human reasoning is limited by human perception and experience. Eve trusted her reason over what God had said and logically concluded that eating the fruit of the forbidden tree was the best choice for her and Adam. *And when the woman saw that the tree was good for food, and that it was pleasant to the eyes, and a tree to be desired to make one wise, she took of the fruit thereof, and did eat, and gave also unto her husband with her; and he did ea*t (Genesis 3:6).

Come, let us reason together (Isaiah 1:18), and look at more examples from the Bible. Is it logical to consider it all joy when you encounter various trials (James 1:2)? Is it logical to believe that God created the earth in six days? Was it logical for Cain to sacrifice fruit of his own work instead of a blood offering? Was it logical for Noah to build an ark where there was no water? Was it logical for men to build the Tower of Babel? Was it logical for Abraham to move away from his family and all he knew, based on what he had heard from an invisible voice? Was it logical for Sarah to have a baby so late in life? Was it logical for Moses to defy Pharaoh and lead the Israelites out of Egypt? Was it logical for Gideon, with the weakest clan (Manasseh), to save Israel from the Midianites? Is it logical to turn the other cheek when someone slaps you? Was it logical for Christ, who was completely without sin, to give His life for us when we are so full of sin? God has every logical reason to punish us for our sins, but in His grace and mercy, He offered us His pardon through His son.

> *Now faith is the substance of things hoped for, the evidence of things not seen. For by it the elders obtained a good report. Through faith we understand that the worlds were framed by the word of God, so that things which are seen were not made of things which do appear.*—Hebrews 11:1–3.

When Dr. John Garr was asked about logic he replied, "Some things with God are supra-logical (not illogical); they go beyond logic into a realm of divine insight that only God fully understands God's ways are beyond man's ways. *By faith we understand that the worlds were framed by the Word of God*—Hebrews 11:3. With God so many things are ineffable: we can understand them only after we have done them."

There is no doubt that God wants us to use our minds. He said, *My people are destroyed for lack of knowledge* (Hosea 4:6), and *Come now, let us reason together.* (Isaiah 1:18). You are reasoning and analyzing now as you read this. The word reason in the Hebrew is a law term used of arguing, convincing, or deciding a case in court.

The Bible encourages knowledge, understanding, and wisdom as virtues to be sought after. We are commanded to get wisdom and understanding (Proverbs 4:5, 7; 16:16, see also Psalm 119:104). Paul prayed for Christ's followers to grow in knowledge, wisdom and understanding (Ephesians1:16–18; Philippians 1:9; Col. 1:9). The Bible speaks negatively of ignorance (Psalm 73:22; Isaiah 56:10; Romans 10:3; 1 Corinthians 14:38; 2 Corinthians 2:11; 2 Pet. 3:5). Paul frequently made the statement, *I would not have you ignorant* (Romans 1:13; 11:25; 1 Corinthians 10:1; 12:1; 2 Corinthians 1:8; 1 Thessalonians 4:13; see also 2 Peter 3:8, 1 Timothy 1:13). The Hebrews, however, never viewed wisdom as merely factual or simply cognitive information. Rather, wisdom was seen as understanding how to apply knowledge to a specific area. Wisdom begins with the ability to see and evaluate all of life from God's point of view (Proverbs 1:7).

Critical thinking is the ability to acquire information, understand it, and then determine how it relates to what one is studying; and it helps one to be able to express ideas clearly and systematically. A critical thinker uses broad, in-depth analysis of evidence to make decisions and communicate his beliefs clearly and accurately. The lessons in the Heart of Wisdom unit studies encourage critical thinking skills through sorting, sequencing, selecting, connecting, rejecting, and classifying the information that has been learned.

If we teach our children to become critical thinkers, do we really need to also teach them formal logic? Logic has limits. Countless problems have been presented to graduate students who arrived at the wrong answer (as defined by the rules of logic) whereas other students arrived at the right answer for the wrong reasons.[1] Logic is not the only means of gaining knowledge and understanding—there is also experience, intuition, direct revelation, and inspiration.

Research on cognitive processes reveals that there is a great difference between everyday reasoning and the logical system devised by logicians. A great deal of everyday thinking is practical, intuitive and emotional. Thinking in formal logical terms requires explicit training, but it is still difficult for highly educated people, even those trained in logic. Wason and Johnson-Laird made an experiment called card-tuning to test the ability of adults in formal thinking. The results are so striking that the vast majority of adults, including trained logicians, not only got the given problem wrong, but usually had given the same logically incorrect answers.[2]

What is Logic and Rhetoric?

Formal logic is the study of the principles and methods of argumentation. The study of logic came from ancient Greek philosophers, Plato, Aristotle, and Socrates. Aristotle (student of Plato, and called "the father of logic") compiled the system of formal logic and wrote a thesis on rhetoric still used in universities today. Aristotle defined rhetoric as the art of persuasion. An argument in logic is a set of statements. Some of the statements serve as premises (or statements of evidence), and others serve as the conclusions that can be drawn from the premises. Syllogism is the most common type of argument form in deductive logic. Example: All German shepherds are dogs. All dogs are mammals; therefore, all German Shepherds are mammals. The *conclusion* is the final statement; the other two statements are the *premises*. Aristotle taught that the syllogism was the main instrument for reaching conclusions. He believed that knowledge of the world could only be obtained through experience.

Dialectic is defined by *Funk and Wagnall's Dictionary* as the art or practice of examining statements logically as by question and answer to establish validity. The Socratic dialectical method was one of cross-examination. In Plato's dialogues, Socrates characteristically argued by means of cross-examining someone else's statements in order to pull out the contradictions in the other's person's position.

Philosophers and educators have occasionally recommended the teaching of formal logic as a means to critical thinking. Not all educators agree with this theory. Robert H. Ennis's book *Philosophy of Education* reports that, although rational thinkers exhibit certain proficiencies, tendencies, and good habits, he explicitly rejected formal logic as a method of teaching rational thinking as "too elaborate."[3]

In Chapter 9, "The Hebrew Educational Model," we explained how Jesus apparently never aimed at a systematic and logical presentation of his teaching. He did not speak to the crowds of fisher folk and peasants in the logical manner of a professor lecturing a classroom. Nowhere do you find definitions of terms used, premises laid down, deductions drawn. He did not attempt to transform men by syllogisms. These things are the mechanics of speech; they are difficult to follow and almost inevitably convey a sense of artificiality. Certainly the deepest things of life are not determined by an argument. Jesus' teaching methods were far superior to the Greek methods used in His day.

Human Reasoning or God's Word?

Based on our worldview, our final authority is either human reasoning or the Bible. The same natural human reasoning that the ancient Greeks so venerated is manifest in today's liberal secular/humanistic thinking. Secular liberals believe that all men are searching for truth and every man gets a portion of it, so nobody is wrong and nobody is right. It doesn't seem rational that God would make a Hell; therefore, they believe that there is no Hell. Reason says, "I don't believe what the Bible says because it does not fit with my rational thinking." Or "I can't believe there is a God of wrath, so there must not be a God of wrath."

Oswald Chambers said, "The salvation of God does not stand on human logic; it stands on the sacrificial death of Jesus. Sinful men and women can be changed into new creatures by the marvelous work of God in Christ Jesus, which is prior to all experience."[4]

Should a Christian Teach Logic?

Logic is not pagan or evil. The God-given ability to reason well is a critical thinking skill that is vital in science, mathematics, law, forecasting, diagnosing, and just about every other circumstance. The ability to reason well is of great importance. Critical thinking skills are not right or wrong. Logic is a skill or a tool like a hammer. A hammer it can be used to build something useful or as a murder weapon. Logic skills can be developed as a tool to defend the Bible or to tear it apart. Are books good or evil? Books can be used to spread the Gospel or promote pornography. Thinking along this line—are cows good or evil?

- In Bible times domesticated cattle were used by the Hebrews in many ways: as a food source (in 1 Kings 4:23 Solomon's daily household ration included thirty cattle and oxen), as sacrificial offerings (Solomon offered twenty-two thousand oxen in 1 Kings 8:63), to pull carts (Numbers 7:3), as pack animals (1 Chronicles 12:40), for threshing (Deuteronomy 25:4) and, together with sheep and goats, for milk products and dung (for fertilizer and fuel for fire).

- On the other hand, the ancient Egyptians worshiped cows. In the wilderness, the Hebrews, looking back to Egypt, built a golden calf to worship. This idolatry brought death to three thousand Hebrews.

- Today the majority of the population in America believes cows are healthy to eat. The average diet includes milk and/or hamburgers. The U.S. beef industry generates an estimated $175 billion in economic activity.

- Other people believe cows are full of harmful antibiotics and hormones and that eating beef will poison their body. Medical reports say eating beef has been linked to heart disease, high blood pressure, and strokes. Drinking milk has been linked to asthma, allergies, intestinal bleeding, and juvenile diabetes. Cutting dairy products out of your diet gives you a greater chance of avoiding bronchial, respiratory, and stomach problems.[5]

- The Hindu religion teaches the sanctity of animal life, and while they themselves usually live in abject poverty, the animals among them are maintained in idleness. Over 50% of India's population is malnourished, while large portions of government funds go for food, shelter and the medical needs of cows.

The answers to our questions will depend on who we ask, and their worldview and their reasoning. Using this example above one can see that a study on worldviews may be more important than a study of formal logic.

We can't always trust human reasoning, especially in moral and spiritual matters—but this fact does not negate the importance of logic nor of reasoning. This book you are reading was outlined in a logical fashion. Each chapter deals primarily with one category, which is necessary because large blocks of information need to be broken down and presented in manageable units. It is essential to adopt the attitudes and dispositions of a critical thinker when studying the Bible.

The question should not be, "Should we use logic?"; rather, the question should be "What is our motivation in using logic?" Basic Bible hermeneutics contains logical principles that must be applied in order to correctly understand the Bible—who is the author, when did he live, what is his point of view, what was the cultural and historical setting of the time in which he wrote, to whom was he writing, and in what language was he writing?

Now, we have validated that reasoning and critical thinking are important skills but we must also recognize that there is an innate weakness in human logic. Logic means correct reasoning, but following logic does not always produce a valid conclusion. If there is not enough information, or wrong information is in the chain of reasoning, the conclusion will be wrong. Paul says, *We know in part.* (1Corinthians 13:9), and we *see through a glass darkly* (1 Corinthians 13:11 KJV). Problems arise when we trust logic more than we trust God or His Word. It is a matter of priorities and balance.

Marvin Wilson describes the difference between block logic and Greek logic in *Our Father Abraham*:

> The use of what may be termed *block logic* is another important contour of Hebrew thought. Greek logic, which has to a large extent influenced the Western world, was different. The Greeks often used a tightly contained step logic whereby one would argue from premises to a conclusion, each step linked tightly to the next in coherent, rational, logical fashion. The conclusion, however, was usually limited to one point of view—the human being's perception of reality.
>
> By contrast, the Hebrews often made use of block logic. That is, concepts were expressed in self-contained units or blocks of thought. These blocks did not necessarily fit together in any obviously rational or harmonious pattern, particularly when one block represented the human perspective on truth and the other represented the divine. This way of thinking created a propensity for paradox, antinomy, or apparent contradiction, as one block stood in tension—often illogical relation—to the other. Hence, polarity of thought or dialectic often characterized block logic.
>
> It is particularly difficult for Westerners—those whose thought-patterns have been influenced more by the Greeks and Romans than by the Hebrews—to piece together the block logic of Scripture. When we open the Bible, therefore, since we are not Orientals, we are invited…to undergo a kind of intellectual conversion to the Hebraic world of the East.
>
> Let us turn, then, to some of the many examples of block logic found throughout Scripture. The book of Exodus says that Pharaoh hardened his heart, but it also says that God hardened it (Exodus 8:15; cf. 7:3). The prophets teach that God is both wrathful and merciful (Isaiah 45:7; Habakkuk 3:2). The New Testament refers to Jesus as the "Lamb of God" and the "Lion of the tribe of Judah" (John 1:29, 36; Revelation 5:5). Hell is described as both "blackest darkness" and the "fiery lake" (Jude 13; Revelation 19:20). In terms of salvation, Jesus said, "whoever comes to me I will never drive away," yet no one can come "unless the Father draws him" (John

6:37, 44). To find life you must lose it (Matthew 10:39). When you are weak, then you are strong (2 Corinthians 12:10). The way up (exaltation) is the way down (humility) (Luke 14:11). "Jacob have I loved and Esau have I hated" (Romans 9:13; Malachi 1:3).

> It is particularly difficult for Westerners—those whose thought-patterns have been influenced more by the Greeks and Romans than by the Hebrews—to piece together the block logic of Scripture.

Consideration of certain forms of block logic may give the impression that divine sovereignty and human responsibility are incompatible. The Hebrews, however, sensed no violation of their freedom as they accomplish God's purposes. Upon a more careful reading of the biblical text, one can often observe that the Bible presents one block from the perspective of divine transcendence—God says, "I will harden Pharaoh's heart"—and the other from a human point of view—"Pharaoh hardened his heart" (Exodus 4:21; 7:3,13; 8:15). The same is often true of Scriptures which deal with the themes of predestination/election and free will/human freedom.

In sum, the Hebrew mind could handle the dynamic tension of the language of paradox, confident that "all is in the hands of Heaven except the fear of Heaven"… Divine sovereignty and human responsibility were not incompatible.

The Hebrew knew he did not know all the answers. His position was "under the sun" (Ecclesiastes 8:17), so his words were few (5:2). He refused to over-systematize or force harmonization on the enigmas of God's truth or the puzzles of the universe. He realized that no one could straighten what God has made crooked (7:13). All things, therefore, did not need to be fully rational. The Hebrew mind was willing to accept the truths taught on both sides of the paradox and recognized that mystery and apparent contradictions are often signs of the divine. Stated succinctly, the Hebrews knew the wisdom of learning to trust God in matters that they could not fully understand.

While philosophical and structural divisions of learning obviously have an important role to play in contemporary education, our Western culture—especially on most levels of secular and Christian instruction—has provided little understanding concerning the nature of Hebrew thought. Thus we have the natural tendency to impose more rational and systematic categories of thought on the Bible.

Both God and his Word have a sovereign unpredictability that defies rational, human explanation. [Not only because of our perceptive inability to see things invisible or to see the forest while we're down here among the trees, but also because God's motives, thoughts, methods and goals are perfect while our hearts and minds have been perverted by the Fall.]

The Semites of Bible times did not simply *think* truth—they *experienced* truth…truth is as much an encounter as it is proposition…. To the Jew, the deed was always more important than the creed. He was not stymied by language that appeared contradictory from a human point of view. Neither did he feel compelled to reconcile what seemed irreconcilable. He believed that God ultimately was greater than any

> The Hebrews of Bible times believed that "walking in the truth" (2 John 4) and "living the truth" (1 John 1:6) were higher priorities than rationally analyzing the truth.

human attempt at systematizing truth. Walking in truth (2 John 4) and living the truth (1 John 1:6) were a higher priority than rationally analyzing the truth. In the words of the renowned biblical scholar Rabbi Joseph Soloveitchikk, "We [Jews] are practical. We are more interested in discovering what God wants man to do than we are in describing God's essence…as a teacher, I never try to solve questions because most questions are unsolvable." He concludes, "Judaism is never afraid of contradictions…it acknowledges that full reconciliation of the two is possible only in God. He is the coincidence of opposites."[6]

Read Hebrews 11. Hebrews 11:4–40 describes many men of great faith. It never mentions anyone of great logic! It is the ancient classical Greek education model that focuses on literature (man's word) and logic. The biblical Hebraic education model focuses on God's Word (the Bible) and faith.

Don't We Need Logic To Defend Christianity?

Do we need to study formal logic to be prepared to answer objections about the Gospels? According to the rhetorical and argumentative standards of Aristotle and the other humanists, every argument had to be answered.

According to God: *Remind them about these things, solemnly calling on them in the presence of God not to argue about words, since that is of no use and tears down those who listen. Do your utmost to let God see that you at least are a sound workman, with no need to be ashamed of the way you handle the Word of Truth. Avoid all that profane jargon, for it leads people still further into ungodliness* (2 Timothy 2:14–16).

Paul was speaking to those who preferred verbal quibbling more than seeking truth. In this passage Paul is deeply conscious that quibbling about words is a waste of time and wished to warn Timothy against this. It is not always recognized that trivial debates are harmful, but Paul uses a strong word here (*ruins*), which emphasizes the disastrous effect quibbling can have on others. The Greek verb translated *correctly handles* really means cutting a straight road and suggests straightforward exegesis.

The philosophers believed that one could do no better than examine the logic of words; they boasted of their notions and their arguments, but the Paul calls them *profane and vain babblings.* The empty talk and arguments over verbal skills of wordy rhetoricians who are unconcerned with truth are worthless. Our goals in defending the Gospel must be to present truth and share Christ in love. Some Christians may try to prove the Bible to natural men by presenting evidences from logic. They assume the problem is merely intellectual and that belief will flow naturally from an airtight presentation of the facts. But the Bible says that man deliberately suppresses the truth (Romans 2:15). The sword of the Spirit does not need to be proved by logic; it needs to be used to penetrate hearts.

Sample of Man's logic: *Now they said: Come now! Let us build ourselves a city and a tower, its top in the heavens, and let us make ourselves a name, lest we be scattered over the face of all the earth!* (Genesis 11:4)

Sample of God's non-syllogistic logic: God said, *Nevertheless, Sara your wife is to bear you a son, you shall call his name: Isaac. I will establish my covenant with him as a covenant for the ages, for his seed after him.* (Genesis 17:19) *Sarah became pregnant and bore Abraham a son in his old age, at the set-time of which God had spoken to him.* (Genesis 21:2) He said: *Pray take your son, your only one, whom you love, Isaac, and go you forth to the land of Moriya and offer him up there as an offering-up upon one of the mountains that I will tell you of.* (Genesis 22:2)

Teaching Critical Thinking

Children learn critical thinking while studying God's Word. God's Word is alive. It does so much more than we can ever comprehend, that any statements I may make about how the Bible affects our intellect would an understatement. Through reading the Bible children learn the capacity to discriminate between truth and error. They learn what is central as opposed to what is peripheral. They learn to make moral judgments and access the meaning of life. They learn to be effective problem solvers, decision makers, communicators and managers.

Basic Bible study teaches how to gather, organize, compare, and analyze information. With Bible study tools students learn the importance of clarifying and evaluating the meanings of words or phrases. They learn to think strategically, see the big picture and consider all sides of an issue. Writing about what is learned through Bible study further develops thinking skills. Through writing assignments students articulate and support their own beliefs while learning note-making methods, essay writing strategies, summarizing, paraphrasing, and outlining.

I used *A Case of Red Herrings*[7] with my children to improve their thinking skills. It's a book on critical thinking that teaches the student to follow lines of reasoning, generate hypotheses, analyze information, test possibilities, and look beyond the obvious. It involved reading short mystery stories where some of the clues gave false leads. It was both fun and educational. The children learned how to note key words and understand critical thinking. We used the book to improve study skills—however, I felt that my children learned thinking skills better as we studied history, science, and Bible in context.

If you want to broaden your child's or your own thinking skills, try studying the literary forms used by the biblical writers. I touched on literary patterns and chiasms (see pages 151-155). Most of us read the Bible as we read any literary work—as a story. But in Hebrew writing, where words, sentences, and paragraphs ran together because there were no capital letters or punctuation, there was a need for literary devices to signal the beginning and end of a thought division. Finding the hidden patterns won't change the meaning of Scripture, but it is fascinating because it will give you deeper more meaningful insight to God's Word. For more information go to http://Homeschool-Books.com and click on Bible Study Tools/Literary Patterns.

Finding the Balance

As explained earlier in this chapter, knowledge and understanding and diligent study are of utmost importance for believers, but we also see the some problems associated with large amounts of time devoted to the study of formal logic.

> If the study of formal logic to defend the Bible takes the place of time spent studying the Bible, we have lost our way.

You may feel lead to teach your child formal logic, if so we urge you to do so in balance. A good test of our priorities is how we spend our time and money. If you have spent curriculum money on books on logic but have no Bible study tools in your library, you need to rethink your priorities. If you spend two hours at night planning logic lessons and an hour each day teaching logic, but only spend 15 minutes in Bible study, you need to rethink your priorities. Pray about priorities and balance. You will never go wrong when you immerse yourself and your children in studying the Word and in solid biblical teaching.

Nothing in our lives—not logic, nor math, nor language, nor literature, not even family or church—should have priority over the Word of God. When any thing replaces the lordship of Christ in our life, that thing can cause us to become idolatrous and susceptible to spiritual disaster.

There is an account of an old recipe for chicken which started out with this instruction: "First catch the chicken." The author of this recipe knew how to put first things first. It all comes down to establishing priorities—we need to put the things that should be in first place in their proper order. If the study of formal logic to defend the Bible takes the place of time spent studying the Bible, we have lost our way.

Section 4

Heart of Wisdom Instructions

In This Section:

Keeping with the cooking analogy this section contains the cooking directions—how to decide on a meal plan, and actually combine and prepare the ingredients, and then present the finished product to your students. In this section you will learn about the Heart of Wisdom four-year plan and philosophies for teaching each subject, as well as how to create your own unit studies.

Chapter 17

An Overview of the Plan

In This Chapter

◆ A two-sided Base: God's Word and God's world.

◆ The four-year plan.

◆ History is taught chronologically.

◆ Science is taught in the order of Creation.

◆ Writing and language skills are integrated into all studies.

The Heart of Wisdom begins with the Bible as the center of education, with all secondary studies examined through the light radiating from God's Word—not the other way around. Academics play an important part, but they are secondary to the study of God's Word. Students spend half of their school day studying the Scriptures, and the other half studying God's world through derived studies—history, science, and life skills—using a unit study approach. Language arts are practiced throughout the day along with the Bible and academic studies. Although we use the phrase "half the school day," we do not mean that there are three hours of Bible study followed by three hours of academics, because students work in the Bible in all studies—hence, half the school day. This approach can be used for all grade levels.

This teaching approach is unique in that it is organized around a two-sided curriculum base: God's Word and God's world. This method is specifically designed for multilevel teaching, and it includes a four-year suggested course of study, designed to be repeated every four years.

GOD'S WORD	GOD'S WORLD
Direct Bible Studies	Studies Derived from the Bible
Bible and Bible study tools.	Thematic unit studies, living books, and the Internet.
The family reads through the Bible each year utilizing Bible study aids while incorporating language skills through writing assignments (narration, summary writing, composition, etc.) and by adding to a Bible portfolio.	History, science, and the arts are filtered through divine truth. History is studied chronologically, and science is studied in the order of Creation. All studies incorporate God's Word. All unit studies incorporate language skills through writing assignments (narration, summary writing, composition, etc.) and by adding to unit portfolios and a timeline book.

God's Word: Direct Studies

With the Heart of Wisdom teaching approach, the Bible is the central subject in the school day. Our approach to Bible study is quite different than the typical half an hour in a workbook approach. With our approach families read through the entire Bible together once each year, using a chronological, daily Bible reading plan.

Each year each student begins a new portfolio. This will provide both you and your children the opportunity to look back through the portfolios and observe their spiritual and intellectual growth over the years. Use a Bible reading plan as a foundation, and then branch off into in-depth historical studies, topical studies or word studies, using other methods as you are led to do so. We recommend the Bible reading plan found in *The Narrated Bible*. This plan is also available on our Web site.

Using the Heart of Wisdom teaching approach, we show our children the importance of God's Word by making it the first priority of the day and continually referring to it throughout the day. The Bible was designed to be stimulating, interesting, delightful, challenging, comforting, and calming. Perseverance on this path will provide you and your children with all of the wisdom you need for life. The decision to study God's Word in order to *do* His Word is a meaningful act of submission and reverence—in short, it is

worship. Study carried out with this motive is
the very essence of biblical learning. This is not
study merely in order to understand—it is
study in order to do.

> Academics play an important part,
> but they are secondary to the study
> of God's Word.

God's World: Derived Studies

Derived studies comprise the three broad categories of history, science, and life-skills
and, combined with living books, cover the following subjects: Bible, religion, history,
government, geography, agriculture, economics, science, art history, literature, and
composition.

You can use the Heart of Wisdom teaching approach with any unit study. You can utilize
Heart of Wisdom unit studies, purchase unit studies from another publisher, or develop
your own.

Heart of Wisdom unit studies are more structured than most other unit studies; each unit
is divided into lessons, and each lesson is divided into four steps. Although the units are
structured, they remain extremely flexible, and planning takes as little as ten minutes per
week.

Language arts skills (including composition, language mechanics, handwriting, spelling,
and vocabulary) are practiced throughout the day, during both Bible and academic
studies, using the methods outlined by Charlotte Mason and Dr. Ruth Beechick.[1]
Students do *not* learn to write by underlining verbs and circling adjectives. Both research
and experience have shown that increased knowledge and understanding of the
mechanics of grammar does not actually improve a child's writing ability. Instead,
children learn to write by writing, correcting, and rewriting their work. We agree with
Ruth Beechick's philosophy—she advocates sparing children endless, repetitive
grammar drills. Instead, we recommend that you correct your child's spelling,
capitalization, punctuation, grammar, sentence structure, subject/verb agreement,
consistent verb tense, and word usage in all of their writing, by marking each error with
a number that corresponds with a rule from a particular writing handbook of your
choice.

Ruth Beechick's book *The Language Wars and Other Writings for Homeschoolers* contains a
series of essays that you will find to be especially useful in helping to evaluate whether
your child needs to work from a curriculum or whether they can learn strictly from real
books—whether they should be taught grammar as a separate subject or whether a
whole language, or living books approach can be used.

A Typical School Day

To gain a full appreciation of a typical Heart of Wisdom school day, or to form a better mental image of this approach, imagine four sets of books: Sets A, B, C, and D.

- Set A includes the Bible, Bible tools (such as a Bible dictionary, a Bible atlas, a customs-and-manners reference, a lexicon, etc.) and a writing handbook.

- Set B includes books related to a historical theme (including reference books and literature).

- Set C contains books related to a scientific theme (including science reference books and science-project books).

- Set D includes books related to life skills (including books on wisdom, self-help, courtship, parenting, interior design, cooking, nutrition, car repair, etc.).

You will use the books from Set A (the Bible and Bible study tools) exclusively during the first hour or two of the school day, depending on your students' ages. The table gives a sample schedule.

There can be variations to this method: Sets B and C can be used in the same day, or Set B can be only used for one to two hours, etc. Or Sets B and C can be used on alternate days of the week (history unit studies Mon., Wed, and Fri. and science unit studies on Tues. and Thurs.)

You will use Sets A and B (history books) during the second half of the school day for a number of weeks. Then, Set C (science books) will replace Set B for a number of weeks. Set D (books about life skills), used with Set A, is not used until the high school years (when the school day is longer).

	1st Semester	2nd Semester
7:00–9:00	Set A	Set A
9:00–12:00	Set A and B	Set A and C
1:00–2:00	Math	Math
2:00–3:00 highschool	Set A and D	Set A and D

Writing, spelling, grammar, capitalization, punctuation, handwriting, vocabulary, phonics, and critical-thinking skills are not taught as separate subjects, but instead are integrated into each study.

The Four-Year Plan

In the Heart of Wisdom curriculum plan, students of all ages can study together, each studying the same topic at their own level. The Bible is read though once every year. History units are studied chronologically, and science units are studied in the order of Creation. Practical life-skills studies are added during the high school years. (Math and phonics are not included in our program, as they need to be taught by level, sequentially.)

Don't worry about the state's requirements! Remember, God's Word will outlast everything that exists. *Heaven and earth will pass away, but my words will never pass away,* Jesus declared (Matthew 24:35). *And the world is passing away... (1 John 2:17);...the form of this world is passing away (1 Corinthians 7:31).* The world system is not only deceptive, it

Overview		
	GOD'S PLAN	**GOD'S WORLD**
YEAR	**HISTORY**	**SCIENCE**
1	Ancient History	Physical Science
2	Early Church–Middle Ages	Earth Science and Botany
3	Early America–American West	The Animal World
4	Industrial Era–Year 2000	Anatomy

is also dangerous. The people who are caught up in the world system think it is safe, solid, enduring and dependable, when, in reality, the world is temporary and passing.

The Purpose of This Teaching Approach

The primary objective of the Heart of Wisdom teaching approach is to encourage parents and students to *seek first the kingdom of God and His righteousness* (see Matthew 6:33). The most important objective must be, as Jesus summed up the entire Law and the Prophets, to encourage every person to love God passionately—with all of his heart, soul, and mind—and to love his neighbor as himself. As A.W. Tozer said: "We are called to an everlasting preoccupation with God."[2] Our goal should be to live within God's kingdom effectively by seeking His wisdom, and becoming hearers and doers of His Word.

It is my prayer that all who read this book will, at a minimum, take away this one piece of advice: Commit to begin each school day in God's Word. I strongly urge you to make a promise to yourself that you will make God's Word your first priority, and never start in any other book before you have spent time in prayer and Bible study. I also pray that each of you will acquire the necessary Bible tools so your entire family can learn about biblical culture, historical settings, and language in order to fully understand God's instruction for life.

Can you imagine the potential results of every Christian homeschooler in America devoting the first part of each school day to studying God's Word? Christ's prayer in John 17:16–17 was that His followers to not follow false loves or the values of this world, but that they would be holy. Time spent in God's Word can produce a spiritual transformation. It is possible for us to produce an entire spiritually mature generation trained and equipped to feed themselves with the Bread of Life—and to be able to discern the sacred and spiritual from the profane and carnal—a generation that would

Heart of Wisdom Four-Year Plan

YEAR ONE

ANCIENT HISTORY	PHYSICAL SCIENCE
Adam to Abraham	Creation
Mesopotamia	Light
Ancient Egypt	Energy
Ancient Israel	Matter
Ancient Greece	Motion
Ancient Rome	Electricity
The Messiah	

YEAR TWO

EARLY CHURCH–MIDDLE AGES	EARTH SCIENCE AND BOTANY
Early Church	Weather
Vikings	Oceanography
Middle Ages	Botany
Renaissance	Geology
Reformation	Astronomy

YEAR THREE

EARLY AMERICAN HISTORY	THE ANIMAL WORLD
Age of Exploration	Marine Biology
Pilgrims to Colonies	Ornithology (Birds)
Colonies to Country	Entomology (Insects)
Civil War and Reconstruction	Earth Zoology
American West	

YEAR FOUR

INDUSTRIAL ERA–MODERN TIMES	ANATOMY
Industrial Era	Cell Design
World War I	Brain/Nervous System
The Depression	Skeletal/Muscular Systems
World War II	Respiratory/Digestive Systems
Holocaust	Heart/Circulatory System
Modern Times (1950 until Today)	Reproductive System

know Truth and be able to boldly answer a false teacher by saying "That's not what that verse means. You are taking it out of context."

Peter said the Word of God is nourishment like milk or meat (1 Peter 3:23). To help you really grasp the importance of this truth I'll ask you to imagine for minute this picture: Visualize a baby starving to death, like those you see on television in third world countries. Now imagine that there is a bottle of rich nourishing milk on the table that would save his life and comfort him, but his mother leaves the bottle sitting on the table because she thinks it's too much trouble to give it to him. Visualize that image every time you feel tempted to skip Bible study. Paul told Timothy that we are nourished by words of faith and good doctrine (1 Timothy 4:6). God's Word contains nourishing life-giving power—don't withhold it from your baby. Feed your children!

> I pray that all who read this book will, at a minimum, take away this one piece of advice: Commit to begin each school day in God's Word...make God's Word your first priority and never start in any other book before you have spent time in prayer and Bible study.

A Biblical Educational Model

As explained throughout this book, the Heart of Wisdom teaching approach is based on a Hebrew educational model rather than the classical Greek model. The Hebrews did not make a significant distinction between secular and spiritual knowledge, for all knowledge is from God and is designed for the human good. In Bible times, the primary purpose of education was to train the whole person for lifelong, obedient service in the knowledge of God (see Proverbs 1:7 and Ecclesiastes 12:13). The aim of learning was to practice holy living and and to be set apart to God in every dimension of life. This holiness required a knowledge of God's acts in history and a commitment to obey His commands, which instructed one in how to live.

Education must contain more than secular facts, theories, and objectives. Biblical wisdom does not depend on secular intellectual knowledge or rationality. God's written Word provides the principles and wisdom we need to live lives that are pleasing to Him. True wisdom rests in our knowledge of and relationship with Jesus Christ, God's incarnate Word. A focus on studying God's Word will transform both the teacher and the student by the renewing of their minds.

> The most important objective must be, as Jesus summed up the entire Law and the Prophets, to encourage every person to love God passionately—with all of his heart, soul, and mind—and to love his neighbor as himself.

Our focus on the Bible does not negate the importance of secular academic studies. God forbid! As parents, we are responsible for training our children to lead the life God has planned for them in this world. Although academics are a secondary focus, students following the Heart of Wisdom curriculum are encouraged in deep study in all academic areas, using living books and delight-directed studies. Through **direct** studies of God's Word, students will:

- Read the Bible daily.
- Read through the Bible with the family once a year.
- Be introduced to biblical languages (at least rudimentary Greek and Hebrew).
- Learn how to use Bible resource tools, including the ability to cross-reference using concordance, lexicons, and Bible dictionaries.
- Learn biblical history and geography.
- Learn the Proverbs and increase practical wisdom.
- Learn about the prophets.
- Learn about the life of Christ.
- Learn about the historical Church.
- Learn about biblical theology.
- Learn the way to righteousness (including a holy life and practical Christianity).
- Become hearers and doers of the Word!

Through **derived** studies of God's world (unit studies), students will:

- Study history while focusing on how the information relates to God's Word.
- Study science while focusing on how the information relates to God's Word.
- Study life skills while focusing on how the information relates to God's Word.
- Writing skills—including context, form, mechanics, editing, and revision.
- Spelling skills—by creating a spelling dictionary, increasing their vocabulary, and creating a personal vocabulary notebook.
- Learn handwriting skills—through the practice of writing out Bible verses and passages from text.
- Study geography, government, economics, the arts, etc., taught within the context of Bible, history, and science studies.
- Learn critical thinking skills—by managing and using information to solve problems, interrelating knowledge, and effectively communicating learning outcomes.
- Learn character development through assignment completion—including attentiveness, commitment, confidence, decisiveness, efficiency, faithfulness, perseverance, promptness, responsibility, and self-control.

Jesus said we are to love the Lord our God with all of our mind. A lack of faith can always be traced back to its unmistakable cause: a lack of knowledge. *My people are destroyed for a lack of knowledge* (Hosea 4:6). *Wisdom is supreme; therefore get wisdom; though it cost all you have, get understanding.* (Proverbs 4:7). Jesus repeatedly asked, "*Have you not read...?*" and told the Sadducees that they were in error because they *did not know the Scriptures or the power of God* (Matthew 22:29). Paul's letters persistently showed that true, functional faith is always built on knowledge. Paul repeatedly asked the question, "*Don't you know...?*" (Romans 6:3, 16; 11:2; 1 Corinthians 3:16; 5:6; 6:2–3, 9, 15–16, 19; 9:13, 27). Philip asked the Ethiopian eunuch, "*Do you understand what you are reading?*" (Acts 8:30).

Learning Stages

Most children learn at different levels according to their ages, and virtually every school system throughout history has recognized three distinct learning stages which appear from ages five or six through the teen years. A Hebrew child in Jesus' day would have been studying the written Torah from the age of five, ready for oral Torah by ten, and at fifteen ready for the study of rabbinic legal decisions. David Mulligan has roughly divided these levels into three categories: knowledge, understanding, and wisdom. It is important to realize that these are approximate levels and will vary for each child.

The knowledge phase takes place in the early grades, approximately grades K–4, in which emphasis is placed on rote learning and exposing the child to a wide range of experiences. Grades 5 through 8 comprise the understanding phase. Students take the knowledge they have acquired in the earlier grades and begin to compare and contrast, to go deeper, making connections and looking for the big picture. Finally, the upper grades, approximately 9–12, comprise the wisdom phase, when both knowledge and understanding are used to discern the proper way to live (practical application). In the wisdom phase, the student learns to evaluate choices and arguments and discovers learning as a way of life.

Students will go through the Four-Year Plan (see page 260) three times at each level. Let's look at the topic of weather to see how a child will view a topic at each level.

Level 1: Knowledge Grade level K/1–3/4 (Proverbs 1:2, 4)—A child can begin to understand the four seasons, why weather is important (effects of weather on agriculture and on our daily lives). They can understand that God provides rain from clouds, and they may be able to grasp the water cycle. They can understand that God's rainbow is the sign of a promise to us. At this stage they learn about observing, recording, and making predictions (e.g., how thermometers measures air temperature), etc.

Level 2: Understanding Grade level 4/5–7/8 (Proverbs 1:2, 5, 6)—Children at level 2 can understand how our world reveals God. God reveals Himself through things like the wind and seasons (Psalms 19:1–3)—They can grasp the layers of the atmosphere, interpret information on weather maps, forecast weather based on cloud patterns, interpret recorded data, recognize various instruments needed to measure weather conditions, identify hazards associated with bad weather, etc.

Level 3: Wisdom Grade level 8/9–12 (Proverbs 1:3–5)—Students at level 3 recognize the masterpiece of creation which eloquently reveals God to every person every day (Psalm 19). They are ready to study meteorology: atmosphere, its composition, structure, and properties, with emphasis on the various processes responsible for weather, climate controls and change, and the impact of atmospheric phenomena on society. They can understand how meteorologist monitor oceanic and atmospheric conditions, air pollution, environmental effects of air pollution, mechanics and impacts of tornadoes, thunderstorms, winter storms, and hurricanes, etc. A student on this level can understand the symbolism of the early and latter rains in the Bible (the early rain softens the soil for planting; the latter rain helps to mature the harvest).

David Mulligan has this to say about these three stages: Wisdom is both an end and a means to an end. Knowledge, understanding, and wisdom are not set up like a three-stage rocket, where each drops off as we are ready for the next stage. Rather, they are three different ways of looking at the world. We see through eyes of knowledge, through the eyes of understanding, and through the eyes of wisdom. One absorbs and reacts with the other. To the young man knowledge and discretion—A man of understanding will acquire wise counsel—A wise man will hear and increase learning (Proverbs 1:4, 5).

Throughout each of these phases, children progress gradually and not necessarily at the same pace. And, a child might reach the understanding phase in one area but still remain in the knowledge phase in another subject. It takes discernment on the part of the parent/teacher to help the child successfully reach phase three. Let's take a closer look at these three levels.

Level 1 Knowledge (Grades K/1–3)

In a child's earliest years, he is extremely curious and seeks as much information as he can possibly gather. This trend continues in a child's formal education throughout the first few years. Children at this age inquire about everything around them—and it is amazing to see how much information they can actually retain. This stage is the first building block toward wisdom—introducing the "raw material" with which the child will later interact through understanding and practical application.

For children in kindergarten to grade three, days should consist of reading aloud, Bible memorization, copy work, oral narration, working on a Bible portfolio and timeline book, various art and crafts, and play. You will follow the four year plan (page 260) by reading aloud daily from the Bible, history, science, and story books.

 The focus of this stage should be the Bible and the three Rs (reading with a strong phonics base, writing, and math). Preplanned history and science unit studies are optional at this age. Go with the child's interest through the history and science topics looking for the spark. If a 6 year-old want to study airplanes or frogs for a month, do it. You are developing a love of learning. Use the four steps to integrate activities and expand the readings. If you are teaching other children with unit studies, you can teach all the children together by watering down the material as needed. Seek and pray—God will lead!

If you are teaching grades K-3 you will need:

1. A Bible and Bible story books (see pages 280–283 and 379).

2. *The Three R's* by Dr. Ruth Beechick (see end of this chapter)

3. A phonics and math program (see Homeschool-Books.com click math or phonics)

4. Living books for history and science (see the Resource section). Children should have access to a variety of highly illustrated information books (plants, animals, how things work, how people live in various time periods, etc.).

5. Access to a variety of story books (see page 482).

As you teach Bible, history, and science, keep the four steps in mind:

1. Begin by discussing what you are going to learn and relating it to something the child already knows about.

2. Read aloud the text, and stop frequently to ask questions.

3. Reinforce with an activity (copy work, illustration or other hands-on activity)

4. Have them tell back what they have learned (narration) with you or another.

Level 2 Understanding (Grades 4/5–8)

After the child has gathered rote knowledge (the basic facts), he may proceed to the second phase of learning, understanding. The basic idea behind the biblical word understanding is "division" or "discernment."

During this phase, children begin to comprehend the meanings behind the things they learned in the knowledge phase. This can be done through definition (as Adam did when naming the animals), through comparison with other similar or dissimilar concepts, and through seeing the facts in the "big picture" or context of things. The learning of facts still plays a role, but these facts are seen as interconnected, in relationship to everything else that is learned.

In grades 5 through 8, the basic subjects that are studied remain the same, but the student begins to view them differently. It is not that the material becomes more complex, per se, but the student is able to approach that material in a different way, and knowledge and understanding begin to grow together toward the ultimate goal: wisdom.

If you are teaching grades 5 through 8 you will need:

1. A Bible and Bible study tools (pages 280–283 and 381–382).

2. *You Can Teach Your Child Successfully Grades 4–8* (see end of this chapter).

3. Heart of Wisdom unit studies (page 377–378) or other unit studies.

4. A grammar and/or writing program (optional decide after reading *The Language Wars* see end of this chapter. See Homeschool-Books.com click on Language arts).

5. Access to a variety of highly illustrated information books (see Resources).

6. Access to a variety of literature (pages 484–486) and biographies (479–481).

7. Life skills resources (pages 472–477). Begin with the *Wisdom Unit Study* (page 376).

8. A foreign language program. (see Homeschool-Books.com click Language Arts)

9. A math program (see Homeschool-Books.com click Math)

Level 3 Wisdom (Grades 9-12)

The final phase, which generally takes place in grades 9 through 12, focuses on wisdom and its lifelong pursuit. The fundamental biblical idea behind wisdom is application of truth. Wisdom must first arise from the student's relationship to God (*The fear of the LORD is the beginning of wisdom*), but it is fed by the previous phases of knowledge and understanding through which the student has passed. Wisdom has been achieved, in the practical sense, when the student consistently makes choices that are pleasing to God and obediently follows God's Word in every area of life.

True wisdom involves a right perspective, a way of looking at things and making decisions about those things that is based on the knowledge of God and the understanding of His will. It is possible for a person to be knowledgeable, even to have great understanding, but not be wise. Wisdom is the principal thing—we must teach our children its importance and then guide them to attain it throughout their lives.

If you are teaching grades 9 through 12 you will need:

1. A Bible and Bible Study Tools (see pages 280–283 and 381–382)

2. Heart of Wisdom unit studies (page 377–378) or other unit studies.

3. Access to a variety of literature (pages 487–489) and biographies (479–481).

4. Life skills resources (pages 472–477). Begin with the *Wisdom Unit Study* (page 376)

3. A math program (see Homeschool-Books.com click Math)

4. A grammar and/or writing program (optional decide after reading *The Language Wars* see end of this chapter. See Homeschool-Books.com click on Language arts).

6. A foreign language program (see Homeschool-Books.com click on Language arts).

Focusing On True Wisdom

We encourage you to continually and prayerfully evaluate your homeschool efforts in order to stay on track. Pray for wisdom daily and reevaluate your schedule monthly. The way to learn to obey Christ and keep from conforming to the world is through the study of the Scriptures: *Do your best to present yourself to God as one approved, a workman who does not need to be ashamed and who correctly handles the word of truth.*—2 Timothy 2:15

True wisdom comes from God: *The fear of the LORD is the beginning of all wisdom, and the knowledge of the Holy One is understanding* (Proverbs 9:10). Wisdom is for the person who sees its value and therefore diligently seeks it. The wise person learns from instruction (Proverbs 9:9) and from God's discipline (Proverbs 3:11), accepts God's commands (Proverbs 10:8), and treasures wisdom as more valuable than silver, gold, or precious jewels.

> *Brothers, think of what you were when you were called. Not many of you were wise by human standards; not many were influential; not many were of noble birth. But God chose the foolish things of the world to shame the wise; God chose the weak things of the world to shame the strong. He chose the lowly things of this world and the despised things—and the things that are not—to nullify the things that are, so that no one may boast before him. It is because of him that you are in Christ Jesus, who has become for us wisdom from God—that is, our righteousness, holiness and redemption. Therefore, as it is written: "Let him who boasts boast in the Lord."*
> —1 Corinthians 1:26–30

In his book *Thinking Christianly*, Dr. Albert Green explains:

Because [having] a Christian mind is more than a mechanical skill, such as driving a car or operating a computer, there is no simple set of steps which can be offered. There are steps to be followed, of course, steps like reading the Bible, prayer, meditation, etc. But the Christian mind is primarily the result of a deepening relationship to God in Christ by the Holy Spirit. It involves the deepest resources of your heart. Here are some suggestions which will help you move in that direction:

• Seek to develop a longing for God. (See Psalms 42:1–2 and 63:1–8.) Come to know Christ as the person who is our only hope of salvation and our only master. It means taking His yoke upon us and learning of Him (Matthew 11:28–30). We do this primarily through learning to hear His voice in the Bible and responding to Him in prayer.

> Biblical wisdom does not depend on secular intellectual knowledge or rationality. True wisdom rests in our knowledge of and relationship with Jesus Christ, God's incarnate Word.

- Endeavor to see His glory and hear His voice in creation. This means a radical break with the popular viewpoint which sees the world as stuff controlled by "natural laws." God made our world and our way of living in it that it should speak to us about Him. We need to learn to hear Him.

- Give increasing thought to what it means to be created in the image of God and what is the task which God has given to all of us in our human lives.

- Pay increasing attention to the biblically sound revelation that truth does not consist of factual information: Truth is a person. Furthermore, truth in the biblical sense is something which must be done to be known (1 John 4:6). Christian knowing is radically different from secular knowing.[3]

Suggested Reading

The Three Rs (Three Volumes) by Dr. Ruth Beechick ⋈
If you have children Grades K to 3 these three small books are jam-packed with practical ideas. *A Home Start in Reading* offers five simple steps for teaching your children to read. *A Strong Start in Language* presents a proven four-step method for teaching writing. And *An Easy Start in Arithmetic* helps facilitate learning by focusing on the "four attitudes" of math education. Includes a phonics/arithmetic chart.

You Can Teach Your Child Successfully Grades 4–8 by Ruth Beechick ⋈
I recommend this book for those concerned with teaching writing and grammar. Thee book also includes a wealth of information on Bible, reading, arithmetic, history, science, music, art, etc. It includes all the details of how to teach writing and grammar (vocabulary, spelling, writing mechanics, etc.) as you read living books (Charlotte Mason approach) and much much more. Learn how to individualize spelling, how to use real books in history, reading, how to make arithmetic meaningful, how to avoid the "grammar treadmill," how to develop advanced reading skills, and much more.

The Language Wars and Other Writings for Homeschoolers by Ruth Beechick ⋈
This book contains a series of essays that you will find to be especially useful in helping to evaluate whether your child needs to work from a curriculum or whether they can learn strictly from real books—whether they should be taught grammar as a separate subject or whether a whole language, or "living" books approach can be used.

Most books are available from Homeschool-Books.com. Books from a Christian perspective are marked with a ⋈

Chapter 18

God's Word:
Bible Study

In This Chapter

◆ A good parent is a good gardener.

◆ How much time?

◆ The importance of both Testaments.

◆ Basic Bible study tools.

◆ Bible study with the four steps

When Jesus was handed the book of the prophet Isaiah in the synagogue at Nazareth (see Luke 4:16), He was expected to read from the set portion of Scripture for that particular Sabbath. It was the tradition of the Hebrews that set portions from the Torah and the Prophets would be read aloud each week. There were two possible cycles for these readings, extending over either one year or three years. The tradition continues to this day.[1] Bible study in the Heart of Wisdom educational program replicates this tradition of reading through the Bible once a year.

It is astounding that for all the commotion we hear regarding Christian education, how little of the Bible actually gets studied. One Gallup survey announced that fewer than half of Americans can name the first book of the Bible, half can't name even five of the Ten Commandments, and only one-third know who delivered the

Sermon on the Mount! In 1997, a Barna Group poll showed that twelve percent of Christians thought that Noah's wife was Joan of Arc, while eighty percent of born-again Christians thought it was the Bible that said, "God helps those who help themselves" (this statement is not in the Bible).[2]

> ...the Bible...contains the mind of God, the state of man, the way of salvation, the doom of sinners, and the happiness of believers. Read it to be wise, believe it to be safe, and practice it to be holy.

Christianity Today survey reported that only 18% of all Christians said they read the Word every day, while another 18% read the Bible between three and six days a week, 37% read it once or twice a week, and 23% said they do not read the Bible at all.

Even in Christian education, the Word of God is only sprinkled into a school day, like a little salt on a meal. Bible study is looked at as an elective. Oh, what a shame! Americans have no idea what they are missing—communication with the Creator and Lord of the universe! Look at Robert Chapman's description of the Bible:

This book contains the mind of God, the state of man, the way of salvation, the doom of sinners, and the happiness of believers. Read it to be wise, believe it to be safe, and practice it to be holy. It's the traveler's map, the pilgrim's staff, the pilot's compass, the soldier's sword. Read it slowly, frequently, prayerfully. It involves the highest responsibility, rewards the greatest laborer, and condemns all who will trifle with its sacred contents.[3]

Andy Butcher's editorial, "Truth Crisis Threatens Churches' Future," states: "There is a growing crisis of Bible illiteracy throughout the West. Churches must not fail to address this drift, acting quickly and persuasively to stem the precipitous slide of its members into an abysmal state of Bible ignorance."

> If the goal of teaching our children is to bring glory to God (and if it is not, then this book is in vain) we must keep the focus of each school day in God's Word.

If the goal of teaching our children is to bring glory to God (and if it is not, then this book is in vain) we must keep the focus of each school day in God's Word: *So whether you eat or drink or whatever you do, do it all for the glory of God* (1 Corinthians 10:31). *And whatever you do, whether in word or deed, do it all in the name of the Lord Jesus, giving thanks to God the Father through him* (Colossians 3:17). *If anyone speaks, he should do it as one speaking the very words of God. If anyone serves, he should do it with the strength God provides, so that in all things God may be praised through Jesus Christ. To him be the glory and the power for ever and ever. Amen* (1 Peter 4:11).

We need the spiritual knowledge that is available in Christ through reading God's Word daily to continuously enlighten and direct us. *In Christ are hidden all the treasures of wisdom and knowledge* (Colossians 2:3). What better can we instill in our children than the direct words of the Creator of the universe? His Word is infallible (see John 10:35); it preserves us (Psalm 119:11) and cleanses us (Psalm 119:9) teaches, instructs and guides us.

> We are to become like Jesus Christ! How does this renewal come about? Through the knowledge of God's Word!

Colossians 3:10 instructs us to *put on the new self, which is being renewed in knowledge in the image of its Creator.* We are to become like Jesus Christ! How does this renewal come about? Through the knowledge of God's Word! The more a person gets to know Christ, the more he or she becomes like Him. As the apostle Paul prayed:

> *I want to know Christ and the power of his resurrection and the fellowship of sharing in his sufferings, becoming like him in his death, and so, somehow, to attain to the resurrection of the dead.* —Philippians 3:10–11

The greatest yearning of Old Testament men and women of God was to know Him. Moses pleaded in prayer, *"If you are pleased with me, teach me your ways so I may know you and continue to find favor with you"* (Exodus 33:13). To know God intimately was the cry of Moses' heart.

We were *formed* in God's image, then *deformed* from God's image by sin. But through Jesus Christ, we can be *transformed* back into the image of God! We must be renewed in the spirit of our minds (Ephesians 4:23). As we grow in the knowledge of the Word of God, we will be transformed by the Spirit of God to share in the glorious image of God (2 Corinthians 3:18). God transforms us by the renewing of our minds (Romans 12:2), and this must involve the study of God's Word. It is the truth that sets us free from the old life (John 8:31–32).[4] It is His Word that brings us to know Christ.

The Heart of Wisdom approach to Bible study is quite different from the usual spend-a-half-hour-in-a-workbook approach. With this new philosophy in place, you, as a family, will use a chronological Bible-reading plan every day, which will guide you in reading through the Bible once each year.

Here are the goals for Bible study embodied in the Heart of Wisdom philosophy of education:

- Families will read through the entire Bible each year in order to gain a view of the whole picture of God's Word.

- Family members will interact as they study together. Children of all ages can learn from each other, as well as benefit from their parents' accumulated wisdom. As an added bonus, parents are often able to learn new things from their children!

- Parents and students will learn to use Bible study tools, such as an atlas, a Bible dictionary, lexicons (for word studies), chronological charts, concordance, etc.

- Each student will document what they have learned, on his or her own level, by creating a portfolio. These portfolios may consist of timelines, summaries, copied and/or memorized Bible passages, essays, paraphrases, colored pages, puzzles, etc. The list goes on. Each year, the student will begin a new portfolio, which will provide both parents and children the opportunity to look back and observe the progress that has been made.

- Families will study God's Word in the light of the ancient Hebrew culture: A Hebrew book is studied; a Hebrew Lord is served (He had Hebrew disciples); and through Christ, we are adopted into a Hebrew family.

A Good Parent Is a Good Gardener

Here lies the secret of parenting that will produce good spiritual fruit in our children: the Parable of the Sower begins with the preaching of the Word, or the planting of the seed in the hearts of people. The seed is God's Word; the different soils symbolize different types of hearts; and the varied results show the different responses to the Word of God. It is our job as parents to sow the seeds lovingly into the hearts of our children.

> It is our job as parents to sow the seeds lovingly into the hearts of our children.

The Word, unlike anything else you teach your children, is *living and powerful* (Hebrews 4:12). It is necessary for the truth of God to be cultivated to take root in the heart before it will bear fruit. In the Parable of the Sower, three-fourths of the seed did not bear fruit, and there was no great harvest.

When you plant the seed (read God's Word), water it with prayer, and share it in love you are causing the seed to be rooted and established in love (Ephesians 3:17). The fruit will be seen in salvation (Matthew 7:16), in good works (Colossians 1:10), in holiness (Romans 6:22), in Christian character (Galatians 5:22–23), in winning others to Christ (Romans 1:13), in sharing (Romans 15:25–28), and in praising God (Hebrews 13:15). To plant this seed lovingly into the heart of your child, you need to have the fruit of love in your own life. It is a circle of life, and you must *impress them* [God's Laws] *on your children* (Deuteronomy 6:7).

> God's Law [instruction] was to be passed on so that godliness and righteousness would be carried down from generation to generation.

This is God's plan for passing on the truth about Himself, from parent to child. As a child matures, he becomes a parent to the next generation, and so on. The seed must come from fruit—fruit from your life—God's love, which is spread abroad in your heart by the Holy Spirit. When your own heart is full of love—as a result of God's Word planted in you—the love of Christ will overflow into the hearts of your children: it will give itself out, give itself away, and enrich the lives of others.

> *But as for you, continue in what you have learned and become convinced of, because you know those from whom you learned it, and how from infancy you have known the holy Scriptures, which are able to make you wise for salvation through faith in Christ Jesus. All Scripture is God-breathed and is useful for teaching, rebuking, correcting and training in righteousness, so that the man of God may be thoroughly equipped for every good work.*—2 Timothy 3:14–17

There is no fruit unless there is hearing first. In Matthew 13 alone, the word *hear* occurs nineteen times. *Consequently, faith comes from hearing the message, and the message is heard through the word of Christ* (Romans 10:17). *Jesus said, "He who has ears, let him hear"* (Matthew 13:9). *"Consider carefully **what** you hear,"* Jesus continued (Mark 4:24, emphasis mine). And, *"Consider carefully **how** you listen,"* He declared (Luke 8:18). In Deuteronomy 6, God told the people that their children were to hear His Word throughout the day from their parents' mouths (verse 7), they were to see it expressed in symbols (verse 9) and in their homes (verse 8). God's Law [instruction] was to be passed on so that godliness and righteousness would be carried down from generation to generation.

So, hearing is the first step. After you read the Word to your children, you need to reinforce what you have read to aid in the learning process (part of the four steps). Using the teaching methods that Jesus used, you need to ask a series of inductive questions to prompt your child to observe (*What does it say?*), to interpret (*What does it mean?*), and to apply the Word you have read (*What does it mean to me?*). Never underestimate the importance of using discussion questions as you study.

Last year I made a commitment to improve my physical health. I began to eat nutritiously. I cut out almost all empty carbohydrates and high-fat foods from my diet. I have walked at least one hour, five days a week, for eleven months. The results have been remarkable. I feel better than I have felt in twenty years. I no longer have arthritis or heartburn. I have tons of energy, and I have lost several pounds, as well as dress sizes! But I did not see these results immediately. A little work was done daily, so little or no progress was seen for many weeks or even months. But I knew if I continued each day the process would work—and it did.

When we don't use our body, our muscles atrophy (deteriorate). It is the same in the area of Bible study. We must feed our spirits and properly work our spiritual muscles daily. We must set apart time to interact with God and hear His precious Word every day. We know if we continue daily, little by little, eventual fruit will come forth!

> *What, then, shall we say in response to this? If God is for us, who can be against us? He who did not spare his own Son, but gave him up for us all—how will he not also, along with him, graciously give us all things? Who will bring any charge against those whom God has chosen? It is God who justifies. Who is he that condemns? Christ Jesus, who died—more than that, who was raised to life—is at the right hand of God and is also interceding for us. Who shall separate us from the love of Christ? Shall trouble or hardship or persecution or famine or nakedness or danger or sword? As it is written: "For your sake we face death all day long; we are considered as sheep to be slaughtered."*

> *No, in all these things we are more than conquerors through him who loved us. For I am convinced that neither death nor life, neither angels nor demons, neither the present nor the future, nor any powers, neither height nor depth, nor anything else in all creation, will be able to separate us from the love of God that is in Christ Jesus our Lord.—Romans 8:31–39*

How Much Time?

Author David Mulligan explains the importance of Scripture-centered curriculum in *Far Above Rubies: Wisdom in the Christianity Community*. He also reveals the surprising hesitancy Christians feel about this approach to curriculum. He states:

> The idea of spending a lot of school time on the study of Scripture may at first be disturbing. We are so used to dividing religious activities from the rest of our time it seems as if Bible study just does not fit, except in a minor way, in our regular school day. We think of Bible study as suitable for family devotions, church services, Sunday school classes, and if the study gets deep, in the seminary. How much Bible can children get without detracting from other studies?

> In asking this question we uncover in ourselves something of the tension that exists in the Western world between learning and religion. We know somehow the question is not right; we should be giving first place to Scripture, but can not quite let go of the other side of things. And rightly so! The other side, God's creation, is

vastly important, but still Scripture should come first, and all other studies find there place in relation to it.

The Importance of Both Testaments

Examining our Hebrew roots does not mean we focus only on the Old Testament—the entire Bible was written by Hebrews! Many people aren't aware that Jesus was a Jew. In fact, the entire first church was Jewish! Remember the famous painting of The Lord's Supper? It's the disciples and Jesus—all Jews—observing Passover. To really grasp the Bible's messages we need to understand the Jewish religion, from which Christianity grew.

Except for a few familiar passages—Genesis 1, Psalm 23, Isaiah 53—the Old Testament remains a closed book to most Christians. Yet it was the only form of Scripture used by Jesus Christ, the Apostles, and the first Christian communities. Jesus referred to the Old Testament consistently. When the words were written, *All Scripture is inspired by God and is useful for teaching, for reproof, for correction, and for training in righteousness* (1 Timothy 3:16), Paul was talking to Christians about what we call the Old Testament—which was the only Scripture in existence at that time. The New Testament had not been written yet.

The majority of God's Word is in the Old Testament. When the Bible is divided into 52 weekly readings, we don't even get to the New Testament until week 41!

The Riches of the Old Testament

The booklet, *Knowing God Through The Old Testament*, describes the riches of the Old Testament:

1. The Old Testament provides the foundation for the whole Bible. The Bible is made up of two Testaments—Old and New. Both are equally part of the Bible. Both tell us about God. Both inform us about basic truths we need to know, but without a grasp of the Old Testament, the New Testament cannot be fully understood or appreciated; and without the New, the Old is left incomplete. The Old Testament established the foundation of truth; the New Testament then built the superstructure.

2. The Old Testament tells us about Jesus Christ. We cannot fully know about Christ and His purpose for coming into our world without studying the Old Testament. It tells us about Him in word pictures and types. It predicts His coming. It puts His ministry into focus. It gives graphic previews of His sacrifice for sin. It goes beyond today to tell us of His coming judgment of the world and kingdom of

peace. In fact, the Old Testament tells us so much about Jesus that some Bible teachers have said Christ can be seen on every page.

3. The Old Testament provides the foundation for faith in Christ. The Christian faith is built on the Old Testament; Erich Sauer, in his book *The Dawn of World Redemption*, said this:

> The Old Testament is promise and expectation; the New is fulfillment and completion. The Old is the marshaling of the hosts to the battle of God; the New is the triumph of The Crucified One. The Old is the dawn of morning; the New is the rising sun and the light of eternal day. If Christianity may be likened to a magnificent cathedral, the Old Testament is its unshakable foundation.

4. The Old Testament helps us to know God. More than anything, the Old Testament tells us about God, His grace and His mercy. It makes Him known in these ways:

1. Factual knowledge: To get to know God personally, we must first know about Him. The Old Testament reveals His character in its record of His mighty deeds.

2. Personal knowledge: The Old Testament brings us past the information stage and brings us to the place where we can know God personally through the experiences and relationships of others who walked with Him.

3. Practical knowledge: Building on a personal knowledge of God, the Old Testament also tells us how to live. It reveals His will and spells out the kind of people He wants us to be. By obeying its commands, thinking as it tells us to think, and accepting the Savior it presents, we can know how to live in our complex world.

Application: The Daily Bible Reading

What you need:

- Your Bible for reading aloud.

- Various Bible translations, including the King James Version.

- Various Bible study tools (discussed in the next few pages).

- A writing handbook.

The King James Bible is an accurate and lovely translation of the preserved Greek and Hebrew text of Scripture. You will need the KJV for comparison and word studies. You may use the KJV for daily read-aloud but the outdated language is not appropriate for English grammar lessons. The antiquated terminology can also be a stumbling block to children.

I recommend reading from *The Narrated Bible in Chronological Order*. It has arranged the Scriptures in the order in which the biblical events took place, and the text is tied together with narrative commentary. It is neither a retranslation nor a paraphrase. The central text is composed entirely of Scripture, using the New International Version.

I recommend The Narrated Bible for many reasons:

1. The central text is composed entirely of Scripture.

2. This chronological arrangement will help readers see how various Scriptures fit with each other and with their historical settings.

3. The modern English used is familiar and easy to understand. Many people have remarked at how easy it is to read through several books of the Bible in one sitting with this story format.

4. Because it is written in everyday English, the text can be used for dictation and copying lessons (thus teaching handwriting, grammar, capitalization, and punctuation).

5. The layout of the book is ideal for teaching students how to outline. Each section includes excellent titles and subtitles that give a concise overview of the theme.

6. The books of Proverbs, Ecclesiastes, and the Song of Solomon are divided thematically. Topic examples include: Discipline, Temper, Patience, Greed, Flattery, Controlled Speech, Wealth, Poverty, etc. We have created a "cause and effect" worksheet, which you can print from our Web site, to use with these readings.

7. The narrative commentary is written in such as way as to be part of an unfolding story, in a separate and distinct typeface and color.

8. A daily Bible reading list, which consists of 360 Bible portions divided into fifty-two weekly readings, is included in the back of the book. The readings have been divided in such a way that the amount of daily reading time is approximately the same each week.

9. For the most part, the narration is written in the present tense in order to heighten the reader's sense of involvement in the lives of those who sought to know God.

This Bible with the same narration is also available in a paperback format with divided by daily readings titled *The Daily Bible*.

You don't have to use *The Narrated Bible* or *The Daily Bible* to follow this approach. There are also chronological Bibles available in the King James version.

Confused About Translations?

At least a portion of the translated Scriptures exists in more than two thousand languages, spoken by over ninety percent of the world's population. Translation of the Bible continues in more than a thousand languages and, even in those languages where it has long been in existence, new translations continue to be made. There are three basic types of Bible translations:

1. Word-for-word

2. Thought-for-Thought

3. Paraphrase

The type of Bible you should use is one that has been translated by a committee of scholars from the oldest existing Hebrew and Greek manuscripts. Paraphrased versions should be avoided because there is a much greater likelihood of misinterpretation.

Bible translations have always been controversial, with extremists believing that the *1611* King James Version is the only authentic Bible. The International Bible Society explains,

> "The King James Version, known in England as the Authorized Version because it was authorized by the king, has become an enduring monument of English prose because of its gracious style, majestic language, and poetic rhythms. No other book has had such a tremendous influence on English literature. However, the KJV translators had access to only a few ancient manuscripts. Since their day many older manuscripts have been discovered, resulting in a more reliable Greek and Hebrew text. In addition, many words in the KJV are now obscure; others cannot be traced back to the most reliable manuscripts.

Dozens of books have been written calling one version over another supreme. Find out for yourself. Get a good parallel Bible and compare the daily readings. *Today's Parallel Bible* is a comparison of four major translations made easy. Each two-page spread contains complete portions of the New International Version, New Living Translation [a paraphrase], King James Version and New American Standard Bible. *The Parallel Bible* allows easy comparison of the standard King James Version and the New International Version.

The accusation that modern versions compromise the truth is completely *false* and shows a lack of understanding of very basic church history. Every Christian should study how the Bible came to us and how translations are made—it is the book we live by, and therefore we should know the history! Did you know Bible translations are one of the largest controversies among Christians? The sad thing is most of the people arguing over this translations don't even know the facts! Read one of the books below to learn how the main translation came into being. Then teach your children how we got the Bible. My suggestions:

- *From the Mind of God to the Mind of Man: A Layman's Guide to How We Got Our Bible* by James Williams. This book has been called "One of the most important books published for believers in the twentieth Century!" If you want to understand the translation issues *you must read this book*! With this book you will learn the true historical facts on the text, transmission, and translations of Scripture.

  The current controversy over the Bible's text and translations is creating confusing division within the ranks of Evangelicalism. A mass of misinformation fuels the debate. Scores of men realize the enormous errors being popularized, but hesitate to engender further debate by speaking out. The confusion, however, is now so pervasive within Evangelicalism that the true, biblical and historical facts on the text, translation, and transmission of Scripture must be restated in layman's terms. In this book, these facts argue eloquently for the unity, not the division of God's people on these issues. Every Christian should read and outline this book.

- *Bible, Babel and Babble* is a free online book from the International Bible Society explaining the Bible translation process.
  http://www.ibs.org/niv/munger/index.php

Resources to use while teaching your children:

- *The Kregel Pictorial Guide to the Story of the Bible* is a wonderful book with full-color illustrations that traces the history of the Bible, how books were written and became part of the canon, and how God preserved His special revelation.

- *How the Bible Came to Us* discusses how the Bible came into being, who wrote it, early and modern translations, monks and manuscripts, and the importance of the Bible.

When you choose a major translation such as KJV, NIV, NASB, or the NRSV, you do not have to be concerned about whether it is really the Word of God. There are some differences between the KJV and the modern translations, but these differences are minor and do not affect or change doctrine. The only real concern is whether or not this is a Bible you will read and study, for if you don't bother to read and study the Bible, the accuracy of the translation is of little importance.

Basic Bible Study Tools

Every home should have the basic Bible study tools on hand. You and your family will be using these tools daily, and they are by far the best investment you can make in the education of your children. Most Bible study tools are available inexpensively at a Christian or a used bookstore. These tools should be a priority among your homeschool purchases. I use the tools listed below at the table with my children. I use some of the same or similar tools in software format (Logos) on my computer for personal study.

> Every home should have the basic Bible study tools on hand for Bible study. You and your family will be using these tools daily, and they are by far the best investment you can make in the education of your children.

The following is a list contains most of my favorite Bible study tools. I should note that I am not in one hundred percent agreement with any of these resources—but I take the good and the bad and analyze it and pray over all of it, agreeing to disagree in a few areas. Books are like watermelons, some contain good fruit but you still have to spit out some seeds. This is how I teach my children not to believe every thing they read. If I run across something in a commentary that I don't agree with, I use it as a springboard for further study. As my children watch, I look up cross-references and writings by other people. My children learn that just because something is in a widely accepted book, it isn't necessarily true, and they learn how to verify the truth.

- **A Bible dictionary or encyclopedia.** *Nelson's New Illustrated Bible Dictionary* is the most comprehensive and up-to-date Bible dictionary available. A wealth of basic study information is found in more than 7,000 entries, plus over 500 full-color photographs, maps, and pronunciation guides.

- **A Bible Timeline.** *The Complete Book of When and Where in the Bible and Throughout History* is a fantastic reference to have on hand. Not only can you look up main Bible events but also the most important Christian and Jewish events from Bible times until the year 2000. The Bible and Christian events are detailed on each page while other important historical events are found on the bottom of each page.

- **A Bible atlas.** A good Bible atlas should contain the following features: maps that show the location of places, groups of people and nations in the Bible, as well as maps that illustrate specific historical events such as the conquest of Canaan under Joshua; geographical information about the various regions of Israel and Jordan, as well as Egypt, Syria, Lebanon, and Mesopotamia; information about climate, weather, travel, and roads; historical geography, including a historical survey of the Bible that shows where and how geography played a role in the history of

Bible times; and a gazetteer, or index, of biblical places. *The Holman Bible Atlas* contains all of these things. A wealth of information in this resource accompanies the visually appealing full-color maps, charts, and diagrams.

- **A Bible Concordance.** This can be found either in the back of a study Bible or in a separate complete concordance such as *Strong's Exhaustive Concordance* or *Young's Analytical Concordance of the Bible.*

- **Commentaries.** *Matthew Henry's Commentary* is an all-time favorite. *Matthew Henry's Concise Commentary on the Whole Bible* includes Matthew Henry's comments in a one-volume edition of his classic devotional commentary. This abridged text preserves all that is most valuable and timely in the original multi-volume edition. *The Teacher's Commentary* by Lawrence O. Richards is an outstanding Christian educational resource; in it, the entire Bible—from Genesis 1 through Revelation 22—is divided into teachable units. There are many "link-to-life" ideas that will help teach each unit to any age group, making it an ideal resource to use in homeschooling your children.

- **Chronology charts.** *Chronological and Background Charts of the Old and New Testaments* illustrate all aspects of the chronology, historical background, and criticisms of the Bible. They cover such topics as weights and measures, social structures, theories of the history of the text, the history of Israel and Rome, and many other subjects.

- **Cross-Reference Tools.** If you're using a study Bible already, you will be familiar with the cross-references usually found in the middle column. *The New Treasury of Scripture Knowledge* contains the most exhaustive listing of biblical cross-references available. It is designed to be used with any edition or translation of the Bible to shed light upon, clarify, or explain the verse that you are consulting.

- **Biblical Lexicons for Hebrew and Greek.** *Thayer's Greek-English Lexicon* of the New Testament coded with Strong's Concordance numbers is one of the best New Testament lexicons available. *Brown-Driver-Briggs Hebrew and English Lexicon* is considered the finest and most comprehensive Hebrew lexicon available to the English-speaking student. Crosswalk.com provides many Bible study tools, including Greek and Hebrew lexicons at no charge!

Two of my favorite books about Bible study are:

- *How to Read the Bible for All It's Worth* is simple yet brilliant in its approach to modern Bible study and understanding, covering everything from translational concerns to different genres of biblical writing. In clear, simple language, it helps the student accurately understand the different parts of the Bible—their meaning for ancient audiences and their implications for us today—so that he or she can uncover the inexhaustible worth that is in God's Word. It divides each of the sixty-six books of the Bible into genres, and then goes into further detail on each genre—that is, its focus, history, application, etc. Each section also contains a caution as to how each genre could be misinterpreted.

- *30 Days to Understanding the Bible in 15 Minutes a Day* is a great visual resource. It helps a student to learn to position the key Bible characters, places, and events into chronological order so that they can think their way through the entire Word of God, with the help of special icons in the book. This resource was a great help to me, and I believe it would be an excellent tool to help your children gain a quick grasp of the entire Bible. See the "12 Eras of Bible History" on page 313.

Some of my favorite Bible study tools to use with children include:

- *Nelson's Illustrated Encyclopedia of the Bible* is like an entire library of Bible background works and historical reference tools—all in one convenient volume! The "Atlas of Bible History" chapter provides an overview of significant turning points in biblical history, with maps, timelines, and special features on key people and places. A "People and Empires" section offers intriguing insights on the nations that influenced the culture of the Jews and early Christians. This information-packed volume also contains a detailed study of the life, ministry, and message of Jesus—plus a comprehensive survey of life in Bible times, including family life, social customs, and religious beliefs and practices from Abraham to the time of the early Church. Contemporary graphics visually enhance the biblical and historical images, making this the most complete, accurate, and eye-appealing Bible encyclopedia you'll find anywhere!

- *The Victor Journey through the Bible* is an easy-to-read, visual exploration of the Bible, which allows children to follow the action from Genesis to Revelation. The stories in Scripture will come alive as you travel story-by-story through Bible lands and times. My children look at the corresponding pictures in this book as I read aloud from *The Narrated Bible*. It's a great book—it includes over 400 colorful pages of photographs, drawings, maps, and charts.

- *The Kregel Pictorial Guide to the Bible.* This fantastic guide is full of color illustrations, maps, and charts, showing life at the time of Jesus, the Jewish festivals, all of the parables and miracles of Jesus, and Jesus' final week in Jerusalem. It includes artists' drawings of clothing styles, houses, a synagogue, a map of Jerusalem, Herod's Temple, and depictions of travel in Bible times. It also includes an Old Testament timeline, ancient writing methods, maps of the tabernacle and Solomon's Temple, and maps that follow the life and journeys of the apostle Paul.

- *The Kregel Pictorial Guide to Bible History.* This full-color book and historically accurate fold-out timeline answers questions such as, When did the Exodus take place? Who was the Roman emperor at the time of Jesus' birth? When did the Jewish exiles return to Judah? and, Who was the king of Israel at the time of the first Olympic games? The timeline also features many events from the contemporary world of politics and the arts, making it ideal for homeschool use.

- *What the Bible Is All About for Young Explorers* is a long-time homeschool favorite. It is a unique resource that shows how everything from Genesis to Revelation actually fits together. It includes information about the writer of each book; special notations listing the meaning of the title and the contents of each book; an outline and list of the main people in each book, to help the reader see the entire book in a nutshell; illustrations, timelines, and maps that show when and where key biblical events took place; and full-color illustrations.

- *Growing Reader Phonics Bible* by Joy Mackenzie. This is a good supplement for children who are learning phonics. It features bright, unique artwork, rhythmic words, and phonics tools designed to help children learn all of the forty-four phonics sounds. These sixty-one stories were designed to help build a child's love of reading, as well as a love for the Bible.

- *The Rocket Read Bible Story Readers.* A comprehensive reading program based on Bible stories. These teaching tools are good for young readers. Each of the books in this expansive series emphasizes one reading skill; younger children will focus on a single letter sound, while older children will learn sight words and writing skills The books area available by level from Prelevel 1 to 4). See Homeschool-Books.com for a list of sets and titles by clicking on the Bible Stories category.

Get Organized!

Keep all of your Bible study tools, pencils, and other supplies on a specific shelf or in a crate or basket near your homeschool area. In my home, we keep the majority of our homeschool books on shelves in my office, but we keep the Bible study tools within reach of the dining-room table (where we conduct homeschool). This prevents us from being interrupted by having to stop and look for a reference book in the middle of a reading. Each student who is old enough should have his or her own study Bible with a wide margin for writing notes, lists, comparisons, etc. Allow them to use colored pencils to mark the text in their own Bibles. If you don't have such a Bible, at least provide each child with a designated spiral notebook for Bible note-taking.

Keep all your materials (writing paper, crayons, regular and colored pencils, markers, scissors, construction paper, etc.) for your Bible portfolio in a large container you can easily bring to the table after each Bible reading. This way the children and work on the Bible portfolios without having to waste time looking for items.

Daily Bible Readings

I recommend following the one-year Bible Reading Plan found in *The Narrated Bible*. There are other one-year plans available on the Internet, if that works better for you. There is really nothing special about the one-year, or 52-week, timeframe. Your students can learn just as effectively, perhaps even more so, by reading through the Bible in two years or more. The suggestions in this book are simply to provide you with a framework to help get you started in your children's education.

As You Rise Up...

I suggest that you read the Bible together as a family each morning and evening. I have found it the most helpful to begin each school day with the Bible. I am committed to never going on to any other subject until I have read what I feel God has led me to read to my children from His Word. In the morning I read chronologically, using *The Narrated Bible*'s daily Bible readings and the four steps explained on the next few pages. In the evening, we usually read something that is applicable to that day's events, the Proverbs for that particular day of the month (for instance, on the eighth day of the month, we would read the eighth chapter of Proverbs), or maybe one of the Psalms. Longer studies or a review of the week's readings can take place on the Sabbath day.

Always begin any time of Bible reading with prayer. Then read the Bible passages together and have a short discussion about what was read, finishing again with prayer.

The Heart of Wisdom approach demonstrates to our children the importance of God's Word by making it the first priority of each day and continually referring to it throughout the rest of the day.

This decision to study God's Word first in order to do His will is a meaningful act of submission and reverence—in short, it is worship. And any study that is carried out with this motive in mind is the very essence of biblical learning. We do not study in order to merely understand—we study in order to do God's will.

Bible Time With Young Children

We begin each school day with Bible study. The best strategy I have found is to begin reading aloud from a Bible story book with my toddler and preschooler while the older children are still gathering supplies and getting settled at the table.

I read aloud from Bible story books or use a book for the pictures and tell the story in my own words. I call this time with the younger children their "school time." This schedule has several advantages:

> The Heart of Wisdom approach demonstrates to our children the importance of God's Word by making it the first priority of each day and continually referring to it throughout the rest of the day.

1. The younger children don't need to sit still during the Bible reading for the older children.

2. The younger children are satisfied and will usually play quietly because they've had Mommy time. (I remind them that they have had their turn and now it's the older children's time.)

3. The other children gain more interest because they hear a "preview" of the story from the Bible story book.

4. The older children see how much is missing from the Bible story book.

After Bible time with the little guys is over, I give them a large Rubbermaid box full of toys (quiet toys, puzzles, blocks, etc.), and that keeps them busy. This special box is never available at any other time. I keep it on a shelf in my pantry and occasionally change the contents. Once I begin Bible time with the older children the little guys are content to play with the toys in their special box and they can listen in to God's Word.

Once after I had spoken at a homeschool conference, two sisters (in their 40s) came up to me and shared about their Bible time with their mother. Every day their mother would read aloud God's Word in her rocking chair. It didn't matter if anyone listened. She read aloud every day as her children played. The sisters told me they remembered quite a bit even though they didn't think they were listening. God's Word promises never to return void!

For younger children (toddlers, preschool, and early elementary school), you may want to use *The Day-by-Day Kid's Bible* (previously titled *God's Story*) by Karyn Henley. The daily Bible readings lead readers ages seven and up through the Scriptures, in chronological order, in one year. *The Day-by-Day Kid's Bible* bridges the gap between a Bible storybook and a full-text Bible since the Scriptures are simplified for young readers.

Creating a Bible Portfolio

The contents of your students' Bible portfolios will vary depending on the ages of the students. Younger children's portfolios will contain more drawings or pictures of crafts, while older students' portfolios will contain more writing assignments. Most of the pages will come as a result of activities discussed in Step 3 (explained later in this chapter). Instructions concerning the creation of a Bible portfolio are included in the "Notebooking" chapter (page 309).

> **IMPORTANT:** The following information is only a guide for you to get the most out of your reading. I repeat: It is only a guide! Use it like a recipe and adapt it to your and your family's preferences. Don't get so concerned about the steps that you neglect the readings. God's Word will never return void. When you are short on time, use the time for just Bible reading and a few questions to be sure the children understand.

The Four Steps and Bible Lessons

I recommend using the same four steps for Bible study that are used for the unit studies. The amount of time for each step will vary from a few minutes to a few hours, depending on the activities you choose to do. These four steps teach to all four learning styles and both brain hemispheres. Studies show that this four-step method motivates students to comprehend the material better and retain the information longer. The steps will occasionally overlap; this is just a general outline for you to use to organize the lessons.

Explain to your children what a privilege it is for us to know the invisible God through the man Jesus, and how relationships are based on communication. God communicates with us through His Word; we communicate with God through prayer. Before beginning the school day, talk to God in prayer. Devote your day to Him and ask for His blessing. During your studies, stop at any time you have difficulty with a passage. Remember that God promises us wisdom when we ask for it (James 1:5); therefore, pray for wisdom. Prayer comes from a humble spirit that is willing to acknowledge its need and ask for assistance. Prayer shows that you recognize your dependence on God (Proverbs 11:2; James 3:5–6).

Step One: Excite (Create an Interest)

Time: 1–5 minutes (rely on the Holy Spirit's leading)

- Both the teacher and the student pray for wisdom and understanding. Prayer is a requirement for Bible study (James 1:5).

- The teacher asks the student questions to find out what he or she already knows about the text they are about to read.

- The teacher shares with the student any personal lessons learned from the story or gives the child a a *mashal* (a metaphor or parable) to help the child relate to the story.

> Start out by seeking a true understanding of the commitment God has made to us through His Son. Then look for His personal commitment to you, and for opportunities for response, service, and maturing in the growth He provides for you.

- The teacher asks the student to recall the highlights from the previous day's reading. (Remember, you are reading chronologically so it's a continuation of a story.)

Step Two: Examine (Find Out the Facts)

Time: Varies—approximately 30–60 minutes. Technically, we can read through the Bible in one year in only fifteen minutes a day, but during Step 2 you will be reading and stopping for questions and discussions as well as looking up things for clarity. Step 2 will often run into Step 3 as you use the Bible study tools along with the readings.

> Technically, we can read through the Bible in one year in only fifteen minutes a day, but during Step 2 you will be reading and stopping for questions and discussions as well as looking up things for clarity.

The reading plan in *The Narrated Bible* consists of 360 Bible portions divided into 52 weekly readings. Each reading is listed by verse and by page number in *The Narrated Bible*. Some portions are very short, and some are very long. The readings are divided up to keep the amount of daily reading time approximately the same each week.

If you are reading the Bible seven days a week, you should average about five pages a day. If you are reading the Bible five days a week, you should read an average of seven or eight pages a day. If you have young children you'll be using the Bible story books reading one story per day. Keep the reading short, between 10–15 minutes, then discuss the passage before reading more.

If reading five to seven pages seems to much back off and try reading through the Bible in two years. Pray about, the Lord will lead. If you decide on the two-year plan, you'll be reading two-and-a-half to four pages a day (depending on how many days per week you read).

You will be reading several portions (stories or topics—like chapters in a book) in each daily passage. You will eventually find out what works best for your family. Either read the entire portion at one sitting, or read one portion, stop and discuss it, and then go on to the next story. If you're teaching several children, you should stop between topics and randomly call on one of the children to narrate (tell back) the story. The teacher can do the reading, but the students should be taking notes.

> One of the main goals of the Heart of Wisdom approach to Bible study is for you to learn to learn. Don't take any man's teaching as truth without questioning it.

As you study the Bible, look for patterns and themes. Start out by seeking a true understanding of the commitment God has made to us through His Son. This is illustrated throughout the Scriptures. Then look for His personal commitment to you, and for opportunities for response, service, and maturing in the growth He provides for you.

Build study and reasoning skills by choosing a section of your reading to study in depth, following these steps:

- Observation: What does it say? Pay close attention to the passage, noticing contrast, repetition, and progression, as well as facts.

- Interpretation: What does it mean? Prayerfully meditate on the content, seeking to find its meaning, particularly from the author's point of view.

- Application: What does it mean to me? Are there promises to be claimed, commands to be obeyed, sins to be repented of? Look for prayer topics for yourself, for others, for your family, for the country, or for the world.

Use questions to probe the passage that you are studying: Who, What, When Where, and Why. Print out WWWW worksheets from heartofwisdom.com/worksheets.htm.

Step Three: Expand (Do Something with What Is Learned)

Time: Varies—approximately 15–60 minutes or more. Choose an activity that appeals to your child's age and interests from the ideas listed below. (See http://heartofwisdom.com for links to Bible crafts pages on the Internet.)

Use the Bible study tools that are available to you! One of the main goals of the Heart of Wisdom approach to Bible study is for you to *learn to learn.* Don't take any man's teaching as truth without questioning it. Be like the Bereans: *Now the Bereans were of more noble character than the Thessalonians, for they received the message with great eagerness and examined the Scriptures every day to see if what Paul said was true* (Acts 17:11). Allow the

Holy Spirit to lead you. Stop when you are prompted by your own interests or your children's questions, and learn using your tools.

Use Bible Study Tools

- Do a word study using the concordance.

- Look up customs and manners in a Bible handbook.

- Look up words in a Bible dictionary.

- Look up the location in a Bible atlas.

- Look up the passage in a commentary.

- Compare different translations.

- Look up cross-references.

Narration, Dictation and Copywork

- Narrate: Have each child tell back the story.

- Have the student record the information as the teacher dictates a portion of the Bible passage.

- Copy or dictate: Assign a passage of the story for copy work or dictate a portion of the story to them to write.

- Have the student copy the Scripture passage directly from the Bible.

Create Art or Drama

- Illustrate the story: The student illustrates the story in any medium, even a cartoon strip or the creation of a storyboard.

- Create a puppet show: Let children retell the story in a puppet show. Older children can write a script or direct the show. Make puppets from household items—old socks, yarn, buttons, paper lunch bags, and crayons. This idea also works well with dolls or paper dolls.

- Act out the story: Allow children to retell the story in a play. Older children can write a script or direct the play. Make costumes from household items—bathrobes, pillowcases, large paper grocery bags, dress-up clothes, fabric or paper scraps, ribbons, costume jewelry, etc. Consider recording the production on video.

- Write a poem, song, or a play.

• Make a craft: Get ideas from a craft book such as *The Big Book of Bible Crafts* or *1001 Ways to Introduce Your Child to the Bible.*

• Create a scrapbook page: Students make a creative story page by using scrapbooking techniques and supplies (memory albums, stickers, die cuts, paper, cardstock, scissors, pens, punches, templates, rulers, idea books, etc.). First have the children draw or cut out photo-size illustrations of the Bible story. Treat the illustrations as photos in a photo scrapbook. Experiment with the layout. Journal below and/or around the illustrations. Apply stickers, frames, etc. Slip the page into a page protector to keep it safe from dirt, dust, spills, and fingerprints. There are literally thousands of scrapbook ideas available on the Internet.

Writing Activities (can also be done verbally).

• Write a newspaper story about the event. Include who, what, when, where, why, and how.

• Contrast the life of the people in the Bible story with the student's own life today. How are they alike and how are they different?

• Write about a character trait the person in the Bible displayed: bravery, honesty, etc. Write about what the student would have done if they had been in that character's place.

• Write an editorial expressing their opinion about an event.

• Compare and contrast the personalities of two different characters.

• Choose a main character or event about which to write a report.

• Write a letter to or from a character in the story.

• Rewrite the story in the student's own words.

• Complete a puzzle: Refer to a puzzle book such as *Through the Year Bible Puzzles*

Record the Facts

• Create an outline.

• Create a mind map about the main event or character.

• Record all new words and their definitions in the vocabulary section of the student's portfolio.

- Record all new customs and manners that helped the student understand the time period.

Fill in a Worksheet. Worksheets are available to download and print from http://heartofwisdom.com/worksheets.htm

- Have the student characterize findings in a Passage Worksheet.

- Have the student characterize findings in an Event Worksheet.

- Have the student characterize findings in a Character Worksheet.

- Have the student characterize cause and effect from the Proverbs in a Cause-and-Effect Worksheet.

Memory Work

- Have the student memorize a passage of Scripture.

Step Four: Excel (Organize and Share Work)

Time: Varies—approximately 20–40 minutes.

The students complete their work and place it in their Bible portfolios and/or share the activity they completed in Step 3 with a family member, a friend, or another group of homeschool students.

- Teacher reviews all writing.

- Teacher and student discuss all grammar, capitalization, and punctuation errors.

- Student looks up appropriate grammar, capitalization, and punctuation rules in Writers Inc. (or a writing handbook on their own level).

If you choose to add this page to the Bible portfolio, continue with the steps below. (Not all written work needs to be rewritten.)

- Student rewrites work with corrections.

- Student adds work to Bible portfolio.

- Student shares work with or uses work to teach another person.

Suggested Reading

1001 Way to Introduce Your Child to the Bible by Kathie Reimer ⌐○
Included is a brief synopsis of each book of the Bible and major people, places, stories from each book with activities to make learning fun and informative. If you looking for more hand-on ideas for Bible reading time, and your children are toddlers to age 12, this book is for you.

Teach Them Diligently: How to Use the Scriptures in Child Training by Lou Priolo ⌐○
There is more to teaching your children the Bible than merely telling them Bible stories. Many parents feel ill-equipped for the task, so they neglect this vital aspect and forfeit many of the greatest blessings of parenthood. A valuable aid for parents seeking help, a wealth of practical, biblical advice to fulfill the mandate of Deuteronomy 6:6–7. As with all Priolo's books this is motivating and encouraging.

The Mission of Motherhood: Touching Your Child's Heart of Eternity by Sally Clarkson ⌐○
Author, speaker, and mother Clarkson uses practical examples, her own personal anecdotes, a challenging vision to give mothers exactly the support they need to persevere in cultivating and sharing their hearts for God, for their children, and for their homes. Every day, as they nurture their children, mothers influence eternal destiny as no one else can. By catching a vision of God's original design and allowing it to shape their lives, mothers can rediscover the joy and fulfillment to be found in the strategic role to which God has called them-for a purpose far greater than they can imagine.

The Ministry of Motherhood: Following Christ's Example in Reaching the Hearts of Our Children by Sally Clarkson ⌐○
By examining the relationship between Jesus and His disciples and incorporating a plan based on a positive and memorable acronym (GIFTS), this book demonstrates how mothers can use each moment of the day to strategically pass on to their children five crucial gifts.

Most books are available from Homeschool-Books.com. Books from a Christian perspective are marked with a ⌐○

292

Chapter 19

God's World: History, Science, and Like Skills Unit Studies

In This Chapter

◆ Teaching language arts: integrating reading, writing, speaking.

◆ Teaching history chronologically.

◆ Teaching science in Creation order.

◆ Teaching life skills as needed.

God's Word must remain paramount in the education of our children, but that does not mean that academic studies are unimportant. Derived studies, or the study of God's world, are also crucial to our children's development, but they must always be filtered through divine Truth.

As explained earlier, the Heart of Wisdom teaching approach is like a meal plan consisting of several recipes. The recipe for studying God's Word is in the previous chapter. In this chapter we will look at philosophies concerning the teaching of language skills, history, science and life skills. The next chapter will give you a unit study recipe to teach history, science and life skills, while blending in language skills. You can follow or adapt my recipe or purchase prepared unit studies. Whichever you choose, you will benefit from reading this section to understand the philosophy behind the Heart of Wisdom teaching approach in these subject areas.

A truly Christian curriculum will not only focus on God, but it will also focus on His works: His creation, His involvement in human history, and the creative and expressive abilities He has given to human beings—in other words, science, history, and the arts. Using a full, well-rounded curriculum can prevent a child from becoming unbalanced, but this does not mean that the homeschooling parent should try to pack as much information into the school day as possible. Rather, it means that the child should be taught how to learn, that opportunities to explore all aspects of God's world should be given, and that the child's imagination should be sparked to study aspects of God and His world that he may only have dreamed were possible.

Language Skills

Language skills are not a derived study, per se, because these skills are incorporated and fostered in all topics presented. Communication skills must first be in place in order to study the Bible—and in order to complete the derived studies of God's world. Communication through language is the most essential tool needed for mastery of any educational pursuit. Language skills have been specifically addressed in the "Writing to Learn" chapter (see page 235), but for our purposes here, let's review the basics: reading, writing, and speaking.

Reading

Ultimately, developing the skill of reading should have as its primary purpose the ability to read God's Word. Many other benefits come from having a skillful ability to read, but proficiency in reading the Bible should remain the most cherished goal.

Reading includes many different types of skills: phonics, comprehension, vocabulary, and memorization (how to teach vocabulary is addressed on pages 319–321). Children learning to sound out words are working in the decoding stage of reading. Some children are naturally fluent readers, but most are not. Most children need guidance, practice and encouragement in order to read smoothly and easily. The best way to get through this is by giving lots of encouragement and explaining that it takes everyone time to learn to read. Valerie Bendt uses a unique approach to teaching phonics in *Reading Made Easy*. She begins with explaining a secret code. This excites and motivates the student as they move through the lessons.

Once children master basic phonics they move into the fluency stage and then into the information stage. Reading is a developmental process and fluency will develop as children increase their sight vocabularies and acquire a repertoire of word-identification strategies. Children in the primary grades generally will increase fluency as they gain more experience reading. The length of time spent in each stage will depend upon the child.

The most important thing you can do to prepare a pre- or beginning reader to read is to read aloud to him. We have baskets of books in almost every room in our home. I read Bible stories aloud to my three- and five-year-old boys every morning and evening and from various picture books throughout the day. We've read the classics such as *Mike Mulligan and His Steam Shovel, The Story About Ping, If you Give a Mouse a Cookie, Caps for Sale, Millions of Cats,* and *Pete's a Pizza,* over and over (and over and over and over...).

I'm not an advocate of either the "better early" or the "better later" teachings. Some of my children began reading at three and others didn't read until six. I believe each child will let you know when he is ready. I work with the five-year-old between fifteen and thirty minutes a day in a phonics program. The three-year-old sits in on the lessons if he is interested (most of the time he is). I learned years earlier not to push. The resource section includes lists of good books for each child's age level.

Over the last twenty years I've tried dozens of phonics programs with my eleven children. My very favorite is *Reading Made Easy* by Valerie Bendt. For years I have recommended using the Bible for phonics reinforcement, and for years I have used the secular book *Teach a Child to Read With Children's Books* by Mark B. Thogmartin, but now *The Growing Reader Phonics Bible* is available. It teaches forty-four sounds using rhyme through sixty-one Bible stories. We offer several good phonics programs under the Language Arts/phonics category at Homeschool-Books.com.

The years between kindergarten and third grade should be focused on teaching the Bible and language skills, and fostering a love of learning. Spend time finding out what your child is interested in, and take many trips to the library to find books around their interests. Free printables for these ages are available at http://www.donnayoung.org.

I strongly believe in Ruth Beechick's methods for teaching language skills. Beechick's books *Language and Thinking for Young Children* and *The Three Rs* should be a standard reading for anyone teaching grades K–3. For students in grades 4 through 8 Beechick offers *You Can Teach Your Child Successfully.* This one book has helped me, with practical every day methods, more than any other book on education. It includes how to avoid the "grammar treadmill," how to develop advanced reading skills, and much more. If you have a reluctant reader, see *How to Get Your Child to Love Reading* by Esme Codell.

Reading Aloud

Research has shown that reading out loud to children is the single most important thing a parent can do to prepare a child for future academic success. Young children learn a great deal when books are read aloud to them. You have the opportunity during your read-aloud time to share in the excitement and emotions as children learn about the structure of stories—how they begin, different types of conflicts, and possible solutions. Children learn to know that events can be seen from different viewpoints, how to use their imagination, and how to view situations from various perspectives. Being read to also helps a child learn the connection between the written and spoken word. Reading aloud to children develops their listening skills and builds vocabulary. And, last but not least, listening to books read aloud helps children develop a taste for excellent literature.

Unfortunately, by the time children outgrow picture books, many parents stop reading aloud with them, but there is no reason to stop reading aloud. Children of all ages enjoy being read to, and they shouldn't be punished for learning to read by losing that special reading-aloud time. We also need to remember that there are whole new frontiers to explore in books even as the children grow older, and children can listen to more advanced books than they can read. I recall several times reading aloud to my eight- to twelve-year-olds, when I didn't think any one else was listening, only to hear later from my much older teenagers remarks about the stories that they had heard when they were eavesdropping on our story time. Every parent should make a set time in their day for reading aloud. Remember, it's never too late to read aloud. (For more on this topic see Reading the Classics in the "Choosing and Using Resources" chapter).

Writing

Skill in writing comes through four different areas: the mechanics of spelling, punctuation, etc.; the science and application of grammar, in which the analysis of language helps a child understand the inner workings of writing and allows him to express himself more clearly; composition, in which the child learns creative expression of his thoughts; and penmanship, in which the child practices the beauty (and legibility!) of communication through the written word. The Heart of Wisdom writing philosophy is covered in the "Writing to Learn" and "Charlotte Mason" chapters (see narration and dictation). How to teach spelling is addressed on pages 321–323.

Speaking

Finally, through oral communication, children learn to organize their thoughts, memorize the content of what they want to say, and ultimately articulate these thoughts in meaningful, expressive ways.

History and Cultural Studies

Cultural studies include the study of God's plan as expressed through history and culture. Culture is the social and artistic expression of man, and history is actually the story of the rise and fall of these various cultures. God is intimately involved in both. It is imperative that children be taught history and culture through the filter of God's Word and a relationship with Him.

Historians divide the past into three major periods: ancient history begins with the appearance of the first human beings on earth and ends with the fall of the Roman Empire in A.D. 476. Medieval history is also called the Middle Ages because it falls between ancient and modern history. The medieval period covers the years between approximately A.D.500 and A.D.150. Modern history is taught by European and American schools as starting at the beginning of the 1500s.

The Heart of Wisdom four-year curriculum plan divides history into four periods:

1. Ancient History

2. Early Church to Middle Ages

3. Early America to the American West

4. Industrial Era to Modern Times

History Resources

The resources we suggest for studying history include information-type reference books, biographies, and novels. Just as God teaches us history through stories of people, history can be taught through biographies and novels for each time period. The Bible is full of biographies of men and women, their families, lifestyles, faith, problems, courage, persistence, etc. While studying a time period, a wonderful way to get a feel for that period is to read about someone who lived through it. There are many wonderful books about interesting people in history, and children will want to hear or read books that secure their attention, interest, and concentration, with little effort from the teacher.

If Charlotte Mason were alive today I believe she would approve of the colorful fact-filled information books available from Usborne, Kingfisher, and Dorling Kindersley. Most of these books include valuable maps, timelines, and photo images of artifacts which can make a time period come alive for children. Combining one of these with a historical novel is an invaluable. While the story books engage the learner, the visual books show how people lived, what their speech was like, how they dressed, etc. Each genre gives information that provides a richer understanding of the period.

See the book lists in the Resources Section for novels, biographies, and information type books about each time period.

Timelines and Maps

Timelines are essential for understanding history. See timeline instructions in the "Notebooking" chapter. *The Complete Book of When and Where in the Bible and Throughout History* by Mike and Sharon Rusten focuses on 1001 events that shaped the religious consciousness of the world. It includes events from Bible times until the year 2000. This book is inexpensive valuable reference book for the teacher. For children Usborne publishes a secular highly illustrated *Timelines of World History* for ages 7–14.

Maps and globes can be just as important visual aids as a timeline. If possible try to hang a world map and a United States map in your home for reference. *The Holman Bible Atlas* is a excellent Bible atlas. It's easy to understand and vividly colored. *Geographica: The Complete Illustrated Atlas of the World* is the Cadillac in map books. Doringly Kindserly publishes a beautiful *Children's World Atlas* for child 8 and up and a nice *My First Atlas* for younger children making geographic concepts easy to understand. Usborne publishes a colorful *Internet-Linked Children's Atlas* (ages 9-12) and an *Internet-Linked First Atlas* for younger children (ages 5-8).

History Year One: Ancient History

Every child has asked, "Why is it important to study stuff that happened so long ago? What difference can it make to me what people did thousands of years ago?" History is the workshop of God. History is significant because it is the story of people, how they came into being, and what they did.

Seventy-eight percent of the Bible focuses on the Hebrew people, and I believe our study of ancient history should have the same focus. Our unit study *Ancient History: Adam to Messiah* focuses on Bible history, as opposed to most ancient history studies—even many Christian-based texts-which concentrate on the pagans in ancient times and ignore God's people. For example, in our *Ancient Egypt* unit the focus is on Joseph, Moses, the Exodus and the Israelites, it includes lessons on the pyramids, mummies and Egyptian religion but the focus is on God's people. Our *Ancient Greece* and *Ancient Rome* units focus on God's people fighting against idolatry under Greek and Roman rule and the beginning of the Church, rather than on Greek mythology, philosophy and Roman gods. We also have an in-depth unit study on *Ancient Israel* and on *The Messiah*. A Christian study of culture and history must include the study of Israel, for she is the foundation of our Christian heritage. Our children must study the Bible directly, but they must also commit to the derived study of biblical history and culture in order to receive a full education.

The Heart of Wisdom four-year curriculum plan recommends studying the following time periods for Year One History:

1. Adam to Abraham   5. Ancient Greece
2. Mesopotamia   6. Ancient Rome
3. Ancient Egypt   7. The Messiah
4. Ancient Israel

People have always had a strong desire to leave records about their activities. Those records—whether chiseled in stone, baked on clay tablets, written on parchment or paper, or fed into a computer—give us a picture of how people have lived. History, then, has two functions: it reveals the life and culture of the past, and it records present experiences. Whether records were written yesterday or thousands of years ago, they are useful in helping us to understand the world in which we live today.

The Bible can be used as a historical reference book. As archaeologist continue to uncover ancient cities and civilizations, their findings have proved the Bible to be true.

The vast majority of ancient history texts written during the twentieth century contain an overwhelming bias in favor of interpreting history from a secular and evolutionary perspective (false doctrine). This bias explains why modern history books rarely attempt to show the relevance of the Bible to their interpretation of historical events or personalities. This humanistic approach to historical interpretation forces students to conclude that our planet, and the life of mankind in general, has no ultimate meaning or purpose.

History Year Two: Early Church to the Middle Ages

Keeping with the theme of focusing on God's people, the second year of Heart of Wisdom's history curriculum encourages an in-depth study of the early Church and growth of the Church through the Middle Ages. One can not overestimate the importance of the changes that took place the Church between the first century and the Reformation.

> We must study Church history all the way back to the first century—not just back to the Reformation.

During the Middle Ages, the powerful authority of the Church led to the regimentation of thought. The Church influenced or controlled political institutions, and expected unquestioned loyalty and absolute faith in its teachings, which had to be accepted as Gospel truth. It hampered economic activities and stunted literary and artistic developments.

The Reformation was responsible for changing the course of history by turning to God's Word instead of following man's traditions.

There are thousands Christian denominations and pseudo-Christian groups (cults), as well as non-Christian religions (which have their sects as well) in the world. Each one distinguishes itself from the others by claiming to know and practice the true religion. The Bible teaches us what God's purpose was for the Church in the first century. We must know when God promised to build it, how the Church started, what pattern He used and how Christians were taught to worship in the New Testament. How can we teach our children to stay away from false teaching unless we understand truth? We must study Church history all the way back to the first century—not just back to the Reformation.

The Heart of Wisdom four-year curriculum plan recommends studying the following time periods for Year Two History:

1. Early Church
2. Vikings
3. Middle Ages

4. Renaissance
5. Reformation

History Year Three: Early American History

America's liberty and prosperity are direct results of America's faith in God—but, believe it or not, Americans have not heard or learned the facts of America's Christian history for over one hundred years. The study of how America came to be is particularly exciting. If you attended public school, you were never taught the following:

- In 1492 Columbus sailed off with two motives: first, to find a new environment to escape the humanistic culture on the European continent, and second, to convert people in other lands to Christianity.

- The colonists fought the seven-year American *Christian* Revolution because they were willing to count and pay the cost of Christian liberty.

- When the first Continental Congress met in 1774, they prayed "fervently for America, for Congress, for Massachusetts...for Boston..." wrote John Adams.

- In times of trouble and need, Congress would declare days of fasting and prayer, humbling themselves before God in repentance and supplication.

- After victories, Congress would declare days of thanksgiving to Almighty God for His aid and assistance.

- The U. S. Supreme Court building is decorated with an eighteen-foot-high sculpture of Moses holding The Ten Commandments.

Today, though the signs of the times may seem disheartening, there is evidence that a change is quietly but surely taking place in our nation. Our unique heritage and founding have again been brought to light, and Americans are again learning about their Christian heritage. Christians are awaking from their national apathy. This rediscovery of the Christian foundations of our country will greatly help to restore Christian leadership in America.

Always remember that your responsibility is more than educating your children—you are constructing the foundation of the nation of tomorrow. Children taught in the public school system are being trained by a program that is committed to secularizing the citizens of tomorrow at the taxpayer's expense. Our public schools are forbidden by the secular courts of the land to teach the faith of our fathers.

It is not only a possibility, but also a responsibility for Christian home educators to restore, in one generation, the family altar, and to reestablish the love of God and country. To do so requires true history books, not secularized public school history books.

> *O my people, hear my teaching; listen to the words of my mouth....I will utter hidden things, what we have heard and known, what our fathers have told us. We will not hide them from our children; we will tell the next generation the praiseworthy deeds of the Lord, His powers, and the wonders He has done....He commanded our forefathers to teach their children so the next generation would know them [His laws], even the children yet to be born, and they would tell their children. Then they would put their trust in God and would not forget His deeds but would keep His commands.*
> —Psalm 78:1–7

Today's public schools teach social science, which is a mixture of censored history, geography, psychology, and sociology. They don't even try to hide it—it's in all the states' scopes and sequences—it is accepted common knowledge.The Heart of Wisdom four-year curriculum plan recommends studying the following time periods for Year Three History:

1. Age of Exploration
2. Pilgrims to Colonies
3. Colonies to Country
4. New Nation
5. Civil War
6. Reconstruction
7. American West

History Year Four: Industrial Era to Modern America

The fourth year is full of stories rich in human drama and tragedy as students study the causes and consequences of political, agricultural, and industrial revolutions during the years of 1700–1900. This was an era of amazing change in a hundreds of different arenas. The invention of the railway locomotive, the steamship, the telegraph and telephone transformed global communications. International commerce grew rapidly. A scientific worldview refocuses Europe's intellectual and cultural orientation to a more secular and rational rather than religious mode.

We continue to examine the events which took place with God's people as we examine changes in the church and men's lives such as John Wesley, Jonathan Edwards, George Whitefield, Charles Finney, C. H. Spurgeon, George Mullar, Hudson Taylor, Karl Barth and Billy Graham. This study moves on to the World Wars, the Holocaust and the Great Depression until modern times. Many wonderful literature resources are suggested for these periods as well as in-depth studies in Church history.

We examine the changes in worldviews during these periods by looking at events that changed the twentieth century—such as the Scope's Monkey Trial and Christian martyrs—more than all the other centuries combined!

The Heart of Wisdom four-year curriculum plan recommends studying the following time periods for Year Four History:

1. Industrial Era
2. World War I
3. Depression

4. World War II
5. Holocaust
6. 1950 to Today

Science

One of the most critical areas of study for the Christian student is the area of science. Rationalist explanations for the existence of the universe abound outside of Christianity, and the idea that mankind evolved from apes is prevalent in the public school systems of America. We must return to teaching science as God intended it to be—the orderly study of His creation.

God created the heavens and the earth to receive and reflect back the glory and honor due Him. All the elements—the sun and moon, mountains and hills, rain and snow, rivers and streams, trees of the forest, grass and flowers of the field, animals, fish and birds—shout out praise to the God who made them.

In each science study students should be given opportunities to get directly in touch with God's creation.

Science and the Bible

Many people believe that the Bible and science contradict each other, when actually the opposite is true. Many scientific discoveries that were written about in the Bible thousands of years before being discovered by scientists (earth's position, sea currents, etc.).

Secular history and science books promote a secular philosophy—even if one overlooks the mention of evolution. How can one possibly study the world and all the marvelous creatures without acknowledging the Creator? The carnal [natural] mind is enmity against God: for it is not subject to the law of God, neither indeed can be... (Romans 8:7) because the god of this world hath blinded the minds of them which believe not(2 Corinthians 4:4); and unless one is born again, he cannot see the kingdom of God (John 3:3). Dr. Albert Green, stated it this way in his book, Thinking Christianly:

> A biblical way of looking at [the] creation will have consequences on your life. As the Holy Spirit grips your heart with the realization that [the] creation reveals God and can be offered back to him in our ordinary daily activities, praise will well up in your heart as never before. Further, you will find your life come [sic] together with new integrity. No more sacred/secular dualism! Christ really is Lord of all! What a glorious message the Gospel is!

> Think of a lovely rosebud in a vase. Where is the beauty of the flower? Is it in the bud itself? A botanist will tell us the flower is simply a bunch of atoms and molecules batting around in empty space. Is the beauty in the retina of our eyes, or in our brains? No, it is God's beauty, reflected back to us from the petals of the rosebud.

> God makes all pleasures. The devil misuses them; he does not make them. If we learn to recognize every pleasure as a shaft of God's glory touching our hearts, that recognition will become an unspoken prayer of praise and worship. Probably that is what Paul means by admonishing us to pray without ceasing.[1]

Various subjects are pursued under the general topic of "science": mathematics, physical science (chemistry and physics), and life science (biology and natural history). Natural history should always include the personal observation of nature directly by the student, often in the form of nature and weather journals.

Heart of Wisdom places a high degree of importance on studying the various areas of science according to the Bible; that is, in the order of creation. Studying science in this way directly refutes the atheistic, evolutionary mindset of our day, and places God back at the center of study. Honoring God in this way acknowledges that He is the Creator of all things, and that we were created with a purpose.

Science Resources

Heart of Wisdom recommends several books that have a Christian view toward studying human anatomy, biology, nature, and science, as well as integrating Bible study with each science subject. As explained in *Understanding the Times*:

Modern science's roots are grounded in a Christian view of the world. This is not surprising, since science is based on the assumption that the universe is orderly and can be expected to act according to specific, discoverable laws. An ordered lawful universe would seem to be the effect of an intelligent cause, which was precisely the belief of many early scientists. The concept that "God is the builder of everything" (Hebrews 3:4) and that Christ "made the universe" (Hebrews 1:2) did not frighten the likes of many great scientists. Most early scientists worked out their scientific views within the theistic Christian belief in a supernatural creator and the doctrine of creation.

Today, scientists still recognize the importance of orderliness in the universe. Physicist Paul Davies, author of *God and the New Physics*, writes: "Science is possible only because we live in an ordered universe which complies with simple mathematical laws. The job of the scientist is to study, catalogue, and relate the orderliness in nature, not to question its origin. But theologians have long argued that the order of the physical world is evidence for God. If this is true, then science and religion acquire a common purpose in revealing God's work."

God had specific reasons for creating the world. God created the heavens and the earth as a manifestation of His glory, majesty, and power. David said, *The heavens declare the glory of God: and the firmament showeth his handiwork*" (Psalm 19:1; Psalm 8:1). By looking at the entire created cosmos—from the immense expanse of the created universe, to the beauty and order of nature—we cannot help but stand in awe of the majesty of the Lord God, our Creator.

> *Let the sea roar, and the fulness thereof; the world, and they that dwell therein. Let the floods clap their hands: let the hills be joyful together.* —Psalm 98:7–8

> *Praise ye the LORD. Praise ye the LORD from the heavens: praise Him in the heights. Praise ye Him, all his angels: praise ye Him, all his hosts. Praise ye Him, sun and moon: praise Him, all ye stars of light. Praise Him, ye heavens of heavens, and ye waters that be above the heavens. Let them praise the name of the LORD: for he commanded, and they were created. He hath also stablished them for ever and ever: He hath made a decree which shall not pass. Praise the LORD from the earth, ye dragons, and all deeps: Fire,*

and hail; snow, and vapours; stormy wind fulfilling his word: Mountains, and all hills;
fruitful trees, and all cedars: Beasts, and all cattle; creeping things, and flying fowl.—
Psalm 148:1–10)

For ye shall go out with joy, and be led forth with peace: the mountains and the hills
shall break forth before you into singing, and all the trees of the field shall clap their
hands.—Isaiah 55:12.

How much more God desires and expects to receive honor and praise from human
beings!

Studying Science in Creation Order

Most evolutionists believe and teach that there is one common ancestor for all life. A
biblical creation perspective on these questions provides an exacting, liberating
framework for biology, and a deeper appreciation for living organisms.

In *The Biblical Classification of Life*, Chard Berndt explains that there exist underlying
questions of greater depth and implication than only "what things are" and "how things
work." Behind all science are questions of meaning and purpose:

> To begin, let me quote from a typical biology textbook: "Flowers are reproductive
> shoots usually composed of four kinds of organs...." While it is true that flowers are
> the reproductive structures of plants, this statement alone, and the discussion that
> inevitably follows, omits two preeminent purposes of flowers revealed in the
> Creation account:

> *And the LORD God made all kinds of trees grow out of the ground—trees that were pleasing*
> *to the eye and good for food.—Genesis 2:9a*

> This passage tells of two original purposes for this major grouping of trees (orchard
> trees, or trees "of the field" in particular): 1. They are pleasing to the eye, and 2. They
> are good for food.

> What would typical biologists or biology teachers say to these higher purposes? For
> one, they would reduce beauty to mere function—the conspicuous petals, they'd say,
> exist to attract pollinators such as bees or wasps. Yet while this is true, do they not
> also attract us? And is it not also true that many less showy flowers also attract
> insect pollinators? What would typical evolutionists say about the higher purpose of
> a fruit being "good for food"? Again, they would reduce it, emphasizing that the fruit
> is essentially a ripened ovary, protecting and eventually distributing the plant's seeds
> for reproduction. Yet while also true, this reduces the fruit to a mere middle function,
> rather than a splendid end in and of itself. We should remember that, in addition to

our enjoyment of pears, apples, mangoes, peaches, avocados, and the like today, the pre-Flood state of the creation provided vegetation (and in particular, vegetative fruits) as humankind's entire diet; there existed no carnivorous activity until God permitted it after the Flood. Incidentally, I gather that before the Fall, humankind's diet included fruits and nuts from trees in greater proportion to the staple foods produced by herbaceous plants (which were the only vegetative kinds specified for land and sky creatures). This distribution was altered largely after the Fall, as evidenced by the fact that although every green plant (both herbaceous and woody) had already been given for food, staple food consumption was mentioned conspicuously as part of the curse:

...and you will eat the plants [herbaceous] *of the field* [those designed for cultivation]. —Genesis 3:18b

So the primary purposes of flowering trees are to provide beauty and to provide food—both for humankind-centered purposes. In a broader sense, biologists and biology teachers typically do the same reducing when discussing leaves as well. The main purpose of leaves, they say, is to produce food for the plant, so it can grow; the liberated oxygen is regarded as a mere by-product of the process of photosynthesis, rather than a purposeful design. But again, the main purpose of leaves is

1. To provided beauty for mankind's enjoyment, and

2. To produce food and oxygen for creatures, and ultimately for humankind.

It is biblical and right for a biologist or biology teacher to regard the beauty and nourishment of a flowering tree as its main purposes, and then to continue explaining how these features also contribute to the plant's survival and reproduction.

The higher purposes in Creation, when acknowledged, open up the book of the Creation further. In addition to instilling wonder in what has been artfully and purposefully created, these purposes instruct us about our own lives and purposes.

The Heart of Wisdom four-year curriculum plan recommends studying the following science topics in the order of the Creation days:

Day 1: Light, Energy, Motion, Matter (Physical Sciences)

Day 2: Air, Water, Weather (Chemistry / Meteorology)

Day 3: Rocks, Minerals, Plants (Chemistry / Botany)

Day 4: Sun, Moon and Stars (Astronomy)

Day 5: Birds and Sea Life (Ornithology / Marine Biology)

Day 6: Land Animals and Human Body (Zoology / Anatomy)

YEAR ONE	YEAR TWO	YEAR THREE	YEAR FOUR
PHYSICAL SCIENCE	EARTH SCIENCE AND BOTANY	THE ANIMAL WORLD	ANATOMY
Creation	Weather	Marine Biology	Cell Design
Light	Oceanography	Ornithology (Birds)	Brain/Nervous System
Energy	Botany	Entomology (Insects)	Skeletal/Muscular Systems
Matter	Geology	Earth Zoology	Respiratory/Digestive Systems
Motion	Astronomy		Heart/Circulatory System
Electricity			Reproductive System

Life Skills

The Hebrew culture, as well as the culture of the American frontier, was practical and regarded hard work to be beneficial to society as a whole, and to the individual as well. In the aristocratic Greek mentality that has invaded our culture in recent years, however, physical work has been regarded as somehow less respected, even relegated to the lower classes. But that is not the biblical view.

According to the Scriptures, work is honorable—even part of the image of God within us. We were commanded to take dominion over the earth, and even before the Fall, Adam worked in the Garden—it was part of his nature to do so.

The husbandry curriculum of life skills studies teach practical skills that all students actually need, but which are very rarely included in the public school education that most children receive. As David Mulligan explains: husbandry subjects include learning how to do the following:

Bake bread	Change a sparkplug	Cut firewood
Build a fire	Change oil	Do laundry
Change a diaper	Cook a meal	File

File	Organize a party	Wallpaper
Fix a leaky faucet	Paint a room	Wash the car
Garden	Prune a tree	Write or cash a check
Lead a Bible study	Sharpen a tool	
Mend clothing	Tie a knot	

Economic studies are related to the life skills topic in that students must learn how to conduct themselves in economic and financial matters. God is greatly concerned about our economic integrity, and much of the Bible is devoted to teachings on financial conduct. We must teach our children to practice not only sound economics, but Christian economics. There are ten skills that our children must be taught (because they are not developed by instinct), in order to follow God's Word in their financial futures.

Each of these areas must be taught in the light of Scripture with scriptural values in place. Economic conduct is no different than behavior in any other area: God requires us to be diligent, to be obedient, and to teach our children to be these things as well.

When we present a curriculum to our students that is well-balanced and based firmly on the Word of God, we will be able to raise godly children in an ungodly world. Heart of Wisdom suggests that students between the 7th to 12th grades study, at a minimum, the following life skills:

1. Wisdom

2. Character of a Proverbs 31 Women

3. Character of a Godly Men

4. Economics

5. Courtship and Marriage

Creating the Notebooks

Notebooking, a practice which allows children to create and update a variety of notebooks as they learn, is a fun and exciting homeschool technique. Notebooks are more than binders used to store a student's work. The notebooking approach is a way to teach students how to learn, as they to plan, develop, classify, categorize, construct, and organize a project for display. Children can create their own notebooks on all the different topics they study.

Notebooks are focused on the areas of the child's interests. School subjects are blended into a theme, in context, so they make sense. School subjects are taught as part of the topic, without the child noticing, resulting in a lifestyle of learning.

George Washington, Benjamin Franklin, and Thomas Jefferson all kept personal learning notebooks. This natural approach to education encourages your students to be life-long learners.

Heart of Wisdom unit studies utilize the four-step system of instruction (referred to in a previous chapter):

- Step 1: Introducing and arousing interest in the topic

- Step 2: Finding out the facts

- Step 3: Doing something with what has been learned

- Step 4: Pulling it all together. Sharing with others

In Step 3 students choose an activity to work on that will become part of their notebook. In Step Four students share their notebook with someone.

The Heart of Wisdom approach recommends that each child develop and maintain the following:

1. Bible Portfolio

2. Unit Study Portfolio

3. Time Line Book

4. Spelling Notebook

5. Vocabulary Notebook

6. Greek and Hebrew Notebook

7. Creation Dairy

Supplies Needed for All Notebooks

- Three-ring notebooks with a clear-plastic pocket cover

- Variety of paper (lined notebook, plain white, colored, cardstock)

- Top-loading sheet protectors (for photos, brochures, maps, etc.)

- A three-hole punch.

Always Include Your Student's Best Work

Some writing may be acceptable in its first draft, but only completed work (rewritten and corrected) should be included in the notebook/portfolio. Our use of the term *portfolio* is not accidental. The portfolio of an artist or photographer is a collection of his or her best work, whether the pages are loose or kept in a 3-ring notebook.

Creating the portfolio will be a reflexive process, as well as a reflective one. Papers may be corrected and rewritten a number of times before they are included. As the papers will define (to an extent) what has been learned, a compilation of these papers will also cause rethinking, reflection, and sometimes, reevaluation.

All work (copy work, letters, summaries, essays, etc) should be placed in either a portfolio or a Drafts Notebook. Only finished work should go into the portfolios. This work should be complete, including all corrections, rewrites, and other improvements. This work will demonstrate correct grammar, punctuation, spelling, and vocabulary usage.

Place all unfinished work into the teacher's Drafts Notebook. This work can stay as drafts or be completed at another time. Writing drafts are works that have not been corrected. Your Draft Notebook can be a valuable teaching tool. Use unfinished work to teach revising and editing in later weeks. Allow students to edit each other's work.

Do not require all work to be finished! For example, in five days of teaching you might have five to ten work items (three to five from Bible study and five from unit study work). Of these items several will be some type of copy work or original writing. Of these items, choose at least one (that's one item per week per subject) to refine to the finished product stage. The other work items should go into the Draft Notebook. You can certainly do more if your student is eager to do so but if you require completed work for every day, both you and your student will be frustrated.

The writing process includes five steps:

1. Prewriting	2. Writing	3. Revising
4. Editing	5. Publishing, or storing the finished product	

The type of work will depend on your child's age and ability. Examples:

K–4	Coloring pages	Dictation	Cut out pictures	Copy work (word to sentence length)
5–8	Illustrations	Dictation	Summary writing	Copy work (sentence to two paragraphs)
9–12	Journal writing	Summary writing	Essay writing	Copy work (two to six paragraphs)

You can be very creative with your portfolios. Some students thrive on creativity. For them we suggest scrapbook supplies (memory albums, stickers, die cuts, paper, cardstock, scissors, pens, punches, templates, rulers, idea books, etc.) Students can decorate papers with illustrations, stickers, frames, etc. See Scrapbooking To Learn later in this chapter.

Organize Your Notebook Supplies

It's important to keep all your notebooking supplies in one convenient place. Don't impede your child's creativity by not having the materials handy. If you homeschool at the dining table, as we do, consider using a basket or even a carry-on suitcase for supplies (they make suitcase-like containers for scrapbookers). Be on the lookout for pages or pictures from magazines or web sites that your children can use to illustrate copy work. Place them in file folders and keep with your notebook supplies.

Any oversized artwork can easily be stored by folding a piece of poster paper in half, stapling the sides perpendicular to the fold (which has now become the bottom), and slipping artwork in through the top.

Label Each Portfolio

You don't want this precious work to be misplaced or lost. Neatly label each portfolio with the student's name, age, address, and telephone number on the inside cover.

Create New Portfolios Each Year

Begin a new portfolio for each child every year. A comparison of the portfolios year by year will allow you to view your child's spiritual and academic growth.

Creating a Bible Portfolio

The Bible portfolio is used to store the student's work as you read through the Bible each year. It will include writing assignments, artwork, small collections, letters, photos, brochures, maps, etc. Begin with a 3-ring vinyl notebook that has clear pockets on the outside so the children can design their own covers.

Each child should have his or her own Bible portfolio. I highly recommend Mother having her own personal Bible portfolio too! The contents of your student's Bible portfolio will vary depending on the age of each student. Younger children's portfolios will contain more drawings or pictures of crafts. Older students portfolios will contain more writing assignments. Mother can use her portfolio to keep a journal of the Bible stories read and reactions of each child to particular stories.

Bible Portfolio Cover

Students can create a cover by drawing on paper with markers or crayons, making a collage, using pictures from the Internet, or enlarging a color photo at a local copy center. Students can then slide the finished product into the pocket covering their notebook. If your student experiences a block in creating a cover design, leave the cover blank until he or she feels inspired.

Understanding the Whole Picture

Teaching the structure of the Bible is the secret to getting a comprehensive overview of the Bible. If you want to build a building you begin with a blueprint. To learn the Bible well, you need to understand its structure. When you try to read through the Bible as one story—or even just the Old or New Testament—it can be overwhelming. There are 66 books in the Bible, which can be divided as follows:

There are 39 books in the Old Testament:

- The first seventeen books are historical

- The next five books are poetical

- The next seventeen books are prophetical

There are 27 books in the New Testament:

- The first five books are historical

- The next thirteen books are Pauline Epistles

- The next nine books are General Epistles

The secret to teaching your children a good overview of Bible chronology is to teach the 12 Eras of Bible History. Using this one simple method from *30 Days to Understanding the Bible* by Max E. Anders has help me understand and teach the chronology of the Bible more than any other technique. Have your children use these eras to create a title page for each section of their Bible portfolio!

The following pages contain instructions to how to divide the Bible portfolio into twelve historical eras. I really like the simplicity of this

> # 12 Eras of Biblical History
>
> 1. Creation Era
> 2. Patriarch Era
> 3. Exodus Era
> 4. Conquest Era
> 5. Judges Era
> 6. Kingdom Era
> 7. Exile Era
> 8. Return Era
> 9. Silence Era
> 10. Gospel Era
> 11. Church Era
> 12. Missions Era

division. In *30 Days to Understanding the Bible* by Anders explains how to study the Bible through these twelve historical eras using helpful pictorial symbols that will give inspiration for title page illustrations.

Anders explains in American history we can view a specific time period in a chart such as the following:

Key Era	Key Figure	Location	Story Line
Colonial	Ben Franklin	Boston	As the 13 colonies long for independence, Franklin leads the formulation of necessary strategy.
Revolution	Jefferson	Philadelphia	Jefferson forges the Declaration of Independence.
Etc.	Etc.	Etc.	Etc.

In the same way, we can study the Bible through charting the main periods (or eras), the central figures, the main locations, and a summary story line. The story line is divided into the twelve main eras with a central figure and main location for each era. This would be a type of overview for each time period. This overview can be placed on the divider page as a list of contents or just inside the divider page. The amount of detail you include is up to you. Below is a sample without the storyline, with a list of major events. Keep it simple enough to get an overview at a glance.

Key Era	Key Figure	Location	Storyline Summary
Creation	Adam	Mesopotamia	Creation Fall Tower Flood
Patriarch	Abraham	Ur to Canaan	Abraham Isaac Jacob Joseph
Exodus	Moses	Egypt	Deliverance Law Kadesh Barnea (12 Spies) 40 Years Wandering
Etc.	Etc.	Etc.	Etc.

Here is a example with a stoyline.

Key Era	Key Figure	Location	Storyline Summary
Creation	Adam	Mesopotamia	Adam created by God, but he sins and destroys God's original plan for man.
Patriarch	Abraham	Ur to Canaan	Abraham is chosen by God to father a people to represent God to the world.
Exodus	Moses	Egypt	Moses delivers the Hebrew people from slavery in Egypt, then gives them God's Law.
Etc.	Etc.	Etc.	Etc.

Your students' Bible portfolios will include essays, reports, stories, poems, songs, Bible verses, journal entries, book reviews, dictation lessons, photographs of projects, computer-produced graphics, memorabilia, recipes, maps, Internet printouts, illustrations, etc. For more creative ideas see Scrapbooking To Learn later in this chapter.

Your children and you will learn as you divide the notebook into the twelve eras with index dividers or colored paper dividers, and make a title page for each section. In addition to the 12 eras, you may want include these sections:

- Poetical Books

- Prophetical Books

- The Epistles

Creating a Time Line Book

In her writings, Charlotte Mason recommended preparing a handmade Time Line Book (originally called a Museum Sketch Book; sometimes called a Book of the Centuries). This activity is based on one of the major keys to motivation—the active involvement of students in their own learning. Students learn by doing, making, writing, designing, creating, and solving. Creating this Time Line Book is a marvelous way for students to be actively involved and pull it all together and grasp the flow of biblical and other historical events.

In a short period of time students can complete an illustrated time line page that tells a story and gives immediate feedback that is satisfying and rewarding. Then, as your

In a short period of time students can complete an illustrated time line page that tells a story and gives immediate feedback that is satisfying and rewarding. Then, as your students learn historical facts, they will make notes and sketches in their books, on the appropriately dated pages, about famous people, important events, inventions, wars, etc. (Work that includes undated information about a time period, such as daily life, education, etc., fits better into a portfolio, but you can combine the books if you wish.)

TimeLine Maker is an innovative tool you can purchase online that allows you to quickly organize events and print stunning timeline charts. Designed with an easy to use and intuitive user interface, data entry is simple and its charts provide an easy, yet powerful way to record and present time based data. Available for download or on CD. See HeartofWisdom.com/Timeline.htm for details.

To Set Up Your Time Line Book You Will Need

- A three-ring notebook with a clear plastic pocket cover
- Blank 8.5" X 11" pages
- Smaller lined pages (8.5" x 11" cut down to 8.5" x 9")
- A three-hole punch
- Glue sticks

One option is to choose a color for the pages of each unit (e.g., peach for Mesopotamia, pink for Rome, blue for Israel, etc.). Decide the units of time you will use (decades, centuries, etc.) to divide your time line into segments. A time line documenting the period from Adam to the Messiah will begin with Creation (before 2000 B.C.) and end with the resurrection and ascension of Christ (c. A.D. 30).

History Divisions

The nice thing about the notebook style time line is that it's cumulative; every year's study can be added in. You can continue this time line as you study later periods by adding pages. As you study each period, there will be times when you will document decades on one page, and other times when you will document several centuries on one page.

> Division for Ancient History Notebook:
>
> 1. Adam to Abraham
> 2. Mesopotamia
> 3. Ancient Egypt
> 4. Ancient Israel
> 5. Ancient Greece
> 6. Ancient Rome
> 7. The Messiah

Place the appropriate section of the time line across the top of each 8.5" x 11" page to represent increments. The shorter lined pages will go in between these pages to hold notes. If there is not enough room on your time line to include all of your chronology, cull some of the dates or add pages with larger segments that leave more room.

In the image area you can add illustrations. There are thousands of illustrations, maps, Christian clip art, etc., available for free on the Internet. A few examples are shown in this chapter. You can also draw your own illustrations, use illustrations from the web, or trace or photocopy illustrations.

On the lined area you can add notes or outlines about key events or people. Write a brief summary for each event, development, or invention. Include: Who did it? When did it occur? What it was. Where it occurred. Why it was important. Write a short biography for each person you research. Information that you may want to include: what they did that was important, birth and death dates, where they were born, where they died, etc.

Unit Study Portfolio

Work from your Bible reading as well as your history and science unit studies can be included in the Time Line notebook, but you will have a lot of work science and life skills topics that will not fit into the Time Line notebook. Make a separate notebook for these. Consider making one notebook for science each year and one for life skills.

Science Portfolio

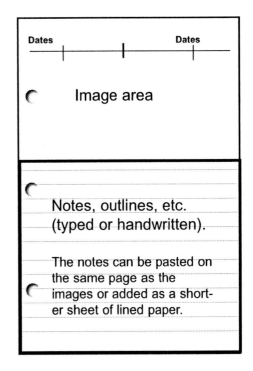

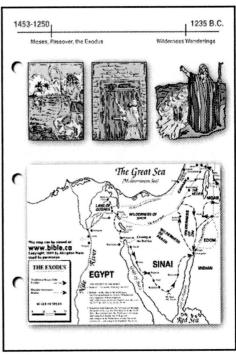

If you want to include a full year of science into one notebook you can divide it into themes such as Heart of Wisdom's first year of science, which is arranged in the order of the days of Creation:

- Creation
- Light
- Energy
- Matter
- Motion
- Electricity

Life Skills Portfolio

A life skills notebook can be divided as follows:

- Wisdom
- Homemaking
- Gardening
- Economics

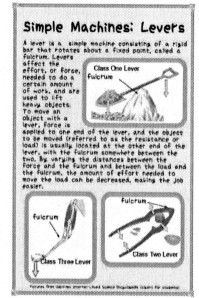

These images are from *Usborne's Science Encyclopedia.* When you purchase Usborne's Internet-linked books (science, history, art, music, etc.) you get access to Usborne links, images, maps, puzzles, quizzes, and coloring pages online. These are excellent options for your portfolio. It's like being able to cut the color picture right out of the book and add it to your portfolio.

See http://www.Usborne-quicklinks.com/

Create the unit study portfolio following the same general directions for the Bible study portfolio. The size (width) of your notebook will depend on your child's interest in the topic and how many topics you place in one notebook. If your family is really interested in studying Creation, you can make a 1" to 3" notebook just on Creation. Possible divisions: Creation Days, Creation vs. Evolution, Darwin, etc. If your daughter is really into cooking, you may want to make an entire notebook for cooking. Possible divisions: main courses, soups, desserts, cooking tips, etc.

Contents will depend on the subject. You can include essays, reports, stories, poems, songs, Bible verses, journal entries, book reviews, dictation lessons, photographs of projects, computer-produced graphics, memorabilia, recipes, maps, Internet printouts, illustrations, etc.

Science unit study notebooks will include: lab reports of experiments, drawings of scientific topics (weather cycles, atmosphere layers, etc.), copy work from science topics, outlines of science chapters, graphs and diagrams on collected scientific information, biographies of famous scientists, summary writing, etc.

The potential content of life skills notebooks is endless. I began a three-ring notebook when we first began building our home. It was a great organizer. Divisions included floor plans, layout, lighting fixtures, kitchen appliances, etc. I had a section titled Progress. Every week I visited the site and took pictures. I documented the progress with my digital camera and compiled photos, from the digging of the basement to completion of our home a year later. What began as an organizer later became a beautiful scrapbook of memories.

Utilize Your Computer

The computer is a great asset for creating notebooks. There are hundreds of images online available at the click of a mouse. With the new digital cameras it's fairly easy to photograph projects, then print them out and include them as illustrations in your notebook.

The advent of computers and desktop publishing software has enabled the aspiring artist to create presentations, brochures, posters, business cards and stationary, and personalized birthday cards. This type work may motivate your student to take a course in desk top publishing. Several online courses are available.

Creating a Vocabulary Notebook

To set up your student's Vocabulary Notebook, divide a spiral notebook into 26 sections (one for each letter of the alphabet), allowing several pages per letter. Read "Improving Vocabulary Skills" in *Writers Inc*. It's best to keep vocabulary in a separate notebook from the unit study portfolios, because many of the new words your student will learn will not be specific to any specific thematic unit.

Vocabulary notebook pages can be helpful for students to observe their progress and to establish increasing awareness in their reading. Research has shown that it is much easier to remember words in context than in simple lists. Computer option: students can keep their vocabulary words in a file on the computer.

Each day, students should make a vocabulary list of unknown words found while reading. At the end of the reading, students will be expected to make vocabulary entries into their notebooks. If the student does not come across any new words, choose new words from the vocabulary section of the current unit study.

Vocabulary Entry	Sample
1. Write the word.	1. Word: intact
2. Include the sentence where the word was first found with the date.	2. Found: "The Lawgiver" p. 239. "The deck was torn and scattered, but the precious engine was intact." (7/9/03)
3. Write the definition of the word from the context.	3. Definition: unharmed, untouched.
4. Write the antonym of the word as derived from the context.	4. Antonym: destroyed, torn apart.
5. Etymology of the word.	5. Etymology: c.1450, from Latin intactus "untouched, uninjured," from in- "not" + tactus, past participle of tangere "to touch"
6. Write a sentence using the word.	6. Sentence: I was pleased to find my house intact after the tornado warnings had passed.

Etymology (Word Roots or Origins)

Etymology is the study of the origins of words. The word *etymology* is derived from the Greek *etumos* which means real or true. The ending *ology* suggests the science study as in biology or geology. Etymology is the study of the origins of words; how they developed.

Etymologist try to reconstruct the history of words from the source, and how their form and meaning has changed. Students should look up the etymology of vocabulary words. It is fun to note the etymology of a word, and noting it helps you understand how the word has come to the modern meaning. One-third of our words are descended from Greek or Latin. For example, the Latin root *tele* means to distance, and this root is found in many English words, such as telephone, telescope, etc. The best way to learn the Greek and Latin roots and prefixes is to learn in context—study the etymology of the words as you come upon them.

The etymology of *grammar.* is from the Greek *grammatike tekhne* "art of letters," from stem of graphein "to draw or write." Middle English *gramarye* also came to mean "learning in general, knowledge peculiar to the learned classes" (c.1320), which included astrology and magic; hence the secondary meaning of "occult knowledge" (c.1470), which evolved in Scottish into *glamour*. A grammar school (1387) was originally "a school in which the learned languages are grammatically taught. In the U.S. (1860) the term was put to use in the graded system for "a school between primary and secondary, where English grammar is taught."

If you have computer access there is a free etymology dictionary online at http://www.etymonline.com. An etymolology dictionary is just as valuable as a English dictionary. A good reference is *The Concise Oxford Dictionary of English Etymology.*

Introduce younger to etymology with a book like *Abracadabra to Zombie: More Than 300 Wacky Word Origins.* This is a fun book explaining the origins of 300 words. Also interesting *Who Put Butter in Butterfly and Other Fearless Investigations Into Our Illogical Language* by David Feldman and *Horsefeathers and Other Curious Words* by Charles E. Funk.

Vocabulary Ideas

Once a week, verbally go over a random list of words. Ask the student to use each word in a sentence. Check off the words that the student masters. Review all words at the end of the semester. Make a checklist of things you want to achieve with your vocabulary notebook. Here are some possibilities by grade level

K–1	Add one word a day into notebook.	Practice and write the letters in the word.	Help Mom think of a sentence with the word.	Tell Dad the meaning of the word.
2–3	Add one or two words a day into notebook.	Copy each word	Dictate a sentence using each word.	Make up a silly sentence with the word.
4–8	Add three words a day into notebook.	Give a synonym for each word.	Help Mom think of a sentence with the words.	Write or tell a silly story with all the words.
9–12	Add five words a day into notebook.	Give a synonym for each word.	Write a sentence using each word.	Look up the etymology.

Creating a Spelling Notebook

To set up your student's Spelling Notebook, divide a spiral notebook into 26 sections (one for each letter of the alphabet). Add any words that the student has trouble spelling. Read "Steps to Become a Better Speller," "Spelling Rules," and "Commonly Misspelled Word List" in *Writers Inc.* Each time you notice a misspelled word in a student's written work, write the word on a list for the student. (Remember to add misspelled words that the spell-checker finds in work written using a word processor.) If the word is again misspelled in written work, the student must add it to his/her Spelling Notebook.

Overcoming Continually Misspelled Words

Has anyone ever told you, "If you can't spell it look it up in the dictionary?" How do look up what you can't spell? *How to Spell It: A Handbook of Commonly Misspelled Words* by Harriet Wittels is an excellent resource. You can look up a word the way they think it should be spelled, then find the correct spelling in the next column in red. Every conceivable spelling of a word is included in this terrific reference that's also a great learning tool. Try using this book with students. Have them place a small mark by each word they look up. You may see a pattern.

If students turn in work with the same words misspelled over and over, you may need to become more firm. Businesses and corporations are continually faced with employees who cannot spell, and use different methods for correcting this problem. One effective example, although a bit extreme, is used by the Orlando Police Department. Police officers in training are required to write lengthy reports (back and front of a page in ink) that are turned in to their sergeants for review. The sergeant reviews the report with a red pen, circling any misspelled words. One error results in the officer rewriting the entire report (back and front). The trainee officers quickly learn to carry a pocket dictionary and carefully proofread reports.

> ### Top 100 Misspelled Words
> acceptable, accidentally, accommodate, acquire, acquit, a lot, amateur, apparent, argument, atheist, believe, calendar, category, cemetery, changeable, collectible, committed, conscience, conscientious, conscious, definite(ly), disappear, discipline, drunkenness, embarrass, equipment, exhilarate, exceed, existence, experience, fiery, foreign, fourth, gauge, generally, grammar, grateful, guarantee, harass, height, hierarchy, ignorance, immediate, independent, indispensable, intelligence, its /it's, judgment, knowledge, leisure, library, lightning, maintenance, maneuver, memento, millennium, miniature, mischievous, noticeable, occasion, occasionally, occur/occurred, occurrence, official, parallel, parliament, pastime, pigeon, possession, preferable, principal/principle, privilege, questionnaire, receive, recommend, referred, reference, relevant, religious, restaurant, ridiculous, rhythm, sandal, schedule, scissors, sensible, separate, special, success, to/too/two, tomorrow, their/ they're/there, twelfth, tyranny, until, vacuum, vicious, weather, weird, you're/your,

We're not suggesting that you use this approach-you don't want to discourage writing-but you can modify this approach by allowing students to use erasable ink. Hand back papers with spelling mistakes and ask for corrections. Encourage students to proofread aloud, always with pencil or pen in hand, and to proofread backwards.

Problem Spellers

I am a poor speller. The running joke in my house is how I am a creative speller. I can think of so many ways to spell a word, and I often include three or four ways to spell one word differently within one article. Amazingly, most of my children are very good spellers-in fact, three of my children have done professional proofreading work-but unfortunately, the misspelling trait has been passed down to two of my other children. We are not alone. William Shakespeare, Thomas Jefferson, F. Scott Fitzgerald, Herman Melville, Woodrow Wilson, and John Irving were also poor spellers. Some people just can't spell.

A recent article in the Washington Post, "Why Stevie Can't Spell," by Steve Hendrix[1] shed light on my spelling problem. In his 14-year professional life as a writer Steve Hendrix has to rely on editors to correct his horrific spelling. A teacher convinced him the problem could be from his schooling and had him try a remedial program. He performed poorly on a pre-test, diligently studied form many weeks, and then did even poorer on a post-test. Steve ended up getting several brain scans. He found out that the recent ability to scan brains demonstrates how poor spellers can usually use the front reading part of their brains, but have a problem accessing the back spelling part. Twenty percent of the population has trouble accessing the spelling part of the brain.

J. Richard Gentry is an expert in spelling instruction. His site is http://jrichardgentry.com. If you or your children have trouble with spelling, get Gentry's book *My Kid Can't Spell!*. In this book Gentry offers timely and practical solutions to many of the problems parents face. It's packed with tools, guidelines, and strategies that parents can use immediately: developmental guideposts to track children's literacy, tips for helping children progress through early spelling stages, a test to determine children's spelling levels, strategies to help children visualize words, ways to identify poor spelling instruction at school, how to recognize if a child has a spelling disability, and much more.

Hebrew and Greek Notebook

Several lessons in Heart of Wisdom unit studies include references to Hebrew or Greek words. Encourage students to look up Hebrew and Greek words in a lexicon. (See our web site for active links to Crosswalk's New Testament Greek lexicon based on *Thayer's and Smith's Bible Dictionary*, and their Old Testament Hebrew lexicon based on *Brown, Driver, Briggs, Gesenius Lexicon*.) Your student should have an assigned place in a notebook to keep these words and their definitions, or in a section of his/her portfolio.

Learning the Greek and Hebrew Languages

It is my hope that learning the Greek and Hebrew words that are sprinkled throughout the Heart of Wisdom lessons will lead you to making a full study of the Greek and Hebrew language, beginning with Hebrew (Greek is much harder to learn).

There has been a recent homeschool renewal of interest in classical education methods and, along with it, a revival of the study of Latin, which can be beneficial in understanding the roots of many English words. We recommend students learn the Greek and Latin roots when they learn the meanings of new words by looking up the etymology of the word. (See page 320).

Learning Hebrew can be very rewarding. Martin Luther said, "…the Hebrews drink from the spring, the Greeks from the stream that flows from it, and the Latins from a downstream pool." Hebrew is the only ancient language still alive today. To know Hebrew is to be enabled to benefit from having direct access to one of the world's oldest cultures. Many people believe Hebrew was the first and only language before the tower of Babel. Jesus both spoke and read Hebrew, and all of the original authors of the New Testament were Jews who spoke and read Hebrew.

Hebrew is the original language of most of the Bible, which continues today to influence, in both direct and indirect ways, much of the world's thought, literature and culture. Learning Hebrew gives you the ability to better understand the original biblical author's words, rather than through a translator's opinion of the author's words. It is very difficult to understand the meanings of the New Testament's messages without having an understanding of the Hebraic mindset of their authors. Major errors in exegesis and consequent doctrine arise because we approach with the Western mindset inherited from the Greek influences on Gentile society.

The Puritans viewed Hebrew as the mother of languages and it figured prominently in the Puritan movement in England. English Puritan emigrants were also instrumental in promoting Hebrew as part of the curriculum in such prominent American universities as Harvard, Columbia, Yale, Brown, Princeton, Johns Hopkins, Dartmouth and Pennsylvania. In fact, Yale, Columbia and Dartmouth still bear Hebrew inscriptions on their seals. In Harvard's early years, more time was devoted to the study of Hebrew than Latin or Greek. This role of Hebrew in the curriculum endured until the 1820s. Graduates of the School of Divinity had to be able to read the Old Testament in the original Hebrew—a practice still required in Denmark.

Understanding the Difficult Words of Jesus by David Bivin and Roy Blizzard, Jr., quotes statistics to show that over 90% of the Bible was written in Hebrew, with about 1% in Aramaic, and the rest in Greek.[2] For more on this topic see writings by Dr. Robert L. Lindsey at http://www.hakesher.org and Jerusalem School of Synoptic Research http://jerusalemperspective.com.

Hebrew is a simple and concrete language. Any seminary student will tell you that Hebrew is infinitely easier than the study of Greek. Hebrew is not a complex language but it is fascinating.

We offer several resources, including *The Greek and Hebrew Tutor* (interactive software) *Jot and Tittle*, at http://Homeschool-Books.com under Language Arts/Languages.

Scrapbooking to Learn

Many homeschooling moms are likely to be familiar with the scrapbooking trend that has swept the nation in recent years. The fastest growing craft industry in the United States, scrapbooking has exploded onto the scene with literally hundreds of new tools, stickers, markers, and decorative scissors, as well as thousands of books full of ideas for recording important moments and memories in scrapbook form.

Fortunately for the homeschool movement, the popularity and the tools and ideas used in traditional scrapbooking can be used to make notebooking an extremely fun and creative outlet for children. Traditional hobby scrapbooking is the practice of combining photos, memorabilia, and stories in a scrapbook-style album. When children are scrapbooking to learn, they follow the same procedures and create scrapbook pages that reflect the topics and subjects about which they are learning.

The Heart of Wisdom approach suggests using scrapbooking methods as a creative outlet for schoolwork. Combine scrapbooking techniques with Charlotte Mason's copy methods for a great display or addition to your unit study portfolio. Scrapbooking is incredibly rewarding. Students show enthusiasm about almost any subject if they are able to scrapbook it.

A Step-by-Step Guide to Scrapbooking to Learn

Scrapbooking to learn is simple when you follow these easy steps:

1. Decide on your paper. Create a border page or colored design paper. You can use crayons or markers to make a border and designs or purchase decorative borders made for scrapbooking. There are several border pages available online to print out for free. You can also purchase special design paper from scrapbook suppliers.

2. Find one to five images to illustrate the concept you are teaching. It is recommended that you use odd numbers of photos on a page. Images are available on clip-art web sites, in magazines, and by photocopying them from books. You can get access to free clip art from *Usborne's Internet-Linked* books.

   One possible source for images, especially on a Bible passage page, is to allow your children to create paper people that will tell the story. They can color and cut out the paper people as you read the Bible story to them.

3. Have your student copy a passage (scrapbookers refer to text as journaling) about the topic—a sentence, a few paragraphs, Bible verses, poetry, etc. Encourage their best handwriting, or let them type up the passage on the computer. (You can be creative with different fonts.) Practice copying the text on notebook paper, making sure the

text is not too long for the space on the scrapbook page. Then, when you are ready, begin writing on the scrapbook page with pencil, then go over it with a black marker, or type the text into the computer, print it, and cut it to fit onto the scrapbook page.

4. Place the images onto the page in a logical sequence or wherever they are visually appealing.

5. Consider adding color to your page by matting images with colored paper. Any paper will do—you don't need to use acid-free, lignin-free paper unless you're working with photos. Use construction paper, special scrapbooking stationery, etc. Or, you could draw a frame around an image with markers, or crop the images in unique shapes.

6. Decorate your page using scrapbooking tools: die cuts, stickers, paper trimmers, borders, etc.

7. Add the page to the student's portfolio. Use a three-hole punch or a sheet protector.

8. Scan the page or take a digital photo in order to share the page with others.

Notebooking—especially when creative scrapbooking and the creation of Bible portfolios are involved—is an easy and fun way to increase learning. You will be amazed at the creative pages your children will produce—and how much they learn in the process!

Sample Pages

Suggested Reading

The Concise Oxford Dictionary of English Etymology
With over 17,000 entries, this is the most authoritative and comprehensive guide to word origins available in paperback making it ideal to use with the students vocabulary notebook. Based on *The Oxford Dictionary of English Etymology*, the principal authority on the origin and development of English words, it contains a wealth of information about our language and its history.

Listening to Languages of the Bible by Lois Tverberg ⊱
This is a perfect book to introduce you to the important of learning Hebrew. It is a guide for discovering the richness of the Scriptures in their Hebraic setting. Using the tools of language and culture, it unearths beautiful nuggets of new meaning from the Bible's ancient words. From seemingly odd phrases, it shares rich insights that do not translate well from culture to culture. The book examines many topics from the perspective of the ancient writers, including prayer, family and the promised Messiah. It also looks at the powerful sayings of Jesus in light of the Jewish culture of his time. The book contains more than 60 brief, illustrated devotional articles that unpack the meaning of a biblical word or phrase for our lives. It is intended both for personal reflection or small group discussion. With many additional references and topical and scripture indexes, it will be useful as a continuing reference for Bible study.

Notebooking! Yes, You Can Be a Binder Queen! by Cindy Rushton ⊱
Filled with ideas to encourage writing and delight-directed learning in all subjects, this book is an in-depth resource to help your children deepen their studies and document learning all along the way. Everything you ever wanted to know about notebooking is in this book. Cindy Rushton, who has become known as The Binder Queen, uses notebooking for everything. She will show you how to begin, whether your child is a toddler or the most skeptical high schooler on the block.

Chapter 21

Scheduling by Faith

Wait for the Lord and keep his way. He will exalt you to inherit the land.
—Psalm 37:34.

In This Chapter

◆ Joshua's three elements for success (scheduling strategies).

◆ Allowing God to chart your course.

◆ Scheduling time to complete a Heart of Wisdom unit study.

◆ Scheduling time for one lesson.

◆ Time management tips.

Throughout this book I have asked you to rethink your beliefs about education. Now I'm asking asking you to consider another paradigm shift—to rethink scheduling. We have asked "What would Jesus do?" And, "How would Jesus teach?" Now let us ask "How would Jesus schedule?" Jesus had obvious long-term goals but He practiced daily as a responder. He prayed daily and allowed the needs of the people around Him to set His agenda. He saw people's needs as opportunities to minister. We need to ask God to help us learn to schedule by faith.

The Heart of Wisdom curriculum plan includes a framework and objectives that requires both structure and flexibility. The four-year plan is a framework you can use as a guide as you schedule your curriculum and time by faith. The basic structure derived from the suggested number of unit studies you'll complete in a year. The unit studies are structured with lessons comprising four distinct, progressive steps. The flexibility is built into the amount of time you will spend in the units and lessons as you follow your child's delight. Heart of Wisdom unit studies include an ample number of lessons to allow you to explore until you discover your child's delight. (If you create your own lessons, you'll be choosing the subject matter of your lessons based on your child's delight.)

> *Teach us to number our days aright, that we may gain a heart of wisdom.* —Psalm 90:12

Keep in mind that the name of our teaching approach came from Psalm 90:12. *Teach us to number our days* is a plea for God to help us recognize how brief our time on earth is so that we might discern the true meaning of life and use our time wisely. The most important part of your planning is giving your schedule to God. *Day and night belong to God* (Psalm 74:16). When you submit your ways to God, He promises to direct your paths. He will lead you. This is a wonderful opportunity for spiritual growth for your entire family. As you lean on Him, I promise that you will see obvious events in your schedule that you will know came directly from God. Marvelous things happen when you wait on Him!

Earlier I stated that reaching the Promised Land is not the end, but a new beginning. Reaching the Promised Land in our homeschool analogy is arriving at a place where you depend on God for all your schooling concerns, including your scheduling.

We turn now to the book of Joshua for insight and encouragement about how to let God give you directions to plan your schedule.

The book of Joshua is the story of how God led the Israelites in the conquest of Canaan. The lessons in Joshua explain how choosing obedience brings victory and blessing, and how disobedience brings defeat.

Joshua was commanded to rid the land of the Canaanites. After the battle of Jericho, the Israelites defeated Ai. The news of Joshua's victories reached the Gibeonites. In their fear, the Gibeonites came up with a plan. They pretended that they came from a far away place (outside of Canaan) and wanted to make peace with the children of Israel. Joshua and his men believed them because of the way they looked (walking by sight/in the flesh), and because they did not ask for God's advice—two big mistakes.

Joshua made a treaty with the Gibeonites and then had to keep his promise to not kill the Gibeonites (once an oath was taken, it could not be revoked). However, he made them slaves. Adonizedec, a Canaan king, heard that the Gibeonites had made peace with Joshua; so he sent word to the other kings and asked for help to kill the Gibeonites. The Gibeonites appealed to Joshua to deliver them from Adonizecec (Joshua 10:6–10). God reassured Joshua that He was with him and the Israelites would win (Joshua 10:7–8).

When the battle began, God sent hail stones to fall on their enemies. He granted Joshua's request, and the sun stood still until they had defeated their enemies!

Joshua's Plan for Success

Three elements combined to give Joshua success in this battle in Joshua 10. These are the same three elements you will use in scheduling your school day:

1. Believing God's promise (v. 8),

2. Using sound strategy (v. 9),

3. Calling on the Lord in prayer (vv. 10–15).

1. Believing God's Promise

The Israelites didn't have to be afraid because God had already promised them victory—and you don't have to fear either, because God has promised to direct your paths. *Trust in the LORD with all thine heart; and lean not unto thine own understanding. In all thy ways acknowledge him, and he shall direct thy paths* (Proverbs 3:5–6). When we live by faith in God and in His promises, we can expect to receive God's help.

2. Using Sound Strategy

I'm not suggesting that you run your homeschool on a whim, but to create your plan with prayer and submission to God. Leaning on God does not negate self-discipline or forming good habits. God has always been working in your life. From before the time you were first formed in your mother's womb. He has been preparing you, just as Joshua was prepared many years for what would belong to him. You will need to plan, but allow time for a variety of unplanned activities; keep some flexible time in your schedule to meet your children's needs and delights; in other words, schedule by faith.

3. Calling on the Lord in Prayer

D. L. Moody said, "Every great movement of God can be traced to a kneeling figure." Prayer is your first step in planning, and the first step in daily Bible study. Use Colossians 1:9–12 as a guide. Ask God:

- To fill you with the knowledge of His will through all spiritual wisdom and understanding;

- That you would live a life worthy of the Lord and may please Him in every way;

- That you would bear fruit in every good work;

- That you would grow in the knowledge of God;

- That you would be strengthened with all power according to His glorious might so that you may have great endurance and patience; and

- That you would joyfully give thanks to the Father, who has qualified you to share in the inheritance of the saints in the kingdom of light.

Worried about having enough faith? Don't worry—the building of your faith is incorporated into the Heart of Wisdom teaching approach because it teaches you to make God's Word is your first priority each day, all day. Learning to lean on God will be part of your daily schedule. Your faith will grow daily because you will be in His Word daily. God will reward your desires when you trust Him and live obediently.

In his book, *Learning to Walk by Faith*, Charles Stanley said, "Faith is not a goal that we must work to achieve. It comes as the overflow of a personal relationship with God. It is as natural as taking a breath of air. Faith is the breath and life of our relationship with God and His Son. A life of faith is one that is dominated by Jesus Christ—not selfish desires. There are three levels of faith—little faith that says, 'God can.' Great faith that says, 'God will.' Perfect faith that says, 'God has done it.'"

Faith Grows

Recently, one of my married daughters and I had a discussion about waiting on God. She commented on the strength of my faith and expressed to me her anxieties about how desperately she wanted faith enough to count on God to lead her in her homeschooling. I explained to her that our faith grows as we consistently walk with the Lord. Faith is a living thing that grows as we see the Lord at work in our lives, and become continually aware of His presence. This year I will turn fifty, and I have gratefully watched God supply my needs and answer my prayers over and over and over for many years. I know I can count on Him because He never changes. This does not mean I am satisfied with the level of faith I now have. I fall very short of the faith God expects from me, as we all do. But I am satisfied with Jesus my Savior, and know that He is doing His work in me.

> *I wait quietly before God, for my hope is in him. He alone is my rock and my salvation, my fortress where I will not be shaken. My salvation and my honor come from God alone. He is my refuge, a rock where no enemy can reach me. O my people, trust in him at all times. Pour out your heart to him, for God is our refuge.*—Psalm 62: 5–8.

Be anxious for nothing, but in everything by prayer and supplication with thanksgiving let your requests be made known to God. And the peace of God, which surpasses all comprehension, will guard your hearts and your minds in Christ Jesus—Philippians 4:6–7.

Fear and faith cannot operate at the same time—they are mutually exclusive. You cannot wait on God to direct your path and then sit around and worry that He won't. Fear comes from trusting in your own ability—faith focuses and depends on God's promises and ability. Because I delight myself in Him, God has promised to direct my paths—and I know He will because He has promised to and because He has done so in the past. My husband pays our bills once a month. I never have to ask him and he never forgets. I know he has promised to take care of it and I don't give it a thought because he has proved himself to be trustworthy—and he is only a man. God guarantees His Word and fulfills His promises. It is when remind ourselves of all He has done, and recognize all He is doing in our lives, that our faith grows.

Faith begets more faith. Developing faith is much like developing muscles; our muscles grow stronger as we use them, and become weaker when we don't use them. Faith comes from prayer and learning about God's ways through studying and obeying His Word; it is through these exercises that we receive the confidence and peace that God gives when we trust Him. Faith is something we must practice continuously. It is a continuing cycle. The more you turn to God, the more your faith is strengthened.

Allowing God to Chart Your Course

Clarence Cranford delightfully illustrates prayer and faith as wind in a sail:

> A sailor was telling a small boy about the sea. He mentioned the wind. "What's wind?" asked the little boy. "I don't know what wind is," replied the sailor, "but I know what it does when I raise a sail." We now know a lot about how to chart the wind's course, but we still can't see it; we can only see what it does. So it is with God's Spirit. We can't see it; we can only see what it does in the lives of those who put their trust in God. The winds of God's grace are always blowing, but we must raise the sail of faith if we want them to propel us toward deeper peace and joy. Prayer is lifting our sails to the winds of God's wisdom and power. We do not tell the wind which way to blow. We learn how to adjust our sail to the wind so it can propel us in the right direction. In prayer we do not tell God how to act. Instead, we lift our praise and concerns so God can fill us with a deeper sense of God's presence and help us steer toward the answer God has in store for us.[1]

Many homeschool mothers want their curriculum plan so laid out that they know what to do every minute of the day. It would be easy to know the charted course before hand and depend on a wind that never changes that would effortlessly take you to your destination! But God doesn't work that way. He wants you to depend on Him moment by moment.

A sailboat without a sail is only driftwood. It is completely dependent upon the wind for its direction and progress. Every morning, before you open your eyes or get out of bed, go to God in prayer. Boldly raise your sail of faith to catch God's sweet Holy Spirit. Ask God to direct your navigation in uncharted waters—come to Him thankfully, willingly, humbly, and absolutely convinced that He is going to propel you in the right direction. The wind is strong—you need only to rightly position your sail for strength and speed. Throughout the day continue to ask Him to direct you. Leave your sails up, and let the Holy Spirit guide your boat. Whenever you feel weary, remember Christ's invitation, *"Come unto me, all ye that labor and are heavy laden, and I will give you rest."* (Matthew 11:28). God will guide your boat and help you weather all storms. Bring to Him any concerns you have, and leave them with Him as you sail toward the destination God has charted for you.

If you do not raise your sail, you have two other choices: aimlessly drift, or row your boat without a rudder or compass to give direction; and the results will be disappointing if not disastrous. Drifting will take you wherever the current of the world goes. Rowing—that is, trying to make progress by your flesh—is just as perilous, because you don't know what the destination is or how to get there, so any rowing effort will be in vain. If you don't let God chart your course you can end up rowing in circles or into dangerous waters. Jonah tried to go his own way instead of following God's direction. He ran from God's will and caused a storm that almost sank the ship he was on, then was thrown into the sea and swallowed by a giant fish. But even after his disobedience, when he repented, God graciously guided Jonah and brought him back on course. Use wisdom and allow God to direct you the first time. Don't cause Him to have to use drastic measures to get you to the proper destination.

It is interesting that the word *knowledge* has a Hebrew root that describes skill in sailing (2 Chronicles 8:18). Your faith will grow daily as you gain knowledge of God's Word. The more Word you have in you, the easier it will be to raise and position your sail. You will be starting your homeschooling each day studying in His Word-reading stories of how faithful God is in every situation, opportunity, and decision. Read Hebrews chapter 11—each person in this faith chapter did something because they believed God.

So then faith cometh by hearing, and hearing by the word of God. (Romans 10:17 KJV). This says that faith *comes* from hearing the Word of God; faith grows by hearing more of the Word, and by applying it and trusting God—watching, waiting, and honoring Him by refusing to indulge thoughts of fear (worry, anxiety, dread, apprehension, etc.).

Charles Stanley said, "When we meditate on God and remember the promises He has given us in His Word, our faith grows, and our fears dissolve. David understood that.

Many times, in the caves hiding from Saul and with from six thousand to twenty thousand men searching for him, David quietly shifted his attention to God. Under the stars or in the darkness of the caves, David focused his attention on [the] God who had equipped him to slay Goliath, who had given him swiftness of body and keenness of mind. He remembered God who had allowed him to avoid Saul's javelin. As he fixed [the eyes of] his inner man on God, his fears and frustrations were soothed by the presence of God. We [will] have our own cave and javelin experiences, and we need to remember His wonderful promises in them."[2]

> *And my God will meet all your needs according to his glorious riches in Christ Jesus.*—Philippians 4:19

God has a design in mind for your homeschool—for you and every member of your family. There are no accidents. He is working in ways unknown to us to bring goodness and hope out of every situation. We must choose to believe that God keeps His promises. Hebrews 11:6 tells us that *without faith it is impossible to please Him, for he who comes to God must believe that He is and that He is a rewarder of those who diligently seek Him.* Anything that is not of faith is sin, because if faith is not our motivation, then by default the fear and pride of the flesh are our motivation, and that's sin.

Remember that God has a special plan for your family, and that it will be different from other families. Don't dwell on the hours you put in and how that compares to others' schedules. This carnal thought pattern can produce either pride or resentment. Focus instead on the wonderful and unique way God is preparing your family. Each night as you pray, ask yourself what your motivation was for the day. Was it to obey God and serve Him by using the gifts and talents He has given you? Or did you try to fulfill objectives outlined by the world, or another person, or a school district? It's so easy to do the latter—I know from experience.

God is in control of your life, ruling over all. He knows your abilities and your weaknesses. He knows your children and their needs. Turn your focus to Christ and place your trust in His might and love. He will never let you down. When we rely on Him we will have *chosen that good part, which will not be taken away*" (Luke 10:42). Absolutely nothing—neither problems, nor circumstances—can take away the wonderful peace and assurance that result from trusting God. Lift your sails to the winds of God's wisdom and power and watch the great and powerful things He will provide.

> *We ought always to thank God for you, brothers, and rightly so, because your faith is growing more and more, and the love every one of you has for each other is increasing.* —2 Thessalonians 1:3

Time Management

One of the greatest problems that homeschooling moms face is that there never seems to be enough time in the day. Fortunately, with a few simple tips and a reassessment of priorities, it is possible to get needed things done and ensure that your children receive the best homeschool education possible. Ephesians chapter 5 has a good message for those whose schedules seem to be filled to the breaking point: *See then that you walk circumspectly, not as fools but as wise, redeeming the time, because the days are evil. Therefore do not be unwise, but understand what the will of the Lord is.*—Ephesians 5: 15–17

Several key phrases in this passage speak to homeschool parents: *"walk circumspectly," "redeeming the time," "do not be unwise,"* and *"understand what the will of the Lord is."* Ultimately, it will come down to a matter of priorities. Everyone has been given twenty-four hours every day—no more and no less—and we must use this time to do the things that God would have us do. To *"walk circumspectly"* and *"not be unwise"* means to refocus your priorities and understand what God's will is for your at this time of your life.

Has God called you to have the most well-kept house in the neighborhood? Has He called you to have your laundry caught up, the windows washed, and every room of your house dust-free? Or has He called you to raise your children according to His Word? One of the first steps to effective time management in any situation, including a homeschool environment, is to reevaluate and then rearrange your priorities, cutting yourself some slack in the areas that don't hold as much importance.

When you feel apprehensive, reread the first section of this book and this chapter. Spend some time in prayer and give your time to God. Trust Him to lead you. This is a special time of opportunity to learn to lean on Him. Following this approach you'll be in the Word daily so your faith will be growing (see Romans 10:17).

Planning Notebook

Create a planning notebook specifically for goals, schedules, and lists. It is much easier to change a working plan than it is to "fly by the seat of your pants." A written plan will help you feel more in control of your time. This notebook is your recipe to create balance and harmony in each of these vital areas: spiritual, family, physical, financial, educational, social, and professional. You can purchase a planner such as *The Ultimate Homeschool Planner* or make a customized planner using a durable three-ring binder and organizational forms from the Internet. The following are possible notebook categories. If you homeschool section is too large you can use another notebook.

- Spiritual (Bible reading checklists, prayer lists, journal entries, etc.)

- Home (annual, monthly, and weekly, and daily chore lists)

- Meals (menu planner, recipes, and master shopping lists.)

- Homeschool (books read lists, books to read lists, annual, monthly and weekly, and daily schedules, library return list, wish lists, unit study planner, etc.)

- To Do (daily and weekly to do lists)

- Honey Do (on going lists of things you need your sweetheart to do)

- Exercise (goals and log)

Make your notebook work for your family by trying different forms and divisions. You'll come up with a system that works for you. See http://organizedhome.com or http://www.donnayoung.org for downloadable forms. At the beginning of each school year, note your priorities and your goals for the next twelve months. Determine your long-term goals first. Set short-term goals based on your long-term goals. Keeping your purpose in mind, break your one year goals in to monthly and weekly goals. Set reasonable goals. You don't want to set yourself up for failure right off the bat by attempting to do too much. Be realistic so you will feel a sense of accomplishment when you reach each of your goals.

Scheduling Units and Lessons

Heart of Wisdom gives you a four-year plan. To plan the units you want to complete each year begin with a calendar. Use our chart as a guide and colored highlighter to mark off the amount of time you will spend in each unit. Once you get a general idea of how many weeks you will spend in a unit, you will need to decide which lessons you want to complete. You can do them all or choose to skip some—**YES you can skip lessons.** School teachers do it all the time and rarely finish a book in a school year. You can skip a full lesson, but please don't skip any of the four steps.

Be flexible. All the Holy Spirit to lead. You may plan on spending four week on a unit and find out it turns in to an eight week unit. You may discover reading through the Bible in one year is too fast and feel better changing to a two year through the Bible reading plan. Continually pray and give your schedule to God.

Here are broad frameworks for first year studies. A typical school year consists of 180 days or 36 weeks. Options 1 and 3 are based on 32 weeks schedule. Options 2 and 4 are based on a year round 48 week schedule. The only difference in Options 3 and 4 is that the history and science units are alternated. All the schedules give you the flexibility to extend any unit for several days or even weeks.

Option 1
Based on a typical 180-day schedule.
2–3 lessons per day (32 weeks)

Adam to Abraham	2 Weeks
Mesopotamia	2 Weeks
Ancient Egypt	4 Weeks
Ancient Israel	4 Weeks
Ancient Greece	3 Weeks
Ancient Rome	4 Weeks
The Messiah	3 Weeks
Creation	2 Weeks
Light	2 Weeks
Energy	2 Weeks
Matter	2 Weeks
Motion	2 Weeks
Electricity	2 Weeks
	32 Weeks

Option 2
Based on a typical year-round schedule.
1–2 lessons per day (49 weeks)

Adam to Abraham	4 Weeks
Mesopotamia	3 Weeks
Ancient Egypt	6 Weeks
Ancient Israel	7 Weeks
Ancient Greece	5 Weeks
Ancient Rome	7 Weeks
The Messiah	4 Weeks
Creation	3 Weeks
Light	2 Weeks
Energy	2 Weeks
Matter	2 Weeks
Motion	2 Weeks
Electricity	2 Weeks
	49 Weeks

Option 3
Based on a typical 180-day schedule.
2–3 lessons per day (32weeks)

Creation	2 Weeks
Adam to Abraham	2 Weeks
Light	2 Weeks
Mesopotamia	2 Weeks
Energy	2 Weeks
Ancient Egypt	4 Weeks
Ancient Israel	4 Weeks
Matter	2 Weeks
Ancient Greece	3 Weeks
Motion	2 Weeks
Ancient Rome	4 Weeks
Electricity	2 Weeks
The Messiah	3 Weeks
	32 Weeks

Option 4
Based on a typical year-round schedule.
1–2 lessons per day (49 weeks)

Creation	3 Weeks
Adam to Abraham	4 Weeks
Light	2 Weeks
Mesopotamia	3 Weeks
Energy	2 Weeks
Ancient Egypt	6 Weeks
Ancient Israel	7 Weeks
Matter	2 Weeks
Ancient Greece	3 Weeks
Motion	2 Weeks
Ancient Rome	7 Weeks
Electricity	2 Weeks
The Messiah	4 Weeks
	49 Weeks

How Much Time for One Lesson?

The time you spent in a lesson should be based on your child's delights. You can spend as little as ten to fifteen minutes in a lesson or several days, or even weeks. Let me use another meal analogy. Some times fast food is quick and easy and sufficient, while at other times it may be appropriate to enjoy a nine course feast. Some days you'll complete two to four lessons, while another lesson may take you a three days. Do not let the amount of available resources and activities make you think you have to spend all day in one lesson. The resources and activities provided are only options to choose from.

Remember, the goal to create a love of learning and to learn how to to learn. Your child will be learning while researching whether the topic is pyramids in Egypt, bread baking, turtles, or car repair. Help them to learn to learn by researching and writing about the topics that interest them. The chart below refers to students grades 4–12.

	Amount of Time	Teacher Involvement
Setp 1	This step usually takes five to ten minutes (unless you choose to watch a video).	The teacher is most active in this step.
Step 2	The resource you choose will determine the amount of time in this step. Heart of Wisdom lessons provide a large number of resource options. You may choose to read a few paragraphs from a resource or an entire book. You might choose to watch a video or use the Internet surfing several pages.	The teacher should interact with younger students (read aloud or use the Internet). Older students can work alone; however most students do better with interaction.
Step 3	The activity you choose will determine the amount of time in this step. Heart of Wisdom lessons provide a large number of activity options. An activity like copying a paragraph will take a few minutes. An activity like writing a research paper will take several days.	The teacher is passive at this step unless the student needs direction. The student is active working on the activity.
Step 4	The activity you choose in Step 3 will determine the amount of time in Step 4. The range will be from ten minutes correcting copy work to place in a notebook or sharing but can be up to an hour or more for rewrites or creating a complex display.	The teacher spends some time assessing the work; the student will spend the most time correcting and sharing the work.

Practical Time Management Tips

Here are some practical tips on how to manage the various tasks that all homeschooling moms face: housework, cooking, teaching, mothering, personal time, and being a good wife—not to mention getting a decent night's sleep every once in a while! For those who need more creative time-management skills, try the following:

- A woodcutter has to come out of the woods to sharpen his ax. Planning saves time. Set a specific time to work in your planning notebook each week (for example, twenty minutes each Monday). Review your notebook plans and make necessary changes. Make prioritized lists and be flexible enough to adapt to changing priorities. It is critical that you take this time to plan. My husband and I make and compare our "To Do" lists often. It only takes ten minutes and it make a big difference on what we get done. Just creating the list removes stress and gives me a sense of direction. Planning is half the battle—use your planning notebook!

- Simplify your life. Put systems in place to keep your house as neat as possible. • Get organized. If you are not not naturally organized, you can learn to be. There are several good books to teach you how to organize your housework, your paper work and your time. De-clutter your home. Find a place for everything, and keep everything in its place. If you can't find a place for it, you may not need it. See the end of this chapter for recommended reading. Above all else, lower your expectations! Everything does not have to be perfect.

- Ask your husband to pitch in. As my Grandmother says, "Many hands make light work." I mange our home well because .my husband helps without being asked. He is a smart man. He knows team work results in a less stressful and happier mom—therefore everyone is happier.

- Enlist the help of your children—especially when they're young! Children like to help. Giving a young child a chore like snapping beans while you're making dinner or dusting when you are cleaning keeps them busy and happy. Don't nag your children about helping around the house. Set firm instructions—with consequences if they are not followed—and then follow through. Make a chore chart for each child.

- Simplify your meals: many times, elaborate, difficult-to-prepare meals are the least healthy for your family. Keep your recipes simple, and use good, wholesome ingredients. Encourage your children and husband to help in the kitchen. Create a menu planner in your planning notebook. List your family's favorite meals on one Master Menu List; from this list make two or three weekly menus you can rotate. Use the weekly menus to make shopping lists. Adapt weekly menus as needed. Consider "freezer cooking:" Make mega portions when you cook chili, spaghetti sauce, vegetable soups, ground beef with onions, etc. to freeze. Several books on freezer cooking are available at Homeschool-Books.com. Click on Woman's Issues/Cooking.

• Don't try to do too much at one time. Focus on one area at a time. Instead of tackling the entire house, work on a room at a time, or one drawer at a time.

• Take a half an hour now and then to do some of the "dirty" jobs that you keep putting off—you know the jobs I mean. Take the time to stop and clean one window or straighten up one drawer, and then get back to your usual schedule.

• Be careful not to waste time—too much television, Internet, shopping, phone conversations, even church work can get out of balance. etc. Learn to say no!

• Begin each school year early to allow time to take breaks when needed, or better yet conduct school year-round. Year round schooling has many advantages.You can take breaks when you need to. Children form habits of learning and don't have to spend one-two months relearning what was forgotten during the summer.

• Don't think that you have to tackle fifty projects a year to be productive. not naturally organized. Prioritize what's most important to you and realize you may only be able to accomplish the top one or two, or that it may take longer than you'd like to get them all done.

• Don't go overboard on field trips or support group meetings. Pray about your outside activities.

• Keep things simple! Allow your children the time they need to learn. Teach one skill at a time and let them practice it, a little at a time, building upon their new skills. This give children confidence in their abilities and makes learning fun.

Review your homeschooling from time to time. Ask yourself these questions:

• Am I overdoing it?
• Is my focus on spiritual development?
• Am I being consistent with the children?
• Do I need to take some time to work on their manners? To teach them to be more responsible?
• Am I unconsciously trying to complicate something simple?

• Am I committed to too many outside activities?
• What can I eliminate in my life right now?
• What is essential?
• Would I do better to postpone certain projects until later? Next month? Next summer? Next year?
• Would Jesus do it differently?

There is no such thing as a perfect homeschool, but with prayer, a refocusing of your priorities, and a determination to follow God's will for your family, it can be done, and it can be done well. And the rewards will be well worth the effort.

Psalm 39 gives a proper perspective of time. In David's protest to God, he said, *You have made my days as handbreadths, and my age is as nothing before You* (v. 5). He meant that, to an eternal God, our time on earth is brief. And He doesn't want us to waste it. When we do, we throw away one of the most precious possessions He gives us. Each minute is an irretrievable gift—an unredeemable slice of eternity.

Suggested Reading

Clutter's Last Stand by Don Aslett
Save your sanity—not your sacks, souvenirs, and old, worn-out shoes. The author shows how clutter can begin to crowd not only our basements and attics, but also our relationships and our personal growth. He gives us the courage to sift, sort, and toss, pinpointing problem areas and offering practical ideas for getting rid of unnecessary clutter and cutting it off at its source.

How to Strengthen Your Faith by Andrew Murray ⊶
Andrew Murray covers every possible reason why you might struggle to obtain the full measure of faith that God has for you, and he explains how to increase your faith until you have erased all doubts. No matter where you are in faith, this book will take you farther along the way to God.

Messie No More by Sandra Felton's
This book includes foolproof strategies that can help even the most frazzled homemaker overcome disorganization. With humor and much-needed affirmation, she sheds light on emotional and physical reasons for messiness and shows why most organizational systems don't work for Messies. Contains the basis for a permanent change in those who long for an orderly home.

More Hours in My Day by Emilie Barnes ⊶
This book is for time-challenged, stressed people who long for even a few extra minutes to take a breath, get focused, and get organized. It's packed with creative ideas gleaned from the thousands of women the author has spoken to at conferences, retreats, and seminars. Based on the foundation that God redeems and blesses our hours when we apply His godly priorities and principles to our lives. Save financial and natural resources, find freedom in daily scheduling, bring order to everything from paperwork to travel details to our prayer lives.

For more on this topic see http://homeschool-books.com. Click on: Christian Living/ Faith and Woman's Issues (see the Home Organization and Cooking categories).

Section 5

Unit Studies and Resources

Creating and/or Purchasing Unit Studies

In the Introduction I used a cookbook analogy to describe the Heart of Wisdom teaching approach. I'll continue this analogy to help you decide between creating or purchasing unit studies. You have three options:

1. Purchase Heart of Wisdom unit studies.

2. Create your own unit studies.

3. Purchase unit studies from another publisher.

You need to invest time and money for your child's education. You can save money by investing time and creating your own unit studies, or you can spend money and save time by purchasing unit studies. However, not all unit studies are alike. Some require minimal preparation, some are only a list of activities or a simple outline and require hours of lesson planning. Deciding to create or purchase a unit studies can be compared to baking a cake.

Cake	Unit Study
If you have the time, creativity and decorating materials, and if you enjoy baking, you can make your cake from scratch.	If you have the time and desire (or limited funds) you can create your own unit studies with lesson plans.
If you lack the time or creativity, you can use a cake mix. You will spend a little more than making your cake from scratch, but you will save time not having to gather and mix the ingredients.	For a small investment you can purchase unit studies that will list activities for you. You create your own lesson plans based on the provided activities. Your time investment will depend on the unit study you choose and and activities it includes.
If you are pressed for time or just don't care for baking, you may find the best solution is to skip the preparation and pick up a cake at a bakery. It will cost more money, but your only time investment is in the shopping and serving	You can invest in a preplanned Heart of Wisdom unit study that is completely laid out, requiring minimal preparation (less than 30 minutes a week).

Creating a Unit Study

Someone may wonder, if all the work has been done for you, why would you want to create a unit study? There are several reasons you might want to create your own study:

- You may find creating your own unit study exciting and challenging.

- You may want or need to save money by creating unit studies.

- You may want to study a topic based on your child's delights that is not in the Heart of Wisdom four-year plan. Examples: quilting, horses, airplanes, trains, baking, holidays, a specific country, presidents, your state, etc.

- You may be ready to work on topics that are not yet available from Heart of Wisdom.

- Parents and children can learn together by creating a unit study together.

There is a television show on the Food Network hosted by Sandra Lee, titled Semi-Homemade. The Semi-Homemade technique of combining fresh ingredients with specially selected store-bought mixes and prepared foods will enable you to create dishes that taste as if they were made 100% from scratch—but are created in a fraction of the time. Sandra's recipes allow you to skip a few steps. I've been writing unit studies for almost twenty years. The methods I once used have changed, and I now have a system that allows you to bypass a few steps, making it easy for anyone to create a unit study.

Involve Your Children in the Preparation

As discussed in the "Hebrew Education Model" chapter children learn best by doing. When a homeschool mother prepares a unit study, she learns a tremendous amount about the topic herself. If you and your child plan the unit together, you both learn a tremendous amount about the topic. In this process children learn to research, classify, sort, reason, organize, connect, etc., by being involved in the preparation step. Granted, it would be easier to plan a lesson by yourself, but you would miss a valuable teaching opportunity.

If you decide to use a preplanned unit study, you can involve your student in the planning process by allowing them the opportunity to participate in choosing the lessons, resources and activities. They will be missing some of the advantages listed above, but will spend more time in the lessons involved in research and writing activities—which is also learning by doing.

Creating A Unit Study: Phases

To differentiate between the steps in creating the unit study and the four-step lessons, I will use the term phase instead of steps. In the next pages I will give you directions and examples for the seven phases involved in planning a unit study.

Phase 1. Pray and seek God's wisdom and guidance.
Phase 2. Decide on a topic.
Phase 3. Decide on a schedule.
Phase 4. Create the list of lessons.
Phase 5. Make a list of resources.
Phase 6. Create vocabulary lists.
Phase 7. Create four steps for each lesson.

Phase 1: The Most Important Step

Before you do anything else, pray for guidance. Ask God for direction on choosing a topic. Ask Him if this is really what He wants you to spend your time on. Should you spend your time creating this unit, or can you find a source that's already created? Is this a topic based on your child's delight? I begin each unit study in prayer seeking direction. God always leads me to wonderful spiritual lessons I would have never dreamed of.

Everything in God's world reveals God—every period in history, every element of creation (science topics). All of creation teaches us something about God and the response He expects from us. Pray for direction and ask God to show you how you and your children can come to know Him better through the unit study. Continue praying throughout your preparation.

Phase 2: Decide On A Topic

The next step is to decide on your unit. You can follow the Heart of Wisdom four-year curriculum plan (page 260) or go off on another topic. Don't let fear keep you glued to a state's scope and sequence. Remember the goal is to create a love of learning and to teach your child based on God's will, not the state's standards. I use the Heart of Wisdom four-year plan as a guide, but have no trouble changing my plan.

For example, I have a friend from Africa who began sharing about her country with my children. I noticed a spark of delight in them, so we began a mini-unit study on Africa. I spent about two hours planning a unit using the methods described here, and we immersed ourselves in Africa for two weeks.

Phase 3: Decide On A Schedule

In the "Scheduling by Faith" chapter we discussed scheduling in depth. How much time do you have to complete this unit study? The number of lessons will depend on your objectives and on the amount of time you plan on spending in the unit. I like to design lessons that usually take between 30 minutes to 2 hours per day (depending on the ages of the children). Remember these are not one-hour school subjects. You will be covering a main subject (history, science, or life skill) as well as Bible, writing, spelling, vocabulary, geography, economics, etc. If you school the typical 180 days, plan on completing two lessons per day (although a delight lesson may take several days). If you school year round you will have much more flexibility. A twenty-lesson unit study should take about two to three weeks give or take. You need to stay flexible to make changes as you work through the studies. There may be days you fly through three lessons, and times one lesson will take three days. Pray as you go and follow your children's sparks.

The "Scheduling by Faith" chapter in this book provides a suggested number of weeks for each unit listed in the Heart of Wisdom four-year plan. This four-year plan is only a guide to help you plan your year. It is based on a 180-day school schedule. You'll need to adapt the four-year plan to add units of delight as we did when we jumped off the schedule to study Africa—we homeschool all year so I can easily add several delight units to the basic plan.

One of the greatest advantages of homeschooling is having the flexibility to follow your child's delights. Once you get into a tasty unit, don't be afraid to extend it for a few days or even weeks once you see the spark. We all thoroughly enjoyed the Africa unit and we all wanted to learn more. Ever since the formal planned unit study has been over my children have continued to read and ask about Africa to this day. By allowing myself the freedom to go off my normal schedule I met one of my main goals—my children are not only learning to learn—they love to learn!

> By allowing myself the freedom to go off my normal schedule I met one of my main goals!—my children are not only learning to learn—they love to learn!

You need not do one unit from beginning to end, either. You can change your schedule based on your family's agenda. The horse unit study example in the next few pages will show you how lessons can easily turn from a two-week study into a two-month study if you see the spark. You also need to stay open to changes based on things happening in the world or in your family. Teaching them along the way (Deuteronomy 6) is about teaching from life. Examples:

- When I found out our support group planned a field trip to a weather station, I delayed our unit study on weather to coincide with the scheduled tour.

- My daughter created a unit study on plants to use with her sons. She began the unit by planting a vegetable garden. The time from planting the garden until they saw the vegetables took several weeks. She had the flexibility to bounce in and out of the plant unit study based on the garden's progress (studying sowing during the planting time and reaping during the harvest time).

- Turn a daily Bible reading into an mini-unit study. Branch off into an in-depth study on a character like David, Samson, Ruth or Paul.

- Turn a problem into a study. A child's weakness in an area may dictate the need to study kindness and mercy, controlled speech, truthfulness, slander, etc. (*The Narrated Bible* divides the Proverbs into these types of categories).

- You may want to change your schedule based on world news. The disastrous 2004 tsunami would have been a good time to teach your children about intercessory prayer, and to focus on world geography, which could lead to a mini-unit study on another country, world religions, natural disasters, etc.

- You may want to plan units around your vacation. A Washington, D.C., trip could lead to a two week mini-unit study before you leave to visit the sites.

- A vacation to the beach with planned museum trips could be a delightful addition to the oceanography or ocean animals units.

- There is no better time to study the reproductive system then when Mother is expecting another baby. Trips to the doctor or midwife can be considered field trip learning adventures.

- An accident such as a broken bone could lead to a study of the skeletal system.

Some people thrive on flexibility, while others feel more comfortable with firm schedules. I'll share with you what broke me from rigid schedules. When I first began homeschooling, I thought we had to do school at home, i.e. sitting at a desk, looking and acting like traditional school. I was so indoctrinated with a public school mentality, it literally took a volcano to open my eyes!

During our second year of homeschooling, my family went to Costa Rica for six weeks. I took suitcases full of textbooks with us and taught school for hours every day. The second week, our school lesson included the topic of volcanoes—and then it dawned on me how ridiculous I was being—we were only a few miles from a large volcano, and there we were, sitting in a small room, reading about a volcano in a textbook! To my children's delight, I packed up all the books and we began exploring Costa Rica. We visited a live volcano, sugar plantations, zoos, ranches, beaches, got involved with the presidential election, shared Christ, began a vacation Bible school, visited fascinating museums and historical sights, and much more. To this day is it remains one of our fondest learning experiences. Breaking out of the traditional school mindset and learning from life is full of rewards. Books are excellent sources of ideas, theories, strategies, etc., but they are only a prelude to, not a substitute for, practical application.

Phase 4: Create a List of Lessons

I can share one valuable secret with you that will show you how to save hours of preparation on a unit study. It's a very simple approach that I wish I had found years ago. Many outstanding book publishers have done the hard part for you by designing and laying out information-type reference books. There is no reason to reinvent the wheel. Instead of spending hours digging through boring scopes and sequences, you can just use a table of contents from a good reference book to make a list of lessons in minutes. By using this method you will cover more material than is listed in any state scope and sequence. Try planning a unit study with this method and then comparing it to a scope and sequence. You'll be surprised at the results.

In the next few pages we'll look at an example unit study using the topic of horses. This is a unit study you might decide to do outside of Heart of Wisdom's four-year plan. The Heart of Wisdom unit study on animals includes a lesson on horses but does not go into the detail you can go into on your own. Start by visiting the Internet or the library and looking through books about horses. Here is an example of the table of contents from *Eyewitness Horses*.

Use the table of contents from a book like this to create a mind map with your child. Once you have exhausted all your own efforts, use the mind map to create a list of lessons and objectives.

There are several options possible, based on the mind map, and depending on your schedule. Begin brainstorming with broad topics and more to more specific topics. If you'd like, you can get into intricate detail.

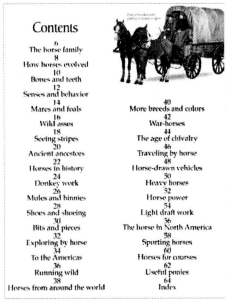

Tables of Contents from *Eyewitness Horses*

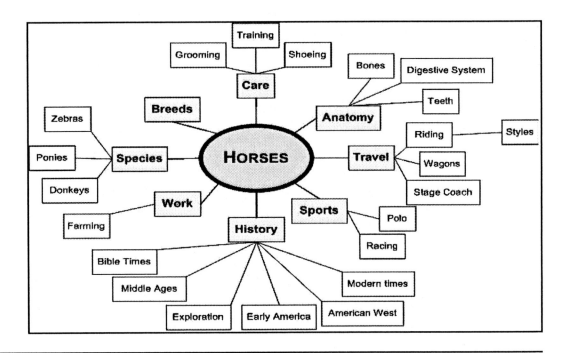

For example, you can make "Horses In History" a topic instead of a lesson, and make a lesson for each time period:

1. Species
2. Breeds
3. Travel
4. Sports
5. Work
6. Anatomy
7. Care
8. Horses in Mesopotamia
9. Horses in Ancient Egypt
10. Horses in Ancient Israel
11. Horses in Ancient Greece
12. Horses in Ancient Rome
13. Horses in the Middle Ages
14. Horses in the Exploration
15. Horses in the Early America
16. Horses in the American West
17. Horses in the Modern Times

If you discover one of the lessons is a real delight for your children you can break it into into more specific lessons. Example: the "Horses in the American West" lesson can be divided into the following lessons:

1. Native Americans (another culture)

2. Pony Express (communication)

3. Stage Coaches (Travel, transportation, communication, shipping)

4. Cowboys or Life on a Ranch (occupations)

5. Wild West Shows (Entertainment, recreation)

Phase 5: Choose Your Resources

Before you divide your lessons into the four steps, you'll need to create a list of the resources you want to use. While you make your list try to include:

1. One or more informational-type reference books (with page numbers and notes)
2. A novel or a biography.
3. A field trip.
4. A movie, video or educational program.

A good basic home library will make your unit study planning much easier. Once our home library was substantial I could find something on almost every topic.

The following is a list of books I found on horses in my home library:

1. *Dorling Kindersley Animal Encyclopedia* (30, 163, 204–206).●━

2. *Kingfisher History Encyclopedia* (70, 74, 120, 134, 146–148, 170–171, 218). ☞

3. *Kingfisher Illustrated History of the World* [earlier version of the above] (100, 101, 162, 131, 181, 192, 209, 230, 292, 362; introduction of horses in America). ☞

4. *Nelson's Encyclopedia of the Bible* (92, 229, 254). ☞

5. *Manners and Customs of the Bible* (95, 272; idolatry).

6. *Unlocking the Mysteries of Creation* (104 horse fossils). ☞

7. *A Closer Look at the Evidence* by Richard Kleiss (105, 169, 173, 356; problems with horse evolution).

8. *What Is Creation Science?* by Henry Madison Morris (52, 73, 98, 131, 143; Huxley estimated the odds against the evolution of the horse are $10^{100,000}$ to one).

9. *Black Beauty* by Anna Sewell. (novel)

10. *Misty of Chincoteague* by Marguerite Henry. (novel)

You probably won't have the number of books in your library as I have in mine (I've been collecting books for a very long time) but those book-marked with a ☞ in the above list are basic reference books I think should be in every homeschooler's library. I include a list of such basic references in the Resource section.

You can use the list in the back of this book to find resources for every age level for the themes listed in the Heart of Wisdom four-year curriculum plan, but you'll have to do a bit more digging if you want to study another topic.

Videos: Here are a few video suggestions from *Learning With The Movies* by Beth Holland. (See details in the "Choosing and Using Resources" chapter.): *Black Beauty, Galent Bess, King of the Wild Stallions, Man from Snowy River, The Horsemasters* and *National Velvet*.

Field Trip Ideas: Assateague Island (island for wild ponies, a two-hour drive from our home), a horse ranch, a stable, tack shop, a rodeo, a horse show, etc.

Experts: Interview people that work with horses: a police officer that rides a police horse, a veterinarian, horse trainer, a jockey a farmer, etc.

Apprenticeship: Offer voluntary services in exchange for learning how to saddle, groom, ride, feed, or exercise a horse. Take photographs for your portfolio.

Phase 6: Create Vocabulary Lists

Create your vocabulary list from the index in the same book you used to create your list of lessons (another big time saver). Or type in "vocabulary words" and the subject topic into a search engine to find words to create your vocabulary lists. You know which words your children aren't familiar with. Once you create a list of words you can make a crossword word puzzle at Discovery School online see http://school.discovery.com/puzzlemaker.

Phase 7: Write the Lessons Using the Four Steps

Once you have your list of lessons, create a list with space to jot down notes for the four steps. You may want to review the "Learning Styles and the Four-Step Process" chapter.

Step 1. Excite! Make it interesting.

Do *not* skip Step 1! What questions can you ask your child to find out what he or she already knows or believes or would like to know about the subject? What else can you think of that will help your child get excited about the topic? Can you share a personal experience? Is there a video or web site from your resources that maybe useful?

Here are a few ideas for Step 1:

- Give a metaphor (mashal)
- Explain metaphor (nimshal)
- Brainstorm and discuss
- Make a mind map

- Watch a video
- Ask questions
- Go on a field trip
- Share experience(s)

- Create a list of questions
- Make a list
- Prepare for an interview
- Contrast and compare

Step 2. Examine. Find out the facts.

Make a list of the resources you will use, beginning with resources you have on hand. Once I decide on a unit study topic, I go through my home library and collect each book that has any mention of that topic. Then I use Post-it notes to mark the relevant pages, or make a list with page numbers and notes. See the next chapter from information on resources (where to get, how to use, etc). Here is a list of the types of resources you'll be using in Step 2:

- Reference books
- Novels
- Historical fiction
- Biographies

- Internet sites
- Videos
- Encyclopedias
- Educational television

- Software
- Interviewing an expert

Step 3. Do something with what was learned.

This is a creative step for the teacher. The following pages give several ideas. It's best to choose two or three options and allow your child to chose from them. Examples:

- Add to a time line book.
- Answer questions.
- Be a TV or radio reporter and give a report.
- Complete a lab sheet.
- Conduct an interview.
- Conduct an investigation.
- Contrast and compare.
- Construct puppets and present a show.
- Cook a dish or meal.
- Copy a Bible passage.
- Copy a paragraph.
- Copy illustrations.
- Create a display using your computer.
- Create a photograph journal
- Create a postcard.
- Create a diorama.
- Create a monologue.
- Create a worksheet.
- Create an outline.
- Create a mini-comic book.
- Define vocabulary words.
- Design costumes for dolls.
- Draw a comic strip.
- Explore and collect.
- Expand your research.
- Find and appreciate art.
- Illustrate a story.
- Illustrate using your favorite medium (colored pencils, chalk, paint, etc.).
- Interview a character.
- Look up words.
- Make a biography box.
- Make a chart.
- Make a children's book.
- Make a collage.
- Make a flow chart.
- Make a game.
- Make a line graph.
- Make a list of character traits.
- Make a map.
- Make a mini-book.
- Make a mobile.
- Make a model.
- Make a poster.
- Make a salt-dough map.
- Make a travel brochure.
- Make a venn diagram.
- Make an educational display.
- Make up questions.
- Narrate verbally or in writing.
- Perform in costume.
- Prepare an oral report.
- Read aloud.
- Read two books on the same subject and compare and contrast them.
- Sketch a picture.
- Take dictation.
- Tell five things you learned.
- Think and discuss.
- Write a biography sketch.
- Write a book review.
- Write a description.
- Write a diary entry.
- Write a full description (physical, emotional, relational).
- Write a job application.
- Write a journal entry.
- Write a letter to a historical person.
- Write a letter to the author.
- Write a scene.
- Write a short story.
- Write a soliloquy.
- Write a story for younger children in picture book form.
- Write a summary.
- Write a summary of your experiment.
- Write a synopsis.
- Write about what you learned.
- Write an article.
- Write an essay.
- Write an obituary.
- Write an original song.
- Write the plot of the story as if it were a story on the evening news.

Step 4. Excel. Pull it all together.

Correct all written work and share what was learned. Sample Step 4 activities:

- Correct all written work to demonstrate correct spelling.
- Record any misspelled words in your Spelling Notebook.
- Correct all written work to demonstrate correct and effective use of grammar and punctuation.
- Add the rules for all punctuation and grammar errors you corrected to your Writing Notebook.
- Add to your Vocabulary Notebook any new words or terms encountered in this lesson, along with definitions.

- Use each word or term in a sentence, either orally or in writing.
- Add corrected written work, maps, or any illustrations to your Portfolio.
- Add any important people or events to your Time Line Book.
- Share with a friend or family member your Time Line Book or Portfolio.
- Share with a friend or family member an activity you completed for this lesson. Explain to them what you have learned.

Help on the Internet

Each Heart of Wisdom unit study contains links to dozens of related Internet resources. If you create your own unit study you can borrow from ideas from theme related sites online that include lesson plans, clip art and activities.

See Heart of Wisdom Theme Links http://Heartofwisdom.com/themes.htm

Choosing and Using Resources

Building a home library will ultimately save you a tremendous amount of time and effort. A well-equipped home library to a homeschooler is like a well-equipped kitchen to a cook. How much time and effort is saved by having the right ingredients and not having to substitute or stop what you're doing to go get the right ingredients? (Is there no end to these food analogies?) Explain this to your husband by comparing it to having the right tool for a job in his toolbox.

A large part of the appeal of unit studies is flexibility. Choosing resources should be as individual as choosing your home décor—it will vary from family to family depending on homeschool budget, time available, the number of children that will be using this program, and personal interests.

Many lessons in Heart of Wisdom unit studies contain enough resource materials in themselves which negates the need for further research. However, several recommendations are included for those who desire to branch out and learn more. We provide hundreds of resources (and a select number of key resources) to choose from. Don't think of this choice as overwhelming—think of it as an opportunity to learn more about your students' interests (delights).

I have been homeschooling for many years with many children and I have used many of the same books over and over through the years. I began using books like the *Kingfisher History Encyclopedia, Reader's Digest ABCs of the Human Body*, and *Usborne Book of Science*, with all my children 15+ years ago, and I continue to use them through the year. I've used *The Narrated Bible, Nelson's Illustrated Bible Encyclopedia* and/or *Victor's Journey Through the Bible* almost daily since they became available.

A $30 investment in a good reference book comes out to pennies per child per year. For example: as of the writing of this book I have four boys at home, ages 13, 11, 5, and 3. I purchased *Dorling Kindersley's Animal Encyclopedia* eight years ago for about $30.00. This wise investment has paid off over and over. I used it as the key resource for an animal unit study with my 13- and 11-year-old eight years ago. Now, my three- and five-year-olds climb on the couch together with this giant book every day, and they ask me to read to them from it every night. It would not be an overstatement to say they spend three to four hours a week looking at pictures in this book. I have not done a formal study on animals with these two boys they can each name more animals and know more about animal classifications and geography than most children their age.

Good homeschool resources are great investments and can be used over and over for generations. Eventually my resources will be used by my grandchildren. One of my daughters married a homeschool student and her mother-in-law gave her many of the books she now uses to teach her three boys! Resources are great investments.

Utilizing the Library and/or Purchasing Resources

Utilizing the library can save you a ton of money and you'll also find lots of interesting resources you may not have thought about. When I first began creating my own unit studies I had four school-aged children and one preschooler. We went to the library often and brought home baskets of books each week but now that we have an extensive home library we don't go have to go to the public library as often.

Remember, library books are only free if you return them on time. I could have bought a few good books for my home library with the money I spent in fines. Try to keep books you check out in one location so they are easy to collect for the return. We use a large wicker basket in the family room. If your library books have cards in the back, remove all the cards when you get home and place a rubber band around them. This helps you know how many books you need to return as well as the date they should returned by.

I have a one important guideline about using the library—I never go to the library with a crawling baby or a toddler because they are too difficult to manage and keep quiet in a public library. (Library trips are doable with small babies though; you can place them in a sling or a stroller to help keep them quiet). Once my older children were old enough to baby-sit, I would leave the toddlers at home with them and run to pick up books by myself.

How do you decide when to use the library and when to purchase the resource you need? First you need to ask yourself, "Do I have enough in my home library to cover the topic adequately?" If you don't have what you need on hand, make a decision about purchasing a book based on the following questions:

1. Can we afford it within our current budget?

2. Is this a book we will use again?

3. Is this a book on a topic that delights my child? (if so, the answer to the second question will be Yes.)

4. Is this resource critical to this unit, but not available from the library or inter-library loan? If so, is there another alternative?

5. Can I borrow the book?

If you don't have enough resources on hand, you can visit the library for resources. If you can't find what you need at the library, ask for an inter-library loan. Also, look in the video section for related videos, and use the library computer to find articles in journals and magazines.

Media resources, including movies, television shows, (available on TV or videos), the Internet, and computer software can enhance your home library.

Reading the Classics

The Heart of Wisdom teaching approach recommends immersing your children in living books, commonly known as classical literature, but we believe you should read the greatest classic—the Bible, which is the only real, literal living book—daily, and attempt to read several classics throughout the year.

What is a classic? The answer depends on who you ask. In a broad sense, the term classic is applied to anything accepted either as a model of excellence or as a work of enduring cultural relevance and value. The books are very different in Heart of Wisdom's classical literature list compared with the classics recommended by classical education.

Classics According to Classical Education

Encarta Encyclopedia defines classical education as the study of Greek and Roman literature, one of the oldest forms of education known. In classical education a classic is any ancient Greek or Roman literary work of the first or highest quality.

The modern classical education approach focuses on "the Great Books of the Western World" (GBWW). Virtually every book in this collection is required reading in liberal arts programs, which include works of art, science, philosophy, poetry, prose and history from the time of the Greeks until the early 20th century. Plato, Herodotus, Virgil, and Aristotle are some of the main authors. This list was originally compiled in 1952 by an editorial board headed by Britannica Editors' Editor in Chief, Mortimer J. Adler. They believed these books to be the core of Western learning and culture. The list includes both the Bible and Quran (Koran). Most of the books in this list were written by non-Christians, men like Aeschylus, Apollonius, Aquinas, Dewey, Euclid, Euripides, Freud, Hippocrates, Homer, Marx, Plato, Ptolemy, Thoreau, etc.

We need to ask ourselves, "Do we want to immerse our children with the ideas and beliefs in books men who promote false gods?" One popular proponent of classical education suggest that students at six years of age listen to a reading of Homer's *Iliad* and *Odyssey.* The *Iliad* and the *Odyssey* are two major epics that have survived from Greek antiquity. In the *Odyssey* Odysseus battles with gods and goddess and one eyed Cyclopes monsters. I see absolutely no value and a good possibility of nightmares in this suggestion. I see no difference in reading the *Odyssey, Harry Potter,* Edgar Allen Poe's or Stephen King's works. Would Jesus read the *Odyssey* to a six-year-old? Exodus 23:13 says *Do not invoke the names of other gods; do not let them be heard on your lips.* Choosing a book for your child is as important as approving of a friend your child will spend time with. Would you allow your child to spend time with a person practicing and promoting witchcraft?

A book labeled a classic by society does not automatically warrent reading it to our children. God's Word says it is wrong for believers to be yoked together with unbelievers. The very nature of the Christian demands that he be separated from that which is unholy. We must not be involved with that which will compromise our testimony or lead us into disobedience.

> ....*come out from among them, and be ye separate, saith the Lord...*—2 Corinthians 6:17

> ...*choose for yourselves today whom you will serve...as for me and my house, we will serve the LORD."*—Joshua 24:15

When you make compromises to lower your standards, usually due to fear (fear of not meeting someone else's standards) you are teaching your children to make the same type of compromises. Such compromises usually start small and insignificant, but then lead to a slow slide to more serious compromises resulting in a weakened conscience. This kind of educational compromise may develop a well trained mind, but what does it have to do with training our children to have mind of the Christ?

I'll repeat here what I said in an earlier chapter: There is one worthy reason to study the "Great Books"—from a critical viewpoint—like a doctor studying to be able to recognize disease. Mature students should learn of the historical implications of the classics from a biblical worldview. You can use *The Great Conversation: A Biblical Analysis of the Great Books of Western Civilization* to incorporate the study of classical authors into the Heart of Wisdom plan; see page 384.

See Three Approaches to Classical Education and Our Alternative on page 99–100.

Classics According to Heart of Wisdom

William Thayer addressed the importance of making wise choices in *Gaining Favor with God and Man*. He begins by quoting Henry Ward Beecher, nineteenth-century author as saying, "Books are the windows through which the soul looks out. A home without good books is like a room without windows. No man has a right to bring up his children without surrounding them with books, if he has the means to buy them. It is a wrong to his family. He cheats them. Children learn to read by being in the presence of books. The love of knowledge comes with reading and grows upon it, and the love of knowledge in a young mind is almost a warrant against the inferior excitement of passions and vices. But to select the books—that is the difficulty. Their number is legion." Thayer comments, "Here is an opportunity to exercise judgment, wise discrimination, and criticism, supplemented by all the good advice parents, guardians, and other friends can bestow. Under these circumstances the choice of books is not easy, but is one of the most important and difficult duties imposed upon the young or old. Yet it must be done, or reading will prove a curse."[1]

Our book selection should be based on Philippians 4:8: *whatsoever is true, honest, just, pure, lovely, of good report; if there be any virtue, and if there be any praise, think on these things*. Some would say Philippians 4:8 teaches against fiction but the word *true* in this passage refers to being honest or having integrity. The Hebrews in Bible times and Jesus used fictional parables to teach about God and integrity.

John Foster said, "Useless books we should lay aside, and make all possible good use of those from which we may reap some fruit."[2] Louisa May Alcott said this about reading: "Reading is a mental trip through an author's mind. Literature allows us to experience many things through the development of imagination. It allows us to go places we might not ever go. It expands the horizons of the mind and heart. It increases our awareness of time—past, present, and future." How well is your "house"—your mind furnished? Do you, like Louisa May Alcott, "enjoy your mind?" Literature helps us furnish our mental homes with permanent fixtures, with things 'wise and wonderful,' with scriptural objects of the beauty, which are the result of study and reflection on God's Word. What do we have in our house? Does it enrich ourself and others?"[3]

Reading Aloud

I strongly encourage reading aloud together daily with all children. Students are never too old to be read to. You should be reading the Bible together daily. Reading aloud is bonding. It strengthens vocabulary, language, grammar and writing. It makes us aware of other places and other lives. It creates life-long readers. Children understand at a higher level than they can read, and listening stimulates growth and understanding of vocabulary and language patterns.

Make reading time a daily habit like brushing your teeth. Hopefully, you have already committed to reading BIble aloud each morning. Choose another time of the day to read other books together. Most books for preschool to age six or so are short and can usually be read in one setting. Short-chapter books can be read in a few settings.

Make reading aloud time fun time. Add sound effects when appropriate, ask questions, etc. My son-in-law makes story time special. He tells my grandchildren Bible stories with different accents (Mexican, Indian, etc.). The accents aren't accurate but they are memorable.

Pre-readers listen to stories with enthusiasm and will ask you to read it again and again. Sometimes they memorize the story. Our family room and bedrooms each have a wicker laundry basket jam-packed with picture- and short-chapter books. We have a set reading time twice a day (before nap time and before bedtime) in which I read aloud five to ten books or stories to my younger children aged 3 and 5: the older children usually listen in. In the afternoon, we usually read aloud from a biography or novel from a theme we are studying.

If you are just starting to read to older children you may get a few groans. Start with something simple and short, reading 15 minutes or less, and increase the time according to the children's response.

Fiction or Nonfiction

For most people the term literature is often considered synonymous with stories. Stories are superb, exciting teaching tools. Historical fiction can make a time period real to a child. But don't discount non-fiction information books.

Boys tend to be reluctant readers more often than girls. According to a 1999 survey of more than 3,000 teens aged eleven through eighteen, fifty percent of girls said they read most often "just for the fun of it," as compared with only thirty-two percent of boys. Eighty-one percent of girls said they would read more if they had the time, as compared with only sixty percent of boys. Twelve percent of girls said they only read for school, as compared with twenty-two percent of boys, [which is] almost double.

My oldest son was a reluctant reader, or so I thought. I invested a huge amount of time trying to get him involved in fiction. I read aloud, I bought books on boys' topics, I took him to the library. I could not interest my son in a novel but he would spend hours in heavily illustrated nonfiction books. I finally realized that he just wasn't interested in fiction and that it was OK. Heavily illustrated information-type books are obviously educational but are almost never found in a classroom. It surprised me that most children prefer nonfiction. Studies dating from the 1950s onward show that most children often prefer nonfiction to fiction (Carter, 1988; Monson & Sebesta, 1991; Norvell, 1950; Purves & Beach, 1972). In *Information and Book Learning*, Margaret Meek stated:

> Critics of children's literature are apt to exclude nonfiction texts from their accounts of what children read. Yet for many young readers, these picture and caption books are their preferred texts. We know too little about how children actually read books with titles like *Roman Britain*, *Stars and Planets*, or *Light*. We need to know much more about how texts teach children about learning. We need critics who are prepared to judge the nature and quality of the engagement required by the nonfiction offered...

> For many students, reading per se is not the problem. What is the problem is the fact that they are forced to read materials that they have no interest in and no voice in selecting. They regard such school reading as an imposition, inconvenience, and interference with current reading interests.

Utilizing the Internet

The Internet has revolutionized education and will be a major part of our future. Students will be using the Internet in almost any profession they choose. The Internet is an open door to an enormous, exciting library. Not only is text information available, but also video clips, audio clips, and entire books.

The wealth of information available on the Internet can be overwhelming because a search for a single topic can lead to thousands of links; but Heart of Wisdom unit studies guide you to the best and most appropriate Web sites for each lesson. Internet addresses, also known as URLs, change frequently, so we have added a special feature on our Web site where you can report dead links and enable us to update them in our files.

Utilizing the Internet can create engaged, involved, and active learners. But remember, sitting in front of a computer reading through Web pages is only part of learning. Studies show that seventy-five percent of students need more than reading to retain information. Heart of Wisdom incorporates the Internet into the four-step process in each lesson. This process motivates students to learn, guides them to activities that help them organize the information that they have learned, and to use it for developing communication skills through writing assignments.

Avoiding the Dangers of the Internet

As wonderful as the Internet is for education, it can also be extremely dangerous. Pedophile predators lurk on children's Web sites looking for prey and pornographic and cultic Web sites are a simple click away. Strictly enforcing the rules below should curtail any potential problems.

Internet Rules:

- The number one rule—Never allow any child access to the Internet in a bedroom or private area. All computers in the home should be in view of all family members.

- Always monitor your child's Internet usage, either in person or with a monitoring device (explained later in this chapter)

- Draw clear guidelines so that children know it is not acceptable to visit sites you consider offensive.

- Check your Internet service provider's parental controls. These controls can block access to certain Web pages, chat rooms, newsgroups and other Internet resources that are not fit for children.

- Purchase blocking software for your computer. These programs block access to objectionable sites and prevent children from disclosing personal information. CYBERsitter and Net Nanny are two popular filtering software systems.

- Help your child pick out a screen name or user name. Avoid names that include a name and/or an age, such as Susie12.

- Never allow your child to use Instant messages and/or chat rooms unless you know the person they are speaking with and/or have monitoring devices in place.

- Advise your child not to give out personal information send pictures or make plans to meet anyone over the Internet.

- Warn your child not to join any mailing lists without your permission.

- Encourage your child not to visit Web sites or respond to any messages that seem strange or scary.

- Encourage your child to speak to you whenever he or she encounters anything that makes him or her uncomfortable.

- Install a monitoring device. Show your child how you can view every site he or she visits. This should discourage any curiosity searches.

Monitoring Devices

The dangers of the Internet are too prominent to simply trust your child. A monitoring device lets your child know that you can see every site and chat he has had on the computer. I believe everyone with Internet access should install monitoring software. Several versions are available; at the time of this writing Spector Pro is the best monitoring software available. It was selected as the Editors' Choice by the experts at PC Magazine. Spector Pro provides the equivalent of a digital surveillance tape so that you can see the exact sequence of everything your children have done on the computer. It contains seven integrated tools that record chats, instant messages, emails sent and received, web sites visited, keystrokes typed, programs launched, and peer-to-peer file searching and swapping. For more information on Spector Pro and more on Internet safety go to HeartofWisdom.com/Spectorpro.htm

In addition to monitoring and recording, Spector Pro has an advanced warning system that will inform you when a PC being monitored has been used in an inappropriate manner. Through the use of keywords that you specify, this program is on alert emailing you an immediate and detailed report of when, where and how a keyword was used—every time it is typed or appears on the PC, on a Web site or in an email.

If you use Internet Explorer or Netscape you might have tried monitoring with the browser's history. It's hard to monitor using this approach because children quickly learn how to erase where they have been. Spector Pro runs in stealth mode and cannot be detected. The only one who can alter the monitoring is the person who has the password.

Using the Internet at the Library

During the writing of this book, I checked out our library's Internet services. I'm glad I did so I can warn you. I was surprised to find two computer rooms. In one room the monitors were upright, but in the other room the monitors were inside a hole in the desk, so only the person using the computer could see the screen. My first thought was,

"How unusual! Maybe they are built like that to avoid neck strain." When I asked the librarian about the rooms, she explained the new situation to me. She said the library is more popular than ever because patrons now flock to public libraries (including the children's sections) to use these computers to access pornography on the Internet. The screens are hidden so as not to expose the pornography to other people visiting the library. Some libraries offer some filtered machines, but I was told that minors are frequently allowed to use unfiltered machines, and parental permission is seldom required.

If you plan to allow your child to use the library's computers for access to the Internet, be sure to find out if the computers have filters and how strict the rules are about allowing minors to use unfiltered machines.

Digital and Personal Video Recorders (TiVo)

Over the years we have tried to control the TV by various means (even getting rid of it) without much success. A new device called TiVo, which is both a DVR (digital video recorder) and a PVR (personal video recorder), is a fantastic resource for doing unit studies. TiVo is a box connected to your computer that records television shows of your choice to a hard drive (anywhere from 30 hours to hundreds of hours). TiVo automatically tunes to the right channel at the right time and records your show. Then you can watch the show whenever you have the time.

TiVo has become the answer for us. It gives you control of your television; you're no longer at the mercy of scheduling (or even commercials). TiVo insulates you from the undesirable features of TV and allows you to automatically record the programs you want for later viewing. We live outside of cable range so we have a satellite dish, and adding TiVo to our regular satellite charge is only six dollars per month—a worthy investment. TiVo also has a season pass option where you can record all the telecasts of a series (such as the *Magic School Bus, Assignment Discovery*, Charles Stanley's program, *In Touch*, or programs like *Mysteries of the Bible*) with a click of a button.

National Geographic, PBS, the Discovery Channel, the Learning Channel, the Science Channel, and the History Channel produce shows such as *NOVA, Assignment Discovery, Newton's Apple, Hands On History, Bill Nye the Science Guy,* and *Magic School Bus,* but it's been almost impossible to plan a schedule around the viewing times. Since we started using TiVo last year, educational television has become a major part of our school day.

For example, for this section on planning a horse unit study I went to my TiVo and typed in the key word "horse" (you can also search by title, actor or genre). Then I clicked "Upcoming Programs" and found the following shows available in the next ten days.

- *That's My Baby*; documentary; a Clydesdale gives birth.

- *Saddle Club*; series; horse information for kids, various topics.

- *Bend of the River*; 1952 movie starring James Stewart; farmers travel by wagon train from Oregon to California during the Gold Rush.

- *Purchasing a Performance Horse*; documentary.

- *Horse City*; national equine events; health issues, training, etc.

- *Down Under Horsemanship With Clinton Anderson*; documentary about working a cow horse ranch; Clinton teaches his horse, Scooter, his "head and poll" exercises.

- *Aiken: Much Ado About Horses*; horse culture in the town of Aiken, S.C.

- *Animal Miracles*; *documentary*; a horse helps a disabled girl.

As I previously mentioned, we recently did an unscheduled mini-unit on Africa. A quick TiVo search of Africa revealed the following shows available for viewing in the next ten days:

- *The History Channel: In Search of History: Dr. Livingstone, I Presume.* A thrilling look at Stanley's journey into Africa.

- *Africa, a Special Presentation of Nature*; a father and his son travel through the Sahara Desert to trade salt.

- *Africa's Deadly Dozen*; the black mamba is the most deadly of a multitude of venomous snakes found in Africa

- *Communities Building Community: Journey to South Africa*; Judy O'Bannon and other Indiana residents travel to South Africa to exchange ideas.

- *Discovery Channel: Nigel's Wild, Wild World.* Nigel Marven traveled to South Africa to meet some amazing and dangerous sharks.

Here is what I got from typing in "Egypt." (Remember, this is only what's showing in the next ten days.) You can see how this new technology can enhance any unit study.

- *Discovery Channel: Building the Great Pyramid.*

- *Curses of Ancient Egypt*; about the "mystery" of the "Ten Plagues."

- *Egypt's Golden Empire*; Egypt is united under Ahmose; Hatshepsut becomes the first female pharaoh; Thutmos III creates an empire.

- *Expedition Egypt*; the Temple of Karnak in southern Egypt; the role of religion in ancient Egyptian society.

- *Mummies: Tales From the Egyptian Crypts*; burial sites along the Nile; constructing the Pyramids; embalming processes.

Some of these programs aired at 2 and 3 a.m. but my TiVo recorded them. Once you record a program, you can keep it as long as you'd like. If you need to make space on your TiVo, you can record the show onto a videotape or DVD. This allows you to use TiVo to record resources months before you start a unit study.

Searching for Educational Television Vai the Internet

You can search educational television channels from their Internet sites for TV listing or worksheets and lesson plans to enhance your studies. We've created a list of links to education television channels and educational shows with Internet sites at http://Heartofwisdom.com/tv.htm

Videos

You can find a video for almost any topic by using *Learning with the Movies: A Guide to Education and Fun*. Beth Holland, a homeschool mom, created her own movie collection by taping movies she thought would be educational for her children. This comprehensive guide lists over 1,000 movies, divided into curriculum categories. Each movie description includes its release year, with a rating of one to five stars, and a brief description. It includes all historical periods, music/arts, biographies, family films, sports, science/nature, horses, medicine, literature, holidays, and more. Simply flip to the section you are studying to find an alphabetical list of videos.

You can also search educational television channels from their Internet sites for TV listing or worksheets and lesson plans to enhance your studies. We've created a list of links to education television channels and educational shows with Internet sites at http://Heartofwisdom.com/tv.htm

Resources

The books in this section are listed by theme with brief descriptions. This literature collection contains all you need to teach Bible, history, science, geography, and literature on every level for a full 12 years (repeating four years three times) with or without Heart of Wisdom unit studies. The Heart of Wisdom unit studies can guide you in using books in these lists with lesson plans and activities or you can create your own lesson plans using the ideas in this book.

We recommend a variety of popular homeschool resources so you can utilize the books already in your home library, and to help you build a good home library. You will have a good chance of finding one or more at your local library or homeschool group. We suggest a number of different books because books sometimes go out of print. Understand, you are never required to use all the resources recommended.

Key resources that we recommend in a homeschool library are marked with a ●—. Books with a ● are books recommended in several Heart of Wisdom unit studies. Books with a ★ are resources recommended in several units in one year. Books noted with a ◆ are resources recommended in several lessons in one unit. The N symbol indicates a novel or story.

If you are looking for a quick and easy way to build a good homeschool library with resources you will use over and over you'll want to invest in books marked with ● and many of the books marked with a ●— and consider all books marked with a ★.

Resources that Refer to Evolution

Whenever possible, you should use books that were written from a Christian worldview. We've marked these with a fish symbol. Unfortunately, there are not many highly visual information books from a Christian viewpoint available, so we have to adapt and use what is available. You can easily skip the evolution pages or use them as opportunities to explain to your children that some people believe in the theory of evolution, how and why they are wrong, and how and why we must be careful of such teachings. You should complete the Heart of Wisdom's *Creation: An Internet-Linked Unit Study* in order to have a good foundational understanding of evolution vs. creation before you have to deal with this topic in other areas.

Disclaimer

The books here and ages levels are listed as a guides. The views and opinions of the authors of the listed resources are not necessarily those of Heart of Wisdom. Please evaluate each book for yourself to see if the book is appropriate for your family's beliefs and your student's age level.

Where to Obtain the Resources

You can obtain resources we recommend at the library, through our Web site, http://Homeschool-books.com or through a homeschool supplier. Resources you will only use once you should obtain from a library.

Have you ever wondered why beautiful full-color books are only available from secular publishers that promote evolution and a secular worldview? In 2002, in the United States, sales of Christian products exceeded five billion dollars. Eighty-eight percent of these sales were made through secular companies. Only twelve percent were purchased from Christian businesses. The reason for this situation is that Christian publishers cannot produce quality materials if they don't have the necessary funds.

Homeschool-books.com was specifically created to bring in revenue to support the development of Christian materials. If Heart of Wisdom has helped you, we would greatly appreciate your patronage. All proceeds go toward the development of Heart of Wisdom unit studies. When you purchase from Homeschool-books.com you receive customer reward points you can apply to save on future purchases.

We encourage you to purchase resources from our site or from any homeschool vendor that has been a help to your family. When you go to a Christian homeschool vendor for help (by phone, email, or articles) and then purchase the product from a secular source, you are hurting the homeschool vendor. During the writing of this book, I watched one of the oldest and largest Christian homeschool vendors go out of business because they could not compete with secular discounters. When you buy homeschool resources from homeschool vendors you are helping Christian families help other families. You may save a dollar or two by purchasing from a secular source, but you are limiting the availability of Christian resources for future homeschoolers (i.e. your own grandchildren).

Series and Award Winners

Once you find an author or series your children like you may want more books in that series. On our site you have the option to browse book by series or theme. Go to Homeschool-Books.com and click on a theme or "Books by Series." Many are available in discount packages.

Illustrated Information Books

Aliki Books: Aliki is the well-loved author and illustrator of many best-selling fiction and non-fiction books for children. She has been the recipient of many honors. Her many books for the *Let's-Read-and-Find-Out* series are familiar to many homeschoolers such as

Mummies Made in Egypt, My Five Senses, A Medieval Feast, Corn is Maize, How a Book is Made.

Bobbie Kalman Books: Kalman is the author and publisher of more than two hundred and twenty quality children's books on history and science topics. Colorful, attractive covers and entertaining text make her books popular.

Dorling Kindersley's Eyewitness Books: DK publishes an extensive range of both adult and children's reference titles that are outstanding in quality and accessibility in both text and design. The award-winning *Eyewitness Books*, DK's trademark series never fail to inform, excite and inspire both children and adults alike. Each Eyewitness book is rich in content and created to help students visualize the subject through a mix of full-color photographs, illustrations, cutaways, 3-D models, cross-section views, and maps. By 2001 the series numbered 117 different titles and has sold over 50 million copies worldwide. The *Eyewitness Guides* are written for ages 8 and up. The *Eyewitness Explorers* (9 titles) and *Eye Wonder Books* (29 titles) are visual information, activity, and guide treats for children ages 3 to 12.

Jean Fritz Books: Mrs. Fritz has written 38 short story colorful popular biographies on historical figures mainly in American history. She never makes up dialogue. Instead, she draws on the real letters, diaries, and journals of those people, using only words that they actually wrote or spoke. This practice can make writing scenes and conversations difficult, but Fritz feels it keeps her writing true to the people involved. Titles include: *George Washington's Breakfast, Why Don't You Get a Horse, Sam Adams, Shhh! We're Writing the Constitution,* and *Then What Happened Paul Revere.* Houghton Mifflin created a site featuring these books at http://shortstories.cjb.net/

I Can Read Books: These books are widely recognized as the premier line of beginning readers. The series has grown to over 200 titles that include mysteries, adventure stories, poetry, historical fiction, and humor. Featuring award-winning authors and illustrators, and a fabulous cast of classic characters, *I Can Read Books* introduce children to the joy of reading and allow them to develop at their own pace.

If You...: Vivid full-color illustrations and a question-and-answer text bring to life traditional life, customs, and everyday worlds in this series covering a rich range of historical events, eras, and peoples. Meticulous research, accuracy of detail, and facts told from a child's perspective convey what it was like to live in another time. Basic concepts of history are made meaningful through details of daily life, putting young readers into the middle of the action. A sample of these titles: *If You Grew up With Abraham Lincoln, If You Sailed on the Mayflower,* etc.

Kregel Pictorial Guides: These beautiful Christian concise guides are as colorful as Usborne and jam-packed with chronological events, timelines, easy-to-follow summaries of key personalities and crucial developments, fully indexed and filled with four-color charts, maps, photographs, and illustrations.

Real Kids/Real Science: This motivating series of inspiration to explore the natural world as a scientist would, through first-hand experience. Each book is full of fascinating colorful photographs. Based on the program of the Children's School of Science of Woods Hole, Massachusetts, the books show children how to go out into the natural world around them. I found each book in this series fascinating. Written for 9- to 14-year olds. Interest level: all ages.

The Magic Schoolbus: The Magic Schoolbus series has been honored with over a dozen awards. Based on a cartoon of the same name, each book includes fun colorful illustrations, side facts, labeling, diagrams, and dialogue bubbles. An informational book that combines fascinating facts and lots of humor to make a "sense-ational" adventure. You can visit Scholastic's Magic School Bus online for games, experiments, and activities based on the episodes. There's a special Parents and Teachers section. http://place.scholastic.com/magicschoolbus/home.htm

Step into Reading: This series offers books at five carefully developed skill levels. This program offers a wide variety of fiction and nonfiction books. Topics of interest and colorful illustrations to make learning to read fun and exciting. The program is designed to give every child a successful reading experience—the grade levels are only guidelines; children can progress through the steps at their own speed, developing confidence and pride in their reading. Sample titles: *Ben Franklin and the Magic Squares; Escape North! The Story of Harriet Tubman; Trail of Tears; Choppers; Alligators; Dolphins.* Random House offers a Teacher site at http://www.randomhouse.com/kids/books/step/

Usborne Books: Usborne Publishing is a multiple-award-winning, independent children's publishing company. Founded by Peter Usborne over 30 years ago, the company revolutionized children's publishing with colorfully illustrated information books that combined very high educational and editorial standards—and made finding out fun. Within months of its first publication, Usborne books were a major international success. Now translated into over 80 languages, the Usborne list has been widely imitated but never bettered, and continues to earn glowing reviews and prestigious prizes. There are now over 200 Usborne Internet-linked books including atlases, encyclopedias, language books and dictionaries. See http://www.usborne-quicklinks.com/

Biography Series

The Childhood of Famous Americans Series: The books in this series were written for grades 3–5. This popular series, with biographies for over 40 different famous

Americans. Reading the Childhood of Famous Americans presents an excellent opportunity to see how our decisions today can affect tomorrow.

Creative Minds Biographies: Biographies of the world's most creative thinkers—ideal for both on-level and reluctant readers. Meet some of the world's most creative minds in story format. These episodic biographies give clear, straightforward accounts of historical figures. Each true story is accompanied by black-and-white illustrations and an afterword. Reading Level: Grade 4. Interest Level: Grades 3–6.

The Sowers Series: Mott Media Biographies offer children a chance to experience the Christ-inspired pathways followed by some heroic men and women. Their impact on our lives, as well as a great deal of factual information, is skillfully presented to the child within the framework of an interest-holding story. Over the years, the Sower Series books have established their appeal with a wide range of readers.

Historical Fiction and Non-Fiction Series

Dear America and My America: Books in these series cover important events or periods of American history and written about those times through the eyes of a young girl ("Dear America") or from the perspective of a young boy ("My Name is America"). Fact and fiction join together in these diaries to give a unique perspective to moments in America's past. The children in this series are from all different backgrounds and each has a different story to tell. The novels also contain "Historical Notes" sections at the end that provides facts, photos, and other material highlighting the actual events that inspired their fictional stories. Written for ages 9 to young adults. Visit http://www.scholastic.com/dearamerica/ to use the writing workshop and fun activities (arts, crafts, puzzles, recipes and more).

G.A. Henty Books: George Alfred Henty (1837–1901) is the prince of storytellers. He began telling stories to his own children. After dinner, he would spend an hour or two in telling them a story that would continue the next day. Some stories took weeks! A friend was present one day and watched the spell-bound reaction of his children and suggest that he write down his stories so others could enjoy them. He did. Henty wrote approximately. 144 books plus stories for magazines and was dubbed as "The Prince of Story Tellers" and "The Boys' Own Historian."

Trailblazer: The award-winning Trailblazer books series of Christian historical fiction for children by Dave and Neta Jackson. Each page-turning book portrays a significant period in a hero or heroine's life and ministry as seen through the eyes of a young person eleven to about fifteen years old. A page in the front of each book explains exactly what is fiction and which events and characters are historical, and a "More About" chapter at the end provides a brief biographical overview of the Christian hero's whole life. As authors, we want kids to learn about pioneer missionaries and other important people in Christian history...and have fun doing it. Easy vocabulary and quick moving story lines will encourage reluctant readers.

Magic Tree House Series: Mary Pope Osborne is the author of this popular series. These are small-chapter books written for young children. Many of her books have been named on best-books lists. Random House has created a Magic Treehouse site were you can get free Magic Tree House Teachers Guides and printer-friendly activity sheets and children can try writing activities. http://www.randomhouse.com/kids/magictreehouse/

Newbery and Caldecott Medal Awards

The John Newbery Medal annual award is given to the author of the book voted the most distinguished contribution to literature for children published in the United States (for children through the age of 14). The Randolph Caldecott Medal annual award is given to the artist of the book voted the most distinguished picture book for children published in the United States. Both awards are presented by the 15-member committee, appointed by the Association for Library Service to Children (ALSC) of the American Library Association (ALA). Both committees cite other books as worthy of attention referred to as Newbery or Caldecott Honor Books. Your local library should have lists of the award-winning books. You can access both Newbery Award winners lists from 1917 and Caldecott Award winners lists from 1938 at http://www.ala.org

When You Finish a Story

Whenever you read a book, it's always good to expand on the study, especially if you see a spark of delight. Watch for teaching opportunities. If you see an indication of interest in a subject, encourage and show your child how to find out more about the time period, author, or subject matter by researching other books or Internet sites.

Examples: The story of *Caddie Woodlawn* can lead to a study on the Western Movement and American pioneers. *The Story of Ping* could lead to a study on China. *Frog and Toad are Friends* could lead to a study on reptiles. *Mr.Popper's Penguins* could lead to a study on credit or penguins.

When the story is over ask your child questions about the story. Use the text in the stories for copy-work, oral and/or written narration, vocabulary, dictionary skills, alphabetizing, art, handwriting , etc. Consider having your children keep reading journals with short book reviews or illustrations.

Teachers' guides, unit studies and/or lesson plans are available for most of the Newbery and Caldecott winners (or for the book's author). Hundreds of guides and activities are available free on line! Type in the title of the book in a search engine and add the phrase "teacher's guide," "lesson plans ," "thematic unit" or "unit study" to find them on the Internet.

See Homeschool-books.com for Bible, history and science packages.

375

Life Skills Unit Study

Wisdom: An Internet-Linked Unit Study by Robin Sampson `4-8` `9-12`
This study is one of the most important things you will ever do with your children. Is your homeschooling on the right path? Are you headed in the right direction? Are you reaching for the right goal? It does not matter how hard you try or how diligent you are if you don't have the right directions.

Suppose you wanted to go to a city in Texas but you were given a map of Florida mislabeled Texas? Following the directions would not work—even if you tried harder or increased your speed. You would still be lost! The problem is not your attitude or effort—the problem is—you have the wrong map. Many homeschoolers are following the wrong map on their homeschool journey: they follow the state's standards, curriculum scope and sequence, or SAT benchmarks. This unique unit study is a map to true wisdom.

A map is not a territory, it is an explanation of certain aspects of a territory. In this study you will learn that true wisdom is understanding and knowing God. The moment we begin to understand and know God—we begin to see His holiness, we see His purposes, His love for men—we know who God is, so there's never any hesitation to obey Him.

> ### Lessons Teach:
> - How to follow the wise path
> - How to stay on it.
> - How to stay off the worldly path
> - How to set wise goals
> - The importance of obedience
> - How to pray for wisdom
> - How to study God's Word
> - How to make wise decisions
> - How to choose friends wisely
> - How to choose counsel wisely
> - How to manage conflict wisely
> - How to have the ultimate relationship with Christ
> - And more!

There are two ways to live life—wisely or unwise. When we follow the path of wisdom the results are joy, peace, contentment, confidence in the presence of God. The results of living unwisely are conflict, discouragement, disappointment, disillusionment, and discontentment. Can you see this information is more important than any academics? Don't homeschool without including this important information! Ebook or paperback.

Customers Comment on Heart of Wisdom Unit Studies

Using Heart of Wisdom Unit Studies has been a life-changing experience for our entire family. We spend more time together in God's Word and are growing in our understanding together! Learning Israel's history has been a tremendous benefit to understanding all of history, past, present, and even future. Also, learning about our Hebrew roots has brought new life to our relationship with God through Jesus Christ. The Science units are wonderful as well, tying it all together in the creation order. We are just beginning the Wisdom unit and are gleaning so much already. I know that God orchestrated Heart of Wisdom becoming part of our homeschooling.

I was drawn to these studies because of the focus on the Bible. But quite honestly, what is keeping me is the quality of content and the ease in lesson preparation!! I plan on staying with these studies as they come out. We are currently doing the Wisdom study and I absolutely think it is outstanding. I would highly recommend Heart of Wisdom to anyone who has been intimidated by the preparation involved in doing unit studies. Robin has done a wonderful job in selecting resources and activities.

This is a great curriculum! We have been putting together our own Bible based unit studies for years. This year due to health problems and less time we would have to purchase something already laid out. I thought I would have to settle for a lesser curriculum. To our relief this curriculum meets and perhaps exceeds our high standards by the many internet links, books lists and more. I have easily adapted it to include our younger students too! Thanks.

Ancient History Unit Studies

Adam to Abraham: An Internet-Linked Unit Study by Robin Sampson
`K-3` `4-8` `9-12` ⮌

Begin your history study with the foundation God gave us—the fascinating stories in Genesis! The first eleven chapters describe Creation, the Fall, the Flood, and the origin of nations. Genesis 12 is the ancestral story beginning with Abram. The focus of this unit study is on the memorable stories from Creation to Abraham entering Canaan and how each of the events foreshadows Jesus, the Messiah! This book is a great way to try out Heart of Wisdom Unit Studies to see if they fit your family. You'll never regret time spent in God's Word. Available in paperback or in the combined volume.

Seven unit studies available individually or in one combined volume.

Mesopotamia: An Internet-Linked Unit Study by Robin Sampson `4-8` `9-12` ⮌

In order to properly understand the various biblical time periods, we must examine the beginnings of culture in the ancient Near East. The *Mesopotamia* unit is central to understanding the beliefs, social norms, and material traits of the Old and New Testament world. Several early civilizations developed in Mesopotamia simultaneously with Egypt. This unit's focus is on Bible geography and the Hebrews' interaction with the Sumerian, Babylonian, Assyrian, and Medo-Persian civilizations of Mesopotamia. Full of maps and activities that will give your student a good grasp of biblical geography!

Ancient Egypt: An Internet-Linked Unit Study by Robin Sampson `4-8` `9-12` ⮌

It is impossible to properly understand the history of God's people without knowing something about ancient Egypt. The children of Israel were taken into Egypt and settled, living there for centuries before becoming an independent nation. Their removal from contact with the people of Canaan and their time of affliction prepared them for inheriting the land promised to their fathers—the land of Israel.

Ancient Israel: An Internet-Linked Unit Study by Robin Sampson `4-8` `9-12` ⮌

As we study how God dealt redemptively with the Hebrews, our spiritual ancestors by faith, we gain insight into the plans and purposes of God for mankind. Three things must be held in common by a society in order for it to be a people: religion, education, and law. In all history, there is only one civilization that bases its religion, education, and law on Scripture—Israel. Secular history books include stories and legends about mythical gods and exclude Israel—the stories from the ultimate living book—God's Word. As you learn about the Hebrew roots of the Christian faith, you will deepen your personal relationship and walk with Christ.

Ancient Greece : An Internet-Linked Unit Study by Robin Sampson `4-8` `9-12` ⮌

Learn about Greece's political history, social systems, cultural achievements, and economic conditions. Also learn how the ancient Greek culture affected the secular view of Scripture and the Church in ancient times and today. These lessons will address the key events, ideas, aspects, and issues of ancient Greek culture to enhance your overall understanding.

Ancient Rome: An Internet-Linked Unit Study by Robin Sampson `4-8` `9-12` ⮌

The history of Rome covers a lengthy era, a massive empire, a rich culture, and a profound philosophical legacy. The New Testament era was influenced by Hellenistic ideas, customs, religion and language, but dominated by Roman law, governmental forms, ideas of class and the military. A study of ancient Rome will give you a better understanding of Jesus and the early Church, because Christ lived His entire human life under the Roman empire. Paul was also a Jew living under the Roman authorities in Jerusalem.

Messiah: An Internet-Linked Unit Study by Robin Sampson `4-8` `9-12` ⮌

All the treasures of wisdom and knowledge are hidden in the person of the Messiah! You'll have the opportunity to investigate ancient prophecies—hidden wisdom—things that people longed to know for centuries before the Messiah came to dwell on earth. You'll be in the privileged position of looking backward through history to see the Messiah as He was described in prophecy, as He dwelt on earth, as He is now, and as He speaks to you through His Word.

Physical Science Unit Studies

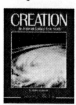

All science unit studies feature easy-to-use four-step lessons, which include discussion starters, demonstrations and lab activities. Certain process skills are woven throughout including observing, making hypotheses, creating and testing models, experimenting, recording and graphing data, making inferences, and forming conclusions. Lessons conform to the National Science Education Standards and SS&C tenets for effective science education.

Creation: An Internet-Linked Unit Study by Robin Sampson **4-8** **9-12** ✏
Does it really matter what you believe about creation? Not only does it matter, it's absolutely vital what we believe! Many Christians fail to realize that the events of Genesis are literal, are historical and are foundational to all Christian doctrine. A believing understanding of the book of Genesis is a prerequisite to an understanding of God and His meaning to man. When you are finished reading this book you will not only know what you believe and why you believe it, you'll also be able to defend it! This is more than a study of Creation—this is a study of Christianity versus humanism.

Light: An Internet-Linked Unit Study by Robin Sampson **4-8** **9-12** ✏
This unit study reveals the mysteries of the light which God created for us. You'll begin with God's words, "Let there be light," then embark on a fascinating journey through the centuries, as your children discover the physical properties of light while they come to understand that the character of God can be comprehended by observing what light is and what it does. Lessons include: photosynthesis, reflection, refraction, electromagnetic spectrum, God's lamp (the menorah), rainbows, particles, waves, photons, lasers, and more.

Energy: An Internet Linked Unit Study by Robin Sampson **4-8** **9-12** ✏
God created for us the ability to further our civilization through industry, travel, food production, and good living standards. In this unit we will discover how central God's creation of energy is to how we live today, as we study sources of energy, types of energy, potential energy, kinetic energy, heat, thermodynamics, conservation and more.

Matter: An Internet Linked Unit Study by Robin Sampson **4-8** **9-12** ✏
God spoke our world of energy and matter into being. Apart from creation of matter our world would have has no structure, no context, no rootage in reality. Since the beginning of the human civilization, people have been curious about matter and its composition. People of the pagan nations of the ancient world believed that matter was eternal and that the gods evolved out of natural processes. Through this study you will learn God created and is involved in all forms of matter: states of matter, the properties, and basic chemistry concepts (atoms, elements, etc.).

Motion: An Internet Linked Unit Study by Robin Sampson **4-8** **9-12** ✏
God is everwhere and intimately involved with His creation. God governs all His creatures and their actions. In this unit study students learn about Newton's laws of motion, simple machines, wheels, floating and sinking, levers, gravity, weight and mass, collisions, friction, centripetal force, and much more.

Electricity: An Internet Linked Unit Study by Robin Sampson **4-8** **9-12** ✏
When God designed our world, He included everything that was needed for electric currents. The natural world has examples of electric power: static electricity shocks us; lightning flashes bright light; the electric eel kills. And yet, throughout thousands of years no one understood how to generate and use electricity. During the Age of Enlightenment scientists began investigating electrical phenomena. Within a few generations, people learned to use electrical devices to take the place of human labor, to communicate, to give light and heat and, eventually, to bring about computers and the information age. In this unit study students learn about electricity throughout history, electric currents, electric charge, batteries, magnets, conductors and insulators, circuits, lightning and more.

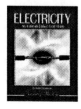

Bible Resources

Bible Story Books

20 Bible Stories Every Child Should Know with CD by Little Man Music **K-3**
A collection of 20 Bible stories that will find its way into your child's heart through words and 20 original Bible memory songs on a full-length CD. ISBN: 0784715866

Abingdon's Bible Story Time Line by Peg Augustine **K-3** **4-8**
Beginning with Creation the time line leads students through the history of the Patriarchs, the United and Divided Kingdoms and their prophets, the Exile and Return, and into the New Testament. Six 16" x 11" charts assemble in a 96" time line. ISBN: 0687096510

The Beginner's Bible: Timeless Children's Stories by Karyn Henley and Catherine DeVries **K-3**
The Beginners Bible contains 95 stories charmingly retold and colorfully illustrated. This is a Bible to be read by early readers or to be read to pre-readers by parents or older brothers and sisters. Full color. ISBN: 0310709628

Bible Story Crafts and Projects Children Love by Group Publishing **K-3** **4-8**
These creative art and craft ideas reinforce 20 Bible stories for elementary-age children. With at least three activities for each Bible story, children will remember what they learn. ISBN: 1559456981

Big Picture Bible Timeline **K-3** **4-8**
Each page is a scene or figure from Bible history. Color each page and then put them together to make a really BIG timeline! ISBN: 0830714723

The Blessing of the Lord: Stories from the Old and New Testaments by Gary D. Schmidt **K-3** **4-8**
Full of drama and wonder, these are fresh retellings of 25 favorite Bible stories. Full-color illustrations give rich visual imagery to each story. ISBN: 0802837891

A Child's First Bible by Kenneth N. Taylor **K-3**
A collection of 125 of the most familiar Bible passages, from both the Old and New Testaments. ISBN: 0842331743

The Child's Story Bible by Catherine F. Vos **K-3** **4-8**
First published more than 50 years ago, this much-loved Bible storybook continues to instruct and delight today's families. ISBN: 0802850111

The Children's Bible in 365 Stories by Mary Batchelor **K-3** **4-8**
A classic collection of Bible stories for every day of the year. ISBN: 0745930689

Children's Illustrated Bible by Victoria Parker and Janet Dyson **K-3** **4-8**
Accessible, lively stories hold the reader's attention and give a uniquely broad and interesting insight into the world of both the Old and New Testaments. ISBN: 0754810968

The Early Reader's Bible by V. Gilbert Beers **K-3**
This Bible features colorful illustrations and over 400 easy-to-read words that will have youngsters saying "I can read it!" ISBN: 0310701392

Egermeier's Bible Story Book by Elsie E. Egermeier **4-8**
Here are 312 stories that cover the Bible from Genesis to Revelation. ISBN: 0871622297

Favorite Children's Bible Stories 4 CD Quad Pack by Media Books **K-3** **4-8**
The incredible drama of the Bible is thrillingly brought to life in this collection of stories told in modern-day English. ISBN: 1578155657

God's Word for Little Ones: Bible Stories I Can Read by Green Key Books **K-3** **N**
A first Bible for young readers, this storybook is packed with colorful illustrations on every page, and stories from the Bible written for beginning readers. Includes memory verses from *God's Word* translation. Full color. ISBN: 1932587411

Bible Story Books continued

The Growing Reader Phonics Bible by Joy MacKenzie **K-3** **N** ⌐
A great book for your 3- to 8-year-olds to practice phonics skills while reading stories from God's Word. Packed with bright illustrations and rhythmic sentences, each story showcases a specific letter or phonics sound—boosting your kids' love of reading and Scripture. ISBN: 0842339175

Hear Me Read Bible Stories Package **K-3** ⌐
Each of the 18 books in this colorful series features a complete Bible story told in 25 different words or less. These books are ideal for children who are "almost but not quite" reading. Young children develop a sight vocabulary as they learn to recognize the simple words. Humor, repetition, and colorful illustrations bring these stories to life for early learners. This package is available through homeschool-books.com.

Learn-to-Read Bible by Paul S. Bellet and Heather Gemmen **K-3** **N** ⌐
Parents can start their children on a lifetime of reading when they are just toddlers. This Bible will delight infants to three-year-olds and offers 101 stories from the Word written especially for toddlers. Full color. ISBN: 0781439752

The NKJV Children's Story Bible by Natalie Carabetta **K-3** **N** ⌐
I recommend this story book because the stories are the actual *New King James Version* text. Seventy-five best-loved Bible stories illustrated in full color using art by Natalie Carabetta bring Bible stories to life for children and their parents. Each story is followed by application questions and a simple prayer. Hardcover. ISBN: 0718009622

The Rocket Reader Bible Story Series **K-3** ⌐
The Rocket Reader books are supplemental level readers designed to launch children who are learning to read into the wonderful world of words using biblical concepts. Each reading level emphasizes a different aspect of reading, using level-appropriate language. Pre-level 1 is for children learning letters. Level 1 teaches alphabet sounds and beginning sight words. Level 2 teaches letter combinations and more sight words, etc. The books within each set are stored in a durable and attractive slipcover case. The colorful artwork is engaging and humorous. Each book includes hands-on faith and reading help for parents, including a Faith Parenting Guide in each book. There are 3 to 5 books in each set and several sets available from Pre-level to level 4. See Homeschool-Books.com for a list of sets and titles in the Bible story category.

Walking the Bible (Children's Edition): An Illustrated Journey for Kids Through the Greatest Stories Ever Told by Bruce S. Feiler **K-3** **4-8** **N** ⌐
On a visit to Jerusalem, Bruce Feiler has a revelation: The stories of the Bible occurred in real places—places he could visit today. So he sets out on a perilous ten-thousand-mile journey retracing the greatest stories ever told. This book is specially crafted for a young audience (not dumbed down). This stunning children's edition of the *New York Times* bestseller is illustrated with black-and-white maps and Feiler's own photographs. ISBN: 0060511176

Who is Jesus?: Children's Bible Basics by Carolyn Nystrom **K-3** **N** ⌐
A simple introduction to the life and mission of Jesus based on passages from the Old and New Testaments. ISBN: 0802478565

The Young Learner's Bible Storybook: 52 Stories with Activities for Family Fun and Learning by Mary Manz Simon **K-3** **N** ⌐
This Bible storybook is an all-in-one resource that's jam-packed with 52 Bible stories and more than 100 parent-child activities and learning fun. ISBN: 0784712778

The Young Reader's Bible: 70 Easy-To-Read Bible Stories by Bonnie Bruno **K-3** **N** ⌐
Each of these 70 stories is short enough to finish in one sitting. Features Scripture references, maps of Bible lands, colorful illustrations, glossary of terms and unfamiliar Bible words, and more.

Bible Study Tools

30 Days to Understanding the Bible in 15 Minutes a Day: Expanded Edition by Max E Anders **4-8** **9-12** ⊳
This is an excellent visual resource that helped me get a grasp of the Bible's chronology. It helps a student to learn to position the key Bible characters, places, and events into chronological order so that they can think their way through the entire Word of God, with the help of special icons. See the "12 Eras of Bible History" on page 317 and more information on page 282. ISBN: 0785214232

Bible Teacher's Commentary by Lawrence O Richards **9-12** ⊳
If you need activity and discussion ideas as you read through the Bible this is an outstanding resource. The entire Bible, from Genesis 1 to Revelation 22, is divided into teachable units with age level link-to-life ideas (lesson activities). I use this book weekly with my children. ISBN: 0781438780

Chronological and Background Charts of the New Testament by H. Wayne House **4-8** **9-12** ⊳
Illustrates all aspects of the chronology, historical background, and criticism of the New Testament. Covers such topics as weights and measures, social structures, theories of the history of the text, history of Rome and Palestine, and many other subjects. ISBN: 0310416418

Chronological and Background Charts of the Old Testament by John H. Walton **4-8** **9-12** ⊳
Charts provide visual organization that is ideal for teaching, learning, and review. Facts, connections, parallels, and contrasts can be grasped easily at a glance. The charts cover historical, literary, archaeological, and theological aspects of the Old Testament, its background, and biblical studies. ISBN: 0310481619

From the Mind of God to the Mind of Man: A Layman's Guide to How We Got Our Bible by James Williams and Randolph Shaylor **9-12** ⊳
This book has been called "One of the most important books published for believers in the twentieth century!" If you want to understand the translation issues you must read this book. With this book you will learn the true historical facts on the text, transmission, and translations of Scripture. ISBN: 1889893382

Greek and Hebrew Tutor CD by Parsons Technology **9-12**
Available individually or as a set. *The Greek and Hebrew Tutors* harnesses the interactive power of multimedia. You'll hear the pronunciation of letters and words as you see them, to learn Greek or Hebrew by sight and sound. Move at your own pace through this engaging, interactive sight-and-sound tutorial. Drills and exercises let you study letters, vocabulary, and grammar and reinforce all you learn. ISBN: 1572640618

Holman Bible Atlas: A Complete Guide to the Geography of Biblical History by Thomas V. Brisco **4-8** **9-12** ⊳
Want to explore the world of the Bible? Use this resource to better understand biblical narratives in their unique cultural/geographic settings. Features 140 color photos, plus charts and maps. ISBN: 1558197095

How the Bible Came to Us by Meryl Doney **K-3** **4-8** ⊳
Read the stories of the people who made it possible for us to have the Bible in our own language. Children learn how to crack a code and make a secret scroll. Bold color illustrations on every page. ISBN: 0745920985

How to Read the Bible for All It's Worth by Gordon D. Fee and Douglas Stuart **9-12** ⊳
This outstanding book helps readers determine what Scriptures meant at the time they were written and how that meaning applies to us today. Covering everything from translational concerns to different genres of biblical writing, *How to Read the Bible for All It's Worth* is used all around the world. In clear, simple language, it helps you accurately understand the different parts of the Bible—their meaning for ancient audiences and their implications for us today—so you can uncover the inexhaustible worth that is in God's Word. ISBN: 0310246040

The Kregel Pictorial Guide to the Bible by Tim Dowley **4-8** **9-12** ⊳
This is a beautifully illustrated full color book on the Bible that answers such intriguing questions as: How do the books of the Bible relate to one another? What was Jewish worship like? What did the Tabernacle and temple look like? What were the Jewish festivals all about? Who were the main characters of the Old and New Testaments? ISBN: 082542464X

Bible Study Tools continued

The Kregel Pictorial Guide to Everyday Life in Bible Times by Tim Dowley 4-8 9-12
Gives readers a real-life glimpse of life in Bible times by examining everything from chariots to clothing, health to hairstyles, plowing to pottery, and work to worship. Full color visual book. ISBN: 0825424658

The Kregel Pictorial Guide to the Story of the Bible by Tim Dowley 4-8 9-12
From the beginning of God's revelation to modern language translations around the world, this popular-level reference book traces the history of the Bible, how books were written and became part of the canon, and how God preserved his special revelation. Full color illustrations throughout. ISBN: 0825424631

Matthew Henry's Concise Commentary on the Whole Bible by Matthew Henry 9-12
A valuable source of reference and sermon material with a clear modern typeface, this classic is a treasure for pastors, students, Bible teachers, and devotional readers alike! ISBN: 0785245294

The Narrated Bible in Chronological Order by F. Lagard Smith K-3 4-8 9-12 ♥ ☞
Chronological accuracy, easy-to-read format. Includes: Moses' laws by subject; Proverbs presented topically; Psalms arranged by sentiment; Paul's teachings integrated into Acts. See page 277 for details. ISBN: 0736902392

Nelson's Illustrated Encyclopedia of the Bible by Nelsonword Publishing Group 4-8 9-12 ♥ ☞
See description on page 282. Great resource. ISBN: 0785246142

Nelson's New Illustrated Bible Dictionary by Nelsonword 9-12
This completely revised and updated edition is the most comprehensive and up-to-date Bible dictionary available. A wealth of basic study information is found in more than 7,000 entries plus over 500 full-color photographs, maps, and pronunciation guides. Includes the Visual Survey of the Bible. ISBN: 0785212175

Old Testament Days: An Activity Guide by Nancy I. Sanders K-3 4-8
More than 80 activities and projects provide insight into life in the Middle East. Children can enjoy a desert picnic, make a loose tunic, eat goat cheese and more. Color illustrations throughout. ISBN: 1556523548

The Student Bible Dictionary by Karen Dockrey K-3 4-8
This concise, easy-to-use Bible-reference book is for students of all ages who seek to learn more about the Bible and its settings. Scores of full-color charts, maps and photos add visual appeal. ISBN: 1577489853

Then and Now Bible Maps: Compare Bible Times with Modern Day by Rose Publishing K-3 4-8
Now you can have full-color Bible maps with clear plastic overlays of modern cities and countries in an 8 1/2" x 11" spiral bound book. This fantastic map book contains maps of the Middle East, the Holy Land, where Jesus walked, Paul's journeys and New and Old Testament time lines. ISBN: 0965508234

Through the Bible in One Year by Allen Stringfellow 9-12
Learn how to analyze all 66 books, which are the most significant chapters, the central purpose, which chief verses to copy and remember, all of which prepare you to meet life's daily challenges. ISBN: 1563220148

The Treasury of Scripture Knowledge by R. A. Torrey 9-12
This classic contains over 500,000 entries which follow the order of the text of the books of the Bible, chronological data, chapter introductions, key word listings, and illustrative notes. ISBN: 0917006224

The Victor Journey Through the Bible by V. Gilbert Beers 4-8 9-12 ☞ ♥
This easy-to-read, visual exploration of the Bible allows you to follow the action from Genesis to Revelation. The stories of Scripture will come alive as you travel story by story through Bible lands and times. One of my favorite resources I use with my children regularly. ISBN: 156476480X

What the Bible is All About for Young Explorers by Frances Blankenbaker and Henrietta C. Mears 4-8
A discussion of the origin, significance, and contents of the Bible, with a book-by-book analysis of events, as well as time lines, photographs, and maps, to pinpoint when and where they happened. ISBN: 0830723633

World History: General

Atlas of World History by Jeremy Black **4-8** **9-12**
With its multicultural orientation and dazzling maps, photos, and artworks, this atlas is a truly global view of world history and mankind's experience on Earth. ISBN: 078944609X

Book of World History by Anne Millard **4-8**
This colorfully illustrated Usborne volume provides a simple introduction to world history from the first civilizations to the early 20th century. The geographical time chart shows what was happening in different parts of the world at similar times. ISBN:0860209598

Encyclopedia of World History by Jane Bingham **4-8** **9-12**
This visually appealing Usborne Internet-linked book is a comprehensive survey of history divided into four sections: Pre-History, Ancient World, Medieval World, and the Last 500 years. It colorfully depicts key figures and the battles, revolutions, and inventions that have shaped today's world. ISBN: 0794503322

First Encyclopedia of History by Fiona Chandler and David Hancock **K-3** **4-8**
This Usborne Internet-linked book covers all the major subjects of world history. A lively introduction to history. Simple text, stunning photographs, detailed illustrations and links to exciting recommended Web sites bring the past alive for young historians. ISBN: 0794503861

The Kingfisher History Encyclopedia by Kingfisher Books **4-8** **9-12** ◐— ♥
Here are all the essential events of world history in one highly illustrated volume. Packed with the people, places, and events that have shaped world history, this book includes essays linked by a chronological time line. ISBN: 0753451948

More Than Dates and Dead People: Recovering a Christian View of History by Stephen Mansfield **9-12** ⌐○
A lively, upbeat look at history as something exciting rather than a boring list of dates to memorize. The focus is on how a Christian worldview affects one's academic interests. ISBN: 1581821182

Penguin Encyclopedia of Ancient Civilizations by Arthur Cotterell **9-12**
A concise but detailed fountain of knowledge of the greatest civilizations of the past. Well-written and fully illustrated, this is a superb value for the price.A wide-ranging, alphabetically arranged overview of the prehistoric world, spanning East and West to study and compare ancient civilizations. ISBN: 140114343

Timeline of the Ancient World: Mesopotamia, Egypt, Greece, Rome by Katharine Wiltshire **4-8** **9-12**
A timeline of ancient history based on the greatest museum collection of antiquities in the world today. The timeline is accompanied by a 32-page book that provides in-depth background information on the four main cultures—Egypt, Mesopotamia, Greece and Rome—and features illustrated articles on the most important people, places, objects and events in the timeline. From the British Museum. ISBN: 1403966095

The Timetables of History: A Horizontal Linkage of People and Events by Bernard Grun **9-12**
The classic history reference, brought completely up to date, linking more than 30,000 events in an overview of 7,000 years of civilization. This is a great resource that distills the essence of civilization, highlighting significant moments in history, politics, philosophy, religion, art, science and technology. ISBN: 067174271X

Usborne Ancient World (Illustrated World History) by Jane Chisholm and Anne Millard **4-8** **9-12**
This superb, lavishly illustrated book contains stories from the first farmers of the Middle East to the rise of the mighty empires of Mesopotamia, Greece, Egypt and Rome. ISBN: 074602760

What in the World's Going on Here? Creation to the French Revolution by Diana Waring **4-8** **9-12** ⌐○
Diana will teach you how to re-evaluate World history from an eternal perspective: God sovereignly ruling over the affairs of men and nations. Four 60-minute tapes: Creation to the Destruction of Assyria, The Rise of Babylon to Jesus Christ, Destruction of Jerusalem to the Fall of Constantinople, The Renaissance /Reformation to the French Revolution.

World History: General continued

A Biblical Analysis of the Great Books of Western Civilization by Dennis Woods 9-12 ● ⊷
As you study history we recommend your high school student study fifty men who affect the world from their graves by using The Great Conversation. It includes fifty biological biographical sketches of classical authors, arranged chronologically. You can easily incorporate the readings with Heart of Wisdom unit studies for your high school students by following order listed below.

Each sketch includes a biography, historical background, summary of teaching, historical implications, biblical analysis and application. A literary timeline helps the student visualize the impact of classical philosophy on corresponding events in world history. The sketches appear in order of publication date giving a good overview of the essential authors. Woods explains that these works are considered classics because of the beauty of their style and the impact they have had on the world, but in many if not most cases that influence has been negative. Their cumulative impact has brought us to a disastrous condition. A student armed with a biblical worldview can evaluate the mistakes of the past as well as the successes.

The Great Conversation Teachers Guide is an essential companion for the busy homeshool mother. It includes answers to the quizzes, as well as answers to 500 short open-ended questions. This is an excellent overview, easy to understand even if you have little knowledge of philosophy; it has been referred to facetiously as the *Philosophy for Dummies*.

The Great Conversation	Heart of Wisdom	Main Characters
The Pagan world	Ancient Greece	Homer, Aristophanes, Socrates, Plato, Aristotle, Cicero, Virgil
The Prince of Peace	The Messiah	Jesus Christ
The Patristic World	Ancient Rome and The Early Church	Constantine, Augustine, Justinian
The Papal World	Middle Ages	Anselm, John of Salisbury, Thomas Aquinas
The Age of Renaissance (1300s-1400s)	Renaissance	William Wallace, Dante Alighieri, Marsiglio of Padua, Niccolo Machiavelli
The Age of Reformation (1500s)	Reformation	Martian Luther, John Calvin, Nicholaus Copernicus, Brutus, Richard Hooker
The Age of Revolution (1600s)	Age of Exploration	Frances Bacon, Edward Coke, Rene Descartes, Samuel Rutherford, John Milton, Thomas Hobbes, James Herrington, Blaise Pascal, John Bunyan, Isaac Newton, John Locke
The Age of Reason (1700s)	The Industrial Era	Jonathan Swift, David Hume, Voltair, Rousseau, Adam Smith, Thomas Pain, Thomas Jefferson, Jeremy Bentham, John Witherspoon, Immanual Kent
The Age of Romanticism (1800s)	The Industrial Era	Karl Mark, Hermn Millville, Michael Behe, Richard Weaver, George Orwell, Cornelius Van Til

Adam to Abraham

A is for Adam: The Gospel from Genesis and *D is for Dinosaur* by Ken Ham and Mally Ham **K-3**
Children will delight in these two colorful books. *A is for Adam* is an ABC book, a coloring book and a devotional. *D is for Dinosaur* teaches about Creation, the Fall, the Flood, salvation, the Gospel, dinosaurs, and fossils. ISBN: 0890512078 and ISBN: 0890511934.

Adam and His Kin: The Lost History of Their Lives and Times by Ruth Beechick **4-8** **9-12**
Drawing on linguistics, archaeology, astronomy, the Bible, and other history, Dr. Ruth Beechick writes an enlightening and entertaining history of Adam and his offspring. Excellent to read aloud. ISBN: 0940319071

The Beautiful World God Made by Rhonda Gowler Greene **4-8**
Simple, rhythmic lines that build into the sweeping story of all creation. Bold, patterned illustrations energetically convey the excitement of all this new life coming into being. A great read-aloud. Will delight and capture the imaginations of children of all ages. ISBN: 080285267-X

Digging up the Past Genesis 3-11 by Kay Arthur and Janna Arndt **4-8**
Join inductive dig team members Max, Molly, and archeologist Uncle Jake in their latest action-adventure as they uncover what happens after God creates a perfect world. Sift through Genesis chapters 3-11, using tools like hieroglyphic decoders, pottery shard puzzles, and scientific experiments. Does the world stay perfect for long? Discover the truth about some of the world's big "firsts"—first sin, first marriage, first civilization, and first genealogy. ISBN: 736903747

Discover Jesus in Genesis: An Illustrated Biblical Theology for All Ages by Larry Edison **K-3** **4-8** **9-12**
You'll want to use this book not only for your personal benefit, but also as a great way to explain the Old Testament and its meaning to your children. You will see Christ come alive through these pages, and your reading of Genesis will never be the same again. ISBN: 1579213898

Genesis: Finding Our Roots by Ruth Beechick **5-8** **9-12**
This dynamic book shows evidence that the writings of Genesis are the most ancient record that we have. Compelling evidence is presented that show that Adam and Noah were real men, and that God did send a world-wide flood. ISBN: 094031911X

In the Days of Noah by Earl & Bonnie Snellenberger **K-3** **4-8**
This spectacular book gives a wide-eyed look into what life must have been like 5,000 years ago. It paints a breathtaking view of God's judgment on a sinful world. Basic questions such as ship size, care of the animals, and many others are answered. ISBN: 0890512051

Noah's Ark by Jerry Pinkney **K-3** **N**
Now, four-time Caldecott Honor recipient Jerry Pinkney captures all the courage, drama and beauty of this ancient story in rich, glorious paintings. Full color. ISBN: 1587172011

The True Story of Noah's Ark by Tom Dooley **K-3** **N**
The adventure of Noah comes to life through dazzling, detailed illustrations. The images of the interior of Noah's ark are like nothing you've ever seen before. The people and cities depicted here are advanced. They invented metals and musical instruments; they were skilled craftsmen; they built grand cities all before the Flood. And this is not fiction; it's all biblically and historically based. ISBN: 0890513880

Song of Creation by Paul Goble **K-3**
The whole earth is in constant prayer, and we can join in. Every element of creation—from the magpie to the minnow—glorifies God in its own way in this bold and brightly illustrated work. ISBN: 0802852718

Tower of Babel by Gloria Clanin **K-3** **N**
One of two 32-page, full-color books follow the storytelling of a grandfather as he leads his grandchildren through two of the great events in Bible history. ISBN: 0890512140

The World That Perished by John C. Whitcomb **9-12**
Photos and detailed descriptive text demonstrate that a global flood disaster is the most reasonable explanation for many natural phenomena. A simple and interesting defense of the Genesis flood. ISBN: 0801096901

Mesopotamia

Ancient Egyptians and Their Neighbors: An Activity Guide by Marian Broida `4-8`
This unique activity book shows what life was like among the Nubians, Mesopotamians, Hittites, and their neighbors, the Egyptians, from 3100 B.C. to 30 B.C. Projects help readers to connect with these cultures. ISBN: 1556523602

Archaeology for Kids: Uncovering the Mysteries of Our Past, 25 Activities by Richard Panchyk `4-8` `9-12`
Includes projects such as making a surface survey of a site and counting tree rings to date a find that teach kids the techniques that unearthed Neanderthal caves, Tut's tomb, and the city of Pompeii. ISBN: 1556523955

Daily Life in Ancient Mesopotamia by Karen Nemet-Nejat `9-12`
The ancient world of Mesopotamia vividly comes alive in this portrayal of the time period from 3100 BCE to the fall of Assyria (612 BCE) and Babylon (539 BCE). Illustrated with timeline and a historical overview. ISBN: 1565637127

Exploring Ancient Cities of the Bible by Michael and Caroline Carroll `4-8` ★ ⊶
Children are introduced to archaeology through photos, maps and interviews with biblical archaeologists. Not only does it explain some of the physical cities in Scripture, but the cultures in which the people lived. Beautifully illustrated with full color illustrations and photos. Hard cover. ISBN: 0781436958

The Magic School Bus Shows and Tells: A Book about Archaeology by Joanna Cole `K-3`
Ms. Frizzle's class is in a Show-and-Tell contest. Arnold brings in an old artifact to show. But since nobody knows what it is, there's nothing to tell! So the class makes guesses as to what the object is, and they go on a wild adventure to find out if their guesses are correct. Full color. ISBN: 0590922424

History Pockets, Ancient Civilizations by Jill Norris `K-3`
If you have children in grades K-3 this is an excellent supplement to *Ancient History: Adam to Messiah!* View sample pages on our Web site. Bring history alive as students make interactive projects while exploring the fascinating past. The projects are stored in labeled construction paper pockets with decorative covers. With *History Pockets*, students are engaged in discovery while creating portfolios for assessment and display. Includes introduction to history; Mesopotamia; Egypt; Greece; Rome; China; the Aztec world. ISBN: 1557999007

Life in the Great Ice Age by Michael and Beverly Oard `4-8` ⊶
Learn the biblical history of the world as you find yourself transported back in time. Discover what life would have been like during the Ice Age and find out the scientific reasons for this puzzling period of time. Colorfully illustrated. ISBN: 0890511675

Mesopotamia and the Bible: Comparative Explorations by Mark W. Chavalas (Editor) `4-8` ⊶
Thirteen scholars explore possible points of connection between the Bible and its ancient Near Eastern context, illuminating the methodologies, contributions, and limitations of both biblical studies and Assyriology. ISBN: 080102420X

Mesopotamia: Find Out about Series by Lorna Oakes `4-8`
Explore the land between the Two Rivers—one of the most ancient of all civilizations—and investigate why the Sumerians, Assyrians and Babylonians were among the first to develop writing, mathematics and the science of astronomy. Grades 3–7. ISBN: 1842159178

Mesopotamia: The Invention of the City by Gwendolyn Leick `4-8`
Painting a colorful picture of everyday lives, this book is an engaging account of the rise and fall of one of the greatest ancient civilizations. ISBN: 0140265740

Ancient Egypt

Ancient Egypt and the Old Testament by John Currid `9-12`
An enlightening guide to Egyptian influences on Israelite history. We do not give the biblical writers enough credit for their knowledge of the ancient Near East and of Egypt in particular. A primary aim of this book is to show many firm point of contact between Egypt and theIsraelites on a variety of levels. Includes illustrations. ISBN: 0801021375

The Cat of Bubastes by G.A. Henty `4-8` `9-12` **N**
Set in 1250 B.C., the time of Moses, this thrilling adventure story offers an evocative look at the ancient Egyptian world. Fascinating details about Egyptian religion and geography, the methods by which the Nile was used for irrigation, how the Egyptians fought wars and how they made mummies. ISBN: 0486423638

Encyclopedia of Ancient Egypt by Gill Harvey and Struan Reid `4-8`
Stunning photographs and detailed reconstructions reveal the fascinating history of one of the world's greatest civilizations with this Usborne Internet-linked book. ISBN: 0794501184

Eyewitness Ancient Egypt by George Hart `4-8` `9-12` ♦ ◐━
A photo essay on ancient Egypt and the people who lived there, documented through the mummies, pottery, weapons, and other objects they left behind. Describes their society, religion, obsession with the afterlife, and methods of mummification. Explore a Pharaoh's tomb, see a mummy up close, and find out about Egyptian gods. A large number of archaeological relics show what life was like for the ancient Egyptians, from how they dressed to the games they played. ISBN: 0756606462

Eyewitness Desert by Miranda MacQuitty `4-8` `9-12`
Superb, full-color photographs of the people, creatures and plants that survive the extremes of temperature of the desert. Learn how sand dunes form, how a mummy can be preserved in sand. Learn which animals never need to drink water, and much, much more. ISBN: 0789458624

Eyewitness Pyramids by James Putnam and Geoff Brightling `4-8` `9-12`
This outstanding collection of specially commissioned photographs tries to answer some of the riddles about the purimids. Discover what archeological finds have revealed about life on the banks of the Nile during the Pyramid Age. A fascinating introduction to colossal structures. ISBN 0756607175

Exodus by Brian Wildsmith `K-4`
Describes how God sent Moses to lead His people out of slavery in Egypt and into the promised land of Canaan. In Wildsmith's hands, the familiar journey of the Exodus comes alive against stunning backdrops. ISBN: 0802851754

The Golden Goblet by Eloise McGraw `4-8` **N**
Ranofer struggles to thwart the plottings of his evil uncle, Gebu, so that he can become a master goldsmith like his father in this exciting tale of ancient Egyptian mystery and intrigue. Newbery Honor Book. ISBN: 0140303359

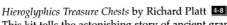

Hieroglyphics Treasure Chests by Richard Platt `4-8`
This kit tells the astonishing story of ancient graphic language symbols. Includes a colorful 32-page book, 27 rubber hieroglyphic stamps, an ink pad, a supply of papyrus templates, an educational Rosetta Stone poster, and much more. Full color. ISBN: 0762415932

History Pockets, Ancient Egypt by Marc Nobleman `4-8`
Students make interactive projects learning about daily life; government and leaders; religion; architecture; language; arts and recreation in ancient Egypt. The projects are stored in labeled construction paper pockets with decorative covers. Grades 4–6. See sample pages on our web site. ISBN: 155799904X

Joseph by Brian Wildsmith `K-3` `4-8` **N**
Sweeping illustrations with brilliant colors and fascinating details bring alive the dramatic biblical story of Joseph and the worlds of ancient Egypt and the Middle East. Brian Wildsmith's vivid retelling of this powerful Bible story engages children with its timeless messages and helps them see the many ways God provides for His people. Full color. ISBN: 0802851614

Ancient Egypt continued

Life in Ancient Egypt: 3,000 Years of Mystery to Unlock and Discover Kit by George Hart **4-8**
Learn about the ancient Egyptians' mysterious art, science, beliefs, daily life, games, and practices. Includes a replica stone necklace, papyrus, hieroglyphic rubber stamp, and more. Full color. ISBN: 1561384623

Lift the Lid on Mummies by Jacqueline Dineen **4-8**
This exploration kit combines lessons in science, archaeology, and anthropology with the experience of creating your very own mummy! The kit includes a mummy figurine, major internal organs with canopic jars for storing them, gauze for wrapping, and more. ISBN: 0762402083

Mara: Daughter of the Nile by Eloise McGraw **4-8**
The adventures of an ingenious Egyptian slave girl who undertakes a dangerous assignment as a spy in the royal palace of Thebes, in the days when Queen Hatshepsut ruled. ISBN: 0140319298

Mummies Made in Egypt by Aliki **K-3**
The Aliki books are like visual candy. This book describes the techniques and the reasons for the use of mummification in ancient Egypt. Full color. ISBN: 0064460118

Mysteries of Egypt (IMAX Video) **9-12** [img]
Surrounding you with spectacular images of colossal monuments and breathtaking landscapes, the IMAX film technology transports you over pyramids, sweeps you to the Nile's turbulent falls, and brings you to rest in burial chambers hidden deep below the scorching desert floor. ISBN: 5555042876

Pharaohs and Kings: A Biblical Quest by David M. Rohl **9-12** ⊳⊂
Pharaohs and Kings reveals the Old Testament to be a true account of the history of the Jewish people. Illustrated throughout. *Pharaohs and Kings* was made into a highly acclaimed television series produced by The Learning Channel. Hard to find but worth looking for. Check your library for the book or video (you may need to request an inner library loan). ISBN: 0609801309

The Pharaohs of Ancient Egypt by Elizabeth Payne **4-8**
Ruled by awesome kings called Pharaohs, ancient Egypt was a land of bustling cities, golden palaces, and huge stone monuments. This astonishing civilization endured for more than 3,000 years. Beginning with the Rosetta Stone, author Elizabeth Payne examines archeological studies that have helped unlock the incredible secrets of Egypt's first kings. ISBN: 0394846990

Pyramid by David Macaulay **4-8** **9-12**
Text and black-and-white illustrations follow the intricate step-by-step process of the building of an ancient Egyptian pyramid. ISBN: 0395321212

Pyramids!: 50 Hands-On Activities to Experience Ancient Egypt by Avery Hart **4-8**
Today's kids can experience the wonders of ancient Egypt in this activity book that includes games, food, clothing and creative ways in which to explore life in an ancient society. Illustrations and photos. Consumable. Another winner from "Kaleidoscope Kids." ISBN: 1885593104

Science in Ancient Egypt by Geraldine Woods **4-8**
Discusses the achievements of the ancient Egyptians in science, mathematics, astronomy, medicine, agriculture, and technology. ISBN: 0531159159

Story of the Nile by Anne Millard and Steve Noon **K-3** **4-8**
Young readers can experience a stunning pictorial journey down the River Nile and learn about the people who settled along its banks. Noon's detailed full-color illustrations capture one of the world's most important ancient cultures. ISBN 0789498715

Tirzah by Lucille Travis **4-8** **N**
A Hebrew slave girl and her family serve the Egyptians until they escape by God's leading through Moses. Then they encounter the desert and its incredible challenges. A clear demonstration of God's faithfulness. ISBN: 0836135466

Ancient Israel

AD Chronicles: First Light, Second Touch, Third Watch by Bodie and Brock Thoene `9-12` **N** ⊱
These three novels transport readers back to the time of Jesus Christ. The Thornes bring these stories to life with detailed historical and biblical research. Opens just after the massacre of Jews before Passover in Jerusalem to citizens are searching for their promised Messiah to return. ISBN: 842375082, 842375090, 842375139

Ancient Israel and Ancient Greece: Religion, Politics, and Culture by John Pairman Brown `9-12` ⊱
John Pairman Brown investigates relationships.of historical religious, linguistic, and cultural connections between between ancient Israel and Greece. ISBN: 0800635914

Ancient Israel: From Abraham to the Roman Destruction of the Temple by Edward Shanks `9-12` ⊱
Immensely readable and digestible in just a few sittings, this book examines the complete history of ancient Israel—from Abraham to the Roman destruction of the Second Temple in A.D. 70. ISBN: 0130853631

Ancient Israel: Its Life and Institutions by Roland DeVaux `9-12` ⊱
Now considered by many to be a modern classic, *Ancient Israel: Its Life and Institutions* offers a fascinating, full-scale reconstruction of the social and religious life of Israel in Old Testament times. ISBN: 080284278X

Behold the Trees by Sue Alexander `K-3`
The history of Israel is told through the story of its trees in this dramatic story. ISBN: 0590762117

Bible History Old Testament by Alfred Edersheim `9-12` ⊱
The Scripture narrative is discussed according to the order of the books of the Bible, chapter by chapter, with biblical references clearly marked to enable the reader to easily find the passages being explained. ISBN: 156563165X

A Biblical Feast: Foods from the Holy Land by Kitty Morse `9-12` ⊱
A fascinating blend of food, history, and traditional recipes updated for today's kitchen, *A Biblical Feast* draws from the original Mediterranean diet—foods that are spoken of in the Bible, recipes in an intriguing cultural context. ISBN: 0898159652

Bless You! Restoring the Biblically Hebraic Blessing by John Garr `9-12` ⊱
A systematic, comprehensive study of the biblically Hebraic concept of blessing. God himself composed and prescribed the blessings for his children, a benediction that also places God's personal name on the one who is blessed. This powerful dynamic can now be experienced in every Christian home
ISBN: 0967827973

A Brief History of Ancient Israel by Victor H. Matthews `9-12`
Drawing on contemporary archaeological findings, this work presents a concise history of ancient Israel from its pre-historic beginnings to the post-exilic period. ISBN: 0664224369

Count Your Way Through Israel by Jim Haskins `K-3`
In counting-book format that teaches about the land, agricultural and manufactured products, history, holidays, symbols, fauna, and peoples of Israel. A pronunciation guide is included. Beautiful watercolor illustrations. ISBN: 0876145586

Chronicles of the King Series by Lynn Austin `9-12` ⊱
Book 1 *The Lord Is My Strength*, book 2 *The Lord is My Song*, book 3 *The Lord is My Salvation*, book 4 *My Father's God*, book 5 *Among the Gods*. Weaving a complex novel of suspense, action, inspiration, and God's enduring grace, Austin brings a new level to biblical fiction. Award-winning series. ISBN: 0834115387.

Families in Ancient Israel by Leo G. Perdue `9-12`
Four top-notch scholars of the Hebrew Bible and early Judaism provide a clear portrait of the family in ancient Israel. The book then draws important theological and ethical implications for the family today. ISBN: 0664255671

Ancient Israel continued

A Family Guide to the Biblical Holidays by Robin Sampson **K-3** **4-8** **9-12** ⌐○
Gives an an extensive look at the nine annual holidays: Passover, Unleavened Bread, Firstfruits, Pentecost, Trumpets, Day of Atonement, Tabernacles, Hanukkah, Purim and the weekly holiday—the Sabbath! Includes historical, agricultural, spiritual, and prophetic purposes of each holiday, showing how each points to Christ. Also projects, crafts, recipes, games, and songs for celebrating each holiday. ISBN: 0970181604

For The Temple by G.A. Henty **9-12** ⌐○
A stirring tale of the last days of the Temple at Jerusalem. Robber bands and political infighting set the stage for the Roman destruction of Jerusalem in A.D. 70. In the face of overwhelming odds, John of Gamala does his best to save God's Temple, harassing Roman work parties, burning Roman camps, defending Jerusalem during the Roman siege, and even fighting Titus himself in hand-to-hand combat—forging a relationship with the Roman leader that lasts until after the war. In spite of fighting a losing battle, John keeps his integrity and honor intact. ISBN: 1887159002

The Gifts of the Jews: How a Tribe of Desert Nomads Changed the Way Everyone Thinks and Feels by Thomas Cahill **9-12**
The author reveals the critical change that made Western civilization possible, in this irresistible exploration of the origins of some of humankind's oldest and most closely held beliefs. ISBN: 0385482493

God's Lamp, Man's Light: Mysteries of the Menorah by John Garr **9-12** ⌐○
God's Lamp, Man's Light is a masterful analysis of the menorah, the only biblical symbol that has the distinction of being designed by God himself. ISBN: 0967827949

A History of the Jews by Paul Johnson **9-12**
A brilliant and comprehensive survey covering 4,000 years of Jewish history. An interpretation of how Jewish history, philosophy, ethics, social and political notions interplay with world history. ISBN: 0060915331

A History of the Jewish People in the Time of Jesus Christ by Emil Schurer **9-12** ⌐○
This classic work includes extensive essays on the Roman political system and its leaders, the political and religious parties of Judaism, Messianic movements, and pertinent Greek and Jewish literature from the centuries before and after Christ. Five volumes. ISBN: 1565630491. Very expensive. Check your library.

Holman Bible Atlas: A Complete Guide to the Expansive Geography of Biblical History by T.V. Brisco **9-12** ◐▬ ♥
This excellent resources is one you'll use over and over for years. Maps, charts and color photographs guide readers through each biblical era, illustrating the land, sites, and archaeology of the ancient world of the Bible. See page 281 for more details. ISBN: 1558197095

The Holy Land by Peter Connolly **4-8**
Spanning a hundred years that culminate in the fall of Masada in A.D. 73, Connolly reconstructs the daily lives—domestic, religious, and military, mostly under the reign of the great King Herod. ISBN: 0199105332

An Introduction to First Century Judaism: Jewish Religion and History by Lester Grabbe **9-12**
Grabbe concentrates on the Second Temple period, objectively summarizing the main currents of scholarship as well as critiquing the available sources in a clear, even-handed way. ISBN: 0567085066

The Kregel Pictorial Guide to the Tabernacle by Tim Dowley **4-8** **9-12** ⌐○
This fully illustrated, full-color pictorial uncovers the significance, services, symbols, and sacrifices of the Tabernacle. ISBN: 0825424682

The Kregel Pictorial Guide to the Temple by Robert Backhouse **4-8** **9-12** ⌐○
Herod's temple in Jerusalem took over eighty years to complete and eventually covered some thirty-six acres. Tragically, this vast complex of colonnades, courtyards, and buildings was destroyed by the Roman army less than ten years after its completion. This is the story of Jewish worship from its early days in the Tent of Meeting at Mount Sinai to the first temple building constructed by Solomon. The enlargement of the second temple building by Herod and the subsequent history of the Temple Mount through the modern era is covered in fascinating detail. ISBN: 0825430399

Ancient Israel continued

Incredible Edible Bible Fun by Nanette Goings `K-3` `4-8`
Each of these 52 recipes ties to a simple, age-appropriate devotion or project. Children will stir up their creations safely and quickly—no sharp knives, hot ovens, or refrigerators are needed, and each recipe takes just 20 minutes from start to finish. ISBN: 0764420011

Israel ABCs: A Book about the People and Places of Israel by Holly Schroeder `K-3`
Jerusalem, Israel's most famous city, is holy to more than half the people in the world. In this ABC tour of Israel, you'll learn all about the wonders of this ancient land. ISBN: 1404801790

Living Emblems: Ancient Symbols of Faith by John D. Garr, Ph.D. `9-12`
Presents explanations of the rich symbolism manifest in the objects and images of Jewish tradition, including the shofar, the menorah, and the tallit. ISBN: 0967827914

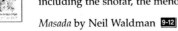

Masada by Neil Waldman `9-12`
Discusses the history of Masada, from the building of Herod's Temple through its use by Zealots as a refuge from the Romans, to its rediscovery in the mid-20th century. ISBN: 1590780639

Masada: The Last Fortress by Gloria D. Miklowitz `9-12`
As the Roman army marches inexorably across the Judean desert towards the fortress of Masada, Simon and his family and friends prepare, along with the rest of the Jewish Zealots, to fight and never surrender. ISBN: 0613979362

Nelson's Illustrated Encyclopedia of the Bible by John Drane (editor) `4-8` `9-12`
See description in page 278.

Our Father Abraham: Jewish Roots of the Christian Faith by Marvin R. Wilson `9-12`
This volume delineates the link between Judaism and Christianity, between the Old and New Testaments, and calls Christians to reexamine their Hebrew roots so as to effect a more authentically biblical lifestyle. See more on page 129. ISBN: 0802804233

A Short History of the Jewish People: From Legendary Times to Modern Statehood by Raymond Scheindlin `9-12`
From the original legends of the Bible to the peace accords of today's newspapers, this engaging, one-volume history of the Jews will fascinate and inform. 30 illustrations. ISBN: 0195139410

Sketches of Jewish Social Life by Alfred Edersheim `9-12`
This classic work on the cultural and social world of Jesus and His apostles continues to be invaluable for students of Scripture. ISBN: 156563005X

Tasty Bible Stories: A Menu of Tales and Matching Recipes by Tami Lehman-Wilzig `K-3`
Stories of Adam and Eve, Noah, Sarah, and other figures are each accompanied by two or three recipes. Each recipe is animated and boldly rendered, surrounded by images of tasty-looking ingredients. ISBN: 1580130801

The Temple: Its Ministry and Services by Alfred Edersheim `9-12`
Jerusalem's temple represented not only the glory of Israel's past but the splendor of its future, when the Messiah would come and reign over God's people. ISBN: 1565631366

The Victor Journey Through the Bible by V. Gilbert Beers `4-8` `9-12`
See description on page 282. ISBN: 156476480X

Your Travel Guide to Ancient Israel by Joseph Sherman `4-8`
Journey to the land of King Solomon, the Dead Sea, and the beginnings of three different religions—Judaism, Christianity, and Islam. Float in the Dead Sea or perhaps in a public bath. See the walls of Jericho, the grand palace of Solomon, or take a walk in the desert—just sure to bring lots of water! Experience what life was like in ancient Israel with this fact-filled travel guide to the past. Reading list, recipes, maps, activities. ISBN: 0822530724

Ancient Greece

Alexander the Great by Robert Green `4-8`
Provides a look into the life of one of the greatest conquerors of the ancient world, and demonstrates the new trade and cultural routes that were created through Alexander's vast conquests in the East. Illustrations. ISBN: 0531157997

Alexander the Great by Ulrich Wilcken `9-12` **N**
Here is one of the greatest biographies of Alexander, in its original form, brought fully up to date with the findings of modern research and criticism. ISBN: 0393003817

Archimedes and the Door of Science by Jeanne Bendick `4-8` **N**
This is a book about the life and work of Archimedes, the Greek mathematician. The author joins together mathematical and scientific principles into a delightful story format. ISBN: 1883937124

Art and Civilization in Ancient Greece by John Malam `K-3` `4-8`
This book helps children understand the past through paintings, murals, sculpture, architecture, and everyday objects highlights ten topics including Athens, religion, and war. Full-color reproductions and photos of sites and artifacts provide additional facts. ISBN: 0872266168

The Birth of Greece by Pierre Leveque `9-12`
An illustrated study of the development of the Greek civilization observes the years from 2000 B.C., when nomads arrived in Greece, through the brilliance of fifth-century B.C. Athens, to 338 B.C., when Philip of Macedon conquered the country. ISBN: 0810928434

A City Through Time by DK Publishing `4-8`
Featuring 12 panoramic illustrations, this book tracks the history of a city, beginning with the birth of a fictional Greek colony and tracing its development over 2,500 years into a vast metropolis. Full color. ISBN: 0756606411

Classical Kids: An Activity Guide to Life in Ancient Greece and Rome by Laurie Carlson `K-3` `4-8`
Travel back in time to see what life was like in ancient Greece and Rome while having fun with such hands-on activities as making a star gazer, chiseling a clay tablet, weaving Roman sandals, and making a Greek mosaic. 100+ line drawings. ISBN: 1556522908

Count Your Way Through Greece by Jim Haskins `K-4`
These beautifully illustrated, interactive picture books introduce children to foreign cultures and languages. ISBN: 0876149735

Eyewitness Ancient Greece by Anne Pearson, Nick Nicholls (Photographer) `4-8` `9-12` ◆ ○—
This look at the culture that most influenced Western society tells how the Greeks made war and worshiped their gods, and examines their legacy of science, medicine, philosophy and art. Full-color photos. ISBN: 0756606497

Greeks Pop-Up by Pam Mara `4-8`
A pop-up book for children to cut and glue and make themselves. Scenes and text tell the story of the ancient Greeks and their place in history. ISBN: 0906212332

The Greek Achievement: The Foundation of the Western World by Charles Freeman `9-12`
Traces the entire course of ancient Greek history across thousands of years—from the Mycenaean and Minoan civilizations of the Bronze Age through the Archaic, Classical, Hellenistic, and Roman periods. This brilliant account celebrates the incredible range of Greek achievement: the architectural marvels of the Athenian Acropolis; the birth of drama and the timeless tragedies of Aeschylus, Euripides, and Sophocles; Homer's epics; the philosophical revolutions of Plato and Aristotle; and the conquests of Alexander the Great. Lavishly illustrated with photographs and maps. provides a rich, contemporary overview of their enduring contribution to world civilization. ISBN: 014029323X

Ancient Greece continued

The Greco-Roman World of the New Testament Era: Exploring the Background of Early Christianity
by James S. Jeffers `9-12`
James Jeffers provides an informative and scenic tour of the various facets of the Roman world—class and status, family and community, work and leisure, religion and organization, city and country, law and government, death and taxes, and the epochal events of Roman history. Here is an eye-opening book that advances our understanding of the New Testament and early Christianity. ISBN: 0830815899

The Greek News by Anton Powell `4-8`
Covering ancient Greece in the form of a daily newspaper written at the time, this innovative book presents historical nonfiction in a unique, child-friendly format. Full color. ISBN: 0763603406

The Greeks by Abigail Wheatley `9-12`
Coins, democracy and the Olympics—ancient Greek civilizations have had an amazing impact on the modern world. Discover what everyday life was like in ancient Greece in this fascinating historical chronicle and reference book. ISBN: 0794504280

Handbook to Life in Ancient Greece by Lesley Adkins and Roy A. Adkins `9-12`
From the beginning of the Minoan civilization, to the fall of the Greek states, to the Romans by 30 B.C., this handy reference provides comprehensive access to over three millennia of ancient Greek history and archaeology. 179 halftones and linecuts. ISBN: 019512491X

Historical Atlas of Ancient Greece by Angus Konstam `9-12`
Lavishly illustrated, with specially designed maps that complement the text this atlas traces the entire historical, cultural, and political progress of the Greeks. ISBN: 816052204

History Pockets, Ancient Greece, Grades 4-6 by Sandi Johnson `4-8`
Students learn about the Greeks military and everyday life in ancient Greece (religion, mythology, work school, art, language, literature, etc.) while creating portfolios for assessment and display. ISBN: 1557999031

Hour of the Olympics by Mary Pope Osborne `K-3`
Jack and Annie are off to ancient Greece, where they race against time to witness the very first Olympic games. Illustrated chapter book. (A "Magic Treehouse" book). ISBN: 0679890629

How Would You Survive as an Ancient Greek? by Fiona MacDonald `4-8`
This transports the reader back to ancient Greece, giving detailed information on aspects of life
Full-color illustrations. ISBN: 0613187555

The Librarian Who Measured the Earth by Kathryn Lasky `K-3` `4-8`
Describes the life and work of Eratosthenes, the Greek geographer and astronomer who accurately measured the circumference of the Earth. ISBN: 0316515264

The Penguin Historical Atlas of Greece by Robert Morkot `9-12`
Charting topics as diverse as Minoan civilization, the Persian Wars, the Golden Age of Athens, and the conquests of Alexander the Great, this volume in Penguin's Atlas series traces the development of a creative and restless people and assesses their impact not only on the ancient world but also on our own attitudes and environment today. Full-color maps and illustrations throughout. ISBN: 0140513353

Science in Ancient Greece by Kathlyn Gay `4-8`
Reveals the large debt owed by modern scientists to the healers, mathematicians, stargazers, explorers, and thinkers of the ancient world. ISBN: 0531159299

The Trojan Horse by David Clement-Davies and Dorling Kindersley Publishing `K-4` **N**
The rich vocabulary and factual panels will set your children on a lifelong path to reading for information in this retelling of how the Greeks used a wooden horse to win the ten-year-long Trojan War. Full color. ISBN: 0789444747

Ancient Rome

Beyond the Desert Gate by Mary Ray 9-12 **N** ∽

Palestine in the first century A.D. was as disturbed and divided as it is today. The Jews had revolted against Roman occupation and as they grew more restive, Rome clamped down harder. The ten Greek cities of Palestine—the Decapolis—wanted only to continue their peaceful trading existence, but they found themselves caught in the middle of uprisings. ISBN: 188393754X

City: A Story of Roman Planning and Construction by David Macaulay 5-8

Text and black and white illustrations show how the Romans planned and constructed their cities for the people who lived within them. ISBN: 395349222

Eyewitness Ancient Rome by Simon James, Nick Nichols (Photographer) 4-8 9-12 ♦ ☞

Explains the customs and daily life of the Romans through a clear, informative text, and features layered illustrations using acetate that reveal the outside and inside of a Roman town house, a theater, an army fort, and the Roman baths. Full-color photos. ISBN: 0756606519

Handbook to Life in Ancient Rome by Lesley Adkins, Roy A. Adkins 9-12

The chapters are arranged thematically, and cover the republic, military affairs, geography, town and countryside, travel and trade, writing, religion, economy and industry, and everyday life. Within each chapter the authors cover an exhaustive range of subtopics. ISBN: 0195123328

Illustrated Encyclopedia of Ancient Rome by Mike Corbishley 4-8 9-12

Designed for young readers, this book describes the ancient Romans and their world. More than 220 informative images detail everyday life in Roman cities and countryside, as well as subjects such as farming, trade, leisure and games, religions, language, technology, and war. Readers will encounter emperors and slaves, writers and soldiers, dictators and gladiators. For ages nine and up. ISBN: 0892367059

The Penguin Historical Atlas of Ancient Rome by Chris Scarre 9-12 ☞

This atlas traces the empire's rise and fall, looking at its provinces and cities, trade and economy, armies and frontier defenses; charting its transformation into a Christian theocracy; and assessing its lasting impact. Full color. ISBN: 0140513299

Pompeii... Buried Alive! by Edith Kunhardt K-4 **N**

A simple retelling of the fateful days in A.D. 79 when Mt. Vesuvius erupted and the people in the ancient town of Pompeii perished. ISBN: 0394988663

Rome Antics by David Macaulay 4-8 **N**

As readers follow the path of a pigeon carrying an important message through the streets of Rome, they discover a fascinating city that has been recycling itself for more than 2,000 years. Macaulay's ingenious vision provides an informative journey through this most wonderful of cities. ISBN: 0395822793

The Search for Ancient Rome by Claude Moatti 4-8

An illustrated look back at ancient Rome discusses the remnants of a once-flourishing civilization—including the Colosseum, the Pantheon, and Diocletian's baths—and its twenty centuries of pillage. ISBN: 0810928396

Science in Ancient Rome by Jacqueline L Harris 4-8

Describes how the Romans put to use and expanded the scientific achievements of earlier civilizations. ISBN: 0531159167

The Young Carthaginian: A Story of the Times of Hannibal by G. A. Henty 4-8 **N**

Set in ancient times, during the Punic wars, this story follows the adventures of young Malchus, an officer in Hannibal's army. Henty describes the army's incredible journey through southern Europe and across the Alps in fascinating detail, providing both a lesson in ancient history and an absorbing story. The balance of power in Europe swayed between Rome and Carthage and the outcome of this struggle would determine the course of Western civilization, even until today. ISBN: 1890623016

The Messiah

AD Chronicles See description in Ancient Israel section. **9-12** **N** ☞

The Bible Jesus Read by Philip Yancey **9-12** ☞
The Old Testament is God's biography, the story of his passionate encounters with people and also a prequel to the story of Jesus. Philip Yancey explores these writings in an effort to know God better. ISBN: 0310245664

The Bronze Bow by Elizabeth George Speare **4-8** **9-12** **N** ☞
A young boy seeks revenge against the Romans for killing his parents, but is turned away from vengeance by Jesus. ISBN: 0395137195

Daily Life at the Time of Jesus by Miriam Feinberg Vamosh **4-8** ☞ ★ ☞
Helps children understand the cultural background of those who lived in Bible times and those who wrote about it. Learn about the people of the time of Jesus, their routines, and their daily life. ISBN: 9652801100

Discover Jesus in Genesis: An Illustrated Biblical Theology for All Ages by Larry Edison **K-3** **4-8** ☞ ★ ☞
You'll want to use this book not only for your own personal benefit, but also as a great way to explain the Old Testament and its meaning to your children. You will see Christ come alive through these pages, and your reading of Genesis will never be the same again. ISBN: 1579213898

Encounter Christ Through the Dramatic Story of Vinegar Boy by Alberta Hawse **4-8** **N** ☞
This is the gripping story of a boy's dramatic encounter with Christ on the Cross. As he brings Christ vinegar to drink, he witnesses the crucifixion and is forever changed. ISBN: 0802465889

He Chose the Nails by Max Lucado **9-12** ☞
The only required act for our salvation was the shedding of blood, yet Jesus did much more. Max examines the symbols surrounding Christ's crucifixion. ISBN: 0849905702

The Four Witnesses: The Rebel, the Rabbi, the Chronicler, and the Mystic by Robin Griffith-Jones **9-12** ☞
How and why each Gospel was written. Mark's Gospel tells the rebel's story of Jesus. Matthew tells of the Rabbi, the long-awaited fulfillment of Jewish expectation. For Luke, Jesus is a heroic, compassionate social revolutionary who confidently and mercifully dies on behalf of all humanity. John's Gospel is a mystic's interpretation of the divinity of Jesus told in powerful poetic language. ISBN: 0062516485

The Hem of His Garment: Touching the Power in God's Word by Dr. John Garr **9-12** ☞
This book gives a comprehensive study of the Jewish tallit commonly worn in Bible days. It has tzitzit (fringes) appended to each corner as a means of calling both the wearer and the observer to remember all the Word of God (commandments).An excellent study, you don't want to miss! ISBN: 0967827906

Jesus by Brian Wildsmith **K-3** **4-8** ☞
In this stunning picture book, Brian Wildsmith portrays the life of Jesus of Nazareth in a series of powerful scenes, framed by gold. ISBN: 0802852122

Jesus the Jewish Theologian by Brad Young **9-12** ☞
Establishes Jesus firmly within the context of first-century Judaism and shows how understanding Jesus' Jewishness is crucial for interpreting the Bible. Upper high school or college level. ISBN: 1565630602

The Life and Times of Jesus the Messiah by Alfred Edersheim **9-12** ☞
This Edersheim classic explores the cities, towns, religious sects, political struggles, customs, and lifestyles of Jesus' day. ISBN: 0943575834

The Life of Our Lord: Written for His Children During the Years 1846 to 1849 by Charles Dickens **K-3** **4-8** ☞
First published in 1934, this simple narrative, written by Dickens for his children during the years 1846 to 1849, expresses the author's great faith and humility by retelling the story of the life, death, and resurrection of Jesus. ISBN: 0684865378

The Messiah continued

The Mind of Christ: The Transforming Power of Thinking His Thoughts T. W. Hunt `9-12`
This book will help Christians understand how God works within them and transforms them, continually renewing and reshaping their minds to reflect the mind of Christ more closely. ISBN: 0805463496

The Miracle of the Scarlet Thread by Richard Booker `9-12`
The Miracle of the Scarlet Thread reveals God's order, sheds light on the Old Testament and demonstrates in clear language how the Old Testament and New Testament fit together. ISBN: 0914903268

More Than a Carpenter by Josh McDowell `9-12`
A hard-hitting book for people who are skeptical about Jesus' deity, His resurrection, and His claim on their lives. ISBN: 0842345523

The Nazarene by Sholem Asch `9-12` **N**
This classic and gripping novel by one of the greatest writers of Yiddish literature tells the unforgettable story of three men: Cornelius, an officer in the Roman garrison of Jerusalem in the first century A.D.; Joseph Arimathea, a young Pharisee student at the time; and Yeshua, a radical preacher from Galilee, better remembered by his Greek name of Jesus. Profound! ISBN: 0786703792

Next Door Savior by Max Lucado `5-8` `9-12`
This book deals with the entire life of Christ, from His birth to His death and resurrection, showing His nature as both God and man. ISBN: 1400303729

The Parables: Jewish Tradition and Christian Interpretation Brad Young `9-12`
While parables have timeless messages, reinterpretations in new contexts throughout the centuries have distorted the original meanings and undermined the essence of what Jesus intended for his initial listeners. Young examines the parables that best illustrate the parallels between the rabbinic and Gospel parables. Upper high school or college level. ISBN: 1565632443

Rabboni Which is to Say Master: by W. Phillip Keller `9-12`
This classic surveys the ministry of Jesus Christ through both the Old and New Testaments in this devotional study. His aim is that Jesus will become more approachable for the reader. ISBN: 0825429919

The Robe by Lloyd C Douglas `9-12` **N**
With more than six million copies sold, this classic is the story of the man who gambled for Christ's robe and won. ISBN: 0395957753

A Shepherd Looks at Psalm 23 by W. Phillip Keller `9-12`
This timeless classic describes a shepherd's view of the love Jesus the Shepherd has for his flock. From the firsthand experiences of one who has developed and managed sheep ranches, this is an inspirational and refreshing look at one of the best-loved portions of Scripture. ISBN: 0310214351

Understanding the Difficult Words of Jesus by David Blivin, Roy Blizzard `9-12`
The authors do an excellent job of placing Jesus in his proper historical context, as highly educated in both the study of the Torah and in the culture of his day. Many of Jesus' sayings contain Hebrew idioms that are meaningless in either Greek or English. This light of understanding reveals the wonders of our Savior's life and teachings. ISBN: 156043550X

The World Jesus Knew by Anne Punton `4-8` `9-12`
If I had known of this book when I wrote *The Messiah* unit study it would have been a key resource (it will be once it's revised so I added a key here). Each chapter covers a distinct aspect of the life of Jesus: his home, childhood, education, clothes, language, prayers, customs, festivals, and much more. This is an invaluable reference tool every Christian should own! It transports readers to the beliefs and customs that

are the background of the Gospels. The author spent 12 years in Israel and lectures extensively on the Jewish roots of the Hebrew faith. Includes over 60 maps and photographs. *Fantastic!* not just for this unit but makes a great read-aloud with Bible study readings when you get to the Gospels. ISBN: 082560042

Early Church

The 100 Most Important Events in Christian History by A. Kenneth Curtis, Lang and Petersen **9-12** ⁀
Traces two thousand years of church history in one concise volume. It highlights the major people, events, and ideas that have shaped the long history of Christianity. ISBN: 0800756444

Christian History Made Easy by Timothy Paul Jones **9-12** ⁀
Mr. Jones' work is a refreshing change in studying Church history. He transitions from one era or event to another makes Church history easy to study. Maps, side-bar quotations, and review learning activities are included. Each of the twelve eras studied (A.D. 64 to 1999) begins with key names, events and terms to remember. It is a thirteen week course with leaders guide. ISBN: 1890947105

Church History in Plain Language: by Bruce Shelley **9-12** ⁀
It's about time that someone wrote church history that tells about people, not just about "eras" and "ages." *Church History in Plain Language* taps the roots of our Christian family tree. It combines authoritative research with a captivating style to bring our heritage home to us. ISBN: 0849938619

Going to Church in the First Century by Robert Banks **9-12** ⁀
This will show you that Church was much, much more than warming a pew Sunday morning—it was a way of life. ISBN: 0940232375

The Early Church ("Penguin History") by Henry Chadwicka **9-12** ⁀
The Church is seen in close relation to its original setting in Jewish and Gentile society, toward which the Christians were indebted, and yet at the same time, with the zeal of martyrs, defiant. ISBN: 0140231994

Early Church History by Verlyn D. Verbrugge **9-12** ⁀
This Zondervan Quick-Reference Library is designed to give the reader a grasp of the history of the early church. Dozens of topics of interest are covered in handy one-page bits of information.ISBN: 0310203953

A History of Christian Thought by Justo L. Gonzalez **9-12** ⁀
Explains the religious culture of the Jews and the Greco-Romans around the time when Jesus Christ came into the world, then outlines the main flow of theology and progression during the first 450 years of the Church through the writings of the Apostolic Fathers and major theologians. ISBN: 0687171822

The Kregel Pictorial Guide To Church History: The Early Church-a.d. 33–500 by John D. Hannah **4-8** **9-12** ⁀
Brings to life the great leaders and conflicts that shaped the early church, as well as the cultural and political developments. Provides easy-to-follow summaries of key personalities and crucial developments in the church's first centuries. Fully indexed and filled with four-color charts, maps, photographs, and illustrations, this concise guide to church history ISBN: 0825427835

Story of the Church by Robert G. Clouse **9-12** ⁀
Follow the church from the beginning, through all of its failures as well as successes. Despite succumbing to the pressure of culture, the church has both survived and thrived. Sure to appeal to a wide range of audiences. ISBN: 0802424813

Timeline Charts of the Western Church by Susan L. Peterson **4-8** **9-12** ⁀
Provides information on theological issues, people and events, the wider culture, and theological texts, all in a time-tested, highly accessible column format. ISBN: 0310223539

A Voice in the Wind ("Mark of the Lion" #1) by Francine Rivers **9-12** **N** ⁀
A.D. 70 Rome comes alive in this tale of the Jewish Christian slave girl Hadassah. Torn between a desire to witness and her fear of persecution, she encourages readers to represent Christ in their world. This book from Moody is similar to the Eyewitness books. Illustrated, index, and maps. ISBN: 0842377506

The Untold Story of the New Testament Church by Frank Viola **9-12** ⁀
Frank Viola casts his gaze back at the birth pangs of first century Christianity in this book. Using a "you-are-there" approach. ISBN: 0768422361

Vikings

Adventures with the Vikings by Linda Bailey K-3 4-8 **N**
Josh and Emma, and their little sister, Libby, stumble into the Good Times Travel Agency and are transported back in time and find themselves as stowaways on a Viking longship. ISBN: 1550745441

Beorn the Proud by Madeleine A. Polland 5-8 9-12 **N**
Beorn, a Viking chief, becomes a better ruler as a result of the influence of Ness, a Christian slave. Ness is in the midst of the action, and exhibits courage, intelligence, and compassion. ISBN: 1883937086

The Story of Rolf and the Viking Bow by Allen French 5-8 9-12 **N**
This turn-of-the-century novel by Allen French is in the style and tradition of the great Icelandic sagas and is set in the time just after Iceland had become Christian. ISBN: 1883937019

Sword Song by Rosemary Sutcliff 5-8 9-12 **N**
A swashbuckling epic of a young Viking swordsman, banished from his home for unintentionally killing a man, who takes up a new life as a mercenary. ISBN: 0374469849

Viking Ships at Sunrise by Mary Pope Osborne K-3 **N**
Their magic tree house takes Jack and Annie back to a monastery in medieval Ireland, where they try to retrieve a lost book while being menaced by Viking raiders. Illustrated chapter book. ISBN: 0679890610

Viking Town by Jacqueline Morley 4-8
Metropolis guides give practical information about life in the cities of the past, including guidebook details for the armchair traveler. ISBN: 0531153800

Viking World: A Guide to 11th Century Scandinavia by Sue Nicholson and Julie Ferris K-3 4-8
Cruise the Scandinavian fjords and rivers and visit a Viking settlement in North America in this historical travel guide to the Norse civilization of northern Europe. ISBN: 0753452375

Viking World Internet Linked by Philippa Wingate and Anne Millard 5-8
An Usborne Internet-Linked book. The Vikings terrorized the people of Europe for three centuries. Raiding, trading and exploring, they sailed fearlessly—as far as Baghdad and the shores of North America. Their irrepressible spirit of adventure is captured inside this fascinating book. ISBN: 0794503543

The Vikings by Ian Heath 9-12
Examine the Viking epic journeys and the ships, their methods of warfare, the organization of their armies, appearance and equipment and history. Includes many fine illustrations and photos. ISBN: 0850455650

The Vikings by Magnus Magnusson 4-8
The Vikings hold a unique place in the history of the West, both mythologically and in the significant impact they had on Northern Europe. ISBN: 0752426990

The Vikings: Come and Discover My World by Two-Can K-3 4-8
Crafts, activities, stories, and historical facts give today's children a close look at youngsters of past cultures. ISBN: 158728071X

Vikings: Raiders and Explorers by Aileen Weintraub 4-8
Written in easy-to-understand language and uses consistently familiar vocabulary to encourage reluctant readers. ISBN: 0516250876

Who Were the Vikings? by Jane Chisholm and Struan Reid K-3
Gives answers to the first questions children ask about history, provoking comparison with life as they know it today. ISBN: 079450177X

Wulf the Saxon by G. A. Henty 5-8 9-12 **N**
When William of Normandy invades England, Wulf is with the English host at Hastings, and stands by his King to the last in the mighty struggle. Altogether this is a noble tale. ISBN: 1887159703

Middle Ages

1,000 Years Ago on Planet Earth by Sneed B. Collard `K-3`
Describes events and cultural developments all over the world 1,000 years ago, including the Americas, Europe, Africa, and Asia. ISBN: 0395908663

Adam of the Road by Elizabeth Janet Gray `4-8` **N**
The adventures of eleven-year-old Adam as he travels the open roads of thirteenth-century England searching for his missing father, a minstrel, and his stolen red spaniel, Nick. ISBN: 014032464X

Atlas of Medieval History (Penguin) by Colin McEvedy `9-12`
This book is a historical and geographical look at the period from the reign of Constantine to the great voyages of discovery. ISBN: 140512497

Castle by David Macaulay `4-8` `9-12`
What David Macaulay can draw—churches, cities, pyramids—he does better than any pen-and-ink illustrator in the world. An impressive Caldecott Honor Book. ISBN: 0395329205

Cathedral: The Story of Its Construction by David Macaulay `4-8`
Superb design, magnificent illustrations, and clearly presented information distinguish all of David Macaulay's books. ISBN: 395175135

Catherine, Called Birdy by Karen Cushman `4-8` `9-12` **N**
Set against a backdrop of life in a medieval manor, here is a young girl's account of her 14th year. Catherine feels trapped because her father is determined to marry her off to a rich man. Newbery Medal winner; ALA 1995 Best Books of 1995; ALA 1995 Best Books for Young Adults. ISBN: 0064405842

Christendom and Christianity in the Middle Ages: The Relations Between Religion, Church, and Society by Adriaan H. Bredero `9-12` ⌐⊂
Though buffeted on all sides by rapid and at times cataclysmic social, political, and economic change, the medieval Church was able to make adjustments that kept it from becoming simply a fossil from the past rather than an enduring institution of salvation. ISBN: 080284992X

Days of Knights and Damsels: An Activity Guide by Laurie Carlson `K-3` `4-8`
More than 100 illustrated crafts, projects, and games help recreate the culture and world of the Middle Ages, when books were handmade and read by candlelight, sundials told the hour, and going barefoot was illegal. ISBN: 1556522916

The Door in the Wall by Marguerite de Angeli `4-8` `9-12` **N**
Set in the fourteenth century, the classic story of one boy's personal heroism when he loses the use of his legs. Classic. Award winner. ISBN: 0440227798

Eyewitness Castle by Christopher Gravett `4-8` `9-12`
Discover the mysteries of the medieval castle and see what life was like for those living within. ISBN: 0756606608

Eyewitness Medieval Life by Andrew Langley `4-8` `9-12` ⦿—
Packed with fascinating facts, *Medieval Life* is a unique and compelling introduction to the people and culture of the Middle Ages. ISBN: 0756607051

Internet-linked Medieval World by Jane Bingham `4-8` `9-12` ⦿—
Lavishly illustrated and crammed with essential information from Usborne. From big battles, kings and warriors to peasants and palaces, the dramatic history of the medieval world is brought to life with lavish illustrations packed with detail and essential information. Links to exciting websites bring history alive with movies, games, sounds and interactivity. Covers period from 500 to 1500. Internet links to exciting websites. ISBN: 0746027621

Middle Ages continued

In Freedom's Cause: A Story of Wallace and Bruce by G. A. Henty. **4-8** **9-12** **N**
Storyteller Henty relates the stirring tale of the Scottish War of Independence. The hero of the tale fought under both Wallace and Bruce, and while the strictest historical accuracy has been maintained with respect to public events, the work is full of "hairbreadth 'scapes" and wild adventure. ISBN: 048642362X

A Knight Of The White Cross by G.A. Henty **4-8** **9-12** **N**
Young Gervaise Tresham leaves England and the turmoil of the Wars of the Roses to become a Knight of St. John. Starting as a page Gervaise quickly attains knighthood and defends Europe and Christendom against the anarchy of piracy in the Mediterranean and the expansion of the Turkish empire. ISBN: 1890623067

Knights and Castles by Alex Martin **K-3** **4-8**
Knights and Castles introduces readers to the exciting world of the medieval knight and his entourage. ISBN: 1587284413

Knights and Castles ("Questions & Answers") by Philip Brooks **K-3** **4-8**
Curious young knaves can find the answers to questions about knights, castles, and medieval times in this exciting book. Full-color illustrations. ISBN: 0753453711

Knights & Castles ("Usborne Time Traveler") by Judy Hindley **K-3** **4-8**
Takes readers back in time to illustrate the exciting happenings of daily life. ISBN: 0794503357

Knights & Castles: 50 Hands-On Activities to Explore the Middle Ages by Avery Hart **K-3** **4-8** **9-12**
Dozens of games and celebrations invite kids to investigate the Middle Ages, while through descriptions of food, clothing and more, they can become part of a time of castles and kings, cathedrals and conquests. Illustrations & photos. Consumable. ISBN: 1885593171

Make This Model Medieval Castle—Usborne Cut-Out Models by Iain Ashman **K-3** **4-8**
There are over ninety pieces to cut out and assemble to make this superb model of a 14th century castle. Surrounded by a moat with a drawbridge which goes up and down, the scene is crammed with accurate historical detail. Require only glue, scissors and a craft knife. ISBN: 0746032927

A Medieval Feast by Aliki **K-3** **4-8**
Aliki books are like visual candy. Each page bursts with color. This book describes the preparation and celebration of a medieval feast held at an English manor house entertaining royal guests. ISBN: 006446050

Men of Iron by Howard Pyle **4-8** **9-12** **N**
In seeking to avenge his unjustly accused father, young Myles Falworth is knighted and wins the friendship of King Henry IV. ISBN: 0890846944

The Middle Ages: An Illustrated History by Barbara A. Hanawalt **4-8**
This book mixes a spirited and entertaining writing style with exquisite, thorough scholarship exploring the history of the Middle Ages, including the merger of Roman, Christian, and Germanic cultures. ISBN: 195103599

Otto of the Silver Hand by Howard Pyle **K-3** **4-8** **N**
Fantastically illustrated tale of the motherless son of a valiant robber baron of medieval Germany. ISBN: 0486217841

Robin Hood: A Classic Illustrated Edition by Evelyn Charles Vivian **4-8** **9-12** **N**
This lavishly illustrated book features over 100 of the best images from the 12th to the 20th centuries, in this classic version of the the adventures of Robin Hood. ISBN: 811833992

Tales of King Arthur: King Arthur and the Round Table by Hudson Talbott **4-8** **9-12** **N**
Retells the story of how the young Arthur became high King of all Britain and assembled his Knights of the Round Table. Talbott's thrilling dazzling paintings bring out this tale of heroism (full color). ISBN: 0688113400

Renaissance

Beware, Princess Elizabeth ("A Young Royals Book") by Carolyn Meyer `4-8` `9-12`
Told in the voice of the young Elizabeth I and ending when she is crowned queen, this second novel in the Young Royals series explores the relationship between a girl who became one of England's most powerful monarchs and her half-sister, Mary Tudor, who tried everything to stop her. ISBN: 0152026592

The Black Death and the Transformation of the West by David Herlihy, Samuel Cohn (Editor) `9-12`
It ravaged a continent for over a century, killed millions of people and decimated economies. The Black Death was the great watershed in medieval history. But Herlihy sees in it the birth of technological advance as societies struggled to create labor-saving devices in the wake of population losses. New evidence for the plague's role in the establishment of universities, the spread of Christianity, the dissemination of vernacular cultures, and even the rise of nationalism demonstrates that this cataclysmic event marked a true turning point in history. ISBN: 0674076133

Brunelleschi's Dome: How a Renaissance Genius Reinvented Architecture by Ross King `9-12`
Brunelleschi's Dome is the story of how a Renaissance genius bent men, materials, and the very forces of nature to build an architectural wonder. Won several awards. National best-seller. ISBN: 0142000159

Doomed Queen Anne ("A Young Royals Book") by Carolyn Meyer `4-8` `9-12`
Meyer's engrossing novel tells Anne Boleyn's fascinating story in her own voice—from her life as an awkward girl, her marriage to King Henry VIII and dramatic moments before her death. ISBN: 0152165231

Eyewitness Renaissance by Alison Cole `4-8` `9-12` ○—
Beautiful, thought-provoking and highly informative guide to understanding the Renaissance. Superb color reproductions of paintings, sculptures and sketches, clear artworks and authoritative text from an established art historian offer a fresh "eyewitness" insight into appreciation of the momentous and influential art of the Renaissance era. A mini-museum between the covers of a book. ISBN: 078945582X

Leonardo and His Times by Andrew Langley `4-8` `9-12` ○—
Here is a stimulating introduction to the world of the Renaissance—from the achievements of Leonardo da Vinci to everyday life in an Italian city-state. Filled with superb, full-color photographs of works of art and beautiful artifacts, Leonardo brings the Renaissance to life, offering a unique view of this exciting period of history. DK Eyewitness Books. ISBN: 0789462907

Leonardo and the Flying Boy by Laurence Anholt `K-3`
A boy under the teaching of Leonardo da Vinci realizes his master is busily working on a mysterious flying machine. Based on true events. Full-color illustrations. ISBN: 0764152254

Leonardo Da Vinci for Kids: His Life and Ideas: 21 Activities by Janis Herbert and Carol Sabbeth `K-3` `4-8`
Presents a biography of this prolific artist and inventor through projects in cartography, animal art, bird observation, and mask-making. ISBN: 1556522983

The Lives of the Artists by Giorgi Vasari `9-12`
Vasari's collection of biographical accounts also presents an informative theory of the development of Renaissance art. ISBN: 019283410X

Katie and the Mona Lisa by James Mayhew `K-3`
At the art museum, while her grandmother dozes, Katie steps into the painting of the Mona Lisa and together they have adventures with the characters from four other well-known Renaissance paintings. Includes information about the artists. ISBN: 053130177X

Morning Star of the Reformation Andy Thomson `4-8` `9-12` ⋈
Wycliffe was the first person to translate the Bible into English. When young John of Wycliffe arrives at Oxford University, he finds it a fascinating and perilous place. With his friend, Sebastian Ayleton, John experiences the terrible plague called the "Pestilence" (the Black Death), and he becomes involved in clashes between university factions as well as riots among the townspeople. ISBN: 0890844534

Renaissance continued

Patience, Princess Catherine ("A Young Royals Book") by Carolyn Meyer **4-8** **9-12** **N**
The fate of Spanish princess Catherine of Aragon becomes uncertain when her betrothed—Prince Arthur of England—dies not long after the wedding. When Arthur's brother takes the throne and becomes Henry VIII, Catherine's resolve to become England's queen remains unshaken. ISBN: 0152165444

The Renaissance by Paul Procter and Rupert Matthews **K-3** **4-8**
This book helps children understand the past through paintings, murals, sculpture, architecture, and everyday objects. Divided into thematic chapters such as how people lived, worked, socialized, fought wars, worshiped, and made new discoveries and conquests. ISBN: 0872266184

Red Hugh, Prince of Donegal by Robert Reilly **4-8** **N**
In 1587, teenaged Hugh Roe O'Donnell, son of the rulers of Donegal, is seized by the English and imprisoned in Dublin Castle for three years before escaping to join in the struggle to rid Ireland of English rule. ISBN: 1883937221.

Renaissance, The: A Short History by Paul Johnson **9-12**
From a legendary historian comes a concise and entertaining survey of perhaps the most revolutionary, and romanticized, era of human history. He explains the economic, technological, and social developments that provide a backdrop to the age's achievements and important figures. ISBN: 0812966198

Robert Boyle: Trailblazer of Science by John Hudson Tiner **4-8** **9-12** **N** ⊷
Biography of how Boyle survived rebellions in Ireland, the English Civil War, the Black Death, the Great Fire and political unrest. He succeeded in making many remarkable discoveries during those difficult times. He lived a devout Christian life, using his science to glorify God. ISBN: 0880621559

Signs and Symbols in Christian Art: With Illustrations from Paintings from the Renaissance **4-8** **9-12** ⊷
Divided into 14 chapters, text and illustrations reveal the symbolism inherent in representations of religious personages, the earth and sky, animals, birds, insects, and flowers. George Ferguson also explores Old Testament characters and events and their symbolic representation in art. ISBN: 0195014324

William Shakespeare and the Globe by Aliki **4-8** **9-12**
Aliki brings to life the world of William Shakespeare, from his birth in Stratford-on-Avon, England to the present day reconstruction of the Globe theater. In her most ambitious work to date, Aliki combines animated words and pictures and quotations from Shakespeare's plays to create a five-act masterpiece that introduces young readers to the playwright and his works. Full-color clever illustrations, as well as architectural drawings. This book introduces the reader to sixteenth-century England, the theater, and provides biographical sketches of Shakespeare and his contemporaries. Award winning. ISBN: 0064437221

Uh-Oh, Leonardo! The Adventures of Providence Traveler **K-3** **N**
Providence Traveler is an imaginative mouse whose hero is Leonardo da Vinci. When she accidentally runs across a design of his for a time-travel machine, she can't resist trying it out. But once she arrives in Leonardo's Renaissance world, how does she get home again? Full color. ISBN: 0689811608

The Vanishing Point: A Story of Lavinia Fontana by Louise Hawes **4-8** **9-12** **N**
In lush, glowing prose, Hawes's historical novel draws readers into the life and art of 16th-century Bologna with a compelling account of Lavinia Fontana, arguably the most famous female painter of the Italian Renaissance. ISBN: 618434232

Reformation

The Bible Smuggler by Louise A. Vernon **4-8** **9-12** **N** ⌐
In this highly readable biography, Vernon explains William Tyndale's work of translating, printing, and distributing the Scripture, focusing on Tyndale's helper, Colin, who begins his work as a carrier boy smuggling in a copy of Luther's New Testament to Tyndale. ISBN: 0836115570

The Boy King: Edward VI and the Protestant Reformation by Diarmaid MacCulloch **9-12** **N**
A vivid picture and fascinating account of an intense period in the battle for dominance between Catholics and Protestants in England after the death of Henry VIII when his son Edward and Edward's advisors aimed to wipe out all manifestations of Catholic idolatry. Illustrated. ISBN: 0312238304

Charts of Reformation and Enlightenment Church History with CDROM by John D. Hannah **4-8** **9-12** ⌐
⌐
Maps, charts, and diagrams, designed by a teacher who learned how hard it is to communicate in a visual world without visuals, provide visual aids for the teaching of Church history from the sixteenth through eighteenth centuries. Includes CD-ROM. ISBN: 0310233178

The Chimney Sweep's Ransom by Dave Jackson and Neta Jackson **K-3** **4-8** **N** ⌐
In this "Trailblazer book," a young English boy is sold to be trained as a chimney sweep and rescued by his brother with the help of John Wesley. ISBN: 1556612680

Debating Calvinism: Five Points, Two Views by Dave Hunt and James White **9-12**
A centuries-old belief system is put to the test as two prominent authors examine the validity of Calvinism. White takes the point position; Hunt, the counterpoint. Gives a good overview of Calvinism. The format features affirmative and denial statements concerning the Reformer's teachings on God's sovereignty and man's free will; followed by response, defense, and final remarks. Lively! ISBN: 1590522737

Duncan's War ("Crown & Covenant" #01) by Douglas Bond **4-8** **9-12** **N** ⌐
In Scotland in 1666, fourteen-year-old Duncan learns the value of being true to his faith while fighting against supporters of England's King Charles II, who oppress the Covenanters—those who believe that only Jesus can be king of the Church. ISBN: 8075527426

Fine Print: A Story about Johann Gutenberg by Joann Johansen Burch **4-8** **N**
Recounts the story of the German printer credited with the invention of printing with movable type. Creative Minds Biography (see our web site for more books in this series). ISBN: 0876145659

God's Bestseller by Brian Moynahan **9-12** **N** ⌐
Moynahan delves into the life of 16th-century scholar William Tyndale, whose attempt to translate the Bible into English incurred the wrath of Sir Thomas More, who proclaimed Tyndale's act heresy, punishable by death. In this lucid biography, Moynahan reveals the English Bible as a labor of love, for which a man in an age more spiritual than our own willingly gave his life. ISBN: 0312314868

Gutenberg: How One Man Remade the World with Words by John Man **9-12** **N** ⌐
Printing was not a widely known trade in the year 1450, but by 1500 millions of books were in print. This is the story of the man responsible for that revolution, Johann Gutenberg, and his invention called printing. ISBN: 0471218235

The Hawk that Dare Not Hunt by Day by Scott O'Dell **4-8** ⌐
Amid political turmoil and threats of plague, young Tom Barton accepts the risks of helping William Tyndale publish and smuggle into England the Bible he has translated into English. ISBN: 890843686

Martin Luther by Martin E. Marty **9-12** **N** ⌐
Describes Luther's long battle with Church leaders—embellished by rich historical background—makes Marty's biography riveting reading. A fascinating history, a story of immense spiritual passion and amazing grace. A balanced view, including Luther's being anti-Semitic in later years. Luther remains intrinsically admirable, a bulwark of conscience as well as faith. (Penguin Life Biography) ISBN: 670032727

Reformation continued

Martin Luther: Martin Luther's Protest Changed the Course of History (Gateway Films) `4-8` `9-12` 🎞 **N**
The dramatic black and white classic film of Martin Luther's life made in 1952. This film was originally released in theaters worldwide and nominated for two Academy Awards. A magnificent depiction of Luther and the forces at work in the surrounding 16th-century society that resulted in his historic reforming efforts. This film traces Luther's life from a guilt-burdened monk to his eventual break with the Roman Church. This film, in spite of its age, continues to be a popular classic to introduce Luther's life. ISBN: 1563646234

Night Preacher by Louise A. Vernon `4-8` `9-12` **N** ⟞⟝
Menno Simons is a Catholic priest who became an Anabaptist in the 1500s. This book is the story of what happened as Menno went about preaching as seen through the eyes of his children, Bettje and Jan. ISBN: 0836117743

The Queen's Smuggler by Dave Jackson `4-8` `9-12` **N** ⟞⟝
Sarah tries to smuggle a New Testament into England in order to save the life of William Tyndale, a man imprisoned for translating the Bible into English. "A Trailblazer Book." ISBN: 1556612214

The Reformation by Diarmaid MacCulloch `9-12` ⟞⟝
At a time when men and women were prepared to kill—and be killed—for their faith, the Reformation tore the Western world apart. In this masterful history, MacCulloch conveys the drama, complexity, and continuing relevance of these events. Weaving together the many strands of reformation and counter-reformation, ranging widely across Europe and even to the New World, MacCulloch also reveals as never before how these upheavals affected everyday lives—overturning ideas of love, sex, death and the supernatural, and shaping the modern age. He offers vivid portraits of the most significant individuals—Luther, Calvin, Zwingli, Loyola, Henry VIII, and a number of popes. ISBN: 0670032964

The Story of Christianity: Volume Two: The Reformation to the Present Day by Justo L. Gonzalez `9-12` ⟞⟝
Beginning with the Protestant Reformation of the sixteenth century, this second volume of *The Story of Christianity* continues narrative history to the present. ISBN: 0060633166

Spy for the Night Riders: Martin Luther by Dave and Neta Jackson `K-3` `4-8` ⟞⟝
Young servant Karl Schumacher is given the opportunity to study under the esteemed Dr. Martin Luther. But Karl fears for his life when Dr. Luther is declared a heretic, and Karl must accompany him to Worms to appear before the Imperial Council. And his fear is heightened when he becomes aware they are being followed. "A Trailblazer Book." ISBN: 1556612370

Traitor in the Tower: John Bunyan by Dave Jackson `K-3` `4-8`
In 1660, after his father is imprisoned in the Tower of London, Richard Winslow goes to stay with his uncle who is in charge of the Bedford jail and there meets and is helped by the Puritan preacher John Bunyan, author of *Pilgrim's Progress*. ISBN: 1556617410

Overall American History

America: A Patriotic Primer by Lynne Cheney [K-3]
The wife of Vice President Dick Cheney introduces the founding principles of America to readers in this alphabet picture book that doubles as a primer of history and a celebration of faith. ISBN: 0689851928

Children's Encyclopedia of American History by David C King [4-8]
With its up-to-the-moment content and engaging style, this major reference book is an essential resource that helps children relate today's news to the events of the past. Focusing on the who, what, when, where, and how, *DK's Children's Encyclopedia of American History* is published in conjunction with the Smithsonian Institution to present a completely unique survey of the story of America. Featuring more than 1,000 stunning photographs, plus maps, charts, and profiles of famous Americans, this book has been painstakingly designed with a cutting edge visual style to pull in even the most reluctant readers. ISBN: 0789483300

The Cod's Tale by Mark Kurlansky [K-3]
Teaches geography, economics, exploration, and American history through a fish: the Vikings, age of exploration, the slave trade, colonial times, and the American Revolution. Very nice ink drawings illustrate the stories. ISBN: 0399234764

Discipling the Nations: the Government Upon His Shoulders by Dennis Woods [9-12]
All Americans recognize the names of our founding fathers—George Washington, James Madison, Thomas Jefferson, Patrick Henry—but few understand the Constitution the founders gave us—neither its strengths nor its critical weaknesses. On these pages you'll explore intriguing questions like, who were the Federalists and the anti-Federalists? Is the U.S. Constitution a Christian document? Why do prominent Christian leaders such as John Eidsmoe, Peter Marshall, David Barton (WallBuilders), and D. J. Kennedy ignore the Constitution's obvious violations of Scripture? Most important, you'll discover why Patrick Henry challenged Washington, Madison, and Jefferson with these words: "I smell a rat!" This book is a refreshing and long-overdue counterweight to the endless procession of "Christian Constitution" releases that have dominated the Christian book market for the past 20 years. It makes a compelling case that America's problems stem not primarily from her departure from the Constitution, but rather from seeds of humanism buried deep within the Constitution itself. Woods goes far beyond a mere critique of the U.S. Constitution to an in-depth exploration of what the Bible says about the foundation, the form, and the function of civil government.The Constitution is deeply flawed in two ways. It ignores the biblical requirement that civil government should confess the supreme authority of Christ ("We the people"). It ignores the biblical requirement that rulers be men who fear God ("no religious test"). Many American history authors in the homeschool movement feel the Constitution must be defended as a Christian document at all costs, to serve as a firebreak against the conflagration of moral/cultural disintegration. Ironically, they end up defending the root cause of the very evil they are trying to eradicate. Woods says, "We need to take what is good from the Constitution, admit the problems, and then move forward to correct them." ISBN: 1880692252

First Book of America by L. Somerville [K-3] [4-8]
In Usborne's colorful comic style this book is filled with entertaining information on people, places and their customs. ISBN: 0746003382

A First Book in American History by Edward Eggleston [4-8]
Stories of great Americans for little Americans, Eggleston draws a more in-depth picture of the development of the United States using the stories of the living and breathing Americans who made it all happen. ISBN: 0965273547

Great Stories in American History by Rebecca Price Janney [9-12]
A selection of events from the 15th to 20th centuries—This collection of stories from American history by Rebecca Price Janney emphasizes the "fingerprints" of God on the persons and events which populate the American saga. ISBN: 0889651469

Overall American History continued

The One Year Book of Christian History by Michael Rusten 9-12
365 inspiring stories about significant people and events from Christian history (one event per day). From ancient Rome to the 21st century, from peasants to presidents, missionaries, and martyrs, this book shows how God does extraordinary things through ordinary people, every day of the year. Each daily reading includes questions for reflection and a Scripture verse. ISBN: 0842355073

Painless American History ("Barron's Painless Study") by Curt Lader 9-12
Middle school students who think that American history is boring, or difficult will be pleasantly surprised with this book. The full span of American history is covered: Columbus, colonization, the Revolutionary War, the formation of a new government, growth and expansion during the nineteenth century, and emergence as a major world power in the present century. Timelines, ideas for fascinating Internet projects, and the author's light narrative style makes this a history book kids will enjoy reading. ISBN: 0764106201

The Penguin History of the United States of America by Hugh Brogan 9-12
It brilliantly captures the dynamic events and personalities that shaped the nation's triumphant progress to global superpower: in Brogan's words, "for good and evil, a power and civilization that surpasses...all empires of the past." In this new edition, Brogan makes numerous revisions to earlier chapters, taking into account the most up-to-date research into American history. ISBN: 014025255X

The Story of America by Allen Weinstein and David Rubel 9-12
Presents the history of the United States not as a parade of facts and dates but as a story with twists and turns, heroes and villains, lovers, saints—and even some comic relief. With the help of more than two dozen eminent colleagues, many of them Pulitzer Prize-winners, the authors give you American history from Columbus to the present not as you've studied it before, but as Americans lived it at the time. It's a fascinating way to understand how America became a world power and the ways in which the nation's past continue to impact its present. With hundreds of brilliant images, and prose as captivating as that of any good novel, *The Story of America* fills in the blanks in your education with tales and observations that delight as they inform. 672 pages from DK. ISBN: 0789489031

The Story of In God We Trust by John Hudson Tiner 9-12
This inspiring and informative series is written for those who have cherished our nation's heritage for many years, as well as our children who are just beginning to appreciate what our country stands for. The US Postal service is now designing posters with the In God We Trust motto to be displayed in over 38,000 post offices across the country. ISBN: 0890513929

The Story of the Pledge of Allegiance by John Hudson Tiner 9-12
Following a legal battle to have the words "under God" removed from the Pledge of Allegiance, President George Bush has now signed a bill to ensure that these patriotic expressions and a recognition of the religious foundation of this country remain a legacy for future generations. ISBN: 0890513937

Wee Sing America Book and CD by Penguin Putnam K-3
Tune in to wholesome family fun with these *Wee Sing* favorites. ISBN: 0843149329 Cassette ISBN: 0843149310

Words That Changed America by Alex Barnett 4-8 9-12
From George Washington to Martin Luther King Jr., to George W. Bush—inspiring speeches from American history. ISBN: 1585748404

We Were There, Too!: Young People in U.S. History by Phillip M Hoose 4-8 9-12
From the boys who sailed with Columbus to today's young activists, this unique book examines contributions of young people in American history. Based on primary sources this handsome oversized volume highlights the fascinating stories of more than 70 young people. Including 160 authentic images. ISBN: 0374382522

Age of Exploration

Around the World in a Hundred Years by Jean Fritz **K-3** **4-8** **N**
These ten true tales of 15th-century explorers bring history to life, with accounts of the exploits of Christopher Columbus, Bartholomew Diaz, Ponce de Leon, and others. ISBN: 0698116380

Christopher Columbus by Bennie Rhodes **4-8** **9-12** **N**
Columbus felt God wanted him to explore the world and find new land and people so that Christ could be proclaimed. Finding boats and money to make the trip turned into a grueling experience in discouragement. He overcame all problems with God's help. ("Sower Series"). ISBN: 0915134268

Eyewitness Explorer by Rupert Matthews **4-8** **9-12**
Here is a new and exciting look at the hazardous world of exploration. Stunning, real-life photographs of famous explorers' equipment and findings. See arrows shot into Livingstone's boat, gold found by Spanish explorers of Central and South America, the flag that flew over the North Pole, what a sailor's life was like, and plant and insect specimens brought back by naturalist explorers. Learn how the first sailors navigated, why Columbus set out on his epic voyage, what kind of food starving explorers ate, discover who first sailed around the world, what the earliest underwater explorers wore, who first crossed the Australian continent, and much, much more. ISBN: 0789457628

Explorers Who Got Lost by Diane Dreher **4-8**
Examines the adventures of such early explorers of America as Columbus, Dias, and Cabot. Includes information on the events, society, and superstitions of the times. ISBN: 0812520386

History Pockets, Explorers of North America, Grades 4-6 by Mike Graf **4-8**
With *History Pockets*, students are engaged in discovery while creating portfolios for assessment and display. Lessons include: Introduction to Explorers of North America: Christopher Columbus, John Cabot, Hernando Cortes, Jacques Cartier, Sir Francis Drake, Henry Hudson, Daniel Boone, James Cook, Lewis and Clark, and John Wesley Powell. ISBN: 1557999058

Magellan: A Voyage Around the World by Fiona MacDonald **4-8**
Follows Magellan's expedition, the first voyage around the world, and describes the adventures that ensued. ISBN: 0613515005

Over the Edge of the World: Magellan's Terrifying Circumnavigation of the Globe by Laurence Bergreen **9-12** **N**
A chronicle of a desperate grab for commercial and political power and more, this captivating tale rivals the most exciting thriller fiction. Despite suffering starvation, disease, torture, and death, they discovered the passageway known today as the Strait of Magellan. ISBN: 006093638X

Pedro's Journal: A Voyage With Christopher Columbus **4-8** **N**
The cabin boy on the "Santa Maria" keeps a diary which records his experiences when he sails with Columbus on his first voyage to the New World in 1492. ISBN: 0590462067

Primary Sources Teaching Kit: Explorers by Karen Baicker **K-3**
Packed with reproducible primary sources from a saga verse written by the Vikings, to an Aztec Codex illustrating small pox victims, this collection of authentic documents will capture students' interest in the events and people of the age of European exploration. Teaching materials provide background information, document-based discussion questions, and reproducibles that help kids analyze and evaluate each historical document. ISBN: 0590378651

The Usborne Book of Explorers from Columbus to Armstrong by Felicity Everett **4-8**
Looks at men and women whose discoveries and achievements have changed the world—charts, diagrams and archival photographs provide detailed historical facts. ISBN: 0746005148

Where Do You Think You're Going, Christopher Columbus? by Jean Fritz **K-3** **N**
Fritz makes history accessible once more in this wry biography of a legendary explorer. A "School Library Journal" Best Book of the Year. Great illustrations. ISBN: 0698115805

Pilgrims to Colonies

The 18 Penny Goose by Sally M. Walker **K-3** **N**
When Letty and her family must flee the farm in 1778 as British soldiers approach, she scribbles a desperate note begging for the life of her beloved goose, Solomon ("I Can Read" book). ISBN: 0064442500

American Family of the Pilgrim Period Paper Dolls in Full Color by Tom Tierney **K-3** **4-8**
Eight dolls and 28 costumes; authentically rendered suits, busks, jerkins, shifts, capes, more. Informative text. ISBN: 048625335X

The Double Life of Pocahontas by Jean Fritz **5-8** **9-12** **N**
A biography of the famous American Indian princess, emphasizing her life-long adulation of John Smith and the roles she played in two very different cultures. ISBN: 0698119355

Hostage on the Nighthawk by Dave Jackson and Neta Jackson **K-3** **4-8** **N**
Faith and history come to life for young readers when viewed through the eyes of fictional teens interacting with historical Christian heroes. ISBN: 0764222651

George the Drummer Boy by Nathaniel Benchley **K-3** **N**
A view of the incidents at Lexington and Concord, Massachusetts, which were the start of the American Revolution, as seen from the eyes of George, a British drummer boy. ISBN: 0060205016

The Great Little Madison by Jean Fritz **5-8** **9-12** **N**
James Madison used his quiet eloquence intelligence to help shape the Constitution, steer America through the turmoil of two wars, and ensure that our government and nation remained intact. ISBN: 0698116216

History Pockets, Life in Plymouth Colony by Marc Tyler Nobleman **4-8**
With *History Pockets*, students are engaged in discovery while creating portfolios for assessment and display. Lessons include: Voyage to the New World, The New World, Building a Village, Home Sweet Home, The Family, Working in Plymouth Colony, Going to School, What Did the Pilgrims Give Us? ISBN: 1557999066

I Am Regina by Sally M. Keehn **4-8** **N**
When Allegheny Indians murder her father and brother and burn their Pennsylvania cabin to the ground, Regina is taken captive. Regina begins a new life with the tribe. Regina never stops wondering about her mother, and whether they will meet again. ISBN: 0698119207

I Walk in Dread, the Diary of Deliverance Trembley, Witness by Lisa Rowe Fraustino **4-8** **9-12** **N**
Deliverance Trembley lives in Salem Village in 1691 Massachusetts. When four young girls from the village accuse some of the local women of being witches, Deliverance finds herself caught up in the ensuing drama of the trials. ISBN: 0439249732

If You Sailed on the Mayflower in 1620 by Ann McGovern **K-3** **N**
Questions and answers describe the voyage of the Mayflower and the Pilgrims' first year in the New World. ISBN: 0590451618

A Journey to the New World: The Diary of Remember Patience Whipple by Kathryn Lasky **4-8** **N**
Twelve-year-old Mem presents a diary account of the trip she and her family made on the Mayflower in 1620 and their first year in the New World. ("Dear America") ISBN: 059050214X

The Journal Of Jasper Jonathan Pierce, A Pilgrim Boy by Ann Rinaldi **4-8** **N**
 A young orphan journeys on the "Mayflower" to a new land full of adventure and mystery. Jonathan strikes out on his own and forms a powerful friendship with the feared Nauset tribe. ("My Name is America") ISBN: 0590510789

The Landing of the Pilgrims by James Henry Daugherty **4-8** **N**
In order to escape religious persecution, a group of English Separatists set sail for America in 1620, hoping to establish a new colony. ISBN: 0394846974

Pilgrims to Colonies continued

A Lion to Guard Us by Clyde Robert Bulla K-3 4-8 **N**
Left on their own in seventeenth-century London, three impoverished children draw upon all their resources to stay together and make their way to the Virginia colony in search of their father. ISBN: 64403335

Off to Plymouth Rock by Dandi Daley Mackall K-3 **N**
Told with the whimsical verse of Dandi Mackall, children will love to hear the story of the Pilgrims' voyage and the Native Americans' guidance that culminated in the first Thanksgiving. Gene Barretta's warm, harvest tones and lively characters add the perfect touch to this story of discovery, compassion, and faith. ISBN: 1400301947

The Pilgrim Village Mystery by Gertrude Chandler Warner 4-8 **N**
When the Alden children spend a week visiting at Pilgrim Village, they uncover the mystery behind the unusual happenings at the historic site. ISBN: 0807565318

The Pilgrims at Plymouth by Lucille Recht Penner K-3 **N**
Life on the Mayflower was harsh. When the Pilgrims reached America, things got even worse. More than half the Pilgrims died the first winter. Luckily, the Pilgrims made friends with the Indians who lived nearby. Thanks to the Indians, the Pilgrims set up the first successful American colony at Plymouth, Massachusetts. ISBN: 0375821988

The Pilgrims of Plimoth: Struggle for Survival by Marcia Sewall K-4 **N**
Chronicles, in text and illustrations, the day-to-day life of the early Pilgrims in the Plymouth Colony. ISBN: 0689808615

The Pilgrims' First Thanksgiving by Ann McGovern K-3 **N**
The Pilgrims' first Thanksgiving lasted three whole days. Ann McGovern's simple text introduces children to the struggles of the Pilgrims during their first year at Plymouth Colony and the events leading to the historic occasion we celebrate today—Thanksgiving. ISBN: 0590461885

Sam the Minuteman by Nathaniel Benchley K-3 **N**
An easy-to-read account of Sam and his father fighting as minutemen against the British in the Battle of Lexington. ISBN: 006020480X

Samuel Eaton's Day: A Day in the Life of a Pilgrim Boy by Kate Waters K-4 **N**
Text and photographs follow a six-year-old Pilgrim boy through a busy day during the spring harvest in 1627: doing chores, getting to know his Wampanoag Indian neighbors, and spending time with his family. ISBN: 0590480537

Sarah Morton's Day: A Day in the Life of a Pilgrim Girl by Kate Waters K-3 **N**
Text and photographs of Plymouth Plantation follow a pilgrim girl through a typical day as she milks the goats, cooks and serves meals, learns her letters, and adjusts to her new stepfather. ISBN: 0590474006

The Sign of the Beaver by Elizabeth George Speare 4-8 **N**
Until the day his father returns to their cabin in the Maine wilderness, 12-year-old Matt must try to survive on his own. During an attack by swarming bees, Matt is astonished when he's rescued by an Indian chief and his grandson, Attean. ISBN: 0440479002

Squanto, Friend of the Pilgrims by Clyde Robert Bulla K-3 4-8 **N**
Tells of the adventurous life of the Wampanoag Indian, Squanto. ISBN: 0590440551

The Story of Thanksgiving by Nancy J. Skarmeas K-3 **N**
Recounts the story of the first Thanksgiving, including the journey of the Pilgrims on the Mayflower and the assistance offered to them by Squanto and the other Indians. ISBN: 0824941640

Pilgrims to Colonies continued

The Story of the Pilgrims by Katharine K. Ross **K-3** **N**
From the dangerous voyage across the Atlantic through the first harsh winter to the delicious Thanksgiving feast, all the excitement and wonder of the Pilgrims' first year in America is captured in this vivid retelling. ISBN: 0679852921

Thanksgiving: A Harvest Celebration by Julie Stiegemeyer **K-3** ⊳
Teach children to give thanks all year long. Connect the tradition of Thanksgiving with the perfect gift of God's love. ISBN: 0758605307

Three Young Pilgrims by Cheryl Harness **K-3** **4-8** **N**
Mary, Remember, and Bartholomew are among the Pilgrims who survive the harsh early years in America and see New Plymouth grow into a prosperous colony. ISBN: 0689802080

The Wampanoag by Katherine Doherty and Craig Doherty **4-8** **N**
Here are vivid descriptions and histories of the lifestyle, customs, and art of major North and South American Indian tribes. ISBN: 0531157652

Who's That Stepping on Plymouth Rock? by Jean Fritz **K-4** **5-8**
Using her trademark humorous style, Jean Fritz tells the story of Plymouth Rock—the granite boulder upon which it was decided the Pilgrims must have set foot upon their arrival in the New World—telling how it came to be the impressive monument it is today. ISBN: 069811681X

The Witch of Blackbird Pond by Elizabeth George Speare **5-8**
In 1687 in Connecticut, Kit Tyler, feeling out of place in the Puritan household of her aunt, befriends an old woman considered a witch by the community and suddenly finds herself standing trial for witchcraft. Award winner. ISBN: 0440995779

Colonies to Country

The American Revolution by Bruce Bliven **5-8**
Presents an account of events leading up to the American Revolution. ISBN: 0394846966

American Revolution, 1700–1800 by Joy Masoff **4-8**
Re-creates the American colonies before, during, and after the American Revolution by describing in words and pictures various aspects of the colonists' lives, including work, food, clothing, shelter, religion, the events leading to the war, and life as a soldier. ISBN: 0439051096

The American Revolutionaries: A History in Their Own Words 1750—1800 by Milton Meltzer **4-8** **9-12**
Acclaimed author Milton Meltzer gathers together a cast of characters in this compelling collage of eyewitness accounts from the American Revolution. Photos and documents throughout make the vivid text come alive. "Will make young readers look at history in a whole new way."—*Booklist*. ALA Best Books for Young Adults. ISBN: 0064461459

Benjamin Franklin by Peter Roop and Connie Roop **K-3** **4-8** **N**
A biography of the noted statesman and inventor, featuring excerpts from his letters, pamphlets, essays, scientific papers, and autobiography. ISBN: 0439158060

Betsy Ross by Peter and Connie Roop **K-3** **4-8** **N**
This is the fascinating story of Betsy Ross—a colonial businesswoman, wife, mother, and American patriot—who sewed the first American flag. ISBN: 0439263212

Calico Captive by Elizabeth George Speare
In 1754 New Hampshire, young Miriam Willard finds herself caught up in the French Indian War, and is captive on a harrowing march north to a life of hard work and perhaps even slavery. ISBN: 0618150765

Fritz Colonial Pack **K-3** **4-8** **N**
Jean Fritz wrote several delightful, exciting books about the Colonial period that are must reads for children of elementary ages. These history-with a-giggle-books are full of facts, well-known as well as the lesser-known details about these historical figures. Package includes: *Can't You Make Them Behave King George?*; *And then What Happened Paul Revere?*; *What's the Big Idea Ben Franklin?*; *Where was Patrick Henry on the 29th of May?*; *Why Don't You Get a Horse Sam Adams?*; and *Will you Sign Here John Hancock?*. Full color fun illustrations on every page. Available individually or in this discount package.

The Courage of Sarah Noble by Alice Dalgliesh **4-8** **N**
Newbery Award-winning true story about an eight-year-old girl in the Connecticut wilderness in 1707. ISBN: 0684188309

Colonial Times, 1600-1700 by Joy Masoff **4-8**
This book describes the colonists' work, food, clothing, shelter, religion, and relationships with Native Americans. Full-color illustrations. ISBN: 043905107X

Colonial Times from A to Z by Bobbie Kalman **K-4**
Delightful text and colorful illustrations highlight colonial life, from clothing accessories to the various trades that occupied the people of the 18th century. Full-color photographs. ISBN: 086505407X

Daniel Boone: Young Hunter and Tracker by Augusta Stevenson **K-3** **4-8**
This exciting fictionalized biography of Daniel Boone—easily read by children of eight and older—sweeps today's youngster right into history. ISBN: 0020418302

Davy Crockett: Young Rifleman by Aileen Wells Parks **K-3** **4-8**
Lively, inspiring, and believable biography looks at the childhood of Davy Crockett, who grew up to become a pioneer, statesman, and hero. ISBN: 002041840X

Early Thunder by Jean Fritz **4-8**
In pre-revolutionary Salem, fourteen-year-old Daniel begins to re-examine his loyalty to the king as the conflict between Tories and patriots increasingly divides the townspeople. ISBN: 140322590

Colonies to Country continued

Eyewitness American Revolution by Stuart Murray `4-8` `9-12`
Readers can be eyewitnesses to the thrilling American war for independence: the battles and leaders, soldiers and heroes, scoundrels and patriots. This ultimate visual guide shows a continental solder's musket, a spy's hollow "silver bullet," Washington's sword, a bullet-riddled battle flag, the Liberty Bell, and the Declaration of Independence. Full-color illustrations. ISBN: 0789485567

The Farm: Life in Colonial Pennsylvania by James E. Knight `4-8`
An indentured servant looks back on his five years of service on the farm of a Pennsylvania German family in the 1760s. ISBN: 0816748012

George Washington and the Founding of a Nation by Albert Marrin `5-8` `9-12` **N**
An esteemed historian offers this absorbing account of the nation's first president's life and times in this *Booklist* Editor's Choice and *School Library Journal* Best Book. Includes photos, maps, charts, prints, and line drawings. ISBN: 0525470689

George Washington's Breakfast by Jean Fritz `K-3` `4-8`
This colorful Fritz book is about George Washington Allen, a boy who never gives up until he finds out what he wants to know, is determined to learn all there is to know about his namesake. ISBN: 0698116119

History Pockets, Colonial America, Grades 4-6 by Marc Tyler Nobleman `4-8`
With *History Pockets*, students are engaged in fun discovery while creating portfolios for assessment and display Pockets include: Introduction to Colonial America, the First Settlements, the Native Americans, homes and villages, daily life, school, work, and memorable people. ISBN: 1557999066

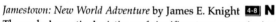
If You Lived in Colonial Times
Brightly illustrated question-and-answer format about what it would be like to live in Pre-Revolutionary War days. What would you eat? where would you live?, etc. ISBN: 059045160X

Jamestown: New World Adventure by James E. Knight `4-8` **N**
Through dramatic depictions of significant moments in American history, this informative series gives young readers a vivid sense of Colonial American life—its farms and villages, cities and ports, and the struggles and dreams of its inhabitants. Illustrated and indexed. ISBN: 0808546589

The Journal of William Thomas Emerson, A Revolutionary War Patriot by Barry Denenberg `4-8` **N**
Set in Massachusetts, this is the story of a boy surrounded by the politics and violence of war, who becomes a spy for the rebel colonists. ("My Name is America"). ISBN: 0590313509

Look to the Hills: Diary of Lozette Moreau, a French Slave Girl, New York Colony, 1763 by Pat McKissack `4-8` **N**
The Newbery Honor-winning author presents this story of an orphaned slave girl who arrives with her French masters in New York Colony at the end of the French-Indian War. ISBN: 0439210380

Love Thy Neighbor: The Story Diary of Prudence Emerson by Ann Warren Turner `4-8` `9-12` **N**
The drama of the American Revolution is brought to life through the eyes of young Prudence Emerson, who tells the story from a rarely heard perspective. ISBN: 0439153085

The Mayflower Secret: Governor William Bradford by Dave Jackson and Neta Jackson `K-3` `4-8` **N**
Teenage Elizabeth Tilley, one of the colonists landing at New Plymouth on the Mayflower, sees her parents die from illness and wonders if God is punishing her for the terrible secret she carries. ISBN: 0764220101

Molly Pitcher: Young Patriot by Augusta Stevenson `K-3` `4-8` **N**
Using simple language that beginning readers can understand, this lively, inspiring, and believable biography looks at the childhood of Revolutionary War hero Molly Pitcher. ISBN: 0020420404

Colonies to Country continued

Noah Webster, Master of Words ("Sower Series") by David Collons **4-8** **N** ◌
One American who seldom receives the attention he rightly deserves. Noah Webster, Jr., does not often come immediately to mind when one considers those who helped the United States during its infancy. His services were many and unique. ISBN: 0880621583

Paul Revere ("In Their Own Words") by George Sullivan **4-8** **N**
This book brings Paul Revere's legendary midnight ride to life, and reveals that Revere was active in many of the events that led to the Revolution. ISBN: 0439095522

Paul Revere: Boston Patriot by Augusta Stevenson **K-3** **4-8** **N**
Using simple language that beginning readers can understand, this lively, inspiring, and believable biography looks at the childhood of patriot Paul Revere. ISBN: 0020420900

The Reb and the Redcoats by Constance Savery **5-8** **9-12**
In an interesting turnabout, the Revolutionary War is seen through the eyes of a British family to whom an American prisoner of war has been entrusted. ISBN: 1883937426

Shh! We're Writing the Constitution by Jean Fritz **K-3** **4-8** **N**
The award-winning Fritz takes readers behind the scenes at the Constitutional Convention for a good-humored history lesson, enlivened by dePaola's quirky colorful illustrations. ISBN: 0698116240

Standing in the Light: The Captive Diary of Catherine Carey by Mary Pope Osborne **4-8** **N**
A Quaker girl's diary reflects her experiences growing up in the Delaware River Valley of Pennsylvania and her capture by Lenape Indians in 1763. Osborne is author of the "Treehouse" series. ISBN: 0590134620

Thomas Edison by George Sullivan **K-3** **4-8** **N**
Inventor Edison explains how he developed ideas and turned them into useful inventions such as the light bulb and hundreds of others. 40 illustrations. ISBN: 0439263190

Traitor: The Case of Benedict Arnold by Jean Fritz **5-8** **N**
A study of the life and character of the brilliant Revolutionary War general who deserted to the British for money. ISBN: 0698115538

Where Was Patrick Henry on the 29th of May? by Jean Fritz **K-3** **4-8** **N**
A brief biography of Patrick Henry tracing his progress from planter to statesman. ISBN: 0698114396

Why Don't You Get a Horse, Sam Adams? by Jean Fritz **4-8** **N**
A brief biography of Samuel Adams describing his activities in stirring up the revolt against the British and how he was finally persuaded to learn to ride a horse. Full color. ISBN: 0698114167

What's the Big Idea, Ben Franklin? by Jean Fritz **K-3** **4-8** **N**
A brief biography of the eighteenth-century printer, inventor, and statesman who played an influential role in the early history of the United States. ISBN: 0698113721

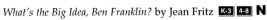

Will You Sign Here, John Hancock? by Jean Fritz **K-3** **4-8** **N**
A biography of the first signer of the Declaration of Independence, outlining all that he did for himself as well as what he did for Massachusetts and his new nation. ISBN: 069811440X

Winter Danger by William O. Steele **K-4** **N**
When a harsh winter hits the mountains, Caje Amis and his father are forced to take shelter with distant relatives...and the experience changes both of them. ISBN: 0152052062

Your Travel Guide to Colonial America by Nancy Raines Day **4-8** **N**
A detailed picture of everyday life provides an accessible context for political and military history, as well as for study of customs and traditions of different societies. ISBN: 0822599082

Civil War to Reconstruction

Abe Lincoln Goes to Washington 1837–1863 by Cheryl Harness `K-3` `4-8`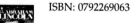
This sequel to *Abe Lincoln: The Frontier Days, 1809–1837* follows Lincoln's life from the age of 28, when he arrives in Springfield, Illinois, ready to take up his post in the state legislature, to his assassination in 1865. Includes six maps researched by the National Geographic Society. Full-color illustrations. ISBN: 0792269063

Abraham Lincoln by David Collins `4-8` **N** ▷
Abraham Lincoln was a most devoted Christian. His entire life reflects a deep personal faith in God. This book will attempt to explore the spiritual side of Abraham Lincoln, relying on his own words and the observations of his family, friends, and historians. For ages 9 to 13. ISBN: 0915134934

Across Five Aprils by Irene Hunt `4-8` **N**
Young Jethro Creighton grows from a boy to a man when he is left to take care of the family farm in Illinois during the difficult years of the Civil War. Newbery Medal. ISBN: 0425102416

The Cabin Faced West by Jean Fritz `4-8` **N**
For Ann Hamilton, life out west was anything but adventurous. She longed for the ease and comfort of the days with friends back in Gettysburg. ISBN: 0698119363

Caught in the Rebel Camp by Dave and Neta Jackson `K-3` `4-8` **N** ▷
A birth defect keeps Danny Sims from fighting with the Union soldiers for the freedom of Blacks, but an adventure soon teaches Danny to be proud of himself just the way God made him. ISBN: 0764222368

Civil War on Sunday by Mary Pope Osborne `K-3` **N**
Jack and Annie are transported by their magic tree house to the time of the Civil War where they meet Clara Barton. A "Magic Tree House" book. ISBN: 067989067X

Color Me Dark: The Diary of Nellie Lee Love, the Great Migration North by Patricia C. McKissack `4-8` **N**
Like many other African-Americans, Nellie and her family move North for a better life and hopefully, to escape racism. Instead, they are faced with a more sinister form of prejudice—hatred within their own race. ISBN: 0590511599

Gettysburg: A Novel of the Civil War by Newt Gingrich, William R. Forstchen and Albert S. Hanser `9-12` **N**
Action-packed and painstakingly researched, the former House speaker and historical fiction author's novel is the first book in a series to tell the story of how a victory for Lee would have changed the destiny of the nation forever. ISBN: 0312309368

Harriet Beecher Stowe and the Beecher Preachers by Jean Fritz `K-3` `4-8` **N**
Harriet Beecher Stowe grew up in a family in which her seven brothers were expected to be successful preachers and the four girls were never to speak in public. Then she penned *Uncle Tom's Cabin* and changed the course of American history. ISBN: 0698116607

Harriet Tubman by George Sullivan `4-8` **N**
From her own childhood as a slave to her establishment of the Underground Railroad that led untold thousands of slaves to freedom, this story of the life of Harriet Tubman draws from her own words, from interviews and accounts from those who knew her. Photos and illustrations. ISBN: 0439165849

Harriet Tubman: The Road to Freedom by Catherine Clinton `4-8` **N**
With impeccable scholarship that draws on newly available sources and research into the daily lives of slaves. ISBN: 0316144924

Hidden in Plain View: A Secret Story of Quilts and the Underground Railroad by Jacqueline L. Tobin and Raymond G. Dobard `5-8` `9-12` **N**
For the first time, the secret codes used in slave quilt patterns that served as maps to escape on the Underground Railroad are revealed—suggesting that there was an organized African-American resistance movement that predated the Abolitionist crusade. Two eight-page color photos inserts. Line drawings. ISBN: 0385497679

Civil War to Reconstruction continued

I Thought My Soul Would Rise and Fly by Joyce Hansen **4-8** **9-12** **N**
The diary of Patsy from South Carolina in 1865. Honor-winning author presents the inspiring story of Patsy, a freed girl who becomes a great teacher. ("Dear America") ISBN: 0590849131

If You Lived at the Time of the Civil War by Kay Moore **K-3** **4-8** **N**
Describes conditions for the civilians in both the North and South during and immediately after the war ("If You" series). Fullcolor illustrations. ISBN: 0590454226

The Journal of James Edmond Pease: A Civil War Union Soldier by Jim Murphy **4-8** **N**
Newbery Honor author Jim Murphy portrays the brave and rigorous army life of a 16-year-old Union soldier who has been ordered by his commanding officer to keep a written record of "G" Company during the most brutal years of the Civil War. ("My Name Is America") ISBN: 059043814X

A Light in the Storm: The Civil War Diary of Amelia Martin by Karen Hesse **4-8** **9-12** **N**
In 1860 and 1861, while working in her father's lighthouse on an island off the coast of Delaware, 15-year-old Amelia records in her diary the Civil War effects. ("Dear America") ISBN: 0590567330

Listen for the Whippoorwill by Dave Jackson and Neta Jackson **K-3** **4-8** **N**
Living as a slave on a plantation, Rosalie Jackson finds herself suddenly alone after the death of her mother her father's escape North. Then, one night, as he had promised, her father returns. ISBN: 1556612729

A Picture of Freedom by Patricia C. McKissack **4-8** **N**
The diary of Clotee, a slave girl in Virginia, 1859. Twelve-year-old Clotee, a house slave, conceals the fact that she can read and write, and her struggle to decide whether to escape to freedom. ISBN: 0590259881

The Red Badge of Courage by Stephen Crane **5-8** **9-12** **N**
Long considered the first great modern novel of war by an American author, this classic work is set in the time of the Civil War and tells a powerful, psychological story of a young soldier's struggle with the horrors—both within and without the war. ISBN: 0553210114

Robert E. Lee: Gallant Christian Soldier ("Sower Series") by Lee Roddy **4-8** **N** ⌐○
Lee's life is well documented from his teen years on and all names, major events and places are real as revealed that Robert E. Lee found the source of his strength and commitment in Christ. ISBN: 0915134403

Sojourner Truth by Peter Roop **K-3**
Truth, a slave born in New York who went on to free herself and her children. As a free woman, she traveled across the country speaking against slavery. Photos. ISBN: 0439263239

Stonewall Jackson ("Sower Series") by Charles Ludwig. **5-8** **N** ⌐○
He was loved in the South and admired in the North. Stonewall Jackson was a great general, a noble Christian and a pure man. ISBN: 0880621575

Stonewall by Jean Fritz **4-8** **N**
A biography of the brilliant southern general who gained the nickname Stonewall by his stand at Bull Run during the Civil War. ISBN: 069811552X

When Johnny Went Marching by G. Clifton Wisler **5-8** **N**
Stories of 49 young people, some as young as ten years old, whose compelling stories of their experiences fighting in the Civil War comprise this impressive album of Civil War heroism. ISBN: 0688165370

When Will This Cruel War Be Over? by Barry Denenberg **4-8** **N**
The diary of a Confederate girl growing up in the Virginia in 1864 during the Civil War reveals the hardships of southern life as the war tore her family and the nation apart. ("Dear America") ISBN: 0590228625

With Every Drop of Blood: A Novel of the Civil War by James Lincoln Collier **4-8** **N**
While trying to transport food to Richmond, Virginia during the Civil War, fourteen-year-old Johnny is captured by a black Union soldier. ISBN: 0440219833

American West

About the American Frontier by Fiona MacDonald **5-8** **9-12**
Presents facts about life for the nineteenth-century pioneers on the American frontier. ISBN: 087226498X

Across the Wide and Lonesome Prairie by Kristiana Gregory **9-12**
In her diary, thirteen-year-old Hattie chronicles her family's arduous 1847 journey from Missouri to Oregon on the Oregon Trail ("Dear America"). ISBN: 0590226517

The American West: An Illustrated History by Liz Sonneborn **4-8** **N**
This thrilling story is told in first person accounts and is accompanied by art depicting people, artifacts, and the changing face of the varied region. ISBN: 0439219701

The American West: Native Americans, Explorers and Settlers by Christine Hatt **5-8** **9-12**
Surveys the settling of the American West, using excerpts from contemporary sources to highlight the original Native American inhabitants, the arrival of fur traders, the Gold Rush, Mormon migrations, the growth of cattle-ranching, and more. ISBN: 1583404430

Andrew Jackson by George Edward Stanley **K-3** **4-8** **N**
This biography of the seventh president of the United States is the fascinating story of how one young man overcame the odds, became a military hero, and rose to the highest office in the land. Illustrations. ISBN: 0689857446

Bandannas, Chaps, and Ten-Gallon Hats by Bobbie Kalman **K-3** **4-8** **9-12** **N**
Bobbie Kalman, author of the acclaimed "Historic Communities and Early Settler Life" series, explores the action and adventure that made the West famous. Bobbie Kalman's colorful book explains how each piece of a cowboy's clothing was specially suited to his work. Authentic period photos feature the clothing of farmers, townspeople, and famous Western characters. ISBN: 0778701050

Boomtowns of the West by Bobbie Kalman **4-8**
The excitement of a goldrush, the arrival of a railroad, or a strong coal deposit could turn a sleepy little village into a boomtown overnight! Children learn about real Old West boomtowns and the businesses, justice systems, and entertainment in these bustling cities that sometimes turned into ghost towns. Full color. ISBN: 0778701107

The Buffalo Knife by William O. Steele **K-3** **4-8** **N**
This classic novel by the Newbery Honor-winning author follows nine-year-old Andy and his family as they brave natural and man-made dangers during a perilous thousand-mile raft trip down the Tennessee River. ISBN: 0152052151

Exiled to the Red River by Dave Jackson and Neta Jackson **K-3** **4-8** **N** ⊷
Fourteen-year-old Spokane Garry is chosen by his tribe to travel thousands of miles to learn about God. What he discovers leads hundreds to faith and makes him a great revolutionary for his tribe (Trailblazer) ISBN: 076422235X

The Forty-Acre Swindle by Dave Jackson and Neta Jackson **K-3** **4-8** **N**
When his father tries to save the family farm in Alabama in 1898 by following the advice of George Washington Carver, fourteen-year-old Jesse struggles to help in his own way. ISBN: 0764222643

Geronimo: Young Warrior by George Edward Stanley **K-3** **4-8** **N**
Young Apache Goyahkla and his friend play games in their village that will prepare him for his role as a hunter and warrior—and the place he will hold in history as Geronimo, fighter for the rights of his people. Illustrations. ISBN: 0689844557

Trail of Tears ("Step-Into-Reading") by Joseph Bruchlac **4-8** **N**
Recounts how the Cherokees were forced to leave and travel 1,200 miles to a new settlement in Oklahoma, a terrible journey known as the Trail of Tears. ISBN: 0679890521

American West continued

The Great Railroad Race: The Diary of Libby West by Kristiana Gregory **4-8** **9-12** **N**
In Kristiana Gregory's third book for the *Dear America* series, a 14-year-old girl records the momentous building of the Transcontinental Railroad ("Dear America"). ISBN: 059010991X

Heading West by Scholastic Books **4-8** **N**
Scholastic's popular series chronicles the great migration Westward. This book is one of four titles that tell stories from a child's point of view in diary form ("Dear America"). ISBN: 0439129419

History Pockets, Native Americans, Grade 1-3 by Karen Lowther **K-3**
With *History Pockets*, students are engaged in discovery while creating portfolios for assessment and display. This book contains nine memorable discovery pockets. The introduction pocket gives an overview of the tribes in North America that are featured. The other pockets focus on food, clothing, shelter, and family life of eight Native American tribes. 1557999015

History Pockets, Moving West, Grades 4-6 by Martha Cheney **4-8**
Students make interactive projects while exploring the fascinating past. Includes: Introduction to Moving West, The New Frontier, Exploring the Wilderness, Missionaries at Work, On the Oregon Trail, The Native American Struggle, Settling the Far West, The Gold Rush, Homesteading the Great Plains, Building the Railroads. ISBN: 1557999023

Homes of the West by Bobbie Kalman **K-3** **4-8**
Examines various types of dwellings in Western Northern America during the nineteenth century, discussing their construction and design as well as the lives of the settlers who lived in them. ISBN: 0778701069

How We Crossed the West: The Adventures of Lewis and Clark by Rosalyn Schanzer **4-8** **N**
Venture through unknown lands beyond the Mississippi with Lewis and Clark, their crew, the slave York, and their guide Sacajawea, told in the actual words of the explorers. Illustrations. ISBN: 0792267265

If You Were a Pioneer on the Prairie by Anne Kamma **K-4**
This new addition to the popular question-and-answer history series invites readers to step back in time to see what it was like growing up 100 years ago on the Great Plains of America. Full color. ISBN: 0439414288

Land of the Buffalo Bones by Marion Dane Bauer **4-8** **9-12** **N**
The diary of Mary Elizabeth Rodgers, an English girl in Minnesota details her family's experiences in their journey from England to the Minnesota prairie, where her father hopes to find religious freedom and fertile land. ISBN: 0439220270

Laura Ingalls Wilder: A Biography by William Anderson **K-3** **4-8** **N**
In these pages we learn what historic events inspired Laura to write her stories and what happened to her after the last *Little House* book was written. For fans who long to know even more about Laura's adventurous pioneer life. ISBN: 0064461033

Lewis and Clark by George Sullivan **4-8** **N**
Lewis and Clark Expedition exploring the uncharted Western wilderness, placing it in its historical context. Includes historic prints, maps, photos, chronology, bibliography, and further reading lists. ISBN: 0439095530

Life on the Ranch by Bobbie Kalman **K-3** **4-8** **9-12**
Examines various aspects of life on cattle ranches in the nineteenth century, describing the reasons for becoming a rancher or a cowboy, the hard work involved, food and living arrangements, and more. ISBN: 0778701034

Life on the Trail by Bobbie Kalman **K-3** **4-8** **9-12**
In the latter part of the 19th century, more than half a million pioneers headed west to carve out a future on an unknown frontier. Some were drawn by the offer of cheap land and the promise of religious freedom while others had high hopes of finding gold. ISBN: 0778701042

American West continued

A Line in the Sand: The Alamo Diary of Lucinda Lawrence, Gonzales, Texas, 1836 by Sherry Garland **4-8** **N**
In the journal she receives for her twelfth birthday in 1835, Lucinda Lawrence describes the hardships her family and other residents of the "Texas colonies" endure when they decide to face the Mexicans in a fight for their freedom. ("Dear America") ISBN: 0590394665

Little House on the Prairie by Laura Ingalls Wilder **4-8** **N**
Laura Ingalls and her family journey west by covered wagon, only to find they are in Indian territory. An ALA Notable Children's Book of 1940-1954. Illustrations. ISBN: 0064400026

The Little House Cookbook: Frontier Foods from Laura Ingalls Wilder's Classic Stories by Barbara M. Walker **K-3** **4-8**
Recipes based on the pioneer food written about in the *Little House* books of Laura Ingalls Wilder, along with quotes from the books and descriptions of the food and cooking of pioneer times. ISBN: 0064460908

My Face to the Wind: The Diary of Sarah Jane Price, a Prairie Teacher by Jim Murphy **4-8** **9-12** **N**
In the late 1870s, many young teachers traveled West. However, the schools were inadequate at best, and many teachers returned home, unable to endure the hardships of prairie life. But Sarah Jane Pryce stayed, braving the rough conditions of the West. Illustrations. ISBN: 0590438107

My Heart is on the Ground: The Diary of Nannie Little Rose, a Sioux Girl by Ann Rinaldi **4-8** **9-12** **N**
Acclaimed historical novelist makes her "Dear America" debut with the diary of a Sioux girl who is sent to a government-run boarding school to learn the white man's customs and language. ISBN: 0590149229

The Journal of Augustus Pelletier: The Lewis and Clark Expedition, 1804 by William Durbin **4-8** **N**
A fictional journal kept by twelve-year-old Augustus Pelletier, the youngest member of Lewis and Clark's Corps of Discovery ("My Name is America"). ISBN: 0439049946

My Little House Crafts Book: 18 Projects from Laura Ingalls Wilder by Carolyn Strom Collins **K-3** **4-8**
18 easy-to-make crafts taken straight from the pages of Laura Ingalls Wilder's *Little House* books. From Laura's corncob doll to Mary's Christmas tassels, and from Ma's button lamp to Charlotte's straw hat. Make homemade crafts that you'll cherish forever. ISBN: 0064462048

On the Way Home: The Diary of a Trip in 1894 by Laura Ingalls Wilder **5-8** **9-12** **N**
Rose Wilder Lane, daughter of Laura and Almanzo Wilder, adds her own remembrances of the remarkable journey from South Dakota to Missouri. Illustrated with photos. ISBN: 0064400808

Patty Reed's Doll: The Story of the Donner Party by Rachel K. Laurgaard **K-3** **4-8** **N**
This story is told from the view of a wooden doll. Recalls the hope with which a group of pioneers begins their journey and the ordeals they face as they travel from Illinois to California. ISBN: 0961735724

Pioneer Life from A to Z by Bobbie Kalman **K-4**
This colorful picture dictionary looks at the life of the hardworking pioneers who settled America. Intriguing objects such as spiders, niddy noddies and hackles that were used by the pioneers are featured. Full color photographs. ISBN: 0865054061

The Pioneers Go West by George Rippey Stewart **4-8** **9-12**
Relates the hardships encountered by a group of pioneers travelling by covered wagon from Iowa to California in 1844. ISBN: 0394891805

Red Fox and His Canoe by Nathaniel Benchley **K-3** **N**
A young Indian boy receives a larger canoe along with some unforeseen complications. ISBN: 0064440753

Seeds of Hope: The Gold Rush Diary of Susanna Fairchild by Kristiana Gregory **4-8** **9-12** **N**
Susanna Fairchild and her family sail from New York to the west, where they plan to start a new life in Oregon. But tragedy strikes when Susanna's mother is lost to the sea. Hearing stories of great wealth, Susanna's physician father decides he wants to join the hordes of men rushing to California to mine for gold. Illustrations. ("Dear America") ISBN: 0590511572

American West continued

Sitting Bull by Peter Roop and Connie Roop `K-3` `4-8` **N**
A proud father and a brave warrior, Sitting Bull wanted the Lakota Sioux to continue hunting buffalo and roaming the Plains. He is remembered for his brave actions and notable accomplishments in this new biography. ISBN: 0439263220

Sitting Bull: Dakota Boy by Augusta Stevenson `K-3` `4-8` **N**
Sitting Bull was admired by friends and enemies alike for his courage, strength, intelligence, and humanity. A great Sioux chief, he fought to preserve his people's homeland and way of life from the encroachment of the white man. Illustrations. ISBN: 0689806280

Small Wolf by Nathaniel Benchley `K-3` **N**
A young Native American boy sets out to hunt on Manhattan Island and discovers some strange people with white faces and very different ideas about land. ISBN: 0064441806

The Railroad by Bobbie Kalman `4-8`
With the westward expansion of the railroad, immigrants from all over the world poured in to settle the land. Children learn about the hard-working people who built the railroads from sea to sea, and how the railroads they built changed the face of western North America forever. Full-color. ISBN: 0778701085

The Story of Thomas Alva Edison by Margaret Cousins `5-8` **N**
The rags to riches story of the great inventor—his unusual life and the valuable contributions he made to modern technology. "Cousins paints a realistic portrait. Recommended."—*School Library Journal*. ISBN: 0394848837

Train (Eyewitness Guide) by John Coiley
Discover the story of railroads. Learn how a steam engine works, how early engineers avoided collisions, how railroads were built, how the railroads crossed America, how subway systems are built, how a driverless train works, and much, much more. ISBN: 0789457563

Wagon Train by Bobbie Kalman `K-3` `4-8` `9-12`
Describes how pioneers set out across the United States and Canada in the nineteenth century looking for a better life in the West—the routes they took, the covered wagons they used, what they ate, the dangers they faced, and more. ISBN: 0778701026

Wagon Wheels by Barbara Brenner `K-4` **N**
A young African-American boy describes the wilderness adventures of his pioneering family in Kansas in the 1870s. ISBN: 0064440524

The Warrior's Challenge by Dave and Meta Jackson `K-3` `4-8` **N** ✎
David and Joseph struggle with the hardships of trail life when their tribe is forced to move west. Can they trust the Moravian missionary who leads them. "A Trailblazer book." ISBN: 155661473X

West to a Land of Plenty: The Diary of Teresa Angelino Viscardi by Jim Murphy `4-8` **N**
The first humorous book in the "Dear America" series, *West to a Land of Plenty* follows an Italian girl's immigrant family as they move from New York City to a utopian community in the frontier west. ISBN: 0590738887

Who Settled the West? by Bobbie Kamman `4-8`
In the 1800s, people in many countries were poor, starving, persecuted, or without land. The unsettled North American west offered the opportunity for a new life. This book looks at the people who already lived in the west and those who made the west their home. Full-color. ISBN: 0778701077

Industrial Era 1700-1900

The Age of Revolution: 1749-1848 by Eric J. Hobsbawm `9-12`
This magisterial volume follows the death of ancient traditions, the triumph of new classes, and the emergence of new technologies, sciences, and ideologies, with vast intellectual daring and aphoristic elegance. ISBN: 0679772537

Alexander Graham Bell ("Snapshots: Images of People and Places in History") by Elizabeth MacLeod `4-8` **N**
Creative, curious and compassionate, Bell was a remarkable man with an amazing lifetime career. This book chronicles his life, from his childhood in Edinburgh, Scotland, to his work with the hearing-impaired in Boston, up until his death in Nova Scotia in 1922. Full-color photos. ISBN: 1550744585

Always Inventing by Tom L Matthews `4-8` **N**
Biography of Alexander Grahm Bell. With photographs and quotes from Bell himself, this photobiography follows this well known inventor from his childhood in Scotland through his life-long efforts to come up with ideas that would improve people's lives. 60 two-color illustrations. ISBN: 0792273915

Buried in Ice: Unlocking the Secrets of an Arctic Voyage by Owen Beattie `4-8` **N**
Probes the tragic and mysterious fate of Sir John Franklin's failed expedition to find the Northwest Passage in 1845. ISBN: 078572477X

The Church in an Age of Revolution by Penguin Books `9-12` ⊃
The Christian Church had to adapt to great changes—from the social upheavals of the Industrial Revolution to the philosophical speculations of Kant's Copernican revolution, to Darwin's evolutionary theories. Some Christians were driven to panic and blind reaction, others were inspired to re-interpret their faith; the results of this conflict within the fabric of the Church are still reverberating today. ISBN: 0140137629

A Coal Miner's Bride: The Diary of Anetka Kaminska by Susan Campbell Bartoletti `4-8` **N**
A diary account of 13-year-old Anetka's life in Poland in 1896, immigration to America, marriage to a coal miner, widowhood, and happiness in finally finding her true love. Her fascinating diary entries give readers a personal glimpse into what life was like in a coal-mining town during a tumultuous time in this country's past. ("Dear America") ISBN: 0439053862

Cut & Assemble Historic Buildings at Greenfield Village by A. G. Smith and Ronald Ted Smith `4-8` `9-12`
Easy-to-assemble popular Railroad and Park model from famed museum village in Dearborn, Michigan. ISBN: 0486256359

Dark Light: Electricity and Anxiety from the Telegraph to the X-Ray by Linda Simon `9-12` **N**
From the invention of the telegraph to the discovery of X-rays, Simon has created a revealing portrait of an anxious age when Americans welcomed electricity into their bodies even as they kept it from their homes. ISBN: 0156032449

Dreams in the Golden Country: Diary of Zipporah Feldman, a Jewish Immigrant Girl by Kathryn Lasky `4-8` **N**
In a vibrant and colorful portrait of a Jewish girl, this is the diary of a Russian immigrant girl who begins a new life on the Lower East Side of New York City. ("Dear America") ISBN: 0590029738

First to Fly: How Wilbur and Orville Wright Invented the Airplane by Peter Busby `K-3` `4-8` **N**
With an inspiring text, original paintings, period photographs, and detailed diagrams, the story of Orville and Wilbur Wright from their earliest challenges to their final triumph in 1903. ISBN: 0375812873

Eli Whitney ("Lives and Times") by Margaret Hall `K-3`
Eli Whitney is best known for his cotton gin. But what was his childhood like? What did he do before starting his company? How can we find out more about him? ISBN: 1403453330

A Head Full of Notions: A Story about Robert Fulton by Andy Russell Bowen `K-3` `4-8` **N**
Carolrhoda's best-selling *Creative Minds Biographies* series appeals to a wide range of readers. Written in story format, these biographies also include inviting black-and-white illustrations. ISBN: 1575050269

Industrial Era continued

Dear America: My Sorrow, the Diary of Angela Denoto, a Shirtwaist Work by Deborah Hopkinson `4-8` `9-12`
Drama and history meet in this moving diary of an Italian immigrant who works in a shirtwaist factory in 1909 New York. Young Angela soon plays a part in the turmoil that erupts as workers begin to strike, protesting terrible conditions in the sweatshops. ISBN: 0439221617

Henry Ford: Young Man with Ideas by Hazel B. Aird `K-3` `4-8`
Using simple language that beginning readers can understand, this lively, inspiring, and believable biography looks at the childhood of inventor and magnate Henry Ford. ISBN: 0020419104

Immigrant Kids by Russell Freedman `K-3` `4-8`
Text and contemporary photographs chronicle the life of immigrant children at home, school, work, and play during the late 1800's and early 1900's. ISBN: 0140375945

The Industrial Revolution by Mary Collins `4-8`
Children can imagine being witnesses to history in the making in this series that explores important events in United States history. ISBN: 0516270362

Industry and Empire: The Birth of the Industrial Revolution by Eric J. Hobsbawm `9-12`
An updated edition of the classic study of the Industrial Revolution. ISBN: 1565845617

The Journal Of Sean Sullivan, A Transcontinental Railroad Worker by William Durbin `4-8`
The story of a fifteen-year-old who goes to Nebraska to work on the Transcontinental Railroad with his father ("My Name is America"). ISBN: 0439049946

Keep the Lights Burning, Abbie by Peter Geiger Roop and Connie Roop `K-3` `4-8`
In the winter of 1856, a storm delays the lighthouse keeper's return to an island off the coast of Maine, and his daughter Abbie must keep the lights burning by herself. Full-color illustrations. ISBN: 0876144547

Make Way for Sam Houston by Jean Fritz `4-8`
Colorful Sam Houston leaps to life in this fresh and funny biography set against the story of Texas's fight for independence from Mexico. ISBN: 0698116461

The Mary Celeste: An Unsolved Mystery from History by Jane Yolen `K-3` `4-8`
The spunky young narrator of this series plans to be a detective. Here she tells the tale of the *Mary Celeste*, which was discovered adrift on the open sea in 1872—with no sign of the captain or crew. What happened? She intends to find out. Full-color illustrations. ISBN: 0689851227

Robert Fulton ("Lives and Times") by Jennifer Blizin Gillis `K-3`
Robert Fulton is best known for his steamboat. But what was his childhood like? What were his interests and hobbies? How can we find out more about him? Read this book to find out. ISBN: 1403453365

Samuel F. B. Morse: Artist with a Message ("Sower Series") by John Hudson Tiner `4-8` `9-12` ⌐○
The inventor of the telegraph set out to be a portrait painter. He succeeded and became one of the most honored artists of his day. He painted the portraits of Presidents of the United States. But his greatest fame came from the years of perseverance in selling the idea of his invention of the telegraph. When asked to sum up his life, Samuel F. B. Morse said, "I agree with that sentence of Annie Ellsworth, 'What hath God wrought!' It is His work. 'Not unto us, but to Thy name, O Lord, be all the praise.'" ISBN: 0880621370

So Far from Home 1847 by Barry Denenberg `4-8` `9-12`
The diary of Mary Driscoll, an Irish mill girl in Massachusetts. Critically acclaimed author Barry Denenberg turns a sharp eye on life for a young Irish immigrant at the Lowell Mill ("Dear America"). ISBN: 0590926675

Industrial Era continued

The Story of Thomas Alva Edison by Margaret Cousins **5-8** **N**
A biography of the great inventor whose creations have contributed to the comfort, convenience, and entertainment of people all over the world. ISBN: 0394848837

A Street Through Time by Anne Millard **K-3** **4-8**
Have you ever wondered what a street was like 100 years ago? In *A Street Through Time* you can actually "see" what happens as you trace its development, spread by spread, through 14 time periods, from the Stone Age to the present day. Full-color. ISBN: 0789434261

Ten Mile Day: And the Building of the Transcontinental Railroad by Mary Ann Fraser **K-3** **4-8**
Chronicles the race to build the first railroad to cross the North American continent. ISBN: 0805047034

Valley of the Moon: the Diary of Maria Rosalia de Milagros: by Sherry Garland **4-8** **9-12** **N**
This diary tells the story of Maria's life as a servant in a Spanish home in California, as she and her brother, orphaned years before, live on a ranch run by the stern Señor Medina. She also offers her account of the war that Alta California ultimately loses to the Americans. ISBN: 0439088208

Victorian Days: Discover the Past with Fun Projects, Games, Activities, and Recipes by David C. King **K-3** **4-8**
American Kids in History™ share the fun, challenges, dreams, and adventures of life in victorian America What would it be like to grow up in New York City during the exciting Victorian era? Travel back to 1893 and find out. ISBN: 0471331228

Voyage on the Great Titanic: The Diary of Margaret Ann Brady by Ellen Emerson White **4-8** **N**
Written from the point of view of a young passenger aboard the ill-fated *Titanic*, this title combines an award-winning series with the disaster of the century ("Dear America"). ISBN: 0590962736

At Work with Thomas Edison: 10 Business Lessons from America's Greatest Innovator by Blaine McCormick **9-12**
McCormick seeks to revive Thomas Edison's forgotten business legacy by giving modern managers the tools they need to break free from corporate America's innovation-squelching mantra of efficiency, standardization and control. Twelve photos and illustrations. ISBN: 1891984357

The Wright Brothers by Quentin Reynolds **4-8** **9-12**
A biography of the two brothers from Dayton, Ohio, who built and flew the first airplane. ISBN: 0394847008

The Wright Brothers: They Gave Us Wings by Charles Ludwig **4-8**
This story is about the Wright Brothers and how relationship affected their decisions...and the course of human history. ISBN: 0880621419

The Wright Brothers for Kids: How They Invented the Airplane, 21 Activities Exploring the Science and History of Flight by Mary Kay Carson **4-8**
How they Invented the Airplane includes facts about these brothers and their invention, plus projects. ISBN: 1556524773

You Want Women to Vote, Lizzie Stanton? by Jean Fritz **K-3** **4-8**
Convinced from an early age that women should have the same rights as men, Lizzie embarked on a career that changed America. ISBN: 0698117646

World War I

Eyewitness: World War I by Simon Adams, Andy Crawford `4-8` `9-12`
Devastating first-hand reports and contemporary photographs of the battles that slaughtered millions, together with a clear account of how nation upon nation sent their men to join the carnage. See the bullet-riddled car of the heir to the throne of Austria-Hungary, everyday life in the dugout, sappers mining tunnels beneath the enemy, and Mata Hari learning the art of spying. Learn how people avoided gas attacks, when periscopes were used, what soldiers wrote home to their sweethearts and mothers, the best way to use a tank, how troops flattened a hillside, and the meaning of Armistice Day. Discover how it felt to go over the top, what happened to all the bodies, how people dealt with shell shock, why war led to revolution, and much, much more. ISBN: 075660740X

The First World War by John Keegan `9-12`
In this definitive account of the Great War, Keegan sheds fascinating light on weaponry and technology, shows the doomed negotiations between the monarchs and ministers of 1914, and takes readers into the verminous trenches of the Western front. ISBN: 0375700455

The First World War by Michael Howard `4-8` `9-12`
Respected historians offers a brief but readable narrative account of WWI, its causes and consequences, and the historical controversies surrounding the origin and conduct of the war. ISBN: 0192804456

The First World War: The War to End All Wars by Geoffrey Jukes, Peter Simkins and Michael Hickey `9-12`
A complete account of the Great War, covering the fighting in each of the major theaters, and examining the impact of war on the soldiers and civilians caught up in it. ISBN: 1841767387

The Forgotten Fire by Adam Bagdasarian `9-12` **N**
Novel of a young boy's journey to survive made all the more powerful because it is the true story of the author's great-uncle during the Armenian genocide of 1915. ISBN: 0789426277

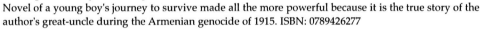

The Oxford Illustrated History of the First World War by Hew Strachan `4-8` `9-12`
From WWI causes to its consequences, and from the strategy of the politicians to the tactics of the generals. Features 140 illustrations, 16 pages of color plates, and seven maps. ISBN: 0192893254

Sgt. York: His Life, Legend & Legacy by John Perry `9-12` **N** ↪
In a world desperate for authentic heroes, the story of Sgt. York reminds readers of the true meaning of heroism. His bravery on the battlefield made him famous, but his life choices made him one of history's greatest Christian patriots. ISBN: 0805460748

Sergeant York: An American Hero by David D. Lee `4-8` `9-12` **N** ↪
Alvin C. York went out on a routine patrol an ordinary, unknown American doughboy of the First World War. He came back from no-man's-land a hero. In a brief encounter on October 8, 1918, during the Argonne offensive, York had killed some two dozen German soldiers and, almost single-handedly, effected the capture of 132 others. ISBN: 0813190282

A Time for Courage: The Suffragette Diary of Kathleen Bowen by Kathryn Lasky `4-8` **N**
As the United States in on the brink of entering World War I, young Kathleen "Kat" Bowen begins recording the activities of the women's suffrage movement in 1917 ("Dear America"). ISBN: 0590511416

True Stories of the First World War by Paul Dowswell `4-8` **N**
Aircraft, submarines, machine guns and tanks, and the generals who fought this war came from an age of cavalry charges and dashing red uniforms. The result was slaughter on a massive scale, making it one of the most troubling wars in history. ISBN: 0794507212

World War I by Tom McGowen `4-8`
Provides an overview of the military battles and political changes that occurred during World War I. ISBN: 0531156605

The Depression

The Bread Winner by Arvella Whitmore **4-8** **N**
When both her parents are unable to find work and pay the bills during the Great Depression, resourceful Sarah Ann Puckett saves the family from the poorhouse by selling her prize-winning homemade bread. ISBN: 0618494790

A Candle in the Dark by Adele Geras, Elsie Lennox **4-8** **N**
Germany in 1938 is a dangerous place for Jews. Clara and her little brother, Maxi, are leaving behind everything they know and going to England to live with a family they have never met. A story set on the brink of the Second World War. ISBN: 0713650761

Children of the Dust Bowl: The True Story of the School at Weedpatch Camp by Jerry Stanley **4-8** **N**
Describes the plight of the migrant workers who traveled from the Dust Bowl to California during the Depression and were forced to live in a federal labor camp, and discusses the school that was built for their children. ISBN: 0517880946

Daily Life in the United States, 1920-1940: How Americans Lived During the Roaring Twenties and the Great Depression by David E. Kyvig **9-12**
Discover what everyday life was like for ordinary Americans during the decades of development and depression in the 1920s and 1930s. ISBN: 1566635845

The Depression Thematic Unit by Sarah Clark **4-8**
Provides lesson plans and cross-curricular activities based on the following pieces of literature: *Children of the Dust Bowl: The True Story of the School at Weedpatch Camp, Out of the Dust.* This reproducible resource is filled with ready-to-use lessons and cross-curricular activities. Also included are creative ideas and a bibliography. ISBN: 1576903648

The Grapes of Wrath by John Steinbeck **9-12**
Forced from their home, the Joad family is lured to California to find work; instead they find disillusionment, exploitation, and hunger. ISBN: 0140186409

The Greatest Generation by Tom Brokaw **9-12**
In this superb book Tom Brokaw goes out into America to tell, through the stories of individual men and women, the story of a generation, America's citizen heroes and heroines who came of age during the Great Depression and the Second World War and went on to build modern America. ISBN: 0385334621

The Journal of C. J. Jackson, a Dust Bowl Migrant, Oklahoma to California, 1935 by William Durbin **4-8**
Thirteen-year-old C.J. records in a journal the conditions of the Dust Bowl that cause the Jackson family to leave their farm in Oklahoma and make the difficult journey to California, where they find a harsh life as migrant workers. ("My Name is America"). ISBN: 0439153069

No Promises in the Wind by Irene Hunt **9-12** **N**
For millions of people in 1932, a job, food to eat, and a place to sleep were simple needs, yet dreams in the midst of the Great Depression. At just 15 years old, Josh has to make his own way through a country of angry, frightened people. ISBN: 0425182800

Out of the Dust by Karen Hesse **4-8** **N**
A poem cycle that reads as a novel, this Newbery Medal winner tells the story of Billie Jo, a girl who struggles to help her family survive the dust bowl years of the Depression. ISBN: 0590371258

Treasures in the Dust by Tracey Porter **K-3** **4-8** **N**
Eleven-year-old Annie and her friend Violet tell of the hardships endured by their families when dust storms, drought, and the Great Depression hit rural Oklahoma. Second to seventh grade. ISBN: 0064407705

When Hitler Stole Pink Rabbit by Judith Kerr **K-3** **4-8**
Recounts the adventures of a nine-year-old Jewish girl and her family in the early 1930's as they travel from Germany to England. ISBN: 0698115899

World War II

The Borrowed House by Hilda Van Stockum `9-12`
When Janna is suddenly summoned from Germany to join her actor parents in Nazi-occupied Amsterdam, she is shocked by the Dutch hatred for the Germans. Her favorite Nordic tales and Hitler Youth indoctrination have not prepared her for the complexities of living in a house requisitioned by a military friend of her parents, nor for the violence she sees on the streets. With her parents preoccupied by their perplexing adult world of careers and relationships, Janna is lonely and full of unwelcome questions. It is the house itself which begins to provide real, if painful, answers to Janna's bewilderment—but not before it adds its own set of mysteries to solve. A well-developed, true-to-life tale for teenagers. ISBN: 1883937469

D-Day: June 6, 1944: The Climactic Battle of World War II by Stephen E. Ambrose `9-12`
This monumental narrative provides a compelling portrait of the strategic dimensions of the invasion that changed the course of World War II, skillfully melding eyewitness accounts of American, British, Canadian, French, and German veterans, materials from government and private archives, and never-before-utilized sources from the homefront. Includes photos and maps. ISBN: 068480137X

Don't You Know There's a War On? by Avi `K-3` `4-8`
This surprising historical novel tells the poignantly humorous story of a young boy's attempt to be a home-front hero during World War II. ISBN: 0380815443

Early Sunday Morning: The Pearl Harbor Diary of Amber Billows by Barry Denenberg `4-8`
Twelve-year-old Amber tells the story of her family's move to Hawaii and her first-person account of the Japanese attack. With a vantage point so close that with binoculars she could see inside the Japanese planes, Amber describes the incessant noise from the low-flying foreign planes, the machine-gun fire, the dull, booming explosions, and the chaos caused by the sneak attack on Pearl Harbor ("Dear America") ISBN: 0439328748

Eyewitness World War II by Simon Adams `4-8` `9-12`
World War II was one of the most destructive episodes in human history. Never before, or since, has the world witnessed such widespread bloodshed. Beginning with the events that led to its outbreak, World War II goes on to introduce the main leaders and highlight the decisive moments. From Pear Harbor, Midway, and the Atlantic to fighting in Russia and in the desert, outstanding and original photography provides a unique glimpse of the tragedies that led to the loss of more than 50 million lives. ISBN: 0756607434

Flags of Our Fathers: Heroes of Iwo Jima by James Bradley and Ron Powers `9-12`
This *New York Times* bestseller, now adapted for young readers, is the unforgettable chronicle of perhaps the most famous moment in American history: the raising of the U.S. flag by Marines at Iwo Jima during World War II. Eight-page photo insert. Maps. ISBN: 0385730640

The Good Fight: How World War II Was Won by Stephen E. Ambrose `4-8` `9-12`
One of today's most preeminent historians presents the story of World War II for young readers. *The Good Fight* brings the most horrific—and most heroic—war in history to a new generation in a way that's never been done before. ISBN: 0689843615

The Journal of Scott Pendleton Collins: A World War II Soldier, Normandy, France, 1944 by Walter Myers `4-8`
A seventeen-year-old soldier from central Virginia records as his regiment takes part in the D-Day invasion of Normandy and subsequent battles to liberate France. ("My Name is America"). ISBN: 0439050138

Mirror Mirror on the Wall: The Diary of Bess Brennan by Barry Denenberg `4-8` N
After Bess is blinded in a sledding accident, she must face a frightening, much-altered world at the Perkins School for the Blind in 1932. ("Dear America"). ISBN: 0439194466

My Secret War: The World War II Diary of Madeline Beck by Mary Pope Osborne `4-8` N
Thirteen-year-old Madeline Beck's diaries, recorded through 1941 and 1942, reveal her experiences living on Long Island during World War II while her father is away in the Navy. Black-and-white photos and illustrations. ("Dear America"). ISBN: 0590687158

World War II continued

One Eye Laughing, the Other Weeping: The Diary of Julie Weiss by Barry Denenberg `4-8` `9-12` N
During the Nazi persecution of the Jews in Austria, twelve-year-old Julie escapes to America to live with her relatives in New York City. ("Dear America"). ISBN: 0439095182

Remember Pearl Harbor: American and Japanese Survivors Tell Their Stories by Thomas B. Allen `9-12` N
Compelling first-person accounts from real-life survivors coupled with dramatic images allow the reader to go beyond the history-book accounts of the day of the attack. ISBN: 0792266900

So Far from the Bamboo Grove by Yoko Kawashima Watkins `5-8` `9-12` N
When the Second World War comes to an end, Japanese on the Korean peninsula are suddenly in terrible danger; the Korean people want control of their homeland and they want to punish the Japanese, who have occupied their nation for many years. Yoko and her mother and sister are forced to flee from their beautiful house with its peaceful bamboo grove. Their journey is terrifying—and remarkable. It's a true story of courage and survival. ISBN: 0688131158

V Is for Victory: America Remembers World War II by Kathleen Krull `K-3` `4-8` `9-12`
A scrapbook of personal stories, photos, posters, letters, and other memorabilia allows readers to share in the experiences of those who lived during World War II. This extraordinary reference book includes profiles of key players, including Roosevelt, Churchill, Hitler, Anne Frank, and Tokyo Rose; photos, including those taken in concentration camps; and much more. ISBN: 0375816003

World War II Days: Discover the Past with Exciting Projects, Games, Activities and Recipes by David C. King `4-8`
Travel back to 1942 and experience first-hand just how exciting and challenging life was for kids in America during World War II. Spend a year with the Donatos and the Andersens, two families working hard to make ends meet while still making time to have fun. Visit eleven-year-old Frank Donato in San Francisco and share in the thrilling sight of warships heading out to sea under the Golden Gate Bridge. Follow twelve-year-old Shirley Andersen through her family's wheat farm in southern Minnesota as they prepare for the autumn harvest. Eager to share the fun, adventure, and hard work of their daily lives, Frank and Shirley will show you how to play their favorite games, make cool toys and crafts, and cook up the yummiest recipes. Create a toy periscope out of a cardboard mailing tube and two small pocket mirrors, cook up a delicious Coney Island hot dog, play the exciting game of Sea Battle, and keep track of the weather with a 3-D cloud chart. Packed with entertaining and easy projects, games, and recipes, *World War II Days* will take you on an exhilirating adventure into one of the most fascinating periods in American history. For ages 8-12. Seventy-five illustrations and photographs. ISBN: 0471371017

World War II for Kids: A History with 21 Activities by Richard Panchyk `4-8`
Packed with information that kids will find fascinating, from Hitler's rise to power in 1933 to the surrender of the Japanese in 1945, this is more than an ordinary history book—it is filled with excerpts from actual wartime letters written to and by American and German troops, and personal anecdotes from people who lived through the war. ISBN: 1556524552

Holocaust

Daniel's Story by Carol Matas **4-8**
In this novel, a young boy tries to remember what normal life was like before the Nazis came to power. The emphasis of the story is on how individuals struggled to survive in the midst of despair. Daniel takes his readers through a journey from his hometown, Frankfurt, Germany, to the Lodz ghetto, then to the Auschwitz concentration camp. His story is the written version of the children's exhibit in the United States Holocaust Memorial Museum in Washington, D. C. If you get a chance to visit this museum do it! ISBN: 0590465880

The Diary of a Young Girl by Anne Frank **4-8** **9-12**
The classic text of the diary Anne Frank kept during the two years she and her family hid from the Nazis in an Amsterdam attic is a powerful reminder of the horrors of war and an eloquent testament to the human spirit. ISBN: 0553296981

The Hiding Place by Corrie ten Boom **9-12**
The true story of two Christian sisters sent to a Nazi concentration camp for helping Jews, and how one of them, Corrie ten Boom, survived. Corrie ten Boom stood naked with her older sister Betsie, watching a concentration camp matron beating a prisoner."Oh, the poor woman, " Corrie cried."Yes. May God forgive her, " Betsie replied. And, once again, Corrie realized that it was for the souls of the brutal Nazi guards that her sister prayed. Here is a book aglow with the glory of God and the courage of a quiet Christian spinster whose life was transformed by it. A story of Christ's message and the courageous woman who listened and lived to pass it along—with joy and triumph! It changed my life. ISBN: 0553256696

No Pretty Pictures: A Child of War by Anita Lobel **9-12**
The author, known as an illustrator of children's books, describes her experiences as a Polish Jew during World War II and for years in Sweden afterwards. This haunting book, illustrated with the author's archival photographs, is the remarkable account of her life during those years. Won several awards. ISBN: 0380732858

North to Freedom by Anne Holm
After escaping from an Eastern European concentration camp where he has spent most of his life, a twelve-year-old boy struggles to cope as he flees northward to freedom in Denmark. ISBN: 0833512897

Number the Stars by Lois Lowry **5-8** **9-12**
In 1943, during the German occupation of Denmark, ten-year-old Annemarie learns how to be brave and courageous when she helps shelter her Jewish friend from the Nazis. ISBN: 0440403278

A Traitor Among Us by Elizabeth Van Steenwyk **4-8**
In the fall of 1944 in Nazi-occupied Holland, thirteen-year-old Pieter, who's part of the Resistance movement, knows there's a traitor in his village. But who is it? ISBN: 0802851576

Tramp for the Lord by Corrie ten Boom **9-12**
The continuation of evangelist Corrie ten Boom's extraordinary journey of hope following the events recounted in her bestseller *The Hiding Place*. ISBN: 0425186296

Things We Couldn't Say by Diet Eman **9-12**
The true story of Diet Eman, a young Dutch woman who, with her fiance, Hein Siestma, risked everything to rescue imperiled Jews in Nazi-occupied Holland during World War II. ISBN: 0802847471

The Upstairs Room by Johanna Reiss **4-8** **9-12**
The autobiographical description of a Dutch Jewish girl's two-and-one-half years spent in hiding in the upstairs bedroom of a farmer's house during World War II. ISBN: 0064470431

Zvi: The Miraculous Story of Triumph Over the Holocaust by Elwood McQuaid
Millions of people have been touched, inspired, and encouraged by this story of a World War II waif in Warsaw, Poland. ISBN: 0915540665

1950 to Today

102 Minutes: The Untold Story of the Fight to Survive Inside the Twin Towers by Jim Dwyer **9-12**
The dramatic and moving account of the struggle for life inside the World Trade Center on the morning of September 11, 2001, when every minute counted. ISBN: 0805076824

1950's: the Music by Dorothy Hoobler and Tom Hoobler **4-8**
In this, Volume 6 of the "Century Kids", the narrative focuses on Matthew, the cousin of Peggy Aldrich. It is the era of communist witch-hunt. Peggy has been labeled a sympathizer, and her son Charley's radio show was taken off the air because he defended her. ISBN: 0761316051

1960': the Rebels by Dorothy Hoobler and Thomas Hoobler **4-8**
"Century Kids" 7, the narrative focuses on Chuck, the son of Charlie (otherwise known as Huckleberry Clown), who is trying to find his own place in his ever-more-famous and growing family while coping with the conditions of a repressive boarding school. ISBN: 076131606X

The 1970's: Arguments by Dorothy Hoobler and Thomas Hoobler **4-8**
"Century Kids" 8, America's involvement in Vietnam adds to the seemingly constant arguing in the Vivante family, whose cousins are among a group of people who have dropped out to live in a commune in Arizona. ISBN: 0761316078

The 1980s: Earthsong by Dorothy Hoobler **4-8**
"Century Kids" 9, The new inventions and gadgets of 1983, such as the personal computer, Swatch watch, and Rubik's Cube, don't distract Suzanne and her friends from confronting the owner of a factory that is dumping toxic chemicals into a nearby lake. ISBN: 0761316086

The 1990s: Families by Dorothy Hoobler and Tom Hoobler **4-8**
"Century Kids" 10, The Aldrich, Vivanti, and Dixon families gather to celebrate Nell and Rocco's one hundredth birthdays as the new century dawns and the specter of the Y2K bug threatens. ISBN: 0761316094

20th Century America: Key Events in History by Robert C. Baron **4-8**
This record of the most significant events in the United States during the 20th century recounts such milestones as the invention of the Model T, man's first flight, the assassination of JFK, and Neil Armstrong's walk on the moon. ISBN: 1555912796

Al Capone Does My Shirts by Gennifer Choldenko **5-8**
Moose Flannagan moves with his family to Alcatraz so his dad can work as a prison guard and his sister, Natalie, can attend a special school. A Newbery Honor book. ISBN: 0399238611

The Atom Bomb Project by Sabrina Crew **4-8**
The easy-to-read text, historic art and photography, suggested activities, and clear, simple maps help bring to life the causes of these events, their effects on people at the time, and their significance today. ("Events That Shaped America") ISBN: 0836834046

Children's History of the 20th Century by Dorling Kindersley Publishing **K-3** **4-8**
This lavishly illustrated, chronologically organized reference gives children an unparalleled overview of this most eventful of centuries. Features include sections on the U.S. government, sports, music, movies, and theater, plus an introduction in which children give their thoughts on the century behind and the millennium ahead. The timeline panels keep you and your child on track as it pinpoints specific events. Each decade has a theme, helping your child commit to memory ten eras of history. Written especially for children, this book is guaranteed to read again and again as your child grows in the new millennium. "An outstanding reference book that's entertaining to simply flip through."—Manchester Journal Inquirer "...It works beautifully as a collection of snapshots, preserving the flavor of the century as it unfolds."—*Biography*. Interesting for all ages. ISBN: 0789447223

1950 to Today continued

Flu: The Story of the Great Influenza Pandemic by Gina Kolata `9-12`
The author examines the Great Influenza Epidemic of 1918 that killed an estimated 40 to 100 million people in the world, and delves into the mystery that still surrounds it. ISBN: 0743203984

Grand Expectations: The United States, 1945-1974 by James T. Patterson `9-12`
A highly readable and balanced work that weaves the major political, cultural, and economic events of the period into a superb portrait of America from 1945 through Watergate, *Grand Expectations* offers a brilliant summation of the years which created the America we know today. ISBN: 0195117972

High Calling: The Courageous Life and Faith of Space Shuttle Columbia Commander Rick Husband by Evelyn Husband, Donna VanLiere `9-12` **N** ⬭
This biography of the commander of the "Columbia,"tragically killed in February 2003 on the ill-fated shuttle mission—is lovingly presented by his wife. His story is not only inspirational but also exhilarating and invigorating, as readers witness the life of a man who pursued his dreams while serving a faithful God. ISBN: 0785261958

A History of the 20th Century: Volume Three: 1952-1999 by Martin Gilbert `9-12`
Accounts of the wars in Korea, Vietnam, and Bosnia; the postwar reconstruction of Europe; apartheid; the arms race; the moon landing; and the extraordinary advances in medical science. ISBN: 0380713950

Homesick: My Own Story by Jean Fritz `K-3` `4-8` **N**
In this Newbery Honor-winning, insightful memory's-eye-view of her childhood (School Library Journal, starred review), Jean Fritz shares some of her own history. ISBN: 0698117824

Isaac's Storm: A Man, a Time, and the Deadliest Hurricane in History by Erik Larson `9-12` **N**
Story of the extreme hurricane that struck Galveston, Texas, in 1900, leaving at least 8,000 dead in its wake. An unforgettable story of the conflict between human hubris and the last great uncontrollable force, "Isaac's Storm" offers a cautionary tale for the millennium. ISBN: 0375708278

The Journal of Patrick Seamus Flaherty: United States Marine Corps by Ellen Emerson White `4-8` **N**
Patrick Flaherty leaves his Boston home when he joins the U.S. Marines and heads for the tumultuous conflict in Vietnam. Scared, but brave, Patrick must deal with all of the emotions of a disturbing war, and chronicles what he witnesses in his journal ("My Name is America"). ISBN: 0439148901

King Came Preaching: The Pulpit Power of Dr. Martin Luther King, Jr. by Mervyn A. Warren `9-12`
A well-developed analysis of Dr. King, the preacher. It traces how King had an influence over black preaching in America. Includes the text to four never-before-heard sermons. ISBN: 0830826580

Leon's Story by Leon Walter Tillage `K-3` `4-8` **N**
"In this riveting autobiography, Baltimore janitor Leon Walter Tillage reflects on his life with all the vitality of a storyteller gathering his audience around him. Roth's dramatic black-and-white collages pay homage to the power of Leon's story, a tale that does more in its gentle way to expose the horrors of racism than most works of fiction ever could."—*Publishers Weekly*. ISBN: 0374443300

Life: Our Century in Pictures for Young People by Richard B. Stolley `4-8` `9-12`
The book spans the 20th century in nine epochs, and nine notable children's authors contribute an essay on each period. ISBN: 0316815896

Lizzie Bright and the Buckminster Boy by Gary D. Schmidt `4-8` **N**
Set in 1912 Maine, this historical novel is based on the true story of a community's destruction. No one in town will let Turner Buckminster forget that he's a minister's son. But when he meets Lizzie Bright Griffin, a smart and sassy girl from a poor nearby island community founded by former slaves, he enters a whole new world. ISBN: 0618439293

1950 to Today continued

A Man on the Moon: The Voyages of the Apollo Astronauts by Andrew Chaikin 4-8
On the night of July 20, 1969, our world changed forever when two Americans, Neil Armstrong and Buzz Aldrin, walked on the moon. Now the greatest event of the twentieth century is magnificently retold through the eyes and ears of the people who were there. Based on the interviews with twenty-three moon voyagers, as well as those who struggled to get the program moving, journalist Andrew Chaikin conveys every aspect of the mission with breathtaking immediacy: from the rush of liftoff, to the heartstopping lunar touchdown, to the final hurdle of reentry. ISBN: 0140272011

Quiet Strength: The Faith, the Hope, and the Heart of a Woman Who Changed a Nation by Rosa Parks 9-12 **N**
This inspiring book on the faith, the hope, and the heart of a woman who changed a nation gives the account of her infamous stand against injustice as well as the lasting impact it has made. ISBN: 0310235871

Rachel's Tears: The Spiritual Journey of Columbine Martyr Rachel Scott by Darrell Scott 9-12 **N**
The Columbine tragedy in April 1999 pierced the heart of our country. In December 1999, we learned that the teenage killers specifically targeted Rachel Scott and mocked her Christian faith on their chilling, homemade videotapes. Rachel Scott died for her faith. ISBN: 0785268480

Remember: The Journey to School Integration by Toni Morrison K-3 4-8
The Pulitzer Prize winner presents a treasure chest of archival photographs that depict the historical events surrounding school desegregation. *Remember* will be published on the 50th anniversary of the groundbreaking Brown v. Board of Education Supreme Court decision ending legal school segregation, handed down on May 17, 1954. ISBN: 061839740X

Spacebusters: The Race to the Moon by Philip Wilkinson 4-8
The U.S. pledged to send a man to the moon before the end of the 1960s. Here is the story of that race against time. Describes the voyage of Apollo 11, its three astronauts, and details of the mission that put the first man on the moon in 1969. (DK Eyewitness Readers: Level 3). ISBN: 0789429616

Standing Next to History: An Agent's Life Inside the Secret Service by Joseph Petro with Jeffrey Robinson 9-12
From Rockefeller to Reagan to the Pope, one of the Secret Service's top agents offers an extraordinary account of protecting the people who made history. 16-page photo insert. ISBN: 0312332211

The Terrorist Attacks of September 11, 2001 by Sabrina Crewe 4-8
This book describes the events of 9/11 and its aftermath, and also explains the international background to those attacks by exploring the relationship between the United States and the Middle East.
ISBN: 0836833996

There Comes a Time: The Struggle for Civil Rights by Milton Meltzer K-3 4-8
Presents an overview of the events in African-American history that culminated in the United States during the 1950s and 1960s and represented a striving for equal rights. ISBN: 0375804145

They Made America: From the Steam Engine to the Search Engine: Two Centuries of Innovators by Harold Evans 9-12
From the steam engine to the search engine, Harold Evans presents an illustrated history of two centuries of American innovators. Vast and beautifully designed, scores of men and women populate this rollicking survey which reveals the surprising truths behind many modern creations, as well as valuable lessons to be gleaned by studying these brilliant entrepreneurs. ISBN: 0316277665

The Unfinished Journey: America Since World War II by William H. Chafe 9-12
This popular and classic text chronicles America's roller-coaster journey through the decades since World War II. ISBN: 019515049X

Where Have All the Flowers Gone?: The Diary of Molly MacKenzie Flaherty by Ellen Emerson White 4-8 **N**
Molly Flaherty's brother is a U.S. Marine fighting in Vietnam while she remains in Boston amid the radically changing political and social landscape. Molly records this disturbing time period in American history in her diary ("Dear America") ISBN: 0439148898

Science Resources for All Four Years

Science General

365 Fascinating Facts from the World of Discovery by Donald B. DeYoung `9-12`
This compilation of short facts will thrill trivia enthusiasts and is designed to help the reader commit them quickly to memory. In this book you will find hours of great reading as the great moments of discovery, both large and small, come to light. ISBN: 0892215003

Amazing Scientists: A Book of Answers for Kids by Jim Callan `4-8`
Discover the moons of Jupiter with Galileo. Uncover the science of radiation with Madame Curie. Travel forward in time with Einstein. Find out how scientists learned to cure diseases, how they discovered gravity, and how they determined the structure of the atom. Fact-filled and fun, this book's question-and-answer format lets you explore the discoveries of some of the world's greatest scientists. ISBN: 0471392898

The Cartoon Guide to Physics by Larry Gonick `9-12`
If you think a negative charge is something that shows up on your credit card bill or if you believe that Newtonian mechanics will fix your car—you need this book to set you straight. Explains velocity, acceleration, explosions, electricity and magnetism, circuits—even a taste of relativity theory in simple, clear, and, yes, funny illustrations. Physics will never be the same. ISBN: 0062731009

Champions of Invention by John Hudson Tiner `9-12`
Inventors like Charles Babbage (computer); Michael Faraday (electric generator); and John Gutenberg (movable type/printing press) gave credit for their achievements to God. Tiner, a science teacher, brings these sometimes-forgotten scientists into our consciousness and demonstrates that legitimate scientists have historically affirmed the Bible's teachings. ISBN: 0890512787

Champions of Mathematics by John Hudson Tiner `9-12`
Gives a readable account of the lives of the founders of mathematics: The story of Pythagoras, Fibonacci, and Newton come alive on these pages. Marvel at the courage of Leonard Euler who continued to make discoveries of the first rank after becoming totally blind. ISBN 0890512795

Champions of Science by John Hudson Tiner `9-12`
Recounts how courageous individuals founded modern science in the face of strong opposition. Copernicus, Kepler, Galileo and others struggled to overcome the widely held belief that the ancient Greeks had all of the answers to scientific matters. ISBN: 0890512809

Dinosaurs and Creation: Questions and Answers by Donald B. DeYoung `9-12`
Donald DeYoung answers fifty questions about dinosaurs, including Where do dinosaurs fit into biblical history? Why were dinosaurs so large? ISBN: 080106306X

The DK Google E.Science Encyclopedia by Dorling Kindersley Publishing `4-8` `9-12`
This visual treat is sure to get your children's interest and help them find a new delight interest! Packed with the latest photographs, artworks, diagrams, and 3-D model the e.encyclopedia science pulls out all the stops to tell and show readers everything about science. A comprehensive and authoritative reference work for children. DK partnered with Google's search engine to actively manage and update dedicated Web sites to take you directly to the most useful, safe, and age-appropriate information online. There are eight core sections to explain and explore over 220 science topics: Matter and Materials, Forces and Energy, Electricity and Magnetism, Space, Earth, Plants, Animals, and Human Body. ISBN: 0756602157

The Earth Science Book: Activities for Kids by Dinah Zike and Jessie J. Flores `4-8`
Explanatory text and experiments present information about the Earth, its seasons, crust, hydrosphere, atmosphere, and life on the planet. ISBN: 0471571660

Exploring Planet Earth: The Journey of Discovery from Early Civilization by John Hudson Tiner `9-12`
Thrilling sagas of the greatest adventures of all time are presented from a Christian background. The book is geared toward the home-school market and can serve as a textbook for fifth grade through junior high level. Illustrated, with end of chapter questions and an index. ISBN 0890511780

Science General continued

Exploring The History of Medicine: From the Ancient Physicians of Pharaoh to Biotechnology by John Hudson Tiner **9-12** ▷
Reveals the spectacular discoveries of men and women who used their abilities to help mankind and give glory to God. Fascinating breakthroughs in medicine come alive in this book, providing students with an educational and entertaining look at the healing arts. Packed with illustrations, end-of-chapter questions and a thorough index. ISBN 0890512485

Exploring the World Around you by Gary Parker **4-8** **9-12** ▷
Researcher and biologist Dr. Gary Parker brings his vast knowledge of ecology to a teaching setting, exploring and explaining ecosystems, population growth, habitats, adaptations, energy problems, and much more. Learn about insect control in California, why mammals have fur, and how sharks maintain friendships with small fish known as remora. Complete with illustrations, chapter tests, and an index. ISBN: 0890513775

Exploring the World of Chemistry: From Ancient Metals to High-Speed Computers by John Hudson Tiner **9-12** ▷
An exciting and intriguing tour through the realm of chemistry. Each chapter unfolds with facts and stories about the discoveries and discoverers. Find out why pure gold is not used for jewelry or coins. Join Humphry Davy as he made many chemical discoveries, and learn how they shortened his life. See how people in the 1870s could jump over the top of the Washington Monument. A wonderful learning tool with many illustrations, biographical information, and an index for easy referencing. ISBN: 0890512957

First Encyclopedia of Science ("Usborne First Encyclopedia") by Rachel Firth **K-3**
Why do things float? What happens to the food you eat? Why is it warm in summer? Find out in this lively book. Simple text, amazing photographs and illustrations, fun science activities and links to exciting recommended Web sites introduce young readers to the wonders of science. ISBN: 0794502733

For Those Who Dare by John Hudson Tiner **9-12** ▷
In this work by popular educational author John Tiner, brief biographies of the most successful, influential, and renowned Christians of all time are presented. Many are scientists and inventors; also includes reformers, statesmen, authors wholly dedicated to God. Discover facts that you didn't know about names you know well. Meet new personalities and learn obscure behind-the-scenes stories about famous inventions and discoveries. This book is a tribute to what God can do with a life given to Him. In this scholarly work by popular homeschool author John Tiner, brief biographies of the most successful, influential, and renowned Christians of all time are presented. ISBN: 0890513759

God Created the World and the Universe with Stickers by Earl Snellenberger and Bonita Snellenberger **K-3**
This combination coloring and sticker book contains information that will help children understand the chronology of Creation, and the reasons we are to care for what God has entrusted us with. The center of each book contains 32 full-color stickers that match the drawings. ISBN: 0890511497

God's Love for Us: Simple Science Object Talks by Heno Head **4-8** **9-12** ▷
Spellbinding science demonstrations impress Bible truths and make them memorable. For classroom use by unscientific teachers, they're fun to do—easy to prepare and present. 24 talks in each book. ISBN: 0784712034

The Handy Physics Answer Book by P. Erik Gundersen **5-8** **9-12**
The sixth book in the "Handy Answer" series, this book explores the lives of those who mathematically proved that things like gravity, torque, elasticity, and electromagnetic waves actually exist. 130 illustrations. ISBN: 1578590582

How Science Works by Judith Hann **4-8**
Tackling the science literary crisis head-on, *How Science Works* is a unique learn-together guide to the basics of science—so simple that even science-phobic parents can confidently share the joy of discovery with their kids. Hands-on experiments. ISBN: 0762102497

Science General continued

The Kingfisher Science Encyclopedia by Charles Taylor (Editor) `4-8`
An illustrated science encyclopedia arranged in such categories as "Planet Earth," "Living Things," "Chemistry and the Elements," "Materials and Technology," "Space and Time," and "Conservation and the Environment." More than 3,500 indexed references. Important events highlighted and illustrated biographies of key figures. 2,000+ full-color photos and illustrations. ISBN: 0753452693

Men of Science, Men of God: Great Scientists Who Believed the Bible by Henry Madison Morris `4-8` `9-12`
Most people are unaware that many of the world's greatest scientists were Christians and ardent creationists who believed the book of Genesis. ISBN: 0890510806

Nature Encyclopedia by Dorling Kindersley `4-8` `9-12` ♥ ☛
describes in outstanding detail the rich diversity of life on Earth. This compelling guide gives fascinating insight into how living things feed, reproduce, and defend themselves. Specially commissioned photographs reveal the lifestyles, anatomy, and behavior of plants and animals from all over the world. Full-color. Explores each major plant and animal group, including flowering plants, birds, reptiles, insects, fish, and mammals. Thematic sections cover topics as varied as reproduction and survival, photosynthesis and communication. Also includes classification charts and a glossary of science terms. ISBN: 0789434113

The DK Science Encyclopedia by Dorling Kindersley `4-8` `9-12` ♥ ☛
This milestone in scientific learning has been rigorously updated to include new scientific advances, from the Internet and CD-ROMs to fresh discoveries in space. Full-color. ISBN: 0789421909

Science and the Bible Volume 1 by Donald B. DeYoung `4-8` `9-12` ☞
Thirty exciting scientific demonstrations that illustrate the laws of nature, as well as teach biblical principles and affirm God as Creator. The use of household objects requires little set-up time. ISBN: 0801030234

Science and the Bible Volume 2 by Donald B. DeYoung `4-8` `9-12` ☞
Techniques to demonstrate both scientific and scriptural principles are presented in this second volume of *Science and the Bible*. Dr. DeYoung introduces thirty new and exciting demonstrations that combine scientific principles and the truths found in Scripture. ISBN: 0801057736

Science and the Bible Volume 3 by Donald B. DeYoung `4-8` `9-12` ☞
This third volume provides even more ideas for demonstrating the order and grandeur of Creation to encourage an appreciation of all God has made. The book's 30 dynamic but simple experiments illustrate the laws of nature, teach Bible principles, and affirm God's power as Creator. Each demonstration has a catchy or unusual result, making the Bible truth unforgettable. ISBN: 080106421X

Science Encyclopedia ("Usborne First Encyclopedia") by Annabel Craig and Cliff Rosney `4-8`
Highly illustrated first reference books. ISBN: 0746030525

A Scientific Approach to Biblical Mysteries by Robert Faid `9-12` ☞
Using his knowledge of science, mathematics, history, archaeology, linguistics, and theology, Faid, a nuclear scientist, presents documented evidence which may help explain how some events—such as the Crucifixion, the Garden of Eden, and the Star of Bethlehem—can be scientifically authenticated. ISBN: 0892212314

A Scientific Approach to More Biblical Mysteries by Robert Faid `9-12` ☞
On the heels of its highly successful predecessor, this book continues the study of Bible questions people have had for centuries. It examines a variety of fascinating subjects, including sightings of Noah's ark, the fate of Pontius Pilate, and the real name of God. An excellent read you won't forget! ISBN: 0892212837

The Usborne Book of Inventors: From da Vinci to Biro by Straun Reid `5-8` `9-12` ♥
Looks at men and women whose discoveries and achievements have changed the world. ISBN: 0746007051

The Usborne Book of Science Experiments by Jane Bingham `4-8`
Over 100 experiments explore basic principles of physics, chemistry and biology. ISBN: 0746008066

Creation

Amazing Story of Creation by Daune T. Gish 4-8 9-12 ⊳◯
The evidence of Creation presented here is entertaining, educational and easy to understand.
ISBN: 0890511209

The Answers Book by Andrew Snelling, Carl Wieland, Kenneth Ham 9-12 ⊳◯
This book addresses 12 of the most-asked questions on Genesis and the creation/evolution issue. Revised and expanded. ISBN: 0890511616

The Case of the Dinosaur in the Desert by Pauline Hutchens Wilson 4-8 ⊳◯
After reading the old *Sugar Creek Gang* books, a new group of kids decide to re-form the old gang. It's not long before the adventures begin. ISBN: 0802486649

The Creation Discovery Series ("Moody Educational Videos") K-3 4-8 📼 ⊳◯
Join zany Professor Walter Schnaegel and his young friends as they discover the fascinating world of plant life, geology, and ecology—all from a biblical perspective. Three episodes: *God's Power Plants*, *God's Rockin' World*, and *God's Earth Team*, each jam-packed with fun, songs, science games, experiments, and adventure. Approximately. thirty minutes each.

D is for Dinosaur by Mally Ham K-3 ⊳◯
A major stumbling block for people when they try to make sense of the Bible and science is the reality of dinosaurs. ISBN: 0890511934

Dinosaur Quest at Diamond Peak by Christina and Felice Gerwitz 4-8 **N** ⊳◯
Rocky Mountain National Park is home to thousands of wild animals, but a dinosaur? Can it truly be possible that the fossilized remains of a Tyrannosaurus rex are millions of years old? Dr. Jack Murphy has been hired to photograph it for a creation science magazine. A turn of events thrusts his teenagers into the middle of this project. It is now up to fifteen-year-old Anna and sixteen-year-old Christian to complete the assignment. ISBN: 0970038569.

Dry Bones and Other Fossils by Gary Parker K-3 4-8 ⊳◯
Join the Parker family on their annual fossil hunting adventure. Dr. Gary Parker and his wife Mary explain to their children what fossils are and how they are formed. They show how fossils support the biblical account of Noah's Flood and contradict evolution. ISBN: 0890512035

The Evolution of a Creationist: A Layman's Guide to the Conflict Between the Bible and Evolutionary Theory by Jobe Martin 9-12 ⊳◯
Dr. Jobe Martin chronicles his personal journey from traditional scientist to creationist. Dr. Martin himself was a traditional evolutionist, but his medical and scientific training would go through an evolution—rather, a revolution—when he began to study animals that challenged the scientific assumptions of his education. ISBN: 0964366509

The Lie: Evolution by Ken Ham 9-12 ⊳◯
Humorous and easy to read, this book powerfully explains the need for Christians to defend their faith. This book will not only strengthen and support the facts of Creation, but is an eye-opening look at the harmful effects of evolutionary thought on modern culture and religion. Ham explains the importance of understanding the true nature of the creation/evolution controversy stating, "If Genesis is only myth or allegory, then Christian doctrines have no foundation." ISBN: 0890511586.

How Majestic Is Thy Name: Delighting in the Grandeur of God by New Leaf Press 4-8 9-12 ⊳◯
Combining the most astounding photography with the most terrific information and the most marvelous Scripture, this is one of the finest and most elaborate gift books published by New Leaf Press.
ISBN: 0892215070

Creation continued

In the Shadow of Darwin by Wayne Jackson, Bert Thompson `9-12` ⋈
A case study of how one Christian writer and speaker has attempted to incorporate long ages and evolutionary theories into the Genesis record. The Ebook is available free online. ISBN: 932859224

Incredible Creatures That Defy Evolution I DVD or Video by Reel Productions LLC `4-8` `9-12` ⊟ ⋈
Are there really creatures that produce fire to defend themselves? How does a giraffe get a drink of water without lethal blood pressure exploding his brain? How can geckos walk upside down and not fall? Powerful evidence proves that animal designs can be attributed only to a creator and cannot be explained by evolution.

Incredible Creatures That Defy Evolution II DVD or Video by Reel Productions LLC `4-8` `9-12` ⊟ ⋈
How can some birds navigate over the ocean and not get lost? How can fireflies and glowworms create pure light that generates no heat? How can great whales dive to the bottom of the ocean without the pressure causing them to implode? Powerful evidence proves that animal designs can be attributed only to a creator and cannot be explained by evolution.

It Couldn't Just Happen: Fascinating Facts about God's World by Lawrence O. Richards `4-8` ⋈
fascinating and entertaining facts about God's world that give us thousands of pieces of evidence to prove that He created and sustains the universe. Delivers solid proof of God's existence and the evidence that He created and sustains the universe. ISBN: 0849935830

The Missing Link: FOUND by Christina and Felice Gerwitz `4-8` **N** ⋈
Follow Anna and Christian who, along with their father, archaeologist and photographer Dr. Jack Murphy face danger and a race against time. In the "Truth Seeker's Mystery" series, you will experience adventure, mystery, heart-stopping suspense, and faith played out first-hand by the Murphy family. ISBN: 970038593

Skeletons in Your Closet by Gary Parker, Jonathan Chong (Illustrator) `4-8` `9-12` ⋈
This picture book for middle graders discusses cavemen, what happened between Adam and Eve and us, missing links, and how God created man. This book supports the creationist view of man's origin. Interest level: All ages. ISBN: 0890512302.

Tyrant of the Badlands by Sigmund Brouwer `4-8` **N** ⋈
Book four of "The Accidental Detectives" series. The Alberta Badlands are famous for their dinosaur discoveries, and Ricky is excited to visit, until his friends vanish. He has to find out who's done the kidnapping before it's too late. ISBN: 0764225677

Unlocking the Mysteries of Creation by Dennis Peterson `4-8` `9-12` ⊶ ⋈
This book captivates and engages those who may not even be prone to read books. Experience an awesome journey of discovery in this unique treasury of historic and scientific knowledge that puts life-changing keys in your hands to understand our world and its amazing past. This book will help you discover the scientific accuracy of the Bible, unveil the fallacies of evolution, and build unshakable confidence in God's Word. Designed to help families build a trustworthy biblical worldview, it introduces a vast treasure of faith-building resources. One of the most user-friendly and comprehensive introductory books ever published on the subject of Biblical creation. Contrasting the biblical case for origins with the evolutionary view, Mr. Peterson skillfully helps both beginner and scholar to "prove all things" and build a worldview that is defined by scripture and enhanced by tangible discoveries. Many observations from the study of life, the earth, and the heavens emphasize God's invitation to "come and let us reason together." 240 pages of beautifully designed photography and artwork amplify the engaging text. ISBN: 0967271304

Yellow and Pink by William Steig `K-4`
Steig's witty dialogue on the nature of existence is now back in print. Two characters who are named for their color discuss their new lives. Full-color. ISBN: 0374386714

Light/Physical Science

Awesome Experiments in Light & Sound by Michael A. DiSpezio `4-8`
Presents over seventy experiments designed to demonstrate the properties of light and sound and explain the science behind them, covering such topics as wavelengths, color spectrums, vibration, and air particles. ISBN: 0806998237

Eyewitness Light by David Burnie `4-8` `9-12` ◐—
Explore the amazing story of light—from ancient sun myths to the latest optic discoveries that have revolutionized modern life. This intriguing book brings to life our exploration of this fundamental energy source. Some of the oldest oil lamps that have been discovered were made out of rocks and shells. Today, we can collect sunlight through solar panels to make electricity to light and warm our houses. Superb full-color photography of original equipment, intricate scientific instruments, revealing experiments, and 3-D models offer a unique eyewitness view to the incredible discoveries that have transformed our world. See how light rays bend; why things glow when they are very hot; what creates a color television picture; how microscopes and telescopes were invented; why a leaf looks green. Learn how fiber optics transmit light; why images are reversed in mirrors; how a liquid crystal display works; what makes a hologram. Discover how some animals can make their own light; what creates a mirage; what a polarizing filter does; why we see rainbows; what a quantum is; how X-rays penetrate our bodies; and so much more. ISBN: 0789467097

Exploring Light and Color by Heidi Gold-Dworkin `K-3`
Engages a child's visual sense with activities that explore such questions as why the sky is blue, what makes a rainbow, and how light bends. ISBN: 071348212

Flicker Flash by Joan Bransfield Graham `K-3`
A collection of poems celebrating light in its various forms, from candles and lamps to lightning and fireflies. ISBN: 039590501X

God's Lamp, Man's Light: Mysteries of the Menorah by John Garr `4-8` `9-12` ◐— ⊶
This is a masterful analysis of the menorah, the only biblical symbol that has the distinction of being designed by God himself. As you read this volume, you'll be enriched by the amazing wealth of understanding manifest in the biblical Hebraic symbols designed by God and by his chosen people Israel. Chapters include: God's Lamp, Man's Light, Divine Design, Pure Gold, One Hammered Work, Clear Consecrated Oil, The Light Motif, Mans Soul-God's Torch, Israel-God's Menorah, You Are the Light of the World, The Tree of Life, A Messianic Portrait, Menorah Mystery Numbers, By My Spirit, Dedication Produces Light, Synagogue, and Church Aflame. Great read-aloud for the entire family. ISBN: 0967827949

Guess Whose Shadow? by Stephen R. Swinburne `K-3`
Teaches young children about how shadows are created, describing night as a shadow on the earth, and giving children tangible reasons for why shadows vary in size, shape, and location. ISBN: 1563977249

Images of God by John Paterson and Katherine Paterson `K-3` `4-8` ⊶
Explores some of the metaphorical images which biblical writers use to teach about God; images include light, rock, and wind as well as a gardener, father, and architect. ISBN: 039570734X

Janice VanCleave's Physics for Every Kid by Janice Pratt VanCleave `K-3` `4-8`
Presents 101 experiments relating to physics using materials readily available around the house. ISBN: 0471525057

Keeper of the Light by Patty Metzer `9-12` ⊶
Christian fiction. The keeper of the light at Highland Lighthouse in Cape Cod life changes when he must travel to Provincetown to find a housekeeper and companion for his ailing sister in 1797. ISBN: 1885904096

Light ("Fascinating Science Projects") by Sally Hewitt `4-8`
Text and activities that explore light and how it works, with quotes from the Bible that encourage the reader to think about the wonders of the natural world. ISBN: 0761317368

Light/Physical Science continued

Light and Color ("Straightforward Science") by Peter Riley **K-3** **4-8**
A straightforward introduction to the key science subjects, this series explains the main scientific principles and shows how they work from our everyday world to outer space. ISBN: 0531153711

Light Fundamentals by Robert W. Wood **4-8**
Provides instructions for a variety of experiments introducing the study of light, its characteristics, sources, and uses. ISBN: 0070718091

The Magic School Bus Makes a Rainbow by Joanna Cole **K-3**
Ms. Fizzle and her class learn about colors and light inside a pinball machine. This is no ordinary pinball machine—it's played with light pulses. ISBN: 0590922513

The Magic School Bus Gets a Bright Idea by Joanna Cole **K-3**
Strange things start happening to Ms. Frizzles' class when they go to see a light show. Friz arrives with the Magic School Bus to help shed some light on the mystery. ISBN: 043910274X.

The Magic Wand and Other Bright Experiments on Light and Color by Paul Doherty and Don Rathjen **4-8**
An educational and entertaining book containing 25 easy-to-perform experiments, illustrated with scores of line drawings, photographs and sidebars. Projects include learning why the sky is blue and the sunset red using a flashlight and a clear box of milky water; exploring reflection by building a kaleidoscope with mirrors, duct tape and cardboard; investigating light waves and refraction by constructing a magnifying lens from a light bulb and fishbowl filled with water.

The Power of Light by Frank Kryza **4-8**
From the days of Archimedes and Leonardo, the earliest efforts to harness the power of the sun have become the stuff of legend. Solar energy expert Kryza recounts the dramatic saga of solar invention, from its optimistic dawning in the mid-19th century to its impending triumph today. Photos. ISBN: 0071400214

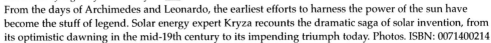

Science Experiments with Light by Sally Nankivell-Aston and Dorothy Jackson **K-3** **4-8**
Explores the properties of light through experiments using materials that are readily available in both homes and schools. ISBN: 0531145778

Sound and Light ("Hands-On Science") by Jack Challoner **K-3** **4-8**
White light and color, recording sound and light, and the light-bending properties of mirrors, prisms, and lenses are all examined in 40 hands-on, fascinating experiments. Full-color. ISBN: 0753453479

The Story of Light by Ben Bova **9-12**
Ben Bova unveils the beauty and science of light as he masterfully explains how it affects us every day of our lives. Includes a holographic, mirrored dust jacket. ISBN: 1402200099

Thomas Alva Edison by Brian Williams **4-8**
Edison's life is discussed in a geographical, social, and historical framework. Answers these questions: What kind of trouble did Thomas Alva Edison have at school? Why did he carry out scientific experiments on a train? How have his inventions changed our lives today? ISBN: 1588109968

Thomas Edison: The Great American Inventor by Louise Egan and Louise Betts **4-8**
Examines the life and achievements of the famous inventor, from his boyhood experiments to his search for electricity. ISBN: 081203922X

Usborne Science With Light & Mirrors **4-8**
This colorful book is packed with exciting scientific activities designed to help young children explore the intriguing properties of light. Real examples show how people exploit the way light behaves for driving mirrors, periscopes, lenses and so on. ISBN: 0746006969.

Energy/Physical Science

Alternative Energy by Christine Petersen **K-3** **4-8**
One of few titles for this age group that covers various forms of alternative energy. ISBN: 0516219448

Awesome Experiments in Force & Motion by Michael A. DiSpezio **4-8**
Provides more than fifty experiments illustrating the properties of force and motion including gravity, inertia, and density. ISBN: 0806998210

Basic Physics: A Self-Teaching Guide by Karl F. Kuhn **9-12**
Here is the most practical, complete, and easy-to-use guide available for understanding physics and the physical world. Even if you don't consider yourself a "science person," this book helps make learning key concepts a pleasure, not a chore. ISBN: 0471134473

Eyewitness Energy by Jack Challoner **4-8** **9-12** ⊶
Here is a spectacular, thought-provoking, and highly informative guide to the fascinating story of energy. Superb full-color photography of original equipment, intricate scientific instruments, 3-D models, and revealing experiments bring to life the ideas and discoveries that have changed our perception of the universe. See plants that bend toward light, alternative energy in action, the first batteries, the food chain, photosynthesis in plants, and how telephones convert the human voice into electronic signals. Learn how energy is measured, how without energy there would be no life at all, why matches burn, why recycling makes the most of energy, how waterwheels work, how efficient light bulbs save electricity, and how geothermal energy creates hot water. Discover the link between friction and heat, the development of steam turbines, how magnets work, how to make air liquid, how to heat coal to produce gas, the difference between renewable energy sources and fossil fuels, why sugar gives you energy, and much, much more. Each lesson in the Heart of Wisdom *Energy* unit study includes suggesting reading assignments from *Eyewitness Energy*. ISBN: 0789455765

Energy from the Sun by Allan Fowler **K-3**
Defines energy and examines how energy from the sun provides us with heat, light, plants, food and other things necessary for life on Earth. ISBN: 0516262556

Energy, Forces and Motion Kid Kit ("Usborne Internet-Linked Library of Science") **4-8**
Stunning photographs and detailed diagrams help demonstrate the use of physics in everyday life. Discover how cars work, why things fall down instead of up, and much more. An ideal revision tool, this book also contains experiments, activities and recommended Web sites designed to enhance learning. This kid kit includes: book, Magne-view magnetic field viewing film, bar magnet, deck of cards, paper airplane cutout marbles, non-hardening modeling dough, matchbox with sticks.I SBN: 1580864120

Heat & Energy ("Science View") by Steve Parker **4-8**
Discover the everyday uses of heat and energy, from warming our homes to fueling the cars we drive. Explore the relationship between kinetic and thermal energy and learn the basics of thermodynamics. (Parker is the author of *Eyewitness: Electricity*) ISBN: 0791082075

Physics the Easy Way by Robert L. Lehrman **9-12**
An introduction to physics for high school students, college-101 courses, or students looking for a self-teaching introduction to this sometimes intimidating science. Uses ordinary language to explain such topics as motion, forces, machines, energy, heat, wave motion, noise and music, electricity, magnetism, electromagnetic waves, the properties of light, and an introduction to nuclear physics. ISBN: 0764102362

Six Easy Pieces by Richard Phillips Feynman **9-12**
Designed for non-scientists, *Six Easy Pieces* is an unparalleled introduction to the world of physics by one of the greatest teachers of all time. ISBN: 0201408252

Matter/Physical Science

Atoms and Molecules: With Puzzles, Projects, and Problems by Phil Roxbee-Cox **4-8** **9-12**
Contains clear explanations, colorful illustrations and fascinating facts for advanced students—includes experiments and projects. ISBN: 0746009887

Chemical Reactions ("Material Matters") by Carol Baldwin **4-8**
This book tells you what happens when materials react together—sometimes with explosive results. There are loads of photos and facts to help you fully understand and find answers quickly. ISBN: 1410909360

Eyewitness Matter by Christopher Cooper **4-8** **9-12** ●━
Everything around us is made of matter—and *Eyewitness Matter* is the perfect way to learn more about it. Discover how the atom was split; learn what happens when matter changes state; find out how glass is created. Focusing on contemporary and historical developments in the study of matter, this book features clear, expertly written text, Superb full-color and black-and-white photos, charts, graphics, and 3-D models—all of which combine to make complex scientific concepts easy to understand. ISBN: 0789448866

Materials ("Usborne Internet-Linked Library of Science") by Alastair Smith **4-8** **9-12**
Taking examples from everyday life, this fascinating Usborne book explores the chemistry of solids, liquids and gases, explaining exactly what they are and how they behave. An ideal revision tool, this book also contains experiments, activities and recommended Web sites designed to enhance learning. Junior Science Prize Award 2002. Collectible series that builds into library of essential reference material. Hundreds of scientific terms clearly defined. Over 100 tested and approved Web sites, free downloadable pictures for projects. ISBN:1580863787

Matter: Solids, Liquids, and Gases ("Science All Around Me") by Karen Bryant-Mole, Mir Tamim Ansary **K-3**
This book explains the basic properties of matter through looking at everyday experiences and direct observation. Topics include: what makes some things heavier than others; how a small object can be heavier than a large one; why it's hard to squeeze a ball filled with air; and, how you can turn a solid into a liquid. ISBN: 1403400539

Metals ("Material Matters") by Carol Baldwin **4-8**
Explores the huge group of materials known as metals. There are loads of photos and facts. Easy to understand. ISBN: 1410909387

Mixtures, Compounds, & Solutions ("Material Matters") by Carol Baldwin **4-8**
Explains how materials join or mix together to make millions of new things. There are loads of photos and facts to help you fully understand the topic and find answers quickly. ISBN: 1410909379

Mr. Tompkins in Paperback by George Gamow, L. McLerran, Roger Penrose **4-8**
George Gamow's *Mr. Tompkins* became known and loved by thousands of readers as the bank clerk whose fantastic adventures lead him into a world inside the atom. ISBN: 0521447712

States of Matter ("Material Matters") by Carol Baldwin **4-8**
This book tells you everything you need to know about solids, liquids, gases, and plasma. There are loads of photos and facts to help you fully understand the topic and find answers quickly. You don't have to be a professor to understand this science book. ISBN: 1410905535

Solid, Liquid, Gas by Fay Robinson **K-3**
The natural world comes alive for young readers with "Rookie Read-About Science." With striking, full-color photos and just the right amount of text, this series immediately involves young readers as they discover intriguing facts about the fascinating world around them. ISBN: 0516460412

What Is the World Made Of?: All about Solids, Liquids, and Gases by Kathleen Weidner Zoehfeld **K-4**
In simple text, presents the three states of matter—solid, liquid, and gas—and describes their attributes. ISBN: 0064451631

Motion/Physical Science

And Everyone Shouted, "Pull!": A First Look at Forces and Motion by Claire Llewellyn **K-3**
Hop on the cart and join the farmyard animals as they find out how to take their heavy load on the hilly journey to market. ISBN: 1404806563

Eyewitness: Force and Motion by Peter Lafferty **4-8** **9-12** 🔑━
Plentiful, appealing color photographs and bits of information skim an enormous range of science history and principles. Discover how Archimedes made water run uphill; why a perpetual motion machine cannot be built; why a spinning top stays upright. Superb full-color photographs of original equipment, 3-D models, and ground-breaking experiments make this a compelling look at force and motion. ISBN: 0789448823

Energy, Forces and Motion ("Usborne Internet-Linked Library of Science") **4-8**
See description in Energy section. ISBN: 1580864120

Experiment With Movement by Two-Can Publishing **4-8**
Physics sounds like a hard topic, but with this science activity book, readers will test and observe basic scientific principles about movement while having fun at the same time. Full-color. ISBN: 1587281163

Forces and Motion Science Fair Projects: Using Water Balloons, Pulleys, and Other Stuff by Robert Gardner **4-8** **9-12**
Why don't you fall out of a roller coaster when it goes upside down? Which is stronger—your arms or your legs? Why do skydivers spread out their bodies when they jump from a plane? All of these questions can be answered by studying the properties of force and motion. These hands-on experiments are easy to carry out and most require simple items that can be found in the home or at school. For those wishing to enter a science fair competition, every chapter contains numerous suggestions and ideas for further exploration.

Janice VanCleave's Physics for Every Kid: 101 Easy Experiments in Motion, Heat, Light, Machines, and Sound by Janice VanCleave **4-8**
Contains 101 fully tested experiments, in each case complete with a discussion of the experiment's purpose, a list of materials, illustrated instructions, a clue to expected results and a scientific explanation in understandable terms. Most of the materials required are available around the house and all experiments are safe. Designed to make the learning of physics a rewarding and fun experience and to encourage kids to seek more knowledge about science

The New Way Things Work by David Macaulay **4-8** **9-12** 🔑━
Caldecott Medalist David Macaulay demystifies the digital age and steers readers successfully into the 21st century Text and numerous detailed illustrations introduce and explain the scientific principles and workings of hundreds of machines. Includes new material about digital technology. This completely updated and expanded edition describes 12 new machines and includes more than 70 new pages detailing the latest innovations. With an entirely new section that guides us through the complicated world of digital machinery, where masses of electronic information can be squeezed onto a single tiny microchip, this revised edition embraces all of the newest developments, from cars to watches. Each scientific principle is brilliantly explained—with the help of a charming, if rather slow-witted, woolly mammoth.

The Physics of Baseball by Robert Kemp Adair **9-12**
A "fascinating and irresistible" ("New York Times Book Review") look at the science behind America's favorite pastime, complete with charts and graphs, baseball lore, and more. ISBN: 0060084367.

The Spinning Blackboard and Other Dynamic Experiments on Force and Motion by Paul Doherty **4-8**
Presents over twenty experiments exploring the principles of mechanics. The experiments are miniature versions of some the exhibits at the Exploratorium, San Francisco's famed museum of science, art, and human perception. ISBN: 0471115142

Electricity/Physical Science

All About Electricity Science Kit by Vincent Douglas **K-4**
Science has never been this much fun. Children learn scientific concepts best with hands-on activities—and that's just what this amazing kit provides. Inside young scientists will find loads of opportunities to explore electricity. ISBN: 1588456110

Battery Science: Make Widgets That Work and Gadgets That Go by Doug Stillinger **K-4**
An introduction to basic electronics with guide and an alkaline battery, light bulb, small motor, and other items that kids can use to master electricity. Wire-O binding. Klutz book. ISBN: 159174251X

Electricity by Becky Olien **K-3**
How does it work? Why does it work? What can I do with it? These are just a few of the questions that young readers will be able to answer after reading this new series of books on basic physics in our world. ISBN: 0736814043

Electricity by Darlene Lauw **K-3** **4-8**
Engaging and safe activities show how electricity works. Fascinating information makes difficult scientific concepts like static electricity understandable for young readers. History boxes feature short biographies of scientists who made the first electrical discoveries ("Science Alive"). ISBN: 0778706079

Eyewitness Electricity by Steve Parker **4-8** **9-12**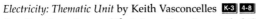
After two centuries of research and experimentation, electricity has revolutionized the way we live and become an indispensable part of scientific progress. Eyewitness Electricity brings vividly to life our exploration of this powerful natural force. It is a vital part of the living world. Our eyes receive light rays and turn them into tiny electrical signals that pass along our nerves to the brain. The chemicals in batteries create power for such things as toys and flashlights. The invention of electric motors enabled the creation of a whole range of household appliances that have shaped the modern world. See how electricity works nerves and muscles and what causes lightning. Learn how electricity can transmit voices and images across an ocean and what makes a silicon chip work. Discover the amazing speed of charged atoms, what happens when you tune in the radio, and much, much more! ISBN: 0789455773

Electricity: Bulbs, Batteries, and Sparks by Darlene R. Stille **K-3**
Beep beep. Zing. Vroom. Electricity makes your computer glow. It makes your toast pop up and your hair dryer blow. Learn how your house is powered in this electrifying book. ISBN: 1404802452

Electricity: Real Science Made Easy by Rob King **K-3** **4-8**
This all-inclusive educational kit provides an exciting and creative introduction to the fascinating world of electricity. ISBN: 1571459685

Electricity: Thematic Unit by Keith Vasconcelles **K-3** **4-8**
A unit on inventors and their inventions is provided. This reproducible resource is filled with ready-to-use lessons and cross-curricular activities. Also included are management ideas, creative suggestions for the classroom, and a bibliography. ISBN: 1557342369

Electricity and Magnetism by E. Humberstone **4-8** **9-12**
Untangles the mysterious properties of magnets, and examines what electricity really is. It delves into the past to reveal some of the most amazing (and sometimes accidental) historical breakthroughs, as well as considering dramatic developments that will radically affect our lives in the 21st century. ISBN: 0746009941

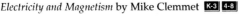

Electricity and Magnetism by Mike Clemmet **K-3** **4-8**
"Fact Finders" series books are based upon a popular BBC educational TV series, are clear and colorful informational books for children 8-12 years of age. ISBN: 0563373083

Electricity/Physical Science continued

Electricity and Magnets by Sarah Angliss **K-3** **4-8**
Conductors and insulators, resistance, circuits, and making magnets are some of the topics explored in this volume of fun-filled facts of electricity and magnetism. Illustrations. ISBN: 0753453495

Electronics by Pam Beasant **4-8** **9-12**
Filled with experiments, each one illustrating an important principle of electronics and demonstrating how different electronic components work. ISBN: 0860208095

Electronics Lab with Book by Brenda Bach **K-3** **4-8**
These action-packed kits contain a 32-page manual with full, easy-to-follow instructions to perform experiments, make observations, baffle the eye, and explore the natural world. Kits come complete with enough supporting components to get any young scientist or curious explorer started. ISBN: 1571454756

Fully Charged: Electricity by Steve Parker **4-8**
Describes how electricity is generated, harnessed, and used, and explains the difference between electricity, static electricity, and electronics. Readers will learn how science is at work all around them, as demonstrated though everyday items. Each spread is dedicated to one concept and features a series of vignettes demonstrating the concept in action in everyday circumstances. ISBN: 1403464197

Gordon McComb's Gadgeteers Goldmine by Gordon McComb **4-8** **9-12**
If you're into high-tech experiments with laser, fiber optics, power supplies, high-voltage devices, and robotics, look no further. This book is one of the most exciting and diverse collections of electronic projects available anywhere. ISBN: 083063360X

How Ben Franklin Stole the Lightning by Rosalyn Schanzer **K-3** **4-8**
Inventive art and superb storytelling bring to life the story of how one of the most famous inventions ever created—the lightning rod—came to be made by the energetic, humorous, and genius Ben Franklin. ISBN: 0688169937

The Magic School Bus and the Electric Field Trip with Bookmark by Joanna Cole **K-4**
Ms. Frizzle's students shrink to the size of atoms and travel through an electrical power plant. From the turbine to the toaster, it's a lightning-fast trip readers will not forget. ISBN: 0590446835

Opposites Attract: Magnetism by Steve Parker **4-8**
Describes what magnetism and magnetic fields are, how they work, and various ways that magnetism is used. "Did You Know" fact boxes present strange-but-true facts while "Try It Yourself" practical projects provide the means for demonstration. Also noted are the people who made significant advances in the study of each concept. ISBN: 1403464219

Shocking Science: Fun & Fascinating Electrical Experiments by Shar Levine **K-3** **4-8**
Children will be "shocked" to learn that with just a few wires, batteries, bulbs, and buzzers they can unlock the mysteries and magic of electricity. These simple and safe experiments will prove enlightening on everything from electrons to circuits to wattage. ISBN: 0806922710

Using Electricity by Angela Royston **K-3**
What is electricity? Where does electricity come from? What is a conductor? Read "My World of Science" *Using Electricity* to find out. Learn about where electricity comes from, where you will find it in everyday life, and how people use electricity. ISBN: 1403400466

Where Does Electricity Come From? by C. Vance Cast **K-3**
Explains, in simple terms, what electricity is and how it is generated. ISBN: 0812048350

Weather/Meteorology

All about the Weather by Bruce LaFontaine **4-8**
Fun-to-color pictures and detailed captions make this introduction to weather ideal for children 8 and older. Forty-four illustrations and diagrams display and explain such phenomena as tornadoes and hurricanes, tidal waves, lightning, El Nino, cloud formation, instruments and more. ISBN: 0486430367

All the Colors of the Rainbow by Allan Fowler **K-3**
This series meets National Curriculum Standards for Science: Earth and Space Science, Physical Science, Science and Technology, Science as Inquiry, Science in Personal and Social Perspectives. ISBN: 0516208012

Can It Really Rain Frogs?: The World's Strangest Weather Events by Spencer Christian **K-3** **4-8** **9-12**
Describes strange weather events such as raining frogs, singing caves, colored rain, and auroras, and discusses weather lore and weather forecasting. ISBN: 0471152900

The Cloud Book by Tomie dePaola **K-3**
Introduces the ten most common types of clouds, the myths that have been inspired by their shapes, and what we can tell about coming weather changes. A Reading Rainbow Book. ISBN: 0823405311

Clouds by Marion Dane Bauer **K-3**
Clouds come in many different shapes and sizes. They can be white and fluffy or dark and scary. But where do clouds come from? The answer is at your fingertips. Just open this book and read about the wonders of clouds. ISBN: 0689854412

The Complete Idiot's Guide to Weather by Mel Goldstein **9-12**
New updated content with expanded coverage of hot topics like extreme weather, global and ocean warming and storm tracking. ISBN: 0028643410

DK Guide to the Weather by Michael Allaby **K-4**
Explores a wide range of weather topics, including climate and seasons, wind and gales, lightning and thunderstorms, hurricanes and tornadoes, solar wonders, and weather forecasting. ISBN: 0789465000

Discovery Channel: Weather by Discovery Publishing **9-12**
Principles of meteorology and explanations of the equipment and techniques used by weather forecasters are combined with practical advice on sky-reading techniques and tools and a field guide to meteorological phenomena. 300+ color photos. ISBN: 1563318024

Down Comes the Rain by Franklyn Mansfield Branley **K-4**
Explains how the water cycle leads to different types of weather patterns. ISBN: 064451666

Exploring the Sky by Day: The Equinox Guide to Weather and the Atmosphere by Terence Dickinson **4-8**
Ideal for children, *Exploring the Sky by Day* offers fascinating insight into such phenomena as lightning, the ten types of clouds, storms, solar haloes, sundogs, and sunsets. Brought to life with dozens of photographs and the color illustrations of John Bianchi, the book provides an excellent introduction to weather and the atmosphere. ISBN: 0920656714

Introduction to Weather & Climate Change by Laura Howell **4-8**
Learn what causes the wild, wonderful and sometimes weird weather we experience every day. Delve into the controversy of global warming, and learn how people may affect the weather. ISBN: 0794506291

It's Raining Frogs and Fishes by Jerry Dennis **4-8** **9-12**
A spellbinding look into the natural world's most fascinating and baffling phenomena, with illustrated explanations of rainbows, meteors, sunsets, hurricanes, the northern lights, and dozens of other curiosities of the sky. 76 line drawings. Answers some of the questions kids ask, that adults would ask if we weren't quite so afraid of sounding childlike. Divided by season into four sections, so it can be used as a kind of field guide. ISBN: 0060921951

Weather/Meteorology continued

The Kids' Book of Weather Forecasting by Mark Breen and Kathleen Friestad **K-3** **4-8**
Kids experience what makes the weather tick in this hands-on introduction to the science of meteorology. ISBN: 1885593392

Lightning and Rainbows by Michael Carrol **K-3** **4-8** ⌒
Introduce the beauty and grandeur of God's creation while teaching your child about wonders in the skies. Children will become aware that God is in control, even of things that might cause them to be afraid. ISBN: 0781430003

The Magic School Bus: Electric Storm by Anne Capeci **K-3** **4-8**
Ms. Frizzle's class learns what makes lightning electric on their fascinating field trip through a thunderstorm. Chapter book with Illustrations. ISBN: 0439314348

The Magic School Bus Inside a Hurricane by Joanna Cole **K-4**
A tropical storm catches the Magic School Bus inside the eye of its hurricane, providing firsthand information on changes taking place in air, sea and land. Science questions and handwritten facts presents basic concepts in the usual lively and fun Magic School Bus manner. ISBN: 0590446878

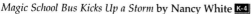
Magic School Bus Kicks Up a Storm by Nancy White **K-4**
When Ralphie imagines that he's a superhero named Weatherman, the Magic School Bus becomes a glider riding an updraft into the storm clouds. Then the kids become part of the storm—turning from ice crystals to rain. It's a science lesson they'll never forget. Full-color. ISBN: 061321949X

Peterson First Guide to Clouds and Weather by John A. Day, Roger Tory Peterson **4-8** **9-12**
This *Peterson First* guide contains easy-to-understand answers to questions about the weather, such as why the sky is blue, what makes it rain, and what causes rainbows. The book also features 116 color photographs that show how to identify clouds, with explanations of what each cloud type tells about the weather to come. ISBN: 0395906636

Rain by Marion Dane Bauer **K-3**
Newbery Honor-winner Marion Dane Bauer explains the wonders of nature in this delightful "Ready-To-Read" that combines inviting art with concise language. Full-color. ISBN: 0689854390

Skywatch West: The Complete Weather Guide by Richard A. Keen **9-12**
Revised and updated, *Skywatch West* offers a clear and interesting way of understanding how weather actually works, from calm and predictable cycles to dramatic and unpredictable events. ISBN: 1555912974

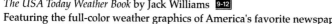
The USA Today Weather Book by Jack Williams **9-12**
Featuring the full-color weather graphics of America's favorite newspaper, here is a newly revised edition of the most readable guide to our nation's weather. It also includes an updated state-by-state guide to weather patterns and scientifically accurate records. ISBN: 0679776656

The Vital Guide to Weather by Brian Cosgrove **9-12**
This is a simple, straightforward look at how weather patterns occur and why weather is constantly changing. Using superb color photos and easily-understood diagrams, this book helps readers understand why the wind blows, why temperature changes, and what about the coming weather conditions can be learned from the clouds. ISBN: 1840372354

Weather by Pamela Chanko **K-3** **4-8**
Photographs and simple text describe some of the activities associated with various types of weather, from ice skating to going to the beach. ISBN: 059010730

Weather/Meteorology continued

Weather ("DK Eyewitness Explorers") by John Farndon `4-8`
Discusses such elements of weather as clouds, wet air, frost, ice, wind, and air pressure. Includes some projects. ISBN: 0789429853

Weather ("Science Alive!") by Darlene Lauw and Lim Cheng Puay `K-3` `4-8`
People are always talking about the weather but did you know that we can create our own weather? Learn how to make clouds and a rainbow, measure humidity, make your own rain gauge, and track a thunderstorm with the experiments in this book. ISBN: 0778706117

Weather and the Bible: 100 Questions & Answers by Donald B. DeYoung `9-12` ⤴
Written from a creationist viewpoint, this question-answer format provides nontechnical explanations for children or adults who wonder about weather phenomena in Bible times and today. ISBN: 0801030137

The Weather Book ("Wonders of Creation") by Michael Oard `4-8` `9-12` ⬤ ⤴
A fascinating overview of all types of weather, across the globe, this book is perfect for a wide audience—Christian and homeschools, and family reading times. Learn why the distance from earth to the moon affects tides, how the Ice Age developed. ISBN: 0890512116

The Weather Detectives by Mark E. Eubank `K-3` `4-8`
Follow the trail of *The Weather Detectives* as they discover pizza-sized snowflakes, see how a sudden temperature change can make a tree explode, and learn how to tell the temperature in the night sky by how fast the crickets are chirping. ISBN: 1586854127

The Weather Wizard's Cloud Book : A Unique Way to Predict the Weather Accurately and Easily by Reading the Clouds by Louis D. Rubin, Jim Duncan, Hiram J. Herbert `9-12`
This book provides weather information quickly and surely, because it focuses upon what is going on directly overhead—the actual clouds now on view in the sky, the actual sequences currently developing. 137 color, 19 black-and-white photographs ISBN: 0912697105

What's So Striking About Lightning by Roger Howerton `K-3` `4-8` ⤴
The latest addition to the "Ask Max" series answers questions about meteorology. Does lightning strike twice in the same place? Can a groundhog predict the weather? Children will love this question and answer book which factually answers their questions about the weather that God created. Lots of information, brilliant illustrations, and fun comprise this wonderful book. Packed with brilliant photos and illustrations, for children ages eight to 12. ISBN: 0890513635

Whatever the Weather by Karen Wallace `K-3`
Simple text, colorful illustrations and photographs of a boy looking out the window introduce different kinds of weather as it changes from day to day. "DK Eyewitness Readers: Level 1." ISBN: 0789447509

Oceans/Oceanography

101 Facts about Oceans by Julia Barnes **K-3**
Why do mountains get bigger? Where is the hottest place on Earth? Why are oceans and lakes changing size? How does a river carve out a valley? Why are tropical rain forests vital for the future of the planet? *101 Facts About Our World* answers all these questions and more about our amazing world. Best of all, these books are packed with spectacular photos that show the stunning beauty of Earth's natural features. ISBN: 0836837096

Air and Water by Tracy Paulus **K-4**
This is a kit with an easel-backed book featuring tons of fun information and instructions for science experiments. Includes: workbook, a mirror, plastic rods, thermometers, compass, magnifying glass, straws, balloons, plastic cup, observation log and more. ISBN: 1588456137

DK Guide to the Oceans by Frances A. Dipper **4-8**
Dramatic digital-terrain mapping and superb photography bring life and color to the exploration of the oceans. A "DK Eyewitness Guide." ISBN: 0789488647

Awesome Ocean Science!: Investigating the Secrets of the Underwater World by Cindy A. Littlefield **4-8** **9-12**
"... activities that illustrate the concepts—how blubber works and how to clean up an oil spill, for example—are creative, illuminating, and easy to follow." ISBN: 1885593716

Bill Nye the Science Guy's Big Blue Ocean by Bill Nye **K-3** **4-8**
The ocean, which makes up an impressive 71 percent of the planet, is still a relatively unexplored area of science. Fascinating facts like this make *Bill Nye the Science Guy's Big Blue Ocean* a compelling and essential read for young science fans. ISBN: 0786817577

The Blue Planet by Andrew Byatt **9-12**
From the depths of the Pacific Ocean, to the icy waters around the poles to lush tropical seas. *The Blue Planet* takes an astounding look at the undersea secrets that are gradually being revealed. ISBN: 0789482657

The Earliest Ships: The Evolution of Boats Into Ships by Robert Gardiner **9-12**
Researching back into prehistory and into the earliest evidence provided by archaeology, this volume explores the varied lines of development from the most primitive watercraft to the first real seagoing ships, from Northern Europe, through the Mediterranean to the Near and Far East. ISBN: 0851779956

First Encyclopedia of Seas and Oceans by Ben Denne **K-3**
Amazing photographs and illustrations combine with lively text to illustrate the basics of our planet's geography, its animals, ocean life and what's out in space. ISBN: 0794501117

In the Sea by Dawn Sirett **K-3**
Beautiful and sturdily made, this "Little Windows" books features easy-to-follow storylines and acetate windows with images visible inside. Readers can look into the deep sea world in this title. ISBN: 0789485710

In the Sea by Helen Orme **K-3**
Imagine yourself in a giant-sized world. This series explores the world of plants and animals through large-scale, close-up photographs. ISBN: 1577685660

Nature Unfolds Oceans by Andy Williams **K-3** **4-8** **9-12**
Children will love poring over two highly detailed fold-out posters in this beautiful book about the world's oceans, their animals, and plants. ISBN: 0778703223

Ocean by Samantha Gray **K-3**
More than 100 captivating photographs show readers the hidden world beneath the waves of the ocean in this title in a new series of reference books that focuses on both science and the natural sciences. ISBN: 0789478528

Oceans/Oceanography

Ocean by Miranda MacQuitty **4-8**
Learn how a monitoring buoy measures temperature, about the world's major currents, why a hermit crab finds a second home, and how the earth's plates form. Discover where the deepest dive was made, the length of a giant tube worm, what fish eat at the bottom of the ocean, how a coral reef is formed, how dead man's fingers got their name, and much, much more. ISBN: 0756607116

The Ocean Book: Aquarium and Seaside Activities and Ideas for All Ages **4-8**
This activity book on the world of the oceans and the living things that inhabit them is filled with experiments, investigations, puzzles, games, and all sorts of fun things to do and learn. ISBN: 0471620785

The Ocean Book with Poster by Frank Sherwin **K-3** **4-8** **9-12**
Where did all of the salt come from? What keeps the oceans from freezing? Why do icebergs float? What minerals are contained in ocean water? What causes the tides and why are they beneficial? How deep are the oceans? Free study guide downloadable from website. ISBN: 0890514011

Oceans by Darlene R. Stille **K-3** **4-8**
An introduction to the ocean describing its physical characteristics, the plants and animals that live in or near it, and its importance to life on Earth. ISBN: 0516215108

Oceans by Kristin Ward **9-12**
Introduces the world's oceans and some of the animals found there. ISBN: 082395532X

Oceans by Neil Morris, **K-4**
Describes the world's five oceans, their movements, effect on weather, lifeforms, and state of pollution. ISBN: 0865058407

Oceans by Philip Sauvain **4-8**
Describes oceans of the world, including the plants, animals, and human use, with case studies of specific areas. ISBN: 1575050439

Oceans and Rivers by Michael W. Carroll **K-3**
Explores oceans, seas, rivers, and lakes, discussing their changing nature, life forms, presence in the Bible, importance for ancient peoples, and environmental aspects. ISBN: 0781430682

Old Man and the Sea by Ernest Hemingway **4-8** **9-12**
The Pulitzer Prize winning short novel about an old Cuban fisherman and his supreme ordeal with a giant marlin far out in the Gulf Stream. ISBN: 0808519328

Seas and Oceans by Felicity Brook **4-8** **9-12**
The Usborne "Understanding Geography" series presents the principles of physical geography and the latest scientific research in an exciting and accessible way. Large, detailed diagrams, realistic illustrations, photographs and maps combine with clear, concise text to make each book a fascinating introduction to its subject. ISBN: 0613130278

Ships That Changed History by A. A. Hoehling **4-8** **9-12**
"Hoehling focuses on the most important seagoing vessels of the past two centuries. (His) text is highly readable."—Publishers Weekly. ISBN: 1568330197

Shipwreck by Richard Plat **4-8** **9-12**
Describes the history of shipwrecks, famous wrecks, causes, navigation and rescue techniques, and underwater archeology and the exploration of wrecks. ISBN: 0789458845

The Ultimate Ocean Glow-in-the-Dark Sticker Book with Stickers by Claire Ellerton **K-3** **4-8**
More than 60 stickers in this amazing book of ocean creatures glow in the dark to bring marine animals from the darkest oceans to life. ISBN: 0789492776

Plants/Botany

America's Deserts: Guide to Plants and Animals by Marianne D. Wallace **4-8**
This fun and lively field guide for all ages illustrates and identifies the plants and animals of North America's four desert regions. ISBN: 1555912680

A Bee in My Begonias by Bernadette McCarver Snyder **4-8** **9-12**
Written by a prolific, bestselling humorist, this book provides an array of prayers and meditations organized around the seasons of a garden year. A warmly humorous take on flowers, and even weeds, as God's gift to us. ISBN: 0764807870

Backyard Explorer Leaf Collector's Kit by Rona Beame **4-8**
Backyard Explorer is the kit that begins with something kids do naturally—picking up leaves, collecting pine cones, stuffing their pockets with acorns, turning it into seasons full of educational fun. ISBN: 0761133194

Bodge Plants a Seed: A Retelling of the Parable of the Sower by Simon Smith **K-3**
Meet Bodge, Big Al, Fat Jim, Stumpy and all their friends. They are here to teach children the parables in a way that is delightful and unforgettable. *Bodge Plants a Seed* is the retelling of the parable of the sower that Jesus told. Book includes text of parable from the NIrV Bible. ISBN: 0310706629

Botanical Gardens Coloring Book by Dorothy Barlowe and Sy Barlowe **4-8**
Detailed and accurate black-and-white line drawings depict the lush beauties of 37 botanical gardens throughout the United States and Canada. Captions. ISBN: 0486298582

Botany Coloring Book by Paul Young **9-12**
An exciting new approach to learning about botany. Teaches the structure and function of plants and surveys the entire plant kingdom. Comprehensive enough for a high school botany course. ISBN: 0064603024

Botany for Gardeners by Brian Capon **9-12**
A bestseller since its debut includes an appendix on plant taxonomy, a comprehensive index, and dozens of photos and illustrations. ISBN: 0881926558

Botany in a Day: The Patterns Method of Plant Identification by Thomas J. Elpel **9-12**
The one-day tutorial included in the text teaches you seven key patterns to recognize more than 45,000 species of plants worldwide. Based on the principle that related plants have similar patterns for identification and that they often have similar uses. ISBN: 1892784157

Corn Is Maize by Aliki **K-4**
"An engaging description of how corn was found by Indian farmers thousands of years ago and how corn is grown and used today. A successful blend of social studies, science, and history...augmented by accurate diagrams and cheerful illustrations."—School Library Journal. ISBN: 0064450260

Discover Nature Close to Home: Things to Know and Things to Do by Elizabeth P. Lawlor
Introduces the three zones of our backyard environment, the canopy, field, and forest floor, and describes the plant and animal life found there. Includes simple experiments and activities. ISBN: 0811730778

Draw 50 Flowers, Trees, and Other Plants by Lee J. Ames and P. Lee Ames **4-8**
Lee J. Ames shows us how to draw a wondrous variety of plants from around the world, including the regal rose and the stunning orchid, but also little-known flowers like the kapok. In these pages you'll find a mushroom, a thistle, a Christmas cactus, and a towering sequoia tree. ISBN: 0385471505

Edible Wild Plants: A North American Field Guide by Thomas S. Elias **4-8** **9-12**
Season-by-season guide to identification, harvest, and preparation of more than 200 common edible plants to be found in the wild. Beautiful color photographs temptingly arranged. ISBN: 0806974885

Eyewitness Plant by David Burnie **4-8**
Learn how plants defend themselves, why flowers are brightly colored, how a plant can climb, why some plants feed on insects, and why some plants have no seeds. ISBN: 0756607159

Plants/Botany continued

Eye Wonder Plant by Fleur Star `4-8`
Examine what a plant is, find out how plants support all other life on the planet, and discover their tricks of attracting pollinators and the secret weapons they use to keep predators at bay. A beautiful book from DK "Eye Wonder" series. ISBN: 0756606187

Exploring Creation With Botany by Jeannie Fulbright `4-8`
This Apologia book uses Charlotte Mason methodology to give elementary school students an introduction to God's incredible world of plants.the student notebook is emphasized in every lesson. Students are told to make illustrations for each lesson and are given notebook assignments to reinforce what they have learned. Assignments include collections of plants from the categories that are being studied, labeling the parts of a flower, making a "comic book" story of a bee pollinating a flower, making bark rubbings, and identifying leaves. Most importantly, of course, a creationist world view is stressed throughout. Time and time again, God is glorified as the Master Creator of all that the students are studying. In addition, sections entitled "Creation Confirmation" provide evidence for young-earth creationism in the context of the topic that the students are studying.

A Field Guide to Trees and Shrubs by George A. Petrides
This "Peterson Field Guide" includes trees and shrubs in the Northeastern and north-central United States and southeastern and south-central Canada. Accounts of 646 species include shape and arrangement of leaves, height, color, bark texture, flowering season, and fruit. Clear, accurate drawings illustrate leaves, flowers, buds, tree silhouettes, and other characteristics. ISBN: 039535370X

A Field Guide to Wildflowers: Northeastern and North-Central North America by Roger Peterson
This "Peterson Field Guide" is grouped by color and by plant characteristics, 1,293 species in 84 families are described and illustrated. Included here are all the flowers you're most likely to encounter in the eastern and north-central U.S., westward to the Dakotas and southward to North Carolina and Arkansas, as well as the adjacent parts of Canada. ISBN: 0395911729

A Friend Planting Seeds Is a Friend Indeed Fun Pack by On the Farm `K-3` `4-8`
It's planting season, and Farmer Bob gives Hercules, Sam, Jenny, and Brandon instructions on how to plant a field, along with a lesson of faith from the parable of the sower. Includes a 30-minute VHS video featuring the voices of Vince Gill and Amy Grant, a 32-page coloring book, and four crayons. ISBN: 1591453097

Fun with Gardening: 50 Great Projects Kids Can Plant Themselves by Clare Bradley `4-8`
By finding out about gardening, children help things grow and watch life develop. Kids will learn how to help the plants become big and strong and how to protect them from the weather and disease. ISBN: 184215138X

The Gardening Book by Jane Bull
Learn how to choose plants and give them what they need to grow, use your craft skills to make a scarecrow or funky yet useful flower container and much, much more. Atmospheric photography, helpful cartoon gardening characters, and easy-to-follow text. ISBN 0789492164

George Washington Carver: From Slave to Scientist by Janet Benge and Geoff Benge `4-8`
Once a kidnapped slave baby, George Washington Carver overcame poverty and racism to become an influential scientist (1864–1943). ISBN: 1883002788

Green Thumbs: A Kid's Activity Guide to Indoor and Outdoor Gardening by Laurie Carlson `K-3` `4-8`
Teach budding gardeners what it takes to make things grow with fun activities that require only readily available materials. Kindergarten to 7th grade. ISBN: 155652238X

Janice VanCleave's Plants by Janice Pratt VanCleave `K-3` `4-8`
Mind-boggling experiments you can turn into science fair projects. Presents facts about plants and includes experiments, projects, and activities related to each topic. ISBN: 0471146870

Plants/Botany continued

Jonny Appleseed ("Sower Series") `4-8` `9-12` 🔊
A first-person narrative of the life of the legendary figure who traveled across the American frontier planting apple trees and carrying the Christian faith to pioneer families. ISBN: 0880621346

Lasagna Gardening: A New Layering System for Bountiful Gardens: No Digging, No Tilling, No Weeding, No Kidding. by Patricia Lanza `4-8` `9-12`
A breakthrough technique designed to yield a lush garden without hours of backbreaking labor. *Lasagna Gardening* is mulch layering to provide a nutrient-dense base for plants. 200 illustrations. ISBN: 0875969623

Learn and Play in the Garden by Meg Herd and Andrew Elton `K-3` `4-8`
It's hands-on activity fun and natural science all in one bright, profusely illustrated book of garden projects. Learn how to make a scarecrow, grow strawberries, make a worm farm, and more. ISBN: 812097807

Like a Garden: A Biblical Spirituality of Growth by Sara Covin Juengst `9-12` 🔊
Sara Covin Juengst explores the use of the garden as a metaphor in the Bible. The discipline of the Christian life, what it means to bear fruit, and the harvest waiting for us in the new heaven and earth. ISBN: 0664256341

Meetings with Remarkable Trees by Thomas Pakenham `4-8` `9-12`
With this astonishing collection of tree portraits, Thomas Pakenham has produced a new kind of tree book. The arrangement owes little to conventional botany. The sixty trees are grouped according to their own strong personalities: Natives, Travellers, Shrines, Fantasies and Survivors. Each tree is a living hisorical monument in its own right and this volume reveals a variety of sacred trees, poets' trees and fantastic trees extraordinary in both their appearance and history. ISBN: 0375752684

The Magic School Bus Plants Seeds: A Book about How Living Things Grow by Scholastic Books `K-3`
Ms. Frizzles' class is growing a beautiful garden. But Phoebe's plot is empty. Her flowers are back at her old school. So the class climbs aboard the Magic School Bus. And, of course, the kids don't only go back to Phoebe's school, but they go inside one of Phoebe's flowers. Follow the kids' adventure and learn how living things grow. ISBN: 0590222961.

Newcomb's Wildflower Guide by Lawrence Newcomb `4-8` `9-12`
A field guide which will help you identify flowering plants. Good for recreational observation and scientific research purposes. User-friendly and accurate. The pictures are printed in black and white because flower color is variable in nature, and color pictures could be misleading. ISBN: 0316604429

Plants Bite Back! by Richard Platt `K-3`
Readers are introduced to stinging plants, poisonous plants and plants that eat animals in more complex sentence structures and colorful photographs. A "DK Eyewitness Reader Level 3." ISBN: 0789447541

Plants That Never Ever Bloom by Ruth Heller `K-3`
Brief rhyming text and illustrations present a variety of plants that do not flower but propagate by means of spores, seeds, and cones. ("Ruth Heller's World of Nature"). ISBN: 0698115589

The Reason for a Flower by Ruth Heller `K-3`
The reason for a flower is to manufacture seeds, but Ruth Heller shares much more about the parts of plants and their functions in her trademark rhythmic style. ("Ruth Heller's World of Nature"). ISBN: 0698115597

Remarkable Trees of the World by Thomas Pakenham
In a handsome paperback volume with flaps, Pakenham embarks on a five-year odyssey to most of the temperate and tropical regions of the world to photograph 60 trees of remarkable personality and presence. A stunning volume" (*Time*) and the most magnificent book on the world's trees published in years. A lavish work and worthy investment that will be treasured for generations. ISBN: 0393325296

Plants/Botany continued

Roots Shoots Buckets & Boots: Gardening Together with Children by Sharon Lovejoy **K-4** **4-8**
Twelve easy-to-implement ideas for theme gardens that parents and kids can grow together. Illustrated throughout by the author's own lyrical watercolors, each garden includes a plan, the planting recipe, seeds, seedlings, and growing instructions spelled out step-by-step and activities such as the Pizza Patch, a giant-size wheel garden planted in "slices" of tomatoes, zucchini, oregano, and basil. ISBN: 0761110569

Seed to Plant by Allan Fowler **K-3**
Beautiful photographs and clear illustrations with easy-to-read text will stimulate inquisitive minds. A "Rookie Read-About Science" book. ISBN: 1550742000

Start Exploring Forests: A Fact-Filled Coloring Book by Elizabeth Dudley **K-3**
Color the world with crayons and imagination. With these fact-filled coloring books for children and adults, anyone can recreate timeless works of art, or take a tour of the human body. Each book features a ready-to-color 17" x 22" poster to hang on the wall. ISBN: 0894717820

Stories Told Under the Sycamore Tree: Lessons from Bible Plants by Samuel J. Hahn **4-8** **9-12** ↰
Examines 52 notable flowers, trees, fruits, and other plants in the Bible. Each lesson includes an informative description based on scientific research and Scripture, a reflection on the plant's symbolism, and a prayer, along with superb color illustrations from award-winning nature artist Scott Patton. ISBN: 0788019724

The Story of George Washington Carver by Eva Moore **4-8**
George Washington Carver was born into slavery but later attend school to receive Master of Science degree in bacterial botany and agriculture. He was an outstanding innovator in the agricultural sciences. He discovered three hundred uses for peanuts and hundreds more uses for soybeans, pecans and sweet potatoes. Carver declined an invitation to work for a salary of more than $100,000 a year (almost a million today) to continue his research on behalf of his countrymen. He received the Roosevelt medal for restoring southern agriculture. This biography follows Dr. Carver's life from childhood to his days as a teacher and discoverer. ISBN: 0590426605

Tree in the Trail by Holling Clancy Holling **K-3** **4-8**
A struggling cottonwood sapling becomes a landmark to travelers, a peace-medicine tree, and after its death in 1834, a yoke which is used on the trail to Santa Fe. ISBN: 039554534X

Trees: Trees Identified by Leaf, Bark & Seed ("Fandex Family Field Guides") by Steven Aronson **4-8** **9-12**
Illustrated, individual die-cut cards feature hundreds of intriguing facts, statistics, and trivia, plus a tree identification guide and a cultural history of trees. 50 cards. Color photos & illustrations. ISBN: 0761112049

A Weed Is a Flower: The Life of George Washington Carver by Aliki **K-3**
Brief text and pictures present the life of the man, born a slave, who became a scientist and devoted his entire life to helping the South improve its agriculture. Full-color illustrations. ISBN: 0671664905

What is a Plant? by Bobbie Kalman **K-3** **4-8**
Plants provide people and animals with food, shelter, and oxygen. *What is a Plant?* introduces young readers to a variety of plant types, including ferns and mosses, and concepts like single-cell organisms, germination, and photosynthesis. Full-color. ISBN: 0865059594

Woods, Ponds, & Fields ("Real Science Real Kids Book") by Ellen Doris **4-8**
Shows you where to look for common plants and animals and how to study them in their natural environment. Hundreds of superb color photos document observation methods, field and rearing techniques to enhance direct experiential learning. Super photos. ISBN: 0500190062

World of Plants ("Usborne Internet-Linked Library of Science") by Laura Howell and Kirsteen Rogers **4-8**
Find out why plants are vital to our survival in this fascinating book. Richly illustrated and informative, it reveals the unseen world of plants and fungi. An ideal revision tool, this book also contains experiments, activities and recommended Web sites designed to enhance learning. ISBN: 0794500862

Rocks/Geology/Earth Science

Crystal Clear: Reflections on Gemstones in Our Lives by Joan W. Randell [4-8] [9-12] ⊶ ⊳
This is the key resource for the rock unit study written by my friend Joan, Bible study teacher and gemologist. She illustrates gemstones' human qualities and ways gems inspire us by their development and natural attributes—both emotionally and spiritually. Gemologists have always used human terms such as the "heart" of a stone, its "face", or even inclusions called "fingerprints" when describing gems. Gemstones, as well as people, go through many stressful conditions. Descriptions of the steps that transform a rough stone into a sparkling gemstone have parallels for us as we seek to overcome obstacles for successful living. *Crystal Clear* includes stories of famous gemstones and their owners, plus interesting insights as to how gemstones have affected history. All of this information is within a biblical context that encourages reflective and enlightened discussion from which we can learn many spiritual lessons. The book is beautifully illustrated with over 60 Full-color photographs, taken by the nation's finest gem photographers. Bound in attractive red leather it is an ideal presentation gift for special occasions. ISBN: 0787210013

Exploring Planet Earth by John Hudson Tiner [4-8] [9-12] ⊳
Combine science and history with this enjoyable overview of earth science topics and exploration from a God-centered view. As you read the 20 chapters, you'll learn about planet and space exploration from Ptolemy to von Braun, as well as navigation, winds, tides, compasses and poles, ocean currents, glaciers, rivers, the atmosphere, flight, and much more. Each chapter has review questions and illustrations. Grades 6-12. IBSBN: 0890511780

Eyewitness Crystal & Gem by R. F. Symes [4-8] [9-12]
Discover the natural beauty of crystals, and their remarkable uses from scalpels to silicon chips. Superb color photographs of crystals, jewels and gemstones of every color, size and shape offer a unique "eyewitness" insight into their extraordinary beauty and variety. ISBN 0756606640

Eyewitness Rocks & Minerals by R. F. Symes [4-8] [9-12]
Here is a spectacular and informative guide to the amazing world beneath our feet. Stunning color photographs of rocks, fossils, minerals, precious metals, crystals, jewels and gemstones give the reader a unique eyewitness insight into the evolution and composition of the Earth. ISBN: 0756607191

Footprints in the Ash: The Explosive Story of Mount St. Helens by John Morris and Steve Austin [9-12] ⊳
In the aftermath of the Mount St. Helens eruption there remained a geologic gold mine for earth scientists. See what was discovered as they reconstructed the sequence of earthquakes, eruptions, avalanches, mudflows, and other geologic processes and unveil their fascinating research findings. Lavishly illustrated picture book is a powerful testament to the Creator and Judge, who forms canyons in just hours, not millions of years. ISBN: 0890514003

The Geology Book ("Wonders of Creation") by John D. Morris [4-8] [9-12] ⊶ ⊳
Whether jutting skyward, or languishing in the murky depths of the deep, rocks and sediments hold our little planet together. Creationist Dr. John Morris takes the reader on a tour of the earth's crust, pointing out both the natural beauty and the scientific evidences for Creation. Profusely illustrated, this book presents an accurate view of earth's natural history. Includes free pull-out poster. ISBN: 0890512817

Geology Rocks! 50 Hands-On Activities to Explore the Earth by Cindy Blobaum [4-8]
Illustrations and instructions help kids design an earthquake-proof building, create a "forming" cave, become a paleontologist, and observe first-hand the effects of water, erosion, acid rain, volcanoes, and earthquakes. Full-color illustrations. ("Kaleidoscope Book") ISBN: 1885593295

The Magic School Bus Blows Its Top: A Book about Volcanoes by Scholastic Books [K-3]
Once again, Ms. Frizzle gets her class right in the thick of things—this time, they're right in the thick ooze of an underwater volcano's magma chamber. As Arnold and Carlos watch from a raft above, the Magic School Bus erupts with the magma and lava, and lands atop a brand-new island. Full-color. ISBN: 0590508350

Rocks/Geology/Earth Science continued

Grand Canyon: A Different View by Tom Vail **4-8** **9-12**
Explore the majesty and beauty of the Grand Canyon yourself, through the photographs and essays in this book. Presents a solid case that the Grand Canyon resulted from the Genesis flood, while showing the holes in the "millions of years" evolutionary theories. ISBN: 0890513732

Hill of Fire by Thomas P. Lewis **K-3**
Every day is the same for Pablo's father. Then one afternoon the ground growls, hisses smoke, and swallows up his plow. A volcano is erupting in the middle of his cornfield. ISBN: 0064440400

Janice VanCleave's Earth Science for Every Kid: 101 Easy Experiments by Janice Pratt VanCleave **K-3** **4-8**
101 fun, safe, low-cost experiments and activities about the earth, sea, and air that can be performed at home. ISBN: 0471530107

Janice VanCleave's Rocks and Minerals by Janice Pratt VanCleave **K-3** **4-8**
Includes 20 fun and simple experiments about rocks and minerals. ISBN: 0471102695

The Magic School Bus Inside the Earth by Joanna Cole **K-4**
On a special field trip in the Magic School Bus, Ms Frizzle's class learns at first hand about different kinds of rocks and the formation of the earth. ISBN: 0590407600

The Magic School Bus Rocky Road Trip by Judith Bauer Stamper **K-3**
The class goes on a wild rock hunt in the wild West to solve a mineral mystery. They take a stagecoach ride, pan for precious gems, and explore an old mine. A "Magic School Bus Chapter Book."
ISBN: 0439560535

Rocks and Minerals ("DK Eyewitness Explorers") by Steve Parker
Youngsters with inquisitive minds can learn about the characteristics of every type of rock and mineral, and also participate in hands-on projects such as crystal collecting. ISBN: 0789416824

Rocks and Mineral ("DK Eyewitness Video") **4-8** **9-12**
Fascinating facts and unbelievably gorgeous photography detailing rocks, gems, and the earth, and especially how we interact with them on a day-to-day basis. ISBN 0789407205

Rocks and Minerals Ultimate Sticker Book by DK **K-3**
Contains over 60 reusable stickers selected from the Eyewitness archive for their visual appeal and annotated with informative labels. ISBN: 0789400073

Rocks: A Resource Our World Depends On by Ian Graham **4-8**
What are meteorites? How do we get metal from rocks? Read this book to find the answers to these questions and more. Each book in the "Managing Our Resources" series examines a valuable natural resource, explaining where the resource is found, how it is extracted and processed, what it is used to make, and how the resource can be used continuously. ISBN: 1403456259

Salt: A World History by Mark Kurlansky **4-8**
In this multilayered masterpiece, Kurlansky explains how salt provoked and financed wars, secured empires, and inspired revolutions. ISBN: 0142001619

The Young Earth by John Morris **4-8** **9-12**
Teach your child geology from a Christian perspective. Geologic evidence for a young earth, fossils, and dating methods are covered. Also, Morris refutes assumptions of the evolutionary theory. Includes 67 pages for duplicating overhead transparencies. Grades 7-12. ISBN: 0890511748

Volcano by Lisa Magloff **K-3**
Discover the inner workings of one of Earth's most terrifying natural phenomena in Eye Wonder: Volcano. How hot is molten lava? How are volcanoes formed under the earth's surface? Learn about famous volcanic eruptions such as the disaster in Pompeii with this unique visual reference. A "DK Eye Wonder" book. ISBN: 0789492709.

Stars and Planets/Astronomy

Absolutely Awesome by Michael W. Carroll and Caroline Carroll K-3 4-8 ▭
This 13-week devotional showcases God's spectacular universe in a way that will captivate tweens.
ISBN: 0842330437

As the World Spins: The Solar System ("Newton's Workshop") 4-8 ▭ ▭
When a space shuttle astronaut visits Trisha's class, it's the first step for Trisha to understanding her place in the cosmos. But leave it to Grandpa Newton to help Trisha learn about the works of Copernicus, Kepler and Galileo and how it all fits together within the framework of the Bible. (Moody Video) ISBN: 1575672219

Astronomy and the Bible: Questions and Answers by Donald B DeYoung 9-12 ▭
Updated answers to 110 questions on astronomy and the universe from a Christian perspective that is informed by Scripture. A useful resource for classroom and home. ISBN: 080106225X

The Astronomy Book by Jonathan Henry 5-8 ▭ ▭
The second book in the highly successful *"Wonders of Creation"* series (following *The Weather Book*), *The Astronomy Book* soars through the solar system targeting middle-school through junior-high levels. The reader will acquire a wealth of knowledge on subjects such as supernovas, red shift, facts about planets, and much more. Enhanced with dozens of color photos and illustrations (including NASA shots), this book gives educators and students a Christian-based look at the awesomeness of the heavens. ISBN: 0890512507

Astronomy Internet Linked by Rachel Firth 4-8
The stars are just a tiny part of what's out in space. Discover some of the amazing things that are out there, many of which you can see with just a pair of binoculars or a small telescope. ISBN: 0794504841

Children's Night Sky Atlas by Robin Scagell K-3 4-8
Featuring the most recent discoveries and state-of-the-art space photographs, this atlas details everything there is to know about the Universe. Contains six acetate overlays. ISBN: 075660284X

The Christian Sky by Mark Edward Dodson 4-8 9-12 ▭
Rediscover the Heavens in the light of the Creator. No equipment necessary. No telescope required. After presenting a few simple but very effective techniques for finding your way through the sky at night, the author takes you on a tour of the Christian constellations. Using new constellations inspired by stories from the Bible, you will be able to locate stars, planets, star clusters, and galaxies during any time of the night and at any time of the year. ISBN: 0976240203

Eyewitness Space Exploration by Carole Stott 4-8
Learn how space probes photograph planets, what causes a meteor shower, what makes Mars red, why the Sun shines, where the moon came from, how the first telescopes worked, the stages in the life of a star, and how the earth's atmosphere sustains life and much, much more. ISBN 0756607310

Exploring Creation with Astronomy by Jeannie Fulbright 4-8 ▭
This Apologia book uses the Charlotte Mason approach to give elementary school students an introduction to our solar system and the universe. Narration and notebooking are used to encourage critical thinking, logical ordering, retention, and record keeping. Each lesson in the book is organized with a narrative, some notebook work, an activity, and a project. Includes the nature of astronomy, major structures of our solar system, earth's moon, the asteroid belt, the Kuiper belt, stars and galaxies, space travel and more. Most importantly, a Creationist worldview is stressed throughout.

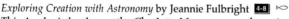

Johannes Kepler, Giant of Faith and Science by John Hudson Tiner 4-8 ▭
Johannes Kepler considered his vast scientific studies as another way of looking into God's magnificent creation ("Sower Series"). ISBN: 091513411X

Journeys to the Edge of Creation by Moody Video 4-8 9-12 ▭ ▭
In the media news, we are reminded of the continuous endeavor of mankind to explore the cosmos. In this series, learn some fascinating discoveries of Science and enjoy images of the world without having to leave the comforts of your own environment. ISBN: 1575672529

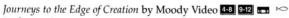

Stars and Planets/Astronomy continued

The Magic School Bus Lost in the Solar System by Joanna Cole **K-4**
On a special field trip in the Magic School Bus, Ms. Frizzle's class goes into outer space and visits each planet in the solar system. ISBN: 0590414291

The Magic School Bus Out of This World: A Book about Space Rocks by Joanna Cole **K-3**
On a trip to outer space, Ms. Frizzle and the gang learn all about shooting stars, meteorites and other space rocks. ISBN: 0590921568

The Magic School Bus Sees Stars: A Book about Stars by Nancy White **K-3**
Keesha and the rest of the class discover what stars are made of, the difference between a young star and an old star, and much more. ISBN: 0590187325

The Moon Book by Gail Gibbons **K-3**
Identifies the moon as our only natural satellite, describes its movement and phases, and discusses how we have observed and explored it over the years. ISBN: 0823413640

Our Created Moon: Earth's Fascinating Neighbor by Don B. DeYoung and John C. Whitcomb **9-12** ▷
Thoughtful and complete, factual explanations about Earth's closest neighbor. Well-known creation scientists Don DeYoung and John Whitcomb share their knowledge in an easy-to-comprehend format. ISBN: 0890514038

Our Solar System by Lawrence T. Lorimer and Peter D. Riley **K-3** **4-8**
Travel among planets, moons, and asteroids on an incredible journey through space. Each turn of the see-through page transports readers from the blazing sun to the distant icy, Pluto and beyond. Information bars on the top of each page highlight important facts about each planet. Full-color. ISBN: 1575842440

Seeing Stars with Cards and Flashlight by Charles Hobson **K-3** **4-8**
Be a storyteller and navigator of the stars with this interactive introduction to the night sky. Ten star punched cards let kids shine a flashlight through them to project constellations onto the wall. Illustrations. ISBN: 0811832058

Starry Messenger: Galileo Galilei by Peter Sis **K-3**
The life and genius of Galileo Galilei are portrayed in this picture book that includes maps, important events, and a world view of Galileo's time period. Full-color. ISBN: 0374470278

Starlight and Time by D. Russell Humphreys **9-12** ▷
The Bible teaches that the universe is just thousands of years old, and yet we can see stars that are billions of light-years away. In this book, Dr. Humphreys explains this phenomenon with his new cosmology including an easy-to-read popular summary and two technical papers. ISBN: 0890512027

Telescope Power: Fantastic Activities & Easy Projects for Young Astronomers by Gregory L. Matloff **4-8** **9-12**
An introduction to the telescope and its uses, including information on setting up the equipment, observation techniques, and a variety of projects and experiments. ISBN: 0471580392

Voyage to the Stars by Richard Bliss **4-8** **9-12** ▷
A beautifully illustrated book on astronomy for junior-high-age students, written in the form of an adventurous trip into space on a space shuttle. The creative design and power of God are made evident throughout. ISBN: 0932766218

Voyage to the Planets by Richard B. Bliss **4-8** **9-12** ▷
A fascinating sequel to the space adventures chronicled in *Voyage to the Stars*. Highly informative on the nature of each planet and its satellites, yet absorbingly interesting and beautifully illustrated. An ideal gift for teens. It honors God and His creation throughout.

The Young Astronomer (Usborne) by Sheila Snowden **5-8**
Practical guides designed for the novice. Filled with helpful ideas about choosing and using equipment. ISBN: 0860206513

Ocean Life/Marine Biology

ABC Under the Sea: An Ocean Life Alphabet Book by Barbara Knox `K-3`
Teach letter recognition and capital and lowercase letters—plus letter names,and sounds. ISBN: 0736816844

The Black Pearl by Scott O'Dell `5-8` **N**
A coming-of-age story in which Ramon learns the family art of pearl diving and respect for the legend that surrounds the giant pearl he finds in a sea creature's cave. "A gripping story that will hold practically any age enthralled."—"The Horn Book." A Newbery Honor Book. ISBN: 0440908035

Commotion in the Ocean by Giles Andreae `K-3`
The sequel to the bestselling *Rumble in the Jungle* is a delightful new collection of poems about creatures who live in and around the ocean. ISBN: 1589253663

Corals by Lola M. Schaefer `K-3`
Simple text and photographs depict corals and how they create coral reefs. ISBN: 0736802444

Crabs by Lola M. Schaefer `K-3`
Rich, vibrant photographs capture readers' interest and provide a realistic perspective that illustrations cannot capture. ISBN: 0736802452

Dolphins and Sharks: A Nonfiction Companion to Dolphins at Daybreak by Mary Pope Osborne `K-3` `4-8`
Fans of the "Magic Tree House" title *Dolphins at Daybreak* can learn lots more about dolphins and sharks with this guide. Includes an illustrated gallery of dolphins and sharks, and more. ISBN: 0375923772

Dolphins At Daybreak by Mary Pope Osborne `K-3` **N**
Their magic tree house takes Jack and Annie deep into the sea, where they meet up with dolphins, sharks, and octopi as they search for the answer to an ancient riddle. ISBN: 067988338X

Dolphins, Whales, and Manatees of Florida: A Guide to Sharing Their World by John Elliott Reynolds `9-12`
For the general public and ecotourists as well as students, teachers, and marine educators, *Dolphins, Whales, and Manatees of Florida* is the primary reference for marine mammal biology and conservation and a guide to wildlife protection laws. ISBN: 0813026873

First Encyclopedia of Seas and Oceans by Ben Denne `K-3`
Amazing photographs and illustrations combine with lively text to illustrate the basics of our planet's geography, its animals, ocean life and what's out in space. ISBN: 0794501117

The Great Shark Escape by Jennifer Johnston `K-3` `4-8`
What starts as a class trip to the aquarium ends up in the ocean where the class has to escape from a great white shark. A "Magic Schoolbus Chapter Book." ISBN: 0439204216

Jellyfish by Martha E. H. Rustad `K-3`
Early readers easily dive into nonfiction texts with the help of this supportive series. Rich, vibrant photographs capture readers' interest and provide a realistic perspective that illustrations cannot capture. This series supports units on oceans and the intriguing world of coral reefs, supports the standard *The Living Environment: Interdependence of Life*, as required by the Benchmarks for Science Literacy: Project 2061. ISBN: 0736816569

Invertebrate Zoology ("Real Kids Real Science") by Ellen Doris `4-8` `9-12`
A beautiful introduction to a vast and diverse group of animals, this book focuses on seven families of organisms, all of which can be easily collected or ordered by mail. Children rear crayfish and spiders, watch flatworms distinguish between light and dark, and more. Almost 200 fantastic color photos. ISBN: 0500190054

Island of the Blue Dolphins by Scott O'Dell `5-8` **N**
An unusual story where an Indian girl spends 18 years alone on a rocky island far off the coast in the early 1800s. ALA Notable Children's Book; 1961 Newbery Medal winner. ISBN: 0440439884

Ocean Life/ Marine Biology continued

The Magic School Bus on the Ocean Floor by Joanna Cole `K-4`
On another special field trip on the Magic School Bus, Ms. Frizzle's class learns about the ocean and the different creatures that live there. Full-color illustrations. ISBN: 0590414313

Meet the Arthropods ("Real Kids Real Science") by Ellen Dorris
Experiments, investigations and discoveries that emphasize direct learning experiences with aquatic arthropods. Investigations include those you can conduct in supermarkets (lobster and crab), field locations seashore (fishing for crabs), salt marshes (horseshoe crabs), beaches (sand crabs), etc. Describes observation, collection, and rearing techniques. Outstanding; especially for young insect collectors who want to put together an exhibit. Over 200 photos in this amasszing visual display. ISBN: 0500190100

Mysteries and Marvels of Ocean Life (Usborne) by R. Morris `K-3` `4-8`
Brings to life many of the unusual and unexpected aspects of creation in Usborne's a beautiful colorful format. ISBN: 0860207536

Nature Unfolds Oceans by Andy Williams
Children will love poring over two highly detailed fold-out posters in this beautiful book about the world's oceans, their animals, and plants. Special emphasis is put on tropical marine life and incredible creatures of the deep. A "Crabtree" book. ISBN: 0778703223

Oceans and Rivers by Michael W. Carroll `K-3`
Ships sailing down river, waves crashing on the shore, and the panoramic view of the wide open sea all hold a fascination with children. But how does the river know where to flow? Who made the seas so big, and deep, and wide? ISBN: 0781430682

Oil Spill!: Investigating Oceanography by Russell Wright `K-3`
Using a combination of reading, writing, and hands-on activities, each uses a real-life event and the research/news stories that accompanied it to make everyday applications of science real for students. ISBN: 0201490900

Orca: Visions of the Killer Whale by Peter Knudtson
The orca, also known as the killer whale, is one of the most intriguing and mysterious animals in the world. This lavishly illustrated portrait of this almost mythical sea mammal offers visions of the orca throughout the ages and across cultures, describing its hunting techniques and refined sonar and communication abilities. ISBN: 1553650344

Pagoo by Holling Clancy Holling and Lucille W. Holling `K-3` `4-8`
An intricate study of tide pool life is presented in text and pictures through the story of Pagoo, a hermit crab. Illustrations. ISBN: 0395539641

Reader's Digest Explores Whales, Dolphins & Porpoises by Readers Digest
This book brings together the latest research findings on the evolution, biology, habits, and behavior of these intriguing creatures. Includes stunning color photographs of 48 species. ISBN: 0895779765

Whales, Dolphins and Porpoises by Mark Carwardine `9-12`
Smithsonian Handbook beautifully illustrated guide to every species of whale, dolphin and porpoise. Covers their identification, evolution, biology, behavior, reproduction and social lives. Includes tips on how and where to watch whales, dolphins and porpoises, and information on their conservation. ISBN: 0789489902

Whales, Dolphins, and Other Marine Mammals by George S. Fichter
A brief survey of the major groups and species of marine mammals: whales, dolphins, porpoises, manatees, dugong, sea lions, walruses, and seals. ISBN: 1582381615

The Wild Whale Watch by Eva Moore `K-3`
The magic school submarinetakes the kids deep into the ocean, where they learn all sorts of fascinating facts about whales. ISBN: 0613275853

Birds/ Ornithology

Audubon Society First Field Guide to Birds by Scott Weidensaul `4-8`
An informative, visual guide to the natural science of birds as well as a field guide to over 150 species found in North America. ISBN: 0590054821

The Backyard Bird Feeder's Bible by Sally Roth `4-8` `9-12`
The A-To-Z guide to feeders, seed mixes, projects, and treats for birds. A stunning full-color reference gives helpful tips and advice for the most popular aspect of bird watching in America today—bird feeding. 400 full-color photos and illustrations. ISBN: 0875968341

Backyard Bird Watching for Kids: How to Attract, Feed, and Provide Homes for Birds by George H. Harrison `4-8`
Entertaining projects to learn about the needs and behaviors of wild birds. Informative text and appealing photos of appealing backyard habitats including feeders, birdhouses and birdbaths. ISBN: 1572230894

The Clown-Faced Carpenter ("Moody Video Science Adventures") `4-8` `9-12`
Integrated with the truths of Scripture this video explain the is woodpecker may look like a clown, but he plays an important role in the forest providing food for the neighborhood. Also on the video, transport to a *Journey to the Stars*, and *Water Water Everywhere*.

Eyewitness Bird by David Burnie `4-8` `9-12`
Learn how birds' bodies are designed for flight, why wings are different shapes and sizes, how birds evolved from their prehistoric ancestors and which are the world's biggest, smallest, slowest and fastest birds. Discover how and where birds make their nests, why eggs are different colors, how many feathers birds have and what each one is for and how to watch birds and attract them to your garden, and much, much more. ISBN: 0756606586

Eyewitness Eagle and Birds of Prey by Jemima Parry-Jones and Eyewitness Books `4-8` `9-12`
Get a bird's-eye view of the amazing world of raptors—from the majestic falcon, hawk, and eagle to the stealthy owl and the formidable vulture. Examines the development, anatomy, mating and nesting habits as well as their techniques for stalking and catching their quarry. Full-color photos. ISBN: 0789458608

Eyewitness Jr: Amazing Birds of Prey by Jemima Parry-Jones `K-3`
Introduces the physical characteristics and habits of birds of prey, including falcons, eagles, vultures, owls, and hawks. ISBN: 0833593056

Fly Away Home: The Novelization and Story Behind the Film by Patricia Hermes `4-8` **N**
14-year-old Amy and her inventor father attempt to teach geese how to fly. Includes a 16-page section of production notes on the making of the film. ISBN: 1557044899

The Life of Birds by David Attenborough `4-8` `9-12`
Based on the spectacular ten-part program that will air on PBS, The Life of Birds is David Attenborough at his characteristic best: presenting the drama, beauty, and eccentricities of the natural world with his usual flair and intelligence. 180 color photos. ISBN: 069101633X

Golden Guide to Birds by Herbert Spencer Zim `K-3` `4-8` `9-12`
A guide to North American birds which gives popular name, describes life and reproduction cycles and feeding habits, and includes a range guide. ISBN: 1582381283

National Geographic Field Guide to the Birds of North America by John Fitzpatrick `K-3` `4-8` `9-12`
This field guide of choice for serious birders combines accurate illustrations with useful maps and text in an easily portable format. Textual information includes notes on identification, behavior, habitat, and song; the illustrations depict individual species in varying plumages. ISBN: 0792268776

Ornithology ("Real Kids/Real Science") by Ellen Doris `4-8` `9-12`
 covers taxonomy, identification, anatomy, nesting, migration, banding, and much more. In addition, there are lots of projects, field trips, ideas, and suggestions to help children study birds in their own areas. Beautiful Full-color photographs. ISBN: 0500190089

Birds/ Ornithology Continued

Ornithology ("Science & Nature") by Corinne Stockley `4-8` `9-12`
Takes an in-depth look at the natural world from a scientific angle. Includes stimulating ideas for practical work. ISBN: 0746006853

Owl Puke: The Book and the Owl Pelet by Jane Hammerslough `4-8`
An owl pellet is regurgitated twice a day by owls, which contains the bones and fur or feathers of at least one owl meal, be it a mouse, vole, shrew, or small bird. Includes a professionally collected, heat-sterilized owl pellet which is illustrated in this book filled with facts and activities about these most amazing birds. It's a hoot! ISBN: 0761131868

Project Puffin: How We Brought Puffins Back to Egg Rock by Stephen W. Kress and Pete Salmansohn `4-8`
Puffins are popular all over the world. But for the past hundred years, puffins along the coast of Maine have been threatened with local extinction. Biologist Stephen Kress decided to try to bring puffins back to Maine with an experiment that had never been attempted before. Stunning color photographs on every page capture each step of this wildlife success story. As you learn about The Puffin Project, you'll also learn all about puffins—how they are so wonderfully adapted to their ocean environment, how they catch fish, socialize, nest in burrows, and raise their young. ISBN: 0884481719

Sibley Guide to Birds by David Allen Sibley `4-8` `9-12`
America's most gifted contemporary painter of birds is the author and illustrator of this comprehensive guide. His beautifully detailed illustrations—more than 6,600 in all—and descriptions of 810 species and 350 regional populations will enrich every birder's experience. An introductory page for each family or group of related families makes comparisons simple. Maps show the complete distribution of every species: summer and winter ranges, migration routes, and rare occurrences. ISBN: 0679451226

Special Wonders of Our Feathered Friends by Buddy and Kay Davis `4-8` ⊷
Did you know that puffins are aquatic arctic birds that only come on land to lay eggs? The bald eagle's nest can be seven feet across and 11 feet deep? The bones of most birds are hollow, having only air spaces and trusses for strength? This book contains God's amazing designs of 30 birds from around the world highlighted in this beautiful and informational book. Full-color photography illustrates the uniqueness of each bird. Information is provided alongside the picture, and the book includes an appendix pinpointing the intelligent design of birds and Glossary. The "Special Wonders" series is a powerful teaching tool. ISBN: 0890512973

Sniffles by Stephen Cosgrove `K-3`
Sniffles, an ostrich, ruins her credibility with the other animals at the oasis by her wild exaggerations of the truth. An inventive way to teach children the dangers of exaggerating. ISBN: 0843138270

Why Noah Chose the Dove by Isaac Bashevis Singer `K-3` ⊷
The animals praise their own special qualities so that each will be assured a place on Noah's Ark. The dove demonstrates meekness and humility. Beautifully illustrated. ISBN: 0374483825

Winged Migration Jacques Perrin (Director) `4-8` `9-12` ▭
This beautiful documentary that follows migrating birds through 40 countries and every continent was captured using planes, gliders, helicopters, and balloons, allowing the filmmakers a spectacularly intimate look at their subjects. Video or DVD. ISBN: 140492308X

Wringer by Jerry Spinelli `4-8` **N**
A boy's tenth birthday marks an event he would rather ignore: the day that he is ready to take his place as a "wringer" at the annual family fest, Pigeon Day. When an unwanted visitor—in the form of a trusting pigeon—arrives on his window sill, the boy realizes that it is a sign to stand up for what he believes. Buckeye Children's Book Award. ISBN: 0064405788

Insects/Entomology

Ant Cities by Arthur Dorros K-4
Dorros provides a beginning look at the fascinating world of ants—the variety of "cities" they build, the job each ant carries out, and the remarkable feats they can accomplish. Includes instructions for building an ant farm. ("Let's-Read-And-Find-Out Science"). Reading Rainbow. ISBN: 0064450791

Bugs in 3-D by Mark Blum K-4
The creepiest, crawliest, and hairiest bugs are featured in this amazing collection of 3-D photographs. Tarantulas, millipedes, flies, bumblebees, beetles, and more loom into view with fascinating detail in this foolproof 3-D experience. Complete with 3-D lenses. 44 color photos. ISBN: 0811819450

Bug Cards by Tina L Seelig
Play card games with an educational twist in each fun and fact-filled deck. Play Crazy Eights, Gin Rummy, Go Fish, Solitaire, and Concentration as you learn the scientific facts about bugs. ISBN: 765145099486

The Bug Safari: Entomology ("Newton's Workshop") K-4 4-8 ⌐○
When bugs invade the Newtons' home, it's time to take action! But not before Wendell recruits Tim and Max for his "Bug Olympics." A bug safari through an old warehouse leads the boys to the heart of the pest problem. It's also where they learn an important lesson in understanding God's plan. (Moody Video).

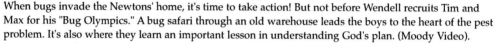

Bugs: Ultimate Sticker Book by DK K-3 4-8
Annotated with factual information, each book contains more than 60 full-color, reusable stickers so children can create their own fun scenes. ISBN: 0756602343

Bug Watching With Charles Henry Turner by Michael Elsohn Ross 9-12
Under the apprenticeship of this 19th-century entomologist, children learn the value of careful observation and persistence (in this case the persistence needed to overcome prejudice). Storyline follows Charles's true-life story as he works toward his goal of understanding the workings of the insect world. Fine blend of multi-cultural and natural history. ("Naturalist's Apprentice Biographies"). ISBN: 157505003X

Butterfly Battle by Nancy White, Joanna and Bruce Degen Cole K-4
Ms. Frizzle takes her students on a butterfly field trip and accidentally turns them all into butterflies. But being a butterfly is not all fun and games, as the students learn when they find that they must battle wind, birds, and even people. Full-color illustrations. A "Magic School Bus Chapter Book." ISBN: 0439429366

City of the Bees ("Moody Video Science Classics") 4-8 ▭ ⌐○
You're about to visit an incredible city, where everyone has a job. A place where there's no need for hospitals or retirement homes—the organized, efficient City of the Bees. You'll learn how these amazing insects live and work. You'll see their police patrols, sanitation squads, and air conditioning systems. And you'll begin to grasp their language, as you watch worker bees describe the direction and the distance of their latest nectar find. You'll be amazed at the harsh law of the hive, which leaves no room for sick or unproductive members. And you'll find out why God's design for human relationships is vastly different from His system for bees. ISBN: 157567033X

Color and Learn Birds, Butterflies and Wild Flowers by Lisa Bonforte, Paul E. Kennedy, and Jan Sovak K-3
A big book of creative coloring fun accompanied by informative, fact-filled captions, identifying names, seasons, habitats, and special characteristics. Additional pages show every picture in full-color to use as an accurate nature identification guide. ISBN: 0486427889

Creepy Crawlies and the Scientific Method by Sally Kneidel K-4 4-8
A collection of experiments to engage the interest of youngsters, to introduce them to the scientific method and to encourage them to understand science by observing small animals in their natural surroundings. Experiments accompanied by easily copied charts and tables encourage scientific understanding as children fill them out. Illustrations. ISBN: 1555911188

Insects/Entomology continued

Entomology ("Real Science Real Kids") by Ellen Doris and Len Rubenstein 4-8 9-12
Beautiful photographs illustrate several major orders of insects. Text gives basic information about each. Includes super field trip suggestions (exploring a pond, observing a beehive, collecting specimens) and explains metamorphosis, pollination, pesticides. A fantastic visual delight. ISBN: 0500190046

Eyewitness Insect by Laurence Mound 4-8 9-12
Learn why bees make honey, how to identify insects, why leaf cutter ants build underground nests, how diving beetles live and breathe in water, and how mosquitoes spread disease. Discover how a wasp's compound eyes work, which insects have ears on their knees, how wasp grubs feed on living caterpillars, how a butterfly can smell with its wings, and much, much more. ISBN: 0756606926

For Love of Insects by Thomas Eisner 4-8 9-12
An absorbing story of Eisner's career as a professor of chemical ecology (a discipline he helped found), interwoven with a passionate celebration of his subject—the lowly insect—and countless did-you-know's from the world of entomology. ISBN: 0674011813

Have You Ever Seen an Ant Who Can't? by Bernadette McCarver Snyder K-3
Explores some of the most unusual and remarkable facts about fascinating creatures on and under the earth while also teaching about the loving and imaginative Creator of all. ISBN: 0877936935

How to Draw Insects by Barbara Soloff Levy K-3
Easy-to-follow guide shows how to create a grasshopper, monarch butterfly, tarantula, caterpillar, cicada, praying mantis, walking stick, centipede, and 22 other insects. ISBN: 0486405893

Go to the Ant Songs from Proverbs for Christian Families by Judy Rogers
Go to the Ant is a collection of Proverbs in song for the whole family. God's wisdom can now be musically rooted in hearts and minds through these scripture-based melodies. You and your children will quickly learn the delightful catchy songs and find the tunes popping into your head when you least expect it. Songs include "Go to the Ant," "Listen My Son," The Tongue," "Seven Awful Things,"and others. CD or cassette tape. A coloring book is also available. ISBN: 5550029081

Insects and Spiders ("Designs for Coloring") by Grosset and Dunlap K-3
In this new selection in Heller's bestselling series, *Insects* takes readers into the fascinating world of these little creatures. Illustrations. ISBN: 0448422506

Insect Invaders by Anne Capeci K-3 4-8
When Wanda brings her ladybugs to school, the whole class ends up on an insect field trip and find out some pretty not-so-nice things about bugs. ISBN: 0439314313

Insects by National Geographic Society K-3 4-8
The world of insects is magnified for readers in this pocket guide that encourages them to investigate the natural world. ISBN: 079226570X

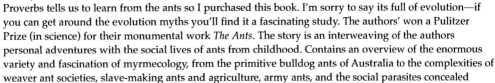

Journey to the Ants: A Story of Scientific Exploration by Bert Holldobler and Wilson 9-12
Proverbs tells us to learn from the ants so I purchased this book. I'm sorry to say its full of evolution—if you can get around the evolution myths you'll find it a fascinating study. The authors' won a Pulitzer Prize (in science) for their monumental work *The Ants*. The story is an interweaving of the authors personal adventures with the social lives of ants from childhood. Contains an overview of the enormous variety and fascination of myrmecology, from the primitive bulldog ants of Australia to the complexities of weaver ant societies, slave-making ants and agriculture, army ants, and the social parasites concealed within anthills. 173 illustrations, 95 in full-color. ISBN: 0674485262

The Magic School Bus Butterfly and the Bog Beast: A Book about Butterfly Camouflage by Nancy Krulik K-3
Ms. Frizzle whisks the class off to a bog full of butterflies to learn what those flying creatures are really like. ISBN: 0590508342

Insects/Entomology continued

The Magic School Bus Gets Ants in Its Pants by Joanna Cole and Linda Ward Beech `K-3`
The Magic School Bus hits the big screen as Keesha directs a movie about social animals for the school science fair, and ends up inside an anthill to observe her subjects firsthand. Ms. Frizzle and friends team up to locate a star, and in the process learn about the cooperative nature of animal social groups. Full-color. ISBN: 059040024X

The Magic School Bus Spins a Web: A Book about Spiders by Scholastic Books `K-3`
Ms. Frizzle's class learns all about spiders. ISBN: 0613054237

More Pet Bugs by Sally Stenhouse Kneidel `K-3` `4-8`
Provides information about the physical characteristics, habitats, and behavior of various insects and tells how to catch and keep them for observation. ISBN: 0471254894

Meet the Arthropods ("Real Science Real Kids") by Ellen Dorris `4-8`
Experiments, investigations and discoveries that emphasize direct learning experiences with spiders, crabs, sowbugs, centipedes, millipedes, aquatic arthropods such as crayfish, and microscopic pond-dwelling arthropods. Divided up by habitats, investigations include those you can conduct in gardens, indoor environments, supermarkets (lobster and crab), field locations (spiders), seashore (fishing for crabs), salt marshes (horseshoe crabs), beaches (sand crabs), ponds and streams (daphnia, cyclops). Describes observation, collection, and rearing techniques. Over 200 photos in this amazing visual display. Also recommended for the *Ocean* unit study. ISBN: 0500190100

National Audubon Society Field Guide to North American Insects and Spiders by Lorus Milne `4-8` `9-12`
Spiders, bugs, moths, butterflies, beetles, bees, flies, dragonflies, grasshoppers, and many other insects are detailed in more than 700 full-color photographs visually arranged by shape and color. Descriptive text includes measurements, diagnostic details, and information on habitat, range, feeding habits, sounds or songs, flight period, web construction, life cycle, behaviors, folklore, and environmental impact. An illustrated key to the insect orders and detailed drawings of the parts of insects, spiders, and butterflies supplement this extensive coverage. ISBN: 0394507630

An Obsession with Butterflies by Sharman Apt Russell `4-8` `9-12`
A luminous journey through an exotic world of passion and strange beauty, this is a book to be treasured by anyone who has ever experienced the enchantment of butterflies. ISBN: 0465071600

One Hundred Hungry Ants by Elinor J Pinczes and Bonnie Mackain `K-3`
Weave a math lesson into your insect unit. One hundred very hungry ants hurry to sample the delights of a picnic, but instead of marching single file, they divide into smaller rows—a lesson in division and visual introduction to math. Full-color. ISBN: 0395971233

Origami Insects by Robert J. Lang `9-12`
Challenging projects: treehopper, spotted ladybug, orb weaver, tarantula, butterfly, grasshopper, dragonfly, praying mantis, more. (Intermediate to advanced level) ISBN: 0486286029

Pet Bugs by Sally Stenhouse Kneidel `K-3` `4-8`
This charming interactive guide explains how to find and keep approximately 25 common insects that are safe to touch and fun to watch. It's a book that will teach kids about the fascinating and complex lives of the world's most abundant creatures—the insects. This book (or book below for older students) would be great for this unit! ISBN: 047131188X

Practical Entomologist by Rick Imes `4-8` `9-12`
Perfect introduction to the world of insects, providing information on the basics of entomology. Includes collection and rearing of insects, insect photography, and use of a field notebook. The book shows you not only what to look for but how and where to look for it—from capturing and keeping live insects to ways of making a collection and taking photographs. Tips on keeping a field notebook are also included. Over 200 glossy photos portray several different insect groups. Useful glossary, listing of resources, and index. ISBN: 0671746952

Animals/Zoology

Animal: The Definitive Visual Guide to the World's Wildlife by Don E. Wilson `4-8` `9-12` ⌐
Unrivaled in its breadth and visual impact, this unique guide sets out to illustrate, describe, and explain the incredible range of creatures that make up the animal kingdom. Exceptional coverage. Animal anatomy, life cycles and the principles of classification are explored. This is followed by a superbly illustrated survey of world habitats and the threats to them. Profiles of over 2,000 individual species. Visually breathtaking. The contents are divided into eight sections: Introduction, Habitats, Mammals, Birds, Reptiles, Amphibians, Fishes and Invertebrates. Each species profile is supported by maps and symbols showing habitat and key information. DK adult reference book produced in cooperation with the Smithsonian Institution and more than 70 expert zoologists. ISBN: 789477645

Animal Life Cycles: Birds, Amphibians, Insects by Jo Ellen Moore `K-3`
These 12 units provide basic science facts and hands-on activities that make science an exciting, successful learning experience. ISBN: 155799093X

Animal Planet: Discover Amazing Facts about Wild Animals from How They Live to the Dangers That Threaten Their Survival by Michael Chinery `4-8`
A stunningly illustrated natural history book that investigates the special characteristics that allow animals to live and survive in the wild. ISBN: 1842158503

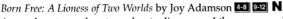
Born Free: A Lioness of Two Worlds by Joy Adamson `4-8` `9-12` **N**
A wondrus true adventure about a lioness and the woman who raised her, then set her free. A story of courage and love. ISBN: 0375714383

The Call of the Wild by Jack London `4-8` **N**
Buck is a dog born to luxury, but betrayed and sold to be a sledge dog in the harsh and frozen Yukon. This is the remarkable story of how Buck rises above his enemies to become one of the most feared and admired dogs in the north. Newbery Honor. ISBN: 0140366695

Case Files of the Tracker: True Stories from America's Greatest Outdoorsman by Tom Brown `4-8` `9-12`
The author of more than 20 books about wilderness and tracking, explains the skills used by trackers and discusses some of his most difficult and fascinating cases. ISBN: 0425187551

The Concise Animal Encyclopedia by David Burnie `K-3` `4-8` `9-12`
This compact marvel covers the animal kingdom from the tiniest protozoan to the mightiest mammal. Organized by classification and packed with vibrant photographs and informative detail, this visual safari covers the gamut of phylums, classes, orders, families, and genuses. ISBN: 0753455900

A Dictionary of Zoology by Michael Allaby `9-12`
Comprehensive reference work on all aspects of the study of animals. Containing over 5,000 entries on everything from animal behavior, ecology, and physiology to genetics, cytology, etc. Includes species and genus names and tells what the different parts of the words mean in Greek or Latin. ISBN: 019860758X

DK Animal Encyclopedia by Barbara Taylor `K-3` `4-8`
I mentioned this book in the last chapter. My children browse it daily. Fully indexed and cross-referenced with 2,000 animal species, this ultimate pictorial reference provides information about the physical characteristics, habits, and behavior of such animals as hedgehogs, peacocks, penguins, salamanders, and snakes. Magnetic for all ages. ISBN: 0789464993

Drawing Mammals by Doug Lindstrand `K-3` `4-8` `9-12`
Offering tips for drawing more than 20 mammals indigenous to North America, this revised reference exhibits each species in several photographs as well as in field sketches. ISBN: 1565232062

Encyclopedia of Animals: A Complete Visual Guide by George McKay `K-3` `4-8`
This is a lavishly illustrated trade reference to mammals, birds, reptiles, amphibians, fishes and invertebrates. Hundreds of glorious photographs, masterful illustrations, and informative maps provide expert and accessible insights into the wonders of the animal world. ISBN: 0520244060

Animals/Zoology continued

Every Living Thing by James Herriot `4-8` `9-12` **N**
For the first time in over a decade, the world's favorite veterinarian, James Herriot, returns us in a twinkle to the rural green enclave of England called Yorkshire for more tales of animals. ISBN: 0312950586

First Animal Encyclopedia by Penelope Arlon `K-3`
This inspiring new edition to the *First Reference* series is loaded with spectacular photos of animals in action showing their habits and habitats. From aardvark to zebra, this book is packed with fascinating facts. ISBN: 0756602270

If My Mom Were a Platypus: Animal Babies and Their Mothers by Dia L Michels `4-8` **N**
Organized by describing 13 different animals, with sections on each covering the topics: birth, growth, knowledge and eating. Each story is told from the baby mammal's view. The 14th and last of the species presented is a human infant. Stunning full-color and black-and-white illustrations. ISBN: 1930775024

James Herriot's Best Dog Stories by James Herriot `4-8` `9-12` **N**
Fifty unforgettable, heartwarming tales about dogs, great and small. With an introduction and notes from James Herriot himself, this tribute to man's best friend will move you to laughter and tears. This is a book that will be treasured for years to come. ISBN: 0312925581

James Herriot's Treasury for Children by James Herriot `K-3` `4-8` **N**
Since the publication of *Moses the Kitten* in 1984, children have found a friend in James Herriot. His award-winning storybooks for young readers bring his farmyard world of Yorkshire, England to radiant life. Now, here is a complete collection of his beloved children's stories. ISBN: 0312085125

Julie of the Wolves by Jean Craighead George `4-8` **N**
The 1973 Newbery Medalist tells the story of a 13-year-old Eskimo girl, protected by a wolf pack while lost on the tundra, who begins to appreciate her heritage. Illustrations. ISBN: 0064400581

The Kingfisher First Animal Encyclopedia by John Farndon `K-3`
A valuable addition to the *Kingfisher First Reference* series, this book offers the perfect introduction to the enduringly popular subject of both wild and domestic animals. Color photos and illustrations. ISBN: 0753451352

The Kingfisher Illustrated Animal Encyclopedia by David Burnie `5-8`
An illustrated encyclopedia describing the physical characteristics, behavior, and habitats of a variety of animals. ISBN: 0753452839

The Life of Mammals by David Attenborough `5-8`
Published in conjunction with a ten-part television series on the Discovery Channel, *The Life of Mammals* brings readers nose-to-nose with mammals in all of their beauty and immense variety. ISBN: 0691113246

The Lord God Made Them All by James Herriot `4-8` `9-12` **N**
In 38 moving chapters, Herriot once again captures the magical beauty of the Yorkshire dales, the joys and sorrows of its inhabitants, and the richly rewarding experiences of a country veterinarian. ISBN: 0312966202

My Friend Flicka by Mary O'Hara `4-8` **N**
A timeless favorite of children and adults. Through his fierce devotion to a young horse named Flicka, Ken comes to assume the responsibilities of growing up and tries to win his father's acceptance. ISBN: 0060809027

National Audubon Society Field Guide to North American Mammals by John O. Whitaker `4-8` `9-12`
Packed with 375 color photos and comprehensive, up-to-the-minute information on the characteristics, behavior and habitats of 390 species that live and breed in the United States and Canada. ISBN: 0679446311

Animals/Zoology continued

The Name Game: Animal Classification ("Newton's Workshop") `K-4` `4-8` ▻○
Grandpa teaches the children about organizing and classifying by checking out a mysterious machine inspired by the father of taxonomy, Carolus Linnaeus. Moody Video.

National Geographic Animal Encyclopedia by National Geographic Society `4-8`
A comprehensive look at the world of animals, their features, behavior, and life cycles, arranged by the categories "Mammals," "Birds," "Reptiles," "Amphibians," "Fish," and "Insects, Spiders, and Other Invertebrates." ISBN: 0792271807

Rikki-Tikki-Tavi by Rudyard Kipling `K-3` N
Kipling's timeless tale of a young mongoose who becomes part of an English family's home in India is adapted and illustrated by beloved award-winning artist Jerry Pinkney. Full-color. ISBN: 0060587857

Scholastic Encyclopedia of Animals by Laurence P. Pringle `K-3`
Highlighting a variety of 140 animals, from alligators to zebras, and many in between, with spectacular photographs of each animal, this comprehensive reference tool presents physical characteristics, behaviors, and habitats of animals. ISBN: 0590522531

Shiloh by Phyllis Reynolds Naylor `4-8` N
When Marty Preston comes across a young beagle in the hills behind his home, it's love at first sight—and also big trouble. ISBN: 0689835825

Snow Leopard by Peter Matthiessen `9-12` N
When Matthiessen went to Nepal to study the Himalayan blue sheep and, possibly, to glimpse the rare and beautiful snow leopard, he undertook his five-week trek as winter snows were sweeping into the high passes. This is a radiant moving account of a journey of the heart. National Book Awards. ISBN: 0140255087

Usborne Internet-Linked First Encyclopedia of Animals by Paul Dowswell `K-3` `4-8`
Which animal has a tongue as long as its body? How does a whale breathe? Why do zebras have stripes? How does a snake see in the dark? These and hundreds of other questions about animals are answered in this beautifully designed encyclopedia. ISBN: 0794502156

Visual Encyclopedia of Animals by DK Publishing `4-8` `9-12`
Perfect for home or school, these *Visual Encyclopedias* are a perfect small format for tossing into a backpack. ISBN: 0789478714

What is a Life Cycle by Bobbie Kalman `K-3`
Introduces the life cycles of plants, insects, amphibians, reptiles, fish, birds, mammals, and humans, discussing birth, growth, parental care, and reproduction. ISBN: 0865058865

Wolves at Our Door by Jim Dutcher and Jamie Dutcher `4-8`
The documentary filmmakers Jim and Jamie Dutcher spent six years living with a pack of wolves in the Idaho wilderness. Their film, "Wolves at Our Door, " garnered two Emmy awards and is the Discovery Channel's highest rated nature documentary ever. ISBN: 0743400496

Zarafa: A Giraffe's True Story, from Deep in Africa to the Heart of Paris by Michael Allin
In 1826, a giraffe that had been captured in the Sudan, was shipped to France. In this story you'll learDK Secret Worlds" Series.n bits of French and Egyptian history, Arabic customs and Parisian ways, geography through a complex web of politics, culture, religion and greed that fueled this phenomenon. ISBN: 0385334117

Zoology Coloring Book by Lawrence M. Elson
For high school biology students and college zoology students, as well as for all students of nature, this coloring book teaches the structure and function of the major animal groups, from simple to complex. Informative texts accompany each drawing. ISBN: 0064603016

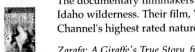
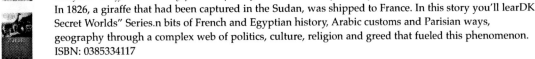

Human Body/Anatomy

The Amazing Pull-Out Pop-Up Body in a Book by David Hawcock [K-3]
Open this book to unfold an illustrated 5-foot-tall, 3-D skeleton complete with bone and muscle details. Pop-up, pull-out flaps allow children to explore the brain, heart, and lungs in detail. Full-color. 9-page foldout. A "DK Amazing Pop-Up Book." ISBN: 078942052X

A.D.A.M. The Inside Story™ [4-8] ● ★
This interactive anatomy and multimedia software tools gives students the gift of adventure and the power of knowledge. Students can explore the body layer-by-layer, then join modern day Adam and Eve as the body's miracles come alive with entertaining animations, video, and sound in their family scrapbook. Has a modesty setting that covers genitals with fig leaves.CD Rom.

The Architecture and Design of Man and Woman: The Marvel of the Human Body by Alexander Tsiaras [9-12]
The human body is a marvel of engineering. From the muscular and skeletal systems of the hand working in concert to allow us to type, eat, and caress, to the circadian rhythms of the heart and digestive system keeping things moving despite our consciousness being elsewhere, our bodies are far more complex and awe inspiring than any man-made creation. This book is an illustrated look at the internal structures and processes that sustain us as living, thinking, social beings. ISBN: 0385509294

Body by Design by Alan L. Gillen [4-8] [9-12] ★ ●— ⊢○
The basic anatomy and physiology in each of the 11 body systems from a creational viewpoint. Every chapter examines different organs and structures giving evidence for theistic design. ISBN: 0890512965

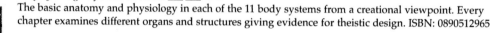
Fearfully and Wonderfully Made by Philip Yancey and Paul Brand [4-8] [9-12] ⊢○
Renowned surgeon Paul Brand and author Philip Yancey explore the human body, a delicate fabric of cells as awesome and mysterious as the galaxies of space. They uncover eternal statements God has made in the very structures of our bodies. ISBN: 031035451X

The Giant Germ by Joanna Cole and Anne Capeci [K-3] [4-8]
Mrs. Frizzle takes the class in Magic School Bus, on a tour of the mini-microbe world where the kids learn first hand that these tiny beings can have huge effects. Full-color llustrations. ISBN: 0439204208

Gray's Anatomy: A Fact Filled Coloring Book by Fred Stark [9-12]
Learn about what makes the body work and just how intricate human beings are—both inside and out. Sixty detailed drawings, designed for coloring, are enhanced by detailed text ISBN: 0762409444

Head to Toe Science: Over 40 Eye-Popping, Spine-Tingling, Heart-Pounding Activities That Teach Kids about the Human Body by Jim Wiese [4-8]
Introduces the circulatory system, muscles, digestion, senses, and other body parts and functions through a collection of activities and experiments which can be developed into science fair projects. ISBN: 471332038

Human Body by Caroline Bingham [K-3]
Specially developed for children ready for their first books about the natural world, this series continues with this title about the human body. Full-color photography and clearly written text help readers with advanced exploration and a stunning new view of the world. A "DK Eye Wonder" book. ISBN: 0789490447

In His Image by Paul Brand and Philip Yancey [9-12] ⊢○
Dr. Paul Brand and Philip Yancey show how accurately and intricately the human body portrays the body of Christ. In five sections—Image, Blood, Head, Spirit, and Pain—they unlock the living lessons contained in our physical makeup. ISBN: 031035501X

The Kingfisher First Human Body Encyclopedia by Richard Walker [K-3]
Colorful diagrams, illustrations and photographs give children an introduction to the makings and workings of the human body. Special fact sections and quizzes invites would-be doctors and nurses to test their knowledge of the body. ISBN: 0753451778

The Magic School Bus Inside the Human Body by Joanna Cole [K-4]
The Magic School Bus, carrying Ms. Frizzle and the entire class, shrinks and is accidentally eaten by Arnold and journeys through his body. ISBN: 0590414275

Human Body/Anatomy/Cells

Amazing Schemes Within Your Genes by Fran Balkwill **K-3** **4-8**
Discusses the structure and function of genes, their adaptations and mutations, and basic genetic processes. ISBN: 0876146353

Blood & Gore by Vicki Cobb **K-3** **4-8**
Electron micrographs create a dramatic journey into the blood, skin, bone, muscle, and nerves of the human body, magnifying the tiniest cells millions of times. ISBN: 0613073746

Cartoon Guide to Genetics by Larry Gonick
Illustrates, simplifies, and humor-coats the important principles of classical and modern genetics and their experimental bases, with amusing anecdotes about how the ancients tried to explain inheritance and sex determination. ISBN: 0062730991

Cells ("Discovery Channel School Science") by Gareth Stevens Publishing **4-8** **9-12**
With an unparalleled array of science topics to choose from, Discovery Channel School Science puts the fascination of the natural world at students' fingertips. ISBN: 0836833678

Cells ("Science Concepts") by Alvin Silverstein and Virginia B. Silverstein **4-8**
Outline key concepts, using charts and color to supplement complex facts. ISBN: 076132254X

Cells Are Us by Fran Balkwill **K-3** **4-8**
Supports the national science education standards Unifying Concepts and Processes: Systems, Order, and Organization; Unifying Concepts and Processes: Evidence, Models, and Explanation; Unifying Concepts and Processes: Form and Function; and Life Science as outlined by the National Academics of Science and endorsed by the National Science Teachers Association. ISBN: 0876146361

Cell Wars by Fran Balkwill **K-3** **4-8**
Explains how cells fight off diseases and viruses in the human body. ISBN: 087614637X

Cell-A-Bration: Cytology ("Newton's Workshop") **K-3** **4-8** 📼 ▷
Using a copy of an old microscope made by Anton Van Leeuwenhoek, Grandpa demonstrates the importance of paying attention to detail, while explaining that there's more to God's creation than meets the eye. Grandpa's make-shift contraptions helps Trisha and Tim better understand the workings of a human cell. Trisha and Tim discover yet another one of God's great miracles.

The DNA Decoders: Genetics ("Newton's Workshop") **K-3** **4-8** 📼 ▷
Grandpa Newton uses Trisha's need for eyeglasses as a lesson about genetics, heredity and DNA. He also show her the difference between natural and artificial selection, proving some things are best left in God's hands.

Germinators: The Immune System (Moody Video "Newton's Workshop") **K-3** **4-8** 📼 ▷
Trisha's brother Tim and his buddy Max create a sci-fi epic using Dad's video camera. Until Trisha comes down with a terrible cold, nobody realizes that Max's dramatic coughing and sneezing do more damage to Trisha than to Tim's movie Grandma and Grandpa Newton's cure for Tricia's boredom is ultraviolet paint, toy soldiers and squirt guns! Using this stuff, they create a sequel to Tim's sci-fi epic that becomes a lesson on the immune system, the miracle of God's design and the wisdom of Scripture. ISBN: 1575672197

Genes and DNA by Richard Walker **4-8**
Explores modern genetics, from an investigation of genes and their function, to forensics, therapy, and cloning. ISBN: 0753456214

Watch Me Grow: Fun Ways to Learn about My Cells, Bones, Muscles, and Joints by Michelle O'Brien-Palmer **K-4**
Explores our bones, joints, muscles, and other connective tissues and how they grow, with sixty hands-on games, experiments, and activities. ISBN: 155652367X

Anatomy/The Brain and Nervous System

The Brain by Seymour Simon `K-3`
State-of-the-art images highlight this fantastic voyage through the wonders of the nervous system, where children learn all about the brain. Full-color photos. ISBN: 0688170609

Brain: Inner Workings of the Gray Matter by Richard Walker `4-8`
Full-color photos and crammed with fun facts, this book takes an in depth look at the brain and how it works. Includes a reference section and web site links. A "DK Secret Worlds" book. ISBN: 0789485281

A Colorful Introduction to the Anatomy of the Human Brain by John P Pinel `9-12`
Make the fascinating world of the brain come alive with this colorful introduction. Readers learn the information in several steps. First they read through the definitions on the left page; then they color the illustration on the facing page; and finally they use the special cover flap to conceal the illustration labels while checking their knowledge until they feel they have completely learned the materials. ISBN: 0205162991

How the Brain Works by Mark Wm. Dubin `9-12`
Provides an introduction to the function (and dysfunction) of the human central nervous system. The book uses nine brief and concise lectures supported by clear illustrations to help the reader understand the relationship between physiology and manifest behavior. ISBN: 0632044411

The Human Brain: A Guided Tour by Susan Greenfield `9-12`
A renowned brain researcher takes readers on a guided tour of the brain to show what today's cutting-edge scientists now know about how that mysterious and fascinating organ works. Readers gain an up-close and personal view of the human brain—what it is, how it works, how mood-modifying drugs find their targets, and more. ISBN: 0465007260

The Human Brain Coloring Book by Lawrence M. Elson and Marian Cleeves Diamond `9-12`
Developed by internationally renowned neurosurgeons, this unique book is designed for students of psychology and the biological sciences, and medical, dental, and nursing students. ISBN: 064603067

It's All in Your Head: A Guide to Understanding Your Brain by Susan L. Barrett `4-8` `9-12`
Discusses the physiology and evolution of the brain, definitions and measuring of intelligence, problem solving, and other related topics. Also includes suggestions for further reading and activities for stimulating creative thinking and other intellectual abilities. ISBN: 0915793458

The Nervous System by Darlene R. Stille `K-4`
Describes the various parts of the nervous system and explains how sensory messages are sent back and forth through nerves between the brain and the body. ISBN: 051626270X

Understanding Your Brain: Internet Linked by Rebecca Treays `4-8`
Lift the lid on what's inside your head. Find out about the pulses of electricity which flash through your brain at high speeds. Lively text, colorful diagrams and comical illustrations help children grasp the basic biological and psychological workings of the brain. Quizzes and tests appear throughout the book to allow readers to study their own brains. ISBN: 0794508537

Anatomy/Muscular and Skeletal Systems

Bend and Stretch: Learning about Your Bones and Muscles by Pamela Hill Nettleton **K-4**
Do you know how your body stands, runs, or jumps? Your bones and muscles allow you to do those things. Find out how they work together to keep you growing and moving in this story about your amazing body. ISBN: 1404802568

Body: Bones, Muscle, Blood and Other Body Bits by Richard A. Walker **4-8**
A full-color, fun, and informative book on the body features easy-to-read narrative text written by a specialist who combines expert knowledge with an entertaining and fresh style. Full-color illustrations. ISBN: 0789479680

Bones: Our Skeletal System by Seymour Simon **K-4**
Award-winning author Seymour Simon continues his fantastic journey through the human body with this stunning new addition. In *Bones*, youngsters will discover the amazing facts about the two hundred and six bones that make up their skeletons, ranging from the smallest, most intricate bones in their feet and hands to the largest, strongest bones in their legs. Blending spectacular full-color photographs and clear, concise text. An intriguing look at human body. ISBN: 0688177212

The Bones Book & Skeleton by Stephen Cumbaa **K-3** **4-8**
This entertaining and educational package pairs a full-color, fact-filled guide to bones (and the body they support) with a 25-piece plastic molded skeleton (designed according to standards set by *Gray's Anatomy*) with actual movable joints. Filled with projects and experiments, it is a curious young anatomist's complete guide to the body. Full-color illustrations. Parents Choice Award. ISBN: 0894808605

Eyewitness Skeleton by Steve Parker,
Starting with the human skeleton, this book explains how each set of bones functions. It examines in detail the construction of the skull, spine and rib cage, hands, arms, legs, and feet. Comparisons are drawn with the bones of birds, reptiles, amphibians, fish, insects, and mammals. See the 206 different bones in the human body, how your skull differs from a lion's or a chimp's, how teeth grow, and what each one is for, and what the inside of a bone looks like. Learn how bones mend themselves when they break, why half the bones in your body are in your hands and feet and how many toes a horse has. Discover which are the smallest bones in the human body, why some creatures wear their skeletons on the outside and what animal once owned the oldest bones ever found on Earth. And much, much more. Note this is (as are all DK's books) from an evolutionary view point. ISBN 0756607272

A Magic Skeleton Book: The Human Body by Janet Sacks **K-3**
Children love finding out about themselves; they're curious about what lies beneath the skin. With a pull of some tabs, and the cool images here, they can find out how oxygen circulates, about the digestive process, and what makes up the inside of a cell. ISBN: 1402712146

Muscles: Our Muscular System by Seymour Simon **K-3**
Nearly 700 muscles control the daily life of a human body. That's just one of the facts kids will learn in this picture book by a best-selling author. Makes complicated science clear and understandable. ISBN: 0688177204

The Skeletal System: Human Body Systems by Helen Frost **K-3**
Simple text, photographs, and diagrams introduce the skeletal system and its purpose, parts, and functions. ISBN: 0736806539

Understanding Your Muscles and Bones: A Guide to What Keeps You Up and About by Rebecca Treays **K-3** **4-8**
See how your skeleton fits together and how your muscles make it move. ISBN: 0746027397

Watch Me Grow: Fun Ways to Learn about My Cells, Bones, Muscles, and Joints by Michelle O'Brien-Palmer **K-4**
See description on page.464. ISBN: 155652367X

Anatomy/Blood and Circulation

101 Questions about Blood and Circulation: With Answers Straight from the Heart by Faith Brynie `4-8` `9-12`
A book that makes blood and the circulatory system understandable. With succinct, evocative and unfailingly interesting answers, Faith Hickman Brynie answers such questions as "Does my heart get tired?" "Is heartburn really heart burn?" "What is blood poisoning?"and more. Appropriate for middle school, high school, and non-physician adults. Includes information on heart action, palpitations, heart attacks, leeches, transplants, blood chemistry, and the importance of diet, exercise, and not smoking in maintaining cardiovascular health ISBN: 0761314555

The Circulatory and Lymphatic Systems by John Coopersmith Gold `4-8` `9-12`
In this informative overview of the circulatory and lymphatic systems, John C. Gold examines the role of these systems in the functioning of the human body. He explores the parts of each system, how they work, and diseases that may affect them. Also addressed are ways to stay healthy and other interesting facts. ISBN: 0766020193

Circulatory System: A True Book by Darlene R. Stille `K-3` `4-8`
Describes the various parts of the human circulatory system and explains how and why blood is circulated throughout the body. ISBN: 0516204386

The Circulatory System: The Human Body by Susan Heinrichs Gray `4-8`
Why does your stomach ache if you eat too much? What makes a cut finger stop bleeding? Basic biology fascinates children, and each book in this kid-friendly collection begins with an engaging narrative to illustrate questions like these. ISBN: 1592960367

The Circulatory System: Human Body Systems by Leslie Mertz `9-12`
Discusses the parts of the circulatory system and how they work together to deliver nourishment, electrolytes, hormones, vitamins, antibodies, heat, and oxygen and remove waste materials and carbon dioxide. Blood pressure, blood type, and fetal circulation are covered. The history of research on the circulatory system is presented. Expensive but may be in your library. ISBN: 0313324018

A Drop of Blood by Paul Showers `K-4`
You've seen your own blood, when you have a cut or a scrape. You can see the veins in your wrist, and you've seen the scab that forms as a cut heals. ISBN: 006009110X

The Heart: Our Circulatory System by Seymour Simon `K-4`
Award-winning author explains the workings of the heart as incredible pump. Weighing only about as much as one of your sneakers, a heart beats over two billion times in an average lifetime, pushing a river of blood that carries nutrients and oxygen through sixty-thousand miles of capillaries to every cell in the body. In stunning photos that will amaze you with their beauty, you can watch while blood cells defeat invading bacteria and see how tiny platelets form blood clots. This journey is as wonderful as any voyage to the stars. ISBN: 0688114083

Martin's Last Chance by Heidi Schmidt `4-8`
German teenager Martin has a serious heart condition. It could lead to an early death unless he obtains a heart transplant. This is the story of how he copes with his predicament and the way in which friends at school react and respond. ISBN: 1857924258

Vital Circuits: On Pumps, Pipes, and the Workings of Circulatory Systems by Steven Vogel `9-12`

Why does dust collect on the blades of a fan? Why should you wear support hose on a long airplane flight? Vogel ranges across physics, fluid mechanics, and chemistry to show how an enormous system of pumps and pipes works to keep the human body functioning. The professor of biology at Duke University makes very complicated biological processes clear and understandable. 64 line drawings. ISBN: 0195082699

Anatomy/Reproduction

The Amazing Beginning of You by Matt Jacobson and Lisa Jacobson K-3 4-8 ⊷
Youngsters discover the amazing truth about their life before they were born and also gain a respect for life, and for the Creator who made each person unique. Illustrations. ISBN: 0310709253

From Conception to Birth: A Life Unfolds by Alexander Tsiaras 9-12
The ultimate visual guide and reference explaining every state of gestation, this is an unparalleled journey through life's origins. Full-color photos. Also see *The Architecture and Design of Man and Woman*. ISBN: 385503180

Beginning Life by Geraldine Lux Flanagan 9-12
The story of the remarkable journey from conception to birth graphically told, hour by hour, then day, by day, then week by week. Peek through a window into the womb, to follow in microscopic detail the progress of our formative weeks. Includes a compelling narrative; a classic work of reference that will surely claim a wide readership from young adults to parents-to-be. ISBN 0789406098

Before I Was Born by Stan Jones K-3 ⊷
Explains, from a Christian perspective, the fundamentals of human sexuality emphasizing that sex is part of God's gift of marriage and family. ISBN: 0891098445

The Endocrine and Reproductive Systems by Susan Dudley Gold and Melissa Kim 4-8
Casual narrative to explain detailed technical facts about anatomy and physiology. Design is open and uncluttered, interspersed with occasional small, helpful, full-color diagrams. Students will find these books non-intimidating. Includes glossary, chapter notes, and bibliography. ISBN: 0766020207

Facing the Facts: The Truth about Sex and You by Stan Jones 9-12 ⊷
Your body and its sexual nature are beautiful and exciting gifts from God that He wants you to understand and appreciate. ISBN: 0891098461

Life Before Birth by Gary E Parker 4-8 ⊷
This sensitively written book with its 85 full-size pages of warm, colorful illustrations allows mom and dad to deal with important reproductive questions while communicating the awesome love of the Creator to children ages 8-12. This excellent work communicates God's plan for reproduction through dialog and illustrations, and reveals beyond any doubt that human life is the result of God's plan, not the result of evolution. ISBN: 0890511640

It's So Amazing! A Book About Eggs, Sperm, Birth, Babies, and Families by Robie H. Harris K-3
With fun, accurate, comic-book-style artwork and a clear, lively text, *It's So Amazing* provides answers about reproduction, babies, sex, and sexuality. Full-color. ISBN: 0763613215

Period: A Girl's Guide by JoAnn Loulan and Bonnie Worthen
Here is everything a young girl needs to know to prepare for her own body's changes, plus a removable Parent's Guide. ISBN: 0916773973

The Reproductive System by Steve Parker 4-8
Explains the parts of the reproductive system and their functions, and provides an overview of human development from birth through adolescence. ISBN: 0817248064

The Story of Me by Stan Jones K-3
This book is designed to help parents answer difficult or embarrassing questions about sex comfortably and truthfully (in age-appropriate terms), and to encourage healthy communication between you and your child. ISBN: 0891098437

What's the Big Deal?: Why God Cares about Sex by Stan Jones 4-8 ⊷
Did you know that God created sex? If He created it, it is a good thing. Here is a book that your parents will read with you, or discuss with you as you read it on your own. They'll answer any questions you might have and help you understand what a beautiful and exciting gift from God your sexuality is meant to be. ISBN: 0891098453

Wisdom

Castle of Wisdom by Rhett Ellis `9-12` ⌐⌐
The hard-to-put down, fictional, fairy-tale type story is a parable about seeking wisdom. It's full of symbols entertaining. Contains material not suitable for young children (sexual references). ISBN: 0967063108

Character in Crisis: A Fresh Approach to the Wisdom Literature of the Old Testament by William Brown `9-12` ⌐⌐
This study demonstrates that the aim of the Bible's wisdom literature is the formation of the moral character of both individuals and the believing community. ISBN: 080284135X

Charles Stanley's Handbook for Christian Living by Charles Stanley `9-12` ⌐⌐
Previously released as *The Glorious Journey*, this practical volume shows readers how to put God's Word to work in their daily lives as it gives biblical answers to life's tough questions. Stanley offers guidance on various aspects of daily living, such as relationships, employment and government, along with teachings on humility, greed and wisdom. ISBN: 0785267026

Discover Your Destiny by Charles F.Stanley `9-12` ⌐⌐
Popular author and pastor Stanley guides readers to unshakable hope based on a personal relationship with Christ. ISBN: 0785263691

God Is in Control by Charles F. Stanley `9-12` ⌐⌐
Inspired by a series of fresh messages from well-known minister Charles Stanley, he compiles some of his most meaningful and thought-provoking sermons and ideas into an easy-to-read book. ISBN: 0849957397

God's Wisdom for Little Boys: Character-Building Fun from Proverbs by Jim and Elizabeth George `K-3` ⌐⌐
Following the success of the bestselling *God's Wisdom for Little Girls*, this wonderful collection of teachings from Proverbs comes to life for boys ages 4-7. Memorable rhymes play alongside watercolors for a charming presentation of truths by which to live. ISBN: 0736908242

God's Wisdom for Little Girls: Virtues and Fun from Proverbs 31 by Elizabeth George `K-3` ⌐⌐
In her first children's book, bestselling author George draws from the wisdom of the Bible's book of Proverbs to encourage young girls to apply the positive traits and qualities illustrated in each verse. Luenebrink's charming watercolors complement the text. ISBN: 0736904271

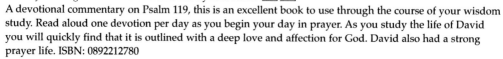

Heart of the King: Meditations on Psalm 119 by Ron Auch `4-8` `9-12` ⌐⌐
A devotional commentary on Psalm 119, this is an excellent book to use through the course of your wisdom study. Read aloud one devotion per day as you begin your day in prayer. As you study the life of David you will quickly find that it is outlined with a deep love and affection for God. David also had a strong prayer life. ISBN: 0892212780

How to Handle Adversity by Charles F. Stanley `9-12` ⌐⌐
When hard times come, we need wisdom to navigate through the shoals of adversity into a safe harbor. And now, in *How to Handle Adversity*, Charles Stanley offers a practical, biblical approach to help us deal with the troubles common to us all. ISBN: 0785264183

How to Listen to God by Charles F. Stanley `9-12` ⌐⌐
Stanley explains that after salvtion, believers discover the joy of hearing God's voice, but often the purity and freshness of that initial experience becomes clouded by the daily routine of life. ISBN: 0785264140

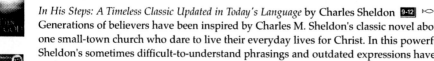

In His Steps: A Timeless Classic Updated in Today's Language by Charles Sheldon `9-12` ⌐⌐
Generations of believers have been inspired by Charles M. Sheldon's classic novel about the members of one small-town church who dare to live their everyday lives for Christ. In this powerful new edition, Sheldon's sometimes difficult-to-understand phrasings and outdated expressions have been beautifully updated in modern language. New notes are included for individual or small-group study. ISBN: 1589199936

Wisdom continued

Introduction to the Old Testament Poetic Books by C. Hassell Bullock `9-12` ⊷
Problems of suffering, the conscience marred by sin, the transience of human life, the passionate love of woman and man. These are some of the subjects dealt with in the five poetical books of the Old Testament surveyed in this well-written introduction. ISBN: 0802441416

Living in His Sufficiency by Charles F. Stanley `9-12` ⊷
Dr. Charles Stanley's new series of Bible study guides features insights and wisdom of this beloved pastor and author. Small groups and individuals who want a Bible study that's spiritually sound and practical will find a wealth of ideas to help them understand and apply the Scriptures to the real world. ISBN: 0785272860

Noah Webster's Advice to the Young by Noah Webster `4-8` `9-12` ⊷
This book contains two historical reprints which founder Noah Webster wrote to "enlighten the minds of youth in religious and moral principles and restrain some of the common vices of our country." Promoting honesty, generosity, gratitude, and more, these works are invaluable today for all ages. ISBN: 092527934X

The Pilgrim's Progress by John Bunyan `9-12` ⊷
This masterpiece of religious allegory that transforms into an intense drama as it represents the passions and trials of the Christian spiritual journey is reissued with a new Introduction. ISBN: 0451528336

Proverbial Wisdom and Common Sense by Derek Leman `9-12` ⊷
A Messianic Jewish approach to today's issues from the Proverbs. This virtual encyclopedia of practical advice from Scripture tackles vital issues, such as family relationships, sexual morality, finances, reputation and gossip, laziness, diligence—and more. ISBN: 1880226782

The Source of My Strength by Charles F. Stanley `9-12` ⊷
Dr. Stanley talks honestly about his own journey through emotional pain and points readers toward the wellspring of strength. He shares his own experiences with grief and shows readers how to overcome pain, understand burdens, confront memories, and discover the courage and strength to live freely in God's love for them. ISBN: 0785205691

A Touch of His Wisdom: Meditations on the Book of Proverbs by Charles F. Stanley `9-12` ⊷
A collection of 31 transforming principles based on the book of Proverbs. Dr. Stanley explores God's perspectives on money, work, marriage, leadership, family, and other everyday concerns. Applying God's wisdom to each of these areas can change failure into success, chaos into order, and fear into trust. ISBN: 0310545404

Walking Wisely: Real Life Solutions for Everyday Situations by Charles F. Stanley `4-8` `9-12` ⊷
The lessons in the *Wisdom* unit study follow the chapters in this book. The truly wise person, Charles Stanley writes, is one whose values, perspectives, career goals, and daily decisions are all shaped by the wisdom found in Christ. ISBN: 0785272984

The Way of Wisdom: Essays in Honor of Bruce K. Waltke by J. I. Packer `9-12` ⊷
A volume of essays on the theme of wisdom written in a scholarly way but with broad appeal to an informed lay reader in honor of Dr. Bruce K. Waltke. ISBN: 0310227283

What Would Jesus Do? by Garrett Ward Sheldon `4-8` `9-12` ⊷
For more than a century, Sheldon's *In His Steps* has been one of the most beloved Christian novels ever. In this retelling of the original story, updated characters and settings shed new light on the question, "What Would Jesus Do?" ISBN: 080540189X

Wisdom Hunter by Randall Arthur `9-12` ⊷
This best-selling novel presents the hypocrisy of Christian legalism and a man's search for the only surviving member of his family. This is an excellent and memorable story. It's the only novel that ever gave me reason to use my highlighter pen. Some adult content (rape reference) not sutable for children. ISBN: 1590522591

Virtuous Women

The Art of Tea and Friendship: Savoring the Fragrance of Time Together by Sandy Lynam Clough 9-12 ⋈
Beloved artist Clough delightfully guides readers in the fine art of blending tea and friendship. Along with her beautiful teaware paintings, she offers a creative variety of ways for friends to gather and savor the fragrance of time spent together. ISBN: 0736910980

Aunt Jane's Hero by Elizabeth Prentiss 9-12 ⋈
First published in 1871. With vivid pictures of life and character, its object is to depict a home whose happiness flows from the living rock, Christ Jesus. It protests also against the extravagance and other evils of the times, which tends to check the growth of such homes, and aims to show that there are still treasures of love and peace on earth that may be bought without money and without price. ISBN: 1879737345

Beautiful Girlhood by Karen Andreola 4-8 ⋈
The book deals primarily with the Christian character development, moral virtues and manners of pre-teen and teenage girls. It's designed to encourage both mother and daughter as they discuss awkward topics, as well as inspiring ones. ISBN: 1883934028

Becoming a Titus 2 Woman by Martha Peace 9-12 ⋈
A book for mothers and grandmothers teaching children. Now more than ever, young women today need to know "*what is good...that the word of God may not be dishonored.*" Peace's in-depth study of Titus 2:3–5 helps you to develop the character that God wants every older woman to have, and fulfill your role as a teacher, counselor, and friend to younger women. Lessons include application questions. ISBN: 1885904177

Becoming a Woman of Beauty and Strength by Elizabeth George 9-12 ⋈
This Bible study explores God's providential guidance as revealed through the story of Esther. You will see God working powerfully through a woman willing to entrust herself to her Him. ISBN: 0736904891

Becoming a Woman of Excellence by Cynthia Heald 9-12 ⋈
These eleven Bible lessons by Cynthia Heald will help you understand what excellence means in such areas as: Surrender, Obedience, Discipline, Discretion, Wisdom, Purity, and A Gentle and Quiet Spirit. ISBN: 0891090665

Big Sister and Little Sister by Charlotte Zolotow K-3
A small girl runs away from her domineering older sister, only to discover how much she is needed and loved. A heartwarming picture book for small girls. ISBN: 0064432173

Christian Charm Course by Emily Hunter K-4 ⋈
With practical guidelines for grooming, dress, politeness, conversation skills, and spiritual growth, this book will help children integrate inner beauty with outer beauty. ISBN: 0890815089

Deal with It!: You Cannot Conquer What You Will Not Confront by Paula White 9-12 ⋈
Dynamic Bible teacher and national speaker White highlights 10 women in the Bible and shows how God transformed their lives and can transform anyone's life who is seeking Him and the answers He provides throughout Scripture. ISBN: 0785261060

Every Woman in the Bible by Larry Richards and Sue Poorman Richards 9-12 ⊶ ⋈
Comprehensive coverage of every woman mentioned in the Bible, both named and unnamed. Profiles individual women, considering their roles, relationships, and lessons from their lives. Fresh insights into their historical/social settings make individual women come alive like never before. Also shows Paul's view of women was not chavenistic. Contemporary, easy-to-follow format and writing style. Over 75 maps, charts, illustrations, and sidebars add important information and visual appeal. ISBN: 0785214410

The Excellent Wife: A Biblical Perspective by Martha Peace 9-12 ⋈
A scripturally based blueprint for the woman who really wants to be the wife God intended her to be. Using the woman in Proverbs 31 as a model, offers detailed practical answers to questions most often asked by Christian wives. ISBN: 1885904088

Life Skills Resources

Virtuous Women continued

Feminine Appeal by Carolyn Mahaney 9-12 ⋈
Laying a foundation of sound doctrine, Mahaney teaches women the specifics of practical living that glorifies God. She joyfully explores home as a place to minister, to enjoy, and to manage, plus helps women cultivate their roles as wives, mothers, and mentors. Her personal anecdotes and illustrations from the lives of others add warmth and humor to this book. ISBN: 1581346158

God's Wisdom for Little Girls by Elizabeth George K-3
Draws from the wisdom of the Bible's book of Proverbs to encourage young girls to apply the positive traits and qualities illustrated in each verse. Luenebrink's charming watercolors complement. ISBN: 0736904271

God's Wisdom for a Woman's Life: Timeless Principles for Your Every Need by Elizabeth George 9-12 ⋈
Bestselling author Elizabeth George includes the Bible's answers to timely questions women have about running their busy lives while doing what is right. ISBN: 0736910611

Having a Mary Heart in a Martha World by Joanna Weaver 9-12 ⋈
This book's fresh approach to familiar Bible stories and its creative, practical strategies are designed to show how readers can draw closer to the Lord, deepening devotion, strengthening service, and doing both with less stress and greater joy. ISBN: 1578562589

A Heart Like His: Intimate Reflections on the Life of David by Beth Moore 9-12 ⋈
In this in-depth look at the life of David, Beth Moore draws spiritual insight and understanding from a man who slayed a giant and saved a kingdom. ISBN: 0805420355

Hidden Art of Homemaking by Edith Schaeffer 9-12 ⋈
This elegant and insightful lady, wife of theologian Francis Schaeffer, reveals the many opportunities for artistic expression that can be found in ordinary, everyday life. ISBN: 0842313982

I'd Be Your Princess by Kathryn O'Brien K-3 ⋈
This picture book encourages godly character, promotes a healthy father-daughter relationship, and illustrates how God's Word is a model for behavior. ISBN: 0784713502

Just Like Mama by Beverly Lewis K-3 ⋈
Charming Amish picture book depicts farm life in Pennsylvania. A book that mothers and daughters of all ages can enjoy, ultimately encourages everyone to be just like Jesus. ISBN: 0736904271

Just Mom and Me Having Tea: A Fun Bible Study for Mothers and Daughters by Mary J Murray 4-8 ⋈
This easy-to-use devotional covers topics that are important in girls' lives, and helps mothers and daughters take a spiritual journey together. ISBN: 0736904263

Let Me Be a Woman by Elizabeth Elliot 9-12 ⋈
The author combines her observations and experiences in a number of essays on male-female relationships. ISBN: 0842321624

Life Management for Busy Women by Elizabeth George 9-12 ⋈
The bestselling author turns her life's experience and gift as a communicator to a subject that will resonate with today's women: taking control of too-busy days and building balanced, godly lives. ISBN: 0736901914

A Little Book of Manners by Emilie Barnes K-3 ⋈
An introduction to the basics of good manners, from meeting and greeting people to proper telephone and mealtime behavior. ISBN: 1565076788

The Mission of Motherhood by Sally Clarkson 9-12 ⋈
Author, speaker, and mother Clarkson uses practical examples, her own personal anecdotes, a challenging vision to give mothers exactly the support they need to persevere in cultivating and sharing their hearts for God, for their children, and for their homes. Excellent! ISBN: 1578565812

Virtuous Women continued

Not Even a Hint: A Study Guide for Women by Shannon and Joshua Harris with Brian Smith **9-12**
Essential for defeating lust and celebrating purity in your own life, this study guide directly addresses the unique temptations you face as a woman. ISBN: 1590523547

Praise Her in the Gates by Nancy Wilson **9-12**
Fulfill your call to Christian motherhood by building a house of grace and joy. Based on the foundation of Proverbs 14:1, Wilson's master plan helps you raise godly children using the tools of love, education, and discipline. Her wise advice will guide you in contributing to God's long-term plan. ISBN: 1885767706

The Princess and the Kiss by Jennie Bishop **K-3**
A resource for parents and is a real delight for children of all ages. Join the princess as she discovers the value of her first kiss, and experiences God's provision in a way she never dreamed! Delightful color illustrations add depth and texture to this story about God's gift of purity. ISBN: 0871628686

The Power of a Praying Woman by Stormie Omartian **9-12**
Best-selling Stormie Omartian's deep knowledge of Scripture and candid examples of her own struggles and epiphanies in prayer provide reassuring guidance for those who seek a greater sense of God's presence in their lives. Each segment of this book concludes with a prayer that women can use as a model for their own prayers. ISBN: 0736908552

The Remarkable Women of the Bible by Elizabeth George **9-12**
Jocebed is an example of a remarkable mother; Deborah's life is an illustration of wisdom; Ruth and Naomi model pure devotion; Hannah demonstrates sacrifice; Esther represents amazing courage. ISBN: 0736907386

The True Princess by Angela Elwell Hunt **K-3**
When the King returns from his long journey, he must use discernment to find his daughter among the multitude of girls who claim to be the true princess. He knows that his daughter will be recognized by that one quality that is evidenced by a true princess—a servant's heart. ISBN: 1591856337

What is a Family? by Edith Schaeffer **9-12**
All the moving, changing shapes of a family, ever in need of work, are shown in Edith Schaeffer's imaginative loving reflections on infancy to grandmotherhood. A heartening view of family life. The family:...a center for the formation of human relationships...a perpetual relayer of truth...a museum of memories...all of these and much more. ISBN: 0801083656

A Wife After God's Own Heart by Elizabeth George **9-12**
The author provides valuable and practical insights on 12 key areas of a marriage. This book can be used alongside *A Husband After God's Own Heart* or as a stand-alone volume. ISBN: 0736911677

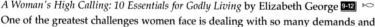

A Woman's High Calling: 10 Essentials for Godly Living by Elizabeth George **9-12**
One of the greatest challenges women face is dealing with so many demands and expectations. What are a woman's greatest priorities? How can she make sure she focuses on what really counts? Drawing on Titus 2:3–5, Elizabeth shares the simple steps a woman can take to make essentials a joyous reality. Offers practical, purposeful advice on living in purity, cultivating personal discipline, managing a home, loving a husband, and more. A study guide for this book is available. ISBN: 0736903275

A Woman's Walk with God: Growing in the Fruit of the Spirit by Elizabeth George **9-12**
Focusing on the gracious habits the Holy Spirit produces, readers discover the attitudes of love and joy; the actions of patience and goodness; and the disciplines of faithfulness and gentleness. ISBN: 0736901884

Godly Men

Be Diligent by Warren W. Wiersbe `9-12`
In this study, Dr. Wiersbe focuses on Jesus Christ the Servant, always on the move, always doing the Father's will and serving others. Mark is the ideal Gospel for busy people who want to discover how to make their lives count for God. Studying Mark's intensely dramatic account of the life and ministry of Jesus Christ will help you appreciate Him as God's Ideal Servant. You will be motivated and encouraged in your own ministry for the Lord. ISBN: 0896933563

Complete Husband by Lou Priolo `9-12`
This ground-breaking, refreshing book encourages men to to give honor to their wives as to the weaker (more fragile and valuable) vessel. The author reminds men that wives come with an owner's manual—the Bible! Priolo shows men how the Bible instructs them to know their wives by discovering their dreams, goals, and desires. It is the husband's job to find out what they are, and cultivate his wife so that she becomes spiritually fertile. The author stresses men to understand, pleasing their wives must be in terms of the whole relationship. Priolo encourages correct biblical thinking will leads to tender actions, which in turn leads to complete fulfillment. Priolo's balanced book motivates a husband to really love his wife—with Christ-like sacrificial love. This book primarily deals with communication and attitudes but one chapter is devoted to the physical aspects of marriage. ISBN: 1879737353

Diligently Seeking God by Gary Henry `9-12`
The book is divided into 366 daily meditations that challenge the reader to take seriously a daily focus upon God. Each reading focuses on different aspects of the character of God, providing compelling reasons to take the seeking of God seriously. ISBN: 0971371008

Bringing Up Boys by Dr. James C. Dobson `9-12`
Boys are different! But with pressure to be "gender-neutral," many try to mold children into a one-size-fits-all model. Dr. Dobson explains why boys are the way they are, how to understand their emotional and physical development, and the best way to motivate them to become godly men. ISBN: 084235266X

Boyhood and Beyond: Practical Wisdom for Becoming a Man by Bob Schultz `4-8`
Bob Schultz, a carpenter by trade, has written a timeless book for boys. Wisdom and common sense are gleaned from short chapters covering topics such as authority, inventiveness, and honesty as well as learning to overcome things like fear, laziness, and temptation. *Boyhood and Beyond* motivates boys to build their lives on a foundation of strong moral principles. Most importantly, these chapters will encourage boys to become the men God wants them to be as they develop a relationship with Him. This is a book designed to be read and lived out in a boy's life, thus becoming one of his building blocks to godly character and, ultimately, manhood. ISBN: 1883934095

The Exemplary Husband: A Biblical Perspective by Stuart Scott `9-12`
Who's your model of an ideal husband? Your father? Your pastor? How about Jesus! Scott takes an in-depth and biblical look at God's expectations for husbands—their walk, Christ-like character, responsibilities, and more. ISBN: 1885904312

God's Wisdom for Little Boys: Character-Building Fun from Proverbs by Jim and Elizabeth George `K-3`
Following the success of the bestselling "God's Wisdom for Little Girls," this wonderful collection of teachings from Proverbs comes to life for boys ages 4-7. Memorable rhymes play alongside watercolors for a charming presentation of truths by which to live. ISBN: 0736908242

How to Build Treehouses, Huts, and Forts by David R. Stiles `4-8`
Finally, a practical guide to building castles in the air! ISBN: 1592281923

A Little Book of Manners for Boys by Bob Barnes and Emilie Barnes `4-8`
An introduction to the basics of good manners, from meeting and greeting people, proper telephone and mealtime behavior, to when it's acceptable to act weird with your friends. ISBN: 0736901280

Godly Men continued

Not Even a Hint by Joshua Harris `9-12`
The author of *I Kissed Dating Goodbye* now calls a generation bombarded with images of sexual sin back to the freedom and joy of holiness. PG-rated book. ISBN: 1590521471

Not Even a Hint: Guarding Your Heart Against Lust on CD by Joshua Harris `9-12`
Harris, author of *I Kissed Dating Goodbye*, calls a generation bombarded with images of sexual sin back to the freedom and joy of holiness in this PG-rated book on 3 CDs. ISBN: 1590522559

Not Even a Hint: A Study Guide for Men by Joshua Harris with Brian Smith `9-12`
Overcoming lust is a process that requires diligent focus and accountability from others—and this in-depth guide helps establish both. It's designed for a variety of settings, from one-on-one accountability partnerships to group study classes. *Not Even a Hint* made the statement that lust is a human problem and that Jesus can free anyone from its power. Going further, this gender-specific study guide features study questions and discussion starters that directly address the unique temptations men face. ISBN: 1590522532

A Passion for Faithfulness: Wisdom from the Book of Nehemiah by J. I. Packer `9-12`
Noted author and theologian Packer looks at the dual themes of how Nehemiah led the people and how God led Nehemiah—all to ultimately build up His Kingdom. As Nehemiah testifies to all God has done in and through him and providing a model for renewal within the body of Christ today. ISBN: 1581342462

Success God's Way by Charles F.Stanley `9-12`
In this bestselling title, Dr. Stanley shows that God sums up success in terms of relationship, character, and obedience. ISBN: 0785265902

A Sacred Foundation by Michael P. Farris and L. Reed Elam `9-12`
Veteran home school parents and authors offer keen insight into the stress points of the home schooling marriage. They guide the reader to a greater understanding of the importance of keeping the marriage bond strong and offer many practical steps that parents can take to keep the foundation of their relationship not merely intact, but strong. ISBN: 0805425888

The Squire and the Scroll by Jennie Bishop `K-3`
As *The Princess and the Kiss* presented purity of heart for girls, this book does for boys. The squire sets out on a quest to recover the Lantern of Purest Light. The dangers he encounters challenge his purity of heart and teach him valuable lessons for his life. ISBN: 1593170793

Ten Boys Who Made a Difference by Irene Howat `4-8`
Would you like to make a difference? These ten boys grew up to do just that—but first they had to change the Church. How did God change them? ISBN: 1857927753

A Young Man After God's Own Heart by Jim George `9-12`
Pursuing God is, and ought to be, an adventurous challenge for a young man. Starting with probing a young man's heart as to, "Where are your desires?", Jim George, who has made a lifetime ministry out of discipling younger men, elevates the pursuit of the desires of teens and men in their early 20's to uncommonly lofty aims. Focuses on getting along at home, choosing quality friends, making wise choices about the future, fighting the battle with temptation, building your faith and more. ISBN: 0736914781

What the Bible Says About Being a Man by J. Richard Fugate `9-12`   f
Fugate explains how we need men who will live by the biblical principles of honesty, courage, loyalty, self-discipline, and above all, godliness. He looks at the past several generations where men have lost a great deal of their masculinity. Parenting, marriage, government, business, and church have been damaged as a result. *Being a Man* explains this demise, the biblical roles of Christian masculinity and the road back to responsible manhood. If you are a Christian man who would like to be a spiritually mature leader, this book is for you. God intends for men to be conquerors in this world. ISBN 1889700290

The Wisdom of Solomon at Work: Ancient Virtues for Living and Leading Today by Charles C Manz `9-12`
The author of *The Leadership Wisdom of Jesus* now ponders the timeless lessons, spiritual views, symbols, and icons of the Old Testament and how they relate to readers' professional lives. ISBN: 157675085X

Christian and Missionary Biographies

Amy Carmichael: Rescuer of Precious Gems by Janet Benge **4-8** **9-12** ▷
Driven by love, sustained by faith and determination, this young woman from Northern Ireland defied the cruel barriers of India's caste system (1867-1951). ISBN: 1576580180

The Autobiography of George Muller by George Muller **4-8** **9-12** ▷
George Muller persistently depended upon the Lord to provide for the needs of thousands of London orphans on a daily basis. Share his experiences in this thrilling account. Muller's unwavering, childlike dependence upon the Father will inspire you to confidently trust the God of the impossible in every area of your life. ISBN: 0883681595

Betty Greene: Flying High by Renee Taft Meloche **K-3** ▷
WWII veteran Betty Greene (1920-1997) combined her love of flying with her love for Christ by helping found the Mission Aviation Fellowship, which still uses airplanes to take the Gospel around the world. ("Christian Heroes: Then & Now"). ISBN: 1576582396

Bruchko by Bruce Olson **4-8** **9-12** ▷
What happens when a nineteen-year-old boy heads into the jungles to evangelize a murderous tribe of South American Indians? For Bruce Olson it meant capture and torture, but what he discovered revolutionized the world of missions. ISBN: 0884191338

A Chance to Die: The Life and Legacy of Amy Carmichael by Elisabeth Elliot **4-8** **9-12** ▷
Elisabeth Elliot, a great admirer of Carmichael produced a balanced biography of this remarkable Christian woman. ISBN: 0800715357

Corrie ten Boom: Keeper of the Angels' Den by Janet Benge **4-8** **9-12** ▷
Relates events in the life of the Dutch woman who survived imprisonment in Nazi concentration camps to become a Christian missionary. ISBN: 1576581365

David Livingstone: Africa's Trailblazer by Janet Benge **4-8** ▷
Braving danger and hardship, David Livingstone crisscrossed vast uncharted regions of Africa to open new frontiers and spread the message of the Gospel to all who would listen (1813-1873). ISBN: 1576581535

Eric Liddell: Something Greater Than Gold by Janet Benge **4-8** **9-12** ▷
A biography of the Scottish missionary and runner who won a gold medal in the 1924 Olympics and went on to do missionary work in China. ISBN: 1576581373

From Jerusalem to Irian Jaya by Ruth Tucker **4-8** **9-12** ▷
An invaluable resource for missionaries, mission agencies, students, and all who are concerned about the spreading of the Gospel throughout the world. ISBN: 0310239370

George Muller: The Guardian of Bristol's Orphans by Janet Benge **9-12** ▷
Sustained by God's provision. George Muller's vision of caring for orphans grew to five large homes that ultimately over ten thousand children would call home (1805-1898). ISBN: 1576581454

Gladys Aylward: The Courageous English Missionary Whose Life Defied All Expectations by Catherine Swift **9-12** ▷
This is the true story of the courageous English missionary who fulfilled her desire to reach the Chinese people for Christ and who proved her commitment by enduring the indignities of Japanese internment with her Chinese counterparts during World War II. ISBN: 1556610904

Hearts of Fire: Eight Women in the Underground Church and Their Stories of Costly Faith by Word Publishing
Eight women from eight very different backgrounds. Yet the struggles they each faced rang with eerie similarity. These courageous women from across the globe—Pakistan, India, Romania, the Former Soviet Union, China, Vietnam, Nepal, Indonesia—shared similar experiences of hardship, subjugation, and persecution, all because of their faith in Christ. Yet all of these women have emerged from adversity as leaders and heroines. ISBN: 0849944228

Christian and Missionary Biographies continued

Heaven's Heroes: Real Life Stories from History's Greatest Missionaries by David Shibley
"God had an only Son and He was a missionary…" With these words, David Livingstone confirmed that he, too, would spend his life telling people in far-off lands about the love of God. This explorer, doctor, author, and missionary longed to see the smoke of a thousand villages, because huddled around African tribal fires were people who might never hear the story of God's love unless missionaries obeyed God's call to serve Him. ISBN: 0892212551

Heavenly Man by Paul Hattaway
Brother Yun has experienced unbelievable persecution, including torture and imprisonment. He has also experienced unbelievable grace and miracles. And in a paradox that continues to confound, he describes how the true church actually flourishes amidst persecution. ISBN: 082546207X

Hero Tales, Volume. 1 by Dave Jackson ▊K-3▊ ▊4-8▊
Drawn from the lives of fifteen key Christian heroes, this book is a treasury of 45 exciting and educational readings designed to help foster Christian character in families with elementary-age children. The book presents a short biography and stories of each hero. ISBN: 1556617127

Hero Tales, Volume 2 by Dave Jackson ▊K-3▊ ▊4-8▊
Life-changing lessons from the lives of real heroes are profiled in Vol. 2 of *Hero Tales*, including Jim Elliot, John Newton, Dietrich Bonhoeffer, Corrie ten Boom, Watchman Nee, and Florence Nightingale. Discussion questions and Scripture verses designed to highlight essential Christian character qualities make this book a perfect tool to teach children ages 6 to 12 lifelong lessons in what it means to live for Christ. Elegantly packaged and illustrated. ISBN: 1556617135

Hudson Taylor: Deep in the Heart of China by Janet Benge ▊4-8▊ ▊9-12▊
A pioneer missionary to China at age 21, Hudson Taylor eventually led 641 missionaries, about half the entire protestant force in China (1832–1905). ISBN: 1576580164

In the Presence of My Enemies by Gracia Burnham
Soon after September 11, 2001, the news media stepped up its coverage of the plight of Martin and Gracia Burnham, the missionary couple captured and held hostage in the Philippine jungle by terrorists with ties to Osama bin Laden. ISBN: 0842362398

Jim Elliot: One Great Purpose by Janet Benge
"Christian Heroes: Then & Now" series have set a new standard of quality in Christian biography. These thrilling true adventures are the best-written biographies for ages 10 and up. Martyred in Ecuador in 1956, missionary Jim Elliot (1927-1956) lived by his words, "He is no fool who gives what he cannot keep to gain what he cannot lose." . ISBN: 1576581462

Jim Elliot Study Guide by Janet Benge ▊5-8▊
These guides turn great adventure reading into an even greater learning experience. With international breadth and spiritual depth, they provide the Christian school teacher and homeschooling parent with countless ways to teach and reinforce diverse curriculum areas as they relate to the life of a Christian missionary. Each unit study is designed for a wide variety of learning styles, grade levels, and abilities and for both individual and group study. ISBN: 1576582043

John Newton: The British Slave Trader Who Found Amazing Grace by Catherine Swift ▊9-12▊ ⊳○
The amazing story of a converted British slave trader who became a well-loved hymnist and a leading abolitionist. A "Men of Faith" biography. ISBN: 1556613059

The Journals of Jim Elliot by Jim Elliot ▊9-12▊ ⊳○
Jim Elliot was part of a team of young missionaries murdered in Ecuador in 1956 by the Auca Indians to whom they were witnessing. Detailing his fascinating missions work this book is a wonderful account of the life of a man who yearned to know God's plan for his life. ISBN: 0800758250

Christian and Missionary Biographies continued

King of the Cannibals: The Story of John G. Paton by Jim Cromarty **4-8** **9-12** ⊷
John Paton willingly risked everything, even his life, so that he might preach Christ as Lord and Savior in a heathen land. His story tells how God protected and cared for one of His faithful servants in the New Hebrides Islands. ISBN: 0852344015

Lottie Moon: Giving Her All for China by Janet Benge & Geoff Benge **4-8** **9-12** ⊷
Each true story in this series by outstanding authors Janet and Geoff Benge is loved by adults and children alike. More Christian Heroes: Then & Now biographies and unit study curriculum guides are coming soon. Fifty-five books are planned, and thousands of families have started their collections. After becoming the most educated woman in the American South, Lottie Moon spent thirty-nine years ministering in China. An annual missionary offering in her name is still taken up today (1840–1912). ISBN: 1576581888

Shadow of the Almighty: The Life and Testament of Jim Elliot by Elisabeth Elliot **9-12** ⊷
"Elizabeth Elliot's account is more than inspirational reading it belongs to the very heartbeat of evangelic witness."—*Christianity Today.* ISBN: 006062213X

Ten Fingers for God: The Life and Work of Dr. Paul Brand by Philip Yancey and Dorothy Clarke Wilson
A biography of Dr. Paul Brand, a leading researcher in rehabilitation for leprosy patients. Dr. Brand's humility and ability to adapt to different cultural and environmental conditions both stem from his love for God and God's creation. Philip Yancey's fine foreword enhances Wilson's portrait of this great man. Excellent reading. ISBN: 0964313707

Through Gates of Splendor by Elisabeth Elliot **9-12** ⊷
After several preliminary overtures of friendship, five young missionary men set out on a crucial January day in 1956 for a meeting with the Auca tribesmen who had reacted with apparent tolerance to earlier gifts and messages. This is the poignant story of their martyrdom told by the widow of one of the slain members of the group. ISBN: 0842371524

Valiant Women in War and Exile: Thirty-Eight True Stories by Sally Keeva and Lynn Kessler **9-12** ⊷
First published in 1987, this profoundly moving collection of women's personal stories crosses political and cultural boundaries, and include stories from pre-World War I Europe to the jungles of Central America in the 1980s. With her new introduction, Hayton-Keeva connects the book's poignant testimonies to contemporary issues of war, and describes a voice distinctively different from the traditional experience of men at war: War is not suspended in time, something outside a woman's experience of life; it is part of life, woven into all the rest. These mothers, daughters, sisters, and wives endured concentration camps, atomic bombs, homeland invasions, terrorism, and guerilla warfare. As nurses, nuns, social workers, soldiers, prisoners, spies, or snipers, they took active command of their lives and did what had to be done. Their accounts convey the lifelong physical, emotional, and spiritual impact of grief, terror, and loss, and reveal that for women, war is not about glory and camaraderie and heroism, but about the quiet valor born of individual suffering and triumph over adversity. ISBN: 087422263X

With Daring Faith: A Biography of Amy Carmichael by Rebecca H. Davis **4-8** ⊷
This is a biography written for children is about the esteemed missionary, Amy Carmichael, who almost single-handedly fought a battle against the practice of child temple prostitution in India in the early part of this century. ISBN: 0890844143

Classics/Grades K-3

Are You My Mother? by P. D. Eastman **K-3**
A baby bird, fallen from his nest, sets out to find his mother. Full-color. ISBN: 0394800184

The Bears on Hemlock Mountain by Alice Dalgliesh **K-3**
A young boy sent on an errand over Hemlock Mountain is not so sure he likes going alone, because there may be bears on the mountain, but with the help of the big iron pot he borrows, he completes his errand. ISBN: 0689716044

Blueberries for Sal by Robert McCloskey **K-3**
Little Sal and Little Bear both lose track of their mothers while eating blueberries and almost end up with the other's mother. ISBN: 014050169X

The Boy Who Held Back the Sea by Thomas Locker **K-3**
Jan had never done anything more heroic than shout for the guard because he'd imagined he'd seen a sea serpent. But when Jan discovered water trickling through a desolate stretch of the dike that protected his low-lying village, he knew he had to act fast. ISBN: 0140546138

Bravest Dog Ever: Story of Balto by Natalie Standiford **K-3**
Recounts the life of Balto, the sled dog who saved Nome, Alaska in 1925 from a diphtheria epidemic by delivering medicine through a raging snowstorm. ISBN: 039499695X

Caps for Sale: A Tale of a Peddler, Some Monkeys and Their Monkey Business by Esphyr Slobodkina **K-3**
A band of mischievous monkeys steals every one of a peddler's caps while he takes a nap under a tree. ISBN: 0064431436

Chicken Little by Steven Kellogg **K-3**
Steven Kellogg's hilarious retelling and irresistible illustrations bring fresh delight to this timeless classic of chai- reaction panic. Full-color. ISBN: 0688070450

The Complete Adventures of Curious George by Margret Rey and H. A. Rey **K-3**
The adventures of the ingenious little monkey who left the jungle to live with the man in the yellow hat. ISBN: 0395754100

The Complete Adventures of Peter Rabbit by Beatrix Potter **K-3**
Beatrix Potter's four stories that feature Peter Rabbit are brought together in one volume, so that Peter's escapades can be read as a continuous saga. The volume includes the complete text and art from *The Tale of Peter Rabbit*, *The Tale of Benjamin Bunny*, *The Tale of the Flopsy Bunnies* and *The Tale of Mr. Tod*. From Peter's mischievous childhood in Mr. McGregor's garden to the time he rescues a family from Tommy Brock's clutches, Peter Rabbit's story is one children will want to hear again and again. ISBN: 0140504443

The Complete Tales of Beatrix Potter by Beatrix Potter **K-3**
This beautiful, deluxe volume contains all 23 of Potter's "Peter Rabbit" tales. Arranged in the order in which they were first published, the stories are complete and unabridged. Full-color illustrations. ISBN: 0723247609

Corduroy by Don Freeman **K-3**
A toy bear in a department store wants a number of things, but when a little girl finally buys him, he finds what he's always wanted most of all. ISBN: 0140501738

The Courage of Sarah Noble by Alice Dalgliesh **K-3**
An eight-year-old girl finds courage to go alone with her father to build a new home in the Connecticut wilderness, and to stay with the Indians when her father goes back to bring the rest of the family. ISBN: 0689715404

Classics/Grades K-3 continued

The Drinking Gourd: A Story of the Underground Railroad by F. N. Monjo **K-3**
Sent home alone for misbehaving in church, Tommy discovers that his house is a station on the underground railroad. ISBN: 0064440427

Family-Time Bible by Kenneth Taylor **K-3**
This collection of more than 120 classic Bible stories makes it easy for parents to teach young children the best-loved stories of Scripture in a way that is easy to understand. Full-color. ISBN: 0842365761

A Family Treasury of Little Golden Books by Ellen Lewis Buell **K-3**
A selection of forty-six stories and poems, each with their original illustrations, previously published as separate editions of Little Golden Books. ISBN: 0307168506

Five True Dog Stories by Margaret Davidson **K-3**
This collection of true dog stories will fascinate young readers. Dox finds jewels and criminals. Grip picks pockets, and Barry rescues people from the snow. Adventure, suspense, and animals are all here. ISBN: 0590424017

Frog and Toad Are Friends by Arnold Lobel **K-3**
Five tales recounting the adventures of two best friends—Frog and Toad. Arnold Lobel has won both Newbery and Caldecott Honor Medals (very unusual for one author) for his books about Frog and Toad. Several teachers guides (some free online) are available to use with this book. ISBN: 0064440206

Henner's Lydia by Marguerite de Angeli **K-3**
An Amish girl living with her family on their farm in Lancaster County, Pennsylvania, tries to finish her hooked rug so that she may take her first trip to market with Father. ISBN: 0836190939

The Hundred Dresses by Eleanor Estes **K-3**
A restored edition of a classic, award-winning book about prejudice and understanding. ISBN: 0152052607

Laddie: A True Blue Story by Gene Stratton-Porter **K-3**
The narrative mode of *Laddie* may prevent an easy suspension of disbelief to some readers. It is told in the first person not by the eight- or ten-year-old Little Sister but from the later position of adulthood. ISBN: 0253204585

The Lion Storyteller Bedtime Book by Bob Hartman **K-3**
A good introduction for younger children to the cultural heritage of many nations. ISBN: 0745946542

Little Visits with God by Mary Manz Simon **K-3**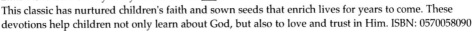
This classic has nurtured children's faith and sown seeds that enrich lives for years to come. These devotions help children not only learn about God, but also to love and trust in Him. ISBN: 0570058090

Mr. Popper's Penguins by Richard Atwater **K-3**
Mr. Popper trains his twelve pet penguins to become stage sensations. ISBN: 0316058432

A New Coat for Anna by Harriet Ziefert **K-3**
Even though there is no money, Anna's mother finds a way to make Anna a badly needed winter coat. ISBN: 0394898613

The Railway Children by Various Authors **K-3**
Three children, forced to alter their comfortable lifestyle when their father disappears, move to a simple cottage near a railway station where their days are filled with adventure. Beautifully illustrated in color by well-known artists such as Quentin Blake and Michael Foreman. Complete and unabridged editions. ISBN: 1843650509

The Story about Ping by Marjorie Flack and Kurt Wiese **K-3**
A little duck finds adventure on the Yangtze River when he is too late to board his master's houseboat one evening. ISBN: 0140502416

Classics/Grades 4-8

The Adventures of Tom Sawyer and *Adventures of Huckleberry Finn* by Mark Twain **4-8**
Newly repackaged and featuring a new Introduction, Twain's classic tales of life on the Mississippi capture the complexities of American life while regaling the boyhood adventures of two of the most popular characters in American literature. ISBN: 0451528646

Anne of Green Gables by Lucy Maud Montgomery **4-8**
When Marilla Cuthbert's brother, Matthew, returns home to Green Gables with a chatty redheaded orphan girl, Marilla exclaims, "But we asked for a boy. We have no use for a girl." It's not long, though, before the Cuthberts can't imagine how they could ever do without young Anne. Gift box edition with eight titles in this series available. ISBN: 0517189682

Ben Hur: Retold for Today's Children by Anne de Graaf **4-8**
Their inherent Christian themes are highlighted and emphazised in short, simple sentences.
ISBN: 8772470038

Big Red by Jim Kjelgaard **4-8**
Story of the friendship between a champion Irish setter and a trapper's son. Together Danny and Red face many dangers in the harsh Wintapi wilderness that they call home. ISBN: 0553154346

Black Beauty by Anna Sewell **4-8**
Written over 100 years ago, Black Beauty remains one of the greatest children's stories of all time. The story, which takes place in turn-of-the-century London, is narrated by Black Beauty himself, and it depicts the horse's prosperity and misfortunes as he relates his owners' whims and his companions' personalities. Featuring full-color illustrations, the tale presents a clear-cut moral about animal treatment and appeals to the sentiments of readers of all ages. It is an ideal and inexpensive way to begin building a classics library. ISBN: 1843650622

The Boxcar Children by Gertrude Chandler Warner **4-8**
No one knows who these young wanderers are or where they have come from. Frightened to live with a grandfather they have never met, the children make a home for themselves in an abandoned red boxcar they discover in the woods. ISBN: 0807508527

The Boxcar Children Volume 5-8 by Gertrude Chandler Warner **4-8**
More adventures. 4 books in one. *Mike's Mystery, Blue Bay Mystery, The Woodshed Mystery* and *The Lighthouse Mystery*. ISBN: 0807508578

The Bronze Bow by Elizabeth George Speare **4-8**
Driven by hatred for the Romans, Daniel has vowed to see their destruction. His leader is amazzing an outlaw force to defeat them, but Daniel has doubts when he hears a teacher from Nazareth preach about the Kingdom of God. ISBN: 0395137195

Caddie Woodlawn by Carol Ryrie Brink **4-8**
Chronicles the adventures of eleven-year-old Caddie, growing up with her six brothers and sisters on the Wisconsin frontier in the mid-nineteenth century. ISBN: 0689713703

Calico Captive by Elizabeth George Speare **4-8**
In the year 1754, the stillness of Charlestown, New Hampshire, is shattered by the terrifying cries of an Indian raid. Young Miriam Willard, on a day that had promised new happiness, finds herself instead a captive on a forest trail, caught up in the ebb and flow of the French and Indian War. ISBN: 0618150765

The Call of the Wild and *White Fang* by Jack London **4-8**
Two of Jack London's best-loved masterpieces, in their entirety. *Call of the Wild* tells a compelling tale of adventure during the Yukon Gold Rush, and fully captures the unquenchable spirit of Buck, a kidnapped dog trying to survive in the harshest of environments. Also set in Alaska, the powerful *White Fang* follows the often savage life of the magnificent title character, a mix of wolf and dog. ISBN: 0553212338

Classics/Grades 4-8 continued

Carry On, Mr. Bowditch by Jean Lee Latham **4-8**
Winner of the 1956 Newbery Medal, this novel tells the story of 18th-century mathematical wizard Nathaniel Bowditch, whose determination to master sea navigation resulted in *The American Practical Navigator*. Illustrations. ISBN: 0618250743

Charlotte's Web by E. B. White **4-8**
E.B. White has created a classic children's tale of responsibility, courage, friendship and trust. Great for reading aloud to the whole family. ISBN: 0064400557

The Cricket in Times Square by George Selden **4-8**
Chester the Cricket, with his friends Tucker the Mouse and Harry the Cat help bring success to a newsstand in Times Square. ISBN: 0440415632

The Endless Steppe by Esther Hautzig **4-8**
A young Polish girl, her mother, and her grandmother, who are taken prisoners by the Russians during World War II and shipped to a forced-labor camp in a remote, impoverished Siberian village, somehow manage to stay together and alive through near starvation and harsh arctic winters. ISBN: 006447027X

Five Little Peppers and How They Grew by Margaret Sidney **4-8**
In a timeless tale of family and survival, Mrs. Pepper and her five lively children handle their difficulties with great courage and cheer. One day the Peppers meet a wealthy gentleman and his young son. Could this finally be the beginning of the good times the children have been waiting for? ISBN: 0694015822

Freckles by Gene Stratton-Porter **4-8**
Orphaned and maimed, Freckles' bitterness about his fate is lessened when he is hired to guard a stretch of lumber in the wild Limberlost, and, after meeting the beautiful *Swamp Angel*, he determines to find out about his past. ISBN: 0253203635

A Gathering of Days: A New England Girl's Journal, 1830-1832 by Joan W. Blos **4-8**
The journal of a fourteen-year-old girl, kept the last year she lived on the family farm, records daily events in New Hampshire, her father's remarriage, and the death of her best friend. ISBN: 0068971419X

Heidi by Johanna Spyri **4-8**
A Swiss orphan is heartbroken when she must leave her beloved grandfather and their happy home in the mountains to go to school and to care for an invalid girl in the city. Illustrated notes throughout the text explain the historical background of the story. ISBN: 0517189674

Island of the Blue Dolphins by Scott O'Dell **4-8**
Left alone on a beautiful but isolated island off the coast of California, a young Indian girl spends eighteen years, not only merely surviving through her enormous courage and self-reliance, but also finding a measure of happiness in her solitary life. ISBN: 0440940001

Johnny Tremain by Esther Forbes **4-8**
After injuring his hand, a silversmith's apprentice in Boston becomes a messenger for the Sons of Liberty in the days before the American Revolution. ISBN: 0440942500

King Arthur and His Knights by James Knowles **4-8**
An idealized Middle Ages, a world filled with violent tests of courage, clamorous and raging battle, adventurous quests, and yearning love of knight and damsel unfolds for the reader. ISBN: 0517189690

Little Princess by Frances Hodgson Burnett **4-8**
This was my favorite story when I was a little girl. Sara Crewe, a wealthy young student at a London boarding school, suddenly finds herself at the mercy of the cruel schoolmistress after tragedy strikes. Overwhelmed by terrible trials, Sara must find the strength to survive. Her story is one of perseverance, bravery, generosity, and imagination. Burnett provides readers with a vivid illustration of the biblical principle that true worth is a matter of the heart. ISBN: 0875527272

Classics/Grades 4-8 continued

Little Women by Louisa May Alcott **4-8** **N**
Chronicles the joys and sorrows of the four March sisters as they grow into young ladies in nineteenth-century New England. ISBN: 0140380221

Newbery Medal Box Set **4-8** **N**
A boxed set of three highly acclaimed, immensely popular Newbery Medal-winning books. Includes *Caddie Woodlawn,* by Carol Ryrie Brink; *A Gathering of Days,* by Joan W. Blos; and *King of the Wind,* by Marguerite Henry. ISBN: 0689718888

Psalm 91 for Children by Peggy Joyce Ruth **4-8** **N** ▷
This book will lay the groundwork for a life of victory over fear, worry and doubt through knowledge of Jesus and His promises to us. Enjoy reading story after story of heart-warming acts of faith by children and the miracles that resulted! ISBN: 089228157X

Robinson Crusoe by Daniel Defoe **4-8** **N**
The life and strange and surprising *Robinson Crusoe* is based,upon the experiences of Alexander Selkirk, who had run away to sea in 1704 and requested to be left on an uninhabited island, to be rescued five years later. ISBN: 0141439823

Sarah, Plain and Tall by Patricia MacLachlan **4-8** **N**
When their father invites a mail-order bride to come live with them in their prairie home, Caleb and Anna are captivated by their new mother and hope that she will stay. ISBN: 0064402053

Secret Garden by Frances Hodgson Burnett **4-8** **N**
Recently arrived at her uncle's estate, orphaned Mary Lennox is spoiled, sickly, and certain she won't enjoy living there. Then she discovers the arched doorway into an overgrown garden. Mary soon begins transforming it into a thing of beauty—unaware that she is changing too. ISBN: 0517189607

Skippack School by Marguerite de Angeli **4-8** **N**
In 1750 in Pennsylvania, mischievous young Eli, recently arrived with his Mennonite family from Germany, tries to adjust to his new life and the teaching methods of his schoolteacher. ISBN: 0836191242

Thee, Hannah! by Marguerite de Angeli **4-8** **N**
Nine-year-old Hannah, a Quaker living in Philadelphia just before the Civil War, longs to have some fashionable dresses like other girls but comes to appreciate her heritage and its plain dressing when her family saves the life of a runaway slave. ISBN: 0836191064

Treasure Island by Robert Louis Stevenson **4-8** **N**
Robert Louis Stevenson's cherished, unforgettable adventure magically captures the thrill of a sea voyage and a treasure hunt through the eyes of its teenage protagonist, Jim Hawkins. ISBN: 0517189631

The Trumpet of the Swan by E. B. White **4-8** **N**
Louis, a voiceless trumpeter swan, finds himself far from his wilderness home when he determines to communicate by learning to play a stolen trumpet. ISBN: 0064408671

Uncle Tom's Cabin: Retold for Today's Children by Anne de Graaf **4-8** **N**
Their inherent Christian themes are highlighted and emphazised in short, simple sentences.
ISBN: 8772470054

Where the Red Fern Grows by Wilson Rawls **4-8** **N**
A young boy living in the Ozarks achieves his heart's desire when he becomes the owner of two redbone hounds and teaches them to be champion hunters. ISBN: 0440412676

The Yearling by Marjorie Kinnan Rawlings **4-8** **N**
A young boy living in the Florida backwoods is forced to decide the fate of a fawn he has lovingly raised as a pet. ISBN: 0020449313

Literature Resources

Classics/Grades 9-12

All Creatures Great and Small by James Herriot `9-12` **N**
Herriot's heartwarming and often hilarious stories of his first years as a country vet perfectly depict the wonderful relationship between man and animal—and they intimately portray a man whose humor, compassion and love of life are truly inspiring. ISBN: 0312965788

The Adventures of Huckleberry Finn by Mark Twain `9-12` **N**
Of all the contenders for the title of The Great American Novel, none has a better claim than *The Adventures of Huckleberry Finn*. More than a century after its publication it remains a major work that can be enjoyed as an incomparable adventure story and as a classic of American humor. ISBN: 0142437174

The Beggar Queen by Lloyd Alexander `9-12` **N**
Chaos reigns in Marienstat as Duke Conrad of Regia, the king's uncle, plots to overthrow the new government of Westmark and bring an end to the reforms instituted by Mickle, now Queen Augusta, Theo, and their companions. ISBN: 0440905486

Ben-Hur: A Tale of the Christ by Lewis Wallace `9-12` **N** ⌐○
From a thrilling sea battle to its famous chariot race to the agony of the Crucifixion, this is the epic tale of a prince who became a slave, and by a twist of fate and his own skill, won a chance at freedom. An historical classic with illustrations, discussion questions, and an introduction to the story behind the story. ISBN: 01561797456

The Call of the Wild, White Fang, and Other Stories by Jack London `9-12` **N**
Four of Jack London's best short stories are included. ISBN: 0140186514

Christy by Catherine Marshall `9-12` **N** ⌐○
Story of a nineteen-year-old girl who goes to teach school in the primitive mountain surroundings of the Smokies to look after and teach its mountain people. Explores the strength of her faith. ISBN: 0380001411

The Cross and the Switchblade by David R. Wilkerson `9-12` **N** ⌐○
A young country preacher ministers to teenage runaways, prostitutes, and gang members.
ISBN: 0515090255

David Copperfield by Charles Dickens `9-12` **N**
Intimately rooted in the author's own biography and written as a first-person narrative, *David Copperfield* charts a young man's progress through a difficult childhood in Victorian England to ultimate success as a novelist, finding true love along the way. Jeremy Tambling's provocative Introduction reveals subtle themes relevant today in Dickens' favorite work. 39 illustrations. Map. ISBN: 0140434941

A Day No Pigs Would Die by Robert Newton Peck `9-12` **N**
To a Vermont farm boy whose father slaughters pigs for a living, maturity comes early as he learns "doing what's got to be done," especially regarding his pet pig who cannot produce a litter. ISBN: 0679853065

A Family Apart by Joan Lowery Nixon `9-12` **N**
When their mother can no longer support them, six siblings are sent by the Children's Aid Society of New York City to live with farm families in Missouri in 1860. ISBN: 0440226767

Fahrenheit 451: The Temperature at Which Book Paper Catches Fire, and Burns by Ray Bradbury `9-12` **N**
A short novel set in the future when "firemen" burn books forbidden by the totalitarian "brave new world" regime. The hero, according to Mr. Bradbury, is "a book burner who suddenly discovers that books are flesh-and-blood ideas and cry out silently when put to the torch." ISBN: 0345342968

Great Expectations by Charles Dickens `9-12` **N**
Great Expectations is at once a superbly constructed novel of spellbinding mastery and a profound examination of moral values. Here, some of Dickens's most memorable characters come to play their part in a story whose title itself reflects the deep irony that shaped Dickens's searching reappraisal of the Victorian middle class. ISBN: 0141439564

Classics/Grades 9-12 continued

Great Stories Remembered II by Joe L. Wheeler `9-12` **N**
Develop values, create empathy and instill kindness in the hearts and minds of children with the second treasury of heartwarming tales from *Focus on the Family*. Each carefully woven story will renew the spirit and provide endearing reminders of the values you treasure. ISBN: 01561796344

Jane Eyre by Charlotte Bronte `9-12` **N**
The classic portrayal of a woman's passionate search for a richer life than that traditionally allowed women in Victorian society continues to endure. ISBN: 0142437204

Joni Eareckson Tada by Kathleen White `9-12` **N**
The remarkable story of Joni Eareckson Tada has become an inspiration to thousands of people around the world. A tragic diving accident when she was a teenager paralyzed Joni immediately. When it was confirmed that she would be a quadriplegic for the rest of her life, she could not understand why God allowed this tragedy. "Men and Women of Faith" series. ISBN: 1556613644

Heart of Darkness With the Congo Dairy by Joseph Conrad `9-12` **N**
In Conrad's haunting tale, Marlow, a seaman and wanderer, recounts his physical and psychological journey in search of the enigmatic Kurtz. Traveling to the heart of the African continent, he discovers how Kurtz has gained his position of power and influence over the local people. Marlow's struggle to fathom his experience involves him in a radical questioning of not only his own nature and values but the nature and values of his society. ISBN: 0140186522

I'll Watch the Moon by Ann Tatlock `9-12` **N**
From an award-winning novelist comes the story of Catherine Tierney, angry at a God whom she no longer believes exists, and her painful journey back to faith. ISBN: 0764227645

The Keeper of the Bees by Gene Stratton-Porter `9-12` **N**
Broken in spirit and body, James Lewis MacFarland, a wounded veteran of World War I, decides to escape from the military hospital before he is sent to a hospital for tubercular patients. He sets out on a great adventure which takes him to the healing sun and ocean of California. ISBN: 025320691X

To Kill a Mockingbird by Harper Lee `9-12` **N**
Two children in the South are introduced to the subject of prejudice when their father defends a falsely accused Black man. ISBN: 0446310786

A Lantern in Her Hand by Bess Streeter Aldrich `9-12` **N**
This is the classic story of a pioneer woman Abbie Deal. Abbie accompanies her family to the soon-to-be state of Nebraska. There, in 1865, she marries and settles into a sod house of her own. Describes Abbie's years of child-raising, of making a frontier home able to withstand every adversity. Aldrich conveys the strength of everyday things, the surprise of familiar faces, and the look of the unspoiled landscape during different seasons. Refusing to be broken by hard experience, Abbie sets a joyful example for her family - and for her readers. This edition includes the author's story. ISBN: 0140384286

Little Britches: Father and I Were Ranchers by Ralph Moody `9-12` **N**
Ralph Moody was eight years old in 1906 when his family moved to a Colorado ranch. Through his eyes we experience the pleasures and perils of ranching there at the dawn of the century. Auctions and roundups, family picnics, irrigation wars, tornadoes, and windstorms provide authentic color. So do adventures, wonderfully told, that prepare Ralph to take his father's place. ISBN: 0803281781

Lord Jim by Joseph Conrad `9-12` **N**
The story of a young, idealistic Englishman who is disgraced by an act of cowardice while serving as an officer on the Patna, a merchant-ship sailing from an Eastern port with a party of Muslim pilgrims. His life is blighted when an isolated scandal assumes horrifying proportions. ISBN: 0140180923.

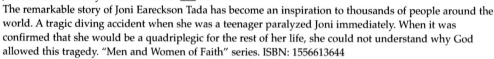

Literature Resources

Classics/Grades 9-12 continued

The Master's Quilt by Michael Webb `9-12` ↜
This compelling historical novel pictures dramatic spiritual conflicts in first-century Israel. Deucalion Quinctus, Commander under Pontius Pilate, has witnessed a miracle—the resurrection of Jesus of Nazareth. Suddenly he finds himself in love with a beautiful outcast named Esther, in possession of a bundle of parchment scrolls—and on the run from demons and men alike. Will the mysterious Watcher, Uriel, be able to protect him from the evil powers that stalk him? ISBN: 192937108X

Moby-Dick: Or, the Whale by Herman Melville `9-12` **N**
Written with wonderfully redemptive humor, *Moby-Dick* is the story of an eerily compelling madman pursuing an unholy war against a creature as vast and dangerous and unknowable as the sea itself. ISBN: 0142437247

The Old Man and the Sea by Ernest Hemingway `9-12` **N**
The Pulitzer Prize-winning short novel about an old Cuban fisherman and his supreme ordeal with a giant marlin far out in the Gulf Stream. ISBN: 0684801221

The Pearl by John Steinbeck `9-12` **N**
When the news of Kino's great find spreads through the small town, no one suspects its power to deceive, to corrupt, to destroy. Kino is a poor diver, gathering pearls from the Gulf beds that once brought great wealth to the kings of Spain and now provide Kino, Juanna, and their infant son with meager subsistence. Then, on a day like any other, Kino emerges from the sea with a pearl as large as a sea gull's egg. With the pearl comes hope, the promise of comfort and of security. ISBN: 014017737X

Pride and Prejudice by Jane Austen `9-12` **N**
Austen's perfect comedy of manners—one of the most popular novels of all time—features splendidly civilized sparring between the proud Mr. Darcy and the prejudiced Elizabeth Bennet as they play out their spirited courtship in a series of eighteenth-century drawing-room intrigues. ISBN: 0141439513

The Story of My Life by Helen Keller `9-12` **N**
The Story of My Life, a remarkable account of overcoming the debilitating challenges of being both deaf and blind, has become an international classic, making Helen Keller one of the most well-known, inspirational figures in history. Originally published in 1903, Keller's fascinating memoir narrates the events of her life up to her third year at Radcliffe College. ISBN: 0553213873

A Tale of Two Cities by Charles Dickens `9-12` **N**
The epic story of two cities and two men. Charles Darnay and Sydney Carton are alike in appearance, very different in character, but in love with the same woman. Darnay, who has abandoned the cruelty of the French nobility for London, must return to Paris during the violent Revolution to rescue his faithful servant from the guillotine. But what part does Carton play in the dramatic events that follow? ISBN: 0140373365

The World I Live in by Helen Keller `9-12` **N**
This sequel to Helen's autobiography remains almost completely unknown. Here, responding to skeptics who doubted that a girl who was blind, deaf, and mute almost from birth could find words to describe her experience, Keller presents a striking word-picture of her reality. It includes Keller's first published essay, written when she was 12 years old. ISBN: 1590170679

Quo Vadis? by Henry K. Sienkiewicz `9-12` **N**
An epic saga of love, courage and devotion in Nero's time, *Quo Vadis* portrays the degenerate days leading to the fall of the Roman empire and the glory and the agony of early Christianity. ISBN: 0781805503

Wuthering Heights by Emily Bronte `9-12` **N**
The passionate love story of stubborn Cathy and wild-as-the-wind Heathcliff has been a favorite since its original publication in 1848. ISBN: 0141439556

See symbol keys on page 370. See pages 355-373 for information about the resources.

Further Information and Support

Heart of Wisdom is a family owned and operated business. With a small staff working on Heart of Wisdom unit studies, each is very busy writing, proofing, laying out books, and addressing all of the administrative and management tasks.

When we first began Heart of Wisdom, we enjoyed answering questions and discussing products with you via the telephone. While we truly enjoyed direct interaction, the time demands associated with day-to-day business operations, homeschooling our children and engaging in other parental activities, we soon realized that we had to provide alternative options to better support you. We are confident that the resources provided on the next page will accommodate most, if not all inquiries about our services and product offerings.

Our primary focus is to create materials to promote God's Word. We made the decision to become wise stewards of our time by providing access to more written information such as sample pages, answers to frequently asked questions, and message boards on our web sites.

We provide an outside answering service to take credit card orders for those who don't feel comfortable ordering online. (Please note, however, that we have never had one problem with online security.) However, it is only an answering service and the operators cannot answer homeschool questions. A shipping company fills our orders. If you have a shipping problem, we will give you the number to call. (They are not involved with our electronic publications.)

Web Sites:

HeartofWisdom.com and HomeschoolUnitStudies.com—contain volumes of information explaining our teaching philosophy and providing examples and resource information. There are hundreds of pages available for download and numerous free sample lessons.

Homeschool-Books.com—our online store, which provides details on each book we carry, our tentative publishing schedule, dozens of sample pages and reviews, and more Frequently Asked Questions (FAQs). Register here to receive news about specials and product announcements.

BiblicalHolidays.com—contains hundreds of pages of information on the holidays in the Bible and Christianity's Hebrew roots.

Message Boards:

Visit our **Homeschool Message Board** to chat with others using the Heart of Wisdom teaching approach at http://www.HeartofWisdom.com/forum

Visit our **Biblical Holidays Message Board** to chat with others about the Hebrew roots of the Christian faith at http://www.BiblicalHolidays.com/forum

Email:

support@HeartofWisdom.com - for general information.

shipping@Heartofwisdom.com - for shipping information.

Remember, we care about you and can answer your questions but ask you to read through the free information and Frequently Asked Questions we provide on our web sites. If you still need help, we are available through email.

End Notes

Preface

1. Harris, R. Laird, Robert Laird Harris, Gleason Leonard Archer, and Bruce K. Waltke. *Theological Wordbook of the Old Testament*, Chicago, IL: Moody Press, 1999, c1980.

Introduction

1. Wood, D.R.W. and I. Howard Marshall. *New Bible Dictionary*, Downer's Grove, IL: InterVarsity Press, 1996.
2. Henry, Matthew and Thomas Scott. *Matthew Henry's Concise Commentary*, Oak Harbor, WA: Logos Research Systems, 1997. (Psalm 90:12)

Chapter 1: Our Homeschool Journey

1. *Merriam-Webster's Collegiate Dictionary*, 10th ed., Springfield, MA: Merriam-Webster, 1996. (Exodus)
2. Strong, James. *Enhanced Strong's Lexicon*, Ontario: Woodside Bible Fellowship, 1996. (#H1350)
3. Thomas Kuhn's book, *Nature of Scientific Revolutions*, popularized the term paradigm, which he described as a set of agreements about how problems are to be understood.) Kuhn, Thomas S. The *Structure of Scientific Revolutions*, 3rd ed., University of Chicago Press, 1962, 1970, 1996. (p. 226)
4. Strong, James. *Enhanced Strong's Lexicon*, Ontario: Woodside Bible Fellowship, 1996. (#1844)
5. Tverberg, Lois A. *Listening to the Language of the Bible: Hearing it Through Jesus' Ears*, Holland, MI: En-Gedi, 2004.

Chapter 2: God Called You to Be a Part of His Plan

1. Wisnewski Jr., Reverend Robert C. "Moses and the Burning Bush," http://www.stjohnsmontgomery.org/lessons/Bible/moses.html.
2. Ibid.

Chapter 3: Focus on God, Not on Circumstances

1 *10,000 Sermon Illustrations*, Electronic ed., Dallas, TX: Biblical Studies Press, 2000.
2. Tverberg, Lois A. *Listening to the Language of the Bible: Hearing it Through Jesus Ears*, Holland, MI: En-Gedi, 2004.
3. Follette, John Wright. *Broken Bread*, Centre Hall, PA: Gospel Publishing House, 1957.

Chapter 4: Only Be Strong

1. Stanley, Charles F. *Advancing Through Adversity*, Nashville, TN: Thomas Nelson, 1997, c1996.
2. Henry, Matthew. *Matthew Henry's Commentary on the Whole Bible* Peabody, MA: Hendrickson, 1996. (Joshua 1:1.)
3. Stanley, Charles. www.InTouch.org.

Chapter 5: What Is Education? What Is Wisdom?

1. Ahern, John. "A Thanksgiving Quiz," Social Studies 82, no. 5: 1991. (pp. 176–178)
2. Daniel Lancaster explains the story behind the Yankee Doodle song as the "Macaroni Principle" on a CD from First Fruits of Zion giving an overview of their Torah Study program explaining the importance of understanding culture. Dan's wife is a homeschool mom who wanted to know what macaroni had to do with hats, so they looked it up and found out.
3. Sampson, Robin. *A Family Guide to the Biblical Holidays*, Stafford, VA: Heart of Wisdom Publishing Inc., 2001.
4. Sampson, Robin. *Wisdom: An Internet-Linked Unit Study*, Stafford VA: Heart of Wisdom Publishing Inc., 2004.
5. *Random House Webster's College Dictionary*, New York, NY: Random House Reference, 2000.
6. Richards, Larry and Lawrence O. Richards. *The Teacher's Commentary*, Wheaton, IL: Victor, 1987.
7. *Random House Webster's College Dictionary*, New York, NY: Random House Reference, 2000.
8. Barclay, William. *Train Up a Child: Educational Ideals in the Ancient World*, Louisville, KY: Westminster Press, 1959.
9. Henry, Matthew and Thomas Scott. *Matthew Henry's Concise Commentary*, Oak Harbor, WA: Logos Research Systems, 1997. (Colossians 2:1)
10. Howshall, Marilyn. *The Lifestyle of Learning: An Introduction*, Arlington, WA: Lifestyle of Learning Ministries, 2000.
11. *Merriam-Webster's Collegiate Dictionary*. (rabbi)

12. Mulligan, David. *Far Above Rubies: Wisdom in the Christian Community*. Marshfield, VT: Messenger Publishing, 1994. (p. 89)

Chapter 6: A Brief History of Education
1. Eldridge, Tom. *Safely Home*, San Antonio, TX: The Vision Forum, 2003.
2. Mulligan, David. *Far Above Rubies: Wisdom in the Christian Community*. Marshfield, VT: Messenger Publishing, 1994 (p. 89)
3. Easton, M.G. *Easton's Bible Dictionary*, (Oak Harbor, WA: Logos Research Systems, 1996. (rabbi)
4. "Fathers of the Church," *Encarta Encyclopedia*, 2005
5. Reed, James E. and Ronnie Prevost. *A History of Christian Education*, Nashville, TN: Broadman & Holman, 1993.
6. Lawson, Kevin. *Introduction to Christian Education: Foundations for the 21st Century*, Grand Rapids, MI: Baker, 2001.
7. Augustine: "Philosophy, Western," *Encarta Encyclopedia*, 2005.
8. Reed, James E. and Ronnie Prevost, *A History of Christian Education*. Nashville, TN: Broadman & Holman, 1993.
9. Mulligan, David. *Far Above Rubies: Wisdom in the Christian Community*. Marshfield, VT: Messenger Publishing, 1994.(p. 79)
10. Ibid.
11. Jones, Timothy Paul, and A. Kenneth Curtis. *Christian History Made Easy*, Torrance, CA: Rose Publishing, 1999.
12. Ibid.
13. Holmes, George, *The Oxford History of Medieval Europe*. New York, NY: Oxford University Press, 1988.
14. Mulligan, David. *Far Above Rubies: Wisdom in the Christian Community*, Marshfield, VT: Messenger Publishing, 1994.
15. McInerny, Ralph. Edward N. Zalta (editor) John "Saint Thomas Aquinas" *The Stanford Encyclopedia of Philosophy*, Stanford, CA: The Metaphysics Research Lab Center for the Study of Language and Information Stanford University, 2005.
16. Woods, Dennis. The Great Conversation: A Biblical Analysis of the Great Books of Western Civilization. Brightrock Press.
17. Reed, James E. and Ronnie Prevost. *A History of Christian Education*, Nashville, TN: Broadman & Holman, 1993.
18. Jones, Timothy Paul, and A. Kenneth Curtis. *Christian History Made Easy*, Torrance, CA: Rose Publishing, 1999.
19. Green, Albert, *Reclaiming the Future of Christian Education*. Colorado Springs, CO.: Association of Christian Schools International, 1998.
20. Jones, Timothy Paul, and A. Kenneth Curtis. *Christian History Made Easy*, Torrance, CA: Rose Publishing, 1999.
21. "History of Education." *Microsoft Encarta Encyclopedia,* Microsoft Corporation, 2005.
22. Green, Albert. *Reclaiming the Future of Christian Education,* Colorado Springs, CO.: Association of Christian Schools International, 1998.
23. Millar, Keith (Ed.) Northwest Nazarene College, Nampa, ID: Christian Classics Ethereal Library Server at Wheaton College.
24. Shenandoah, April. *History of America's Education: Universities, Textbooks and Our Founders*, Sierra Times, April, 2002.
25. Tan, Paul Lee. *Encyclopedia of 7700 Illustrations,* Garland, TX: Bible Communications, 1996, c1979.
26. Wesley, John. *Sermons, on Several Occasions,* Oak Harbor, WA: Logos Research Systems, Inc., 1999.

27. Law, William. *A Serious Call to a Devout and Holy Life,* (original 1728) Vintage 2002.
28. Green, Albert. *Reclaiming the Future of Christian Education,* Colorado Springs, CO: Association of Christian Schools International, 1998.
29. Stern, David H. *Jewish New Testament Commentary,* Clarksville, MD: Jewish New Testament Publications, 1992.
30. Childs, John L. *American Pragmatism and Education: An Interpretation and Criticism*, New York, NY: Holt, Rinehart, and Winston, 1956. (pp. 18–19)
31. Reed, James E. and Ronnie Prevost. *A History of Christian Education*, Nashville, TN: Broadman & Holman, 1993. (311)
32. Ibid. (312–313)
33. Clouse, Robert G. (Ed.) *The Meaning of the Millennium*, IV Press, 1977; Ladd, G.E., "A Historical Premillennial Response." (p. 93)
34. Scores are according to studies by Lawrence M. Rudner, Ph.D., director of the ERIC Clearinghouse on Assessment and Evaluation, as well as studies by Dr. Brian D. Ray, president of the National Home Education Research Institute (1997)
35. Dr. John Wesley Taylor's nationwide study revealed that the self-concept of homeschool students was significantly higher than that of public-school students for the global and all six subscales of the Piers-Harris Self-Concept Scale. The Galloway-Sutton Study (performed in 1997) showed that from five success indicators (academic, cognitive, spiritu-

al, affective-social, and psychomotor), comparing with public- and private-school students, "in every success category except psychomotor, the home-school graduates excelled above the other students."

36. "Learning from the Greeks," *Commentary Magazine* Vol. 106, August 1998, No. 2.

37. Hanley, Mark Y. *Beyond a Christian Commonwealth: The Protestant Quarrel with the American Republic*, 1830–1860 Chapel Hill, NC: University of North Carolina Press, 1994.

38. Ibid.

39. Wirt, William. *The Life and Character of Patrick Henry*, Hartford, CT: S. Andrus & Son, 1849. (p 400, 403)

40. Mulligan, David. *Far Above Rubies: Wisdom in the Christian Community*. Marshfield, VT: Messenger Publishing, 1994.

41. Earl and Diane Rodd, "Questioning Secular Classical Education", *Homeschool Digest*. Covert, MI. http://www.homeschooldigest.com/

42. Ibid.

43. Tan, Paul Lee. *Encyclopedia of 7700 Illustrations*, Garland TX: Bible Communications, 1996, c1979.

Chapter 7: Christian Versus Secular Worldviews

1. For more information see www.Christianworldview.org.

2. Walsh, Brian J. and Richard Middleton. *Transforming Vision: Shaping a Christian Worldview*, Downers Grove, IL: Inter Varsity Press, 1984.

3. 60II: *Unconventional Wisdom*, 60 Minutes, February 20, 2002. http://www.cbsnews.com/stories/2002/02/19/60II/main329882.shtml

4. Ibid.

5. Ibid.

6. Ibid.

7. Ibid.

7. Patton, Francis Landey. Memorial address, May 2, 1921.

8. During his lifetime Warfield also wrote: *An Introduction to the Textual Criticism of the New Testament* (1886); *The Gospel of the Incarnation* (1893); *Two Studies in the History of Doctrine* (1893); *The Right of Systematic Theology* (1897); *The Power of God unto Salvation* (1903); *The Lord of Glory* (1907); *The Plan of Salvation* (1915); *Faith and Life* (1916); *Counterfeit Miracles* (1918); and many others.

9. Piper, John. *Future Grace*, Sisters, OR: Multnomah Books, 1998.
   (p. 176)

10. John Grebe is a chemist and founder of the Creation Research Society. www.creationresearch.org

11. Cohen, I.L., *Darwin Was Wrong: A Study in Probabilities*, Greenvale, NY: New Research Publications, 1984.

12. Denton, Michael. *Evolution: A Theory In Crisis*, Bethesda, MD: Adler & Adler, 1985. (p. 264) The author is a molecular biologist and, in this book he sets out, on a purely scientific basis, the weaknesses of the Darwinian model of evolution. It presents no pro- or anti-religious bias, but certainly contains a most comprehensive collection of scientific evidence demonstrating the shortcomings and failures of the Darwinian model. The complexity of the simplest known type of cell is so great that it is impossible to accept that such an object could have been thrown together suddenly by some kind of freakish, vastly improbable event. Such an occurrence would be indistinguishable from a miracle. (p. 13)

13. Jackson, Wayne. "The Big Bang Theory vs. God's Word," *Christian Courier*, December 1, 1999. <http://www.christiancourier.com/feature/december99.htm> (accessed July 2003)

14. Asimov, Isaac. *In The Beginning*, New York, NY: Crown, 1981. (p. 13)

15. Grant, George. *Grand Illusions: The Legacy of Planned Parenthood*. Cumberland House Publishing, 2000.

16. National Home Education Research Institute, www.nheri.org.

17. Noebel, David A. *Understanding the Times: The Religious Worldviews of Our Day and the Search for Truth*. Manitou Springs, CO: Summit Ministries. 1991.

Chapter 8: Greek Versus Hebrew Worldviews

1. Kurtz, Paul. *Humanist Manifesto*, Buffalo, NY: Prometheus, 1979

2. Krauthammer, Charles. "Education: Doing Bad and Feeling Good," *Time*, 5 February 1990. (p. 78)

3. Dowgiewicz, Mike and Sue Dowgiewicz. *Restoring the Early Church*, Colorado Springs, CO: Empowerment Press, 1995. (Available at http://www.restorationministries.org/html/booksCD.html)

5. Barrett, William. *Irrational Man*, Garden City, NY: Doubleday, 1958.

6. Benner, Jeff A. *The Ancient Hebrew Culture: Hebrew Thought*, Ancient Hebrew Research Center [http://www.ancient-hebrew.org/12_thought.html] Accessed November 2004.

7. Wiersbe, Warren W. *The Bible Exposition*

Commentary, Wheaton, IL: Victor, 1996.

8. Dowgiewicz, Mike, Sue Dowgiewicz. *Restoring the Early Church*, Colorado Springs, CO: Empowerment Press, 1995. (Available at http://www.restorationministries.org/html/booksCD.html)

11. Roberts, Dr. Mark D. "Developing a Biblical Worldview in 2004," January 2004. http://www.markdroberts.com/htmfiles/resources/worldview.htm (accessed November 2004)

12. Youngblood, Ronald F., Bruce, F.F., Ed. *Nelson's New Illustrated Bible Dictionary*. Nashville, TN: Thomas Nelson, 1997.

13 Walsh. Brian J., Richard Middleton. *Transforming the Vision: Shaping a Christian Worldview*. Downers Grove, IL: InterVarsity Press, 1984.

14. MacArthur, John, Jr. *How to Study the Bible*, John MacArthur's Bible Studies, Chicago, IL: Moody Press, 1996, c1982.

Chapter 9: Hebrew Education

1. Mishnah, Avot 5:21
2. Philo, of Alexandria, and Charles Duke Yonge. *The Works of Philo: Complete and Unabridged*, Peabody, MS: Hendrickson Publishers, 1996, c1993.
3. Josephus, Flavius, and William Whiston. *The Works of Josephus: Complete and Unabridged*, Peabody, MS: Hendrickson Publishers, 1996, c1987.
4. Strong, James. *Enhanced Strong's Lexicon*, H4720, Ontario: Woodside Bible Fellowship, 1996. (miqdash)
5. Ibid. (ma'at 4592)
6. Ibid. (yarah)
7. *Encarta Encyclopedia*, 2005.
8. Tverberg, Lois A. *Listening to the Language of the Bible: Hearing it Through Jesus' Ears*, Holland, MI: En-Gedi, 2004.
9. Wiersbe, Warren W. *Wiersbe's Expository Outlines on the Old Testament*, Wheaton, IL: Victor Books, 1993. (Deut. 1:1.)
10. Mulligan, David. *Far Above Rubies: Wisdom in the Christian Community*. Marshfield, VT: Messenger Publishing, 1994.
11. Edersheim, Alfred. *Sketches of Jewish Social Life*, Peabody, MS: Hendrickson Publishers, updated edition, 1994.
12. Israel High-Tech & Investment Report December 2004, http://ishitech.co.il
13. Cantor, Norman. *The Sacred Chain: The History of the Jews*, New York, NY: Harper Collins, 1994.
14. Wilson, Marvin.R. *Our Father Abraham: Jewish Roots of the Christian Faith*. Grand Rapids, MI: William B. Eerdmans Publishing Company, and

Dayton, OH: Center For Judaic-Christian Studies, 1989.

15. Pryor, Dwight. "Learning for Life," Jerusalem Perspective Online, Jerusalem School of Synoptic Research.

16. Barclay, William. *Educational Ideals in the Ancient World*, 1959.

17. Johnson, Ashley S. *Condensed Biblical Cyclopedia*, Blue Letter Bible. "Time Given to Religion." 2002.

18. Branscomb, Harvie. *The Teachings of Jesus*. New York, NY: Abingdon Press, 1931.

19. Joseph Klausner, *Jesus of Nazareth*. New York: Macmillan Company, 1925.

20. Mulligan, David. *Far Above Rubies: Wisdom in the Christian Community*. Marshfield, VT: Messenger Publishing, 1994.

21. Curry, Jeffery L. T*he Parable Discovery: First Century Discipleship*. Roanoke, TX: See Again Press. 2004.

22. Mulligan, David. *Far Above Rubies: Wisdom in the Christian Community*. Marshfield, VT: Messenger Publishing, 1994.

23. Bivin, David. "Jesus' Education" Jerusalem Perspective Online. JerusalemPerspective.com 1987–2005.

24. Hegg, Tim. *The Letter Writer: Paul's Background and Torah Perspective*. Littleton, CO: First Fruits of Zion, 2002.

25. Abbott, Lyman. *The Life and Letters of Paul the Apostle*, Cambridge, MA: The Riverside Press, 1898.

26. Tertullian, De praescriptione haereticorum. Circa A.D. 200.

Chapter 10: Why Christians Reject Hebrew Ways

1. Easton, M.G. *Easton's Bible Dictionary*, Oak Harbor, WA: Logos Research Systems, Inc., 1996, c1897.
2. Carson, D. A. *New Bible Commentary:* 1970. Leicester, England; Downers Grove, IL: InterVarsity Press, 1994.
3. Henry, Matthew and Thomas Scott. *Matthew Henry's Concise Commentary*, Oak Harbor, WA: Logos Research Systems, 1997.
4. Garr, John. *Restoring Our Lost Legacy*. Atlanta, GA: Golden Key Books. Restoration Foundation. 1998
5. Kimel, Alexander. *A Primer of Anti-Semitism*, http://www.kimel.net
6. Grobman, G. *The Holocaust: A Guide for Pennsylvania Teachers*, Millersville, PA: Millersville University, 1990.
7. Stern, David H. *Jewish New Testament Commentary: A Companion Volume to the Jewish New Testament*, Clarksville, MD: Jewish New Testament

Publications, 1992.

8. Wagner, Clarence H. Jr., *Jerusalem Courier*, Volume 10, No. 4, 1992.

9. Dowgiewicz, Mike, Sue Dowgiewicz. *Restoring the Early Church*, Colorado Springs, CO: Empowerment Press, 1995. (Available at http://www.restorationministries.org/html/booksCD.html)

10. *The Holocaust Chronicle* © 2002 Publications International, Ltd.

11. Poole, Chris M. *A Christian Apology.* 2002 http://christianactionforisrael.org/antiholo/apology.html

12. Luther, Martin. *About the Jews and Their Lies*, Wittenberg, 1543.

13. Converted Jews were called Converso—Spanish or Portuguese Jews who converted outwardly to Christianity in the late Middle Ages so as to avoid persecution or expulsion, though often continuing to practice Judaism in secret.

14. The term marrano appears to be derived from the color of the robes of a Roman Catholic Bishop; Jews who converted were placed under the direct tutelage of that bishop.

15. Grossman, Rafael G. *9–11 and Anti-Semitism.* Arutz Sheva 2001. http://christianactionforisrael.org

16. Chesler, Phyllis. *The New Anti-Semitism: The Current Crisis and What We Must Do About It.* Indianapolis, IN: Jossey-Bass. 2003.

17. Flannery, Edward H. *The Anguish of the Jews: Twenty-Three Centuries of Antisemitism.* Toronto: Collier-MacMillan, 1965.

18. Brickner, Al. Executive Director for Jews for Jesus. Http://WWW.Jewsfor Jesus.org

19. Garr, John. R*estoring Our Lost Legacy.* Atlanta, GA: Golden Key Books, Restoration Foundation, 1998.

Chapter 11. Learning Styles and the Four-Step Process

1. McCarthy, Bernice. *The 4MAT System: Teaching to Learning Styles with Right Brain Processing Techniques* Barrington, IL: Excel, Inc., 1987.

2. For more on this subject, listen to the tape by Jonathan Lindvall, "Psychology vs. Christianity," tape #303.
http://www.boldchristianliving.com/

3. McCarthy, Bernice. *The 4MAT System: Teaching to Learning Styles with Right Brain Processing Techniques* Barrington, IL: Excel, Inc., 1987.

4. Ibid.

5. James Strong, *Strong's Exhaustive Concordance of the Bible,* Peabody, MS: Hendrickson Publishers,1988. (shaman, #8150)

6. Ibid. (shen, #8128)

Chapter 12. Delight-Directed Studies

1. Harris, Greg. *The Christian Homeschool,* Brentwood, CA:: Wolgemuth & Hyatt, 1988.

2. Howshall, Marilyn. *Wisdom's Way of Learning Book 1,* Arlington, WA Lifestyle of Learning Ministries, 2000.
http://www.lifestyleoflearning.org

3. James Strong, *Strong's Dictionary of the Hebrew Language*

4. Camp. Terry. *Ignite the Fire!* Pocahontas, IA. *2000*

5 Schank, Roger. *Engines for Education*, Lea Publishing, 1995

Chapter 13. Unit Studies

1. Harro Van Brummelen, *Stepping Stones to Curriculum: A Biblical Path* (Seattle, WA: Alta Vista College Press, 1994)

2. Anderson, Robert H. "The Return of the Nongraded Classroom." *The Multiage Classroom.* Palatine: IRI/Skylight Publishing, 1993.

Chapter 14. Charlotte Mason's Philosophies

1. Worldwide Education Service pamphlet.

2. King, Jenny. *Charlotte Mason Reviewed.* Arthur H. Stockwell Ltd, 1981.

3. Mason, Charlotte M. *School Education.* London, England. Kegan Paul Trench, Trubner, and Co., Ltd., 1907.

4. Michael Sadler as quoted by Catherine Levison in *A Charlotte Mason Education.* WI: Champion Press, 1999.

5. Ibid.

6. Ibid.

7. These prints can be purchased from the National Gallery of Art www.nga.gov/

8. Mason, Charlotte M. *School Education.* London, England. Kegan Paul Trench, Trubner, and Co Ltd. 1907.

9. Mason, Charlotte M. *A Philosophy of Education.* London: Kegan Paul Trench, Trubner, and Co., Ltd., 1907.

10. Charlotte Levison, *Why Home Schoolers are Turning to Charlotte Mason Methods* http://www.christianity.com/CC_Content_Page/0,,PTID61309%7CCHID452240%7CCIID,00.html [Accessed September 2004.]

Chapter 15. Writing to Learn

1. Cohen, Cafi. *And What About College?: How Homeschooling Can Lead to Admissions to the Best Colleges & Universities*, Holt Associates, 2000.
2. Catherine Copley, *The Writer's Complex*, Empire State College, 1995. http://www.esc.edu/html-pages/writer/copley/hmpg.htm.

Chapter 16. Critical Thinking and Logic

1. Halpern, Diane. *Critical Thinking across the Curriculum: A Brief Edition of Thought and Knowledge*. Mahwah, NJLawrence Erlbaum Associates, 1997. (p. 80).
2. Wason, P.C., Johnson-Laird, *Psychology of Reasoning: Structure and Content*. London: Batsford, 1972.
3. Robert H. Ennis, "A Conception of Rational Thinking," in Jerrold R. Coombs, *Philosophy of Education*, Normal, IL: Philosophy of Education Society, 1974. (pp. 3–30).
4. Chambers, Oswald. *My Utmost for His Highest*, Grand Rapids, MI: Discovery House Publishers, 1993, c1935.
5. Oski, Frank A. *Don't Drink Your Milk: New Frightening Medical Facts About the World's Most Overrated Nutrient*. Teach Services. 1992.
6. Wilson, Marvin R. *Our Father Abraham: Jewish Roots of the Christian Faith*, Grand Rapids, MI: William B. Eerdmans Publishing Company, with Dayton, OH: Center For Judaic-Christian Studies, 1989.
7. The term red herring came from the practice of using smoked herring to distract dogs following a scent trail; the strong smell would obscure the real trail. Being used when an irrelevant topic is introduced to divert the attention away from the topic that's being discussed, or an argument where the premises are not logically connected to the conclusion. It is also referred to as changing the subject.

Chapter 17. An Overview of the Plan

1. For further details, see *You Can Teach Your Child Successfully* by Dr. Ruth Beechick.
2. A.W. Tozer, *Rut, Rot, or Revival: The Condition of the Church*. Camp Hill, PA: Christian Publications, Inc. 1992.
3. Green, Albert. Thinking Christianly, Seattle, WA: Alta Vista College Press, 1990.

Chapter 18. God's Word: Bible Study

1. de Lange, Nicholas. "Jewish Approaches to the Bible," Cambridge University Press Fathom Knowledge Network. http://www.fathom.com/feature/122097/
2. Barna Research Group, OmniPollTM, conducted each January. http://barna.org
3. *10,000 Sermon Illustrations*. Dallas: Biblical Studies Press, 2000.
4. Wiersbe, Warren W. *The Bible Exposition Commentary*. Wheaton, IL: Victor Books, 1996, c1989.
5. Bivin, David and and Roy Blizzard, Jr., *Understanding the Difficult Words of Jesus*. Destiny Image Publishers. 1995.

Chapter 19. God's World: Unit Studies

1. Green, Albert. *Thinking Christianly*, Seattle, WA: Alta Vista College Press, 1990..
2. Berndt, Chard. *Biblical Classification of Life: A Framework and Reference for Authentic Biblical Biology*, Elihu Publishing, 2000.

Chapter 20. Creating the Notebooks

1. Hendrix, Steve. "Why Stevie Can't Spell," *Washington Post*, February 20, 2005.
2. Bivin, David, Roy Blizzard, Jr., *Understanding the Difficult Words of Jesus*. Destiny Image Publishers, 1995.

Chapter 21. Scheduling by Faith

1. Cranford, Clarence W. *Cups of Light : And Other Illustrations*. Willow Grove, PA: Woodlawn Publishing, 1988.
2. Stanley, Charles F. *The Glorious Journey*. Nashville, TN: Thomas Nelson Publishers, 1997, c1996.

Chapter 23. Choosing and Using Resources

1. Thayer, William. *Gaining Favor With God And Man*. originally written in 1893. Reprint Mantle Ministries.1998.
2. Slater, Rosalie J. *A Family Program for Reading Aloud*, San Francisco, CA. Foundation for American Christian Education. 1991.
3. Ibid.

Biblography

10,000 Sermon Illustrations, Dallas, TX: Biblical Studies Press, 2000.

Abbott, Lyman. *The Life and Letters of Paul the Apostle*, Cambridge, MA: The Riverside Press, 1898.

Abramson, Glenda, Tudor Parfitt (eds). *Jewish Education and Learning*. Chur, Switzerland: Harwood Academic Publishers, 1994.

Aharoni, Yohanan. *The Land of the Bible: A Historical Geography*, Philadelphia PA: Westminster Press. 1967.

Anders: Max E. *30 Days to Understanding the Bible*, Brentwood, TN: Wolgemuth & Hyatt Publishers Inc. 1988. ☙

Angus, S. *The Environment of Early Christianity*, New York: C. Scribner's Sons. 1915.

—. *The Religious Quests of the Greco-Roman World: A Study in the Historical Background of Early Christianity*, New York: Scribner's Sons. 1929.

Anthony, Michael J. *Introducing Christian Education: Foundations for the Twenty-first Century*, Grand Rapids, MI: Baker Academic. 2001.

Bacon, Earnest. Spurgeon, *Heir of the Puritans, Arlington Heights*. IL: Christian Liberty Press, 1996.

Barclay, William. *Train up a Child: Educational Ideals in the Ancient World*, Philadelphia, PA: Westminster, 1959.

Bar-Illan, David. *Egypt Against Israel*. Commentary, September, 3. 1995. http://www.questia.com/.

Barrett, William. *Irrational Man*. Garden City, NY: Doubleday, 1958.

Bean, E. William. *New Treasures: A Perspective of New Testament Teachings Through Hebraic Eyes*, Oak Creek, WI: Cornerstone Publishing. 1995. ☙

Beckett, John D. *Loving Monday: Succeeding in Business without Selling Your Soul*, Downers Grove, IL: InterVarsity Press, 2001.

Beechick, Dr. Ruth. *Teaching Primaries: Understanding How They Think and How They Learn*, Denver, CO: Accent Books, 1985. ☙

—. *You Can Teach Your Child Successfully: Grades 4-8*. Pollock Pines, CA: Arrow Press, 1993. ☙

—. *The Language Wars: and Other Writings for Homeschoolers*, Pollock Pines, CA: Arrow Press, 1995. ☙

Berthold, Fred, Alan W. Carlsten, and Klaus Penzel, eds. *Basic Sources of the Judaeo-Christian Tradition*, Englewood Cliffs, NJ: Prentice Hall, 1962.

Blizzard, Roy. U*nderstanding the Difficult Words of Jesus: New Insights from a Hebraic Perspective*, Destiny Image, Shippensburg, PA, 1995. ☙

Bloch, Abraham P. *The Biblical and Historical Background of Jewish Customs and Ceremonies*, New York, NY: KTAV Publishing House, Inc., 1980.

Branscomb, Harvie. *The Teachings of Jesus: A Textbook for College and Individual Use*, Nashville,TN: Cokesbury, 1931.

Bruce, F.F. *New Testament History*, Garden City, New York: Doubleday-Galilee Book, 1980.

Brummelen, Harro Van. *Steppingstones to Curriculum: A Biblical Path*, Seattle, WA: Alta Vista College Press, 1994.

Brummelen, Harro Van. *Walking with God in the Classroom: Christian Approaches to Learning & Teaching*, Seattle, WA: Alta Vista College Press, 1988.

Burtness, Bill. *Judah Bible Curriculum*, Education for Liberty, Urbana, IL: Judah Bible Curriculum, 1988.

Butts, R. Freeman. *A Cultural History of Western Education: Its Social and Intellectual Foundations*, 2nd ed. New York, NY: McGraw-Hill. 1983.

Cammilleri, Joseph P. A *Generation Which Knew Not the Lord*, North Greece, NY: Carmen Publishing, 1995.

Cantor, Norman. *The Sacred Chain: The History of the Jews*, Harper Collins, 1994.

Carroll, Joyce Armstrong Ed.D. and Ron Habermas Ph.D.*Jesus Didn't Use Worksheets: A 2000 Year old Model for Good Teaching*, Houston, TX. Absey and Co. 1996

Carson, D. A. *New Bible Commentary*, Downers Grove, IL: Inter-Varsity Press, 1994.

Castle, E.B. *Ancient Education and Today*, Harmondsworth: Penguin, 1961.

Charles Silberman. *A Certain People: American Jews and their Lives Today*, Summit Books, 1985.

Childs, John L. *American Pragmatism and Education: An Interpretation and Criticism*, New York, NY: Holt, Rinehart, and Winston, 1956.

Clark, Donald Lemen. *A Study of Ancient Rhetoric in English Renaissance Education*, New York, NY: Columbia University Press, 1948.

Clarke, M. L. *Classical Education in Britain, 1500-1900*, Cambridge, Eng.: University Press. 1959.

Clarkson, Clay and Sally. *Educating the Whole Hearted Child: A Handbook for Christian Home Educators*, Walnut Springs, TX: Whole Heart Ministries, 1996. ☙

Coder, S. Maxwell. *First Steps To Knowing God's Will: Everything You Need to Live A Christian Life*, Meridian Publication, 1996.

Cohen, I.L., *Darwin Was Wrong: A Study in Probabilities*, Greenvale, NY: New Research Publications, 1984.

Cohn-Sherbok, Dan. *The Crucified Jew: Twenty Centuries of Christian Anti-Semitism*, London: HarperCollins Publishers, 1992.

Coke, Karl D., Ph.D. *Restoring The Home As The Center For Spiritual Growth*, Charlotte, NC: Family Restoration Fellowship.

Colson, Charles W. *How Now Shall We Live?*, Carol Stream, IL: Tyndale, 1999.

Crenshaw, James L. *Education in Ancient Israel: Across the Deadening Silence*, New York: Doubleday, 1998.

—. *In Search of Wisdom*, Louisville, KY: Westminster John Knox Press. 1993.

—. *Old Testament Wisdom: An Introduction*, Atlanta, GA: John Knox Press. 1981.

Cubberley, Ellwood P. *The History of Education: Educational Practice and Progress Considered as a Phase of the Development and Spread of Western Civilization*, 1920.

Curry, Jeffery L. *The Mysteries of the Kingdom: The Literary Path to Wisdom*, Roanoke, TX: See Again Press. 2004.

—. *The Parable Discovery: First Century Discipleship*, Roanoke, TX: See Again Press. 2004.

—. *Parallels and Prophecy: Hidden Treasure*, Roanoke, TX: See Again Press. 2004.

—. *The Mysteries of the Kingdom*. Roanoke, TX: See Again Press. 2004.

—. *The Parable Discovery*, Roanoke,

TX: See Again Press. 2004.

Davis, Moshe, ed. 1956. *Israel: Its Role in Civilization*, New York: Harper.

Deporter, Bobbi and Mike Hernacki. *Quantum Learning: Unleashing the Genius in You*, New York, NY: Dell Publishing, 1992.

Dobson, J. F. *Ancient Education and Its Meaning to Us*, New York: Longmans, Green and Company. 1932.

Donfried, Karl P., Peter Richardson (eds). *Judaism and Christianity in First Century Rome*, Grand Rapids MI: Eerdmans Publishing. 1998.

Dowgiewicz. Mike and Sue Dowgiewicz. *Restoring the Early Church*, Colorado Springs, CO: Empowerment Press. 1996.

Dorsey, David A., *The Literary Structure of the Old Testament: A Commentary on Genesis–Malachi*, Grand Rapids, MI: BakerAcademic. 1999.

Dowley, Dr. Tim, Org. Ed. *Eerdman's Handbook to the History of Christianity*, Grand Rapids, MI: Wm. B. Eerdmans Publishing Company, 1988.

Easton, M.G. *Easton's Bible Dictionary*, Oak Harbor, WA: Logos Research Systems, Inc., 1996, c1897.

Ebner, Eliezer. *Elementary Education in Ancient Israel: During the Tannaitic Period*, New York: Bloch Publishing Co., 1956.

Edersheim, Alfred. *Sketches of Jewish Social Life at the Time of Christ*, Hendrickson Publishers, 1994. ❧

———. *The Temple: Its Ministry and Services*. Peabody, MA: Hendrickson Publishers, Inc.,1994. ❧

Elboim-Dror, Rachel. *Israeli Education: Changing Perspectives*, Israel Studies 6, no. 1: 76-100. 2001.

Eldridge, Tom. *Safely Home*, San Antonio, TX: The Vision Forum, 2003.

Elston, D. R. *Israel: The Making of a Nation*, London; New York: Published for the Anglo-Israel Association by the Oxford University Press. 1963.

Enns, Paul P. *The Moody Handbook of Theology*, Chicago, IL: Moody Press, 1997, c1989.

Feder, Don. *A Jewish Conservative Looks at Pagan America*, Lafayette, LA: Huntington House Publishers, 1993.

Feldman, Abraham J. *Contributions of Judaism to Modern Society*, New York: The Union of American Hebrew Congregations.

Flannery, Edward H. *The Anguish of the Jews: Twenty-Three Centuries of Anti-Semitism*, New York: Macmillan Company, 1965.

Flusser, David. *Jewish Sources in Early Christianity*, Tel-Aviv, Israel: MOD Books, 1989.

Follette, John Wright. B*roken Bread: A Devotional Classic for Developing Christian Character*, Springfield, MO: Gospel Publishing House, 1957.

Freeman, James M. *Manners And Customs of the Bible: A Complete Guide to the Origin and Significance of Our Time-Honored Biblical Tradition.*

Frymer-Kensky, Tikva, David Novak, Peter Ochs, David Fox Sandmel, and Michael A. Signer, eds. *Christianity in Jewish Terms*, Boulder, CO: Westview Press, 2000.

Gammie, John G. *In Search of Wisdom: Essays in Memory of John G. Gammie*, Louisville, KY: Westminster John Knox Press. 1993.

Garr, John. *Bless You: Restoring the Biblically Hebraic Blessing*, Atlanta, GA: Restoration Foundation. 2003. ❧

———. *Family Sanctuary: Restoring the Biblicall Hebraic Home*, Atlanta, GA: Restoration Foundation. 2003. ❧

———. *Restoring Our Lost Legacy*, Atlanta, GA: Restoration Foundation. 1999. ❧

Gartenhaus, Jacob. *Traitor?: A Jew, a Book, a Miracle: an Autobiography*, Nashville, TN: Thomas Nelson, 1980.

Gill, Mohammad Akram. *Reverse Logic in the Philosophy of God*, Free Inquiry, Spring, 62. 2002.

Goldberg, Harvey. *Jewish Passages: Cycles of Jewish Life*, University of California Press. Berkeley CA. 2003.

Gonzalez, Justo, L. *A History of Christian Thought: From the Beginings to the Council of the Chalecedon*, Nashville: TN: Abington Press. 1970, 1987.

Goodman, L. E. *God of Abraham*, New York: Oxford University Press. 1996.

Goodman, Martin, ed. *Jews in a Greco-Roman World*, Oxford: Oxford University. 1998.

Green, Albert. *Reclaiming the Future of Christian Education*, Colorado Springs, CO.: Association of Christian Schools International, 1998. ❧

———. *Thinking Christianly*, Seattle, WA: Alta Vista College Press, 1990. ❧

Grollenberg, L. H. *Atlas of the Bible*, London: Nelson. 1956.

Gruber, Dan. *The Church and the Jews: The Biblical Relationship*, Hagerstown, MD: Serenity Books. 1997.

Guignebert, Charles. *Jesus*, London: Knopf. 1935.

Harris, Gregg. *The Christian Home School*, Brentwood: Wolgemuth & Hyatt, 1988.

Harris, R. Laird, Robert Laird Harris, Gleason Leonard Archer, and Bruce K. Waltke. *Theological Wordbook of the Old Testament*, Chicago, IL: Moody Press, 1999, c1980.

Hawkins, O. S. *In Sheep's Clothing: Jude's Urgent Warning about Apostasy in the Church*, Neptune, NJ: Loizeaux, 1994.

Haycock, Dr. Ruth C. *Encyclopedia of Bible Truths for School Subjects*, Association of Christian Schools International.

Hayford, Jack. *Everyday Wisdom for Everlasting Life : A study of Proverbs*, Spirit-Filled Life Bible Discovery Guides. Thomas Nelson: Nashville 1997, c1996.

Hegg, Tim. *The Letter Writer, Paul's Background and Torah Perspective*, First Fruits of Zion, Littleton, CO. 2003.

Henry, Matthew. *Matthew Henry's Commentary on the Whole Bible* Peabody, MA: Hendrickson, 1996.

Heschel, Abraham Joshua. *God in Search of Man*, Farrar, Straus, and Giroux, 1976).

———. *Man's Quest for God: Studies in Prayer and Symbolism*, New York: Charles Scribner's Sons, 1954

Horne, Herman. *Jesus the Teacher*, Revised by Angus M. Gunn. Grand Rapids, MI: Kregel Publications, 1998. Originally published as *Jesus: The Master Teacher*, 1920.

Howshall, Marilyn. *The Lifestyle of Learning: An Introduction*, Lifestyle of Learning Ministries, 2000.

Hubbard, David A. *The Wisdom of the Old Testament*, Messiah College Occasional Papers, no.3 Grantham, PA: Messiah College, August, 1982.

Jacoby, Russell. *Dogmatic Wisdom: How the Culture Wars Divert Education and Distract America*, New York, NY: Doubleday, 1994.

Jamieson, Robert, A. R. Fausset. *A Commentary, Critical and Explanatory, on the Old and New Testaments*, Oak Harbor, WA: Logos Research Systems, Inc., 1997.

Jones, Timothy Paul, A. Kenneth Curtis. *Christian History Made Easy*, Torrance, CA: Rose Publishing.

Josephus, Flavius and William Whiston.

❧ Indicates Recommended Reading

The Works of Josephus, Peabody: Hendrickson, 1996, c1987.

Juster, Dan. *Jewish Roots: A Foundation of Biblical Theology,* Shippensburg, PA: Destiny Image, 1995.

Karleen, Paul. *The Handbook to Bible Study:* Oxford University Press: New York, 1987.

Kent, Charles Foster. *Biblical Geography and History,* New York: Charles Scribner's Sons, 1911.

Kimel, Alexander. *A Primer of Anti-Semitism,* http://www.kimel.net

Kimeldorf, Martin. *Creating Portfolios: For Success in School, Work, and Life,* Minneapolis, MN: Free Spirit Publishing, 1994.

Koch, Robert and Remy Koch. *Christianity: New Religion or Sect of Biblical Judaism?,* Palm Beach Gardens, FL: Messenger Media. 2000.

Kuhlman, Edward L. *Agony in Education: The Importance of Struggle in the Process of Learning,* Westport, CT: Bergin & Garvey, 1994.

Kuhn, Thomas S. *The Structure of Scientific Revolutions,* 3rd ed., University of Chicago Press, 1962, 1970, 1996.

Lapide, Pinchas E. *Hebrew in the Church,* Grand Rapids: William B. Eerdmans Publishing Co., 1984.

Lawson, Kevin. *Introduction to Christian Education: Foundations for the 21st Century,* Grand Rapids, MI: Baker, 2001.

LeFever, Marlene D. *Creative Teaching Methods: Be an Effective Christian Teacher,* Colorado Springs, CO: Cook Ministry Resources, Colorado, 1996.

Levenson, Jon D. *The Hebrew Bible, the Old Testament, and Historical Criticism: Jews and Christians in Biblical Studies,* Louisville, KY: Westminster/John Knox Press. 1993.

Limburg, James, ed. *Judaism: An Introduction for Christians,* Minneapolis, MN: Augsburg Publishing House, 1987.

Lindsey, Robert. *Jesus, Rabbi, and Lord: The Hebrew Story of Jesus Behind Our Gospels,* Oak Creek, WI: Cornerstone Publishing, 1990.

Luther, Martin. *About the Jews and Their Lies,* Wittenberg, 1543.

MacArthur, John, Jr. *How to Study the Bible,* John MacArthur's Bible Studies, Chicago, IL: Moody Press, 1996, c1982.

MacArthur, John. *Rediscovering Expository Preaching,* Dallas, TX: Word Pub., 1997, c1992.

MacDonald, William ed. *Believers Bible Commentary: A Thorough, Yet Easy To Read Bible Commentary That Turns Complicated Theology Into Practical Understanding,* Nashville, TN: Thomas Nelson Publishers, 1995.

Manz, Charles C., Manz, Karen P., Marx, Robert D., Neck, Christopher P., *The Wisdom of Solomon at Work: Ancient Virtues for Living and Leading Today,* San Francisco,CA: Berrett-Koehler Publishers, 2001.

Martin, Ralph P. *Worship in the Early Church,* Grand Rapids, Michigan: Wm. B. Eerdmans Publishing Company, 1974.

Marx, Karl and Friedrich Engels. *Basic Writings on Politics and Philosophy,* New York: 1959.

Mason, Charlotte. *Original Homeschooling Series,* origanally published in London: England, 1906. Reprint Wheaton, IL: Tyndale House Publishers, Inc., 1954.

Mathis, James and Susan. *Foundations of A Christian World View,* Gainesville, FL: Christian World View Publishing, 1993.

McCarthy, Bernice. *The 4MAT System: Teaching to Learning Styles with Right/Left Mode Techniques,* Barrington, IL: Excel, Inc. 1981, 1987.

Merriam-Webster's Collegiate Dictionary, 10th ed., Springfield, MA: Merriam-Webster, 1996.

Meyers, Carol. *Discovering Eve: Ancient Israelite Women in Context,* New York: Oxford University Press. 1991.

Miller, J. Maxwell and John H. Hayes. *A History of Ancient Israel and Judah,* 1st ed. Philadelphia: Westminster Press. 1986.

Miller, M.S. and J.L. Miller, *Harper's Bible Dictionary,* New York: Harper and Row Publishers, 1973

Miller, Patrick D. *The Religion of Ancient Israel,* Louisville, KY: SPCK. 2000.

Minear, Paul Sevier. *Eyes of Faith, a Study in the Biblical Point of View,* Philadelphia, PA: The Westminster Press, 1946.

Morgan, Robert and John Barton. *Biblical Interpretation,* Oxford: Oxford University Press, 1988.

Moseley, Ron. *Yeshua: A Guide to The Real Jesus and The Original Church,* Hagerstown, MD: Ebed Publishing, 1996. ☙

———. *Spirit of the Law,* Ebed Publishing, Hagerstown, MD. 1995. ☙

Mosley, Steven R. *Glimpses of God: Finding the Father Who Fills Your Every Need,* Sisters, OR: 1998. ☙

Mulligan, David. *Far Above Rubies: Wisdom in the Christian Community,* Marshfield, VT: Messenger Publishing, 1994. ☙

———. *Worldviews in Conflict: Choosing Christianity in a World of Ideas,* Grand Rapids, MI: Zondervan. 1992.

Murray, Andrew. *Abiding in Christ,* Minneapolis, MN. (original 1895). 2003. ☙

———. *How to Strengthen YOur Faith,* Springdale, PA: Wicker House (original 1898). 1997. ☙

———. *Waiting on God,* Springdale, PA: Wicker House (original 1897). 1981. ☙

Neusner, Jacob. *Judaism in the Beginning of Christianity,* Philadelphia, PA: Fortress Press, 1984.

Orlinsky, Harry M. *Ancient Israel,* New York: Cornell University Press, 1954.

Overman, Christian. *Assumptions that Affect our Lives,* Simi Valley, CA: Worldview Matters 1996.☙

Packer, J. I. *A Quest For Godliness: The Puritan Vision of the Christian Life,* Wheaton, IL: Crossway Books, 1994.

Panikkar, Raimundo. *A Dwelling Place for Wisdom,* Louisville, KY: Westminster John Knox Press, 1993.

Parkes, James. *The Foundations of Judaism and Christianity,* Chicago: Quadrangle Books, 1960.

Peterson, E. H. *The Message: New Testament with Psalms and Proverbs,* Colrado Springs, CO: NavPress, 1995.

Pfeiffer, C. F. *The Wycliffe Bible Commentary: New Testament,* Chicago, IL: Moody Press, 1962.

Phillips, John. *Exploring the World of the Jew,* Neptune, NJ: Loizeaux, 1993.

Phillips, Michael, *Make Me Like Jesus: The Courage to Pray Dangerously,* Colorado Springs, CO: Waterbrook Press. 2003. ☙

Philo, of Alexandria, and Charles Duke Yonge. *The Works of Philo,* Peabody: Hendrickson, 1996, c1993.

Piper, John. *Future Grace,* Sisters, OR: Multnomah Books, 1998.

Postman, Neil and Charles Weingartner. *Teaching as a Subversive Activity,* New York, NY: Delta Publishing.1969.

Power, Edward J. *Religion and the Public*

Schools in 19th Century America: The Contribution of Orestes A. Brownson. New York: Paulist Press, 1996.

Prilol, Lou. *Teach Them Diligently: How to Use the Scriptures in Child Training,* Woodruff, SC: Timeless Texts. 2000. ❦

Pryor, Dwight. *Learning for Life,* Article Jerusalem Perspective Online, Jerusalem School of Synoptic Research.

Punton, Anne. *The World Jesus Knew,* Chicago, IL: Moody Press. 1996. ❦

Purinton, Carl E. *Christianity and Its Judaic Heritage: An Introduction with Selected Sources,* New York: Ronald Press Co. 1961.

Ramachandra, Vinoth. *God's That Fail: Modern Idolatry and Christian Mission,* Downers Grove, Il: Intervarsity Press. 1996.

Reed, James E. and Ronnie Prevost. *A History of Christian Education,* Nashville, TN: Broadman & Holman, 1993.

Reinhold Niebuhr. *The Nature and Destiny of Man,* New York: Westminster, John Knox Press, 1941.

Richards, Larry. *The Bible Reader's Companion,* Wheaton, IL: Victor Books, 1991.

Richards, Lawrence O. *Christian Education: Seeking to Become Like Jesus Christ,* Zondervan Publishing House Grand Rapids MI. 1931, 1975.

———. *The Teacher's Commentary: Explains and Applies the Scriptures in a Way That Will Help You Teach Any Lesson From Genesis to Revelation,* Wheaton, IL: Victor Books, 1987. ❦

Riches, John. 2000. *The Bible: A Very Short Introduction,* Oxford: Oxford University.

Riese, Alan W. and Herbert J. La Salle. *The Story of Western Civilization: Greece and Rome Build Great Civilizations,* Cambridge, MA: Educators Publishing Service, 1990.

Rogers, Jay. *A Brief History of Christian Influence in Christian Colleges.*

Roland De Vaux. *Ancient Israel: Its Life and Institutions,* New York: McGraw-Hill, 1961.

Rossel, Seymour. *Introduction to Jewish History: Abraham tot he Sages,* West Orange, NJ: Behrman House, 1981.

Rousseau, Richard W. *Christianity and Judaism: The Deepening Dialogue,* Scranton, PA: Ridge Row Press.

Rudin A James and Marvin Wilson. *The Jewish Role Shaping America Society,* Grand Rapids, MI: William B. Eerdmans Publishing Co., 1987.

Sampson, Robin. *A Family Guide to the Biblical Holidays,* Stafford, VA: Heart of Wisdom Publishing Inc., 1997. ❦

———. *Ancient History: Adam to Messiah,* Stafford, VA: Heart of Wisdom Publishing Inc., 2001. ❦

———. *What Your Child Needs to Know When,* Stafford, VA: Heart of Wisdom Publishing Inc., 2001. ❦

———. *Wisdom: An Internet-Linked Unit Study,* Stafford, VA: Heart of Wisdom Publishing Inc., 2004. ❦

Saucy, Robert. *Scripture: Its Power, Authority and Relevance,* Nashville, TN: Word Publishing. 2001. ❦

Schaeffer, Edith. *Christianity is Jewish,* Wheaton, IL: Tyndale House Publishers Inc., 1975. ❦

Schaeffer, Francis A. *How Should We Then Live? The Rise and Decline of Western Thought and Culture,* Wheaton, IL: Crossway Books, 1983. ❦

———. *The Complete Works of Francis A Schaeffer,* Westchester, IL: Crossway Books, 1982.

Schank, Roger C. and Cleary, Clip. *Engines for Education,* The Institute for the Learning Sciences, 1994.

Schurer, Emil. *The History of the Jewish People in the Age of Jesus Christ,* Edinburgh: T&T Clark LTD, 1973.

Seeskin, Kenneth. *No Other Gods,* West Orange, NJ: Behrman House. 1995. ❦

Shenandoah, April. *History of America's Education: Universities, Textbooks and Our Founders,* Sierra Times. April, 2002.

Sire, James W. *The Universe Nextdoor: A Basic Worldview Catalog,* Downers Grove, IL: InterVarsity Press. 1997.

Slater, Rosalie J. *A Family Program For Reading Aloud,* San Francisco, CA: Foundation For American Christian Education, 1991.

Smalley, Beryl. *The Study of the Bible in the Middle Ages,* Oxford: Blackwell, 1952.

Smith, Barbra and Douglas Smith. *Teach Me Lord That I May Teach,* Arnold, MD. Third Floor Publishing. 1995 ❦

Smith, James E. *The Wisdom Literature and Psalms,* College Press Pub. Co.: Joplin, Mo, 1996.

Spurgeon, Charles Haddon. *Faith's Checkbook,* Devotional, August 5.

Stamps, Don. *The Full Life Study Bible* KJV, Life Publishers International, 1992. ❦

Stanford, Miles J. *The Green Letters: Principles of Spiritual Growth,* Grand Rapids MI: Zondervan Publishing House. 1975. ❦

Stanley, Charles F. *Advancing Through Adversity,* Nashville, TN: Thomas Nelson, 1997, c1996.

Stein, Robert H. *The Method and Message of Jesus' Teachings.* Louisville, KY: Westminster/John Knox Press, 1994.

Stern, David H. *Jewish New Testament Commentary,* Clarksville, MD: Jewish New Testament Publications, 1992. ❦

Strayer, Debbie. *Gaining the Confidence to Teach,* Melrose, FL: Common Sense Press, 1997.❦

Swift, Fletcher. *Education in Ancient Israel: From Earliest Times to 70 A.D,* Chicago: Open Court, 1919.

Thayer, William M. *Gaining Favor With God and Man,* Mantle Ministries reprint. 1893. ❦

Tverberg, Lois A. *Listening to the Language of the Bible: Hearing it Through Jesus Ears,* Holland, MI: En-Gedi, 2004. ❦

Wagner, Clarence H. Jr., *Jerusalem Courier,* Volume 10, No. 4, 1992.

Walsh, Brian J. and Richard Middleton. *Transforming Vision: Shaping a Christian Worldview,* Downers Grove, IL: InterVarsity, 1984.

Waltke, Bruce K. *The Way of Wisdom,* Zondervan Publishing House, Grand Rapids, MI, 2000.

Walvoord, J. F. *The Bible Knowledge Commentary: An Exposition of the Scriptures,* Wheaton, IL: Victor Books, 1983-c1985.

Ward, Kaari, ed. *Jesus and His Times,* Pleasantville, NY: Readers Digest Association, Inc., 1987.

Waring, Diana. *Beyond Survival: A Guide to Abundant-Life Homeschooling,* Lynnwood, WA: Emerald Books, 1996. ❦

Weiss, Randall A. *Jewish Sects of the New Testament Era,* Cedar Hill, TX: Cross Talk, 1994.

Whitaker, Richard. ed., *The Abridged Brown-Driver-Briggs Hebrew-English Lexicon of the Old Testament,* Oak Harbor, WA: Logos, 1997.

Wiersbe, Warren W. *Be What You Are: 12 Intriguing Pictures of the Christian from the New Testament,* Wheaton IL: Tyndale House, 1996, c1988. ❦

Wiersbe, Warren W. *The Bible Exposition Commentary,* Wheaton, IL: Victor

❦ Indicates Recommended Reading

Books, 1996.

Wiersbe, Warren W. *Wiersbe's Expository Outlines On The Old Testament,* Wheaton, IL: Victor Books, 1993. (Pr 12:1)

Wilson, Douglas. *Recovering The Lost Tools of Learning: An Approach to Distinctively Christian Education,* Wheaton, IL: Crossway Books, 1991.

Wilson, Marvin R. *Our Father Abraham: Jewish Roots of the Christian Faith,* Grand Rapids, MI: William B. Eerdmans Publishing Company, and Dayton, OH: Center For Judaic-Christian Studies, 1989. ❦

Woods, Dennis. *Discipling the Nations: The Government Upon His Shouders,* Franklin, TN: Legacy Communications. 1996. ❦

————. *The Great Conversation: A Biblical Analysis of the Great Books of Western Civilization,* Brightrock Press. ❦

Wright, G. Ernest, ed. *The Bible and the Ancient Near East,* Garden City, NY: Doubleday, 1961.

Wurmbrand, Richard. *Tortured for Christ.* Bartlesville, OK: Living Sacrifice Book Co., Voice of the Martyrs, 1967, 1998.❦

Young, Brad H. *Jesus the Jewish Thelogian,* (Forewords by Marvin Wilson and Rabbi David Wolpe), Peabody, MS: Hendrickson Publishers 1995. ❦

————. *The Parables: Jewish Tradition and Christian Interpretation,* Peabody, MS: Hendrickson Publishers 1998. ❦

————. *Paul the Jewish Thelogian: A Pharisee Among Christians, Jews, and Gentiles.* Peabody, MS: Hendrickson Publishers 1996. ❦

Youngblood, Ronald F., Bruce, F.F., ed. *Nelson's New Illustrated Bible Dictionary,* Nashville, TN: Thomas Nelson, 1997

Zondervan *Pictorial Encyclopedia of the Bible,* Grand Rapids, Michigan: Zondervan Corporation, 1975.

Printed in the United States
30225LVS00002B/1-28

9 780970 181671